THE COMING TO POWER
Critical Presidential Elections in
American History

The Coming to Power
Critical Presidential Elections in American History

ARTHUR M. SCHLESINGER, JR., EDITOR
Albert Schweitzer Chair in the Humanities
City University of New York

Fred L. Israel, Associate Editor
Department of History, City College of New York

William P. Hansen, Managing Editor

CHELSEA HOUSE PUBLISHERS

CHELSEA HOUSE PUBLISHERS
Harold Steinberg, Chairman & Publisher
Andrew E. Norman, President
Susan Lusk, Vice President

A Division of Chelsea House Educational Communications, Inc.
133 Christopher Street, New York 10014

Contents

The Critical
Presidential Elections

by Arthur M. Schlesinger, Jr.

This book contains a selection of essays from the four-volume work *History of American Presidential Elections* published in 1971 by Chelsea House and McGraw-Hill. The pieces reprinted here deal with what the editors, after painful and prolonged reflection, decided were the most critical fifteen of the forty-six presidential elections held in the United States from 1789 to 1968. The choice was not easy. We do not expect everyone to agree with this particular list; but disappointment over omissions may be readily assuaged by reference to the longer work.

1.

Why these fifteen elections? The essay on the elections of 1789 and 1792 was inevitable. Here the young republic, in twice voting for George Washington, established the first set of precedents by which the American people (or at least the adult white males among them) could choose their chief magistrate. The election of 1800 was almost equally vital in the shaping of the process. The new nation, in selecting Thomas Jefferson, the head of the Republican opposition, over the Federalist incumbent, John Adams, accomplished the task, so difficult for young countries, of transferring power peacefully from one political party to another.

The election of 1800 consolidated the role of the party system. It also represented a new infusion of democracy into the process. The election of 1828, coming as the nation expanded toward the West, strengthened the democratic impulse and precipitated the changes associated with the age of Jackson. Jeffersonian Republicans now evolved into Jacksonian Democrats; the Whigs arose in place of the Federalists as the party of those whom Alexander Hamilton had called the "rich and well-born"; and the party system entered a new phase. But parties had not only to develop organization; they also had to meet issues. The bafflement of the new party system before the question of slavery led to political upheaval. By 1856, our next critical election, the Whig party had broken up, and a new party, the Republican, made its national debut. The 1856 election reminds us too that the electoral process does not always produce men capable of rising to the challenge of crisis. James Buchanan, the victor in 1856, became an impotent spectator in the White House as the nation drifted toward civil war.

Eighteen-sixty brought in the first Republican President, Abraham Lincoln; and, with his election, southern states began to secede from the union. The next election, 1864, subjected the process to new and unprecedented strain: a presidential contest in the midst of a civil war. Eighteen-seventy-six brought still another new challenge, when Samuel J. Tilden, the Democratic candidate, appeared to have won both the popular and electoral vote, but an electoral commission, encouraged by Republican concessions to southern pressures, gave disputed electoral votes and the Presidency to Rutherford B. Hayes.

Conservatism generally prevailed in the White House for the thirty years after the Civil War. But accumulating protest against business rule found expression in William Jennings Bryan's campaign as Democratic and Populist candidate in 1896. The Republicans under William McKinley turned back this revolt. The demand for reform, however, continued to rise. In our next critical election, 1912, this demand ruled the canvass, with the eloquent Democrat Woodrow Wilson and the fiery Progressive Theodore Roosevelt setting the tone and with even the Socialist candidate, Eugene V. Debs, polling nearly a million votes. Four years later, war in another continent intruded itself into a presidential election for the first time in more than a century; this began the immersion in international power politics with which the voter would be dismally familiar in the later twentieth-century.

The Democratic interlude of Wilson was followed by a resumption of Republican control until the election of 1932. Seizing the opportunity created by the Great Depression, Franklin D. Roosevelt now popularized new ideas of affirmative government and constructed a new majority coalition. In 1940 he even overcame the old and powerful tradition against third terms (and, during the life of the Twenty-second Amendment, will be the only President ever to serve more than two elected terms). The election of Dwight D. Eisenhower in 1952 brought the Republicans back to the White House, but Eisenhower failed to build a new majority; and in 1960 the Democrat John F. Kennedy, in the first election dominated by television, defeated the Republican Richard M. Nixon. Nineteen-sixty-four, the last of our critical elections, has assumed increasing significance in retrospect because of its relationship to American involvement in the war in Indochina.

The choice, I say, was not easy. One found it hard to leave out the election of 1812, the first held in wartime; the election of 1832, with the beginnings of national mass political organization; the election of 1844, which led to the acquisition of Oregon and to the Mexican War; the election of 1884, with the return of the Democrats under Grover Cleveland in a campaign of unusual scurrility; the election of 1900, with the debate about American imperialism; the election of 1944 and the fourth term; the election of 1948 and the most dramatic upset in the history of presidential elections; and the election of 1968 with the Republican resurgence after the disaster of 1964. But these elections, and all the others, receive careful treatment in the four volumes of the *History of American Presidential Elections.*

So much for the elections chosen for this book. Incomplete as this selection is, it covers, I believe, the turbulent range of American political history from the young republic with its land area of 865 thousand square miles and its population of four million to the great contemporary nation with its three and a half million square miles and its 200 million people. The selection also illustrates the permutations and vicissitudes of the presidential process and raises the crucial issues in our system of presidential choice.

2.

We often forget the audacity of the political undertaking conceived by the fathers of the American republic. The attempt at self-government by nationalist revolutionaries in thirteen ex-colonies straggling along the eastern seaboard of the American continent was unprecedented at the time. More than half a century after the Declaration of Independence, democracy remained a most perilous experiment. Alexis de Tocqueville, the acute young Frenchman who visited the United States in 1831–32 in order to find out what democracy was all about, wrote almost with wonder about the way Americans chose their Presidents:

> For a long while before the appointed time has come, the election becomes the important and, so to speak, the all-engrossing topic of discussion. Factional ardor is redoubled, and all the artificial passions which the imagination can create in a happy and peaceful land are agitated and brought to light. . . . As the election draws near, the activity of intrigue and the agitation of the populace increase; the citizens are divided into hostile camps, each of which assumes the name of its favorite candidate; the whole nation glows with feverish excitement; the election is the daily theme of the press, the subject of every private conversation, the end of every thought and every action, the sole interest of the present.
>
> It is true that as soon as the choice is determined, this ardor is dispelled, calm returns, and the river, which had nearly broken its banks, sinks to its usual level; but who can refrain from astonishment that such a storm should have arisen?

If the nations of Europe had thus to choose their leaders, Tocqueville noted, few "could escape the calamities of anarchy or of conquest every time they might have to elect a new sovereign." But the American democracy, rejecting the principle of hereditary succession, had invented a means by which, in spite of ominous hullabaloo, a new head of state could take over from a predecessor — by which, even more strikingly, the opposition could succeed the party in power. How formidable an achievement this was we can well understand today when we consider the way the problem of succession convulses so many of the nations of our own day.

When Tocqueville made these observations, the United States of America was well established as a nation. Half a century earlier the situation of the newly liberated colonies, each with its own interests, each endowed by the colonial experience with a mistrust of central control, had been far more precarious. The new nation then faced the hard question whether it could survive at all. Disputes over the location and devolution of power could become a threat to survival both by feeding division within the country and by offering foreign empires their chance, as James Madison put it at the Constitutional Convention, "to mix their intrigues & influence with the Election." The solution of the 'succession' problem — the problem, that is, of how the authority of government was to pass from one set of men to another — was therefore a vital part of the quest for stability.

Marcus Cunliffe in his essay on "The Elections of 1789 and 1792" recalls the complex debates which finally produced Article II, Section 1, of the Constitution. This article confided the choice of the President neither to the Congress, as some had proposed at Philadelphia, nor directly to the people, as favored by others, but to a group of "electors," designated in each state for the single, specific and temporary purpose of choosing the chief magistrate. The electors, exercising their independent judgment in their respective states, would cast their votes for President, a majority to prevail; and, since no one supposed that any individual (after General Washington) would easily obtain a majority, it was expected that the House of Representatives would ordinarily make the final choice from the five highest in the list they received from the Electoral College. The second man in the House vote would become Vice President.

Defending this system in the 68th *Federalist,* Alexander Hamilton laid particular stress on the importance of affording "as little opportunity as possible to tumult and disorder" in the election of the chief magistrate. Selection of the President by the Congress would be an invitation to "cabal, intrigue, and corruption . . . chiefly from the desire in foreign powers to gain an improper ascendant in our councils"; moreover, it was essential that "the Executive should be independent for his continuance in the office on all but the people themselves." But direct selection of the President by the people would expose the process to "heats and ferments" arising from mass emotion. While "the sense of the people" had to be expressed in the choice, Hamilton said,

> the immediate election should be made by . . . a small number of persons, selected by their fellow-citizens from the general mass, [who] will be most likely to possess the information and discernment requisite to such complicated investigations. . . . The choice of *several,* to form an intermediate body of electors, will be much less apt to convulse the community with any extraordinary and violent movements, than the choice of *one* who was himself to be the final object of the public wishes.

This "mode of appointment," Hamilton added, ". . . is almost the only part of the system, of any consequence, which has escaped without severe censure, or which has received the slightest mark of approbation from its opponents." His satisfaction turned out to be remarkably misplaced. The united desire of the electors to make Washington President at first concealed the defects of the process; but it really only worked once — in the election of 1796. Thereafter the electors stopped exercising independent judgment and began casting party votes; and, as Noble E. Cunningham, Jr., explains in his discussion of "The Election of 1800," the Jefferson–Burr imbroglio in the House of Representatives led to the first substantive modification of the Constitution when the 12th Amendment in 1804 required electors thereafter to vote separately for President and Vice President.

3.

The original process got into trouble because of one of the few notable miscalculations by the Founding Fathers — their failure to realize that the competition for the Presidency would generate the formation of political parties; indeed, their larger failure to see that their splendid plan of government could hardly work at all without a party system.

This was an understandable failure. The eighteenth-century world was without experience of political parties in the modern sense. Burke was almost alone in defining party favorably — "a body of men united for promoting by their joint endeavors the national interest upon some particular principle in which they are all agreed" — and contending that a party system could be a good thing. The American experience in particular had been from colonial days with family cliques or local juntos. Given the concern over national survival, the Founding Fathers saw such groupings as gratuitous sources of instability and condemned them as "factions." Washington summed up the feeling in his Farewell Address, where he warned, as he put it, "in the most solemn manner against the baneful effects of the Spirit of Party." While acknowledging that this spirit, "unfortunately," was inseparable from human nature and that it broke out in all forms of government, Washington said that in popular governments "it is seen in its greatest rankness and is truly their worst enemy."

Yet the very intensity of his language proceeded from his recognition that the spirit of party was already beginning to rise in American politics. The reasons for the appearance of the party system were manifold. Basically party competition reflected the economic diversity of the new republic and first appeared in the debate over Hamilton's fiscal program. Madison in the 10th *Federalist,* after the customary denunciation of factions, went on reluctantly to concede that "the various and unequal distribution of property" was "the most common and durable source of factions" and that the "regulation of these various and interfering [economic] interests . . . involves the spirit of party and faction in the necessary and ordinary operations of the government." Moreover, the commitment of the Fathers to the idea of a balanced government itself soon implied a role for parties; in 1792 Madison, while still determined to oppose the spirit of party, wrote that the evil could be mitigated "by making one party a check on the other, so far as the existence of parties cannot be prevented." The revolutionary government in France, to which the Hamiltonians and the Jeffersonians responded in sharply different ways, accelerated the political division; it "kindled and brought forward the two parties," Jefferson said in 1793, "with an ardour which our own interests merely, could never excite." The argument over foreign policy also helped insure that the party system, as it crystallized, would be a *two*-party system (though this also corresponded with John Adams' view that "in every society where property exists, there will ever be a struggle between rich and poor" and Jefferson's view that "men by their constitution are naturally divided into two parties" — those who distrusted the people and those who had confidence in them). By 1794 John Taylor of Caroline could write a pamphlet entitled *A Definition of Parties.* "The existence of two parties in Congress," he said, "is apparent"; he then added, in the vein of the times, that this was "extremely perilous" because "truth is a thing, not of divisibility into conflicting parts, but of unity. Hence both sides cannot be right."

The Constitution, the Congress and disputes over foreign policy thus created a *national* politics; the party distinctions arising in Congress made contact with political groupings already existing in the states; and there developed rather quickly the first real party system known anywhere in the modern world. It was, as Walter Dean Burnham has emphasized, an "experimental" system. It had no models and no precedents; organization was rudimentary; the essential links in party communication were provided by the press. Because this was the first generation to have parties at all, the factor of traditional party loyalty, later to become so central in American politics, had little weight. And undercutting the whole enterprise lingered the conviction that a party system was somehow bad.

The great test of the American solution to the succession problem came in 1800. The thought of a Jefferson victory appalled many Federalists. But, when the horrid moment arrived, they accepted the result with astonishing equanimity, and power passed tranquilly from one side to the other. The Federalist party now entered a slow decline, compromised itself by toying with the idea of secession during the War of 1812, saw many of its policies taken over by its opponents after the war and failed to come up with any new policies of its own. When it finally disappeared as a national party after the election of 1816, the restoration of a one-party system seemed no more than a return to basic principle. "Now is the time to exterminate the monster called party spirit," General Andrew Jackson wrote President-elect James Monroe in 1816; and Monroe, presiding over the Era of Good Feelings, described parties to Madison in 1822 as "the curse of the country."

4.

But already the party system was moving into a new phase — a phase in which, ironically, Jackson was to be both beneficiary and master. The evolution of the party system registered changes in the nation itself. By the 1820's the equalitarian impulse was beginning the transformation of American politics. In 1824 nearly all adult white males could vote in seven-eighths of the states; and in three-quarters of the states presidential electors were now chosen by popular vote rather than by the state legislature. The deferential order of the early republic was fading away. The union was rushing on into the frontier west. New democratic energies were seeking expression.

And a new breed of political leaders now appeared to guide and exploit these energies. They were professional politicians; the party was their vehicle, their domicile and almost their religion; and they were prepared to challenge fundamentally the old ideas about the baneful influence of party spirit. While such men could be found all across the country, they emerged in the most notable and articulate way in the state of New York. Here Martin Van Buren and the Albany Regency legitimized the political party as a democratic association ruled by its members, and defended it, in effect, as an end in itself, controlled by discipline and consecrated in loyalty. Moreover, Van Buren and his friends saw the strife between parties as absolutely proper and necessary in a democratic republic. In a certain sense, despite John Taylor of Caroline, both sides, they felt, could be right.

As usual, the presidential contest precipitated the crystallization of party division. In 1824 four candidates, all nominally Republicans, competed for the White House. Jackson led both popular and electoral vote but lost in the House of Representatives; and one consequence was a deep sense of political frustration. Moving into the vacuum, Van Buren assumed leadership of Jackson's campaign for 1828. Jackson's victory then, repeated in 1832 and confirmed in Van Buren's own success in 1836, brought about the re-establishment of the two-party system.

The new system not only legitimized but democratized party conflict. Some of the democratization was symbolic, but much of it was real; and the essence of the period was the incorporation of the mass of voters into the party system. In this undertaking the Democrats led the way; the National Republicans and their successors the Whigs resisted for a time, but eventually went along. Jackson, of course, was peculiarly identified with the effort to include the people in national politics. His celebrated veto in 1832 of the bill to recharter the Bank of the United States was a deliberate (and successful) attempt to circumvent established political institutions and leaders and appeal directly to the voters. His lieutenants meanwhile devised the machinery to institutionalize this appeal.

The democratization effort ushered in the most inventive period in American history in the field of political structure and technique. The nomination of presidential candidates by congressional caucus was discredited after 1824; nomination by state legislatures proved an unsatisfactory substitute; and in the 1830's the politicians came up with the national convention to provide for popular participation in the nominating process. Conservatives resisted this innovation. "I find these assemblies dangerous," John Quincy Adams told Tocqueville. "They usurp the place of political bodies and could end by completely thwarting their action." Tocqueville himself, while regarding the convention as — at least for the French — "a dangerous and impracticable consequence of the sovereignty of the people," acknowledged that in such meetings "men have the opportunity of seeing one another; means of execution are combined; and opinions are maintained with a warmth and energy that written language can never attain." The first national conventions were improvised and unrepresentative gatherings; and the professional politicians soon became as adept at managing conventions — especially as a consequence of the two-thirds rule in the Democratic convention — as they had once been at managing caucuses. But nonetheless conventions became for a time the nerve center of the system, and they spawned a whole network of subsidiary structures.

For America, as Tocqueville so often remarked, was indeed the land of voluntary association. The political party rapidly provided the national genius for organization a major outlet. In 1840 the Democratic convention first adopted a national platform, an example followed by the Whigs four years later, and in 1848 the Democratic convention appointed the first national chairman, Benjamin F. Hallett of Massachusetts, and the first national committee. American politics was now acquiring an elaborate apparatus of conventions and committees at all levels, designed not only to mobilize voters but to raise funds and churn out party propaganda, the whole enterprise bound together by the glue of federal patronage.

The transformation of structure was accompanied by a transformation of style. Political campaigns came into their uproarious own, above all at the time of presidential elections. The candidate himself was still expected to stay above politics, but he could make his presence felt, as Jackson so effectively did, by receiving delegations and sending out public letters. When, however, Jackson was rash enough to attend a barbecue in Kentucky in 1832, the opposition *National Intelligencer* in Washington expressed the repugnance of the older school: "This is certainly a new mode of electioneering. We do not recollect before to have heard of the President of the United States descending in person into the political arena." The ordinary citizen, however, suffered no such inhibition. "His concern for politics," said Tocqueville, ". . . is his biggest concern and, so to speak, the only pleasure an American knows. . . . Even the women frequently attend public meetings and listen to political harangues as a recreation from their household labors. Debating clubs are, to a certain extent, a substitute for theatrical entertainment." In the absence of competing amusements, the political rally was rivalled only by the religious revival as a source of color and excitement amidst the monotony of daily life. And, as a man belonged to his father's church, so now he tended to belong to his father's party.

The statistics of voter turn-out, as compiled by W. D. Burnham, suggest the success of the Jacksonian two-party system as an agency for political mobilization. In 1824, 27 per cent of those eligible voted in the presidential election; four years later, the figure shot up to 58 per cent; by 1840, it was 80 per cent; in 1860, it was 81 per cent. But a party system must not only turn out the vote; it must also meet the problems of the country. In this regard the political order as reconstituted in the thirties eventually got into trouble.

For a generation, indeed, one point of the new system was precisely to dodge the question of slavery. When the question proved undodgeable, when, in another irony, Van Buren, the supreme political professional of the twenties, broke with the system by becoming the Free Soil nominee in 1848, the parties, like nearly every other national institution, began to disintegrate. The Whig party faded away after the Kansas-Nebraska Act of 1854. Then the emergence of the Republican party in 1856 expressed the frustration of a growing body of voters and foreshadowed, as so often in American history (as perhaps the Anti-Masonic party had in the late twenties), the beginning of a new political era.

5.

If the period before the Civil War could be considered the time of the rise of the two-party system, the period after the war was clearly that of the system's apogee. Voter turn-out continued at high levels; it did not fall under 70 per cent in a single presidential election between 1864 and 1900. In spite of the isolation of life on the farm, the rural voter displayed no symptoms of political apathy; and the urban machine reached its height of accomplishment in marshalling and suborning the voter in the city. Burnham estimates that two-thirds of the potential electorate were regular voters, only one-tenth were intermittent and peripheral, and about one-quarter remained outside the process. Moreover, within the active electorate, the political party itself had probably never, before or since, commanded the continuing loyalty of so large a proportion of the voters.

The period, however, saw few changes in political structure or style. Party organization, as inherited from pre-war years, underwent little development; only new and gaudier methods of manipulation and corruption strengthened the hold of the professionals on the process. The single striking experiment in campaign techniques was attempted early in the era when Stephen A. Douglas in 1860 introduced the notion that the presidential candidate should take an active role in his election. Desperate to hold the crumbling union together, he ignored public criticism and stumped large parts of the country. Horatio Seymour made a "swing around the circle" eight years later, and in 1872 Horace Greeley delivered almost 200 speeches in eleven days. Probably because the pioneers were all losers, the innovation failed to catch on. While William Jennings Bryan traveled 18,000 miles up and down the nation in 1896, William McKinley stayed comfortably at home, read statements from his front porch to visiting delegations and won the election. Though Theodore Roosevelt had campaigned actively as a vice-presidential candidate in 1900, he went into purdah as President four years later, complaining bitterly a few weeks before the vote, "Of course a President can't go on the stump and can't indulge in personalities, and so I have to sit still and abide the result." The inhibition apparently weighed less, however, on candidates than on incumbents; and in 1908 William Howard Taft, in spite of strong temperamental disinclination, campaigned extensively in the East and Middle West. Thereafter even Presidents were expected to play some personal role in the campaign.

Still, if there were few changes in structure or style, there were significant changes in the composition of the parties. The emergence of the Populists in 1890 foreshadowed a period of reshuffle; and the election of 1896 left Republican strength concentrated in the urban North and East, Democratic strength in the agricultural South and West. "Excluding the special case of 1912," Burnham writes, "84.5 per cent of the total electoral vote for Democratic presidential candidates between 1896 and 1928 was cast in the Southern and Border states." The sectional line-up produced a decline in two-party competition in large areas of the country; and this development, along with the enlargement of the passive electorate through growth in the newly naturalized immigrant sector and, later, through the 19th Amendment and votes for women, led to a marked reduction in voter turn-out. In no presidential election in the twentieth century has the proportion of turn-out exceeded 65 per cent.

The twentieth-century two-party system thus suffered badly by comparison with the nineteenth-century in terms of voter mobilization — this in spite of spectacular improvements in transportation and communication. The decline in two-party competition also meant that in one-party areas conflict began to take place within rather than between the parties. This soon resulted in a demand for direct primaries and created new opportunities for the outsider to challenge the organization. So the efforts of the parties to strengthen their support often led to a weakening of party structures.

The primary movement quickly affected the system of presidential choice. A number of states in the Progressive period passed laws providing for presidential preference primaries or for the election of delegates to the national convention, either of which constituted an invitation to presidential candidates, or their backers, to enter the state. In 1912, Theodore Roosevelt became the first man to seek the presidential nomination via the primary routes. He carried nine of the twelve primary states (La Follette carried two of the other three); but Taft nevertheless controlled the Republican convention and ended as the candidate.

The primary enthusiasm was still high, and in 1913 Woodrow Wilson in his first annual message urged "the prompt enactment of legislation which will provide for primary elections throughout the country at which the voters of the several parties may choose their nominees for the Presidency." He added that this legislation "should provide for the retention of party conventions, but only for the purpose of declaring and accepting the verdict of the primaries and formulating the platforms of the parties." Wilson further suggested that the conventions should consist not of delegates chosen for this single purpose but "of the nominees for Congress, the nominees for vacant seats in the Senate of the United States, the Senators whose terms have not yet closed, the national committees, and the candidates for the Presidency themselves, in order that platforms may be framed by those responsible to the people for carrying them into effect."

This singularly imaginative proposal was too late, or perhaps too early. After TR's frustration in 1912, the primary movement began to lose its first momentum. Though 26 states had presidential primary laws in 1916, eight had repealed their laws by 1935. Only one state — Alabama — was added to the list between 1920 and 1949. Candidates, in the main, ignored the primary. In 1928, for example, Herbert Hoover and Alfred E. Smith allowed their supporters to enter their names in a few states but did not take primaries seriously enough to enter the states themselves (though by this time, once they had the nominations, they were prepared to stump in the general election). Franklin Roosevelt followed their example in 1932.

6.

If the two-party system was measurably less effective in the early twentieth than it had been in the nineteenth century, it had nevertheless by 1930 beaten back the presidential primary, and the mode of presidential choice remained much as it had been three quarters of a century earlier. The composition of the parties, however, was once again in flux. The urban coalition of business and labor put together by McKinley and Mark Hanna in 1896 began to fall apart when the Republican party, after disgorging Theodore Roosevelt in 1912, concentrated thereafter on ministering to the whims of the business community.

The character of the post-TR Republican policies gave Democrats their chance to split off the working class in the Republican urban strongholds, a tendency intimated by Wilson in 1916, greatly advanced by Smith in 1928 and, as the business cult collapsed into the rubble of the great depression, triumphantly concluded by Franklin Roosevelt in the 1930's.

The result was a new majority coalition, now based on classes rather than on sections. The Roosevelt era brought about a distinct resurgence in voter turnout, if not to the levels of the late nineteenth century. And the ferment stirred by the New Deal led in time to an apparent revitalization of the two-party system. This development, made possible by the commitment of the Democratic party to a militant civil rights program, nationalized political competition and, by the 1970's, practically abolished one-party states. Yet it remained unclear whether this apparent revitalization represented a genuine resurgence of the two-party system or only the hectic flush before a final illness. For a number of developments in the years since the New Deal had deprived the parties of many of their functions and threatened to weaken the very bases of the traditional political order. Indeed, if the 1870's could be said to have seen the maturation of the two-party system, the 1970's might well be the period of the crisis of that system.

An enumeration of lost functions will suggest the contemporary dilemma of the parties. We have already seen how the parties had receded as instruments of voter mobilization. The waning of immigration ended the Ellis Island role as an agency of acculturation. The advent of the welfare state finished the party as the patron of the unemployed, sick and old. The city boss was in many respects a casualty of the New Deal. In that classic novel of urban politics, Edwin O'Connor's *The Last Hurrah,* a character observes that it was Franklin Roosevelt who

> destroyed the old-time boss. He destroyed him by taking away his source of power.... The old boss was strong simply because he held all the cards. If anybody wanted anything—jobs, favors, cash—he could only go to the boss, the local leader. A few little things like Social Security, Unemployment Insurance, and the like—that's what shifted the gears, sport. No need now to depend on the boss for everything: the Federal Government was getting into the act. Otherwise known as a social revolution.

The more intelligent or younger bosses, sensing the drift of things, tapered off their old ties with businessmen and crooks and came to terms with the social revolution. But their status was diminished. They were no longer delivering the goods themselves; they were only claiming a free ride on a government process which delivered the goods in their stead. By the 1970's, the remaining city bosses — Mayor Richard Daley of Chicago was perhaps the last of the Mohicans — were anachronisms.

On the larger stage, the professional politicians began to lose control of vital parts of the political machinery. To this the abolition in 1936 of the two-thirds rule in the Democratic convention and, more especially, the revival of the presidential primary made important contributions. For thirty years after 1912 the primary had been a negligible factor in the presidential calculus. Then Wendell Willkie, who had won the Republican nomination in 1940 without entering a single primary, lost it in 1944 by running last in the primary in Wisconsin. This proved at least the veto power of the primary. Four years later Harold Stassen, beginning his perennial quest for the Republican nomination, demonstrated that the primary could become an effective recourse for candidates who lacked organization support; and Thomas E. Dewey was able to secure renomination only by showing he could beat Stassen in Oregon. Though neither Robert A. Taft, a Republican, nor Estes Kefauver, a Democrat, won nomination in 1952, the consequence of their impassioned primary efforts was to reawaken public interest in the primary system. New laws were passed. New states joined the primary rolls.

At the same time, changes in the means of communication, and especially the spread of television in the 1950's, reinforced this process. Television, for example, made the viewer an intimate and daily participant in primary contests. It fostered the expectation that candidates for the presidential nominations would be familiar faces, not distant 'favorite sons' or unknown 'dark horses'; otherwise the presidential choice would appear to have been conjured up by bosses out of smoke-filled rooms. By 1956 it seemed that only a sitting President, or his personally chosen candidate, could escape the primary test. Adlai Stevenson that year, John F. Kennedy in 1960, Barry Goldwater in 1964, Richard Nixon in 1968 — all settled the nomination in the primaries and, in effect, presented *faits accomplis* to the conventions. Not after 1952 did a convention require more than a single ballot to choose its candidate. And the probability of humiliating defeat in the Wisconsin primary in 1968 was unquestionably a major factor in Lyndon B. Johnson's decision to bow out of the presidential contest that year. By 1971 so many new states were rushing to join the primary parade that, to some observers, it seemed inevitable that the nation would have a *de facto* national primary system without knowing it. Sixty years later, the conditions were becoming ripe to enact Wilson's vision of 1913.

The impact of television on the nominating process was only part of the deeper impact of the new electronic world on politics. Together television, the public opinion poll and the computer began to devastate the traditional political structure. For a century a cluster of institutions — the political machine, the farm organization, the trade union, the ethnic federation, the trade association, the chamber of commerce — had mediated between the politician and the voter, interceding for each on behalf of the other and providing the links that held the party system together. The electronic age was severing these links. Television presented the politician directly to the voter; public opinion polls presented the voter directly to the politicians. The political brokers began to lose their jobs, and the mediating agencies, in so far as they had political functions, were confronted by obsolescence.

The parties, cut loose from old moorings, sailed vaguely on in uncharted waters. Reform movements arose to rescue them and, in trying to do so, further diminished the power of the professionals. Thus the reconstruction of the nominating process, carried out for the Democrats by the McGovern Commission after the disastrous Chicago convention of 1968, increased citizen participation in the party but at the expense of the permanent party structure. The effort in 1970 and thereafter to abolish that vestigial survival, the electoral college, and choose the President by direct popular vote threatened further to enfeeble state organizations.

In short, the political process the professionals once thought they owned had turned in their hands into a set of ceremonies. What had happened to the electoral college in 1800 now appeared to be happening to the national convention: it was increasingly a forum, not for decision, but for ratification. Political competition in the future, as James David Barber remarked, would revolve increasingly around access to the electronic media. And, if advertising agencies did not quite practice the black arts their own mythology assigned to them, still American politics was entering a time when election specialists, hired out as mercenaries, would play a larger role in mobilizing the voters.

7.

The functional depletion of party organization was accompanied by changes in the character of the electorate. The fastest-growing group in American society was the one defined by the Bureau of Labor Statistics as "professional, technical and kindred workers." In 1900 that group constituted 4 per cent of the labor force and as late as 1940 less than 8 per cent. By 1970 it was more than 12 per cent, and it was continuing to increase at more than twice the average for other fields of employment. If one added to this group those defined as "managers" and "officials" in the BLS category of "managers, officials and proprietors, excluding farm," the cumulative figure approached 20 per cent of the labor force.

This group, moreover, had a political zeal and sophistication which gave it influence far exceeding its numbers. Its members were predominantly college-educated — and by the middle seventies, according to current estimates, more than 40 per cent of the electorate would have gone to college. They lived predominantly in the suburbs — and, as the 1920 census showed that the cities outnumbered the countryside, the 1970 census showed that the suburbs now outnumbered the cities. If this professional-technical-managerial class were by no means unified in its views or values, its unprecedentedly high level of education and aspiration generated both an informed interest in issues and a formidable commitment to public affairs — and this at just the time that, as a consequence of the electronic revolution, the old politics of the mediating institutions was giving way to the new politics of instantaneous mass involvement.

The politicians, having lost their protective mantle of mediating agencies, now began to stand eyeball-to-eyeball with a diffuse, frustrated and aggressive public opinion. The United States in the 1970's would never (at least since the 1790's) have so large a proportion of well-informed, independent, discriminating and, to use the jargon, 'issue-oriented' voters, or so many determined to influence the course of history. In his great work on *Public Opinion* half a century ago, Walter Lippmann had written that the power of opinion was "for all practical purposes the power to say yes and no." As Samuel Lubell emphasized, that had now drastically changed. People

> are unwilling to be limited to "yes" or "no"; nor are they content to channel all their interests and emotions through the parties. Instead there has developed a sharp struggle for political visibility—by the voters to make themselves seen and felt, and by presidents and other managers of society to control or shape what should become visible.

The general competition for visibility was probably set off by the success of the black revolution. The civil-rights movement stimulated a host of spinoffs and imitations, organizing women, students, Indians, Mexican Americans, Italian Americans, convicts, homosexuals in their own crusades of self-assertion. Even when the self-asserters stayed within the two-party system, they operated through citizens' and volunteers' associations, which they formed with rapidity and skill, if sometimes with limited attention span; these, along with the mercenary specialists, were displacing the party organization as sources of publicity and manpower. Increasingly they regarded the old party system with automatic mistrust, rallied to candidates who inveighed against it, voted split tickets or for minor parties and otherwise drove the old politics even more against the wall.

Compounding the crisis of the two-party system was the evolution in the substance of political issues. Psephologists, in their preoccupation with quantity and structure, have tended to underrate the impact on politics of the policy choices forced upon the state. Yet such choices, as we have seen in the case of slavery in the 1850's and social justice in the 1930's, remain in the end the most powerful determinants of political development. A number of changes had taken place in the substance of political questions since the last great creative period in national policy during the 1930's, and the two-party system of the sixties and seventies showed few signs of a capacity to absorb and digest these new issues.

One such issue was the growing sense of the incipient fragmentation of the social order. A series of tensions had begun to strain the national fabric: tensions between young and old, between poor and rich, between black and white, between educated and uneducated. "Of all dangers to a nation," Walt Whitman had once written, ". . . there can be no greater one than having certain portions of the people set off from the rest by a line drawn — they not privileged as others, but degraded, humiliated, made of no account." The urgent task of contemporary American politics — the task identified especially with John and Robert Kennedy and neglected since their murders — was to give the alienated groups a feeling of membership in the national process. The alienated groups consisted of two sorts — the estranged and the excluded. The estranged were those who in the past had formed part of the national community — the intellectuals, the young, the lower-middle-class whites, for example — and were disaffected on recent and particular grounds: the intellectuals and the young because of the Vietnam war; the lower-middle-class whites because of student violence and the black revolution. The excluded were those — the structurally poor, the blacks, the Indians, the Chicanos, the Puerto Ricans — who had never been full members of the nation. The domestic imperative of the seventies was to bring these groups into the national community.

For this mission, the two-party system had thus far been inadequate. The rise of such anti-system movements as the George Wallace party of 1968 and the black nationalist organizations might well foreshadow, as other third parties had in the past, the recombinations which usher in a new political era. In addition, the problems of government in the high-technology society were becoming, or at least were appearing, increasingly technical in nature and therefore inaccessible to traditional party policies or solutions. And world affairs, for the first time since the 1790's, were a continuous and sometimes decisive issue in domestic policy; and this too consistently eluded the two-party system because of the power inexorably exercised, regardless of the party in office, by the foreign policy and military establishments.

The experience of a century and a half had left the popular impression that the two-party system was ordained by Providence for Americans to elect their Presidents. Yet it was by no means clear that this system was permanent and irrevocable. A process formed in the relatively simple America of the 1830's might not necessarily meet all the needs of the diversified and explosive America of the 1970's. Much evidence confirmed the view that the two-party system, if not in decay, was at least in crisis. Party lines and loyalties had never been so fluid. Political disaffiliation was high, especially among the young, who would, after all, be the voters of the future. The electronic world had sapped much of the vitality of the traditional political structures. The "tumult and disorder," the "extraordinary and violent movements," feared long ago by Hamilton now seemed an inseparable part of the public process. Tocqueville's river, instead of sinking back to its usual level after the electoral storm, seemed ever more likely to overflow its banks.

Presidential elections remained the moments of truth when the electorate had its chance to affirm or alter the direction of national policy. But, for the two-party system to work, it had to present effective choices; the outcome had to make a difference; no vital group could feel unrepresented in the party duel. It has been a while since the two choices quadrennially presented to the people held out much hope of satisfying, or even containing, the energies of national frustration, rancor and despair. Only the most extraordinary leadership, it appeared, was likely to save the two-party system in its present form. Should such leadership not emerge, the United States could anticipate, at the least, extensive upheaval and realignment within the existing parties and, quite possibly, the multiplication of parties in response to the urgent diversity of public interests and concerns. Would the nation see the crystallization perhaps of a three- or four-party system, as portended, for example, by the possible abolition of the electoral college as 'politics without parties'? Could there even be a gradual evaporation of parties in their traditional sense and by proposals for public financing of presidential elections, whether by income tax check-off or other means? The age of experimentation in political structure might well have come again.

"Before my term is over," John F. Kennedy said in 1961, "we shall have to test anew whether a nation organized and governed such as ours can endure. The outcome is by no means certain." The outcome seemed even less certain a decade later.

THE COMING TO POWER
Critical Presidential Elections in
American History

Elections of 1789 and 1792

by *Marcus Cunliffe*

The nature of the presidential office proved to be the most recalcitrant of all the issues that confronted the delegates at the Philadelphia convention in 1787. There were, James Madison reported to Thomas Jefferson, "tedious and reiterated discussions" on whether the executive should "consist of a single person, or a plurality of co-ordinate members, on the mode of appointment, on the duration in office, on the degree of power," and on whether the President should be eligible for reelection. True, a majority of the delegates fairly soon reached agreement on the need for a single executive. But the other problems concerning the office were more intractable. Within the whole tangle, as Madison later recollected, a key difficulty was that "of finding an unexceptionable process for appointing the Executive Organ of a Government such as that of the United States . . . ; and as the final arrangement of it took place in the latter stage of the Session, it was not exempt from a degree of the hurrying influence produced by fatigue and impatience in all such bodies."

The Philadelphia convention began on May 25, 1787. Within a week the delegates had declared themselves in favor of a single "Executive Magistracy" who was to be elected by the national legislature for a term of seven years and then to be "ineligible a second time." By July 26, having so far consumed the greater part of eight days in discussing the election and term of office of the President, the delegates were still on record (by the votes of seven states to three) as supporting the original broad method proposed in Edmund Ran-

3

dolph's resolution of May 29. Such harmony was, however, far more apparent than real; it signified that, for the moment, they could see no ideal solution to the complexities which they had explored.

Randolph's "Virginia plan" seemed to provide the only workable means of election. In 1787 only a few states, including Massachusetts, New Hampshire, and New York, relied upon the popular election of their governors. Arguing the point on July 17, Roger Sherman of Connecticut thought that "the sense of the Nation would be better expressed by the Legislature, than by the people at large. The latter will never be sufficiently informed of characters, and besides will never give a majority of votes to any one man. They will generally vote for some man in their own State, and the largest State will have the best chance for the appointment." In the same debate, George Mason of Virginia concurred: "It would be as unnatural to refer the choice of a proper character for chief Magistrate to the people, as it would, to refer a trial of colours to a blind man. The extent of the Country renders it impossible that the people can have the requisite capacity to judge of the respective pretensions of the Candidates." Charles Pinckney of South Carolina and Hugh Williamson of North Carolina were of the same opinion. Then and subsequently, certain delegates (Madison and Gouverneur Morris of Pennsylvania among them) preferred the idea of popular election. But they could not disguise their uneasiness at the prospect of an election on so diffuse a scale; their recommendation was not so much out of enthusiasm for the principle of popular suffrage, but rather out of resistance to other principles for which they felt still less enthusiasm.

Nor did alternative proposals immediately commend themselves. Elbridge Gerry of Massachusetts, for example, made no headway on June 9 with a resolution "that the National Executive should be elected by the Executives of the States whose proportion of votes should be the same with that allowed to the States in the election of the Senate." Replying to Gerry, Edmund Randolph of Virginia maintained that in such a method the big states would secure the appointment; that even so, bad appointments would result, "the Executives of the States being little conversant with characters not within their own small spheres"; that a President selected under state auspices would be unlikely to defend the national interest against state encroachments; and that state governors would not willingly support a national executive — "They will not cherish the great Oak which is to reduce them to paltry shrubs."

John Dickinson of Delaware found equally little support for a suggestion (July 25) that the people of each state should nominate a "best citizen. . . . [They] will know the most eminent characters of their own States, and the people of different States will feel an emulation in selecting those of which they will have the greatest reason to be proud—Out of the thirteen names thus selected, an Executive Magistrate may be chosen," either through the national legislature, or electors appointed by it. More attention was paid to sundry proposals for electors chosen by state legislatures. But these and other expedients failed to unite a convinced majority of delegates. "There are objections," said Madison (July 25), "against every mode that has been, or perhaps can be proposed." His fellow-Virginian, Colonel Mason, wearily echoed the observation (July 26): "In every Stage of the Question relative to the Executive, the difficulty of the subject and the diversity of the opinions concerning it have appeared. Nor have any of the modes of constituting that department been satisfactory."

At this phase of the convention, on the eve of a ten-day recess, the delegates revealed a sort of fatigued dullness—the dullness that comes when men feel that they have explored every possible alternative and are dissatisfied with all. To some extent, also, they seemed to have become the prisoners of the initial formulation: election by the national legislature for a single seven-year term. Every time the executive came up for discussion this basic premise was reiterated and voted on. One reason for the frustrating sense of impasse, as J. R. Pole explains, was that "the delegates wanted the new head of state to have some of the attributes of a prime minister but some of the attributes of a king; and they allowed themselves to be confused by their own terminology." British precedent both impressed and alarmed them. They did not fully understand the respective, and changing, roles of the Crown and the chief minister in the British system—in part because of their own sensitivity to the charge that they might, deliberately or otherwise, saddle the United States with a monarchy or an aristocracy, or both. They were groping for a means of establishing an executive element that was to be much more than a formal head of state.

Gradually, and thanks largely to the lucid interventions of James Madison, the logic of their wishes disclosed itself. One of Madison's most persuasive speeches was delivered on July 25. The President, he said, must be elected either by some existing authority under the national or state constitutions, or by some special authority derived from or directly exerted by the people of the United States. Under the national constitution the two existing authorities would be the legislature and the judiciary. The judiciary was clearly unsuitable. As for the legislature, Madison continued, summarizing views already expressed in the convention and adding some of his own, it too was an unsuitable agency. A major objection was that the election would seriously "agitate & divide the legislature." The effect upon a presidential candidate would be equally undesirable. He would "intrigue with" the legislators, would owe his appointment to "the predominant faction," and would be "apt to render his administration subservient" to the controlling faction. Moreover, as the cases of the Holy Roman Emperor and the elective Polish monarchy showed, such a claustrophobic method of election would encourage foreign powers to meddle: "No pains, nor perhaps expence, will be spared, to gain from the Legislature an [appointment] favourable to their wishes."

If appointment within the national sphere would be unsatisfactory, what of the state level? Neither governors nor the judiciary would be desirable. As for state legislatures, they were unreliable bodies with a propensity for "pernicious measures." One of the purposes of a national legislature was to offset this. And one of the objects of creating a national executive was to control the national legislature (through the veto power), "so far as it might be infected with a similar propensity." But such a check would be impossible if the executive were chosen by a legislative body, at whatever level.

There remained accordingly the mode of popular election, either "immediately" or by means of electors popularly chosen. Madison himself preferred the notion of a mass popular vote, though he admitted that there were snags — notably "the disposition in the people to prefer a Citizen of their own State," which would confer an advantage on the larger states. He was also responsive to the idea of selection by specially chosen electors. But he admitted that the device, having already been rejected by the convention, would probably not win approval.

On this occasion Madison's reasoning did not prevail. But he stimulated a fruitful discussion. Here was one of the days when instead of negating and perplexing each other the delegates seemed collectively to think their way forward. Some, it is true, reverted to the stale issue of whether ineligibility for reelection would be an adequate safeguard against undue legislative influence upon the President, or whether that would not excessively hamper the executive freedom of maneuver. But other delegates were more alertly constructive. Williamson suggested that if popular election were sanctioned, the claims of candidates from the smaller states could be recognized by allowing every voter to choose three names. One of the three would probably be a man from his own state; the other two might well be drawn from other states. Gouverneur Morris liked the idea, suggesting as an amendment that "each man should vote for two persons one of whom at least should not be of his own State." Madison also warmed to the amended suggestion. A plethora of favorite sons would be likely to yield the election to some universally admired second choice. There was the risk that each citizen might throw away his second vote on some obscure figure, in order to improve the chances of his favorite candidate. "But it could hardly be supposed," said Madison, "that the Citizens of many States would be so sanguine of having their favorite elected, as not to give their second vote with sincerity to the next object of their choice."

The decisive advance was still some way off. On August 24, when the delegates again scrutinized the executive provisions of their draft constitution, they were still committed to election through Congress (as it was to be called). They wrangled over the question of whether the President was to be chosen by one or both houses of Congress. Faced with the prospect of an interminable task, and increasingly restive, they agreed however to place all such unfinished business in the hands of a committee made up of one delegate from each state.

Now the leaven worked. The committee comprised some of the ablest members of the Philadelphia convention, and some of those most firmly persuaded of the need for a strong executive. On September 4 they introduced a set of proposals in almost the form with which we are familiar. They had concluded that the principle of a separation of powers made it impossible to elect the executive entirely in the legislature. Once this was affirmed, there was likewise no overriding need to limit the executive to a single term, since the

President would be immune to excessive congressional influence. Nor need his term of office be lengthy if he could be reelected: four years would be preferable to seven. The method of election recommended, in line with some of the previous suggestions of delegates, was via a body of presidential electors, to be chosen as each state legislature determined. The number of electors would equal the number of federal senators and representatives to which each state would be entitled. The electors would meet in their respective states (not in one central place, which might have exposed them to corruption, and which would have been a laborious and expensive procedure). They would vote for two persons, "one of whom at least shall not be an inhabitant of the same State with themselves." Their votes would be transmitted to the presiding officer of the Senate, under whose chairmanship the Senate—balloting among themselves if there were no clear majority—would decide the outcome. The person coming second in number of votes should become Vice-President, and would then act as President of the Senate.

An intricate debate followed, and continued next morning (September 5). "The greater part of the day," noted James McHenry of Maryland, whose appetite for constitution-making had become sated, was "spent in desultory conversation on that part of the report respecting the mode of chusing the President—adjourned without coming to a conclusion." He was too despondent. The delegates were very near to completing their task. Except for the few who were uneasy over the whole tenor of the convention, opposition to the committee's proposals focused mainly on the prominence given to the Senate. By September 6 the draft had been amended to meet the chief objections.

In the event of a tie, or the absence of a clear majority of votes, the House of Representatives (one vote per state) was to choose a President by ballot. At last the convention had a formula commanding the assent if not the enthusiasm of the majority of delegates. They probably assumed that the election would nearly always be determined in Congress; this had certainly been their contention when the plan was to let the Senate be the arbiters. Still, they had hit upon a pattern that would in theory allow the voice of the people to be heard. If all went well, the principal persons nominated ("candidates" is perhaps the wrong word) would be worthy characters, hopefully of nationwide repute; they would not have been picked by any small conclave or cabal; and Congress would thus be obliged to make its choice from among citizens chosen by the citizenry.

An additional comment should be made on the invention of the Vice-Presidency, an office not mentioned in the Philadelphia proceedings until the committee report of September 4. It had previously been implied that the President would also act as President of the Senate, hardly an acceptable provision if the separation of powers was to be observed. Yet this was not the main reason for creating a Vice-President; indeed Elbridge Gerry and George Mason were among those who complained that "the office of vice-President [was] an encroachment on the rights of the Senate; . . . it mixed too much the Legislative & Executive, which . . . ought to be kept as separate as possible." Roger Sherman of Connecticut defended the innovation by remarking that if the Vice-President were not to preside over the Senate he would have nothing to do; and—an argument with a shade more force—that if some senator were to preside, he would automatically be deprived of his voting rights: a deprivation that would as a result halve the voting strength of one state. The chief rationale for the Vice-Presidency was mentioned by Hugh Williamson, who thought it a superfluous office: it was "introduced only for the sake of a valuable mode of election which required two to be chosen at the same time." He was more or less correct. The genesis of the office appears to lie in Williamson's own proposal of July 25, as amended by Gouverneur Morris. They hoped to avoid jealousies between the states, and a sense of impotence among the smaller ones, by permitting more than one vote for the Presidency. Once the idea was implanted, duties could readily be found for the man who was runner-up; and there were equivalent figures (lieutenant-governors and the like) in the organization of state governments. At any rate the Vice-Presidency was established, belatedly, consequentially, and somewhat perfunctorily. Yet the comments of Madison and others on the niceties of plural voting indicated that American politicians would be quick to master the tactics appropriate to a dual vote.

Both at Philadelphia and in the ensuing months, Americans of every viewpoint seem to have assumed that there was only one man who could and would inaugurate the presidential office: General Washington. When the convention first broached the idea of a single executive on June 1, there was a "considerable pause" before the debate got under way. Among the reasons for this hesitation was no doubt a certain embarrassment at discussing the proposal in the presence of the presiding officer: George Washington. Three days later, on June 4, Pennsylvania's venerable delegate Benjamin Franklin offered some gloomy predictions as to the eventual aggrandizement of the executive branch. He conceded however that "the first man, put at the helm will be a good one." Such observations crop up again and again in private correspondence, in pamphlets and in the newspapers. The Philadelphian Dr. Benjamin Rush, not present at the convention but alert to catch stray rumors that filtered through its closed doors, was enthusiastic over the prospects. "The new federal government," he told Timothy Pickering on August 30, "like a new Continental waggon will overset our state dung cart . . . and thereby restore order and happiness to Pennsylvania. . . . General Washington it is said will be placed at the head of the new Government, or in the stile of my simile, will drive the new waggon." An unidentified correspondent, writing to Thomas Jefferson on October 11, 1787, also from Philadelphia, in the same general spirit as Rush, explained the reasons why the Constitution would and ought to be ratified. Thus, Washington was still vigorously alive, and "as he will be appointed President, jealousy on this head vanishes." The General's associates were writing to him in the same strain. David Humphreys, a Connecticut soldier-diplomat, and one of the General's most devoted admirers, wrote, "What will tend, perhaps, more than anything to the adoption of the new system will be an universal opinion of your being elected President of the United States and an expectation that you will accept it for a while." Washington's wartime friend Lafayette chimed in from Paris, "You cannot refuse being elected President."

Even those with deep misgivings on the "new system" concentrated their criticism upon other features of the Constitution, or—like Franklin—upon the hazards that would befall America after Washington had gone. The Virginian Richard Henry Lee, a one-time president of the Continental Congress, was convinced that the Philadelphia document was fraught with danger. A reeligible President, he argued in January, 1788, "will have no permanent interest in the government to lose, by contests and convulsions in the state, but always much to gain, and frequently the seducing and flattering hope of succeeding. . . . [This] will be the case with nine tenths of the presidents; *we may have, for the first president*, and, perhaps, one in a century or two afterwards . . . *a great and good man, governed by superior motives*; but these are not events to be calculated upon in the present state of human nature." Pierce Butler, a former delegate, admitted in May, 1788, that the considerable powers entrusted to the executive would not have "been so great had not many of the members cast their eyes toward General Washington as President; and shaped their Ideas of the Powers to be given to a President, by their opinions of his Virtue."

The expectation that General Washington would become President Washington was voiced in the press within a few days of the adjournment of the convention. Newspapers favoring the Constitution, such as the important *Pennsylvania Packet*, repeatedly sang his praises. Washington, they assured their readers, would not have lent his name to the convention if its intentions had been dubious; and with him at the head the new government's success was beyond doubt. The Fourth of July celebrations in 1788 came at the climactic moment of the struggle over ratification. Though the news took some time to reach every corner of the Union, the necessary nine states (including Washington's Virginia) had already ratified. At many places the national holiday was seized upon as an occasion to pay tribute to the future President. Toasts and songs embroidered the sentiment—

— Farmer Washington—may he like a second Cincinnatus, be called from the plow to rule a great people

— May the Saviour of America gratify the ardent wishes of his countrymen by accepting that post which the voice of mankind has assigned him.

— Great Washington shall rule the land/While Franklin's counsel aids his hand.

Whatever the nation expected of him, or friends urged upon him, George Washington was far from reconciled to the apparently inevitable. Well-informed Americans were worried by what Jefferson called Washington's "vast reluctance," though like Jefferson they clung to the conviction that Washington "will undertake the presidency if called to it." Alexander Hamilton was only the most persistent of several correspondents in pressing the General to signify his willingness. They appealed to his pertinacity, his patriotism, his personal sense of duty, his standing with posterity, the parlous state of the country. Hamilton was particularly subtle in his reading of Washington's psychology; he never resorted to such overblown statements as that of the General's old friend John Armstrong, who seemed to feel that divine providence was in charge of the impending election.

George Washington's hesitations were understandable. Fifty-six years old in 1788, he felt that he had already given up some of the best years of his life to the service of his country. After eight and a half years as Commander-in-chief he had, at the end of 1783, resigned his commission with unfeigned relief. His own affairs, above all the management of his Mount Vernon estate, absorbed his energies — energies which he felt to be waning. Moreover, in quitting public service he had stressed the finality of his retirement. If he now came back at the head of affairs he could, he wrote Alexander Hamilton, be accused of "inconsistency and ambition." He well knew from the tenor of the Philadelphia convention, and from the abundant subsequent criticisms of the Constitution, that Americans were highly suspicious of the corrupting effect of high office.

As he frequently remarked, he dreaded the "new fatigues and troubles" of undertaking an immense new responsibility for which he did not think himself properly equipped. Soldiering had been onerous enough; the entire weight of executive responsibility would be almost unendurable.

One aspect of his uneasiness was thus a matter of propriety. Even if he were firmly to decide that he was ready to stand, he could see no acceptable way of making this known without seeming presumptuous. Certainly he could not declare himself, or do more than make plain his support for the new Constitution as a whole, while its ratification remained uncertain: that would be to anticipate events to an unthinkable degree. And in the second half of 1788, when ratification had been assured (at least by eleven of the thirteen states: North Carolina and Rhode Island still held aloof), the delicacy of his position continued to preoccupy him. It was surely not his task to inform the nation that he would agree to be President, before or even after the meetings of the presidential electors in the various states. He may well have reflected that it would be egotistical even to announce in advance that he would *not* serve; for that would be to indicate that he saw himself as a likely occupant of the office. Other men might not have shown so much punctilio in his shoes. But from 1787 to 1789 no other men were remotely close to standing in his shoes; Washington's situation was unique, and therefore — for him — uniquely painful. He was neither running for office nor able to run away from it.

A second cause for uneasiness shaded from the first. Almost nine months elapsed between the close of the Philadelphia convention and the knowledge that the Constitution had passed muster, in some instances by a narrow majority in state ratifying conventions. Prominent citizens in his own state — George Mason, Edmund Randolph, Patrick Henry — were outspoken in criticism of the new instrument of government. Nine more months were to elapse before the results of the first presidential election would be formally announced, though they had been unofficially bruited about several weeks earlier. In this long, dragging period the extent of opposition was a source of increasing dismay to Washington. He confided to Hamilton that he found some consolation in the faint hope that "the Electors, by giving their votes in favor of some other person, would save me from the dreaded Dilemma of being forced to accept or refuse." It had become objectively apparent that Washington was the only person being spoken of for the Presidency. But the actual operation of the Electoral College was conjectural. No one could accurately predict whom the electors would be; they were not even to be chosen, so dilatory were the workings of the old moribund Congress, until the first Wednesday in January, 1789. Washington's anxiety shifted to the possibility that his consolation might instead prove a form of humiliation. In the same letter, he went on to ask:

> If the friends to the Constitution conceive that my administering the government will be a means of its acceleration and strength, is it not probable that the adversaries of it may entertain the same ideas? and of course make it an object of opposition? That many of this description will become Electors, I can have no doubt of . . . . It might be impolite in them to make this declaration *previous* to the Election, but I shall be out in my conjectures if they do not act conformably thereto—and from that the seeming moderation by which they appear to be actuated at present is . . . a finesse to lull and deceive. Their plan of opposition is systemised, and a regular intercourse, I have much reason to believe between the Leaders of it in the several States is formed to render it more effectual.

Such a development would obviously be humiliating if it led to a spread of votes in which some other man was preferred to Washington. That however was most unlikely, unless by some fluke distribution of electoral preferences; the only American who could be ranked with George Washington in universal esteem was Benjamin Franklin, but Franklin was eighty years old and in failing health. One gains the impression that, for Washington, any semblance of a contest between him and some other man or men would be extremely disagreeable. He did not want to be President. Yet if he must be President, he wanted to be chosen *nem.con.* In other words, he could not seriously have supposed that someone else would get more votes than he. What perturbed him was the possibility of any sort of competition. A challenge of that kind would stigmatize his good name, and indicate alarming dissensions within the country.

Washington's perplexity was aggravated by the sluggishness of the newly-elected Congress. The twenty-two senators and fifty-nine members of the House converged on New York (the temporary seat of the Federal Government) with agonizing slowness. The presidential electors duly met on the first Wednesday in February, 1789, and the presidential inauguration had been set for March 4. But the electoral votes could not be counted until there was a quorum of both houses. By March 4 only eight senators and eighteen representatives had shown up; and the last laggard legislator required to make the necessary quorum did not arrive in New York until April 5. Washington was still parrying the congratulations and importunings that each post delivered to Mount Vernon. In effect he had consented to stand, and to become President. He must have been cheered to learn that "Federalists" (i.e., men ready to defend the Constitution) had secured a commanding position in the elections for the Senate, and a sizeable share of the House of Representatives. But one of the few clues to his own acquiescence in the apparently inevitable came when his followers consulted him on a suitable person for the Vice-Presidency. His answer could be interpreted as a definite though hardly enthusiastic commitment on his own part. Washington intimated that any "true Foederalist" capable of commanding the votes of true American would not be "disagreeable" to him. Whoever the hypothetical person might be, "I would most certainly treat him with perfect sincerity and the greatest candor in every respect. I would give him my full confidence and use my utmost endeavors to cooperate with him, in promoting . . . the national prosperity; this should be my great, my only aim."

An assurance in a private letter was about the nearest that Washington came to a declaration of his readiness to serve if elected. Candidates in future presidential elections would make gestures toward the Washington style of stately, reluctant immobility. But never would a hat float so spectrally into the ring. Nor would any future putative President add, as Washington did in the same letter, his "fixed and irrevocable resolution of leaving to other hands the helm of the State, as soon as my services could possibly with propriety be dispensed with." He would serve, that is true; but he would not bind himself for a full term if a chance of escape came his way.

Since none of the Anti-Federalists made any move to deny the Presidency to General Washington, partisan calculations were confined to the Vice-Presidency. Even at this rudimentary stage of presidential electioneering, both sides were swift to see the utility of uniting around one name instead of allowing the scatter of choices envisaged by the Philadelphia delegates. (Perhaps this quick development owes as much to the primacy of Washington as to controversy over the Constitution and the means by which it had been introduced. If more than one man had appeared outstandingly qualified for the Presidency, it is at any rate conceivable that the electors, and politically active Americans, would not have drawn any sharp distinction between the two people whom they desired to see in executive office.) With Washington as the universal nominee for the first office, the situation of the second office engrossed attention.

Among the leading Federalists, the initial problem was to agree upon a suitable associate for General Washington. To name another Virginian would be to lose the 10 votes of the Virginia electors, who would be debarred from giving both their sets of votes to men of their own state. But in any case sectional strategy dictated the choice of a Northerner, presumably from the powerful state of Massachusetts (which also had ten electors), since the comparably powerful states of New York and Pennsylvania had no one of outstanding eligibility.

Massachusetts possessed an ample share of prominent citizens. Among those who had become associated with Washington during the Revolutionary War were Henry Knox and Benjamin Lincoln. Hamilton referred to both, though somewhat incidentally, in canvassing opinion.

Another man with a national reputation, Samuel Adams, was ruled out because of his brusque temperament and his supposed antagonism to the Constitution. He had remarked, on the occasion of the Massachusetts ratifying convention: "As I enter the building I stumble on the threshold. I meet with a National Government, instead of a Federal Union of Sovereign States." A more plausible candidate, certainly in his own eyes, was Governor John Hancock, who had appropriated much of the credit for his state's ratification. Hamilton seems to have been prepared at one point to back him. At length, though, Hamilton and his cronies concluded that John Adams was their best bet.

Adams had a long record of public service—a delegate to the First and Second Continental Congresses (1774–78), Commissioner to France (1778), delegate to the Massachusetts Constitutional Convention (1780); and under Franklin and Jay, a negotiator of the Paris Peace Pact (1783)—and a considerable if slightly equivocal reputation as a political theorist. The first volume of his *Defence of the Constitutions of the United States of America*, written while he was American minister in London, appeared just in time to be consulted by the Philadelphia convention. Returning home in 1788, Adams, now fifty-three years old, soon made it clear, in spurning an offer of election to the Senate, that he wished for either a high office or none at all. He had not displayed ecstatic admiration for the new Federal Constitution, and he could never be said to possess a lovable disposition. But his assets far outweighed his disadvantages.

Several scholars feel that Adams was the victim of complex machinations on the part of Hamilton. There is no doubt that Hamilton did express only a grudging readiness to recommend him, and that he did his best to reduce the vote for Adams. Replying to Theodore Sedgwick in October, 1788, Hamilton showed that he was not yet entirely willing to agree that Adams should be the man. He mentioned theories that Adams was "unfriendly in his sentiments to General Washington," and might form an alliance with the Virginia Lees that would greatly embarrass a Federalist executive.

Once the selection had narrowed to Adams, within the Hamiltonian circle, Hamilton worked busily to ensure that Adams would poll appreciably fewer votes than Washington. The reason he gave was "that defect in the constitution which renders it possible that the man intended for Vice-President may in fact turn up President." The probability, he said, was that Washington would be a unanimous choice. But so might Adams. Either through accident or "Anti-Foederal malignity," the transfer of a handful of votes could place Adams in the Chief Magistracy. It was therefore advisable to "throw away a few votes," say 7 or 8, that would have gone to Adams, and distribute them among "persons not otherwise thought of." Hamilton instructed at least two people along these lines—James Wilson of Pennsylvania and Jeremiah Wadsworth of Connecticut. The outcome was much as Hamilton had foreseen it. In later years Adams got wind of Hamilton's intervention, and complained bitterly of the "dark and insidious manner" in which Hamilton, "like the worm at the root of the peach," had intrigued against him.

Hamilton's inner motives can only be guessed at. There is no proof that he acted out of malice, though within a few years he and Adams were to become intensely suspicious of one another. Nor, on the scanty evidence, are we entitled to assert that his conduct was underhand, though it was certainly staged—as it had to be—under cover. In defense of Hamilton, one might note that he was not alone in doubting the suitability of John Adams. James Madison, at this juncture a staunch supporter of the Constitution, provided a similar estimate of vice-presidential candidates in October 1788:

> Hancock is weak, ambitious, a courtier of popularity, given to low intrigue, and lately reunited by a factious friendship with Samuel Adams. John Adams has made himself obnoxious to many, particularly in the southern states, by the political principles avowed in his book. Others, recollecting his cabal during the war against General Washington, knowing his extravagant self-importance, and considering his preference of an unprofitable dignity to some place of emolument . . . as a proof of his having an eye to the presidency, conclude that he would not be a very cordial second to the General, and that an impatient ambition might even intrigue for a premature advancement.

Such opinions suggest that Hamilton may merely have been voicing reservations shared by a number of Adams' contemporaries. It should also be added that Hamilton's own ambitions, while they included President-making, probably did not run to making himself President. In this respect he was not a rival to Adams. Madison's comments are a reminder of how deep were the distrusts of the day, and how sharp the memory remained of wartime "cabals." There is a further worry that may legitimately have concerned Hamilton, as it seemed to concern Madison. Washington's dream of an early retirement was presumably known to all of his associates. They may have indulged him in the idea that it might be feasible, in order to strengthen his resolve to submit to the electoral will. Suppose Washington, once in office, persisted in the idea? According to the somewhat hazy constitutional notions of succession held in 1788–1789, John Adams would then merely be acting President. But he might be difficult to dislodge. Madison's letter suggests that he contemplated the possibility; so perhaps did Hamilton. In a memorandum of May, 1792, describing a conversation with Washington concerning retirement from office, Madison noted that he had in 1788 "contemplated, & I believe, suggested" to the General "a voluntary retirement to private life as soon as the state of the Government would permit," in order to demonstrate the sincerity of previous announcements about remaining a private citizen.

On the matter of "losing" votes that would otherwise have gone to Adams, Hamilton's intentions may likewise not have been "dark and insidious," and the problem may have been anticipated by others. At Philadelphia, after all, Madison had speculated that in an undifferentiated two-vote system the second vote might be the winning one. Subsequent experiences revealed that Hamilton was quite correct in describing the two-vote mechanism as defective; the 12th Amendment recognized the fact. With so much at stake, and so much uncertain, there was a strong argument for making sure that Washington came first. If through mischance the General came second, the consequences might be appalling. Washington would clearly not consent to fill the role of Vice-President; whoever was installed as President would be regarded as an interloper, if not a usurper; and the new Federal Government might well collapse under the strain. It is perhaps significant that John Adams' son-in-law, William Stephens Smith, writing to Jefferson on February 15, 1789, showed no sign of believing that there had been any treachery: "It is Generally believed here [Boston] and in the middle states, that Mr. Adams will be the Vice President, he had the unanimous Vote of Massachusetts and New Hampshire and 5 out of 7 of the electors of Connecticut. That he had not the whole there, originated from an apprehension, that if the state of Virginia should not vote for General Washington that Mr. A. would be President, which would not be consistent with the wish of the country and could only arise from the finesse of antifoedral Electors with a view to produce confusion and embarrass the operations of the Constitution, against which many have set their faces, both in this and some of the other states."

While Hamilton and other Federalists were at work, the "Anti's" were equally though less masterfully preoccupied with their own exercises in electoral arithmetic. They too, accepting that General Washington would be President, wanted a northerner as Vice-President. The most conspicuous possibility was Governor George Clinton of New York, whose anti-Constitutional onslaught had gone down to a narrow defeat in the state ratifying convention. Like Governor Patrick Henry of Virginia, he talked of summoning a new national plenary convention to reopen the affair. "Mr. Henry," a Virginia correspondent told Madison in November, 1788, "is putting in agitation the name of Clinton for vice-president." The main activity on behalf of Clinton went on in New York and Virginia, with feelers put out to other areas. Early in the new year, St. John de Crèvecoeur, the author of *Letters from an American Farmer*, then in New York as French consul and in outlook a rather bewildered Federalist, reported to Jefferson: "'tis proposed in Virginia to Vote for Govr. Clinton as a President, some back Counties in Pensilvania Will unite as well as this State." Henry was one of Virginia's presidential electors, and in fact gave his second vote to Clinton, who also collected 2 other Virginia votes. But this meager total of 3 was all that Clinton garnered in the electoral college. His New York enemy Hamilton rightly discerned that Clinton's challenge was negligible. Clinton could nibble away a few votes in the South; a few more might have been forthcoming in New York, but a dispute over the method of selecting electors led to a failure to choose any, so that Clinton's own state had no say in the 1789 presidential election. Indeed, as Hamilton explained to Madison, Clinton's candidacy could actually benefit the federal cause: "if pains are taken the dangers of an Antifoederal vice President might itself be rendered the instrument of Union."

The New York electoral fiasco wrecked whatever hopes Clinton and his friends may have nourished. The "Federal-Republican" clubs they had founded and the circular letters they had sent counted for little at this juncture. Even with better fortune it is hard to see how the Anti-Federalism of 1788–1789 could have been organized into a coherent opposition. There was a real case against some aspects of the Constitution, mixed up with a miscellany of fears and grudges. In ratifying, six of the eleven states had submitted lists of proposed amendments, and two other states had withheld ratification. Clinton was presented as a plain, hearty Republican who inside the new government would speak for the dissatisfied. But as yet the situation supplied no leverage. The new government could not be attacked until it had been given a reasonable opportunity to display itself, and to honor the understanding that amendments would be incorporated in the Constitution. What could an Anti-Federalist Vice-President hope to accomplish, especially when he dare not, and had no reason to, impugn the good faith of the man destined to be President?

The first part of the process, the choosing of electors, passed off fairly smoothly in most of the states, though not without some excitements—not surprisingly, since at the same time elections for Congress were also under way. Only in New York was there a total fiasco. In part this reflected the Clintonian-Hamiltonian division, in part the weaknesses of a method involving a bicameral legislature, when the two houses were of two minds. For in New York, as in Connecticut, Delaware, Georgia, New Jersey, and South Carolina, presidential electors were to be chosen by the legislature. The Assembly, the lower house, was Clintonishly Anti-Federalist; the Senate, the upper house, was predominantly though not overwhelmingly Federalist in tone. The Assembly proposed a joint ballot, the Senate a concurrent one: in other words, an arguing match. The details are unimportant for our purposes; each house calculated that its own method might yield the desired results in the shape of a batch of faithful Federalist (or Anti-Federalist) electors. Since neither would agree to compromise, New York deprived itself of its presidential ballots—and, incidentally, also of its pair of senators during the first session of the new Congress.

A dispute of similar proportions threatened a similar outcome in New Hampshire. Here the nomination of electors was left to popular choice, but the actual appointment to the legislature. It had not been explained how the appointment should be determined. The lower house wanted a joint ballot; the upper house insisted on a veto power, on the same lines as its power to negate bills and resolutions emanating from the lower house. After prolonged contention the lower house gave way, under protest. New Hampshire ended up with five presumed Federalists for electors.

There was a certain electricity in the atmosphere of two other states, Pennsylvania and Maryland, where the choice of electors depended directly upon a popular vote. Citizens of those states feared or hoped, according to temperament, that there would be an Anti-Federalist majority. Two "tickets" were disclosed in Pennsylvania. That of Lancaster, representing the sentiment of eastern counties, listed ten men known to be staunch supporters of Washington and the Constitution. The Harrisburg ticket, representing the suspicions of the western counties, listed a phalanx of men who had resisted the ratification of the Constitution. The Lancasterians triumphed though: all 10 of the Pennsylvania electoral votes went to Federalists. In Maryland too there were rival tickets, addresses, accusations of fraud. A few electoral nominees in Baltimore, whose leanings were in doubt, issued cards declaring that if chosen they would cast their votes for Washington and Adams. The same thing was done in Philadelphia. As in Pennsylvania, Federalism—or at least Washingtonism—gained the victory.

There were some scuffles in Virginia, of the kind taken for granted on election day. Otherwise, the first Wednesday in January, 1789, went off tranquilly. No troubles were reported, for instance, in Massachusetts, where two electors were chosen at large, and the eight others were picked by the legislature from twenty-four names produced by the state's congressional districts. In the nation as a whole, sixty-nine electors were chosen: with New York the number would have been seventy-nine, and of course larger still if North Carolina and Rhode Island had come within the rubric.

The electors duly met a month later, cast their votes, and prepared to transmit the sealed figures to Congress as soon as there was an adequate Congress to count them. Their lips were less sealed. As we have seen, the verdict was accurately though unofficially tabulated long before the official announcement. The electors clearly did not feel that their ballots were secret, and indeed there was no reason why they should, except out of courtesy to Congress.

It goes without saying that none of the men who received an electoral vote had delivered himself of a manifesto, or of a promise as to how he would act if elected. General Washington had scrupulously declined to commit himself, not only to being a candidate but also to considering the claims of those who wrote to him about possible federal appointments. Naturally enough, though, those who labored in support of particular candidates allowed themselves to think that loyalty would not go unrewarded. Benjamin Rush, for example, was actuated by more than simple benevolence when he wrote to John Adams in January, 1789:

> You will perceive by the Philadelphia papers that your friends *here* have not been idle. You will I believe have every vote from this state, and pains have been taken to secure the same unanimity in your favor in several of the adjoining states. I assure you, sir, that friendship for you has had much less to do in this business . . . than a sincere desire to place a gentleman in the Vice-President's chair upon whose long-tried integrity, just principles in government, and firm opposition to popular arts and demagogues, such a dependence could be placed as shall secure us both from a convention and from alterations falsely and impudently called by some of our state governors *amendments*.

A month later, Rush had the embarrassment of accounting to Adams for something less than the "unanimity" of which he had boasted. Two of Pennsylvania's vice-presidential votes had gone to John Hancock, although Adams acquired the other 8. All of Delaware's 3 votes had been diverted from Adams to John Jay, and Maryland's 6 to Benjamin Harrison.

Rush turned the difficulty to advantage. The conduct of Delaware and Maryland in "throwing away their votes for a vice-president" was he suggested due in part to "a jealousy of the New England states, which has been revived . . . by their vote in favor of the meeting of the first Congress in

New York." Philadelphia was the true "headquarters of federalism." The set-back to Adams was thus explained—and linked with a broad hint that his friends had rallied to him in the belief that he would be their champion. "There is an expectation here," Rush asserted, "that your influence will be exerted immediately in favor of a motion to bring Congress to Philadelphia."

A foretaste of interest politics? But in 1789, so far as Adams was concerned, there was no deal. Pennsylvanians like Rush and William Maclay supported him in the hope that he would use his weight to bring the national capital to their state. Philadelphia did become the temporary capital, but this was a mere sop. They were soon disabused. Like a second Washington, apparently, Adams supposed that votes would accrue to him as of right; he would not bargain for them.

So came April 6, when the electoral votes were opened in Congress, in the presence of both houses. The result amazed few men, though it gratified George Washington and chagrined John Adams. Every one of the sixty-nine electors, even the disaffected Patrick Henry, had given a vote to Washington. While Adams had no serious rival, he had gathered only 34 votes (Henry's other vote, it will be recalled, went to Clinton).

STATE	WASHINGTON	ADAMS	JAY	HANCOCK	OTHERS
New Hampshire	5	5			
Massachusetts	10	10			
Connecticut	7	5			2
New Jersey	6	1	5		
Pennsylvania	10	8		2	
Delaware	3		3		
Maryland	6				6
Virginia	10	5	1	1	3
South Carolina	7			1	6
Georgia	5	—	–	–	5
	69	34	9	4	22

A few of the also-rans—Jay, Hancock, John Rutledge of South Carolina (who collected 6 of his state's 7 votes)—were men of some stature. Others such as John Milton and Edward Telfair, whose fellow-Georgians gave 2 votes and 1 vote respectively, were in no sense national figures. However the verdict was interpreted—and Adams thought his own treatment "scurvey . . . an indelible stain on our Country, Countrymen and Constitution"—it was clear that in 1788–1789 Washington was *hors de concours*, and that any who stood against him would be ignominiously placed *hors de combat*.

The final stroke of the electoral mechanism consisted of notifying Washington and Adams that they had been chosen. A messenger brought the summons to Adams on April 12, as he fidgeted in his Braintree home, his bags already packed. Charles Thomson, the elderly Secretary of Congress, had a more difficult journey to Mount Vernon, and did not therefore arrive with the news until April 14.

I have now, sir, to inform you that the proofs you have given of your patriotism and of your readiness to sacrifice domestic separation and private enjoyments to preserve the liberty and promote the happiness of your country did not permit the two Houses to harbour a doubt of your undertaking this great, this important office to which you are called not only by the unanimous vote of the electors, but by the voice of America, I have it therefore in command to accompany you to New York where the Senate and House of Representatives are convened for the dispatch of public business.

The formal notification, which old Thomson also delivered, while it was briefer and reminded the General that the support he commanded was that of "a free and enlightened people," was in the same mode of solemn compliment. The vocabulary of such addresses suggested that the first President had received an "election" almost more in the religious than in the political sense of the word.

Four years after his first qualms about undertaking the office of President, Washington found himself embroiled in the same cycle of painful uncertainties. The renewed demands upon him were to lead to the same conclusion: reelection by a unanimous vote for a second term, and reelection by a divided vote of Vice-President John Adams.

Much had, however, changed in the meantime; and the changes both increased and made more illusory Washington's desire to liberate himself from the shackles of responsibility. He celebrated his sixtieth birthday in February, 1792, and felt older than his years. He had survived serious illnesses in 1790 and 1791. He was, he complained, growing deaf; his eyesight was deteriorating; and his memory was beginning to be defective. The detailed and far from absentminded letters that he wrote on Sundays and sent to his agents at Mount Vernon on points of farm management reveal that he was perhaps not so much tired of life as tired of being President. The Federal Government had moved headquarters from New York to Philadelphia in the autumn of 1790, but though Washington was now less than a week's coach-ride away from Mount Vernon, and managed to spend some time there in 1791 and 1792, it was still too far away to suit him. His concern for his plantations increased; in the summer of 1792 his nephew-manager George Augustine Washington fell into a wasting illness (from which he was to die in February, 1793). Uncle Washington knew that his nephew's decline and the decline of the estate would go hand in hand.

He was concerned too for his own reputation. To judge from correspondence he had not yet overcome the scruples of four years before. In fact they were augmented. If he had then fretted over the impropriety of taking office, despite previous declarations of a final retirement, he now feared that he might appear still more disingenous if he did not decisively honor his old pledge. Moreover, the hope of resigning before the end of his first term had proved illusory. But he had surely given enough of himself by enduring the weight of one whole term?

Nor could this first term be regarded as pleasurable. There were solid accomplishments in which he could take pride. Some Anti-Federalist grievances had been removed by the ten amendments to the Constitution that formed the so-called Bill of Rights. North Carolina and Rhode Island had entered the Union and so had two new states—Vermont and Kentucky. He had drawn some of the country's most brilliant men into his Administration —notably Alexander Hamilton as his Secretary of the Treasury and Thomas Jefferson as his Secretary of State. Edmund Randolph, his Attorney-General, had become a firm supporter of the Constitution. The Secretary of War, Henry Knox, was staunchly loyal to his old military chief.

Yet there were fresh, bitter, and growing dissensions. Hamilton's financial measures—the funding and assumption of state and national debts, the establishment of a national bank under federal auspices, an excise tax—had generated fierce opposition, and indicated the persistence or the emergence of deep sectional and economic cleavages. His opponents maintained that the legislation he had pushed through Congress confirmed what they had suspected ever since 1787, or even earlier: the move toward a "consolidated" government was a move toward dictatorship by a selfish, "aristocratic" minority. Such assertions filled the columns of "Republican" newspapers. The most truculent of these, the *National Gazette*, had begun publication in 1791 in Philadelphia under the very nose of the national Government. Worse still for Washington's ease of mind, the controversy radiated from within his executive circle. Hamilton and Jefferson were, as Jefferson later remarked, pitted against one another like two fighting-cocks. Both men had a gift for friendship, and Jefferson in particular was temperamentally averse to personal quarrels. But their friends were more and more grouped in rival camps (they resorted to pseudonymous journalism to attack one another), and Jefferson was accused of having treacherously and improperly established the *National Gazette* in order to undermine the Administration. There was no denying that its editor, Philip Freneau, was on the payroll of Jefferson's State Department in a minor capacity.

Some of the most disagreeable feuding was still to come when in May, 1792, the President summoned James Madison on a confidential matter. Madison, a member of the House of Representatives, was already a critic of Hamilton's financial policy and was to develop into a leading Jeffersonian. Washington, however, still relied upon Madison's political acumen, and wanted to reopen a question on which he had hitherto sought Madison's advice: "the *mode* and *time*" for announcing to the nation that he would not again consent to be President. He had already consulted Jefferson, Hamilton, Knox, and Randolph, though apparently not John Adams. They had all "made pressing representations" to induce the President to reconsider his decision. What he wanted from Madison was a draft of a suitable Farewell Address, and an opinion as to how he should deliver it. As in 1788, Washington was fretted by a logical paradox. He could not retire without saying so; but if he said so, he might seem to be "arrogantly presuming" that he would be reelected. The timing also was difficult. The opening of the next session of Congress, in November, would be "an apt occasion" in itself. But it would be perhaps too close to the election, and the reply that Congress would make to his Farewell Address "might entangle him in further explanations."

Apart from such questions of protocol, Washington revealed to Madison something of the much heavier burdens that oppressed him. For example, popular discontents were showing themselves more and more; and while "the various attacks against public men & measures had not in general been pointed at him, yet in some instances it had been visible that he was the indirect object." In spite of Madison's counter-arguments, the President gave no indication that he had relented, or would do so.

As in 1788, a combination of gloomy reluctance and bashful *hauteur* inhibited Washington from making any direct statement, positive or negative, during the second half of this election year. His dismay at continuing in office was no doubt magnified by further evidence of the gulf between Hamilton and Jefferson, and of factions throughout the nation. The stirrings of a "whiskey rebellion" in western Pennsylvania at the end of the summer could be taken as a symptom of a widespread unruliness. Washington and his associates were ready to believe that disaffection was being fomented by the enemies of the Administration. Hamilton, in his pamphleteer-role, asserted that one of the principal enemies might be inside the Administration — the Secretary of State. Edmund Randolph, writing to Hamilton early in September, was perturbed enough to begin his letter: "Persuaded as I am, that the last effort for the happiness of the United States must perish with the loss of the present Government." The President, in correspondence with Randolph at about the same time, revealed his angry alarm at the effects of newspaper polemics — "those attacks upon almost every measure of government with some of the Gazettes are so strongly pregnated; & which cannot fail, if persisted in with the malignancy they now team, of rending the Union asunder. . . . In a word if the Government and the officers of it are to be the constant theme for Newspaper abuse . . . it will be impossible, I conceive, for any man living to manage the helm, or to keep the machine together." And while the abuse was only obliquely aimed at him (by comparison with the salvoes sent against John Adams, he was immune) he took it personally.

However, the worse things became, the more he was open to the insistence of his contemporaries that he alone could save the nation. Randolph had not meant to say in his lament to Hamilton that the United States was doomed, but only that it would be if the Federal Government allowed the situation to get out of hand. The men whom the President consulted about his retirement all returned the same answer: it would be a black day for the country, at the present juncture. They also, and perhaps inconsistently, attempted to reassure him that things were not so bad, and might with luck and good management soon vastly improve. One reason for this, no doubt, was a desire to convince the President that this time he might escape without having completed his term. The crisis was coming to a head, Jefferson told him in May, 1792, and must shortly be settled. If so, Washington might retire "without awaiting the completion of the second period of four years. I cannot but hope" — Jefferson added a flattering flourish — "that you can resolve to add one or two more to the many years you have already sacrificed to the good of mankind." Two months later, in almost identical language, Hamilton begged

the President to "make a further sacrifice. . . . I trust that it need not continue above a year or two more—And I think it will be more [eligible] to retire
from office before the expiration of the term of an election, than to decline a
reelection." But that there *was* a crisis Randolph direly insisted: "Should a
civil war arise, you cannot stay at home. And how much easier will it be, to
disperse the factions, which are rushing to this catastrophe, than to subdue
them after they shall appear in arms? It is the fixed opinion of the world"
—again an appeal to Washington's self-esteem—"that you surrender nothing
incomplete."

The condition of the outside world, especially in western Europe, was in
itself enough to demand continuity and stability in the American Government.
The ferment of militant French republicanism might have the gravest consequences for the United States. But in the midsummer of 1792, as Washington
sought the relative tranquility of Mount Vernon, domestic and personal factors were probably foremost in his imagination. One point developed by Madison may well have struck home. Eventually there would of course have to be
a successor to Washington; but who could succeed him at the moment? Madison reviewed the options, with a "Republican" emphasis that could be discounted to some extent but not entirely dismissed. The three likeliest successors were Jefferson, Adams, and John Jay (who in a close-fought election had
just been robbed of the governorship of New York by Clinton, in circumstances discreditable to Clinton). Of these, Jefferson wanted to quit public life
for the peace of his Monticello home; and in any case he could not command
enough support in the North. Adams was unacceptable because his views
were too "monarchical" and because he was unpopular in the South. "It
would not be in the power of those who might be friendly to his private character, & willing to trust him in a public one, notwithstanding his political principles, to make head against the torrent." As for Jay, he had succeeded in
becoming unpopular with groups throughout the Union; "his election would
be extremely dissatisfactory on several accounts." Washington might not feel
that such an estimate was altogether fair, but he could not deny that it was
essentially correct. There was no plausible alternative, or none to be risked at
a time of unrest. He was the only person who could command a national following.

This was reinforced by the remarkable harmony of viewpoint expressed
by Hamilton and Jefferson. Agreeing, it appeared, on almost nothing else,
they were at one in wishing Washington to remain in office. Could he though
expect that the rest of the nation would concur? Even if no one could come
near him in electoral votes, might there not be a contest of sorts, and of an
ugly character? Hamilton reassured him, exactly as in 1788: "The dread of
public indignation will be likely to restrain the indisposed few. If they can cal-
culate at all, they will naturally reflect that they could not give a severer blow
to their cause than by giving a proof of hostility to you. But if a solitary vote or
two should appear wanting to perfect unanimity, of what moment can it be?"

Thus for Washington on this issue the wheel had come full circle. In 1792,
as in 1788, he yearned to avoid the inevitable, while friends implored him to

yield to it. Not knowing what else to do, he kept silent—though his friends fancied they could read between the lines. They and the nation took his silence for consent. By November, 1792, when Congress reassembled and the President offered no indication of impending withdrawal, it was taken for granted that next March would witness his second inauguration. As in 1788, the political horoscope then shifted to a subsidiary yet highly intriguing question: who would qualify as his Vice-President?

For those who were generally in sympathy with the development of American affairs, and approved of Hamiltonian policies, it seemed obvious that John Adams should remain as the President's deputy. Though his office was, as he complained, relatively insignificant, it made him known to every member of Congress. Even overshadowed by Washington, he was unquestionably a national figure. The warmest support not surprisingly came from his own section, New England. But he could count on the personal esteem of men throughout the Union, whether or not they shared his political opinions. He enjoyed for example a fluctuating but basically firm friendship with Thomas Jefferson, who thought that in the coming election "the strength of [Adams's] personal worth and his services will . . . prevail over the demerits of his political creed," and so actually recommended Adams to one of the Virginia electors. Leading Federalists such as Charles Carroll of Maryland, Oliver Wolcott of Connecticut, and Rufus King of New York, all gave him their imprimatur. Hamilton, perhaps a little ambiguously, also bestowed a blessing; certainly he did not contemplate any other candidate within the Federalist persuasion.

Jefferson himself held aloof from electioneering in 1792. Others in the Republican camp made fitfully strenuous efforts to turn the vice-presidential contest to their advantage. When the struggle was over, the Federalist Theodore Sedgwick observed that the "Opposition has been as busy as the Devil in a gale of wind." One tack was to denounce Adams for monarchical leanings. Undoubtedly he was a tempting target. He had made himself somewhat ridiculous in the first session of Congress by advocating semi-regal designations ("His Highness") for the President. His *Defence of the Constitutions*, written in 1786–87 and stretching to three volumes, made plain his conviction that the executive branch must be separate and powerful, and that there was much to be said for a hereditary instead of an elective chief of state. He argued on the same lines in his *Discourses on Davila*, which he regarded as a sequel to the *Defence*. The *Discourses* were written as a series of letters in John Fenno's Federalist newspaper the *Gazette of the United States* in 1791. They provoked so much "Jacobinical" complaint that Adams terminated the series before he had exhausted his argument—though not before he had trailed his coat in thirty-two issues of the *Gazette*. Freneau's rival publication, the *National Gazette*, thundered against "those monarchical writers on Davila, &c., who are armed with long wigs, long pens and caitiff printers ready to disseminate their. poisoned doctrines." Admirers of Adams countered, sometimes in dinner-table exchanges, by asking his critics whether they had read his works, or merely heard about them. Patrick Henry was challenged in this way. So was the vehement Virginia Republican William Branch Giles, who was forced to admit that his knowledge of Adams' "monarchal" doctrines was confined to newspaper accounts and random extracts. Jefferson observed (in code) to Madison about Adams that the presidential title affair was "superlatively ridiculous. . . . It is a proof the more of the justice of the character given by Dr. Franklin of my friend, 'always an honest man, often a great one, but sometimes absolutely mad.'" In short, Adams' idiosyncratic and skeptical ruminations weakened his popular appeal; yet their very idiosyncrasy prevented them from doing fatal damage, since his attitudes were complex and hard to disentangle.

Thrusts at John Adams were merely incidental; the Republicans needed a candidate to set against him. As in 1788, George Clinton was the most obvious person. His reputation suffered in the unedifying dispute over the vote-count in the New York gubernatorial election of 1792 — an episode prefiguring in miniature the disputed presidential election of 1876. Jefferson feared that it might weaken "the cause of republicanism." There were subsequent rumors that if Clinton succeeded in ousting Adams he would continue to be Governor of New York while also acting as Vice-President — a pluralism calculated to cast contempt upon the Federal Government. The affair, again according to rumor, put Clinton at odds with New York's junior senator Aaron Burr, who together with Senator Rufus King was asked to adjudicate in the controversy.

Nevertheless by June it seemed certain that the Republicans were agreed on backing Clinton. "You are I presume aware," Hamilton told Adams, "that Mr. Clinton is to be your Competitor at the next election. I trust he could not have succeeded in any event, but the issue of his late election will not help his cause." Hamilton added "Alas! Alas!" with less than heartfelt sincerity. At the same time, of course, the Republicans were making a determined effort to run strong candidates in the forthcoming congressional elections.

Adams' own reaction, somewhat akin to that of Jefferson, was an unhappy (and incomplete) detachment. The news that reached him of maneuvers afoot heightened his old distaste for "electioneering" (a word which, incidentally, was already current). In his native Massachusetts, his cousin Samuel Adams and John Hancock were said to be promoting the Anti-Federalist interest. Fisher Ames, the Massachusetts Federalist — "the colossus of the monocrats and paper [money] men" in Jefferson's phrase — was being sharply challenged. Ames in turn, urging New Englanders to give "zealous support" to Adams, expressed his regret at the tone of anti-Adams propaganda; it was sad that "a life of virtue and eminent usefulness should be embittered by calumny." Adams, who in selfrighteous moments felt the same way about himself, decided to remain in seclusion on his Quincy farm, and not to expose himself to the factious atmosphere of Philadelphia until well after the beginning of the next session of Congress in November. Alarmed by the report, the tireless Hamilton, claiming it was "the universal wish of your friends," implored him to show himself "as soon as possible at Philadelphia."

> I fear that this will give some handle to your enemies to misrepresent — and though I am persuaded you are very indifferent personally to the . . . election, yet I hope you are not so as it regards the cause of good

Government. The difference . . . is in my conception between the success of Mr. Clinton or yourself; and some sacrifices of feeling are to be
made.

Others in Philadelphia, including the Vice-President's son Thomas Boylston
Adams, wrote in the same vein. But John Adams stayed put, and did not set
out from Quincy until the end of November. By the time he reached the federal capital the presidential electors had met and cast their votes. No one
would be able to say that John Adams had stooped to conquer.

In the meantime there had been a flurry of behind-the-scenes activity
among the Republicans, especially between key men in New York, Pennsylvania, and Virginia. Two busy personages in Pennsylvania were Dr. Benjamin
Rush, and John Beckley, the clerk of the House of Representatives, who in
recent years has been shown to be a significant agent in the formation of a
fully-fledged Republican party. Rush, previously a good friend of Adams, had
become temporarily hostile to what he thought Adams portended. Gripped in
the hectic emotions of a period when both America and Europe saw before
them a tremendous drama of choices, Rush opted for the side of liberty and
republicanism—as he interpreted it. With the knowledge of Madison and
Jefferson, Beckley traveled to New York at the end of September. He bore a
letter of introduction from Rush to Aaron Burr. Burr's own opinions had not
hitherto seemed to place him firmly in one camp or the other. He was not on
good terms with Clinton. On the other hand he could be presumed not to be in
collusion with Hamilton, since he had captured the Senate seat of Hamilton's
father-in-law Philip Schuyler. Apparently he was now reckoned to be a Republican, and a talented and promising one; for Rush wrote that his "friends
everywhere look to you to take an active part in removing the monarchical
rubbish of our government. It is time to *speak out*—or we are undone." Rush
also encouraged Burr to extend the network into New England: "The association in Boston augurs well. Do feed it by a letter to Mr. Samuel Adams."
Apart from pseudonymous printed polemics, it would seem most of the speaking out was done in private, almost conspiratorially.

Beckley, back in Philadelphia, informed Madison that Burr was ready to
"support the measure of removing Mr. A" and replacing him with Mr. C. But
a Philadelphia Republican, John Nicholson, had already suggested a better
candidate in the shape of Mr. B—namely, Senator Burr. "The people here,"
said Nicholson, understood that Clinton wished to withdraw. They thought
Burr might prove a more popular candidate in some areas. They would back
either man, and would like "a communication with their Southern Brethren on
the subject." Burr sent an emissary to Nicholson: and in the same crowded
interval a letter signed by two New York Republicans arrived in Virginia,
addressed to Madison and to James Monroe and delivered by hand to Monroe. The bearer, Monroe told Madison, "was intrusted with a similar [commu-
nication] for some [gentlemen] in Penn'a & elsewhere, particularly to the
south." The message was more or less that imparted by Nicholson. Monroe
was not enthusiastic. He thought Burr too young, and the scheme somewhat
presumptuous, and probably launched too late. It was difficult to know how
best to proceed; in a straight contest, he would not hesitate "to aid Burr in

opposition to Adams." Madison wrote back to express his general agreement, but proposed that he and Monroe should first meet in Fredericksburg, Virginia, and jointly "weigh the subject in every scale." When they were able to reply to the New Yorkers, they stated that "the Republican interest, so far as the voice of this State may be estimated, requires that things should be kept to the course which they have in a manner spontaneously taken." In short, Virginia preferred Clinton. "Warmly supported by sundry influential characters," he was more likely "to unite a greater number of electoral votes." When they wrote, a meeting had in fact already taken place in Philadelphia between Pennsylvania Republicans and one of the New York spokesmen, Melancton Smith. They had firmly decided to "exert every endeavor for Mr. Clinton and to drop all thoughts of Mr. Burr." Smith volunteered to make the decision known, and to take an immediate trip into New England to spread the word for Clinton. John Beckley, present at the meeting, begged Madison and Monroe to display similar energy in Virginia and other southern states. The chronology of the episode, which was squeezed into about a fortnight, indicates the sense of urgency of those involved, and their capacity to move swiftly despite the handicaps of distance.

So ended the brief flare of Burr's candidacy. Clandestine though it had been, it soon came to the ears of Rufus King. He wrote in alarm to Hamilton: "If the enemies of the Government are secret and united we shall lose Mr. Adams." Burr was "industrious in his canvass." In Connecticut Burr's uncle Pierpont Edwards, a prominent lawyer, was busy on his behalf; and maneuvers were in train elsewhere. The danger was not so much that Burr would win, but that he could get so many votes that Adams might out of pique "decline the Office." For a few weeks Hamilton seems to have been seriously worried. Or at least, he appears to have lost his usual coolness, perhaps out of the personal antipathy to Burr that was to grow with the years and eventually to cost him his life on the dueling ground at Weehawken. He conveyed the gist of King's letter to several correspondents, including Charles Cotesworth Pinckney, a leading citizen of South Carolina, John Steele, a congressman from North Carolina, and—perhaps the clearest indication of his loss of composure—to President Washington, who may have thought Hamilton's letter indiscreet and best left unanswered. In nearly identical phrasing Hamilton, in his other letters also, offered a ferocious assessment of Burr. Clinton was bad enough—"a man of narrow and perverse politics, . . . steadily opposed to national principles." Burr was potentially far more dangerous—a man "whose only political principle is, to *mount at all events* to the highest legal honours of the Nation and as much further as circumstances will carry him."

Hamilton revealed himself too to be in the grip of an oddly unrealistic conviction about Jefferson. In the course of his *nom-de-plume* newspaper onslaughts against the Republicans he had asserted that Jefferson was scheming to become President through jealousy of Hamilton. In so doing he seems to have given unwitting proof of his own jealousy of Jefferson. At any rate he speculated in this batch of letters as to whether Clinton or Burr, or both, might be run by the Republicans "as a diversion in favour of Mr. Jefferson." Perhaps he was genuinely mystified by the Republican tactics. Perhaps he honestly believed that votes might be steered to Jefferson, though such a plan would not have made much sense. Even more than the clash of personality, however, Hamilton's reaction points to the intensity of emotion and suspicion aroused by the political divisions of the era. Where so much was at stake, each group understandably assumed that the other group would act without scruple in order to secure an advantage. Hamilton and others of the Federalist "interest" watched their opponents like hawks. And Hamilton, for political as well as personal reasons, must have been vastly relieved when it was clear that the Burr candiacy had been abandoned. Once this was apparent, it could be seen as evidence of Republican confusion rather than collusion. And once Hamilton had regained his composure, he was convinced that Adams would be safely reelected.

In March, 1792, Congress approved a new law regulating the presidential succession, and the method of establishing the electoral vote. The electors were to be appointed in the month preceding the first Wednesday in December, on which day they were to meet in their states and vote by ballot for two men—making no mark on their papers to disclose which of the two they preferred for President or Vice-President. A certificate from each state was to be sent to the presiding officer of the Senate before the first Wednesday in January, 1793; and the votes were to be counted in Congress on the second Wednesday in February. No elector was pledged in advance. Each camp read the successive signs—the trend in congressional and state elections, the political coloration of the men chosen as presidential electors, the analyses published in the press or conveyed in private letters—and toted up provisional scorecards. The Republican interest gained appreciably in Congress, though they would not take their seats until the fall of 1793 and so could not influence the immediate pattern of events in Philadelphia. However, Republican morale was high, and Adams for one disclosed his uneasiness in a Christmas letter to his wife Abigail. The Burr following had swung behind Clinton; Burr's New England uncle Pierpont Edwards had turned up in Philadelphia and closeted himself with Jefferson. Ready for the moment to think the worst of his friend, Adams professed to be "really astonished at the blind spirit of party which has seized on the whole soul of this Jefferson. There is not a Jacobin in France more devoted to faction." The public seem to be carried away "with every wind of doctrine and every political lie." He believed that the Federalists must fight the enemy on every literary front: "reasoning must be answered by reasoning; wit by wit. . . ; satire by satire; . . . even buffoonery by buffoonery."

The war of pamphlets continued, with Hamilton as an army in himself. The votes came in slowly; corroboration of those from the new state of Kentucky apparently did not reach Philadelphia until March 1. But every sophisticated citizen knew before the close of 1792 that there would be no startling surprises. The only uncertainty was the exact margin of Adams' lead over Clinton. In mid-October Hamilton accurately forecast the outcome. Adams, he said, would have a "nearly unanimous vote" in New England. In New York, the Republican majority in the legislature would pick Clintonian electors. Adams would get all the votes of New Jersey, and probably sweep the

board in Pennsylvania. Delaware and Maryland were fairly secure. Virginia
and Georgia were Republican territory; North Carolina might be. Adams
would get some votes in South Carolina, but Hamilton confessed he did not
know how many. By December 18, he wrote of the election as a thing of the
past. "The success of the Vice President," Hamilton informed John Jay, "is
as great a source of satisfaction as that of Mr. Clinton would have been of
mortification & pain to me." He protested that he would "relinquish my share
of the command, to the Antifederalists if I thought they were to be trusted
— but I have so many proofs of the contrary as to make me dread the experience
of their preponderancy." When the tally was complete, it confirmed a unanimous vote for Washington: 132 in all. Adams had 77 votes, Clinton 50. The
ghost-candidacies of Jefferson and Burr were commemorated in a couple of
eccentric gestures: 4 for the former, the product of Rhode Island's obscurely
wayward practices; and a single stray South Carolina vote for Aaron Burr.
Otherwise the scattering of 1789 had disappeared, giving way to a
significantly more disciplined alignment. Each "interest" could draw some
satisfaction from the result, although — a perhaps apocryphal story — Adams is
said to have reacted to the news of the final vote with a furious "Damn 'em,
damn 'em, damn 'em! You see that an elective government will not do." One
Republican, writing to Madison on December 24, 1792, felt that their newspaper campaign against Federalist iniquities had started too late. A Massachusetts Federalist, David Cobb, described the result in his state in somewhat odd — perhaps jocular — language: "Our Elections are unanimous for the
old King and his second." The Republicans had failed to make any real impact
on Pennsylvania. On the other hand, they had swung obediently behind Clinton,
for all the peculiarities of his candidacy; they had the makings of a solid southern bloc; and the link between New York and Virginia was emphatically
pictured in the following voting table.

The two presidential elections of 1788–89 and 1792 possess an obvious
fascination as the forerunners of a long and still flourishing sequence of such
contests. They hold something of the pride of place, the nostalgic appeal that
in the history of aviation is accorded to those few precarious seconds when the
Wright brothers first became airborne over the dunes at Kitty Hawk. By
analogy, we may say that in the first try-outs the federal electoral mechanism
took wing. It *worked*, if not very well; optimists, of whom on the whole
George Washington was one, could feel reasonably confident that with time
the machinery would work a good deal better. The electors were chosen
— apart from the New York muddle of 1789 — just as the blueprint prescribed.
Having been chosen, the electors chose; and their choices were nationally
accepted. No elector was assassinated or kidnapped or browbeaten, though a
certain amount of psychological pressure was doubtless brought to bear upon
them. In this respect the two Washington-Adams elections set the vital precedent.

Yet in other respects they furnish only a shadowy precedent. Seen in the
perspective of later elections, they may appear strikingly different, even aber-
rant. The gap between them and subsequent campaigns is indicated indeed in
that word, since the events of 1788–1792 were not "campaigns" in the famil-

iar American understanding of the term. The lines were not clearly drawn, the performers were (by later standards) singularly reluctant and uncommunicative, their supporters secretive and maladroit. Absent were the characteristic features of a campaign in any modern sense: the prolonged search for candidates, the nationwide activities of professional politicians, the crowded and ritualized conventions, the banners and songs and slogans and processions, the convergence of a mass electorate on the polling stations on a specified day in November. The profound divisions that existed in 1788–1792 were not yet focussed and polarized. To the extent that they found a political outlet, they were expressed rather in state and congressional elections than in the presidential one. While this was most conspicuously evident in the states where the legislature picked the electors, it applied also in states where the electors had to submit to a popular vote. So we may argue that the subsequent presidential elections are linked to the first ones not so much by direct as by a kind of collateral descent. *Lucus a non lucendo?*

STATE	WASHINGTON	ADAMS	CLINTON	JEFFERSON	BURR
New Hampshire	6	6			
Massachusetts	16	16			
Connecticut	9	9			
New Jersey	7	7			
Pennsylvania	15	14	1		
Delaware	3	3			
Maryland	8	8			
Virginia	21		21		
South Carolina	8	7			1
Georgia	4		4		
New York	12		12		
North Carolina	12		12		
Rhode Island	4			4	
Vermont	3	3			
Kentucky	4	4			
	132	77	50	4	1

A major difference, as has been noted, was created by the unique situation of George Washington. This factor alone would be enough to explain much that was atypical in 1792. Though James Monroe was to be unopposed in 1820, and to receive every electoral vote except one, he owed his elevation to the temporary disappearance of the party system, not to any widespread belief that he was a second Washington. Washington was the automatic and universal nominee, *pater patriae*, the father of his people, even if some men grumbled privately at the dangers of excessive adulation, and if these murmurings found their way into print toward the end of his second Administration. Because he was above the battle, the Presidency did not yet become the principal strategic feature of the political battleground. Because of this, the Vice-Presidency likewise did not serve as a genuine symbol around which to rally; for the office in its nature lacked an autonomous reality. Its meaning was conditional upon the meaning attached to the Presidency. Adams understood this and once remarked, "I am nothing, but I may be everything." While Washington was President, Adams was a cipher, the occupant of what he termed "the most insignificant office that ever the invention of man contrived or his imagination conceived." No wonder that the effort to beat him in 1792 had a slightly half-hearted quality. He was blanketed, so to speak, by Washington's aura; while Washington was President, there was no great point in mounting a large-scale operation to capture the post of Vice-President.

Viewed thus, Washington inhibited and delayed the political evolution of the Presidency, like a man who will not allow a match to be put to a fire that has been laid. If such a parallel had been suggested to him, he might well have replied that he had indeed no intention of risking a conflagration before the house was fireproof. But leaving aside for the moment the question of party politics, it can be argued that Washington's mere presence may have inhibited the growth of highly undesirable forms of electioneering. If there had been a free-for-all contest, there might have been vicious wrangling over the methods of choosing electors, and an overwhelming temptation to buy and sell them. John Adams, culling his examples from the sadly corrupt history of mankind in all epochs, insisted that this was the inevitable tendency of government by the few. "Awful experience," he said in 1790, had convinced him "that Americans are more rapidly disposed to corruption in elections than I thought they were fourteen years ago." Adams nourished a belief, which became more and more heretical in the American context, that it would be safer to appoint an executive and an upper house for life than to plunge the country into the machinations of an elective system. "First magistrates [i.e., Presidents] and senators had better be made hereditary at once, than that the people should be universally debauched and bribed, go to loggerheads, and fly to arms regularly every year." One does need to accept the Adamsite thesis in order to concede that presidential elections were open to abuse. To the degree that Washington's reputation spared him such fevers, he may have provided his country with a beneficial lull, during which electioneering was muted. This, and the fact that the Presidency was not yet the major prize of political competition, may explain why there was so little discussion in the Washington era of the possibility that a handful of men would arrange the business between them, a point touched on, for instance, by historian James Schouler. The 1788–89 election, he writes, "showed that though [the] State colleges might act independently of the people, they were exposed to the yet greater danger of secret cabals among party leaders. In fact the machinery of this election, with all its simplicity of choice, was turned by a crank over which a few party Federalists presided."

Washington's primacy may also have minimized the serious inadequacy of the constitutional device of naming two men without separating the functions for which they were being named. True, the confusion was to produce an alarming deadlock in the 1800 election, that had to be resolved by the 12th Amendment. At any rate Washington's lead over all other potential candidates postponed the crisis for a few years, until Americans were more habituated to their new Government. Simply by being President, he may also have saved the United States from the divisive confusion that could have been caused by competition between a multiplicity of candidates. Such a competition had been envisaged when the Constitution was drawn up. But one can imagine the delay, bewilderment and dissatisfaction that would have followed if the first presidential elections had had to be decided in the House of Representatives.

Suppositions of this kind should not be taken too far, though; they ignore another equally crucial factor, the relative absence of national party politics during 1788–1792. The matter may be put the other way round: without Washington, party politics might have emerged earlier. Parts of the problem remain conjectural, though much has been clarified by the recent investigations of Joseph Charles, William N. Chambers, Noble E. Cunningham, and others. It is difficult to relate national to state considerations, and organization to ideology. It is difficult to make definite pronouncements about motivation in 1788–1792, except over the question of continuity of ideas and personnel between the anti-federalism of 1787–88 and the republicanism of the 1790's, on which most present-day writers seem to agree that essentially new elements underlay the rise of the Democratic-Republican persuasion. These difficulties are increased by the near impossibility of knowing what men of the period meant when they used a word like "party." What are we to make, for instance, of the following statement?

> In all public bodies there are two parties. The Executive will necessarily be more connected with one than with the other. There will be a personal interest therefore in one of the parties to oppose as well as in the other to support him. Much has been said of the intrigues that will be practiced by the Executive to get into office. Nothing has been said on the other side of the intrigues to get him out of office. Some leader of party will always covet his seat, will perplex his administration, will cabal with the Legislature, till he succeeds in supplanting him.

It occurs in a speech by Gouverneur Morris at Philadelphia in 1787. Is it remarkably prescient vision of the future course of presidential politics, or merely Morris's version of English parliamentary tactics, with their alternation of "ins" and "outs"? The latter seems more likely; Morris seems to confine his notion of party behavior to what goes on inside the government.

What is clear is that though many Americans of the era expected parties to emerge, few rejoiced in the prospect and fewer still could perceive the shape that they would take. If by a "party" we mean an interconnected structure operating at national, state, and local level, with a program of sorts, a self-conscious identity of name and sentiment, and a sustained determination to capture the federal executive branch, then obviously such a phenomenon did not exist in the period under review. "Opposition" claimed but was not granted legitimacy. Party labels tended to be anachronistic ("Anti-Federal"), and pejorative rather than honorific, terms of abuse rather than badges of identity. They have been loosely employed in this essay, but with the partial justification that they were loosely employed at the time. The word "interest" perhaps comes closest to conveying both the limited, manipulative nature of political groupings, and the conception that Madison, Hamilton, and others actually had of their own activities.

Yet such groupings—cliques, cabals, juntos, connexions, all with an eighteenth-century flavor of politics as a game played by family alliances —were not incompatible with a passionate if uneven and intermittent response to ideological issues. The presidential politics of the 1790's were, starting in 1793, to be powerfully swayed by ideology, though these heady emotions did not last. The elections of 1788–89 and 1792 mark a transitional zone. The elements that were to make the capture of the Presidency a central aim of party politics were already in being, but not as yet brought together. Washington could still endeavor to conduct himself as a "disinterested" *head of state*; most of his successors would owe their election and their subsequent fortunes to the fact that they had also been designated *head of a national party*. Perhaps the process was inevitable, once a federal government was a going concern. E pluribus unum: the many depended upon some single focus; in unity was strength. The differences between these two primordial elections and the style of a fully developed presidential system are substantial. Most of the enduring precedents set by Washington belong to quite other realms of statecraft. Yet there are continuities to be discerned, in the amorphous but coalescing affiliations between New York and Virginia, and even in the various things that Washington and Adams did *not* do.

A final analogy may help to summarize the situation: in children's drawing books there are pages made up of apparently miscellaneous dots, each dot with a number. They are transformed into recognizable pictures —say of a donkey or an elephant—by joining up the dots in numbered order. From 1788 to 1792, so far as presidential elections were concerned, the dots were all there. The diagram, however, had not yet been completed, and only some of the dots bore numbers; others were puzzlingly blank. So, within the scope of the diagram, a different though not totally different picture could have emerged.

Election of 1800

by *Noble E. Cunningham, Jr.*

Looking back on the election of 1800 Thomas Jefferson spoke of "the revolution of 1800" and affirmed that it had been "as real a revolution in the principles of our government as that of 1776 was in its form; not effected indeed by the sword, as that, but by the rational and peaceable instrument of reform, the suffrage of the people." Although Jefferson exaggerated when he spoke of a revolution, the election of 1800 was indeed one of the most significant elections in American history. The transfer of control over the executive and legislative branches of the national government from the Federalists to the Republicans in 1801 marked the first such transfer of power in the national government from one political party to another; that this was accomplished in a peaceful and orderly fashion demonstrated the maturity of the nation's first system of political parties. The election of 1800 was the first test of strength of the two national parties that had been formed in the course of the 1790's, and, more than any Presidential election that had preceded or would follow for at least a generation, it was a *party* contest for control of the national administration and for determining the direction and the management of national policy.

The two principal candidates who faced each other in seeking the Presidency in 1800 were the same men who had stood in contest in 1796, but their situations had greatly altered in the four years since John Adams had won the office by a margin of three electoral votes over Thomas Jefferson. In 1796 Adams had been Washington's Vice-President, promising to follow in the first

President's footsteps; in 1800 he was the President with the record of his own Administration to defend. In 1796 Jefferson, beginning his third year in retirement at Monticello, was genuinely reluctant to have his name brought forward for the demanding office, and he remained inactive throughout the campaign. In 1800 Jefferson as Vice-President was deeply involved in politics, not as part of the Administration in which he was Vice-President but as the active leader of the Republican opposition seeking to remove Adams and the Federalists from command of the national government.

Adams and Jefferson had first met in Philadelphia in the summer of 1775 as delegates to the Continental Congress. The Massachusetts-born (1735) graduate of Harvard College (1755) was seven years the senior of the Virginian who had graduated from the College of William and Mary (1762) and read law under George Wythe. In 1800 Adams was sixty-four, Jefferson fifty-seven. Each had served his political apprenticeship as a member of his respective colonial assembly. In the wartime Congress, Jefferson and Adams found themselves on the same side of debates, and they served together on the committee to draft the Declaration of Independence. Alterations that Adams suggested in his own hand on Jefferson's draft of the famous document linked the two men together in a great moment of history, and neither could have then imagined the roles of antagonists into which their political futures would lead them.

In the postwar years both men served in key diplomatic posts in Europe, Adams as Minister to Great Britain and Jefferson as Minister to France. Both were at these European posts during the Constitutional Convention of 1787, but both returned in time to become members of the first Administration under the Constitution, Adams as Vice-President and Jefferson as Secretary of State. As the Republican interest emerged, Adams, who had attracted considerable unfavorable publicity during the first Congress by favoring titles for executive officers, became a symbol of aristocratic tendencies, and there was an organized but unsuccessful attempt in 1792 to unseat him as Vice-President. As early as 1791 Jefferson had expressed his opposition to the "political heresies" which he found in the writings of Adams, but it was Alexander Hamilton rather than Adams who most alarmed Jefferson; and in 1797 Jefferson considered the possibility of his Republican followers coming to some understanding with the newly elected President as to the best means of preventing Hamilton from getting into office in the future. The possibility of an accommodation with Adams, however, soon appeared only as a passing thought, and Jefferson as Vice-President almost immediately found himself assuming the leadership of the Republican opposition. He was to spend much of the next four years mobilizing the party for the campaign of 1800.

That Jefferson and Adams had developed different outlooks on government since they had stood together during the Revolution was clear by the time they joined Washington's Administration. In his three-volume *A Defence of the Constitutions of the Government of the United States of America* Adams emphasized the need for balance between the forces of aristocracy and democracy. "In every society where property exists, there will ever be a struggle between rich and poor," wrote Adams. "Mixed in one assembly, equal laws can never be expected. They will either be made by numbers, to plunder the few who are rich, or by influence, to fleece the many who are poor. Both rich and poor, then, must be made independent, that equal justice may be done, and equal liberty enjoyed by all."

On the other hand, Jefferson avowed an unqualified faith in the people. In addressing his neighbors in Albemarle County, Virginia, before leaving to take up his duties as Secretary of State, Jefferson spoke of "the holy cause of freedom" and affirmed, "It rests now with ourselves alone to enjoy in peace and concord the blessings of self-government, so long denied to mankind: to shew by example the sufficiency of human reason for the care of human affairs and that the will of the majority, the Natural law of every society, is the only sure guardian of the rights of man. Perhaps even this may sometimes err. But its errors are honest, solitary and short-lived.—Let us then, my dear friends, forever bow down to the general reason of the society. We are safe with that, even in its deviations, for it soon returns again to the right way."

In the heat of the first election contest between Jefferson and Adams in 1796 these differences were made to appear by Jeffersonian partisans as the differences between "a firm Republican" and "an avowed Monarchist"—a choice between "the uniform advocate of equal rights among citizens" and "the champion of rank, titles and hereditary distinctions," between "the steady supporter of our republican constitution" and "the warm panegyrist of the British Monarchical form of Government." While such bold contrasts of the political characters of Jefferson and Adams never disappeared from the campaign literature, by 1800 the Republicans had added to their arsenal of campaign ammunition a major new weapon—the record of the Adams Administration.

John Adams alone, of course, did not write the record of his Administration, for it was written in part by Congress, which did not always follow the President's lead, and in part by his Cabinet, which for most of Adams' Presidency was more loyal to Hamilton than to the President. But the record was that of the Federalist party, to which all members of the Cabinet claimed allegiance and which had a majority in Congress. The Republican opposition had no reason to draw distinctions between moderate Federalists and ultra-Federalists, between friends of Adams and backers of Hamilton, for Republicans were excluded from the Administration and from offices in the government. For the first time under Adams the nation experienced a party Administration, however divided that party may have been; and for the first time in 1800 a party would have to stand on the record of an Administration.

To a large extent the record of the Adams Administration was written in response to the pressures of foreign affairs growing out of the crisis in French relations which greeted him when he took office and which, before it was settled, led to decisions in domestic policy more controversial than those in foreign affairs. Soon after his inauguration Adams summoned a special session of Congress to deal with the French problem. In reaction to the United States' acceptance of the Jay Treaty with Great Britain, France had begun an

aggressive campaign against American shipping and had refused to receive
Charles Cotesworth Pinckney as Minister from the United States. While calling upon Congress to provide measures for defense, Adams announced the
appointment of a commission (John Marshall, Elbridge Gerry, and Charles
Cotesworth Pinckney) to attempt further negotiations. The outcome of this
effort was the famous XYZ crisis which broke upon the country in April,
1798, when Congress released for publication the dispatches from the envoys
to France. The immediate effect was a wave of anti-French feeling throughout
the country, extensive measures for defense, and an undeclared naval war
with France. Federalist popularity soared, and Federalists increased their
majority in Congress in the congressional elections of 1798–99. At the same
time, the Federalist response to the difficulty with France provided the basis
for the major issues raised by the Republican opposition during the campaign
of 1800.

In preparing for defense Congress created the Department of the Navy
and began the building of a naval force. The regular army was expanded, and
the President was authorized to raise a provisional army. These decisions
extended beyond the immediate crisis with France and raised broad questions
of policy in regard to naval power, standing armies, and reliance on the militia
for defense. When Hamilton was appointed Inspector General, second to
Washington in command of the army, questions were raised in the minds of
Republicans as to the purposes of the increased military establishment. The
clear preference given to Federalists over Republicans for commissions in the
army created additional concern. The increased military expenditures required new measures of taxation and government loans, thus supplying other
issues for political debate. Above all, the French issue provided the occasion
for the passage of the most controversial domestic legislation of Adams' Presidency: the alien and sedition laws and the naturalization act of 1798. These
laws raised the issue of whether they were necessary for the internal security
of the United States or whether under the guise of patriotic purposes they
were designed to cripple, if not destroy, the Republican opposition. The alien
and sedition laws also took on increased significance in the political contest
between Federalists and Republicans both in respect to the manner in which
they were enforced against Republican newspaper editors and in regard to the
basic constitutional and civil-liberties issues involved in the legislation. Moreover, the alien and sedition acts provided the occasion for the issuance of the
Kentucky Resolutions, secretly drafted by Jefferson, and the Virginia Resolutions, secretly authored by Madison. These resolutions of 1798 not only
posed fundamental questions of constitutional interpretation and state rights,
but they also became campaign documents to be used in the Republican effort
to dislodge the Federalists from their command of the national government.

The Presidential election of 1796 had been extremely close, and in exam-
ining the results of that contest Republican party managers had been struck
by the fact that Adams' three-vote margin of victory in the electoral college
could be attributed to 1 vote from Pennsylvania, 1 from Virginia, and 1 from
North Carolina. In each of these states the Republicans had won an impres-

sive victory, amassing in the three states a total of 45 electoral votes. The loss of 3 votes in these strongly Jeffersonian states was due to the district method of electing Presidential electors. In looking for ways to improve their chances for victory in the next presidential election, Republican managers thus turned their attention to state election laws. No uniform system of selection of presidential electors prevailed. In some states electors were chosen by the state legislature; in others they were elected on a general ticket throughout the state; in still others they were elected in districts. This meant that the party which controlled the state legislature was in a position to enact the system of selection which promised the greatest partisan advantage. Thus, in January, 1800, the Republican-controlled legislature of Virginia passed an act providing for the election of presidential electors on a general ticket instead of by districts as in previous elections. By changing the election law, Republicans in Virginia, confident of carrying a majority of the popular vote throughout the state but fearful of losing one or two districts to the Federalists, insured the entire electoral vote of the Union's largest state for the Republican candidate.

When Virginia Federalists protested the change, Republicans replied that "the same game is playing off in New England, and some other Eastern States." And, indeed, it was. In Massachusetts, Federalists feared that Jefferson might carry as many as two districts in that state under the system previously employed. Thus, the Federalist-controlled legislature of Massachusetts changed the laws of that state to provide for the selection of presidential electors by the state legislature in place of popular election by districts. In New Hampshire a general ticket was similarly replaced by a legislative choice of electors. In New York, Republicans introduced a measure to move from legislative choice to election by districts, but the proposal was defeated by the Federalists, an outcome which ultimately worked to the advantage of the Republicans when they won control over the legislature in the state elections of 1800. In Pennsylvania, a Republican House of Representatives and a Federalist Senate produced a deadlock over the system to be used to select electors, and the vote of that state was eventually cast by the legislature in a compromise division of the 15 electoral votes, eight Republican and seven Federalist electors being named. This solution essentially deprived Pennsylvania of a voice in the presidential election of 1800.

When all changes in electoral procedures had been completed, in only five of the sixteen states were presidential electors popularly elected: Rhode Island, Maryland, Virginia, North Carolina, and Kentucky. With the naming of Presidential electors in the hands of the state legislatures in approximately two-thirds of the states in 1800, the elections of members to the state assemblies became a major aspect of the presidential election. "It is perfectly well understood," wrote Thomas Boylston Adams to his brother John Quincy Adams in Berlin, "that the tiral of strength between the two Candidates for the chief magistracy of the Union is to be seen, not in the choice of electors by the people, but in the complextion and character of the individual legislatures." These elections coming at various times during the year meant also that the campaign of 1800 would extend throughout the year and that the results of an election in one state might influence later elections in other states.

The organization of political parties was incomplete in 1800, and in contrast with later refinements party machinery was still rudimentary. But a system of competing national parties did clearly prevail in 1800, a condition which had not existed when Washington took office little more than a decade earlier. Formal party machinery was most extensive in 1800 in those states in which Republicans and Federalists were most evenly balanced and party competition was keenest. The Middle Atlantic States best displayed these conditions. New York and Pennsylvania had the most extensive networks of party committees, with systems of county committees, township committees, and city ward committees. The Republican party was better organized than the Federalist party and tended to take the initiative in devising party machinery and new campaign techniques. As the party in power, the Federalists enjoyed advantages which the Republicans sought to overcome through better organization and more effective campaigning. Federalists commonly attempted to duplicate Republican machinery wherever it appeared and, in fact, had more machinery than they were willing to admit, since they tried to leave the impression that they were superior to such devices.

The presidential election of 1800 led to the introduction of formal party machinery for the first time in several states. Virginia offers the best example of this and also illustrates the type of party organization developed by this early date. When, in January, 1800, the Virginia legislature changed the state presidential election law from a district system to a general ticket, the state was faced for the first time with a statewide election, since the governor was chosen by the legislature and congressmen and assemblymen were elected in districts. Under the new law each voter, who in the past had voted for 1 presidential elector from his district, was now required to vote for 21 electors from the state at large. To conduct such a statewide campaign demanded party machinery. In January, 1800, Republican machinery to meet this need was initiated by what was reported in the newspapers to have been "a meeting of ninety-three members of the Legislature and a number of other respectable persons." This was a party caucus, composed primarily of state legislators but also open to other Republican party leaders. The machinery created by this caucus consisted of a central committee of five members in Richmond and county committees, also usually of five members, in nearly every county in the state. The central committee, headed by a state chairman, coordinated the campaign throughout the state, publicized the slate of electors in the press, and kept up regular correspondence with the county committees, supplying them with copies of the ticket and information to be used in the campaign. Federalists in Virginia in 1800 copied the Republican organizational structure and formed a similar, though less extensive, network of committees. In other states where formal party machinery had been introduced by 1800, similar patterns of committees of correspondence and campaign committees tended to be followed. But although parties, especially the Republican party, had made major strides in building formal machinery by 1800, party organization in many states still depended upon the informal direction of party leaders and small groups of party activists.

National party organization rested primarily on the informal association of party leaders and particularly on the members of each party in Congress. By 1800 both Federalists and Republicans had instituted the congressional nominating caucus. As will be described below, a caucus of Republican members of Congress in 1800 decided that Aaron Burr should be supported as the Republican vice-presidential candidate to be run on the ticket with Jefferson, and the results of the election would demonstrate how effective this caucus had become. The Federalist members of Congress also held a caucus in 1800 in which they agreed to support John Adams and Charles Cotesworth Pinckney as the Federalist candidates.

In 1800 the congressional nominating caucus was vigorously attacked. "If any thing will rouse the freemen of America," exclaimed one political commentator, "it must be the arrogance of a number of members of Congress to assemble as an *Electioneering Caucus*, to control the citizens in their constitutional rights. Under what authority did these men pretend to dictate their nomination? Did they receive six dollars a day for the double purpose of *caucussing* and *legislating*? Do we send members to Congress to *cabal* once in four years for President?" But, though denounced in 1800 and repeatedly challenged as long as it survived, the caucus system of nominating presidential candidates introduced in 1800 was employed by the Republican party until 1824, and until 1824 every presidential candidate nominated by the Republican caucus would win election. Thus, by 1800 the Republican party had instituted the basic mechanism of party organization on the national level.

When the Philadelphia *Aurora* announced in its issue of January 20, 1800, that "the electioneering campaign has already commenced," this was hardly news to the members of Congress who had been sitting since early December. While Federalists charged Republicans with "canvassing for the Election of Mr. Jefferson at the expense of $1,000 per day," the Speaker of the House was counseling Federalist friends that "in all our measures, we must never lose sight of the next election of President." Indeed, as one contemporary observed, Congress appeared as "a conclave of cardinals, intriguing for the election of a Pope." The President's son Thomas Boylston Adams called the session "altogether and exclusively, an Electioneering Cabal and Conspiracy."

During the campaign of 1800 national attention shifted from one state to another as critical elections determining the electoral votes of key states were held at widely separated times. By April all eyes were focusing on the election in New York, where the control of the legislature which would cast that state's electoral vote was at stake. A victory there would give an important psychological boost to the successful party. Republicans were particularly anxious to win in New York, since Adams had carried that state's 12 electoral votes in 1796, and an early Republican victory there might be of great influence on elections elsewhere. Besides, Republican leaders were not at all sure that they could win without New York. Jefferson calculated that if the Federalists carried New York the Republicans would have to carry both New Jersey and Pennsylvania and "we could not count with any confidence" on doing that. In March, 1800, Jefferson thus regarded a Republican victory in New York as essential to his election. The key to success in New York, party leaders on both sides agreed, was to win in New York City. The strength of the two parties throughout the rest of the state indicated the election of a legislature so nearly balanced that the thirteen members from New York City could be expected to give a majority to whichever party carried the city. Thus, both Federalists and Republicans concentrated their greatest efforts on the city election.

The initial advantage appeared to rest with the Federalists, since they had elected their entire slate in the state election of the previous year. Moreover, the Federalist effort was being directed by Alexander Hamilton, who had greatly impressed Republicans as a campaign manager in a recent election by attending "*all* the polls of this city, *daily* and *hourly*." To counteract Hamilton's leadership, Republicans relied on more broadly organized party machinery, consisting of party committees in each ward of the city and a general committee composed of deputies from the respective ward committees, and on the management of Aaron Burr. At the height of the 1800 campaign in New York, Burr was described by a close associate as "a man whose intrigue and management is most astonishing." What appeared to many contemporaries as "intrigue and management" was in fact skillful planning, organization, and effective campaign direction. Burr in 1800 was not some devious plotter, but an aggressive, practical party organizer.

Burr's basic plan for victory in New York City rested upon maintaining Republican unity and framing a slate of candidates that would represent all elements of Republican strength and at the same time present a list of distinguished and influential candidates. What Burr had in mind was for the Republican ticket to contain the names of such prominent persons as former Governor George Clinton, General Horatio Gates, and Judge Brockholst Livingston—all as candidates for the state assembly. None of these men wished to be nominated, and it required Burr's best persuasive efforts to get their agreements. "But for the matchless perseverance of Colonel Burr," said one of the Republican committeemen who called on Clinton, "the ticket, as it stood, never could have been formed." In arranging for Republicans to nominate a number of influential and well-known persons whose names alone would attract votes, Burr was following the example of Virginia Republicans who had nominated a slate of presidential electors including such prominent figures as George Wythe, James Madison, and Edmund Pendleton. Having formed the ticket, Burr was careful to keep his strategy a secret until after the Federalists had announced their ticket. The Federalist slate was published in the New York newspapers on March 29. On April 16 notices appeared in the papers calling a Republican meeting on April 17 to make nominations. This "numerous meeting of Republicans" placed a ticket in nomination, and from the newspaper reports it appeared to be the spontaneous action of a party meeting. But the slate of candidates named was that which Burr had carefully put together and for which he had already secured the backing of other party leaders.

Burr's accomplishment in framing a strong ticket inspired the lesser party leaders to greater effort. "Never," said one of them, "have I observed such an union of sentiment; so much zeal and so general a determination to be active." In marshaling support for the Republican ticket, Burr worked through the network of party committees linked together by the general committee, rather than through the Tammany Society as frequently assumed. Some Republicans thought that Burr's leadership was indispensable. "If we carry this election," wrote Matthew L. Davis to Albert Gallatin, "it may be ascribed principally to Col. Burr's management and perseverance." Burr's success depended on mobilizing the regular party machinery into an effective campaign organization. This Burr was able to do.

The Republicans, Abigail Adams thought, "laid their plan with much more skill than their opponents," while the Federalists nominated "men of no note, men whol[l]y unfit for the purpose; only two names of any respectability graced their list." Federalists, nevertheless, were extremely active in the campaign. Hamilton's dislike of Adams did not lessen his efforts to defeat the Republicans, though some men were later to make that charge. One friend of Adams felt that Hamilton "was as industrious at the Election as was consistent with his Rank" and assured Mrs. Adams that he had heard Hamilton at a public meeting denouncing Jefferson as "an atheist, a modern french Philosopher, overturner of Government, etc.," while speaking most respectfully of President Adams.

Electioneering by both parties continued until the final hours of voting. When the polls opened on April 29, both parties were predicting victory, but neither side was prepared to relax its efforts. The polls remained open for three days, and considerable last-minute campaigning took place at or near the polling places. Although candidates themselves did not campaign at the polls, party leaders on both sides went from ward to ward, while other party activists stationed themselves at the various voting places. Both Hamilton and Burr were active throughout the three days of voting and were reported to have engaged in some brief public debates when they accidently met at polling places. On the last day of the voting, Burr was reported to have remained at the poll of the seventh ward for ten hours without interruption, and one of his lieutenants was kept so busy that he went without eating for fifteen hours. Hamilton's supporters were equally vigorous. "I have been night and day employed in the business of the election," wrote Federalist Robert Troup after the close of the polls. "I have not eaten dinner for three days and have been constantly upon my legs from 7 in the morning till 7 in the afternoon."

The New York polls closed at sunset on May 1. By midnight enough votes had been counted to indicate a Republican victory, and Republicans quickly dispatched letters to Philadelphia announcing the victory. "We have labored hard but the reward is great," wrote Edward Livingston to Jefferson. The final returns showed that the Republicans had carried their entire ticket for the assembly in New York City, and a Republican majority in the legislature appeared to be assured. Most knowledgeable New York Republicans were willing to give Burr the principal credit. James Nicholson, a leading New York Republican, confided to his son-in-law Albert Gallatin that the election "has been conducted and brought to issue in so miraculous a manner that I cannot account for it but from the intervention of a Supreme Power and our friend Burr the agent. . . . His generalship, perseverance, industry, and execution exceeds all description, so that I think I can say he deserves anything and everything of his country."

Burr's reward was not long in coming. As soon as the news of the New York victory reached Philadelphia, jubilant Republican members of Congress commissioned Gallatin to obtain "correct information of the wishes of the New York Republicans" in regard to the vice-presidential nomination, which had not yet been determined. Republican consensus made Jefferson the party's presidential nominee in 1800, as it had in 1796, but some means of formal nomination was required to concentrate Republican electoral votes on a second candidate. Republican members of Congress in 1796 had attempted to decide on the vice-presidential nomination in a party caucus, but they had failed, and as a result the second ballots of Republican electors were widely scattered. Republicans in 1800 were thus anxious to avoid the difficulties of 1796, and party members in Congress hoped to make a nomination for the second office that would enable Republicans to elect both the President and the Vice-President. After the New York victory, there was general agreement that the vice-presidential nomination should go to a New Yorker. The most likely candidate appeared to be either George Clinton or Aaron Burr. Which did New York Republicans prefer? After conferences with Clinton, Burr, and other Republican leaders, Nicholson reported back to Gallatin that Clinton declined being considered and that Clinton and all of the Republicans with whom he had consulted agreed that "Burr is the most suitable person and perhaps the only Man." Their confidence in Burr, Nicholson concluded, was "universal and unbounded."

This was all that the Republicans in Congress needed to know, and soon after the report reached Philadelphia a Republican caucus was held. Forty-three Republican members were reported to have attended the caucus that met on May 11, and they unanimously agreed to support Burr for Vice-President. This first congressional nominating caucus established the method by which the Republican party would nominate the party's presidential and vice-presidential candidates down to 1824, and it demonstrated as early as 1800 the dominant role which Republican members in Congress played in providing national organization for the party.

If the New York election had a powerful effect on the Republican party, it also had a similar effect on the Federalists. "Yesterday they were arrogant and certain of our defeat," Republican Edward Livingston wrote on the day after the election. "Today, there is a most auspicious gloom on the countenances of every tory and placeman." So despairing were New York Federalists that at least two of them wrote to Federalist Governor John Jay urging him to call a special session of the legislature before the terms of the Federalist majority ended on July 1 in order to change the election law from a choice of electors by the legislature to election by districts. One of these Federalists was Alexander Hamilton; the other was his father-in-law, General Philip Schuyler. Hamilton argued that "in times like this in which we live, it will not do to be overscrupulous. It is easy to sacrifice the substantial interest of society by a strict adherence to ordinary rules . . . . They ought not to hinder the taking of a *legal* and *constitutional* step, to prevent an *atheist* in Religion, and a *fanatic* in politics from getting possession of the helm of State." Jay, who had resigned from the Supreme Court of the United States to become governor of New York, was not persuaded by Hamilton's reasoning and endorsed Hamilton's letter: "Proposing a measure for party purposes, which I think it would not become me to adopt." Thus, the newly elected Republican majority in the New York assembly could be expected to choose electors pledged to Thomas Jefferson.

Shortly after the Federalist defeat in New York, Hamilton also sent off an urgent appeal to Federalist members of Congress to resolve to support Charles Cotesworth Pinckney as a Federalist candidate on an equal basis with John Adams. "To support *Adams* and *Pinckney* equally is the only thing that can possibly save us from the fangs of *Jefferson*," he wrote on May 4 to Theodore Sedgwick, the Federalist Speaker of the House of Representatives. "It is, therefore, essential that the Federalists should not separate without coming to a distinct and solemn concert to pursue this course *bona fide*." Hamilton's proposal was based upon the fact that the Constitution did not provide for separate balloting for President and Vice-President but specified that each elector cast two ballots without distinguishing between the two offices. The candidate with the highest number of votes, provided it was a majority, became President; the second highest candidate became Vice-President. The success of Hamilton's plan rested upon the expectation that the vote of South Carolina would be cast for Jefferson and Pinckney, a native son, just as in 1796 the South Carolina vote had gone to Jefferson and to Thomas Pinckney, another native son. In 1796 the second ballots of Federalist electors had been widely scattered, so that Jefferson had become Vice-President; but it was expected that in 1800 both parties would give more attention to the second office. If Federalist electors in all states except South Carolina voted for Adams and Pinckney, and South Carolina electors voted for Jefferson and Pinckney, Pinckney rather than Adams would be the highest Federalist candidate. In all probability he would also be higher than Jefferson and thus be elected President.

It seems clear that Hamilton had already discussed this plan with other Federalists leaders, since the Federalists in Congress met in a caucus immediately after the news of the New York defeat was received and before the arrival of Hamilton's letter. Sedgwick reported a few days later: "We have had a meeting of the whole federal party, on the subject of the ensuing election, and have agreed that we will support, *bona fide*, Mr. Adams and General Pinckney." The leading Federalist to oppose this scheme in the caucus was Samuel Dexter of Massachusetts, who argued that whatever opinion Federalist leaders might have of Adams, "as he is viewed by the great majority of federalists, he is the most popular man in the United States, and deemed best qualified to perform the duties of President." Dexter reasoned that should Pinckney be elected over Adams it would "crumble the federal party to atoms." But many Federalists in Congress agreed with Timothy Pickering that "the only chance of a federal President will be by General C. C. Pinckney," and all except Dexter reportedly consented to support the scheme "as far as their advice and influence would go." Theodore Sedgwick privately stated that at the time of the caucus the Federalist members form South Carolina gave assurances that, whatever electors were chosen in that state, the popularity of Pinckney was such that the vote would be either for Adams and Pinckney or for Jefferson and Pinckney.

In May, 1800, Hamilton was not prepared publicly to oppose Adams' reelection, but privately he made it clear that he would "never more be responsible for him by my direct support, even though the consequence should be the election of *Jefferson*. If we must have an *enemy* at the head of the government," he wrote, "let it be one we can oppose, and for whom we are not responsible, who will not involve our party in the disgrace of his foolish and bad measures." By May, 1800, it was also clear that Adams was prepared to seek reelection without Hamilton's support. Indeed, the decisiveness with which Adams moved after the Federalist defeat in New York suggests the reaction of a shrewd politician, which Adams himself would never have admitted being and which some historians are reluctant to concede. In this connection, a review of the sequence of events following the defeat of the Federalist ticket in New York is instructive.

The news of the outcome of the New York election arrived in Philadelphia on Saturday morning, May 3. On Saturday evening the Federalist caucus met and agreed to support Pinckney equally with Adams. On Monday, May 5, President Adams summoned Secretary of War James McHenry, one of the Hamiltonian clique in the Cabinet, and demanded his resignation, which McHenry presented the following day. On Saturday, May 10, Adams sent a letter to Secretary of State Timothy Pickering, the leading Hamiltonian in the Cabinet, requesting his resignation by the following Monday morning so that he could send the nomination of his successor to the Senate before Congress adjourned. Pickering's reply was in Adams' hands early on Monday morning, May 12, for Adams in his own hand endorsed the letter "Rec'd at 9 O'Clock, May 12, 1800." Pickering's letter was a lofty refusal to resign, and Adams immediately sent him a note informing him that he was "hereby discharged from any further service as Secretary of State." The nomination of John Marshall to be Secretary of State was sent to the Senate the same day; his appointment was confirmed the following day, and Congress adjourned on May 14.

The speed with which Adams moved after the New York election seems significant. The split between Adams and the key members of his Cabinet was not a sudden development. By retaining Washington's Cabinet in taking office, Adams had begun his Administration with subordinates who gave first loyalty to Hamilton, and tensions between Adams and his department heads had increased as time passed. The split in the Administration came out into the open early in 1799, when Adams decided, over the objections of the Hamiltonians, to send a second peace mission to negotiate with France. Yet, despite the fact that as early as 1799 there was an irreparable breach between Adams and Hamilton's supporters in the Cabinet—Timothy Pickering, Oliver Wolcott, and James McHenry—Adams was apparently unwilling to risk the political consequences of the further alienation of the Hamiltonian leaders that would follow the dismissal of Hamilton's friends from the Cabinet. After the Federalist defeat in New York, Adams no longer felt compelled to deal gently with Hamilton, who could no longer deliver the New York vote either for or against him. The best hope for political success would therefore appear to have been for Adams to seek to win support among moderate Federalists in such states as Maryland and North Carolina, where the electors would be popularly elected. The appointments of John Marshall, a moderate Virginia Federalist, as Secretary of State, and of Samuel Dexter, who opposed the movement to support Pinckney, as Secretary of War, were well designed to make such an appeal.

Republicans were quick to see the implications of Adams' moves and charged him with electioneering, a charge against which Mrs. Adams was prompt to defend her husband, arguing in private letters that "if popularity had been his object, he would not have sought it by a measure that must create two Enemies to one friend." But, it might be asked, after New York was lost would those enemies be in a position to cost Adams the votes that he might lose by maintaining an alliance with the ultra-Federalists? The ultras might attempt to get Federalist electors in New England to throw away votes from Adams to favor Pinckney, but unless Adams could pick up sufficient votes south of New York to balance the New York loss he had no chance of winning. Mrs. Adams might deny that any political considerations were involved in the Cabinet dismissals, and the President himself would never have admitted, even to himself, that he was acting like a politician, but a political interpretation seems a more reasonable conclusion than the explanation that Adams simply lost his temper when he fired McHenry. It is undoubtedly true, from McHenry's report on his interview with Adams, that the President lost his temper. But what triggered this? The news of the New York election, followed by the meeting of the Federalist caucus, must surely explain why Adams no longer felt compelled to maintain the patience with which he had for so long tolerated the obstruction of McHenry and Pickering. Adams' only hope for victory after the loss of New York was to seek support from moderate Federalists and to win votes south of New York; his actions suggest that he saw this as clearly as did his Republican opponents.

In contrast to his role in 1796 when he made no effort to promote his own election, Jefferson in 1800 worked systematically to bring about a Republican victory. In drafting the Kentucky Resolutions of 1798 to protest against the Alien and Sedition laws, Jefferson not only raised issues for constitutional debate but also launched the Republican campaign to drive the Fed-

eralists from power. Early in 1799 he explicitly set down the Republican platform for the election of 1800 in a letter to Elbridge Gerry (quoted below), and
as the year advanced Jefferson's political activities quickened. In February,
1799, he wrote to Madison suggesting that "this summer is the season for systematic energies and sacrifices. The engine is the press. Every man must lay
his purse and his pen under contribution. As to the former, it is possible that I
may be obliged to assume something for you. As to the latter, let me pray and
beseech you to set apart a certain portion of every post day to write what may
be proper for the public. Send it to me while here, and when I go away I will
let you know to whom you may send, so that your name shall be sacredly secret."

During the campaign of 1800 Jefferson appealed to other political friends
to write political tracts and pieces for the newspapers, though he himself adhered faithfully to an earlier resolve not to write anonymously for publication.
Jefferson also aided Republican newspaper editors who supported the Republican cause, including financial aid to James Thomson Callender, probably the
most abusive opponent of John Adams in the country. Jefferson later indicated
that his gifts to Callender were meant as charities rather than as encouragement to his writings, but on at least one occasion he suggested that Callender's *The Prospect Before Us* "cannot fail to produce the best effect." When
Republican newspaper editors were indicted under the sedition law in prosecutions that appeared to the Republicans to be carefully timed to coincide
with the election campaign, Jefferson came to their aid. "I as well as most
other republicans who were in the way of doing it, contributed what I could to
the support of the republican papers and printers," he recalled in 1802, "paid
sums of money for the Bee, the Albany Register, etc. when they were staggering under the sedition law, contributed to the fines of Callender himself, of
Holt, Brown and others suffering under that law."

Jefferson was also active in helping the Republican party in the distribution of political pamphlets. In sending a dozen such tracts to James Monroe in
February, 1799, he suggested: "I wish you to give these to the most
influential characters among our country-men, who are only misled, are candid enough to be open to conviction, and who may have the most effect on
their neighbors. It would be useless to give them to persons already sound.
Do not let my name be connected with the business." In the course of the
campaign of 1800 Jefferson made considerable use of this method of campaigning. In April, 1800, he sent to the chairman of the Republican state
committee in Virginia eight dozen copies of Thomas Cooper's *Political
Arithmetic*, a pamphlet protesting against commercial expansion and well suited
to the farmers and planters of Virginia. Jefferson requested that one copy
of the pamphlet be sent to each county committee in the state. "I trust yourself only with the secret that these pamphlets go from me," he wrote to the
Virginia chairman. "You will readily see what a handle would be made of my
advocating their contents. I must leave to yourself therefore to say how they
come to you."

Throughout the campaign of 1800 Jefferson took special precautions to guard against the possibility of any of his private letters falling into Federalist hands for use against him. Convinced that "the postmasters will lend their inquistorial aid to fish out any new matter of slander they can gratify the powers that be," he avoided the discussion of political subjects in correspondence except when writing to trusted friends in letters sent by private conveyance. He left many of his letters to close political associates unsigned. But, although guarded in writing any letter that might reach the public, Jefferson had made clear his position on the issues before the public, and his party kept his platform before the voters.

It is interesting to note that Vice-President Jefferson in the spring of 1800 considered making a public visit to Governor James Monroe of Virginia. Although he disapproved of "pomp and fulsome attention by our citizens to their functionaries," he was concerned about the reports of "a great deal of federalism and Marshalism" in Richmond and thought "republican demonstrations" might help to counteract it. "Sometimes it is useful to furnish occasions for the flame of public opinion to break out," he suggested. Governor Monroe, however, advised against the visit, and Jefferson abandoned the idea. Could it be that Jefferson had heard that President Adams was planning to visit the new capital at Washington after the adjournment of Congress?

Adams was not so active as Jefferson in 1800 in the types of campaign activities in which Jefferson engaged — letter-writing, circulating political pamphlets, urging friends to write pieces for the press, assisting Republican newspaper editors, and encouraging Republican followers throughout the country to assist in the party cause. But Adams enjoyed the advantages of being the President of the United States, and, whether consciously or not, he allowed his candidacy to benefit from these advantages. After the adjournment of Congress in May, 1800, Adams did make a trip to Washington to inspect the new capital to which the offices of government were to be moved by June 15. He journeyed to Washington by way of Lancaster and York, Pennsylvania, and Fredericktown, Maryland, receiving along the way the attention that his station commanded. "How is it he has taken the route . . . *fifty* miles out of the strait course?" asked the Republican Philadelphia *Aurora*. After inspecting the new capital, Adams went to pay his respects to Mrs. Washington at Mount Vernon, where six months before General Washington had died. On his return trip northward, Adams stopped at Baltimore, before speeding home to Quincy for the summer. If Adams did not recognize the political advantages of such a trip, his Republican opponents did, as did also the anti-Adams Federalists within his own party. "The great man has been south as far as Alexandria, making his addressers acquainted with his revolutionary merits," wrote Fisher Ames, "and claiming almost in plain words at New London, office as the only reward."

Spending the summer in Massachusetts in the center of Federalist infighting, Adams noted that the Boston Federalist leaders did not make their accustomed calls at Quincy; and those party leaders noticed that at a dinner in Faneuil Hall in July Adams volunteered a toast to "the proscribed Patriots Hancock and [Sam] Adams." "It is evident Mr. Adams calculates upon engaging the passions and prejudices of the populace on his side, and with this reinforcement to overcome or beat down his federal opponents," observed George Cabot, in noting that Adams "has lately toasted men he has hated or despised these fifteen years." Fisher Ames thought that "no measures will be too intemperate that tend to make the Citizens revolutionary enough to make the man of 1775 the man of 1800." So many opponents of Adams called attention to the efforts of Adams and his friends to recall his revolutionary service that it is impossible not to consider such tactics as campaign strategy. Whether or not the tactics originated with Adams, he lent himself to the efforts. There can be no doubt that Adams wanted to be reelected in 1800, and, as a man active in politics all of his life, he could hardly have been unaware of the political consequences of his movements and actions during the campaign of 1800. If, as Adams' biographer Page Smith has concluded, Adams "often threw away political advantage quite deliberately," there is little evidence that he did so during the election of 1800.

"Never was there a more singular and mysterious state of parties," wrote Fisher Ames in July, 1800. "The plot of an old Spanish play is not more complicated with underplot." The underplot to which Massachusetts Federalist Ames referred was the struggle within the Federalist party over whether or not to dump John Adams and openly to try to elect Charles Cotesworth Pinckney. Publicly, the Federalist party was committed to support the reelection of Adams for President, but privately many of the most influential leaders of the party were opposed to Adams' reelection. When the Federalist caucus in Philadelphia in May, 1800, agreed to recommend the support of Adams and Pinckney equally, it was the intention of Hamilton and other anti-Adams Federalists that this scheme would promote the election of Pinckney and the defeat of Adams. The public argument, however, was that this was the best plan to insure a Federalist President and prevent the election of Jefferson, and it was on this ground that Adams' friends had agreed to the caucus decision. In private letters the ultra-Federalist leaders freely avowed their opposition to Adams, but they hesitated publicly to denounce their party's nominee, who in the public mind was the Federalist candidate for President and who was also the President of the United States. "Of those who forsee the exclusion of [Adams]," wrote Ames in June, 1800, "few yet dare, and fewer think it prudent or necessary, to avow their desire of such an event of the election."

Massachusetts was the center of much of the Federalist plotting and counterplotting. Some believed that the transfer of the choice of presidential electors from a popular vote to the legislature was designed to insure that all electors would vote for both Adams and Pinckney, but neither side was certain that this was true, or satisfied, in any case, to accept it. As early as June, 1800, Secretary of the Treasury Oliver Wolcott, a Hamiltonian, was urging his ultra-Federalist friends in Massachusetts to work to obtain electors who would vote *only* for Pinckney. "If General Pinckney is not elected," he wrote, "all good men will find cause to regret the present inaction of the federal party." On the other hand, George Cabot reported in July that "great efforts are making to persuade our people that they ought to throw away votes at the election, lest Mr. P[inckney] should be made President." Cabot suggested that "there are even men among the federalists who prefer Jefferson to a *federal* rival of Mr. A[dams], and there are some certainly who prefer Mr. J[efferson] to Adams."

In June Hamilton returned from a trip to Massachusetts, New Hampshire, and Rhode Island convinced that there would be Federalist electors in these states but that there was "considerable doubt of perfect union in favour of Pinckney." As the summer advanced, Hamilton moved further and further in the direction of an open break with Adams and an all-out public effort to elect Pinckney. He was strongly supported in this by Oliver Wolcott, who felt that the Federalists "ought in the first place to decide on one object and then avow and pursue it in an open and explicit manner." But Hamilton's closest followers in Massachusetts argued against any last-minute effort to drop Adams. "We shall be greatly embarrassed, if at this late period. after our sentiments are extensively known, there should be a new or different ground taken," George Cabot wrote to Hamilton; and to Wolcott, Cabot explained, "I am, and have long been, as fully convinced as you are, that Mr. Adams ought to have been abandoned by the federal party, whom he has sacrificed. But it seems a majority were not brought to this opinion in season, and the present half-way system was the consequence . . . . but still I do not see how it will be practicable to discard Mr. Adams as a candidate at this period without confounding us in this quarter, and consequently exposing the whole party to a defeat."

Throughout the summer of 1800 as anti-Adams Federalist leaders debated in their private letters the course which they should take, the wisdom of an open attack on Adams was widely questioned. From New Jersey, Richard Stockton reported that a "public avowal of a design to drop and oppose" Adams would endanger the chance of Federalist success. It was impossible to expect the Federalist members of the state legislature suddenly to drop the man that they had for four years been holding up "as one of the wisest and firmest men in the United States." "But if we use a prudent silence we shall get in our ticket of electors, and if I am not deceived, they will be men who will do right in the vote; they will go on the basis of securing a federal president. Mr. P[inckney] will be the man of their choice. They will act, at all events, in conformity with the plan proposed, in Philadelphia, and if the eastern states will unite in a more direct and decisive system, they will not desert them. But they will not be prepared to say that they prefer J[efferson] to A[dams]; they would effectually destroy themselves in public estimation if they did."

Although most of the advice that reached Hamilton from party workers active in key states opposed an open avowal of the movement to elect Pinckney, Hamilton by August confessed, "I have serious thoughts of giving to the public my opinion respecting Mr. Adams, with my reasons, in a letter to a friend, with my signature." By the end of September such a letter had been drafted. Printed for private circulation among Federalist leaders, a copy fell into Republican hands, and near the end of October it was before the public.

In the *Letter from Alexander Hamilton, Concerning the Public Conduct and Character of John Adams, Esq., President of the United States*, Hamilton attacked Adams more devastatingly than any Republican had ever done. Adams "does not possess the talents adapted to the *administration* of government," said Hamilton, and "there are great intrinsic defects in his character, which unfit him for the office of chief magistrate." "He is a man of an imagination sublimated and eccentric; propitious neither to the regular display of sound judgment, nor to steady perseverance in a systematic plan of conduct; and . . . to this defect are added the unfortunate foibles of a vanity without bounds, and a jealousy capable of discoloring every object." Hamilton did not publicly advise that votes be withheld from Adams, but he suggested that if the Federalists who shared his opinion of Adams were willing to vote equally for Adams and Pinckney, the least they could expect would be for the friends of Adams not to withhold any votes from Pinckney, especially since by voting for both men "they will increase the probability of excluding a third candidate, of whose unfitness all sincere Federalists are convinced." Hamilton's letter appeared too late in the campaign to be of much help to the Republicans, but they made the most of it in the time that remained. Its publication was a sensational event in an election year filled with dramatic developments.

The campaign of 1800 was conducted both at the level on which issues were discussed and alternatives provided and at the level where parties appealed to the emotions, prejudices, sectional attachments, and selfish interests of the voters. Although these two levels of argument were often inseparable in the partisan literature of the campaign, it is useful for the purposes of analysis to separate them. At the same time, since there is no way to determine whether a voter made up his mind through a reasonable evaluation of the issues or an emotional response to the campaign, or a combination of both influences, all levels of campaign rhetoric must be examined.

The Republican party did offer the voters a platform in 1800. Although the term *platform* was not used nor was any statement officially adopted by any agency of the Republican organization, a clearly defined party program was formulated and repeatedly presented to the electorate. The basic principles of the Republican platform were well understood by Jefferson, who stated them precisely in letters to a number of correspondents as the election of 1800 approached and reiterated them as the campaign continued. With the election won, he would repeat this same broad statement of principles in his first Inaugural Address. In a letter to Elbridge Gerry in January, 1799, Jefferson provided his best expression of the Republican platform. He began by affirming his attachment to the Constitution and continued:

> I am for preserving to the States the powers not yielded by them to the Union, and to the legislature of the Union its constitutional share in the division of powers; and I am not for transferring all the powers of the States to the general government, and all those of that government to the Executive branch. I am for a government rigorously frugal and simple, applying all the possible savings of the public revenue to the discharge of the national debt; and not for a multiplication of officers and salaries

merely to make partisans, and for increasing, by every device, the public debt, on the principle of its being a public blessing. I am for relying, for internal defence, on our militia solely, till actual invasion, and for such a naval force only as may protect our coasts and harbors from such depredations as we have experienced; and not for a standing army in time of peace, which may overawe the public sentiment; nor for a navy, which, by its own expenses and the eternal wars in which it will implicate us, will grind us with public burthens, and sink us under them. I am for free commerce with all nations; political connection with none; and little or no diplomatic establishment. And I am not for linking ourselves by new treaties with the quarrels of Europe; entering that field of slaughter to preserve their balance, or joining in the confederacy of kings to war against the principles of liberty. I am for freedom of religion, and against all maneuvres to bring about a legal ascendancy of one sect over another: for freedom of the press, and against all violations of the constitution to silence by force and not by reason the complaints or criticisms, just or unjust, of our citizens against the conduct of their agents.

"These, my friend," Jefferson affirmed, "are my principles; they are unquestionably the principles of the great body of our fellow citizens."

The summary of the Republican position which Jefferson here offered in a private letter corresponded to the public positions that Republicans took in response to the measures of the Adams Administration. A series of resolutions adopted by Republicans in Dinwiddie County, Virginia, in November, 1798, and published in the Richmond *Examiner*, December 6, 1798, placed emphasis on many of the same points. These resolutions may serve as an example of the public statement of Republican arguments against Federalist policies, which Republicans made the principal issues of the election of 1800. The major points of these resolutions were:

(1) Opposition to standing armies. "A militia composed of the body of the people, is the proper, natural, and safe defence of a free state," it was declared in resolving "that regular armies, except in case of an invasion, or the certain prospect of an invasion, are not only highly detrimental to the public welfare, but dangerous to liberty. . . . Military establishments are in their nature progressive, the vast expense attending them, producing discontent and disturbances, and these furnishing a pretext for providing a force still more formidable; thus finally occasioning the oppression, the ruin, the SLAVERY of the people."

(2) Opposition to great naval armament "because it enlarges still more the fund for increasing executive influence: because the expense is incalculable . . . because this country cannot hope to protect its commerce by a fleet . . . or to guard from invasion a coast fifteen hundred miles in extent. . . . When therefore the navy of the United States is competent to the protection, not of our extensive coast, nor of our commerce throughout the world, but of our sea ports and coasting trade, from privateering and piratical depredations, it has attained the point, beyond which it ought not to go."

(3) Opposition to "an alliance with any nation on earth." Republicans "reprobate therefore the practice of maintaining ministers resident in foreign countries, in the extent to which it is carried by the executive of the United

States; because it adds still more to the already enormous mass of presidential patronage; because every important political view might be accomplished by a single minister advantageously stationed, and every valuable commercial purpose might be effected under the ordinary consular establishments; and because at a time like this, when money is borrowed to supply the deficiency of the taxes, every expense not absolutely necessary ought to be avoided."

(4) Opposition to increasing the national debt on the grounds that "the only proper way to raise money for national purposes, is by taxes, duties, excises and imposts, and that the power of borrowing money, ought not to be exercised except in cases of absolute necessity; that if money be really wanted, the people ought to be taxed to pay it; if not wanted, it ought not to be raised."

(5) Opposition to the alien act as "unnecessary, repugnant to humanity, and contrary to the constitution."

(6) Opposition to the Sedition Act as "a daring and unconstitutional violation of a sacred and essential right, without which, liberty, political science and national prosperity are at an end." "Freedom of the press is the great bulwark of liberty and can never be restrained but by a despotic government."

Various versions of this platform were published during the course of the campaign in party leaflets and in the press. The Philadelphia *Aurora* printed a popularized version listing the alleged Federalist record and the proposed Republican program in parallel columns, urging voters to "Take Your Choice" between "Things As They Have Been" and "Things As They Will Be."

In answer to the question "What do the republican interest want by so zealously attempting a change of men?" Charles Pinckney, who managed the Jeffersonian campaign in South Carolina, explained in a pamphlet: "Never to have such acts as the alien and sedition laws; or unnecessary embassies; or too intimate a connexion with any foreign power; but a just and impartial conduct to all—so that peace may be established, and wars avoided, with all their dangerous and expensive armaments and consequences—the public expense reduced, so that our revenue may be employed in paying and lessening the public debt, and an end put to heavy additional yearly loans, at the rate of eight per centum—no direct tax on the landed and agricultural interests only, but strict economy in all our expenditures . . . these are among the objects of the republican interest in endeavouring to place men in power in whom they can confide to accomplish them effectually."

While the Republicans thus presented a clearly identifiable platform, the Federalists essentially ran on their record, and in this they took pains to link together the Administrations of Washington and Adams and to lay a party claim to the accomplishments of the first President. Federalist literature stressed the "present prosperous situation" of the nation as a result of "the sage maxims of administration established by the immortal Washington, and steadily pursued by his virtuous successor," and argued against change. "An unvarying course of prosperity, like the even tenor of health, makes no impression, while we betray a quick sensibility to the slightest misfortune or pain," declared the Federalist state committee of Virginia. "We forget that our government has preserved us from two impending wars, the foundation of which was laid before its existence, with the two most powerful nations of the world, armed to the full extent of their powers; and that, without any sacrifice of the national interest, or of the national honor. We forget that we have been preserved from a close alliance with either of those nations, which would have been the worst, and the most inevitable, consequences of a war with the other; and that we remain, if we will, completely free and independent. But the fleet, the army, the taxes, all the little evils which were necessary to the attainment of these great and invaluable objects, make a strong impression, and are attributed as crimes to the government."

In a similar vein, a Federalist address to Rhode Island voters argued: "The land tax has afforded a topic of declamation to the opponents of government. It has been charged upon the administration when it ought to have been charged to the war in Europe, and the depredations which have been committed on our commerce by the powers at war. A Navy has become indispensable to the existence of our commerce, and the prosperity of our agriculture." Repeatedly, Federalists defended their record, and they expected voters to "value the blessings of good government too well to risque a change."

However clearly and reasonably the two parties presented their positions, as they did on numerous occasions, neither party rested its case on the restrained presentations of policy differences. Both parties appealed to the voters' emotions and prejudices, to their hopes and fears, and to their personal, class, and sectional interests. Although there was a note of restraint in most official party publications, whether Republican or Federalist, an emotional appeal rang through many campaign handbills, leaflets, and endless columns of newspaper print. "We ought . . . to bring our arguments home to their feelings," advised one Republican; while a Federalist urged his party to "sound the tocsin about Jefferson," arguing that "the hopes and fears of the citizens are the only source of influence, and surely we have enough to fear from Jefferson."

"*Is it not high time for a CHANGE?*" asked a Republican campaign leaflet addressed to the voters of New Jersey. And throughout the country Republicans painted a shocking picture of the state of the nation: "Our agriculture is oppressed by taxation. Our manufactures are superceded by British productions. Our commerce subjected to the spoliations of foreign cruisers. . . . We are struggling under a direct tax, with heavy imposts; raising money on loan at *Eight* per cent. — And our expenditures are encreasing, while our national debt is accumulating." On the outcome of the election, voters on Long Island were told, "will depend whether the present system of war, debt, and encreasing taxation shall continue to be pursued, or a new line of conduct shall be adopted." Republicans published long lists of figures showing governmental expenditures and the increase in the national debt. They compared the six-and-a-half-million dollar appropriation for the Army and Navy in 1800 with the total expenditure of nine hundred thousand dollars during Washington's first year in office and suggested that "if we want to return to the best days of Washington's presidency, let us elect Jefferson, who was his principal minister in those days." A New Jersey Republican committee urged voters to vote against "the present administration, under which your *taxes* and *public debt* have been greatly increased, in a time of peace; under which the number of federal officers hath been greatly increased, and mercenary armies attempted to be raised; which is not barely an unnecessary expense upon the people, but highly alarming and dangerous to their liberties."

A New England Federalist observed that the Republicans "have a certain number of sounds, thrown into the form of regular and well connected sentences, which they can on all occasions utter with the utmost facility and volubility. In these sentences the words British Influence—Standing Army—Direct Taxes—Funding System—Expensive Navy—Commerce can support itself—Congress have too high wages—Aristocracy—and Washington's Grave Stones, are ever and anon distinctly heard." Although Republicans directed their campaign rhetoric primarily against the record of the Federalist Administration rather than against Adams personally, there were charges of monarchist leveled against the President. One Republican writer, hoping that Americans "will never permit the chief magistrate of the union to become a *King* instead of a president," attempted to prove "that there is a monarchical party in the United States, and that Mr. Hamilton and Mr. Adams belong to that party." Republicans also tried to picture Administration leaders as British sympathizers. "We have seen with regret," declared a Republican state convention in September, 1800, "*British subjects* raised to posts of honor and profit, to the exclusion of *honest Americans*, who braved the perils of a long and bloody war. We have seen old tories, the enemies of our revolution, recommended as the guardians of our country."

Campaign literature frequently appealed to local prejudices and sectional attachments. Federalists in New England suggested that "the great and powerful State of Virginia seems to take the lead in the present opposition to the measures of administration. The plausible and specious cry that the liberties of the people are in danger, and that aristocracy is creeping into our government, originates in and emanates from that State. But will New-England-men, with arms in their hands, ever confess that they are in danger of slavery?" In a similar vein the *Connecticut Courant* insisted that the freemen of Connecticut should not stoop "to learn the principles of liberty of the slave-holders of Virginia." And one reader agreed: "We want no *Southern lights* in these parts: We have northern lights,—we have gospel light, and political light, sufficient to exterminate Jacobinism."

Republicans likewise shaped their appeals to the particular interests and sentiments of the voters addressed. "Why should you hear any more of the Alien Law?" they asked Pennsylvania Germans. In Rhode Island, they called particular attention to Jefferson's devotion to religious toleration and attacked Adams as a champion of established religion. In Pennsylvania, Republicans proclaimed that "to religious men, Mr. Jefferson has indisputably been the most useful character, since *William Penn*," and as President he would promote "the sound *practical Equality* of the Quaker" and "the *equal Brotherhood* of the Moravian, the Mennonist, and the Dunker." In New Jersey, Republicans accused Federalists of attacking Jefferson on religious grounds simply "because he is not a fanatic, nor willing that the *Quaker*, the *Baptist*, the *Methodist*, or any other denominations of Christians, should pay the pastors of other sects; because he does not think that a catholic should be banished for believing in transubstantiation, or a jew, for believing in the God of Abraham, Isaac, and Jacob."

In some regions, Republican campaign literature frequently referred to Jefferson's agrarianism, and a passage was widely quoted from his *Notes on the State of Virginia* in which he had written that "those who labor in the earth are the chosen people of God." The farmers of Rhode Island were told, "He has not fawned on great cities for support. He has declared, that 'if ever God has a chosen People, it is the cultivators of the soil.' Cultivators of the Soil—friends of peace, humanity, and Freedom: give him your support. He will not betray you." At the same time, Republicans in the cities appealed to the "mechanics" and other city dwellers, and Jefferson was held up as the "friend of the people." An editorial in the New York *American Citizen*, April 3, 1800, concluded that "*Thomas Jefferson* is the enlightened citizen, the patriot, the philosopher, and the friend of man, to whom the republican attachment and affections of this country ought to be directed." Republicans in the cities thus found ample ground for praising Jefferson without calling attention to his agrarianism.

Everywhere Republicans pointed to Jefferson as the author of the Declaration of Independence. "Let us therefore," urged one campaign broadside, "taking the Declaration of Independence in our hands, and carrying its principles in our hearts, let us resolve to support THOMAS JEFFERSON, whose whole life has been a comment on its precepts, and an uniform pursuit of the great blessings of his country which it was first intended to establish." Republicans also praised Jefferson for his "talents as governor of his native state, as an ambassador abroad, as legislator and secretary of state," and lauded him as "the adorer of our God; the patriot of his country; and the friend and benefactor of the whole human race." Concluded the Republican state committee of Virginia in its official address to the voters: "As a friend to liberty, we believe Jefferson second to no man, and the experience of no man has afforded better lessons for its preservation."

The Federalist picture of Jefferson was, of course, quite different. "You have been, Sir, a Governor, an Ambassador, and a Secretary of State," a writer in the *Gazette of the United States* addressed Jefferson, "and had to desert each of these posts, from that weakness of nerves, want of fortitude and total imbecility of character, which have marked your whole political career, and most probably will attend you to your grave."

One recurring theme in much of the anti-Jefferson literature was that his election would bring to the United States the disorders that the French Revolution had brought to France. Wrote "A North Carolina Planter": "Against the dangerous principles of Mr. Jefferson's philosophy . . . to warn you, my fellow citizens, I have only to direct your view to that ill fated country France, and bring to your recollection the history of the horrid government of their philosophers, who professed similar principles. . . . From the government of such philosophers, may the beneficent father of the universe protect us." A writer signing himself "A Christian Federalist" warned in *A Short Address to the Voters of Delaware*: "Can serious and reflecting men look about them and doubt, that if Jefferson is elected, and the Jacobins get into authority, that those morals which protect our lives from the knife of the assassin—which guard the chastity of our wives and daughters from seduction and violence—defend our property from plunder and devastation, and shield our religion from contempt and profanation, will not be trampled upon and exploded. Men are the same in their natures in different countries and at different times. . . . Let these men get into power, put the reins of government into their hands, and what security have you against the occurrence of the scenes which have rendered France a cemetery, and moistened her soil with the tears and blood of her inhabitants?"

The issue that received most attention in newspapers and pamphlets was Jefferson's religion. "The Grand Question Stated," as the Philadelphia *Gazette of the United States* repeatedly proclaimed, was: "At the present solemn and momentous epoch, the only question to be asked by every American, laying his hand on his heart is 'shall I continue in allegiance to

GOD—AND A RELIGIOUS PRESIDENT;

Or impiously declare for

JEFFERSON—AND NO GOD!!!' "

In newspapers, pamphlets, and handbills, Jefferson was charged with being a deist, an atheist, and an enemy to religion. The accusations were often voiced in the most vehement language. In the widely circulated pamphlet *Serious Considerations on the Election of a President: Addressed to the Citizens of the United States*, the Reverend William Linn of New York charged Jefferson with "disbelief of the Holy Scriptures" and the "rejection of the Christian Religion and open profession of Deism." Citing passages from *Notes on the State of Virginia*, Linn concluded that "the election of any man avowing the principles of Mr. Jefferson would . . . destroy religion, introduce immorality, and loosen all the bonds of society. . . . The voice of the nation in calling a deist to the first office must be construed into no less than a rebellion against God." Federalist editors reprinted long passages in their papers; the pamphlet, said the editor of the *Gazette of the United States*, "convicts Mr. Jefferson of scepticism, deism, and disregard of the holy scriptures."

It is evident from the number of replies to Linn's pamphlet that the Republicans were sensitive about this issue. They countered with their own passages from Jefferson's *Notes on the State of Virginia*, which offered abundant proof, they suggested, that Mr. Jefferson was not a deist. One Republican pamphlet argued "that the charge of deism, contained in such pamphlet, is false, scandalous and malicious—That there is not a single passage in the Notes on Virginia, or any of Mr. Jefferson's writings, repugnant to christianity; but on the contrary, in every respect favourable to it." Republicans also stressed Jefferson's authorship of the act for establishing religious freedom in Virginia and his efforts to promote toleration in religion. "Religious liberty, the rights of conscience, no priesthood, truth and Jefferson," promised the Philadelphia *Aurora's* version of the Republican platform.

"Jefferson is pretty fiercely attacked in different parts of the Continent on the ground of his religious principles," wrote Federalist Robert Troup of New York in September 1800. "It is not probable, however, that all that has been, or will be, written on this subject will deprive Jefferson of a single vote, so irrevocably bent is his party on forcing him into the President's chair." Republicans were, however, taking no chances, and they saturated the country with defenses of their candidate's religious principles.

Most of the campaign issues were debated within the context and procedures of state elections for members of the legislatures which would choose the presidential electors in two-thirds of the states. While presidential electors were popularly elected in only five of the sixteen states in 1800, the evidence is overwhelming that state elections were dominated by the presidential contest.

In Maryland, where under existing legislation presidential electors were popularly elected, a simultaneous campaign went on for members of the legislature. The election for the legislature was to be held on the first Monday in October, and Federalists campaigned on the promise to transfer the choice of electors to the state legislature before the election of presidential electors would be held on the second Monday in November. "We deem it a sacred duty to pursue every *proper and constitutional* measure to elect John Adams president of the United States," a group of Federalist candidates for the assembly announced in a joint statement.

There was more open campaigning in Maryland than in any other state in 1800. It took place wherever people gathered, "at a horse race, a cock-fight, or a Methodist quarterly meeting," explained one observer. "Here, the Candidates for political honors or preferment, assemble with their partizans —they mount the Rostrum, made out of an empty barrel or hogshead, Harrangue the Sovereign people—praise and recommend themselves at the expence of their adversary's character and pretentions." The Baltimore *Federal Gazette* on July 28, 1800, reported two large meetings where "the different candidates for elector of president and members of assembly attended and harangued the voters. . . . After panegyrising the character of Mr. Jefferson, and defending it against the charges of pusillanimity and deism," the Republican candidate for the assembly "discanted on the official conduct of Mr. Adams. He declared several acts of congress unconstitutional and offered himself as a member of the next assembly, to forward the election of the former and to oppose the re-election of the latter." A Republican candidate for elector also attempted "to prove the necessity of turning Mr. Adams out of the presidency and of electing Mr. Jefferson in his place." He was answered by a Federalist spokesman who solemnly replied "that the measures of the present administration were conceived in wisdom, and executed with firmness, uprightness and ability—that the path laid down by Washington had been faithfully pursued by Adams—and that the latter had done all that could be done, and no more, to ensure *justice* from abroad and *tranquillity* at home."

While Federalists attempted to associate Washington's name in the popular mind with Federalism, Republicans were unwilling to permit an exclusive claim to the young nation's greatest hero. "Consummate your reverence for the memory of Washington," suggested the Republican state committee of Virginia, "not by employing it as an engine of election, but by declaring, that even his name shall not prevent the free use of your own understandings." And the title page of a Republican pamphlet containing extracts from Jefferson's writings on religion ran a quotation from Washington: "The path of true piety is too plain to want political direction."

In private letters during the summer and fall political leaders on both sides arrived at similar conclusions about the outcome of the election. They agreed that, except for uncertain Rhode Island, the New England states would be Federalist, though whether they would be unanimous for Adams and Pinckney even Hamilton could not predict. New York would be Republican; Pennsylvania probably would not cast a vote; Delaware would be Federalist; New Jersey would be close. "We think we have an equal claim with the federalists, to the whole of New Jersey," Burr wrote in July. "The republicans of that State speak most confidantly of a republican legislature at the approaching election in October." From the Federalist side, Hamilton wrote in August: "The State of New Jersey is more uncertain than I could wish. Parties will be too nicely balanced there. But our friends continue confident of a favorable result."

Maryland was uncertain. If the district system prevailed, the 10 electoral votes would be divided. Burr in July claimed 4 certain, and 2 possible, Republican districts. Federalist James A. Bayard in August would concede but 3 Maryland districts to Jefferson. All agreed that Virginia would be unanimous for Jefferson; or, as Bayard expressed it, "Virginia is sold, and past salvation." North Carolina, where electors would be elected by districts, would be divided. Nathaniel Macon, who, a friend noted in passing along his prediction, was "too proud to promise on slight grounds," reported that Republicans could be sure of 8 votes out of 12 from that state. Bayard advised Hamilton to count 7 North Carolina votes for Jefferson. Kentucky, Tennessee, and Georgia were counted in Jefferson's column, but South Carolina had everyone guessing.

Burr predicted in July that if Pennsylvania did not vote Jefferson would have 63 votes, or a majority of 2. Hamilton refrained from an exact prediction but concluded in August that "there seems to be too much probability that Jefferson or Burr will be President." Bayard, however, predicting South Carolina for Pinckney and Jefferson, thought there was still "no reason to despond, unless the Eastern states play a foul game." At the end of November, Jefferson calculated that, excluding Pennsylvania, Rhode Island, and South Carolina, the Republicans would have 58 electoral votes and the Federalists 53. "Both parties count with equal confidence on Rhode Island and South Carolina," he said. "Pennsylvania stands little chance for a vote. . . . In that case, the issue of the election hangs on South Carolina." From Washington, D. C., two days earlier, Oliver Wolcott had written in much the same vein to a Federalist friend: "The issue of the election of a President, is, at this time, as uncertain as ever; all depends on the vote of South Carolina, and this is claimed and expected by both parties."

As elections in various states were decided and the party complexion of the electoral vote determined, it became clear that the election was, indeed, to be finally settled by South Carolina. Without that state's vote, the last to be reported, the Federalists had all of the New England electoral votes. They also won New Jersey and Rhode Island, carried 5 of 10 districts in Maryland, and elected 4 of the 12 electors in North Carolina. In Pennsylvania a compromise was reached on December 1 by which the Republicans secured 8 electors and the Federalists named 7 – a net gain of but 1 for the Republicans. These victories gave the Federalists 65 votes. On the other side, the Republicans won the entire vote of New York, Virginia, Georgia, Kentucky, and Tennessee, which together with 8 electors from Pennsylvania, 5 from Maryland, and 8 from North Carolina, gave the Republicans a total of 65 votes also. Thus, with South Carolina unrecorded, Republicans and Federalists stood equal. Some Federalist editors now began to predict a Federalist victory, though all agreed that the outcome rested upon South Carolina.

One person who had been convinced all along that "the choice of a President would in a great measure depend upon this States vote" was Charles Pinckney, Republican senator from South Carolina who had devoted himself to winning the state for Jefferson since returning home after the adjournment of Congress. Since June, Pinckney had been actively "sprinkling," as he put it, "all the southern states with pamphlets and Essays and every thing I thought would promote the common cause against what I well knew must be the Consequence if the federalists succeeded." Despite Pinckney's efforts, Federalists carried 11 out of the 15 seats from Charleston, and the composition of the state legislature appeared so doubtful that Pinckney himself, not a member of the assembly but a United States senator, decided to go to the capital at Columbia for the climactic meeting.

The assembly convened on the last Monday in November (November 24), and Presidential electors were to be chosen on the first Tuesday of December (December 2). In a week of political maneuvering Pinckney worked frantically to get a slate of electors for Jefferson and Burr. The presence of a native son, General Charles Cotesworth Pinckney, the Federalist candidate and a member of the state senate, further complicated the situation. At two evening caucuses Republicans named their slate. In a report to his partner and co-editor Seth Paine of the Charleston *City Gazette*, Peter Freneau described the situation in Columbia on November 27, three days after the opening of the session. "There have been two meetings of the republicans at the School House," he wrote, "and 69 have signed their names to support the Jefferson and Burr Ticket, and it is believed that there are 12 to 20 more who will Vote for it. It is the general opinion of the republicans here that all will go right, and this is my opinion if some arts are not successful between this and tuesday; every thing that can be done by the other party will be attempted. There is to be a meeting at the Presidents of the Senate this evening. There are 142 members present, we suppose there will be 150, of course 75 is equal, we count from 84 to 86, some say 90. I hope we are not mistaken still I am not confident as there are some of this number which do not like to give up P[inckney]. I have heard that the drift of the meeting this night is to offer a compromise, while others say that the General will not suffer his name to be run with Mr. Jefferson. At any rate I think things look favorable."

When Republicans caught wind of a Federalist plan to send speakers to the final Republican caucus the night prior to the balloting, they canceled the meeting. As Republicans understood the scheme, Federalist spokesmen hoped to appeal to state loyalty and propose a compromise ticket of Jefferson and Pinckney. If this were the case, no Federalist ever admitted it, and Federalists repeatedly claimed that General Pinckney had firmly resisted all attempts to form a ticket with Jefferson.

On December 2 the legislature elected all the Republican candidates by majorities of from 13 to 18 votes. Freneau hurriedly sent the news to Paine in Charleston: "Our Electors are chosen . . . rejoice and let the good news be known. Our Country is yet safe. The vote tomorrow will be Jefferson 8. Burr 7. Clinton 1. This I am told—it is not the wish to risque any person being higher than Jefferson. I know not what I am writing I am so rejoiced." Freneau gave much of the credit for the victory to Charles Pinckney; and from Pinckney's own letters to Jefferson written immediately after the South Carolina victory the clear implication was that Pinckney had made some promises of patronage. While the report went out that 1 vote would be withheld from Burr in South Carolina, the electors met in Columbia and cast 8 votes for Jefferson and an equal number for Burr.

In New York, Federalist Robert Troup wrote on December 4 to Rufus King in London: "This is the day appointed for the election of President and Vice President. The calculations now are that Adams and Pinckney will outrun Jefferson and Burr. . . . This opinion is based upon the votes of the States, now known, and, that, in South Carolina, all our accounts agree that the last election of members of the Legislature terminated in the triumph of the federalists, and that the electors appointed by them will of course be decidedly federal. General Pinckney who wrote to General Hamilton after the election, and before the event was certainly known, puts much confidence in the appointment of federal electors and says that they would vote honorably according to the agreement in Philadelphia for Adams and himself. It is this success in South Carolina that determines the event of the election."

Troup's optimism was shared by numerous Federalist editors, one of whom announced that "the non-election of (*Citizen*) Jefferson is now certain." The news of the actual South Carolina vote thus came as a blow to many Federalists. "I have never heard bad tidings on anything which gave me such a shock," a New England clergyman confided in his diary. The Republicans, too, got a jolt when the outcome in South Carolina was known and all the votes were tallied. The final count was Jefferson 73, Burr 73, Adams 65, Pinckeny 64, and Jay 1. The shock was not that the Republicans had won, but that Jefferson had not actually been elected President. Instead, the equal vote given to Burr forced the election into the House of Representatives, in the first of only two such occasions in American history.

PRESIDENTIAL AND CONGRESSIONAL ELECTIONS, 1800

	Electoral Vote					*Members Elected to House of Representatives*	
	Jefferson	Burr	Adams	Pinckney	Jay	Republicans	Federalists
New Hampshire			6	6			4
Vermont			4	4		1	1
Massachusetts			16	16		7	7
Rhode Island			4	3	1	2	
Connecticut			9	9			7
New York	12	12				6	4
New Jersey			7	7		5	
Pennsylvania	8	8	7	7		10	3
Delaware			3	3			1
Maryland	5	5	5	5		5	3
Virginia	21	21				18	1
North Carolina	8	8	4	4		5	5
South Carolina	8	8				3	3
Georgia	4	4				2	
Kentucky	4	4				2	
Tennessee	3	3				1	
	73	73	65	64	1	67	39

(*Italics* indicates states in which presidential electors were elected by popular vote.)

In analyzing the election returns, historians have frequently pointed to the fact that outside New York Adams received 7 more votes in 1800 than in 1796. That is true, but 6 of those 7 votes came from Pennsylvania, where the deadlocked legislature prevented an actual test of strength and divided the state's electoral vote 8 for Jefferson and 7 for Adams. Jefferson had carried 14 of the 15 electoral votes of Pennsylvania in 1796; in 1799 the Republicans won the governorship of the state, and in 1800 Republicans carried 10 out of the 13 districts in the congressional elections. It is thus evident that the Pennsylvania vote in 1800 did not reflect the true strength of parties, and no significance should be attached to the increase in Adams' electoral vote in that state. The observation that Jefferson could not have won without New York should not be used to suggest that Jefferson's victory reflected no real nationwide strength and that it resulted merely from the Republican success in New York City. This overlooks the clear evidence that Jefferson's strength in Pennsylvania was not reflected in the electoral vote, and it also ignores the impressive proof of Jeffersonian strength displayed in the congressional elections.

Any analysis must take into consideration the congressional elections, which, because of the manner in which the electoral system operated in 1800, more adequately reflected the preferences of the electorate. Congressional returns demonstrated that the Republican party was stronger in 1800 than the presidential electoral vote indicated and that there was a clear popular verdict in favor of the Republican party and its candidates. While the margin in the electoral vote between Jefferson's 73 and Adams' 65 electoral votes was narrow, in the elections for Congress the Republicans won 67 out of 106 seats in the House of Representatives.

The congressional vote also showed that the operation of parties and the basis of support of both parties were more national in scope than the electoral returns suggested. In New England (New Hampshire, Vermont, Massachusetts, Rhode Island, and Connecticut) where the entire electoral vote of 39 went to the Federalists, Republicans elected 10 of the 29 representatives. In the middle states (New York, New Jersey, Pennsylvania, and Delaware) the electoral vote was divided, 20 Republicans and 17 Federalists; and the congressional vote was divided, 21 Republicans and 8 Federalists. In the South (Maryland, Virginia, the Carolinas, and Georgia) the electoral vote was 46 Republicans to 9 Federalists, while the congressional representation was 33 Republicans to 12 Federalists. In the two western states (Kentucky and Tennessee) both the electoral vote of 7 and the congressional membership of 3 were unanimously Republican.

In assessing the outcome of the election, Federalists put a great deal of emphasis on the split in the Federalist party. Adams himself suggested that he sacrificed his chances for reelection by alienating the Hamiltonian leaders when he decided to send a second peace mission to France. An analysis of the election returns, however, fails to reveal that the Federalist split was in fact responsible for Adams' defeat. The divisions in Federalist ranks were the most serious in New England, but Adams lost not a single electoral vote in any New England state. The loss of New York cannot be attributed to Hamilton's opposition, for Hamilton worked to maintain Federalist control over the New York assembly. If Federalist control had been maintained, it might then have been used to promote Pinckney over Adams; but a Republican legislature would offer no hope, as Hamilton's frantic appeal to Governor Jay indicated. Adams carried New Jersey and Delaware, and the vote of Pennsylvania was determined by the deadlock in the legislature between the Republican house and the Federalist senate. In the southern and western states there is reason to believe that Adams was helped more than he was hurt by his repudiation of the ultra-Federalists. In Maryland, where Adams had won 7 electoral votes in 1796, he received 5 in 1800; in North Carolina, Adams' vote went from 1 in 1796 to 4 in 1800. In these two states, then, Adams had a net gain of 1. In Virginia, where Adams had received 1 electoral vote in 1796, there was no chance of winning any in 1800 because of the change in the method of electing presidential electors. Elsewhere in the South and the West Adams had won no votes in 1796. The best hope for increasing his vote in 1800 was in South Carolina, which had voted for Thomas Pinckney and Jefferson in 1796. It was Hamilton's hope that South Carolina might vote for Charles Cotesworth Pinckney and Jefferson in 1800 and give Pinckney the Presidency, but this, of course, did not occur. Still, there is no reason to conclude that Federalist divisions or Hamilton's opposition to Adams kept South Carolina from going either to Adams and Pinckney or to Jefferson and Pinckney. Although one New York Federalist reported that letters from "respectable federalists in South Carolina" asserted that Hamilton's letter attacking Adams had "accomplished the democratical majority in the South Carolina Legislature," it is clear from surviving records that the events in South Carolina were not so easily explained.

A comparison of the presidential electoral vote in 1800 with that of 1796 suggests the acceptance of two-party competition in American politics by 1800 and a tightening of party discipline and control. In 1796 thirteen candidates received votes, though most of the scattering of electoral votes was in the second ballots (for Vice-President). In 1800, with the exception of one Rhode Island elector, all Presidential electors cast their votes for the Republican ticket of Jefferson and Burr or the Federalist slate of Adams and Pinckney.

The possibility of a tie vote between Jefferson and Burr had been considered by Republican leaders during the campaign, but no definite plans had been completed to insure that it did not occur. James Madison, one of the Virginia electors, recalled that "it was with much difficulty that a unanimous vote could be obtained in the Virginia College of Electors for both [Jefferson and Burr] lest an equality might throw the choice into the House." But he "had received assurances from a confidential friend of Burr that in a certain quarter votes would be thrown from B[urr] with a view to secure the majority for Jefferson." Thus, Virginia electors were persuaded to vote for Jefferson and Burr in order to strengthen the New York-Virginia alliance within the Republican party. In 1796 Burr had received only 1 vote in Virginia, and he had indicated in 1800 that "after what happened at the last election . . . it is most obvious that I should not choose to be trifled with." Both Jefferson and Madison worked to secure an unanimous vote for Burr in Virginia, relying on the withholding of votes in some other state. This expectation rested more upon reports, assurances, and rumors than on clear arrangements, and none of the rumored plans to withhold votes from Burr materialized. Instead, there was an unprecedented display of party regularity. As a result. the election was left to the House of Representatives—and not the newly elected body that the Republicans were sweeping into power but the Federalist-controlled House elected in 1798 at the height of Federalist popularity following the XYZ incident. "The Federalists in the legislature have expressed dispositions to make all they can of the embarrassment," wrote Jefferson, "so that after the most energetic efforts, crowned with success, we remain in the hands of our enemies by the want of foresight in the original arrangements."

In the election by the House of Representatives, voting was by states, with each state casting one vote. Although the Federalists had a majority, they did not control a majority of the state delegations; but neither did the Republicans. Two state delegations were equally divided, and the Republicans needed 1 of these to command the 9 states necessary for a majority. The Federalists were thus in a position to block the election of Jefferson or prevent a decision before Adams' term of office ended on March 4. From the beginning of the contest, Hamilton urged the Federalists to support Jefferson rather than Burr, whose "public principles have no other spring or aim than his own aggrandisement." But the Federalists in Congress ignored Hamilton's advice and threw their support to Burr. They did not have the votes to elect Burr, but by supporting him persistently enough they might persuade some Republicans to switch from Jefferson to Burr in order to decide the election before Adams' term expired.

Burr early issued a statement declaring that anyone who knew him ought to know that he would utterly disclaim any competition with Jefferson and that he would never be an instrument in counteracting the wishes and expectations of the people of the United States. He publicly maintained this position throughout the contest, but he never clarified it, and he never issued the one statement that would have ended all Federalist hopes. Burr never declared that if elected he would refuse to accept the Presidency. Federalists thus circulated the word that Burr's statement was to be ignored and that he was willing to accept the office. Just what Burr was attempting to do behind the scenes cannot be fully determined. But it seems clear that Burr did not need to resort to intrigue to obtain Federalist support; this he already had. What Burr needed was Republican support. By not issuing a statement promising to resign if elected, Burr, many Republicans concluded, was actually seeking the Presidency for himself.

The election law required that the certificates of the electors be opened in a joint session of the two houses of Congress on the second Wednesday in February, and thus the election could not be decided before February 11, 1801. As soon as the returns were counted by Congress on February 11, balloting by states began in the House of Representatives. On the first ballot Jefferson received the votes of 8 states: New York, New Jersey, Pennsylvania, Virginia, North Carolina, Georgia, Kentucky, and Tennessee. Burr had the votes of 6 states: New Hampshire, Massachusetts, Rhode Island, Connecticut, Delaware, and South Carolina. Two states, Vermont and Maryland, were divided. This vote differed from the breakdown by states of the vote in the electoral college. There Jefferson had carried 8 states but had not carried New Jersey and had won South Carolina; Vermont's electoral vote had gone to Adams, and Maryland's vote had been equally divided.

By midnight of February 11, the first day of balloting, nineteen ballots had been taken. On each the result was the same. Balloting continued for nearly a week with no changes except for a few within state delegations that did not alter any state's vote. With the end of Adams' term only two weeks away, the deadlock was creating a major crisis. Governor James Monroe of Virginia assured Jefferson that if any unsurpation were atempted, he would immediately convene the Virginia assembly. There were rumors in Virginia that the Federalists planned to turn over the Presidency by legislative act to Secretary of State John Marshall until another election could be held. "If that party wish to disorganize, *that* is the way to do it." said Monroe. "If the union could be broken, that would do it." As Monroe implied, what was being tested by this crisis was nothing less than the peaceful transfer of political power in the national government from one party to another.

As tensions mounted, the Federalists yielded. On February 17, on the thirty-sixth ballot, Jefferson received the votes of 10 states and was elected President. This resulted from the Federalist members from Vermont and Maryland either not voting or putting in blank ballots so that those 2 states which had been divided went to Jefferson. The votes of Delaware and South Carolina were cast as blank ballots, so that no Federalist-controlled delegation actually voted for Jefferson. On the final ballot, Burr thus received only the votes of 4 New England states. The manner in which the Federalist vote was cast in this final ballot was arranged only a few minutes before the vote was taken, but the crucial decision was made when James A. Bayard, who as the only member from Delaware cast that state's vote, announced to a Federalist caucus that he was prepared to throw his vote to Jefferson to end the deadlock. That Bayard, who had been under pressure from Hamilton to support Jefferson from the beginning, did not reach this decision until all efforts to elect Burr had failed destroys the common assertion that Hamilton's influence was decisive in throwing the election in the House to Jefferson.

Why did the Federalists finally decide to give up Burr? Jefferson thought the Federalists saw the impossibility of electing Burr and "the certainty that a legislative usurpation would be resisted by arms, and a recourse to a convention to re-organize and amend the government." "The very word convention gives them the horrors,". he wrote, "as in the present democratical spirit of America, they fear they should lose some of the favorite morsels of the constitution." On the other hand, some Federalists later indicated that they had secured guarantees as to future policy from Jefferson before permitting his election. Five years after the election Bayard testified that he had received assurances on certain points of policy and in regard to officeholders from Samuel Smith of Maryland on the authority of Jefferson. When questioned, Smith affirmed that he had given Bayard assurances and that he had conferred with Jefferson. However, Smith insisted that he had not acted on Jefferson's authority and that there had been no bargains. Indeed, he later affirmed that he had conferred with Jefferson "without his having the remotest idea of my object."

While there is no reason to question Smith's testimony that he did not tell Jefferson he was seeking assurances to be passed on to the Federalists, it seems unlikely that Jefferson did not realize that his discussions with Smith might be shared with others. At the same time, it is evident that Jefferson did not regard Smith as an emissary seeking to negotiate a contract. During the balloting Jefferson wrote Monroe that "many attempts have been made to obtain terms and promises from me. I have declared to them unequivocally that I would not receive the government on capitulation, and that I would not go into it with my hands tied." There is no reason to doubt Jefferson's declaration, and it is clear that, regardless of whatever satisfaction the Federalists may have obtained from Smith's reports, Jefferson in no way entered office with his hands tied.

"I hope you will have the cannon out to announce the news," said a message dispatched by express from Washington to Richmond reporting the final ballot in the House, and Republicans throughout the country were soon caught up in a wave of festivities celebrating the inauguration of Jefferson as President on March 4. For the moment, Burr, who was elected Vice-President, was still in Republican favor; but as Republicans reviewed the contest their confidence in him evaporated, and Burr was soon, in effect, read out of the Republican party. After the victory celebrations faded away, Republicans also remembered the anxiety of the months of crisis that resulted from the Jefferson-Burr tie, and this concern brought about the adoption of the 12th Amendment in 1804, prior to the presidential balloting of that year. Providing for the separate balloting by presidential electors for President and Vice-President, this amendment was a clear recognition of the existence of the party system in American politics.

The election of 1800 was truly a critical election in American history. It not only tested the operation of the political mechanisms that the Constitution and political parties had created, but also produced a meaningful change in the management of the national government. When Republicans replaced Federalists in control of the federal administration, they brought both new men and new policies. Although the campaign of 1800 was no pure contest of principles, there is ample evidence to conclude that voters had general conceptions of what to expect if the Federalists continued in office and what changes to anticipate if the Republicans were victorious. Above all, the election demonstrated that control of the vast political power of the national government could pass peacefully from one political party to another. Subsequent repetition of this accomplishment cannot diminish the significance of this first success.

Election of 1828

by *Robert V. Remini*

When the presidential contest of 1824–25 ended in the election of John Quincy Adams, the defeated candidate, Andrew Jackson, took his loss with all the grace and dignity one might expect from this enormously self-assured and imposing westerner. At a reception given by President Monroe on the night of the election in the House of Representatives, Senator Jackson stepped up to the President-elect and without the slightest trace of disappointment in his voice, said, "How do you do, Mr. Adams. I hope you are well, sir."

"Very well, sir," replied Adams, "I hope General Jackson is well!" And with that the two men parted. About the election, there was not a word, not even one of congratulations from the defeated candidate. Jackson accepted his loss and seemed to pay no further heed to it. He might never have said much more about it had not Adams, shortly after their meeting, announced his intention of appointing Henry Clay his Secretary of State. The news convulsed Jackson. His well-known temper blazed up in all its terrible fury. He was transfixed with anger and soon convinced himself that he had been cheated of the Presidency by Adams and Clay. He, who had won a popular and electoral plurality in the fall election, he declared, had been swindled in the House by conniving politicians who would not hesitate to set aside the popular will to satisfy their ambitions. In Jackson's mind, and indeed in the minds of many other politicians, the selection of Adams had been arranged prior to the House election by a "deal" in which Clay promised to throw his enormous support among the representatives to Adams in return for an appoint-

ment as Secretary of State, a position which historically led straight to the
Presidency. There had been rumors of such a "deal" but no proof. Now, with
Clay's appointment, Jackson claimed he had all the evidence he needed to
prove that a "corrupt bargain" had been struck to prevent his election as
President. He returned to his home in Tennessee, resigned from the Senate
and poured out his wrath in a series of letters to politicians all over the country about how the people's will had been thwarted and how chicanery and
fraud now ruled in Washington. With uncanny skill and instinct he had
touched upon the one issue his friends could use to attack and embarrass the
new Administration. It was the issue they would superbly develop to elect
Jackson President in 1828.

In Congress the "corrupt bargain" cry was taken up by the General's followers and rung through a thousand changes. Clay was accused of seeking out
several candidates until he finally found the one who agreed to give him what
he wanted. John Randolph of Roanoke, the eccentric senator from Virginia,
fired off a speech in the upper chamber which amused the Jacksonians but
horrified the friends of the Administration. He described the coalition of
Adams and Clay in terms of two notorious characters from Fielding's novel
Tom Jones. Said he: "I was defeated, horse, foot, and dragoons—cut up—and
clean broke down—by the coalition of Blifil and Black George—by the combination, unheard of till then, of the Puritan and the black-leg."

Clay, understandably sensitive to the charge since he had indeed arranged the election and his own appointment, though not by fraud or corruption, challenged Randolph to a duel in the hope of silencing his critics. The
two men met on the southern shore of the Potomac River and exchanged single shots. Both shots missed. At that point Senator Thomas Hart Benton of
Missouri, who had been watching the duel, tried to intervene and bring the
fight to a halt. Clay brushed him aside. He insisted on a second shot. Randolph airily agreed to the demand but whispered to Benton that he would not
return the fire. On the second exchange Clay put a bullet through the senator's coat, while Randolph blithely discharged his pistol into the air. Randolph
then came forward, hand outstretched, which Clay readily grasped. "I trust
in God, my dear sir, you are unharmed," said Clay. "After what has occurred I would not have harmed you for a thousand worlds." "You owe me a
coat, Mr. Clay," came the reply. "I am glad the debt is no greater," said the
Secretary.

So ended this ridiculous duel, but it silenced neither Randolph nor other
Jacksonians in their efforts to discredit the Administration. Indeed, it served
as a reminder of how the election had been decided and of Clay's inordinate
need to stifle all reference to it. Rumbling throughout the entire campaign of
1828 was the charge of a "corrupt bargain" along with Jackson's impassioned
cry that the "will of the people" had been thwarted.

Apart from creating the leading issue of the campaign, the announcement
of Clay's appointment produced an immediate political effect. No sooner did
the President indicate his selection for the State Department than the new
Vice-President, John C. Calhoun, along with a number of his friends, marched

straight into the camp of General Jackson. Obviously, the Adams-Clay coalition would now block the road to the Presidency for many years, perhaps as long as sixteen; so the impatient Calhoun, who could not wait that long for his own turn to come around, decided to abandon his neutral position and join forces with Jackson in the expectation that he would succeed to the Presidency four or possibly eight years hence. Even before Jackson left Washington for Tennessee, Calhoun and "other members of the South Carolina delegation" dined with him and agreed to form a party "to oppose Mr. Adams' administration."

The initial formation of an opposition party inaugurated with Clay's appointment was accelerated by the President's first annual message to Congress delivered on December 6, 1825. In a bold and forthright assertion of the Government's responsibility to develop the country and its resources, Adams outlined a program of public works that showed his personal commitment to Henry Clay's American System, a system which advocated protective tariffs, internal improvements, stable currency, distribution of federal surpluses to the states, and a sound banking system. "The great object of the institution of civil government," Adams contended, "is the improvement of the condition of those who are parties to the social compact, and no government, in whatever form constituted, can accomplish the lawful end of its institution but in proportion as it improved the condition of those over whom it is established." Accordingly, he proposed the building of roads and canals, the establishment of a national university as well as an astronomical observatory, the exploration of the western territories and northeastern coastline, the building of a naval academy similar to West Point, and the adoption of a uniform standard of weights and measures—all at government expense. "The spirit of improvement is abroad upon the earth," he proclaimed, and the United States must take the lead in furthering it." Unfortunately, in closing his message, Adams committed the unpardonable political blunder of telling Congress not to give the rest of the world the impression "that we are palsied by the will of our constituents."

The message, when read to Congress, produced quite a jolt, particularly among those of the Republican party who supported the candidacy of William H. Crawford in the presidential election of 1824. This faction was known as the party of "Old Republicans" or "Radicals" because of its deep commitment to a highly conservative interpretation of the Constitution and their equally conservative approach to a definition of governmental-powers. The Old Republicans advocated states rights; by the same token they opposed a strong central government in Washington; they called for rigid economy in budgeting national expenditures; they opposed protective tariffs and internal improvements; in fact they opposed virtually everything the American System espoused. To them, therefore, Adams' entire message was a declaration of war and they agreed almost at once to do everything in their power to wreck the President's legislative program.

Because Crawford suffered a paralyzing stroke during the 1824 campaign the Old Republicans were now led by the junior senator from New York,

Martin Van Buren, known to some as the "Little Magician" because of his unparalleled skill as a political manipulator and compromiser. Van Buren had been raised in the rough and tumble school of New York politics where he learned how to survive in an arena of cutthroat politicians. After a long, hard fight with De Witt Clinton for control of the New York Republican party, Van Buren won out and forced Clinton into retirement. He then created a state-wide machine, called the Albany Regency, to govern New York while he was absent in Washington. Basically, this machine was a governing council of approximately half a dozen adroit politicians, operating out of Albany and dispensing patronage and instilling discipline among party regulars.

To someone like Van Buren, who was intellectually committed to the Jeffersonian philosophy of states rights and who was also the political leader of a state involved in the expensive building of the Erie Canal, it is no wonder that he and his "Radical" friends objected to President Adams' call for a national program of internal improvements. But apart from these "philosophic" considerations was Van Buren's own extremely shrewd appraisal of the developing political scene. He knew that the election of 1828 would be limited to Adams and Jackson, and of the two men he certainly preferred Jackson. Not only was the President's policy offensive to the Old Republicans, but Adams himself was devoid of popular appeal and seemingly indifferent to his public image. To many, he was an unattractive, intellectual, hard-nosed Puritan; and while he had enjoyed a distinguished career as minister to the Russian Court, as commissioner who assisted at Ghent in writing the peace treaty that ended the War of 1812, and as Secretary of State under Monroe, he was not the man to attract politicians to his cause. Professional politicians measure the size of a man's coattails. And Van Buren reckoned that Adams had no coattails at all.

Jackson, on the other hand, was obviously popular with the voting masses, as seen in the election results of 1824. Much of his popularity was based on his extraordinarily successful military record. After an interesting but by no means outstanding civilian career as a lawyer, judge, storekeeper, and legislator in Tennessee, where he emigrated from the Carolinas, Jackson took up soldiering just prior to the outbreak of the War of 1812. Elected general of the Tennessee militia he was sent against the Creek Nation in the South and won a tremendous victory that forever crippled Creek power. He then proceeded to New Orleans where he repelled a British invasion and inflicted on the invaders a devastating defeat. It was the greatest victory of the war and gave the American people a sense of national pride they had rarely experienced before. Known to his men as "Old Hickory," Jackson now became the affectionate "Hero of New Orleans" who proved to the world that independence was something the United States had earned and could keep.

In 1818 Jackson added to his reputation by defeating the Seminole Indians and seizing Florida from the Spanish. Though his actions brought a demand by nearly all the members of Monroe's Cabinet to censure him, they eventually led to the purchase of Florida by the United States. This was due mainly to the efforts of John Quincy Adams, the only member of the Cabinet to defend Jackson. Adams convinced the President to stand behind his General and press the Spanish to sell Florida.

Jackson's appearance on the national scene in larger-than-life size was indeed fortuitous. He arrived just as the country was undergoing profound economic and political changes, when a new generation of men was coming forward to seize leadership from an older social and political elite. These men saw in Jackson a symbol of their own ambitions; they also saw in him a living example of the self-made man. Surely if an orphan boy from the backwoods could make good, there was no reason why they too could not aspire to wealth and social status by relying on their own talents to get what they wanted.

Furthermore, this was an age of developing professionalism in all fields — including politics. In the 1820's, men were hard at work perfecting the techniques of winning elections. They built machines to manage the popular vote; they believed in organization; and they were determined to rule. As sharp-nosed professionals, like Van Buren, they were quick to sense the response the General's popularity produced among the "rising" classes of Americans and to realize that association with Jackson might be crucial to their future position in politics, both nationally and locally. Small wonder, then, that Van Buren decided in the winter of 1826–27 to move into the Jackson camp and to bring with him as many of the Old Republicans as he could influence. "If Gen Jackson & his friends will put his election on old party grounds," Van Buren wrote to one Radical, "preserve the old systems, avoid if not condemn the practices of the last campaign we can by adding his personal popularity to the yet remaining force of old party feeling, not only succeed in electing him but our success when achieved will be worth something."

Since Jackson had resigned his Senate seat after his House defeat and was therefore not in Washington, Van Buren went to Vice-President Calhoun, who was now openly allied to the General, and offered him Radical support for the election of Jackson in 1828. Van Buren promised to swing over the Richmond Junto, the Virginia political machine, through his influence with Thomas Ritchie, editor of the Richmond *Enquirer* and a leader of the Junto. He also promised to tour the South and do everything possible to bring the entire Old Republican faction into the new coalition, even to the extent of seeing Crawford and winning his support. During their conversation about this alliance, Calhoun and Van Buren also discussed the possibility of holding a national nominating convention to replace the outmoded caucus system, but nothing definite was decided at this time.

In a subsequent letter to Ritchie, Van Buren clearly stated that his concern for the political scene went further than a single election. He urged the Radicals to join him in this new coalition, not simply to defeat Adams but to achieve "what is of still greater importance, the substantial reorganization of the Old Republican party." He called for a revival of the two-party system and for a renewal of Jefferson's old North-South alliance, between what he termed the "planters of the South and the plain Republicans of the North." For Van Buren, like many other politicians of the day, recognized that the political system of the 1820's had failed to respond to a changing society and that unless something were done right away it might collapse altogether.

Because of the efforts of many men to restructure the system, the election of 1828 witnessed the reemergence of the two-party system in American politics. The Jackson-Calhoun-Van Buren coalition eventually became known as the "Democratic" Republican party, or simply the Democratic party, while the Adams-Clay combination was called the "National" Republican party. With respect to party principles—not that they were much discussed in the campaign of 1828—the Democrats tended, when prodded, to restate the doctrines of Jefferson, particularly those emphasizing the rights of the states and the importance of the ordinary citizen. The National Republicans, on the other hand, affirmed the need for a strong central government in advancing the material well-being of the nation. Although there continued to be personal factions and cliques operating within the system, and while party organization did not advance in every state with equal rapidity, still in 1828 there was the beginning of a genuine, nationally organized, two-party system, a system that came of age in the 1830's.

The work of Calhoun and Van Buren—particularly Van Buren—was essential to the creation of the Democratic party, but it should be remembered that their efforts were efficacious only insofar as Jackson's primacy within the party was acknowledged. This was so obvious that for a long time the new coalition was called simply the "Jackson party." Not until 1832 was "Democratic party" used regularly as a substitute. Indeed, the General by his own actions proved that he regarded himself as the head of the emerging party. After his renomination for the presidency by the Tennessee legislature in October, 1825, he toiled relentlessly for the next three years to win the Presidency. He supervised the establishment and direction of a central committee in Nashville, composed of such loyal friends as John Overton, William B. Lewis, Alfred Balch, and George W. Campbell. They corresponded with other Jackson committees in the different sections of the nation. The General also engaged in an enormous personal correspondence with party leaders in every state; moreover, he directed the activities of a small band of men, such as John Eaton and Major Henry Lee, who travelled about the country eagerly campaigning for him.

In Washington a cadre of congressmen committed to the General started holding regular caucus meetings to map strategy for defeating the National Republicans. Soon a wide channel of communication between Nashville and Washington was opened through an exchange of letters between the leading Jackson congressmen and the Nashville Central Committee. And the Hero himself took great care that the factions merging into his party would have no difficulty in adjusting their principles to his political views. Displaying ever improving qualities of political skill, he exercised extreme caution in defining his position on leading issues. He acknowledged himself a friend of the states but he warned against interpreting his words as hostile "to domestic manufactures or internal works." While he frowned on public works sponsored by the Federal Government, he did think surplus revenues could be distributed to the states to permit them to undertake their own improvements. With respect to the tariff, he placed himself on the side of a "careful Tariff," one that pursued a "middle and just course" — wherever that was. Similarly he did not disclose his strong prejudice against banks and paper money or his highly conservative views about credit and specie. On one point, however, he was emphatic. As President, if elected, he would "purify the Departments" and "reform the Government." He informed Amos Kendall, one of his most important supporters in Kentucky and the editor of the *Argus of Western America*, that all men in office "who are known to have interfered in the election as committeemen, electioneers or otherwise . . . would be unceremoniously removed." Furthermore, he would remove "all men who have been appointed from political considerations or against the will of the people, and all who are incompetent." During the campaign the Jackson newspaper editors assured their readers that the General's political headhunting was in fact a crusade to purge the Federal Government of corruption and privilege.

The importance of party newspapers during this campaign cannot be overemphasized. The creation of a vast nationwide newspaper system to inform the electorate of political affairs was one of the most important accomplishments of the two parties. On the Democratic side, it was understood that a congressional caucus had agreed to sponsor "a chain of newspaper posts, from the New England States to Louisiana, and branching off through Lexington to the Western States." So rapid was the appearance of these newspapers that Hezekiah Niles, editor of *Niles Weekly Register*, reported that by 1828 there were six hundred newspapers published in the country, fifty of them dailies, one hundred fifty semi-weeklies and four hundred weeklies. The cost of publication for all these papers, approximating one thousand of each, was placed at a half-million dollars a year.

Among Democratic sheets the most influential was the *United States Telegraph* edited by Duff Green. Green, a close friend of Calhoun's, had been brought from St. Louis to run the paper. He turned it into a slashing, hard-hitting, vigorous newspaper whose influence extended to every Democratic organization within the states. Also important were the Richmond *Enquirer*, edited by Thomas Ritchie; the Albany *Argus*, the mouthpiece of the Albany Regency, edited by Edwin Croswell; the *Argus of the West*, edited by Amos Kendall; and the New Hampshire *Patriot*, edited by that state's most energetic organizer Isaac Hill. These newspapers barraged the public with cries against the "corrupt bargain" that had cheated Old Hickory in 1825. At the same time they insisted that "Andrew Jackson is the *candidate of the People*," the candidate of the ordinary citizen in opposition to the candidate of the aristocracy. Democrats contended that the contest was basically a struggle for "free principles and unbiased suffrage," between the few and the many, the rich and the poor. "The Aristocracy and the Democracy of the country are arrayed against each other," pontificated one New Yorker.

John Quincy Adams, on the other hand, was rapped as the darling of the rich who believed that the will of the majority counted for nothing and that the "few should govern the many." Democrats feigned horror at his "kingly pretensions." As President, they said, he strolled about the White House like a ruling monarch. Nor was Henry Clay any better. He pretended devotion to his "American System," but in the State Department he used fancy English writing paper in all his communications. "O fie, Mr. Clay," mocked Duff Green in the *Telegraph*, "—*English* paper, *English* wax, *English* pen-knives, is this your *American* System?"

In their efforts to capture votes, Democratic newspaper editors even stooped to invoking religious bigotry or national prejudice. They trifled with minority groups by concocting lies about Adams and they intimidated recent immigrants by playing on their fears. For example, the Administration was accused of speaking rudely of the Dutch, "calling them '*the Black Dutch*,' '*the Stupid Dutch*,' '*the Ignorant Dutch*' and other names equally decorous and civil." At another time immigrants were warned that John Adams, the father of the incumbent, was the "author" of the Alien and Sedition Acts, a series of laws aimed specifically at hobbling an immigrant's progress toward naturalization. To please the Irish and Scotch-Irish it was pointed out that Jackson was "the son of honest Irish parents. . . . That natural interest which all true-hearted Irishmen feel in the fame of one who has so much genuine Irish blood in his veins, has drawn upon the head of that devoted people, the denunciations of the partisans of Messrs. Adams & Clay."

On the religious issue, Duff Green was not loath to accuse John Quincy Adams of anti-Catholicism. "Mr. Adams denounced the Roman Catholics as bigots, worshippers of images, and declared that they did not read their bibles." Or Adams was lambasted as a "Unitarian," which in some parts of the West was as good as calling a man an "atheist." Isaac Hill criticized him in New England for "travelling through Rhode Island and Massachusetts on the Sabbath. . . ." It was bad enough that he desecrated the holy day by touring but it was worse because he was seen "in a ridiculous outfit of a jockey." Jackson, of course, was praised for his firm adherence to the Christian faith and the diligence with which he performed his devotions regularly with his family at a Presbyterian Church. "Does the old man have prayers in his own house," asked Martin Van Buren of a friend visiting the General. "If so, mention it modestly." Isaac Hill was not so discreet in telling his readers about the Hero's religious practices. He assured them that Jackson said prayers "every morning and night, also table prayers."

In addition to creating a large and effective press which poured out all kinds of propaganda to blacken the reputation of the Administration and its friends, the Jacksonians developed and improved techniques for raising money to pay for the campaign. As in most elections, the regular costs incurred in the 1828 campaign were absorbed at the local level. Large contributions were solicited and, in addition, fund raising committees were established in many counties to pay for expenses. Also, delegates to conventions and local meetings were taxed a fixed amount to meet printing costs. One county in Ohio requested each ward within the county to "appoint a fund committee . . . for the purpose of receiving . . . contributions . . . and that the same be paid over to the treasurer of the general committee of the county." Elsewhere, public dinners and banquets were held to defray costs. But one of the most

burdensome items—the expense of mailing newspapers and other propaganda
—was deftly shifted to the Federal Government through the franking privilege. The cost of mailing, running to the hundreds of thousands, was easily
disposed of by Jacksonian congressmen who franked anything and everything
that had to go out in the mails. Thomas Ritchie even noted that Democrats
were franking wrapping paper which was then distributed to committees to be
used as needed. Hezekiah Niles figured that something like $2,250,000 a year
was involved in the privilege.

It has been estimated that to win election to the House of Representatives from a western state in 1828 cost somewhere in the neighborhood of
three thousand dollars, exclusive of mailing expenses. In the East, especially
New York and Pennsylvania, the amount was higher by a thousand dollars or
so. Because of the unusual efforts to stir popular interest in the candidates
exerted in this campaign, and the resulting expenses connected with these
efforts, the cost of a presidential election soared appreciably. Estimating
roughly, and including the franking expense in the estimate, it probably
cost close to one million dollars to elect Jackson President of the United
States.

Campaign costs were high because this was the first presidential election
in which the great mass of American people were encouraged to express their
preference at the polls. From 1824 to 1828 the number of persons eligible to
vote soared because many states removed the last remaining restrictions to
the suffrage, mainly property qualifications. Moreover, most states had terminated legislative selection of presidential electors. By 1828, only two states
—South Carolina and Delaware—had failed to provide popular selection of
electors. With these changes politicians recognized the necessity of changing
with the time. They sensed a need to bring the people closer to the Government
and its operation, to root the party not simply in sectional alliances or alliances
between states or economic interests but in the great mass of the American
electorate. In adjusting to a new and essentially more popularistic society
they reckoned their political future depended on their ability to bring the national party into a closer relationship with the people. "Our true object," said
Duff Green, "is to . . . induce all aspirants for office to look to the
people . . . for support." "Contending as we are against wealth & power,"
wrote one Kentucky politician, "we look for success in numbers."

The necessity of building a party based on numbers forced politicians to
concern themselves with convincing the masses to vote the party ticket. What
they did was to improve and perfect the committee system which managed
the details of a campaign, details such as raising money, providing party propaganda, arranging parades and dinners, and corresponding with committees in
other parts of the state and outside the state. A vast number of these committees were set up at all political levels, from the local ward to the state central
committee. Normally, the central committee directed the functions of local
groups within the state and communicated with central committees in other
states for purposes of coordination and cooperation. The extensiveness of
these committees can be seen in a report written by one politician to Andrew

Jackson. "I therefore originated," he wrote, "and with the cooperation of half a dozen, intelligent and zealous friends, carryed into full and successful operation last year, a plan, or System of Committees, from a Principle or Central Committee . . . down to Sub Committees into every ward of the Town, and Captains Company in the Country."

Also important in the development of party organization were the state conventions. These conventions were especially useful in generating party discipline and loyalty. They were usually called to name the state ticket and endorse the national candidate. But they were also important in dictating the party line for the campaign. "As party spirit increased more and more," wrote one man, "the necessity of some mode of concentrating the party strength became more and more apparent. . . . An attempt at this was early made . . . by introducing the convention system of nominating candidates."

The directions of the state convention were most effectively carried out by the local ward committees, which, during the 1828 campaign, were frequently called "Hickory Clubs." These clubs were principally concerned with exciting voter interest in the candidates and in getting them to the polls to register their interest. The techniques normally employed to build mass support included rallies, barbecues, town meetings, parades, hickory pole raisings, and street demonstrations. In the 1828 campaign the raising of a hickory pole in the town square was particularly popular with the local ward committees. These ubiquitous monuments appeared "in every village," reported one, "as well as upon the corners of many city streets. . . . Many of these poles were standing as late as 1845, rotten momentoes /sic/ of the delirium of 1828." One "Grand Barbecue" for Jackson held in Baltimore was arranged by Roger B. Taney to climax a celebration commemorating the successful defense of the city against British attack during the War of 1812. "I am told by a gentleman who is employed to erect the fixtures," Jackson was informed, "that three Bullocks are to be roasted, and each man is to wear a Hickory Leaf in his hat by way of designation." At this celebration there was also a parade, the firing of cannons, speeches, and the singing of songs in praise of Old Hickory. These scenes of enthusiasm for the party's candidate supposedly helped to build popular majorities. At least the leading Democratic politicians seemed to think so. "Van Buren has learned you know," said an Administration man, "that the *Hurra Boys* were for Jackson . . . and to my regret they constitute a powerful host."

To encourage the "Hurra Boys" and whip up even greater excitement for Jackson, some politicians even toyed with the idea of bringing the General himself to their meetings, although this clearly violated tradition and ran the risk of provoking resentment. "You *must*, yes I say, you *must* visit us next autumn in person," wrote an Ohio organizer to Jackson. But Old Hickory vetoed all such proposals—all, that is, except one. He chose to accept an invitation of the Louisiana Central Committee to attend a ceremony in New Orleans on January 8, 1828, to commemorate his victory over the British in 1815. Although the celebration was ostensibly "non-political" there were representatives from many state delegations along with a group of leading national Jacksonians. The occasion, widely reported in the press, was "the most stupendous thing of the kind that had ever occurred in the United States," said one man. It served to remind the American people the debt they owed General Jackson. The welcoming ceremony, the speeches, parades, and dinner were unlike anything ever seen before. "The World has never witnessed so glorious, so wonderful a Celebration," exclaimed a participant, "—never has *Gratitude & Patriotism* so happily united, so beautifully blended—& it will form a bright page in American history."

In comparison to the Jackson party, the National Republican party of Adams and Clay was sadly deficient in such essentials as organization and leadership. Only in the matter of program and principles was the party superior. Its goals were relatively clear, straightforward and unambiguous. Supporting the American System, the National Republicans called for a federal program of aid to all partners of the social compact. Such support included public works, the establishment and development of cultural and intellectual institutions, aid to domestic manufactures, and higher tariffs.

But a party needs more than a program and so the labor of erecting a national organization behind Adams fell mainly to Henry Clay. Unfortunately, Adams would do nothing to assist his reelection, not even help his friends in purging the Government of those appointees who actively opposed his Administration. He admitted he had been "reproached" by his supporters "because I will not dismiss, or drop from Executive offices, able and faithful political opponents to provide for my own partisans." Nor would he abandon the candidate's traditional silence, adopt the role of President as party leader, and encourage popular support. A brooding introvert, he reacted coldly to any public display of affection, as though he could hardly care less whether the electorate approved of him or not. "I am a man of reserved, cold, austere and forbidding manners," he wrote in a deadly accurate self description. "My political adversaries say, a gloomy misanthrope, and my personal enemies an unsocial savage. With the knowledge of the actual defects of my character, I have not the pliability to reform it."

Under the circumstances, Clay and other National Republican organizers such as Daniel Webster of Massachusetts worked as best they could to amalgamate a party behind the President which would be responsive to the changing times. They raised money to subsidize a favorable press, recognizing its propaganda value. Said Clay, "The course adopted by the Opposition, in the dissemination of Newspapers and publications against the Administration and supporting presses leaves to its friends no other alternative than that of following their example, so far at least as to circulate information among the people." And, by and large, the National Republicans had an excellent press. In Washington they were supported by the *National Intelligencer* edited by Joseph Gales and William W. Seaton, and the *National Journal* edited by Peter Force. Elsewhere they received the strong backing of the New York *American*, Cincinnati *Gazette*, Virginia *Constitutional Whig*, the Baltimore *Weekly Register*, the Massachusetts *Journal*, and the Missouri *Republican*.

Like the Democrats, the National Republicans held local rallies, county meetings, and state conventions. "Political meetings are continually taking place in the different Towns of the State" [New Jersey] explained one Administration man, "where Resolutions are passed and Delegates appointed to attend at Trenton to fix on the Electoral Ticket." At the conventions central committees and correspondence committees were appointed. In addition, an address to the public was usually written to extol the virtues of Adams and urge his reelection. At several such conventions Richard Rush of Pennyslvania was selected to run with Adams. Rush had had a very respectable diplomatic career, serving as Secretary of State *pro tem* when the Rush-Bagot agreement was signed neutralizing the Canadian border, and as minister to Great Britain when the English first suggested a joint resolution to prohibit foreign influence into Latin America. Although Rush seemed to have the support of most National Republicans, some state conventions left the second slot vacant and simply instructed their electors to vote for that man most acceptable to the majority of Adams men within the state.

Despite the efforts of many politicians to erect a national organization the results were woefully uneven throughout the country. In some states the Adams supporters were exceedingly slow in setting up party machinery, resulting occasionally in no machinery at all. When Clay sent out a detailed paper on the necessity of large committees of vigilance he received an acknowledgement from one state leader that questioned the advisability of such a committee. "It was apprehended by some," the letter read, "that the appoint. of such a comm. would excite the animadversions of our adversaries." No wonder the party suffered from organizational deficiencies in the West and South when such politicians feared to arouse the "animadversions" of the Democrats.

Still, as a party with a specific course of action to offer the people—one united behind a man of proven talent and experience—the National Republicans reckoned they had a fighting chance to win the election, despite weaknesses. For example, in calculating the electoral vote, they believed they had a slight edge over the Democrats. By counting all of New England as reasonably safe for Adams, they began with 51 electoral votes. Then they added Kentucky, Ohio, and Missouri, all won by Clay in 1824, which brought the total to 84. Thus if they could pick up a substantial number of votes from New Jersey, Delaware, and Maryland—all of which were leaning heavily toward Adams—the election could be successfully concluded in New York and Pennsylvania, two states highly susceptible to the tariff argument. Unfortunately, this extremely important and useful issue was lost to the National Republicans by the aggressiveness and astuteness of the Jacksonian leaders in Congress.

When the Twentieth Congress convened in December, 1827, the friends of the General had won control of both houses. The previous fall elections had gone to the Jacksonians largely because of their superior organization.

For their part, the National Republicans were still unable to match their opponents in this vital political sector. "We are in the same disjointed state here as formerly," wrote one Administration man from the middle states, "a great many well wishers . . . but no organization." Out West, an Adams man reported the Democrats as "an organized corps, active and well disciplined," while in the South one of Clay's advisers predicted, the "organization of the other side . . . *will be* stronger than all." All of this was reflected in the fall elections of 1827, resulting in Jacksonian control of Congress. So complete was that control that one senator remarked, "The opposition party constitute in fact the *administration.* Upon it rests the responsibility of all legislative measures."

For the next several months of the session the Democratic leadership in Congress addressed itself to a single difficulty, that of providing electorally important states with substantial reasons for voting for Jackson in 1828. Nothing was more indicative of their efforts at political brokerage than the passage of the Tariff of 1828, more popularly known as the Tariff of Abominations.

One major difficulty respecting protection was the sharp sectional difference it automatically triggered. In the North there was strong demand for increased rates from most manufacturers, but in the South such action was regarded as ruinous. The problem was complicated by the opposition of certain northern commercial groups to the tariff; furthermore, westerners required protection for their raw materials which not all manufacturers approved. Thus, it was a tricky business to put together a tariff schedule that could operate to the credit of the sponsoring party and win electoral votes. The astuteness and cynicism with which the Democrats managed this feat was a remarkable performance of political legerdemain.

What they did was to draw up a bill that laid heavy duties on imported raw materials, particularly hemp, iron, and sail duck. All of these items struck most heavily against New England commercial interests; at the same time they pleased the agrarians in the West. In addition, a duty of ten cents per gallon was levied against molasses, while that on distilled spirits was raised ten cents—again injuring New England by penalizing her distillery industry. In order to attract Pennsylvania's support, a high duty was placed on iron products. But the most important schedules in the bill related to raw wool and woolen products. In effect, the Democrats safeguarded the producers of raw wool, but only offered token protection to the manufacturers of woolen commodities. Thus the tariff was "arranged" to appeal to western voters, particularly those in Kentucky, Ohio, and Missouri, who had voted for Clay in 1824, and secure the favor of the protectionist farmers in New York and Pennsylvania. Only New England distillers, shipbuilders, and woolen manufacturers were discriminated against, for New England was written off as unalterably attached to President Adams. Unfortunately, the high protectionist rates also offended southerners, but the Democratic leadership felt they could afford this offense because the southerners could not retaliate and vote for Adams since the President was regarded as the "acknowledge leader" of all manufacturing interests. Southerners would support Jackson under any circumstance, high tariff or no.

The bill passed the House of Representatives despite strong opposition by New England and southern congressmen. However, in the conservative Senate the opposition had proportionately greater strength, and was prepared to kill the tariff unless altered. To prevent this, the Democratic leadership, in a cynical move, agreed to a single amendment which raised the tax on all woolen manufactures to a 40 per cent ad valorem rate with a 5 per cent increase each year until it reached 50 per cent. This change was just enough to satisfy some New England senators to win their votes and in so doing squeeze the bill through. Now farmers from the middle and western states had protection for their raw materials, Pennsylvania had its duty on iron, and New York the duty on raw wool. Hopefully, they would reciprocate this Democratic generosity by voting the Jackson ticket in 1828. As one senator feared, the tariff was "changed into a machine for manufacturing Presidents, instead of broadcloths, and bed blankets."

Southerners were outraged by the passage of the message and some of them threatened secession if their demands continued to go unheeded. John C. Calhoun returned home and wrote an "Exposition and Protest" which enunciated the doctrine of nullification. It was the Vice-President's argument that a state enjoyed the privilege of voiding a federal statute if that law was deemed injurious to the state. But despite this near-violent reaction the South stayed with Jackson, believing that as President he would redress the wrong and lower the tariff. Even so, a number of southerners loudly criticized the Democratic leadership in Congress for having stooped to deception to get the tariff passed. Senator Littleton W. Tazewell of Virginia supposedly cornered Van Buren one day immediately after the passage of the tariff and said: "Sir, you have deceived me once; that was your fault; but if you deceive me again the fault will be mine."

Regrettably, there was a great deal of deception in this election. There were double-dealing and gutter tactics. Indeed, the election of 1828 was probably the "dirtiest," coarsest, most vulgar election in American history. Jackson, on the one hand, was publicly labeled an adulterer, murderer, and traitor; Adams, on the other, was called a pimp and a gambler. The charges against Jackson had been cited before, but in this election they were given greater publicity and sharpened to a finer political point. The charge most often discussed concerned his marriage to his wife Rachel.

Rachel Donelson Jackson was previously married to Lewis Robards, from whom she separated after a series of bitter quarrels. A neurotically suspicious man, Robards believed he had been cuckolded by Jackson, who, for a time, lived in the same house with Robards and his wife. Whether Jackson was guilty of the charge is impossible to say; in any event Rachel could stand the accusations no longer and fled with Jackson to Natchez, chaperoned by the elderly Colonel John Stark. Later, when the couple heard that Robards had begun legal proceedings to obtain a divorce on the grounds of adultery and desertion, they waited a decent interval and then were married in August, 1791. Unfortunately, at the time of their marriage Robards had not yet received the divorce. All he had was an enabling act from the legislature permitting him to bring suit against his wife in a court of law. Not until September, 1793 did Robards actually go through with his suit and win a divorce. A few months later, on January 17, 1794, Jackson and Rachel married a second time.

In the 1828 campaign, Charles Hammond, editor of the Cincinnati *Gazette* spent a great deal of time "researching" the curious circumstances of the marriage. Then, in lurid detail, he spread the results of his investigation in the pages of his newspaper and did not hesitate to use such words as "bigamist" and "adulterer" to make his points. "Ought a convicted adultress and her paramour husband to be placed in the highest offices of this free and christian land?" he asked. The shocking manner in which Jackson's marriage was described forced the Nashville Central Committee to issue a detailed report on the circumstances of the technical bigamy to explain how it had accidentally occurred. Both Jackson and Rachel were deeply injured by this publicity — and Rachel mortally so, according to her friends, for she died of a heart attack shortly after the election. The General himself believed that Henry Clay was behind the attack, had subsidized Hammond's "research" trip, and supplied him with evidence. This was denied several times by the Clay's allies but Jackson remained unconvinced. Later, when the story was reprinted in the Washington newspapers, he blamed the President for doing nothing to prevent its publication. He felt the Administration could have intervened had it not wanted to take full advantage of the scandal. Jackson never forgot how the newspapers had abused him, and blamed much of the abuse on Clay and Adams.

The depth to which this campaign sunk in repeating or creating stories to vilify the candidates is best exemplified by the indecent assault on Jackson's mother. "General Jackson's mother was a COMMON PROSTITUTE," said one piece, "brought to this country by the British soldiers! She afterwards married a MULATTO MAN, with whom she had several children, of which number GENERAL JACKSON IS ONE!!" It is reported that when the Hero read this story he broke down in tears and his body shook with grief. Seeing his distress, Rachel asked him what was wrong. Jackson pointed to the offending newspaper and said, "Myself I can defend. You I can defend; but now they have assailed even the memory of my mother."

Jackson's reputation as a duelist and gunfighter was also given considerable play in the newspapers. He was maligned as a bully and a ruffian, a street brawler, cockfighter, and gambler. His famous gunfight with the Benton brothers and his duel with Charles Dickinson were narrated in great detail and with much distortion, necessitating a full and "accurate" account of the incidents by the Nashville Central Committee. Also noticed, were the military executions that took place under his command, especially the six militiamen shot during the Creek War in 1813. These men were charged with mutiny, desertion, inducing others to desert, and stealing military supplies. They were tried, found guilty, and executed. But the Administration newspapers in 1828 saw the incident as savage brutality. The men, declared the newspapers, had legally completed their military service and desired to return home. Instead of their being returned home, as was their right, they were murdered by Jackson. John Binns, editor of the Philadelphia *Democratic Press*, printed a handbill to dramatize the incident. The names of the six "victims" were printed at the top, and under each name a picture was drawn of a large, black coffin. Below that came a narrative account of the "murders." The entire handbill was enclosed in a black border. Called the "Coffin Hand Bill," it proved to be a very effective propaganda tool which the National Republicans believed would convince the American people that Jackson was a wild man under whose charge the Government would collapse.

Jackson was also criticized for his involvement in Aaron Burr's western conspiracy. Indeed, the impression was distinctly given that his participation was suspiciously treasonous. It was claimed that he had levied troops for Burr by calling on governors of the several states to supply militiamen. It was documented that he built flat boats for Burr to carry soldiers down the Mississippi River. It was also contended that these soldiers meant to attack New Orleans, and that·Jackson was therefore a chief officer in the conspiracy. Finally it was noted that the General testified for Burr at his treason trial despite clear evidence that Burr was guilty of a major crime. Naturally the Democrats vigorously denied the charges and insisted that the first tangible evidence that President Jefferson received about a western conspiracy came from Andrew Jackson. And, inasmuch as Henry Clay had defended Burr concerning his western activities before a grand jury in Kentucky, the Democrats were able to counter any accusation against Jackson in this matter with equally fraudulent accusations against Clay.

The mudslinging that typified this election was not confined to the National Republicans. The Democrats gave as good as they got. One of the nastiest (if not funniest because it is so absurd) stories circulated at the time was the accusation that John Quincy Adams once procured an American girl for the Czar of Russia when he was minister to that country. The charge was certainly untrue, but some men chose to repeat it, adding that the reasons for Adams' fabulous success as a diplomat had at last been uncovered. Adams' wife was also attacked for having indulged in premarital relations with the President, but the charges brought against her in no way compared to those leveled at poor Rachel.

Democrats were especially effective in repeating the charge that Adams was an aristocrat. They accused him of assuming the manner of a monarch, with the White House as his palace. "We disapprove the kingly pomp and splendour that is displayed by the present incumbent," editorialized several newspapers. To prove the charge of "royal extravagances," a report was published that public funds had been expended to equip the East Room with gambling furniture, in particular a billiard table, cues and balls, and a set of expensive chessmen made of ivory. Something like twenty-five thousand dollars was supposedly spent on the gambling equipment, cried the Democrats, an expenditure unheard of in a republican country.

But the most telling accusation against Adams was the "corrupt bargain" charge. This was repeated over and over and no amount of denials by Clay or the National Republicans could hush the story. Even Jackson took to repeating it regularly to the many politicians who visited him at his home in Tennessee. He said he received the details of the notorious deal from "a congressman of high respectability." This congressman turned out to be James Buchanan of Pennsylvania, who, when pressed, was unable to produce substantiating evidence.

Clearly the election of 1828 devolved into a contest of personalities. No real national issue was discussed. It seemed as though politicians believed the people preferred scandalous stories to intelligent debates on the important issues. However, there were two movements that appeared toward the end of the campaign which tried to force a discussion of several important questions. These movements began in New York and Philadelphia and had long-range effects.

In New York there was a sudden release of violence in the western counties of the state as a result of the disappearance and reported death of a man named William Morgan. Morgan was a stonemason who settled in Batavia, New York, and joined the order of Freemasonry. He was not an especially personable man and in time got into a heated quarrel with his fellow Masons. Swearing revenge for the injury he believed he had suffered, Morgan set about writing a book revealing the secrets of the order. He talked David C. Miller, editor of the Batavia *Advocate*, into publishing the manuscript, at the same time refusing to listen to the pleas of other Masons that he abandon his project and destroy the manuscript. Since Morgan was deaf to their entreaties his former friends decided to teach him a lesson. They had him arrested for allegedly stealing a shirt and a tie, seized the page proofs of his book, and set fire to Miller's establishment.

But Morgan was a stubborn man and not easily intimidated. The charge against him was not sustained, so he was released. Since Morgan had every intention of pursuing his project he was rearrested almost immediately after his release for a debt owed to another Mason. Then someone paid his bail. As Morgan emerged from the jail he was seized, hustled into an awaiting carriage, and taken to Fort Niagara, where, according to one account, he was held captive for several days and then drowned in the Niagara River. However the only source which attempts to account for Morgan's death is open to some doubt, so it will probably never be known what really happened to him, or how and when he met his death.

Even so, there was no question that Morgan had disappeared, and to most New Yorkers the Masons were guilty of a ghastly crime. Within weeks, the western counties of the state were ablaze with demands to apprehend the kidnappers and obliterate the Masonic Order. Westerners convinced themselves that the fraternity was a conspiracy against ordinary citizens. It was an

elitist group, made up of aristocrats, they said, to control everything—the
government, the courts, and business. If anyone opposed them, like poor
Morgan, they did not hesitate to exterminate him.

Sensing the dimension of this outburst, the governor of the state, De Witt
Clinton, ordered an investigation of Morgan's disappearance. Soon there were
public meetings calling for the dismissal of every appointed Mason in office
and the defeat of those who held their positions at the hands of the electorate.
As one man, a judge of the court of appeals, said: "Believing that the shocking oaths, which the members of the Masonic fraternity took, on entering it,
were subversive of good order, impediments in administering justice and enforcing execution of the laws, and also encouraged and even enjoined the
commission of murder, I became an anti-Mason, and did what I could to put
an end to Masonry in this country." Because the Masons denied equal opportunity to other citizens, the order had to be eliminated, said its attackers. New
Yorkers seemed willing—nay anxious—to use their vote to rid society of this
"aristocratic" institution. All of which said something about the desire of
most people in 1828 to remove any obstacle which seemed to militate against
the equality of all.

Not long after the disappearance a body was washed up on the shores of
Lake Ontario. Morgan's widow inspected the remains and to her horror she
recognized her late husband because of the "double teeth all around." However, several more bodies were later fished out of the lake—usual around election time—and all were identified as the decomposed Mr. Morgan. "Some
dead body is always dug up and examined," complained one man, "two or
three times, in order to excite into activity all the old prejudices against the
masons and masonry."

While it is very difficult to understand the sudden and explosive outbreak
of anti-masonry, it would appear that it was partially caused by the "disturbed and unsettled state of the public mind" during a period of rapid economic and political transition. It was a spontaneous release of violence in
which deep pyschological and perhaps religious forces were at work. Most of
the initial "infection" was concentrated in the western parts of the state where
Bible-oriented, pious Yankees had recently moved from New England. Perhaps their unsettled state and their deep commitment to the Puritan ethic had
something to do with the severity of the explosion.

In any event, it did not take long for sharp-eyed politicians to see an opportunity to direct this agitation, particularly since it seemed naturally bent on
entering the political arena. Thurlow Weed, for example, took advantage of
the movement and established the Anti-Masonic *Enquirer* in Rochester and
soon had the assistance of an able young lawyer by the name of William H.
Seward. These and other men began to direct the emerging state party by calling a convention and nominating candidates for state offices, including the
gubernatorial office. Since Andrew Jackson was a Mason of very high rank,
Weed tried to move the new party into the Adams camp, particularly since
the President had categorically denied any association with Freemasonry. "I
state that I am not, never was, and never shall be a freemason," wrote Ad-

ams. However, some of the political advantage of the President's disclaimer
was lost because his Secretary of State, Henry Clay, was known to be a high-
ranking Mason.

As the Anti-Masonic party expanded it soon spilled over the borders into
neighboring states; and as it grew it turned more and more toward demanding
freedom of opportunity for the individual and the elimination of all institutions
and practices which impeded, threatened, or denied that freedom.

Another movement advocating wide social reforms that began during the
campaign of 1828 centered around the demands of the laboring man. The
Mechanics Union of Trade Associations founded in Philadelphia in 1827 and
the Workingmen's party which appeared late in 1828 in that city were two
expressions of this important new movement. These organizations consisted
of a wide range of social and professional classes, from laborers, physicians,
intellectuals, and merchants to speculators, lawyers, and politicians. One of
their most insistent demands called for the restriction of the power of the state
legislature to create corporations by special charter. Such action, in the minds
of these Workingmen, tended to concentrate the "wealth producing powers of
modern mechanism" in the hands of a few and thereby injure the small businessman who could not compete under this increasingly monopolistic system.
The Workingmen were particularly concerned about the granting of bank
charters. As hard money men (as most of them were) they objected to the
bank-issued paper currency whose value was frequently unstable. Moreover,
banks were less willing to lend money to small capitalists because of high risk;
yet it was the small businessman who was most in need of financial support.

In addition, the Workingmen urged the passage of mechanics lien laws
which would force employers who went bankrupt to recognize the legitimate
claims of workers, just as they did other creditors, and pay them a portion of
their wages out of whatever funds were available. They also demanded laws
to prevent employers from declaring themselves bankrupt in order to avoid
paying workers' salaries. Furthermore, the mechanics were most forceful in
urging the abolition of imprisonment for debt. They argued rather logically
that it helped no one to imprison a debtor and thereby keep him from earning
the money he needed to pay his debt. The practice hurt both debtor and credi-
tor. Besides, the practice was seen as having its cruelest impact on the poor
and served to lock them in a perpetual state of poverty.

The Workingmen also advocated improvements in general education in
order that their children might acquire a free, public education without the
parents having to humiliate themselves by openly acknowledging their indig-
ence. The improvement and expansion of public education was just beginning
in the United States at this time, and it would take several more decades before free education was generally available at both the primary and secondary
levels. Moreover, the mechanics urged the reform of the auction and lottery
systems and an end to the issuance by banks of large amounts of paper money.
They also opposed the "excessive distillation of liquor."

While the Workingmen's movement attracted considerable support from
middle-class capitalists, it did include a bona fide labor group contending for

the interests of the wage earner. Late in 1828 the movement developed into a political party in Philadelphia and soon spread to other large cities, most notably New York, Boston, and Baltimore. Although more a local phenomena than a unified national movement, the party was most effective in urging social and economic reform during the Jacksonian era. Whenever necessary to gain approval for its reforms, the Workingmen's party shifted its support within the states from the Democrats to the National Republicans, crossing political lines at will.

In Philadelphia in 1828 all the candidates of the Workingmen's party who also ran on the Jackson ticket were elected. Indeed, the Democrats proved quite strong in many cities, not simply Philadelphia. Of course they had an extremely popular figure as their candidate. But they also had an energetic and aggressive party machine that knew how to go after the popular vote. However, the organization was not evenly developed in all the states. Such states as New York, Pennsylvania, New Hampshire, Virginia, North Carolina, Ohio, Kentucky, and Indiana had the most effective organizations. Many others had already made notable starts in erecting the party apparatus. All were exhorted to turn out the vote and see to it that those "who can get to the polls, shall go there, and vote /for Jackson/." One southern politician described the extent of party activity to get the masses to the polls. "Considerable pains were taken to bring out the people," he said; "flags were made and sent to different parts of the country, and the people came in in companies of fifty or sixty with the flag flying at their head, with the words, 'Jackson and Reform' on it in large letters." In the *Telegraph*, Duff Green pleaded for a massive turnout. "To the polls," he cried. "To the Polls! The faithful sentinel must not sleep—Let no one stay home—Let every man go to the Polls—Let not a vote be lost—Let every Freeman do his duty; and all will triumph in the success of

JACKSON, CALHOUN AND LIBERTY."

Balloting in the election extended from September to November. In most states, voting occurred over a period of several days. The states did not provide an official ballot; instead, the parties printed their own ballots, distributing them to friends and employing high-pressure party hacks at the polls to get the voter to accept the ticket. It was not unusual for a person to be accosted by several hawkers at once and threatened with bodily harm unless he accepted the proffered ballot.

The procedures for voting varied considerably throughout the twenty-four states. Delaware and South Carolina were the only states whose legislatures chose the electors. In all other states, they were chosen from a general or district ticket by an electorate that was roughly equivalent—except in Louisiana, Virginia, and Rhode Island—to the adult, white male population. Maryland, Maine, Illinois, Tennessee, and New York were the states using the district system, which meant that their electoral votes could be split between the candidates on a proportional basis. In all other states where the general ticket was employed, the candidate with the highest popular vote received all the electoral votes. Only Rhode Island and Virginia continued to restrict suffrage with property qualifications, and Louisiana maintained tax payments as a voting requirement.

When the election ended and the ballots were counted, it was clear that Jackson had won a stupendous victory. Out of a total of 1,155,022 popular votes cast, John Quincy Adams received 507,730; Andrew Jackson won 647,292 or just a little better than 56 per cent of the entire vote. This was an extraordinary achievement by Jackson, a veritable landslide. In percentages it was unequalled in any presidential election during the nineteenth century. And his total represented substantial support from all sections of the country, including New England.

The total popular vote in the election represented an increase of nearly eight hundred thousand over the previous election in 1824. In Pennsylvania alone, the number rose from forty-seven thousand to 152,000 four years later. There were several reasons for this spectacular rise. In the first place, the two-party system had been reestablished, if unevenly, and where in 1824 there were several candidates running for the Presidency there were only two in 1828. Second, there was considerable interest in the election generated to a large extent by an exciting, if not scurrilous, campaign initiated by both the Democratic and National Republican parties. Third, there was a concerted effort on the part of many politicians to get out the vote at election time; and finally, four states, representing a considerable electorate, changed their laws and transferred the selection of electors from the legislature to the people.

In the Electoral College, Jackson's victory was even more impressive. He won a total of 178 electoral votes to 83 for Adams. He swept everything south of the Potomac River and west of New Jersey. Adams carried New England (except for a single electoral vote in Maine), Delaware, New Jersey, and most of Maryland. Adams and Jackson shared New York, with the General taking 20 of the state's 36 electoral votes. All the remaining states went to Old Hickory. The election was relatively close in New Hampshire, New York, New Jersey, Maryland, Kentucky, Louisiana, Ohio, and Indiana. In the final analysis, what made the difference in virtually every one of these states was superior party organization.

In the Vice-Presidential race, Calhoun won an easy reelection over Richard Rush, but received 7 fewer electoral votes than Jackson, because Georgia, which resented Calhoun's treatment of William H. Crawford when they sat in Monroe's Cabinet together, awarded 7 votes to Senator William C. Smith of South Carolina.

Aside from the importance of party in producing Jackson's triumph there was also his own popularity and charisma. He was a living, authentic legend, the victor of New Orleans, the man who won over the British the greatest feat of arms in American history. Moreover, there was a dignity and bearing about him that bespoke leadership and authority. He was "presidential-looking," more so than any other public figure of the day. He inspired confidence among the largest mass of voters despite his lack of education and his reputation as an untamed westerner. In that sense Jackson himself was the essential issue in the campaign, just as he would be again in 1832, and the people in "vast numbers" crowded to his side.

Recently, however, some historians have questioned the vastness of the 1828 victory. Comparing the statistics of this election with previous state elections and future presidential elections, one historian has raised serious doubts as to whether the people poured out to the polls to express their confidence in Jackson. Perhaps it is possible to make meaningful comparisons between a presidential election and a state election for local officers held at different times or two presidential elections separated by a dozen or more years. And perhaps not. But in any event the fact remains that no matter how the statistics are analyzed or interpreted the people themselves who lived at the time believed that Jackson's election represented a great surge of popular support for the General. They believed that the ordinary citizen, the so-called "common man," who were farmers, workers, frontiersmen, and the like, had seized the opportunity to express their political opinion by voting for Jackson. And what is believed by the electorate is frequently more important than the objective reality. Many Democratic politicians, of course, saw the contest as one between "farmers & mechanics of the country" on one hand and the "rich and well born" on the other, "between the *aristocracy* and democracy of America." Thus when they read the returns from such states as Pennsylvania, Virginia, North Carolina, Ohio, and elsewhere they were astounded by the figures and therefore convinced of the truth of their own propaganda.

Not only did the Democrats see the election as a victory produced by the "vast numbers" of American people, but the National Republicans thought so too. That is what is even more astonishing. "Well," sighed one of them, "a great revolution has taken place. . . . This is what I all along feared but to a much greater extent." "It was the howl of raving Democracy," wrote another, "that tiped /sic/ Pennsylvania & New York & Ohio—and this will be kept up here after to promote the ends of the /Democratic party./" "All our efforts," said one of Clay's friends, "have not withstood the Torrent." Hezekiah Niles in his newspaper credited Jackson's "triumphant victory" to the "ardor of thousands." And Edward Everett of Massachusetts, one of Adams' most dedicated supporters in Congress, explained to his brother that the General won "by a majority of more than *two* to *one*, an event astounding to the friends of the Administration and unexpected by the General himself and his friends. . . . /They/ are embarrassed with the vastness of their triumph and the numbers of their party."

Generations of historians, therefore, have interpreted Jackson's election in 1828 as the beginning of the "rise of the common man" in American history. Of course, such an easy and sweeping generalization does not take into consideration the fact that the "common man" had been rising for generations, and had made notable political advances long before Jackson appeared on the scene. Yet this election seemed to symbolize the people's arrival to political responsibility. Whether or not this was objectively true hardly mattered; what mattered was an expressed sense of participation in the electoral process experienced by ordinary citizens and that because of it a true "man of the people" had at last been elected President of the United States.

The notion of a popular "uprising" in Jackson's favor was strengthened by the scenes that occurred during his inauguration as President on March 4, 1829. Some twenty thousand people from all parts of the country converged on Washington to witness the triumph of their candidate. It was "like the inundation of the northern barbarians into Rome," wrote one, "save that the tumultuous tide came in from a different point of the compass." Daniel Webster was dumbfounded at the scene. "I never saw such a crowd here before," he said. "Persons have come five hundred miles to see General Jackson, *and they really seem to think that the country is rescued from some dreadful danger.*"

The ceremony itself was staged out-of-doors and the people massed themselves in front of the Capitol to see for themselves the "inauguration of popular government." The press of the crowd was so great that a ship's cable had to be stretched about two-thirds of the way up the flight of stairs leading to the portico. "Never can I forget the spectacle which presented itself on every side," said one observer, "nor the electrifying moment when the eager, expectant eyes of that vast and motley multitude caught sight of the tall and imposing form of their adored leader, as he came forth between the columns of the portico." As Jackson appeared, the mob began to scream and shout, and shake the very ground beneath them. Then, "as if by magic," the "color of the whole mass changed. . . all hats were off at once, and the dark tint which usually pervades a mixed map of men was turned. . . into the bright hue of ten thousand upturned and exultant human faces, radiant with sudden joy."

When the ceremony ended, the throng rushed through the streets and avenues to get to the White House, where a reception was scheduled to permit the people to meet their new President. But what was planned as a function of proper decorum turned into a wild mêlée. The mob poured through the White House looking for Jackson and the refreshments that had been promised them. They were "scrambling, fighting, romping" from one room to the next. "The President," wrote Mrs. Samuel H. Smith, "after having been *literally* nearly pressed to death & almost suffocated & torn to pieces by the people in their eagerness to shake hands with Old Hickory, had retreated through the back way or south front & had escaped to his lodgings at Gadsby's." It was a "regular Saturnalia," said one congressman who watched the scene. The mob "broke in, in thousands. . . in one uninterrupted stream of mud and filth." The danger to the White House—to say nothing of life and limb—grew so great that the liquor was taken outside to the garden to draw the crowd from the house. Men jumped through the windows in their haste to reach the alcohol, thus instantly easing the pressure inside the mansion. So began the Administration of the "people's President," an Administration baptized by the screams and shouts of a wildly enthusiastic public.

The election of 1828 was in some respects the first modern presidential election. Democrats launched a national campaign of song, slogan, and shouting to attract the largest possible number of votes. It was the first campaign which witnessed a concerted effort to manipulate the electorate on a mass scale. Hereafter the major parties sought presidential candidates with wide popular appeal — frequently war heroes — then backed them with an engine of ballyhoo in order to create the numbers which would provide success. In the 1828 election, barbecues, parades, tree plantings, and the like were extensively used as part of the popular entertainment. Such techniques had been employed in previous elections but not on such a lavish scale. When they proved so effective by virtue of Jackson's extraordinary victory they became standard techniques in subsequent elections, receiving their biggest display in 1840.

But Jackson's impressive showing was not so much the result of the campaign ballyhoo as it was the organization that provided it, plus the General's widespread popularity based on his military exploits. The organization in time became an elaborate party machine through which the ordinary citizen could control the operation of Government and shape public policy. But the major importance of Jackson's election was the conscious and concerted effort of many politicians to organize an effective popular majority. In the process, the two-party system slowly reemerged after a hiatus of nearly sixteen years. So ended the political disorder of the Era of Good Feelings. A new party system had begun.

Election of 1856

by *Roy F. Nichols*
and *Philip S. Klein*

The Inaugural Address of a President has often focused attention upon promises and hopes by which the voters would judge the success of a Chief Magistrate and his party. Franklin Pierce entered the White House in March, 1853, with a clear popular mandate. He had carried all but four of the states and polled six times the electoral vote of his Whig opponent Winfield Scott. The Free Soil party, such a frightening threat in 1848 and during the sectional crisis of 1850, seemed to have run its course, for in 1852 it had attracted only 150,000 voters in a presidential poll of over three million, and Pierce's Democrats captured a 2 to 1 majority in both the House and the Senate. While both Whigs and Democrats had accepted the "finality" of the compromise measures of 1850, some of the Whigs hedged on their promise and called for a repeal of the Fugitive Slave Law, whereas the Democrats stood firm on the compromise. The simple question seemed to be whether the country wished to reopen the agitation about slavery or to end it, and Pierce's triumph left no doubt that most voters wished to end it.

In his Inaugural Address Pierce reflected this national sentiment. He first emphasized Manifest Destiny, quite frankly admitting that he thought it eminently important, if not essential, to acquire more territory. However, Pierce showed his deepest concern over the slavery question. In an emphatic conclusion, he expressed his love for the Union, and his fears that sectionalism rooted in the slavery issue might destroy it. The President stated his beliefs that the Constitution recognized slavery in the states; that the Government had to enforce the rules relating to slavery like any other constitutional guarantees (that is, the Fugitive Slave Law, resting on Article 4, Section 2 of the Constituion); that the compromise measures of 1850 should be strictly enforced; and that the constitutional rights of the South should be respected as resolutely as those of any other section. Concluding, Pierce appealed for maintenance of the status quo. The fearful crisis of 1850 had been surmounted, he said. "Let the period be remembered as an admonition, and not as an encouragement . . . to make experiments."

In his first message to the new Congress in December, 1853, Pierce renewed his hope that the question of slavery might quietly pass out of the national view. He spoke of a present "bright with promise" because the apprehensions of 1850 had been quieted by distinguished citizens of all parties who had sacrificed their private views, and had "restored a sense of repose and security to the public mind." Pierce pledged that this repose would "suffer no shock during my official term, if I have power to avert it."

The country, indeed, seemed to have regained control of itself and looked confidently to the future. The Democrats, by a policy of flamboyant diplomacy, proposed to direct public attention away from domestic issues which had so recently raised sectional passions. An aggressive and adventurous foreign policy which promoted domestic financial and commercial interests might serve to strengthen the national aspect of the party as it had under President Polk.

With the rules regarding slavery finally fixed by federal law over every square mile of the territorial domain, recurrent discord in Congress over this divisive subject might be considered at an end, and with political peace and stability the economic opportunities appeared unlimited. Trade boomed as American clipper ships raised the merchant marine to the height of its career. The gold found annually in California amounted to more than the entire revenues of the Federal Government. Men looking westward found opportunity at every step from the Mississippi to China. The negotiations with Mexico would provide a low level route for a transcontinental railroad through the Gila River Valley, a region soon to be acquired by the Gadsden Purchase. Several steamship and railroad promoters were canvassing ways to achieve quick and safe transport to California via central America, by rail in Panama, steamship in Nicaragua, and by plank road across the Isthmus of Tehuantepec. Commodore Perry was opening the door to trade with Japan, and explorers in the Pacific were searching out coaling stations and guano islands to claim for the United States. In the Caribbean the United States acted as the protector of tiny republics from European influence. Pierce planned, as a major policy, to consummate the acquisition of Cuba, and also sought land from Mexico and Santo Domingo. All these hopes and activities reflected the bouyant optimism and exuberant confidence in the future which Pierce was able to associate with his party's favorite slogan—"Young America."

The Whigs shared in the economic prosperity, but could not make political capital of it, for their leadership had collapsed. Harrison and Taylor, the

Whig ex-Presidents, had died, as had the party's greatest leaders, Webster and Clay. The election of 1852 had rendered Scott ridiculous, and only Fillmore and Crittenden remained to give high-level direction to the remnants of the party. Their management made the image of the Whigs stodgy and old fogyish, and no match for the appeal of the Democrats under their "Young Hickory of the Granite Hills." Indeed, General Scott's nomination and his miserable showing in the 1852 election seemed to have consigned the Whig party to oblivion. Scott's free-soil proclivities destroyed the Whig party in the South, split its northern supporters, and terminated its national appeal. Except for the stirrings of some nativists, the Democrats seemed securely in control of the country and in all probability would renominate and reelect President Pierce in 1856. So, at least, it appeared as Congress met in December, 1853.

A month later the whole political outlook had changed. In January, 1854, Senator Stephen A. Douglas reported a bill out of the Committee on Territories, of which he was chairman, proposing to divide the Nebraska Territory into two parts which, when ready for statehood, would be "received into the Union, with or without slavery, as their Constitution may prescribe at the time of their admission." Since 1820 the Missouri Compromise had excluded slavery in the Louisiana Purchase region north of latitude 36°30'N. The Kansas-Nebraska bill explicitly repealed the Missouri Compromise, and after an acrimonious congressional debate, the new law passed in May, 1854. By opening a vast region to slavery where it had long been excluded, the law immediately destroyed the concept of "finality" which had gained respect for the 1850 Compromise. It also brought to a sudden end the "sense of repose and security" which Pierce had promised to protect.

The passage of the Kansas-Nebraska Bill again brought the slavery controversy to the center of the national political stage and raised sectional passions to white heat. It would have been hard to find a worse place in the United States than Kansas to hold a plebiscite on slavery. The territory not only lay at the junction of North and South equally accessible to crusaders from both sides, but it symbolized the country's hopes, and therefore invited a major contest for control between powerful forces within the nation. Political control of Kansas meant opportunities in real estate, transportation, and mining. It might alter the political balance and determine the future supremacy of a party or a section. The great question in Kansas was not what would be done there; all were agreed on that. There would be new towns, railroads, homesteads, cattle, military supply contracts, and all manner of fortune hunting. The big question was whether northern or southern settlers would control the local government and grant or withhold crucial privileges.

It was no doubt a delusion for anyone to have believed in 1852 that the problem of slavery had been settled, but the delusion did exist. With the heat of controversy beginning to subside for the first time in twenty years, why did Douglas introduce the explosive Kansas-Nebraska bill? And why did President Pierce abandon his pledge of maintaining the status quo on slavery and risk his political reputation by making this bill an Administration measure and giving it his signature?

The election of 1856 would revolve largely around the assignment of blame or guilt for the Kansas-Nebraska Act and the tumult and bloodshed which followed its passage. In fact, the attribution of criminal responsibility to Pierce and his party became a major platform plank of the new Republican party created by the bill. Political propaganda would oversimplify the answer, declaiming that the "Nebraska infamy" was a typical action of the aggressive slave power whose leaders dominated the Democratic party and the Federal Government and who planned to spread slavery throughout the land. Historically many factors combined to bring the Kansas tragedy into being.

The Congress itself was inexperienced, only eighty members of the 234 having served prior to December, 1853. Almost everyone was a newcomer. The westward push of population kept up unceasing pressure to open new lands to settlement and establish territorial governments. Developments in the California and Far Eastern trade and the rapid stride of transportation technology made promoters confident that roads and railroads would soon tie the Mississippi with the Pacific and that the population needed to be distributed along such lines. These men thought the bill a natural step of economic development. Senator David R. Atchison, coming up for reelection in Missouri, faced a stiff fight with his rival, Thomas Hart Benton. He wanted the political advantage gained by promising to open Kansas to eager settlers of Missouri without restrictions on slaves. Atchison brought pressure for the Nebraska bill, while Benton opposed it, foreseeing clearly its dangers.

Douglas, however, was the main mover of the bill. His motives were mixed and pragmatic. As chairman of the Committee on Territories it was his business to inaugurate the steps leading toward statehood. As a businessman, he had important interests in real estate and in railroading which would develop as population moved west. As a politician, he recognized that the West would become a new center of gravity in national politics; it was a region which, in alliance with any other, might exercise control and place him in the White House. He had hoped for this in 1852, but discovered that his important role in maneuvering the Compromise of 1850 had alienated the South.

That section had permitted California to enter the Union as a free state, thus terminating the balance of slave and free states which had prevailed since 1820 and giving the free states a majority of senators. In exchange for this relinquishment of its power to veto hostile legislation in the Senate, the South had demanded an expression of the North's intent to enforce the fugitive slave clause of the Constitution in good faith. The importance which the southern leaders attached to this obligation was emphasized by the "Georgia Platform" which announced to the world that the continued existence of the Union depended specifically upon "faithful execution of the Fugitive Slave law." In short, the South had placed itself in subject political status to the North when it admitted California as a free state, making sixteen free to fifteen slave states; and the South could assume that in the future no more slave states would enter the Union. This condition would remain tolerable only so long as the North used the power of its majority to guarantee scrupulously the legal and constitutional protections to slavery. But the North had not observed the Fugitive Slave Law; most northern states adopted local procedures which essentially nullified the federal statute, and the South legitimately considered that it had been swindled by the North in the 1850 Compromise. For this they had Senator Douglas to thank. Douglas had to counter this point of view among southern politicos. The Kansas-Nebraska bill was, in part, his response to these events.

Douglas had repeatedly introduced territorial bills into Congress only to find them blocked by southerners because areas of free population grew so much faster than slave regions. In 1854 he saw his chance to serve multiple interests; the doctrine of popular sovereignty, applied in 1850 to New Mexico and Utah Territories, had not raised any serious outcry. To apply the same doctrine to Kansas and Nebraska would be consistent with past policy and would require no further debate since the issue had been thoroughly thrashed out four years before. It would also open to the South the means and possibility of recapturing their parity with the North in the Senate. Douglas correctly assumed that this proposal would receive bipartisan support from southerners, and that enough northern Democrats could be mobilized to its support that the bill would pass.

The Kansas-Nebraska bill quickly passed the Senate, but in the House enemies of Douglas and of the slavocracy placed an explicit repeal of the Missouri Compromise in the text. Prior to this, slavery would have been forbidden during the territorial period, but might have been approved at the time of adopting a state constitution. If the Missouri Compromise was repealed, however, then slaves might be taken into the territory in the months or years before statehood. The latter proposal was the signal for a bitter congressional battle which soon spread all over the country. The antislavery fire, which had been running out of fuel, was suddenly rekindled by the passionate oratory and outraged cries of people who had come to think of the Missouri Compromise as next to the Constitution in importance.

The gauge of battle suddenly shifted. After the Compromise of 1850 the North had appeared to be the region contemptuous of the Constitution and the section faithless to its given word, but now the South was forced into the role of villain. The repeal amendment altered the character of the territorial bill. It diverted emphasis from the opening of the West and toward the expansion of slavery; it gave a new lease on life both to aggressive abolition and aggressive slavocracy; it split the Democrats, killed the Whig party, offered a new role to native Americans, and created a new Republican party pledged to resist the extension of slavery into any territory. The bill created such unanticipated confusion and righteous anger that its passage could no longer be predicted, and Douglas, to protect his own reputation and future prospects, had to use party discipline to guarantee the necessary votes. In this effort, he had to seek help from President Pierce. The latter initially balked, for he foresaw the dangers of the bill, but Douglas, backed by southern senators, threatened to withhold support from important presidential diplomatic and patronage plans and forced Pierce into line. Thus, the entire weight of the Administration was thrown behind the bill, and the Democratic leadership had to accept responsibility for the bill and its consequences.

The antislavery men, handed a better propanganda tool than they had ever been able to forge, seized upon the bill as clear proof that the slave power wanted more than the protection of southern slavery discussed in 1850; they wanted it spread abroad into once free areas. In mid-January, a number of congressmen—Joshua Giddings of Ohio, Gerrit Smith of New York, Senator Salmon P. Chase of Ohio, Senator Charles Sumner of Massachusetts, and two others—drafted an "Appeal of the Independent Democrats in Congress to the People of the United States." All these men were antislavery spokesmen, some of them were Free Soilers in 1848 and abolitionists. Giddings and Chase did most of the writing, and the others signed the finished document which labelled the Kansas-Nebraska Act as "part and parcel of an atrocious plot" to trample free labor and to make the great West into a "dreary region of despotism inhabited by masters and slaves." They pointed out that the idea of popular sovereignty had never been accepted as a general rule, applicable anywhere; that it had no bearing on the Missouri Compromise since New Mexico and Utah lay outside of the Louisiana Purchase Territory; that Douglas had projected the popular sovereignty idea into the Nebraska region in defiance of logic, to support his own self-interest; and that Henry Clay, were he alive, would have indignantly condemned such bad faith. The document used the classic propanganda devices of inflammatory rhetoric and passionate denunciation. The bill was "a gross violation of a sacred pledge"; a "criminal betrayal of precious rights"; it perpetrated a "monstrous wrong"; it extended "legalized oppression and systematized injustice" over a vast area; it inspired "indignation and abhorrence" and called for resistance by any and every means, "for the cause of freedom is the cause of God."

The "Appeal to the Independent Democrats" profoundly stirred the nation. It was widely reprinted in the press and led directly to the formation of the Republican party. It proved to be the catalytic agent, and provided a powerful attraction at a critical juncture, to dedicated antislavery people like the abolitionists and Free Soilers. In addition it drew thousands of people whose conscience had been agitated by the Fugitive Slave Law, by Mrs. Stowe's effusive *Uncle Tom's Cabin*, and by a continual onslaught from the pulpit. Thus, the "Appeal" brought into the same camp, under the anti-Nebraska banner, every shade of northern antislavery sentiment—from the most moderate to the most extreme, and cloaked all with an aura of righteousness and Divine blessing. By shifting the focus of public attention from peace and prosperity to morality and the need to fight to the death against an evil slavocracy, the framers of the "Appeal" had seized the initiative, inaugurated an emotional crusade, and cut to shreds the old party loyalties.

Among the Democrats there were now anti-Nebraska people calling themselves Independent Democrats, southern or slave Democrats who identified with Pierce and maintained a rudimentary structure in the North sustained by officeholders, and a third force—largely within the party of the North—trying to repair the split.

If the Kansas-Nebraska Bill disrupted the Democrats, it completely overset the Whigs. The followers of Millard Fillmore, that is the old "Silver Greys" or "Nationals" who represented the northern commercial people and nearly all the southern Whigs, gave up the party name and tried to take control of the growing nativist movement known as the Know Nothing party. The other whig faction led by William H. Seward and known as the "Conscience" Whigs or "Woolly Heads" represented the anti-slavery people. An exclusively northern fragment, this faction actively sought union with other anti-Nebraska voters of the North, promoted fusion tickets for the 1854 congressional elections, and ultimately became the core of the newly emergent Republican party. The Silver Greys remained strongest in the Northeast and the Woolly Heads gained power fastest in the Midwest, but each state showed a different pattern and the movement of Whigs into the ranks of the Know Nothing or Republican parties was fitful and uncertain. With eyes on the election of 1856, Whig leaders had either to effect a merger between nativists and anti-slavery Republicans, or choose between them, for they despaired of running candidates under the tattered Whig banner.

Native Americanism had for many years exercised political influence in the United States and grew rapidly after the mid-1840's in response to the heavy influx of Germans and Irish Catholics. Anti-Catholic riots and church burnings afflicted many eastern seaboard cities where foreigners were concentrated, and hundreds of local nativist clubs sprang up throughout the country. Dedicated to the preservation of white, Anglo-Saxon, Protestant values which the nativist clubs identified as "100 per cent American," these groups thrived on hysteria. Their cause was strengthened by the boast of Archbishop John Hughes of New York in 1850 that the Pope planned to convert all inhabitants of the United States to Catholicism. By 1853 the people had become so excited that when the papal nuncio, Gaetano Cardinal Bedini, visited America to iron out some difficulties of domestic Catholic Churches he detonated riots in almost every city he visited, was burned in effigy, and was nearly assassinated.

Until this time the nativist clubs had not made politics their primary interest, but in 1852 the New York-based Order of the Star Spangled Banner came under the management of James W. Baker, who devised techniques to use nativism as a political force. New members pledged themselves to obedience and secrecy, and took an oath to oppose Catholics or foreigners for any public office, regardless of their party affiliation. When admitted to membership, the initiate learned the secrets of the Order—a kind of ritual apparatus borrowed partly from Masonry—including passwords, signs, grips, signals of recognition and distress, and requirements to progress through the several degrees within the order. As branches spread into all the surrounding states under the new name, the Order of United Americans, it began to control local elections by choosing designated candidates from the regular tickets without running any candidates of its own. In fact, no one knew who belonged to the Order because members, if questioned, replied, "I know nothing about it." Although the political nativists had generally adopted the name "American Party" by 1853, most people called them "Know Nothings."

The nativists had a strong bent toward national patriotism, conservatism, and respect for the Constitution; in this they agreed generally with the Silver Grey or National Whigs. As the Kansas-Nebraska controversy splintered the Whigs in the spring of 1854, leaders of the National or Fillmore faction contrived the idea of joining the nativist organization, gaining control of it, renaming it, and using it as a new political engine, and they succeeded. While the original thrust of nativism had been xenophobic and anti-Catholic, the new Whig managers tried to alter its goals to make it an anti-Democratic and anti-sectional party in which the Union-loving, nationalist Fillmore Whigs might feel at home.

The fight over the repeal of the Missouri Compromise fragmented, disrupted, and changed the aspect of the Democratic, Whig, and Know Nothing parties, and raised a new sectional party out of the ensuing chaos. The birth of the Republican party signaled the almost self-evident fact that the slavery issue could not possibly be kept out of sight and forgotten. Despite bipartisan claims that the 1850 measures had finally settled the slavery question, and President Pierce's hopeful proclamations that agitation about it had ceased, never to be revived, the Kansas-Nebraska proposition did revive the controversy, instantly, bitterly and with unprecedented vehemence. It exposed the delusion that the issue would disappear, and provided northerners, who generally abhorred slavery but tolerated it as the price of Union, with a chance to speak their conscience at last without seeming to be unpatriotic.

The tap root of the new party was antislavery sentiment, strengthened by the Kansas-Nebraska Bill. Free Soilers and abolitionists provided the initial impetus to unite all men opposed to the further extension of slavery. This was a cause which had a powerful moral influence throughout the North, but other forces attracted people to this nucleus for reasons entirely apart from slavery. The Republican party, as it slowly took shape, became a strange coalition of moral crusaders, religious fanatics, disgruntled politicians, favor-seeking businessmen, land-hungry farmers, temperance leaders, and other seceders from the ranks of Democrats, Whigs, or Know Nothings. Those who would create a new party of such disparate elements had to keep public attention focused on some dynamic issue. The Republicans tried to keep emotions highly charged about the anti-slavery cause. The Know Nothings sought to attract bolters from other parties by focusing on anti-Catholicism and anti-foreignism. Horace Greeley predicted in 1855 that of the two, nativism would prove a transitory political force and antislavery a permanent magnet for votes.

At the time Douglas introduced his explosive territorial bill, party loyalties had already weakened and serious dissension existed in all the groups. Northwestern Democrats had never forgiven southern party leaders for giving up half of Oregon while taking all of the Mexican southwest, for defeating rivers and harbors bills, or for withholding support from Cass in 1848. Northeastern Democrats had protested the party's low tariff policy since 1833. Democratic Administrations since Jackson had opposed the rapid opening of the West through land grants or homestead acts while ex-President Van Buren in 1848 had drawn many Democratic supporters to his Free Soil movement. These people became the Anti-Nebraska and Independent Democrats of 1854.

To old Jacksonians, it appeared as if the regular Democratic party had become a tool of the slavocracy. Thus, one had to be anti-Democratic to be antislavery. This was not true but it was a powerful argument in 1854 and 1855. The Whigs of the East had split into "National" and "Conscience" factions, the former eventually moving into the Know Nothing ranks and the latter joining the antislavery Republicans. In the West, however, where the Know Nothings had little appeal, almost all of the Whigs became Republicans. It might be more accurate to say that the Whigs of the Northwest agreed to change their name to Republican. There were fewer switches of Know Nothings to the Republican ranks, because these two groups were rivals in seeking the support of disaffected Democrats or homeless Whigs. But groups of humanitarian crusaders, primarily temperance people and the Maine Law promoters of state prohibition, tended to gravitate into the Republican coalition, as did the old Liberty party supporters.

The antislavery adherents began fusing a new political organization at Ripon, Wisconsin on February 28, 1854, under the leadership of Alan E. Bovay. On July 6, a state meeting at Jackson, Michigan, chose the name "Republican" for the new party and named party candidates. A variety of names had been used and would continue to be locally employed, such as Independent Democrats, Anti-Nebraska party, People's party, Reform party, Fusion party, and the like, but by midsummer of 1854 the name "Republican" had received official recognition. On July 13, anniversary of the Northwest Ordinance, Republicans of Ohio, Indiana, and Wisconsin held state conventions and placed tickets before the public.

The results of the 1854 election confounded nearly everybody and are still not clearly understood. The Democrats were overwhelmed throughout the North, but the reasons remained obscure. The anti-Nebraska people claimed a victory over the slavocracy, but much evidence pointed to the probability that the Know Nothings, acting in secret concert, brought their solid phalanx to bear against the Democrats. Many northern Democrats had quietly become Know Nothings and voted their party at the polls. The anti-liquor crusade weighed heavily in particular states like Pennsylvania against the "Rum Democrats," as they labeled the opposition.

The campaign for congressional and state candidates started with the New Hampshire and Connecticut elections in May, before the Kansas-Nebraska bill had been passed, and continued furiously through the fall of 1854. The Democrats found their hands tied, for they had to adopt the policy of Douglas and the Administration on the question. This gained them no added support in the South, and divided their northern partisans; they also had to support the immigrants to protect their control of the cities. These stands were hard to defend in the North, and were not needed to keep control in the South.

Iowa held the first election after the passage of the Kansas-Nebraska Act. A strongly Democratic state in the past, it now elected a free-soil Whig for governor and a legislature which chose a Republican for United States senator. In this state, where Democrats had never before been defeated, they were not to carry a state election again for thirty-five years.

The normally routine mid-term elections aroused more physical violence and verbal fury than had been known in a generation. Cardinal Bedini's visit in the early months of 1854, when the Kansas-Nebraska act was being debated, stirred riots in half a dozen cities and stimulated a rush of applications for induction into the Know Nothing lodges. Senator Douglas, cursed as a Benedict Arnold or Judas Iscariot, was burned in effigy from one end of the North to the other, and was booed and stoned from the speaker's rostrum in his native Chicago as he tried to defend his territorial bill. Few newspapers could make any enthusiastic defense of the repeal of the Missouri Compromise, but scores of them employed their most vivid imagery in condemning this as an outrage, perfidy, swindle, enormity, craven surrender, or atrocious plot. Anti-Nebraska stump speakers indulged themselves in the most irresponsible utterances, and used all the talents they possessed to stir up righteous indignation. During the week of the passage of the Nebraska bill, the entire North resounded to the savage attack of an antislavery mob on the federal courthouse in Boston in an attempt to free a fugitive slave, Anthony Burns. State and federal troops had to be mobilized to move him out of the city to shipboard, while thousands lined the streets, hissing and groaning at the enforcement of this part of the federal Constitution. Pierce's orders to use all necessary military power to enforce the law was consistent with his oath of office, but coming at the very moment of the passage of the bill opening the West to slavery, it made the President's name anathema in New England, and apparently provided proof that slaveholders controlled the Administration and that the Fugitive Slave Law and the Kansas-Nebraska Law were cut of the same cloth.

The refueled antislavery fire burned across Pierce's home state of New Hampshire and prevented the selection of the man Pierce had endorsed for senator. The summer's events intensified the struggle between New York's Democrats. The "Hards" had supported Pierce's policy, but the "Softs" had declined to endorse the Kansas-Nebraska move, and the President, using patronage to punish them, widened the rift. In the early fall election in Maine, a traditional Democratic bastion in New England, the opposition won the governorship and the congressional contest, and the Democrats dropped one-third below their usual poll. Pierce attributed this to the anti-liquor party and the Know Nothings, but others claimed the triumph for the Republicans under the leadership of apostate Democrat Hannibal Hamlin, who had rejected Pierce's policies.

In October, the opposition carried Ohio, Indiana, and Pennsylvania, and the Democrats suffered a net loss of thirty-one congressmen. The November elections, coming just after the *New York Herald's* publication of a garbled version of the Ostend Manifesto, brought defeat for the Democrats in New Jersey, Delaware, and Massachusetts. Wisconsin and Michigan went against Pierce, and New York and Illinois delivered important offices to candidates of the fusion parties. Six months after the passage of the fateful Kansas-Nebraska Bill the Democrats had lost their majority in the House. Pierce had carried all but two northern states in 1852; in 1854 his party lost all but two of these states and gave up sixty-two seats in Congress. The implications of such a massive shift in public opinion projected themselves immediately to the coming presidential election. One of the Administration leaders wrote that the elections had convinced every intelligent Democrat "of the utter impossibility of the re-election of General Pierce." New Hampshire Democrats proposed Sam Houston as a good prospect for the 1856 nomination, and the friends of James Buchanan, who had hoped for the nomination since 1844, began to circulate his name. Douglas, of course, stood ready, though temporarily unnerved by the course of events.

The precise meaning of the political upset of 1854 puzzled all the experts. Opposition to the Democrats seemed clear enough, but no one knew the identity of the opposition. The voters had been offered many tickets under many names — People's party, Republican, Anti-Nebraska, Fusion, Union, Know Nothing, American, Temperance, Maine Law, and others — all of them anti-Democratic, but not otherwise unified in objective. Fusion occurred in many states, but local conditions determined which groups would combine their support of one ticket, and what part of the coalition would exert leadership or command a major place on the ballot. Surface observation indicated that the Know Nothings had constituted the significant force. American Protestants had responded emphatically to the Catholic threat, highlighted by Pierce's appointment of a Catholic to the Cabinet, Archbishop Hughes' provocative address, Cardinal Bedini's untimely visit, and the riots in the cities. Many looked forward to the American party developing as a national organization, successor to the Whigs. Opposed to sectionalism, quiet on the slavery issue, stressing patriotism and love of the Union, such a party had a chance to inherit the Whig constituency.

But other evidence pointed in a different direction. Strong antislavery leaders had been sent to the Senate. New York elected William H. Seward; New Hampshire, John P. Hale; Vermont, Jacob Collamer; and Illinois, Lyman Trumbull. These men were among the most outspoken leaders of the antislavery movement; no hint of Know Nothing influence could account for their selection by the respective state legislatures.

The Know Nothings had confused the issue. Astute politicians planned to use the period before the next presidential election to achieve clarification. For the Whig leadership, now ensconced high in the councils of the American party, this meant constructing a national party organization, and this in turn meant taking no position on any issue involving slavery. For the antislavery people of the North, it meant focusing all attention and energy upon Kansas where the hated Kansas-Nebraska Act would be implemented, and devising means to make that region a showcase of violence, corruption, horrors, and atrocities which could be attributed to slavocrats or Democrats. Chaos in Kansas, which kept public interest alert and emotions charged, would bring strength through publicity to the Republicans, while it would divide and weaken every other political group.

As the year 1855 developed, and Kansas began rapidly to fill up with settlers, most of them from the free states, it began to look as if the natural operation of popular sovereignty would soon make Kansas free. This would vindicate Douglas, and northern Democrats cultivated the idea that these results would follow. Excitement diminished as it seemed unlikely that slavery actually would move north of latitude 36°30′N. The Know Nothing party benefited from the abatement of the uproar, but suffered from lack of unity and backbone among its own leaders. They blundered in Virginia, losing the governorship to Democratic Henry A. Wise. In June, at a Philadelphia meeting to strengthen national organization of the party, the slavery question came up in the form of a resolution to restore the Missouri Compromise. Its defeat brought the secession of the Ohio and Massachusetts delegations, and foreshadowed the future difficulty of avoiding such divisive questions.

The Republicans rather than the Know Nothings seemed to be the transitory party in the early months of 1855, but there were several encouraging signs. In New York, Seward formally carried his Woolly-Head Whigs into the Republican party, bringing with him Thurlow Weed, Horace Greeley, Henry J. Raymond, and the organizational and publicity machines they controlled. The shift was especially significant because Raymond was an enemy of the Know Nothings. The New York Republicans proposed to stand alone, without any need for fusion except on their own terms. In Ohio, the Republicans forced Salmon P. Chase on the coalition ticket with Know Nothings as candidate for governor. Chase was vehemently against slavery, and for this reason obnoxious to Know Nothings and National Whigs who participated in the party fusion; but the Republicans managed to nominate and elect him and thus to encourage their associates elsewhere to resist absorption and to take command of coalitions against the Democrats.

Public apathy remained the greatest threat to the Republicans, and to counter it they had to keep passions high by an incessant newspaper barrage of propaganda about frauds and atrocities committed by the Administration party in Kansas. There was a great deal of fraud and violence, and the term "Bleeding Kansas" was appropriate, but both sides printed exaggerations and lies about events there, with the Republicans commanding the better writers and the wider circulation of newspapers. The battle of Kansas, so essential to Republican survival as a party, was fought almost as fiercely in Congress and in the Republican press as it was on the western plains.

Popular sovereignty might have worked in Kansas had normal immigration been permitted and the settlers allowed to work out their political destiny without outside interference. But control of the area quickly became symbolic of the whole struggle between anti-and pro-slavery forces. Abolitionists formed the Emigrant Aid Societies to mobilize and speed unnatural migration of free-state settlers, while southerners also moved in settlers like troops, though on a smaller scale. Missourians rushed in to participate in the election of the first territorial legislature in March and carried the day for the slavery faction. Since the Kansas boundary line had not yet been surveyed, no one could prove, however, that the presumably fraudulent voters resided actually in Missouri rather than Kansas. The free-state settlers cried fraud and called the territorial legislature a bogus assembly. Governor Andrew Reeder sided with them and by the end of July had to be removed by President Pierce. The free-state people then privately organized their own legislature, appointed Reeder the congressional delegate from the free-state government, and drafted a free-state Constitution at Topeka which was ratified in December, 1855, by a rump vote restricted to free-state men. This document, which excluded all Negroes from Kansas and sought to erect a white man's state, was submitted to Congress for approval. In the meantime, Pierce sent a new governor to Kansas, Wilson Shannon, who tried but failed to bring some order to the growing chaos. Early in January, 1856, the Free State party, operating under the rules of the Topeka Constitution, elected its own governor and legislature. Thus two government establishments, each with officers and military forces, confronted each other in Kansas, one the creation of President Pierce through his appointed officers, and the other existing without any connection with the national Administration.

As the election year 1856 dawned, Kansas faced civil war. President Pierce would have been glad for some backing in Congress, but the House of Representatives, meeting in December, 1855, with the congressmen who had been elected in the fall of 1854, discovered that no party held a majority so that it was inpossible to choose a Speaker. For two months a strange assortment of faction-ridden Democrats, Republicans, Whigs, Know Nothings, and victors of fusion tickets who knew no way to identify themselves tried, without success, to choose a Speaker. Not until February 2, three weeks before the first of the presidential nominating conventions, did the antislavery forces in the House succeed in naming Nathaniel Banks of Massachusetts to the Speaker's chair.

In the meantime, Pierce had to deal with Kansas. On January 24 he proclaimed the proslavery legislature, which rested on a legal base even though tainted by election frauds, as the recognized and official government of Kansas Territory, and condemned the Topeka government as revolutionary and treasonable. A few weeks later he denounced illegal methods used by partisans of both Kansas governments, but his words and threats had little effect; both continued to rule where their guns could control and neither paid any attention to Washington. The southerners, based at Lecompton, and the northerners at Lawrence and Topeka, kept up sporadic guerilla warfare.

The Presidential campaign of 1856 formally began on Washington's Birthday when the Republicans held their first national organization meeting at Pittsburgh, Pennsylvania, and the Know Nothings on the same day met at Philadelphia to nominate their candidates for President and Vice-President. The simultaneous meetings of these two groups was not accidental, and reflected a mutual belief that some kind of collaboration between the two would have to be established in the presidential canvass. The Republican meeting, promoted by Chase to perfect party organization and prepare for a summer nominating convention, drew such a heterogeneous group of delegates that no body of principles could be agreed on. The conservatives took control, decided not to attempt agreement on any antislavery proposal, and appealed to a variety of special interest groups: businessmen, laborers, farmers, clergymen, temperance people, nativists, and German and Irish minorities. Inconsistencies between the factions were waved off as the leaders appealed to the broad hopes of each group without affronting any in specific matters. Despite its heterogeneous membership, the convention was remarkably harmonious and adjourned after setting up national and state committees and calling for a nominating convention at Philadelphia on June 17.

The Know Nothings, now formally called the American party, held their nominating convention at Philadelphia on February 22. The very fact of such a meeting publicized the obvious but recent development that secrecy, once a major attraction of the party, no longer prevailed. So many people, including enemy infiltrators and spies, had joined that everyone knew the once mysterious rituals and procedures. The leaders still tried to govern by edict, passing orders from the national to the local lodges and anticipating obedience. The National Council came to Philadelphia several days early to draw up the party platform emphasizing loyalty to the Union and restraints on foreigners. "Americans must rule America," read the third article. The convention of 227 delegates from twenty-seven states—there were no representatives from Maine, Vermont, South Carolina, and Georgia—quickly fell into an angry controversy over slavery. The northern faction offered a resolution that no candidates should be nominated who did not favor prohibiting slavery north of latitude 36°30'N. When this proposal was laid on the table, most of the antislavery delegates withdrew, mainly from New England, Pennsylvania, Ohio, Illinois, and Iowa. The main convention, now mostly a southern body, proceeded to nominate Millard Fillmore for President and Andrew J. Donelson for Vice-President and adjourned.

The seceders organized themselves as a separate party, called the North Americans. These "Northern Bolters" or "Republican Sympathizers," called for a nominating convention in New York in June, about the same time as the Republican convention in Philadelphia, a clear indication that an alignment between the two was in preparation. These results showed, even before the usual season for Presidential nominations, that the once-feared Know Nothing movement had fractured at the Mason and Dixon line over the pervasive slavery issue, and could not possibly play a serious role, by itself, in the coming presidential canvass. In the South, the Americans would swallow the Whigs and form the major anti-Democratic party; but in the North their members could do little but sell themselves to the Democrats or the Republicans for the best price they could get. The seceding North Americans had already designated their choice.

The Democrats scheduled their convention at Cincinnati on June 2. The party, weakened in the North by the outburst against the repeal of the Missouri Compromise, remained the strongest political force in the nation. Lacking effective leadership, it had developed feuds and splits in many states, and between the major sections, but the party had a Jacksonian tradition of invincibility, a large number of nationally important public figures, control of federal patronage, and the backing of a nearly solid South and a loyal portion of the North and West. No other party could claim as much.

President Pierce, encouraged by his official family, hoped for renomination. Senator Douglas, the most assertive policy maker of the party, anticipated that he might receive the prize. He counted on the support of the southern members of the party for whom he had suffered much because of the Kansas-Nebraska fracas. Northern Democrats rejected both of these obvious prospects, and preferred James Buchanan, who had been safely in England as minister to the Court of St. James throughout the entire Kansas controversy. He offered the security of broad political experience, a conservative approach to crisis situations, and a nonsectional background. There were other hopefuls, notably Lewis Cass of Michigan who had lost to Taylor in 1848, but most of the pre-convention planning revolved about the first three men.

Pierce and Douglas agreed early that the two should pool their strength to prevent Buchanan from capturing the nomination. Pierce would run first; if he failed to progress he would throw his strength to Douglas; and if that politician could not succeed, the two would hold off Buchanan until they could settle on a dark horse candidate who might, as Polk in 1844 and Pierce in 1852, break the deadlock. All these plans had been roughly worked out some weeks before the convention assembled. Buchanan had made no advance plans for his own convention strategy, having only returned from England at the end of April, and he might well have been outmaneuvered; but several sensational events just a week before the convention worked against Pierce and Douglas and in Buchanan's favor.

In the Senate on May 19 and 20, Charles Sumner delivered a theatrical "extemporaneous" speech which he called "The Crime against Kansas." Actually, Sumner had prepared a dramatic script which he had carefully rehearsed for days before the delivery. The result was a personal attack which many thought he intended to provoke by his vulgar and coldly insulting diatribe. Senator Sumner mixed his attacks on Pierce's Kansas policy with filthy allegations against Senator Andrew Pickens Butler of South Carolina, a man whose character was so far removed from Sumner's crude allegations that no one could make any sense of the insults, especially since Senator Butler was not in the Senate Chamber. Sumner's philippic was such a tour de force of classical scholarship, used to so juvenile a purpose—that is, to shout dirty names at an absent senator from South Carolina—that Douglas frankly said he thought Sumner's object was "to provoke some of us to kick him as we would a dog in the street." Cass called it "the most un-American and unpatriotic" speech he had ever heard. Predictably, a nephew of Butler's, Congressman Preston Brooks, obliged Sumner by coming to the Senate and beating him nearly to unconsciousness with a heavy rubber cane. Intellectual vulgarity had called up its physical counterpart.

Sumner's speech gained wide currency as a Republican campaign document throughout the North. The day after its delivery, the proslavery forces in Kansas invaded the free-soil town of Lawrence and sacked it on trumped up charges. Preston Brooks rubber-caned Sumner the next day, on May 22. Two days later, John Brown and his murderous party raided the homes of proslavery settlers along the Osawatomie in Kansas, dragged five men from their beds, split open their skulls with a broad axe, cut off their hands, and laid open their bowels. Brown proclaimed he was acting for "God and the Army of the North." These vicious and crazy acts, immediately preceding the Democratic nominating convention, brought unaccustomed sobriety to many of the delegates.

The Buchanan managers, notably Senators John Slidell and Judah P. Benjamin of Louisiana, James A. Bayard of Delaware, and Jesse D. Bright of Indiana, gained control of the convention from the outset, electing their candidate for permanent chairman and controlling the committees. Buchanan, Pierce, and Douglas, in that order, led the voting for presidential nominee for 14 ballots without any one receiving a simple majority, much less the necessary two-thirds. The Pierce men, abandoning hope for him, then switched to Douglas according to prior agreement. They expected Douglas to hold on until some new name could be introduced on which they could unite, but the Douglas supporters, laying the groundwork for his nomination in 1860, suddenly withdrew his name and Buchanan received the nomination on the seventeenth ballot. A young friend of Douglas, John C. Breckinridge of Kentucky, received the vice-presidential place on the ticket.

The outcome, achieved by a temporary union of northern and western Democrats, displeased the southern wing of the party, which distrusted Buchanan on the slavery issue. They had hoped, by a convention deadlock, to carry a compromise candidate more sympathetic to their views. The platform fell short of their hopes, and the convention had rejected their vice-presidential preference, John A. Quitman of Mississippi. They left Cincinnati disgruntled, though not to the point of rebellion. The Democrats had settled on candidates and policies which represented their wish merely to hold the old structure together. No new faces or policies would be offered to the public; the course of the past decade would remain unaltered and the voters, nervous and fearful of the future, would be offered security, experience, and a continuation of the status quo.

The renegades from the February Know Nothing Convention, that is the North Americans or Free Soil segment of the party, held a nominating convention in New York from June 12–15. Delegates came from all the northern states except Ohio, though many of them represented no particular constituency. They were Know Nothings more in name than in fact, and since they were much stronger on antislavery policy than on nativism, it seemed apparent to all that the major object of the convention was to work up some kind of an arrangement or union with the Republicans. Weed and Greeley were much in evidence, trying to patch up all prior differences. As the Republican inner council had already decided that John C. Frémont might be their best candidate, the North Americans wished also to nominate him with the thought that it might strengthen him in Philadelphia, but it seemed more likely that the opposite reaction might occur. The convention finally nominated Nathaniel Banks, Speaker of the House and a close friend of Frémont, with the understanding that after the Republicans had made Frémont their candidate, Banks would retire and direct the North Americans to give Frémont their votes. A good many of the delegates wanted merely to maintain the party's election machinery which later could be offered for sale without reserve, with the Republicans as the only possible bidder. A reporter wrote of this: "May his Satanic Majesty have a place specially hot and sulphurous wherein to roast such humbuggery."

Two days after the North Americans adjourned in New York, the Republicans assembled for their first national nominating convention in Philadelphia. Nearly one thousand delegates came, representing all the free states and four of the border slave states. Many important and astute politicians participated, such as Charles Francis Adams, David Wilmot, Francis P. Blair, Joshua R. Giddings, Horace Greeley, Thurlow Weed, Thaddeus Stevens, Henry Wilson, and Henry S. Lane, who became permanent chairman. But mostly, the delegates comprised young reformers and dedicated crusaders, a group which was, in contrast to the other conventions, committed, enthusiastic, passionate, optimistic, uncompromising, and imbued with a sense of religious mission. The convention was sectional, evangelical, and radical. The politicians and the crusaders soon disagreed on whether to bow to the realistic requirements of trying to win a presidential election, or to demonstrate their courage and firmness of purpose by audaciously going all out on the antislavery issue.

The platform, reported by David Wilmot, brought something new to the political scene, calling for no extension of slavery into any free territory, and asking Congress to prohibit polygamy and slavery in the territories, to admit Kansas promptly as a free state under the Topeka Constitution, to plan for a Pacific railroad, and to appropriate more money for rivers and harbors bills and other accommodations to business. A provocative tradition-breaking resolution accused adherents of the Pierce Administration of "murders, robberies, and arson," and pledged that the Republicans, when elected, would punish the offenders. In a blanket indictment of all Pierce Democrats, the platform pledged that the Republicans would bring these people "to a sure and condign punishment hereafter." The formal pledge of one party, if elected, to treat members of the other as condemned criminals formed an unprecedented aspect of the 1856 contest. It also threatened an end to the elective system, for it repudiated compromise and the idea of peaceful coexistence between opposing parties.

The major Republican leaders had caucused enough in the months before the convention to make it nearly certain that John C. Frémont would emerge as the party's nominee. Frémont had been approached by the Democrats in 1855 as the answer to their need. He was a young and romantic figure, entirely free of any complicity with the Kansas mess; but he could not approve either the Fugitive Slave Law nor the Nebraska Act. The Know Nothings also had approached him without success. Late in 1855, at Blair's estate in Silver Spring, Maryland, the leading antislavery men, including Chase, Sumner, and Banks, concluded that Frémont would be the ideal Republican candidate. Chase doubtless deserved the nomination for his energetic promotional work, and Seward would have had the most prestige of anyone; but since the practical politicians did not anticipate victory on the first trial they preferred to save these stalwarts for a later day and to permit someone outside professional politics to lead the party to defeat.

Frémont's name achieved increasing publicity throughout the spring of 1856. Seward and Chase still had many supporters who thought that the nominee should, in honesty, be someone who had worked and suffered for the antislavery cause. But both these men had taken too strong a stand against slavery and it was thought that they would give an abolitionist tinge to the new party and drive off all the moderates. Seward, furthermore, had aroused the hatred of the Native Americans. One other man stood between Frémont and his nomination by acclamation, possibly on the first ballot. Justice John McLean of Ohio, over seventy and an uninspiring old fogy, had the merits of years of experience; a moderate stance on all the public issues, which meant that he had created few bitter enemies; and strong support in the important states of New Jersey, Pennsylvania, and Illinois. If the young crusaders would go for McLean, he would draw into the fold most of the old National Whigs and the northern business community, which did not like the Democrats but had grown very skittish about antislavery extremists. They hoped to win with Frémont running second on a McLean ticket. As the convention organized, it became apparent that the young aggressive antislavery Republicans controlled the issue. Early in the balloting, delegates rose in succession to withdraw from contention the names of Seward, Chase, and McLean; and Frémont was then chosen.

The convention nominated W. L. Dayton of New Jersey for Vice-President, and in so doing committed what many believed to be its major blunder. Thurlow Weed and others equally perceptive thought that Simon Cameron of Pennsylvania, if awarded second place on the ticket, would have seriously threatened Buchanan's hold on his native state. Cameron had been a Buchanan henchman for years, knew all the trade secrets of the Democrats, and furthermore had ingratiated himself with the Know Nothings. But the decision had been made; the convention responded with wild excitement and unprecedented noise, confusion, and enthusiasm, and the Young Republicans, chanting their slogan "Free Speech, Free Soil and Frémont," prepared to go before the country in a headlong assault against all rivals.

The candidates for President in 1856 — Buchanan, Fillmore, and Frémont — gave the voters a choice between two old fogies and a young American, or between two experienced but unexciting elder statesmen and a military man innocent of political sophistication. Buchanan had earned the largest measure of prestige by serving in national office for nearly half a century as congressman, senator, minister to Russia and to Great Britain, and Secretary of State during the Mexican War. Originally a Federalist, he had gone over to the Jackson party in the disputed election of 1824. A lawyer by profession, Buchanan put great stock in orderly procedure and the solution of problems by the use of reason and compromise. Temperamentally, Buchanan was cool and reserved, without passion and almost always firmly self-controlled. As a bachelor, he acquired a stronger belief in the efficacy of reason as an arbiter of human affairs than most married men. Friend of the golden mean, foe of fanatics, Buchanan had no use for reformers, especially temperance people and preachers playing at politics. He had been an enemy of slavery since his college days, but had more reverence for the Constitution and Union than he had antagonism to slavery; in a clear choice he would put the Union first and the antislavery cause second. He disliked the popular sovereignty principle because it placed before untrained voters a question which had baffled the best wits of every national leader; he predicted in 1850 that settlers, on this principle, would rush into a territory and murder each other; and events in Kansas had borne out his prophecy. In accepting the Democratic nomination, he publicly stated that he would submerge his private misgivings about this feature of the Kansas-Nebraska Act and be "the representative of the Cincinnati Platform."

Buchanan's greatest assets to his party as a candidate in 1856 were his lifelong aversion to sectional politics; the fact that he had fortuitously escaped association with the four great crises of his era—the Compromise of 1820, nullification, the Compromise of 1850, and the Kansas-Nebraska Bill—which had weakened all the major participants; his political experience; and the unassailability of his personal life. His weaknesses before the electorate were his age, sixty-five in 1856; his lack of dramatic and emotional appeal; and his sane, unexciting record. As logic was his principal political tool, his actions always were predictable to any logical person, and thus he never held the gauge of battle on anyone or gained the advantage of an ambush, a surprise attack, or a sudden witty move that upset an opponent. Buchanan had been in England as United States minister from 1853 until a month before his nomination and thus had escaped the mud bath which had spattered every prominent participant in the Kansas struggle. He came before the public in the role of the wise trustworthy and experienced old captain, the kind of man to whom the ship of state could safely be entrusted in a storm.

Millard Fillmore, candidate of the Know Nothings, was a man much like Buchanan. Trained as a lawyer, he appealed to people not by showmanship or emotion, but by logic, simple exposition, and reasonableness. He was dignified, restrained, devoted to the American Union, and a loyal and unselfish servant to the Whig party. Like Buchanan, he saw compromise as the major technique of national survival, and for this reason as President had encouraged the adoption of the 1850 measures. Thereafter he used all his efforts to preserve the national base of the Whig party. When the Whigs under

Scott suffered their disastrous defeat in 1852, Fillmore gave up hope that the party could survive and transferred his interest to making over the new Know Nothing movement into a bastion of Union sentiment. Fillmore's Silver Greys instituted the new Union Degree and shifted Know Nothing policy away from anti-Catholicism and anti-foreignism to anti-sectionalism. Fillmore did not so much seek the Know Nothing nomination as to permit himself to be used in the cause of Union.

The Republicans had the most colorful candidate, though no one knew very much about him politically. John C. Frémont's life had been involved in passion and adventure from the day of his adulterous conception. Raised in South Carolina, he early engaged in topographical work and explorations. Before the Mexican War he had aided in trans-Mississippi explorations ordered by the War Department. Back in Washington, he met and fell in love with the beautiful, vivacious young Jessie Benton, daughter of gruff Senator Thomas Hart Benton of Missouri; she responded impetuously to the handsome young explorer, but her parents forbade the marriage. In 1841 they were secretly married by a Catholic priest in Washington; she was seventeen and he twenty-eight. Senator Benton stormed when the news leaked, but his threats were vain.

Frémont explored the Rocky Mountains, and was in California at the time of the Mexican War. Between then and his nomination to the Presidency he had been on almost half a dozen major western explorations, earning the title of "The Pathfinder" and achieving some public notice through the publication of illustrated reports on the western country. Interestingly, in the year before Frémont and Jessie Benton eloped, Senator Buchanan had been young Jessie's escort to Washington functions. He greatly admired her, and aided Colonel Frémont by inducing Congress to appropriate funds for the wide circulation of his exploration reports. That the impoverished young naturalist and the already elderly Senator would meet as opposing presidential candidates some two decades later seemed then beyond the wildest flight of imagination.

Frémont, unlike Buchanan or Fillmore, was a man of impetuosity and passion, who often acted first and thought later. Such a trait brought him devoted friends and bitter enemies; few could fail to respond one way or the other. He knew no middle ground, whereas his presidential rivals perceived no ground but the middle. He was sincere and essentially simple in his political outlook, but his quick enthusiasm and his rash impulsiveness were dangerous. He tended to judge people and problems swiftly and offhandedly, and often judged badly. He was neither hero nor villain, victor nor vanquished, but much of his life oscillated close to these extremes rather than proceeding more moderately between them.

He could not be counted on to distinguish the political subtleties, but he spoke straight and clear on the main issues. He opposed nativism and the extension of slavery. In accepting his nomination, he made a brief statement against filibustering and recommending the admission of Kansas as a free state. Under advice from his political mentors, this was his first and last public statement in the 1856 campaign. His greatest advantage was his youth. As Harrison in 1840 had stolen the Jackson thunder, so Frémont in 1856 repeated the trick, stealing the image of "Young America" under which Pierce had won.

The battle for the Presidency was fought on two fronts, in Congress and before the public. Kansas formed the center of the congressional battle; the Democrats wanted to defuse this powder keg and the Republicans hoped to blow it sky high. As the original Kansas-Nebraska Bill spelled out no detailed procedure to inaugurate statehood, Whig Senator Robert Toombs of Georgia proposed an enabling act defining in great detail the mechanics of calling a constitutional convention and holding the plebiscite on slavery. Douglas approved, and the Senate passed this bill by a large majority on July 2. The bill was eminently fair; Toombs alleged that southerners would welcome Kansas as a slave or a free state, as long as the result came from a fair vote. Seward admitted that it gave both sides an equal opportunity but denied that the proslavery group deserved an equal chance. The Republicans, denying that there could be more than one side on the issue of human freedom, declined the Democratic invitation to amend the bill in any way they desired, and stated that they would not support the bill in any form. In short, they demanded the immediate admission of Kansas as a free state regardless of the terms of the Kansas-Nebraska law.

On July 3, the day after the Senate sent the Toombs bill to the House, the latter, completely ignoring the Senate action, passed its own bill admitting Kansas as a free state under the Topeka Constitution, the product of a government which Pierce had proclaimed revolutionary and treasonable. The Senate killed this bill. Just before the end of the session, when it was learned that Pierce planned to send federal troops to Kansas to enforce the local law and keep the peace, the House killed the whole military appropriations bill by a rider forbidding the army to be used for law enforcement in any territory. Pierce had to call a special session which, in order not to leave the nation wholly defenseless, finally passed the army appropriations. Congress adjourned on August 30, with Kansas still in anarchy and producing excellent campaign propaganda for the Republicans, as they had intended it should. The actions of the two houses of Congress during July and August displayed to the public the basic character of the contending parties. The Democrats and leading southern politicians in the Senate seriously feared that the Republicans intended a disruption of the Union and announced their willingness to compromise all the practical issues in Kansas to avert such a catastrophe. The Republicans in the House responded that they would deal with Kansas on no terms except their own, regardless of any laws or the effect on the Union. One party accepted negotiation as a political device; the other insisted on its own way as the only acceptable one, despite any consequences.

The campaign before the public was remarkable in that only one half the nation became involved. Scarcely any contest developed in the South because the Republicans did not even run tickets in the slave states, and it was assumed that Fillmore would run weakly and that Buchanan would carry the 108 southern electoral votes by default. The whole contest centered in the

North, and even here the struggle would be concentrated, for knowledgeable observers assigned 114 electoral votes to the Republicans—those of the New England states, New York, Ohio, Michigan, Wisconsin, and Iowa. The doubtful states, where campaign money and energy needed to be spent, were Pennsylvania with 27 electoral votes, Indiana with 13, Illinois with 11, Maryland with 8, New Jersey with 7, and California with 4, or 70 in all. Maryland would probably be the one state which Fillmore might capture, but since 149 electoral votes would create a President, Pennsylvania and any other state with a dozen votes might put either Buchanan or Frémont into the White House. Thus, in the South the campaign was dull and uninteresting. The important southern campaigners came north to work. In the North both parties concentrated on the doubtful states, and both worried about Fillmore's candidacy. The Republicans feared he might take away their possible margin of victory, as the Liberty party had defeated Clay in 1844. Buchanan, while he thought that the Old Whigs would give him their suffrage, recognized the chance that the Fillmore vote might throw the election into the House.

The Democrats took as the keynote of their canvass Buchanan's warning: "The Union is in danger and the people everywhere begin to know it. The Black Republicans must be, as they can be with justice, boldly assailed as disunionists, and this charge must be re-iterated again and again." The Democrats must publicize the statements of "the abolitionists, free soilers and infidels against the Union," to show that the Republicans had become traitors to it. "This race," said Buchanan, "ought to be run on the question of Union or disunion."

The Democratic press and campaign literature stressed this theme usually by quoting for their shock value the alleged statements of Republican leaders. Ohio's Joshua Giddings had announced: "I look forward to the day when there shall be a servile insurrection in the South; when the black man . . . shall assert his freedom, and wage a war of extermination against his master." New York's William H. Seward asserted that "There is a higher law than the Constitution," and hoped that he could soon "bring the parties of the country into an aggressive war upon slavery." Speaker of the House Nathaniel P. Banks, Know Nothing presidential candidate who had retired in favor of Frémont, announced that he was willing to let the Union slide. Judge Rufus Spalding said that if he had to choose between tolerating slavery and dissolving the Union, he was for dissolution of the Union. Editor James Watson Webb expected the Republicans would have "to drive back the slavocracy with fire and sword," while Horace Greeley editorialized in the *New York Tribune* that "the free and slave states ought to separate" and that the Union was not worth maintaining if the South remained in it. A Republican preacher in Poughkeepsie prayed from the Pulpit "that this accursed Union may be dissolved, even if blood have to be spilt." Groups of Republicans sent petitions to Congress requesting "the speedy, peaceful and equitable dissolution of the existing union." H. L. Raymond told an audience in Boston's Faneuil Hall, "Remembering that he was a slaveholder, I spit on George Washington." (Hisses and applause.) "You hissers are slaveholders in spirit!"

Scores of such quotations filled the Democratic newspapers day after day and ran the rounds of the exchanges. The strategy performed its function of making moderate northerners shun the radical new party as a hotbed of irresponsible revolutionaries; but it had the further effect of fixing this image of the Republican party in the mind of the South, for this was the main material which circulated there. While the Democrats published such quotations to condemn the disloyalty of Republicans, the Republicans republished the same excerpts in their own columns as inspiring slogans of their glorious crusade. Getting rid of slavery *was* more important than preserving the nation; destroying slaveholders *was* a more righteous work than cooperating with them. With talk of disunion battering the public from all sides, the idea began to take hold.

Southerners, both frightened and inflamed by northern threats and bravado, responded in kind. Southern unionists at last now began to believe that the election of Frémont involved the dissolution of the Union and that "it would be for mutual advantage of the parties to have a Southern Confederation." John Forsyth of Alabama wrote simply that the South should not submit to rule by the Republicans and that with Frémont's election, "the government of the United States will be at an end." Senators Slidell and Mason echoed the same sentiment, insisting that the South could not remain in a Union controlled by its avowed enemies, and the major Democratic newspapers predicted immediate disunion if Frémont should be elected. Buchanan worried primarily about this, stating that all issues of the election were trifling "when compared to the grand and appalling question of union or disunion." He too, believed that a Republican triumph would bring "immediate and inevitable" disunion.

Although other issues were trifling, they were not ignored by the Democrats. Northern Democrats broadcast the notion that Buchanan would achieve fair play in Kansas, and would bring it in as a free state. The widespread northern slogan was "Buchanan, Breckinridge and Free Kansas." This obviously would not serve in the South. There, the Democratic line pledged a quick and fair settlement which would end the turmoil of Bleeding Kansas and bring an end to the Republican party.

Frémont posed no problem for the Democrats as an individual. They ridiculed his inexperience and passed him off as "a man whose only merit, so far as history records it, is in the fact that he was born in South Carolina, crossed the Rocky Mountains, subsisted on frogs, lizards, snakes and grasshoppers, and captured a woolly horse." In comparison with ex-President Fillmore and the old public servant, Buchanan, Frémont's candidacy was laughed at by many Democrats as a farce and a burlesque. But others saw danger, particularly in the fusion of Know Nothings with Republicans and tried to break up this alliance by attacking Frémont as secretly a Catholic. They trumped up a long list of allegations, most of which were absurd. Some of them, however, were true and these managed to raise suspicions, even if they did not prove anything—that his father had been Catholic, that he had been married by a Catholic priest, and that he had sent a niece to a Catholic school. The Catholics, because they believed Frémont to be a candidate of the Know Nothings, solidly opposed him, but this, oddly, did not undermine the charges that he himself was a Catholic. The Democrats used the religious allegations with considerable effect in Know Nothing areas and probably diverted some votes by it.

Frémont's life exposed him to considerable mud-slinging by Democratic editors who manufactured unsavory details about his admittedly clouded birth. He was held up as a drunkard, a cruel and rapacious exploiter of Mexicans in California, a man guilty of using his official position for private gain in the West, and attacked with many other commonplace election-year canards.

The whole Democratic campaign assumed a negative cast. It was mainly a campaign of the printed word, appealing to conservatives and older people to rally to the defense of ancient heroes and traditional values. The Democrats as a party had become habit-bound; over the years, the managers and the local electioneering methods had become stale and routine, and the 1856 repetition did not stir much excitement among the faithful.

The Republican campaign had a wholly different aspect. It offered fervor, youth, novelty and a positive, aggressive approach. Rather than the "Don't rock the boat" outlook of the Buchaneers, the Republicans ordered "Full speed ahead." Their rallies assumed the form of wild jubilees or camp-meeting revivals. Their multiple campaign songs dwelt on the inspirational concept of the committed underdog, "We shall overcome." They made much fun of Buchanan as a superannuated bachelor, and of Fillmore as merely super-aunnuated, and celebrated their handsome young bearded candidate and his still lovely consort, Jessie. Lithographs, in color and black and white, poured from the northern presses showing Frémont planting the national flag on a mountain top, or leading his men through the western wilderness, or simply in portrait pose. The Republicans mobilized eastern clubs of Wide Awakes, and "Bear Clubs" in California to signalize Frémont's leadership in the Bear Flag revolt. They held rallies and torchlight marches often punctuated by floats, transparencies, and "White Negroes"—that is, whites painted black. In some eastern cities factories closed on Republican rally days. They organized fife and drum corps, glee clubs, picnics, and rallies, and pressed all their notables into service on the stump.

In the East, Banks, Chase, Greeley, Sumner, Hale, Emerson, Bryant, and Wendell Phillips gave political speeches, and in the West audiences listened to Carl Schurz, Schuyler Colfax, Abraham Lincoln, and others. Poets such as John Greenleaf Whittier and Thomas Buchanan Read ground out campaign rhymes. Women, instead of staying at home, moved out to join parades and meetings, and clergymen gave political speeches for Frémont from their pulpits. The Republicans had seized the offensive; they became, as one of their leaders phrased it, "the charging party," and forced their opponents into the role of the defensive or resisting party. The Republicans laid effective claim to youth, morality, religion, and commitment, portraying their enemies as old fogies, tired, politically bankrupt, brutal, and corrupt.

The American party, with Fillmore as its candidate, had little alternative except to play the part of spoiler. There were a few who deluded themselves that Fillmore might actually win, and others who more realistically thought that he might prevent an election and force the issue into the House of Representatives as in 1825. There, anything might happen. By midsummer it seemed clear that Fillmore could not beat Buchanan in the South, and that he might, by drawing off votes of the National Whigs, defeat Buchanan and thus elect Frémont. As that fear deepened, the influential Whig Rufus Choate announced that he thought the first duty of his party ought to be "to defeat and dissolve the new geographical party," and that he would vote for Buchanan. The northern Whigs then began a general movement to the Buchanan side. Fletcher Webster and James B. Clay, sons of the former Whig leaders, and a host of others, denounced the Republicans and publicly joined in rallies and stump appearances for Buchanan.

Some of the old guard rejected such action and called a political convention of Old Line Whigs on September 16 in Baltimore with delegates from twenty-five states. After many speeches, the delegates pledged eternal fealty to the Union, endorsed the candidacy of Fillmore, and called for "a spontaneous rising of Whigs throughout the country" to elect him. The press mostly ignored this ludicrous and melancholy effort to restore to life the already dead Whig party. A Republican reporter put his finger right on the basic truth, not yet generally comprehended, when he wrote: "These gentlemen are evidently incapable of the idea that the process now going on in the politics of the United States is a *Revolution*."

The national rather than sectional appeal of the Democrats and the adherence of so many Whigs to Buchanan's cause seemed to guarantee success in November. But in September, Maine, the Democratic stronghold in New England, went Republican by a towering majority. Buchanan had not counted on winning Maine, but he anticipated a close vote rather than a smashing defeat. The unanticipated result sent the Democrats into a frenzy of action, and they concentrated on Pennsylvania, which now seemed to hold the key to success or failure. But every October state now assumed crucial importance, and Buchanan hurriedly, though belatedly, dispatched a strong letter to California in favor of a Pacific railroad, thus hoping to neutralize the Republican promises there.

Speakers from both sides converged on Pennsylvania. Charles Dana wrote: "I suppose there are about two hundred orators, great and small, now stumping Pennsylvania for Frémont." The Democrats summoned their best speakers from afar to carry their message. Howell Cobb of Georgia made ten speeches in ten days from Philadelphia to Erie. The Buchanan managers ordered concentration of all the force of the party upon the Pennsylvania election upon which everything hinged. The efforts cost both sides money, which they tried to extract mainly from frightened New York businessmen. Each side made wild accusations about the financial operations of the other. The Republicans may have done better in Wall Street, selling Frémont's election as a profitable undertaking with tariffs and business subsidies as the payoff; whereas the Democrats had the advantage of friendly connections with financially influential men like W. W. Corcoran, Augustus Schell, S. L. M. Barlow, Royal Phelps, August Belmont, and others. They also were in power and could assess their officeholders, which they did.

At length, on October 14 Pennsylvania's state election day arrived and brought a Democratic victory. As an added bonus, Indiana also responded to the worn but still effective tools of Democratic campaigning. That state went Democratic and rendered Buchanan's election in the November balloting a practical certainty. Buchanan's state ticket in Pennsylvania had brought in a small majority over the Union ticket combining Whigs, Know Nothings, and Republicans. In the presidential poll in November, the Democrats would meet the Republicans alone and were sure to win.

The presidential election returns brought the result which the professionals had predicted. Buchanan, in a total poll of about 4 million, beat Frémont by one-half million votes and Fillmore by 1 million. The Electoral College gave Buchanan 174 votes, Frémont 114, and Fillmore 8. The popular vote was 1,832,955 for Buchanan, 1,399,932 for Frémont, and 871,731 for Fillmore. The statisticians quickly discovered many interesting and some ominous features of the returns. The change of only a few thousand votes from Buchanan to Fillmore in Kentucky, Tennessee, and Louisiana would have given those states to Fillmore. With this result, no candidate would have acquired a majority and the decision would have gone to the House of Representatives. Frémont had carried all but five of the northern states, eleven in all, and come within thirty-five electoral votes of winning. If the Republicans could have captured Pennsylvania and nine more votes, they could have won the Presidency, even though their candidate had not received a single vote in twelve of the states, all in the South. For the future, this raised the fear that the anti-slavery party of the North would soon be able politically to control the South. What then would become of the Union?

Although the Republicans gained 33.1 per cent of the popular vote to 45.3 per cent for the Democrats, the latter won in 1,067 counties of the nation, to 362 for the Republicans. This disparity, a four to three ratio of Democratic popular votes over the Republicans, contrasted with their three to one superiority in the county units, suggested a significant political change. The Republicans were gaining power in areas where population was dense, whereas the Democrats held their influence in the more numerous rural counties. The election of 1856 demonstrated the isothermal theory dramatically, for the Democrats scarcely carried a county north of the forty-first parallel, and the Republicans did not carry one south of the Mason-Dixon line. In sectional terms, the Republicans had shown their strength in New England, New York, and the Midwest. The Americans had captured their 21.6 per cent of the popular vote mainly in the South, but they held a balance of power in the Middle Atlantic region. The Democrats were strongest in the South, the Far West, Pennsylvania, and the Ohio River regions of the Midwest. They polled respectably in every county of the nation, and remained the only party able to command victories in all the major sections except New England.

The sudden rise of the Republicans, the coming to maturity of a party so geographically limited and so ideologically hostile to a large part of the nation, revived the efforts of southerners to organize a secession movement. Governor Henry A. Wise of Virginia had called a conference of southern governors at Raleigh just before the election to consider procedures of separation should Frémont win. Other governors failed to attend, but the campaign material of both major parties in 1856 raised to the level of a real probability the ultimate separation of the slavery and antislavery portions of the Union. From this time on, the idea of disunion seemed less treasonable and acquired a kind of respectability through simple repetition.

The election of 1856 marked the end of an era in United States history. The personalities, the parties, and the principles which had grown directly out of observation of the founding fathers—Washington, Hamilton, Jefferson, and their contemporaries—all had played out by the time Buchanan took office. The President-elect himself was one of the few survivors of a bygone generation—that of Jackson, John Quincy Adams, Webster, Calhoun, Clay, and Polk. The Whig party had disappeared, the Democratic party with its Jeffersonian heritage had lost its youthful Jacksonian frenzy and become complacent and corrupt. The only dynamic, idealistic, and crusading political aggregation in the country was the new Republican party, barely two years old, without experience or restraint, and with little regard for the kind of government and society which others valued. The principles of rule by compromise, of mutual respect between contesting political parties, and of regard for constitutional requirements seemed in 1856 to have run their course. The Republicans enunciated a new principle that they would attain their ends by any means. It was evident in the election of 1856 that the prophecies of disunion which had alarmed patriots since the Missouri Compromise of 1820, had come dangerously close to actuality. More than an election, the campaign of 1856 was a final warning.

Election of 1860

by *Elting Morison*

For sheer drama the election of 1860 is one of the less successful in our history. Few if any imaginative devices, such as log cabins and hard cider, attracted the public fancy; few if any catch words caught on, like "Tippecanoe and Tyler too," or "He kept us out of war"; no disastrous ineptitudes, such as "rum, Romanism and rebellion"; and no striking explosions of feeling, as when the Bull Moose brought down the house with the Battle Hymn of the Republic, or when the galleries who wanted Willkie finally got him.

The conventions—there were four of them—produced, as conventions usually do, some moments of excitement, but quite often they bogged down, more often than conventions normally do, into argument over procedure and technical questions. The same was true of the subsequent campaign. One of the candidates really said and did nothing. Two others said very little and said it flatly and dully. The fourth conducted a campaign unusual for the times, moving feverishly about the whole country. He spoke often, he had something important to say, and he spoke with his familiar intensity. But since he had stated his case before, and since none of the other candidates paid any attention, there was about as much tension in the performance as in an exhibition of shadow boxing. Finally, in the minds of many citizens of the country, the results of the November election were foreordained from the 18th of May, when the Republican convention selected its candidate and adjourned.

There is not much here to command attention. The meaning of the election of 1860 lies outside the usual mechanics of a political canvass—the conventions, the campaigns, the actual balloting. The country was in turmoil and the election was like the eye of a hurricane, a moment of dreadful calm intensified by the memory of the wild events that had preceded it and by the foreboding sense of the greater storm to come.

Measured by many of the ordinary indicators and most of the usual statistics, it seemed, and still seems, extraordinary that in the year 1860 the country found itself in such disorder. Vitality, health, and growth could be demonstrated in almost every area of national life.

The total population according to the 1860 census was 31,443,790. This represented an increase of 35.6 per cent during the previous decade and the greatest increase in any single decade of the previous half century. Almost every other area of the nation's life revealed an equally startling advance. The number of banks, the amount of capital owned by banks, the extent of money deposited in banks—all about doubled in the years between 1850 and 1860. The value of real estate and personal property had risen 26.40 per cent in the same period. And in the same decade, railroad mileage in the United States had expanded almost four times—from 8,500 miles to 30,500 miles. Similar impressive gains were registered in what the census called the products of industry, which in 1860 reached a value of almost $2 billion. Likewise, the number of steam engines, the new prime mover, increased by 68 per cent. In fact, wherever one looked—at iron founding, soap and candles, illuminating gas, musical instruments, boots and shoes—the output had increased, in some cases doubling and tripling. Judging by these signs the United States was riding high, even higher than a half century before, on a flood tide of successful experiment. Indeed it appeared that the country might well have gone beyond the experimental stage to a period of rapid, sustained and fairly orderly growth. In spite of some financial disturbances, there was recurring evidence that during the 1850's Americans began to coordinate the various parts of the huge plant they had thus far been building in a haphazard fashion.

Most dramatically of course the railroads had tied various sections of the country and the varied life within each. But there were other less visible and dramatic indications that the men building the nation were learning the skills required by a complex integration of activity. The system of credit, for instance, was greatly strengthened and expanded by the founding of the New York Clearing House in 1853. Also, the various components of the iron industry—the coking plants, blast furnaces, forges, and foundries—that in the earlier days of the Republic had been scattered throughout the countryside in the fifties began to be concentrated on sites which were close to the sources of material, supplies of power, and means of distribution.

The energy—human and mechanical—in the whole system was immense; the natural resources available both in variety and extent were equally immense; and the space for expansion seemed boundless.

Considering these favorable conditions and opportunities, it would seem that the energy, skill, and imagination of the nation's citizens should have been fully engaged. Also, it would seem that this expanding system would produce, besides opportunity, certain problems for those who sought in 1860 to manage the explosive energy in the society. Indeed it did. Major issues were before the people of the country: the shape of the banking structure, the extension and financing of internal improvements (especially the indispensable railroads), the organization of the new territories to the west, the determination of the tariff schedules, the training and education of the citizens in a free society, and so forth. These problems, which have to do with the nourishment of a growing society, laid heavy claims upon the attention of the citizens, the statesmen, and candidates for public office, especially the Presidency. The further and fuller development of this marvelous social organism should have been enough of a challenge to engage the combined efforts of all those who had anything to do with it. The fact is that it was not. In 1860 the national mind was preoccupied, and the political process was crippled by a single issue; states' rights, the "peculiar institution," secession, slavery, however it was phrased. The question was whether and under what conditions the system of intellectual, social, economic, and physical energies that had been developing for over four score years could be sustained; whether the Union as it had evolved could be preserved.

The candidates in the election of 1860 were truly representative of the state of the nation that year. That there were four of them indicates that the political processes which had slowly become a two party system had broken down. Each of the four expressed a distinct opinion on the central issue. John Bell sought no solution at all; Stephen A. Douglas worked for an ingenious compromise; John Breckenridge felt that the difference was irreconcilable; and Abraham Lincoln argued that the Union must be preserved at all costs. In spite of their differences on the issue of slavery, the four candidates did represent the state of the country on almost every other matter. It is interesting, for instance, that all four came from the same part of the country, a part where almost all the energy of our national life was at work.

A compass stretched to give a radius of 150 miles and swung around Vincennes, Indiana, as the central point would encompass the homes of all of them. This area was a kind of microcosm of most of the variety of economic and social life in America—industry, farming, trading, free men, slaves, big time operators, and middle men. It was also an area populated by people who were familiar with and influenced by the habits of mind and behavior of the Eastern Seaboard, still moved by frontier aspirations and, in 1860, stirred by the energy pouring into the West from the older regions. It was an area which had the sense of a lively future. Tennessee, John Bell's home state, and Kentucky, where John Breckenridge was born, were two of the fastest growing states in the South. Illinois, the birthplace of both Stephen A. Douglas and Abraham Lincoln, was in many ways the fastest growing state in the North. The four candidates faithfully reflected these characteristics.

It is often the custom to write off John Bell and John Breckenridge as marginal candidates, but even though neither was as well-known or as significant a political figure as Stephen A. Douglas was at the time, nor as famous and powerful an historical symbol as Abraham Lincoln later became, both were men of ability and experience.

The four together offered an impressive field from which to choose. Breckenridge, thirty-nine years old in 1860, was the son and the grandson of unusual men who had served Kentucky and the United States as lawyers and public servants. He himself became a lawyer, practiced for a time in Iowa, and then returned to his native state to become a successful lawyer in Frankfort. During the Mexican War he joined the Army and afterwards entered political life by running as a Democrat for Congress from Ashland, Henry Clay's old district. He served several terms in Washington and quickly established himself as a leader both in Kentucky and in Congress. In 1856 he was nominated for and elected Vice-President in the Administration of James Buchanan. Along with the way Breckenridge acquired a reputation as a man with an open mind and liberal spirit, a man of "intellectual power and stalwart character." On the disputed issue of how to organize the territories he had in the early fifties supported the idea of popular sovereignty, a rare opinion for a man who lived as far south as he did.

John Bell, the candidate of the Constitutional Union party, also entered politics as a Democrat, but he grew restless over Jackson's attack on the Bank during his early years in the Congress and joined the Whigs in 1834. He soon took over the leadership of the party in his home state, where the party then became the central political influence in Tennessee. Elected to the Senate in 1847, he distinguished himself as a powerful agent of the Whigs' national program. He supported the Compromise of 1850, and in 1858 he disregarded the instructions of his state legislature and voted against the entry of Kansas as — for all intents and purposes — a slave state. Early in his career he had supported John Quincy Adams in his defense of the right of petition against those who sought to prevent the Congress from considering any slavery petitions. Sixty-three years old in 1860, he was a man of large spirit, independent judgment, and action.

Stephen A. Douglas, far better known than the other two, had been an active figure in American political life for almost twenty years before the election of 1860, and more recently had become the leading spokesman of the Democratic party. He had sought to increase the industrial expansion of the country and had been dominant in the attempt to create and organize new territories, and tireless in his search for healing accommodations among the sections. Forty-seven-years old in 1860, he was probably the leading figure in American politics.

It now seems incredible that of the four men Abraham Lincoln was the least known and least experienced. He had served in a small and local Indian war, in the Illinois legislature, and then had served an undistinguished term in the House of Representatives. He subsequently dropped out of politics, returning only in the mid-fifties to deliver a series of speeches in various parts of the country. In these speeches he increasingly sharpened the differences between the North and South, and left a clear impression that no accommodation was possible, that houses divided do not stand, and that a nation could not exist half slave and half free. On this issue he was the clearest of the four candidates and this tended to distinguish him from the others; yet all in all the four

men shared a great many attitudes and feelings. At a time when the country
had become divided and local attachments seemed paramount, all four maintained the national view. They were inheritors of the vision of Henry Clay
rather than of the restricting allegiances of Calhoun or Sumner. Their collective concern had always been to support those legislative acts and public policies that would develop and strengthen the whole country. And in the decade
of the fifties, when dissension spread, they reiterated their faith in the Union.
In 1859, for instance, John Breckenridge delivered before the Senate such an
eloquent and reasoned plea for the preservation of the Union that some
senators were moved to tears. And during the campaign he told a Kentucky
audience that he was "an American citizen, a Kentuckian, who never did an
act nor cherished a thought that was not full of devotion to the Constitution
and the Union." Nothing in his career could be used to undermine the force
and essential truth of those words.

So also with the slave owner John Bell, who sought in the closing years
of the fifties to bring the new Republicans and the old southern Whigs together. Opposing secession "both as a Constitutional right and as a remedy for
existing evils," he ran on a platform in support of "the Constitution of the
country and the Union of the States." When the Civil War began, he remained in the South, his spirit broken, pacing the floor lamenting the conflict
and reasserting his faith in the United States. As for Douglas and Lincoln,
they had in a score of speeches and in a hundred different ways affirmed and
reaffirmed their devotion to the Union.

It is strange that the country so torn by confusion and tension nominated
four such sound men, who, if the essential needs of the country were reckoned in terms of railroads, tariffs, stable currency, commerce, industrial and
agricultural development, would have been in agreement, men who had repeatedly proved their faith in the Union. It seems probable that their selection
represented the conscious and reasonable views and expectations of most of
their countrymen, east and west, north and south—an expression of what
Americans still believed was appropriate and still hoped was possible in a rational world.

But by 1860 problems had reached a stage defying rational responses. The
country was shaken to its foundations. As with the neurotic, the flow of normal rational responses was broken by atavistic urges and long repressed un-
conscious drives. Tariffs, railroads, crops, counting houses, credit systems—all
the stuff of reality—were shoved aside as irrelevant.

This strange condition had been produced by the only issue that counted in
1860—slavery—and by all the economic, political, and social forces that
clustered around it. Because of its predominence as an issue in 1860, and because nothing that happened in that year is intelligible without some understanding of its role in the development of the nation, it would be helpful here
to trace the evolution of the "pecular institution."

The Declaration of Independence asserts that all men are created equal
and are endowed with the inalienable rights of life, liberty, and the pursuit of
happiness. These assumptions were the philosophies or moral base of the

Revolution. They were put forward as articles of faith shared by all members of a society that was said to be "one people." But the document containing these ideas was not a direct expression of this people, nor of any single agency acting for this people. It was instead specifically a "Unanimous Declaration of the Thirteen United States of America, in Congress." There was, in other words, an unstated assumption that each state was the primary agent for its own citizens and that the whole population became one body only when the individual states acted in voluntary concert.

This primacy of the individual state was a product of history. From the beginning, settlement had been divided among the several colonies. Typically, a citizen's political awareness developed within the framework of his colony. The resentment toward the mother country which grew between 1764 and 1776 had been given form and expression by the several colonies. When these colonies became states they were still viewed as the familiar and reliable agencies for political action. They were large enough to give weight to local interests and small enough to be responsive to the social and economic needs of the communities they represented. They were also of a size to be comprehended by the affections of the citizens.

The feeling for the individual state in 1776 was therefore greater than the feeling for some less definable sum of all the states. This feeling was intensified by the fact that the Revolution which followed the Declaration of Independence was conducted by the several states acting as independent but cooperating agencies.

Given such a background, it follows that the first attempt to form a government that would secure for Americans the rights enumerated in the Declaration of Independence would start from the assumption of the essential integrity of the individual state. The fact that the Revolution had been fought to free each state from the restraining authority of a central government did not diminish the force of this assumption. As a result, the Articles of Confederation began with the following words: "Each state retains its sovereignty, freedom and independence and every power, jurisdiction and right which is not by this confederation expressly delegated to the United States in Congress assembled."

Five years' experience was enough to demonstrate that from such sovereign elements no union could be made that was strong enough to provide for the national defense, promote the general welfare, and secure the blessing of liberty for all citizens. Each state tended to put its own local and immediate needs before the claims of national interest. The sobering experience of these years yielded information and understanding that led to a significant conclusion: what was required was a more perfect union in which citizens of all the states would become one people organizing and administering their affairs through a central government that would in many matters be superior to the governments of the several states.

The Constitution was, in great part, simply a definition of these matters. By its terms, responsibilities and powers were defined and allocated to the Federal Government on the one hand and to the state governments on the other. In many instances, where spheres of interest were separable, the Constitution was both clear and precise; in others, where interest intertwined, it prescribed the means for mutual accommodation; in still others, where clear definition was impossible, it had to resort to more general phrases that were open to various interpretations.

The Constitution is an amazing work of reason, art, and judgment. From independent elements it shaped a federal system that worked. But, as the 10th Amendment suggests, it had to leave unresolved some problems of jurisdiction. Residual powers not assigned to the Federal Government and not prohibited to the states were reserved, by the terms of this amendment, for the states or for the people. Amid such negatives and alternatives there was room for difference of opinion.

The great question was: at what points did the power of the Federal Government leave off and at what points did the power of the states begin? In the first seventy years of our history this was a subject of continuing speculation and debate. As time passed two opposing views were developed and fully elaborated. On the one hand it was argued that the Federal Government was the product of a compact among the several sovereign states that had declared their independence, fought the Revolution, maintained the Confederation, and ratified the Constitution. As an agency which existed before the Union, any single state had the right of final review of any act of the Federal Government and the right to interpose its will and to resist a federal act when it collided with the legitimate interest of the state. On the other hand it was argued that the Federal Government was the product of the will to union of all the people. From this it followed that any federal act taken in accordance with the procedures laid down in the Constitution was taken in the interests of the citizens as one people, and since the interests of the whole people were superior to the interests of any particular state, such an act was not subject to legitimate review or resistance by any state or group of states.

The debate produced by the collision of these two views gave American political life a unique intellectual substance and quality. In part this was because the Constitution provided a framework for the discussion; it put intellectual bounds upon the tension rising between the opposing parties. In part it was because the debate took place, on the whole, in the formal surroundings of legislative bodies, particularly in the United States Senate at a time when it contained some of the ablest men in the society. In part it was simply that it was a great subject. In the course of the half century of argument the basic concepts of political science which are often obscure—the nature of sovereignty, the purpose of government—were thoroughly exposed. During the debates public officials expressed their views in disquisitions on the state as a necessary agent for the protection of a minority, on the Union as an almost mystical means for the expression of the will of the majority, on the nation as an unfinished experiment in self-government. The disquisitions were not prompted by a scholarly or philosophical concern for political theory; practical considerations demanded their promulgation. As the nation grew it acquired a set of national interests. To serve these interests the power of the

Federal Government was gradually increased by legislative intent, judicial decision, and executive act. Such perceptible extension of the federal authority naturally disturbed those who believed in the sovereignty of the states or who advocated what came to be called "states rights." And the disturbance was the greater because the action of the Federal Government, taken for the assumed good of the whole, at times created inequities among some of the parts. The trouble was that the population did not cohere into one people. Diverse influences—accidents of terrain, climate, technology and history —produced differentiation in the society. In one sense this was all to the good; by virtue of the differences the society became increasingly resourceful and interesting. But as time passed the forces producing variety became concentrated, making one section of the nation different from another. By the middle of the nineteenth century the United States was less a union of one people than a union of three different regions. In the South men raised cotton, in the North they made and sold goods, in the West they farmed and traded and moved even farther west.

The problem of creating national policies that served equally the needs of three different sections was difficult. Men like Henry Clay had majestic schemes for putting the parts together into an American system, but they fell short of achieving this objective because hard money did not mean the same thing in all sections, and because internal improvements did not do the same thing in all parts of the country. The argument for states' rights took account of this sectional differentiation and of the fact that sections were made up of states with similar interests. It was not used in support of a theoretical concept of how the Union was made, but rather as a practical means of expressing political opposition, as a way of giving regional matters weight against the adverse influences of the national government.

At different times, each region made use of the states' rights argument. In 1798 Kentucky and Virginia asserted the right to review and resist federal laws they could not sanction, laws which in the particular case of the Alien and Sedition Acts they had good reason to oppose. In 1815 representatives of the New England States asserted in almost identical language a similar right. The object here was to resist the federal embargo cutting off trade on the Eastern Seaboard. In 1830 western senators started a great debate on the powers of state within the Union by charging that the eastern region was attempting "to check the settlement and prosperity of the West by seeking a federal restriction on the sale of public lands." And one year later South Carolina brought the discussion to the verge of armed conflict by claiming the right to interpose her will, to resist a federal tariff that was damaging the economy of the whole South.

The succession of such episodes afforded the opportunity to develop and refine both sides of the argument. Also their recurrence produced among the debaters an increasing tension, a growing sense of foreboding about the future of the Union. But in the first half century of American history the internal pressures arising from the differences in sectional concerns were always accommodated. Sometimes the cause of the disturbance passed with time, as in

1798 and 1812. Sometimes the occasion yielded to the threat of force, as in 1832 when President Jackson said he would take up arms against South Carolina. Sometimes the issue was resolved by practical adjustment, as in 1833 when Henry Clay arranged an acceptable compromise in tariff schedules.

In such experiences the men in power in this country searched out the location of the points where federal authority might leave off and the authority of the states, acting as agents for the sectional interest, might begin. In this exercise they acquired not only the dialectical skill that gave distinction to the argument, but also the understanding, patience, and sense of necessary accommodation that made continuing resolution of the problem possible. It seems probable, especially since all concerned shared a profound commitment to the idea of the Union, that the conflict between the Federal Government and the states would have been worked out satisfactorily had it not been for the existence of some special circumstances.

One of these circumstances was slavery. What in the beginning had been only one of several ways to obtain small increments of labor or service in any part of the country became in time an institution peculiar to a single section. This came about not so much by forethought or conscious intention as by accidents of climate, market demand, and mechanical invention. The result was that the South began to do its work in a different way from the rest of the nation—and with a difference for which it was difficult to find accommodation. When men fall out over tariffs on the sale of public lands or cheap money there is, ordinarily, a chance for sensible trading. In the matter of rates and schedules, opposing elements can look for the bargain that will leave both sides with some degree of satisfaction. But in the matter of slavery there was far less room for maneuver. The Constitution might count a full slave as three-fifths of a citizen to give more weight to delegations of Congressmen from particular states, but it was harder to find the fraction of liberty in the condition of servitude that would make a man in slavery also free and equal to other men. In fact it was impossible. If the state of bondage became subject to compromising modification the peculiar institution would cease to exist.

And if slavery ceased to be, the South would lose its shape. On the peculiar institution had been constructed a way of living that was also, in the national context, peculiar. While men in the North were saying that things were in the saddle, men of the South were trying to give serious place to many interests that others—more puritanical or grasping—looked upon as irrelevant or unseemly diversions. In the South, for example, men were prepared to accept without undue constraint the evidence of the senses, to make provision for the excitement of feeling, to create surroundings that had actual physical charm. Furthermore in a society that sought to smooth off the signs of human difference, they made a great point of the distinctions caused by birth, breeding, and sex. They thought and spoke of themselves as "ardent," "magnanimous," "brave," and "giving." They set more store by the instinctive response than by the findings of reasoned analysis. Seeking to take the organization of life beyond prudential calculations of profit and loss, they developed a set of attitudes—a style—to govern the conduct of their affairs. To maintain this style they invested most of their energy and the greatest part of their feeling. Any change in the shape of this society would therefore change not only how men did the day's work but also what they thought of themselves. On such a matter it was also difficult to discover any way to strike a compromise.

And in the particular event it was doubly difficult. This conception of a style of life that went beyond the schemes of the market place has had in retrospect, a persistent attraction for the succeeding generations that have grown up in an industrial democracy. But, even at the time, it had its considerable defects. Among them was the fact that in almost any given fiscal year the South was hard up, without the means to support the way of life it had set for itself. What in the conception had a kind of casually ordered grace became, quite often in the reality, a rather tacky charm. Much of the energy of the section therefore went into the effort to demonstrate the value of the substance by keeping up the appearance. To endure the painful changes in reality the South sought to project a sustaining image of what it conceived itself to be, and in such straits men do not often compromise on the terms of the illusion.

Finally, slavery, unlike a tariff schedule or a rate of exchange, forced men to take positions on a question of good or evil. In the beginning this aspect of the matter was put somewhat to one side, as something to be accepted or gotten around until time and new conditions wore it away. But time and the new conditions served only to fix slavery in the society as a primary fact. Concerning this fact two distinct views gradually developed. Those without slaves concluded on the whole that slavery was an evil, while those with slaves came, on the whole, to the stated conviction that slavery was not only a necessity, it was, in the conditions, "a good, a positive good." Here again, on such a matter, it was difficult, indeed impossible, to find a point where one could strike a compromise.

Thus by a series of historical misfortunes a set of conditions were created that lay outside the workings of the political process as it had developed in this country. The process was designed to take into account minority opinion in general dispersion throughout the country; but here was a minority that had become the impacted majority of one part of the country. The process was also designed to accommodate variety produced by differences in degree within a common scheme; but here variety was produced by a totally different kind of scheme. The process was further designed to give a practical context for the day's work, to supply, by trade and bargain, workable conclusions on the extent of the gold reserve, the height of a wool duty, the size of the pork barrel; but here a public decision was required on the moral content of American life. Such decisions, in the ordinary course, were taken, unexamined, as the given assumptions in the hearts of the founders, or they were left, again by design, to the private conscience.

In such conditions the success with which the different sections dealt with this problem within the political process in the first half of the nineteenth century was truly remarkable. One favoring circumstance was that throughout this period the country was growing, not just increasing in population but

acquiring and settling new land. Because of this the slave power which was
not subject to modification by changes in its nature could at least be brought
within territorial accommodation and limit.

Much of the debate in these years dealt with the problem of the extension
of slavery into the new western lands in ways that would satisfy both sides.
There were two reasons the South wished to expand. The first was economic.
The section lived by cotton and cotton exhausted the ground it grew in. In the
Southwest there was fresh soil for the indispensable crop. The second reason
was political. To protect its interests the South needed to maintain its
influence in the Congress. By extending slavery in the territories the region
could insure the creation in time of new slave states that would give additional
weight to its votes in the House and Senate.

The problem presented to the country therefore was to devise means that
would give the agrarian South some economic security within the developing
mercantile and industrial society and that would also preserve an equilibrium
as between the slave power and the free states in the determination of national
policies.

For fifty years these ends were accomplished by a series of ingenious
compromises. From 1802 to 1819 the political balance was maintained by
admitting alternately a slave and then a free state to the Union. In 1819 the
opposing elements were each represented by eleven states. In that year Missouri applied for admission as a slave state formed from part of the land acquired in the Louisiana Purchase. Its application put in jeopardy the established equilibrium in the Union and raised the further question of the place of
slavery in the remaining territory of the Louisiana Purchase. After much debate in the Congress it was decided to admit Missouri as a slave state and
balance it by admitting the free state of Maine at the same time. It was also
decided to settle the future organization of the remaining territory by permitting slavery below the line 36°30' while prohibiting its spread above this line.

For a quarter of a century this solution provided a measure of peace and
satisfaction. But after the Mexican War the country confronted once again the
necessity to organize a vast tract of new land. Once again there was much
debate before a satisfactory compromise was reached. The crucial territorial
provisions in the final settlement were as follows: California was admitted as
a free state while the territories of New Mexico and Utah were organized
without any restriction on slavery. This last condition meant that any states
formed from the new land would be "received into the Union with or without
slavery as their constitutions may prescribe at the time of admission." This
opportunity for residents in the territories to decide for themselves what they
wanted was called popular or squatter sovereignty.

By this Compromise of 1850 the question of slavery within our continental limits seemed to many Americans to be settled for all time. East of the
Mississippi, history had already fixed the conditions in the several states;
west of the Mississippi the line 36°30' held for the land drained by the Missouri and the Platte while in the old colonial empire of Spain—from Texas to

the Pacific—the matter was left to the desire of the inhabitants. It is possible that, if all other things had remained equal, the arrangements that held the Union together in 1850 would have served to continue it forever.

This was possible but by no means certain. The expansion which permitted successive accommodations of the slave power also insured its continuation as a disturbing element in the society. Though room for the difference between the North and South could be given by ingenious compromise, no compromise could reduce the fact of difference. Indeed time served only to accentuate the things that came between the sections. In the North trade and growing industry were producing a varied, turbulent society, while the South was becoming more firmly fixed in the rigidity of a single-crop system. Furthermore the balance between North and South that had been continued by the wit of men in Congress was tipped slowly away from the slave power by natural causes. Throughout the first half century the South was losing ground, in terms of population, money, and political power, to the free regions of the country. So the Cotton Kingdom developed the mood of an oppressed minority. There was also for both sides the terrible fact of slavery. As time went on it became increasingly difficult for the South, whether by historical analogy, the plea of necessity, or nicely conceived logical argument, to justify itself before the North. And at the same time it became increasingly difficult for the North to express with patience or tolerent understanding its views of the South. Indeed by 1850 it seemed difficult, in spite of ever more positive assertions on both sides, to believe that either one was in real communication with the other. In such circumstances the points of political and economic differences became armed with the passion produced by fear, self-righteousness, guilt, uncertainty, and continuing frustration. Beneath the surfaces of workable compromise remained a turmoil of emotion that could not find adequate discharge.

That such was the case became apparent only four years after the great Compromise of 1850, when Stephen A. Douglas presented to the Congress what is now called the Kansas-Nebraska Act. The essential terms of his bill were provisions for organizing the remaining land acquired in the Louisiana Purchase. Douglas proposed that in the two new territories the question of slavery was to be left to a vote of the inhabitants. In other words, he wished to replace the line of the Missouri Compromise, which five years before he had called "a sacred thing," by substituting the idea of squatter sovereignty. Using all his matchless powers as a politician he obtained the passage of the bill and in so doing supplied the place where the turmoil of natural emotions could be discharged. Men from the North and the South poured into the area in an effort to obtain a majority for their positions. What they produced was Bleeding Kansas and a conflict that reopened the whole question of slavery and the future of the Union.

Why Douglas, a most adroit politician, a man devoted to the idea of the Union, was moved to introduce this bill has remained one of the most persistent unanswered questions in our history. It has been said that he was very anxious to build a railroad to the West which would have a terminus in Chicago, where Douglas had large real estate holdings. To this end it would be necessary to organize the Nebraska territory, and to get approval for this organization it was necessary to obtain southern votes. It was also said that the bill was an effort on the part of the Illinois senator, "a simply, selfish, ambitious" effort to attract enough southern votes to win him the Presidency in 1856. He might also have done it simply to show he could do it. He was a full-blooded, impulsive, exciting man in a Senate from which the great men — Clay, Calhoun and Webster — had just departed. He was also working within the feeble time-serving Administration of Franklin Pierce and within a party of conflicting councils and divided spirit. Amid such frustrating circumstances, this restless, passionate man may have felt the need to demonstrate that he could do something rather extraordinary.

Or he may have been moved by the hope that he could supply a more sensible base for his party that was in such disarray. The pattern of agreement between the North and the South, while apparently serving the purpose of preserving a working relationship, certainly contained some arbitrary elements — most notably the boundary of 36°30′. If the Missouri Compromise were repealed, the South, as Douglas said, could "no longer crouch behind a line which Freedom could not cross." By his proposal of popular sovereignty he may well have hoped that he was offering a more natural means, a means much more appropriate within the normal workings of the traditional democratic process, for solving the problem so vexing to the country.

Whatever his purpose or mixture of purposes, the results of his actions were dreadful. There was, in the year following, the long, continued bleeding in Kansas marked by persistent disorder, political chicanery, double dealing, and the lurid excursions of John Brown and his followers, who, "in support of their principles had been guilty of many dastardly crimes, including robbery and murder." The impact of these dangerous and frightening episodes reverberated throughout the country, starting up rival passions in both North and South. Things went from bad to worse as it became increasingly obvious that the enfeebled Buchanan Administration could supply no useful solution to the difficulties. And, as the Democratic party, under the burden of the President's feckless actions, gradually disintegrated, the last great unifying and stabilizing agency was withdrawn from the political life of the country. Then, shortly after, the Dred Scott decision turned years of effort and experience upside down by setting the slavery question in the territories beyond the reach of all the political and legislative adjustments that had so far served.

What followed was hardly unexpected. When the standard patterns of accommodation were broken up, when the familiar political institution — in this case the Democratic party — had splintered, when oversimplifying passions had made their way to the surface, the extreme solutions were increasingly put forward.

The nature of these extremes as set out in the years from 1856 to 1860 was surprisingly simple considering all the social, economic, and political rhetoric that had gone into the making of the issue in the previous thirty years. It came down in the end to a disagreement over the power of Congress to regulate slavery in the territories. In the South it was contended that Congress had no right of regulation beyond the constitutional obligation to protect the life, liberty, and property (that is slaves) of citizens living in the territories. In the North it was contended that Congress had the power "to prohibit the spread of slavery into the territories."

The implications of these rather simple extremes were however considerable. It could be argued in the South that, by guaranteeing the existence of slavery in the western territories, one guaranteed also the future admission of slave states which in turn would guarantee the continuation of slavery and the continuation of southern economic and political power within the country. It could be argued in the North that, while Congress could not interfere with slavery in states where it already existed, it was certain that by preventing its extension into new territories the institution would, in a famous phrase, be put in the course of ultimate extinction. And, with the setting of that course, would follow also the inevitable reduction of the economic and political power of the South within the Union.

Furthermore, both in the South and in the North in the years from 1856 to 1860 it was increasingly affirmed that these points were not negotiable. William L. Yancey during this period became the great and gifted articulator of the southern view. Contained in manner, calm in tone, he said he would not argue with men who proposed to take all the territories for themselves while "they take from the South the privilege of forming more slave states out of the vast and magnificent domain in our common country. Now friends," he went on, "we do not stand upon compromise. We stand on something far higher than compromise, something more sacred than compromise. We stand upon the Constitutional compact made by our fathers with your fathers. [The South] must have and she will have a recognized equality in the Union, or she will take it out of it."

And on the other side it was Lincoln who in these years most effectively organized and defined the argument of the North. Roused from a long continued lethargy by the passing of the Kansas-Nebraska Act, he laid out with much historical documentation and skillful logic not only the right of Congress to prohibit slavery in the territory, but the operational necessity to put it in the course of ultimate extinction because he believed "this government cannot exist half slave and half free."

So things had reached this pass—that the two sides were divided by differences, differences it was agreed not to be modified by compromise or negotiation, which could be resolved only by the acceptance by one side of the other's total view, or by withdrawal of one side or the other. Thus stated, things seemed bad enough, a poor environment in which to try to settle the intractable differences by suasion or argument on the merits. But a further condition further complicated the situation. It was not just that each side was separated by difference; it was that in the differences were involved matters of right and wrong, indeed of good and evil. As Lincoln said "Now, I confess myself as belonging to the class in the country who contemplates slavery as a moral, social, and political evil, having due regard for its actual existence among us and the difficulties of getting rid of it in any satisfactory way, and to all the constitutional obligations which have been thrown about it; but nevertheless, [I] desire a policy that looks to the prevention of it as a wrong, and looks hopefully to the time when as a wrong it may come to an end."

To all the ordinary problems that arise when parties fall out were therefore added in this case the inflaming points of damaged self-respect, implied moral superiority, self-doubt, guilt, and pride. It was quite a burden to let loose upon the overburdened country in the year 1860. That the differences as put by the extremes engaged the whole country, or even most of the citizens, appears improbable. Extremes rarely do attract majorities. It seems quite clear that, as the year turned, the preponderant number, north, south, east and west, still hoped and desperately searched for some compromise, some saving accommodation and were still devoted to the idea of the Union. There was, of course, a compromise position, most often and most effectively stated by Stephen A. Douglas. On the matter of the Federal Government's power, whether through the Congress or the Supreme Court, to regulate slavery in the territories, he maintained that his own solution of popular sovereignty — the determination of the condition of slavery by the citizens living within the territories — was the only possible solution. Whatever the Congress or the Court decided, the opportunity to bring slaves into a territory became "barren and worthless" unless sustained, protected, and enforced "by appropriate police regulations and local legislation." It was a practical argument unsupported by the appeals to history or political theory that filled out and buttressed the southern position as explained by Yancey, or the northern position as put forth by Lincoln. Slavery wouldn't work if the local people didn't want it to. Douglas also sought to draw the fire from the opposing views by saying that he didn't care whether, in the territories, slavery was voted up or down. Again the practical argument — if the people wanted it and by due process expressed and obtained their desire — he would not undertake to judge whether it was an evil or a positive good they were obtaining.

But in 1860 those who commanded the public attention appeared uninterested in practical solutions or further search for the middle ground. They seemed instead, or many of them did, captivated by the opportunity to speak out in the most violent terms about the most extreme alternatives. There was much talk about the South protecting herself "out of the Union if not in it"; about "the harlot slavery," about "irrepressible conflicts," about "black hearted scoundrels" and "nigger-stealing thiefs" and men "axle deep amid the enslaved and mangled and bleeding bodies of human beings."

There was, in other words, much wild, violent, frenzied talk and some violent personal or local action, but if the disordered mood prevented men from looking for reasonable compromise, it also did not lead, as yet, to decisive general action — or indeed to mob action of any sort. The lurid statements hurled about may well have given some temporary relief to raw feelings, but they also merely described deeds — secession, rebellion, civil war — that neither the speakers nor those who heard them were yet prepared to undertake. So the country lay as paralyzed as a ship in irons.

The whole occasion can be summed up or symbolized by the events that took place in the House of Representatives at the beginning of the first session of the Thirty-Sixth Congress in December 1859. The first order of business was the selection of the chief presiding officer, the Speaker. After one inconclusive ballot the members of the House fell into shrill discussion of a book — *The Impending Crisis* — that had been written by a man named Hinton Helper two years before. The essential point of the book was that the South was in bad shape. The text was indeed heavy with surprising statistics in support of the proposition — as, for instance, that the northern hay crop in a recent year had been worth more than all the cotton, tobacco, rice, hay and hemp grown in all the southern states. The question presumably at issue was whether or not a man who had read or recommended this book was fit to be Speaker of the House.

From this point of departure the talk ran on to a consideration of what the South was like and what the North was like and what they both might become. There were dreadful threats ("as the stroke follows the lightning's flash" we "will act so help us God"); there were extraordinary episodes (one member pulled a revolver on another in debate); there were sporadic hand-to-hand encounters all over the floor of the House. In time the assembled representatives degenerated into "a great unruly mob." Every now and then a ballot would be cast in a vain attempt to elect a Speaker and then members would return to their strange deliberations. All this went on for two months before the eyes of the dismayed and tentative clerk who was supposed to act temporarily as the presiding officer. At last a majority was mustered in support of one candidate — William Pennington, a new member, a sober, gracious man who had been elected by something called the People's party. He stood for little, represented few, was without legislative experience, offended in no way those committed either to the North or South, and turned out to be an inadequate presiding officer.

It was in such conditions that the parties met in the spring of 1860 to nominate their candidates for President. The Democratic party met first in Charleston on April 23. The leading candidates were James Guthrie of Kentucky, R. M. T. Hunter of Virginia, Andrew Johnson of Tennessee, and Stephen A. Douglas of Illinois. Douglas, as the leading member of the party for a decade, as the candidate who had stepped aside four years before at Cincinnati to permit the nomination of James Buchanan, was beyond all doubt the favored candidate among the aspirants. But he came to the convention severely weakened within the party by the great struggle he had engaged in with Buchanan over the admission of Kansas. Buchanan, feeble and indecisive in the administration of public affairs, had proved unyielding in his efforts to destroy the senator from Illinois. The attempt had not been wholly successful; Douglas remained the most powerful single man in the party, but by his effort, Buchanan had sharply divided — indeed broken up — the party structure, and because of his curious southern sympathy, had created the party division along the lines of North and South. Douglas came to the convention therefore with an unstable, small majority in support of him and a ponderable minority of southern interests against him. This minority had been carefully nourished and well-organized by William Yancey and other southern extremists like Robert Barnwell Rhett and Robert Toombs. It was, obviously, because of the weakened condition of the party their big chance to capture control of the party mechanism.

They almost succeeded. The Committee on Resolutions, in which each state had one vote, brought in a majority report based on the principles of the Dred Scott decision and asserting the right and obligation of the Federal Government, the Congress, to protect slavery in the territories. A minority report upheld the principle of squatter sovereignty but was somewhat qualified by a commitment by the party to accept any later Supreme Court decisions on the questions of constitutional law.

When these minority and majority reports were put before the convention as a whole, the minority or Douglas proposals were adopted by a vote of 165 to 138. Immediately the delegations from Alabama, Mississippi, Texas, and Florida, and a majority of delegates from Virginia, South Carolina, Georgia, and Arkansas withdrew from the convention. The delegates who remained, working under the two-thirds rule, then proceeded to the task of nominating a candidate. Throughout 57 ballots Douglas maintained a solid majority but never succeeded in obtaining the necessary two-thirds of the remaining delegates. So on May 3 the convention adjourned to meet in Baltimore on June 18.

While this was going on the delegates who had withdrawn were conducting an informal convention of their own. They agreed to retain the party name, approved the idea of seeking a common Democratic platform and adjourned to meet in Richmond June 11.

Naturally throughout these stirring days what is often called pandemonium reigned, and in the weeks that followed confusion mounted. Much of the confusion was caused by the problem of which delegates originally elected to the Charleston convention should attend the Baltimore convention. Interminable, bitter wrangles on this question ensued in the opening sessions at Baltimore, as they always do over contested delegations. The Douglas forces succeeded in establishing dominance in the matter, and on June 23 the senator from Illinois was nominated by a vote of $181\frac{1}{2}$ over John C. Breckenridge who obtained $7\frac{1}{2}$ votes. The dissidents, both those who had come to Baltimore and been disappointed and those who had been left over from Charleston, then withdrew to Maryland Institute Hall to nominate John C. Breckenridge. Thus the great party that for thirty years had acted as a stabilizing influence in American politics was finally, after five years of internal struggle, split apart on the single issue of slavery and on that small segment of the issue which had to do with the power of the Federal Government to regulate the institution within the western territories.

Sometime earlier, on May 9, the Constitutional Union party had met in Baltimore to select a presidential candidate. Twenty-one states were represented by men who, on the whole, had been members of the old Whig party. Like that party it drew its strength from both the South and North. Its leading candidates were chiefly moderate southerners—John Bell of Tennessee, John Botts of Virginia, Sam Houston of Texas, John J. Crittenden of Kentucky. On the second ballot Bell was nominated. It was a simple platform the convention constructed for its candidate: an opening paragraph stating that whereas other party platforms usually had the effect of misleading and deceiving the people they were resolved to recognize "no political principle other than the Constitution of the country, the union of the States and the enforcement of the laws." That was about all there was to it.

One week later, on May 15, the Republicans met in Chicago at the Wigwam. William H. Seward was the best known man in search of the nomination among a field which included Abraham Lincoln, John McLean of Ohio, Simon Cameron of Pennsylvania, and Salmon P. Chase of Ohio. Seward came to Chicago believing that he would be chosen by the convention. He had constructed a successful and impressive career in the politics both of his state and the nation. Now sixty years old, he was intelligent, suave, and articulate. He had a dedicated following and he was the author—or most distinguished user—of the resounding phrase about an "irrepressible conflict." But he had been around a long time and had accumulated enemies—in the South of course, but also in the North where the Know-Nothings disliked him, where those who hoped for honest government distrusted him because of the support he obtained from Thurlow Weed, the great New York boss, and where Horace Greeley frankly opposed him. Also he had at the beginning of the year 1860 made a long speech in the Senate in which he seemed to take back almost everything he had said about irrepressible conflicts two years before. It was no more than many other men who aspired to the Presidency had done before and after him, but it made him look a little like a subtle time server, if not tricky, at a time when men were preparing to follow trumpets that gave out more certain sounds.

That was the first great asset of Abraham Lincoln. In 1854, as noticed, he had come out of a profound and prolonged depression during which, politically, he had practically sunk from sight. What roused him was the Kansas-Nebraska Bill, which gave him an issue that stirred him to his depths. He believed that the extension of slavery in the territories by any means was both politically and morally a mistake. He also believed it was an issue that, properly developed, might lead him to the Presidency. Douglas by his great miscalculation refueled what William Herndon called the little engine of Lincoln's ambition. And for the next five years Lincoln built his case against slavery and also, of course, against the South. He built it up with painstaking historical documentation, with remarkable demonstrations of logic, with, especially in the early days, some few maneuvers left over from his time as a trial lawyer, but never rhetorical flourishes or flamboyant predictions. As he went on, the case against slavery as inconsistent with the founders' intent, as a perturbing element in the body politic, as an ultimately destructive evid if not set in the course of ultimate extinction, became ever more gravely and eloquently stated and ever plainer to the public view.

That was his first great asset. His second was that in the four years before 1860 he started to do the ground work and establish the connections that men in search of office must. He gave speeches in the right places, he did the party's dog work, he wrote notes to the right people, he made himself available, he put himself forward but not too far and not too fast. By 1860 he had a solid base in the area he came from and recognition as a force in other sections of the country.

Finally among his assets he had David Davis and Norman Judd. Davis alone would probably have been enough. He weighed three hundred pounds, was a judge on the Eighth Circuit, an old friend of Lincoln, wealthy, funny, vastly energetic, extremely shrewd. He was the head of the organization that handled the Lincoln campaign in the search for the nomination at the Wigwam, the architect of the organization that made the deals that brought Indiana to his side, that made the arrangement with Simon Cameron that brought in Pennsylvania, that provided the extra tickets that packed the hall with wildly shouting Lincoln supporters. Davis was the man who took the responsibility for all these and countless other smaller maneuvers after he received a telegram from Lincoln saying "I authorize no bargains and will be bound by none." Observing that "Lincoln ain't here," he went forward skillfully to pick up the necessary support.

And so at the end of the third ballot when the Ohio delegation changed 4 votes after a whispered promise from Joseph Medill that, if the change were made, Salmon P. Chase could have anything he wanted, Abraham Lincoln was nominated as the Republican candidate for the Presidency. And as Judge W. D. Kelley of Pennsylvania remarked, "Well, we might have done a more brilliant thing, but we certainly could not have done a better thing."

The campaign that followed the work of these conventions, insofar as it advanced the discussion of the issues or opened up the possibility of new solutions to the familiar problems, was, as has been said, not very useful or interesting. It was the custom in those days for candidates to remain in dignified retreat from the active canvass. Following this convention John Bell was scarcely seen or heard, Breckenridge gave one speech in his home county in September, while Abraham Lincoln, asserting that he had already made his position clear on every issue, limited his remarks to the greetings he gave the delegations who came to pay their respects. About the only public campaign maneuver he engaged in during these months was the well-remembered decision to grow a beard after a young girl, Grace Bedill, wrote him that "all the ladies like whiskers."

There was, of course, action by the other party members. John J. Crittenden worked and spoke tirelessly for John Bell; William Yancey moved through the North dropping in his serene way his incendiary proposals: "Governments should not be changed for light and transient causes, but whenever the whole property of an entire people is swept away by a policy that undermines it or deals it a death blow directly"; "If Abraham Lincoln . . . shall undertake to use Federal bayonnets to coerce free and sovereign states in this Union, I shall fly to the standard of that state", "Don't be impatient gentlemen, and above all things keep your temper. This is not the time to fight certainly."

And for the Republicans all the big guns — Seward, Chase, Bates — appeared in the northern states in behalf of Abraham Lincoln. Lesser party leaders organized the usual festivities — barbecues, torch-light parades and so forth. A novelty was added by the Republicans in the creation of the Wide Awakes, young men in capes and helmets who snake danced under flashing lights through various northern city streets.

Stephen A. Douglas alone of the four nominees took his case to the people. This shocked a good many citizens, a candidate pleading his own cause. But it seemed to Douglas, at first, the only way he could proceed. He began with some confidence that he could win, but deprived of the momentum of a whole party by the calculated hostility of President Buchanan and the calculated initiative of Yancey and the other fire eaters, he understood that he himself would have to do much of the work that parties do. He therefore went into the North and the South in the early days of the campaign to reassert the merits of popular sovereignty and to answer as directly as he could the difficult questions put to him. For instance: On Lincoln's election will the South be justified in seceding? Answer: No. If the South secedes before an overt act of Lincoln will you advise resistance by force? Answer: The duty of the President is to enforce the laws and Douglas would support him in so doing.

As time went on Douglas began to have increasing doubts about his success and increasing anxiety about what would happen if he failed. Those questions about southern secession in the event of Lincoln's election, the wild stories that began to circulate around the South about slave revolts and uprisings and massacres if the Republicans won, troubled him deeply. It is fair to say that at that time he knew the whole country better than any of the other candidates and that during the campaign he took more trouble to learn the temper of the country — north, south, east and west — than any of the others. And what he discovered touched his essential self in ways he had not been reached before by public views. When in August the Republicans achieved substantial victories in local elections in Maine and Vermont he could read the signs of the times. And when he read the telegram in October telling of impressive Republican victories in Pennsylvania he is supposed to have said to his secretary, "Mr. Lincoln is the next President. We must try to save the Union. I will go South."

Bone-tired after months of feverish action, looking at times like a "way worn back woods traveller," certain of his own defeat, physically sick, he went out again to do what he could to prevent the public catastrophe he now foresaw. His argument was almost exclusively in defense of the Union; no contemporary inequity or the election of no one man was sufficient course to break up the Union. The night before election he was saying these things in Mobile, Alabama, the home state of William L. Yancey.

The next day the country cast 1,766,452 votes for Abraham Lincoln, 1,376,957 votes for Stephen A. Douglas, 849,781 votes for John Brecken-

ridge and 588,879 votes for John Bell. The electoral vote was Lincoln 173,
Breckenridge 72, Bell 39, and Douglas 12. This suggests that the extreme po-
sitions for slavery or against it attracted the most votes South and North.
Lincoln, for instance, took every northern state but New Jersey while Breckenridge carried all the southern states save Tennessee. Bell did best in the
Border States which shared both southern and northern influences. In the
North, save in Pennsylvania where there was a fusion ticket, Breckenridge did
not do very well, and in the South Lincoln received virtually no votes at all.
Clearly the extreme view was the way to win a section, and indeed the national
election if the section was big enough. Lincoln's understanding of this situation
was correct. But something may be said for the moderate people in between.

For one thing Bell and Douglas between them polled 100,000 more votes
than Lincoln. And for another these votes were distributed more evenly
around the country than was the support for either of the other two candidates.
This is especially striking in the South where in virtually every state, if broken
down county by county, it can be seen that Douglas and Bell had in certain
areas considerable support, often together—as in large parts of Georgia,
North Carolina, Virginia, Tennessee, and Kentucky—outpolling Breckenridge. Even in Alabama, Arkansas, Mississippi, and Louisiana there were
regions of some size where the two together had greater support than Breckenridge. This is suggestive that the states of the South were not so solid for the
extreme position, for rupture, secession, rebellion, and the act of violence as it
may sometimes be made to seem. It suggests too, though the fraction may
well be an exaggeration, that, as *The New York Times* said in June, 1860,
popular sovereignty, with all that implied of a middle ground, had a strong hold
upon nine-tenths of the American people.

It is clearer now than it could have been to Judge Kelley that the Republican convention in May 1860 did in fact a brilliant thing. It selected the mind
and spirit which over the next four years in various texts gave us our most
satisfying statement of what this country is all about, and in so doing, supplied
an enduring focus for the truest poetry in our being. But this question remains
of whether the convention could have done some better thing. Abraham Lincoln was elected and the South seceded and the war did come.

Maybe it would be sensible just to leave it there. As Dwight Dumond
said, it would seem presumptuous to say that without William L. Yancey there
would have been no Confederate States of America even though he believed
it was probably so. In a situation so complex it is not very bright to make any
one man the special minister of any single fate: since Lincoln was elected the
conflict became irrepressible; since Douglas was not, there was a needless
war and so forth. These men and all their fellows—R. B. Rhett, John Brown,
Charles Sumner, Robert Toombs, W. L. Garrison, J. J. Crittenden, Harriet
Beecher Stowe, and the rest—were agents of special forces in a great field of
force that may well have developed its own inertia and determined its own
direction. Still there may be room for a little further reflection and speculation
about this single gross malfunction in our system.

What Lincoln did up to the time of his election was to say that what the

South was doing, in spite of some apparently legitimizing history, was contrary to the intention of the men who started this country. It was, in spite of the ingenious and extremely interesting political theory developed in the South, based upon an erroneous concept of the nature of the Constitution and the Union. It was also, in spite of repeated assertions and learned justifications to the contrary, evil. It was also, in spite of some apparently legitimizing history and some honest hopes for the future, a source of fundamental difference between the North and the South which had continuously disturbed the Union and, if left ungoverned, would destroy it.

This much had often been said before in whole, or more frequently, in several parts. Lincoln, unlike many of those before him, did not put it as an insulting accusation to win a local following. Nor did he, again unlike many of those before him, put it with the lopsided passion of the abolitionist who professed to speak for a just and angry God. He laid it out simply, clearly, and with remorseless logic. He also stated that because in due time what the South was doing would destroy the Union what it was doing must be stopped. Not right now and altogether. But, in his single concession, by prohibiting its further extension which, as he said, would put it in the course of ultimate extinction.

It was beyond much doubt this final proposition, confirmed overwhelmingly by the North in the election of 1860, that drove the South out of the Union. Lincoln said it again and again. He had not suggested that popular sovereignty was a way out; he had not sought ingenious ways around the Dred Scott decision. He had not talked grandiloquently of higher laws and irrepressible conflicts and then backed away into the contemplation of more cheerful alternatives. He had gone on saying it a long time; and when the North elected him the leaders of southern opinion reached the conclusion that the life of the South had been set upon the fatal course and that its days were numbered.

Long before the election of Lincoln, sensible men in the South could have figured this out for themselves. For one thing the section, as has been noticed earlier, had a very hard time making ends meet. "Only the most efficient plantations enjoying the benefits of the most fertile land made money year in and year out." And such money as was made got so tied up in the maintenance of the labor force that capital of any kind for any other endeavor was in very short supply. By all the usual indicators the South in the years immediately before the war was losing ground rapidly to the East and West. Hinton Helper wasn't so far wrong.

Then, too, anyone who could perceive reality understood that whatever the Dred Scott decision said, whatever the Democratic platforms said, whatever the powers of Congress were assumed to be, even the smallest extension of slavery as it had developed in this country was really just about impossible. For years men had been saying in Congress and out of it that they would not dream of trying to legislate slavery into existence in land where God had placed his ordinance against it—by which they meant places like Nebraska, or Utah, or New Mexico, where the conditions of climate made the plantation form of slavery impossible.

These were the palpable pressures on the South in 1860. They could not generate within their system the economic resources to compete effectively with other sections of the Union, and they could not extend that system into other territories to give them the balance of political power they needed in the Union. There were impalpable pressures of equal force. They were virtually surrounded by other parts of the country containing a vigorous, changing, free-wheeling society which was doing different kinds of things and which thought the South was wrong. They were also surrounded by a whole world which for reasons economic, social, and moral was dismantling the system which the South was so desperately trying to shore up. Slavery in its various formal expressions from Portugal to Turkey, from Brazil to Russia, was finished or in the course of ultimate extinction.

Carl Schurz in a tremendous speech at St. Louis in 1860 put it all together very well. In the middle of the nineteenth century, he said, the world was developing a new kind of society where the human mind was seeking out new and wonderful powers and the last remnants of feudalism were disappearing. This new society accepted change, believed in progress, and was sustained by free inquiry. It was a great humming system of railways, dynamoes, prime movers, telegraphs, and machines that transformed the work of the world, expedited the free movement of men through all the reaches of the social structure, and acted in support of "progressive advancement." In such a world, which could only be operated by free men, educated citizens, and inquiring minds, the thought of maintaining a slave power with all its special restrictions and contrived protections was impossible. This, he said again to the South, was the nineteenth century; look around you and see how lonesome you are in this wide world of ours.

Precisely because they were so lonesome, no doubt, the leaders of the South could not look out into the great humming world too far, nor too closely into the antiquated society they had constructed upon their peculiar institution. Obviously threatened, comfortable only in their own surroundings, appalled by the brashness and ill-organized energy in the world developing around them, maddened by the condemnation of those not subject to the same temptations, forced constantly to rejustify to others and to themselves the fact of slavery, confronting a diminishing future in an expanding world, proud—they sought desperately to shore up their case with threats and accusations of their own, with legalisms and devices, myths and illusions. And the greater the pressure on them, and the more serenely complacent the admonitions to come and join the nineteenth century, the more alert became the instinct for self-protection and the more fixed became the illusions.

One of the fundamental elements in the democratic process as it has worked out in this country is that it produces means for dealing with the ambiguity created by different opinions over what to do and how to do it. From the array of opinion, what makes sense and what is appropriate is slowly sifted out. And from the siftings it becomes possible ordinarily to form enough solid ground for agreement not so much on what is ideal or even best but on what, given the variety of interests to be served, is possible at the moment. When the differing opinions define real imbalances or unfulfilled needs in the society,

and when the proposed corrections have some substance, the process can ordinarily produce compromise adjustments that satisfy the majority and serve
the interests of the whole. Over time the views of the Knights of Labor, or
Single Taxers, or Socialists, having acted in the process of adjustment to
sharpen the public sympathies and enlarge the general understanding, are
brought within some saving accommodation.

Some differing opinions do not have much clarifying definition and not
much useful substance; they are like nativism, religious bigotry, John Bircherism or McCarthyism, simply intractable modes of feeling or aberration dispersed through the body politic. The democratic process, as developed in this
country, has been designed to hold even such aberrations in neutralizing
suspension until those who possess such views wear themselves out, or come
round, or grow up.

The essential condition of the democratic process is the acceptance of the
fact that in the daily ordering of affairs there are more matters to be solved by
striking compromises among reasonable differences than by forcing or imposing outright choices between one kind of thing and another kind of thing. The
emphasis is upon means rather than ends, upon the process by which all sorts
of men and conditions are taken into account and brought to accommodation
rather than upon the product or the particular nature of the accommodation to
be achieved. And this process seeks, on the whole, pragmatic sanctions; it
sets what will work in a given moment somewhat ahead of the good, the ideal,
the beautiful, and the absolutely true.

Of all those contending for presidential office in the election of 1860 Stephen A. Douglas was working most closely within our traditional democratic
process. The scheme of popular sovereignty, the suggestion that over time
local regulations have more influence than a federal court decision, the insistence, even though he believed as a private person that slavery was evil, that
as a public policy it made no difference if it was voted up or down as long as it
was voted on—all these things put him within the essential spirit of the American political process. Had he won the election and sustained this spirit it is
possible that, as in all other grave differences in our history, time would have
allowed the enormous issue to work itself through to saving accommodation
and the South would have entered the nineteenth and twentieth centuries
without the heavy, still continuing expenditures of blood, tears, and treasure.
Considering only the terrible alternative that occurred one can certainly wish
that Douglas had been given his chance.

There are, however, other considerations. Some are political, some functional, some clinical. As for the political, even had Douglas been elected, the
party he represented had been split in two, in part by the vindictiveness and
fecklessness of James Buchanan, but in part also by the very issue Douglas
would have to deal with as President. In trying to deal with this issue, therefore, he would have been deprived of the machinery to get things done and
the stabiliizing influence that great political parties, which draw their strength
from all sections and classes, can supply.

As for functional considerations, slavery and the South were like no other problem that had been put through our historic political processes. By patient search and skillful maneuver and, in the earlier years, favoring conditions, it had been possible to reach salvaging compromises on the physical limits or the kinds of protection to be given the southern way of life, but it had never been possible to achieve agreements that would modify the essential character of that way of life and it was the continuation of the essential character that was held to be at stake in 1860. Furthermore, the issue of the South, unlike nativism, or McCarthyism, or the John Bircherism, did not appear in small nodes of feeling dispersed throughout the society. It was a concentration of imposing geographical mass, economic weight, comprehensive social structure, and self-sustaining scheme of values. Historically it had proved difficult to hold in neutralizing suspension in the hope that it would wear itself out and the prospect for the years after 1860 was certainly no better. Indeed, as can now be seen, far worse, for those years demonstrated with what high resolve and remarkable energy the South could sustain its own case in conditions of mounting adversity.

As for the clinical considerations, it seems possible that the country as a whole could no longer find the intellectual and emotional resources to continue the ordinary processes of political decision in this matter. Things were at the ragged edge. Too much shouting across the border about harlotry, mangled bodies, sin, evil, and positive good. Too many loud, loose claims of getting out or not retreating one inch. Too many insistent demands to lay it on the line and to be heard. Too much blood in Kansas, too much madness at Harper's Ferry, too much frenzy in Mobile and Boston, and too much paralyzing disorder in Washington. Maybe, whatever the prospect, the people North and South just could not stand it any more and like overburdened neurotics could find release from terrifying frustration only in some violent discharge.

The actual prospect offered by Lincoln and confirmed by the election of 1860 was the apparent cause of the violent discharge that did take place. It is by no means clear that Lincoln believed that such would be the consequence of his intent. Understanding the South less well than Douglas he said in August, 1860, that he thought the section "had too much common sense and good temper to break up" the Union.

But it is not clear either that, even had he fully recognized the consequences of his argument, he would have changed it. Indeed all his subsequent actions suggest he would not have done so. And even if he did not fully take in the possible consequences, he still may have offered the best of a very bad set of solutions. His primary objective was to preserve the Union, that practical and mystical source of the political process he put beyond all other considerations. Things having gone so far he calculated that he could not obtain his great objective by any of the customary means. So he was prepared to save the Union by military measures trusting that in the end might could be used to make right.

It has proved to be a hard choice between what Douglas might have accomplished and what Lincoln did achieve—which is another way of asking whether there was a way to maintain the states united without going to war.

Many people have asked this question and tried to answer it. It does not seem very useful to try to answer it here once again. As with so many sentimental investigations of what might have been, not much that is illuminating can come from the effort to weigh so clouded a non-event against so ponderable a reality. Any judgment must come down to anybody's guess. My own guess. for whatever it may be worth, is that things could not have been held together by any other means than those that the country was finally forced to use. For seventy years, continuous efforts had been made to resolve the difference separating the North and South. All reasonable possible grounds for compromise – geographical, legislative, economic, and constitutional – had, in those years, been thoroughly explored and skillfully used. The end result of all this effort was that in 1860 the sense of difference was sharper than ever, while the apparent cause for division was becoming less and less real. Men fell out and parties split up over a meaningless point – the power of Congress to control the development of slavery in areas where it could not exist. When things had reached such a pass it must seem that all the negotiating room had been used up. The country found itself in an unbearable state of tension, which, beyond much doubt, could not be resolved by means that had failed in better times and which, in the absence of any real prospect of resolution, could not be long endured. The only way out, it must seem, was to let "the erring sisters" depart in peace or to seek to continue the Union by what Clausewitz called other means.

Election of 1864

by *Harold M. Hyman*

"Of the canvass of 1864, from our point of view little may be said," Charles Francis Adams, Jr. advised historians thirty-five years after Appomattox. In Adams' judgment, the 1864 election was an infertile research field because, in the "altogether exceptional" wartime context, little popular energy or interest existed for calm analysis of public issues. But Adams did not realize the relevance of the Civil War to America's ongoing political processes. Voters at that time responded sensitively and appropriately to much more than battles on the field. By 1864 they had learned that the amassed votes of the individuals would shape the fates of armies and fleets, of forms of government, and of races and nations; that, by their interaction, battles and leaders gave form to the issues about which individuals balloted. Contrary to Adams' estimate, the 1864 election deserves historical respect and scholarly attention.

The most remarkable fact about the 1864 election is that it occurred. A century ago, even the handful of nations where elections normally decided matters suspended balloting during wars. But in 1864, Americans voted almost as in peacetime.

In a mechanical sense, there were no alternatives. National and state constitutions set inexorable calendars for elections no matter how inconvenient or dangerous the moments were. During the Civil War some conservative theorists, despairing of democracy's ability to survive a war, suggested extraordinary plebiscites or referenda as substitutes for elections. But in politically practical terms, these suggestions for delaying, canceling, suspending, or reversing elections, proved to be duds. Here and abroad, America's rigid electoral rhythms were accounted basic flaws in her constitutional-political arrangements, increasing the odds against the Union. Defeatists believed the theory of intrinsic defects borne out by the South's secession and the North's dispiriting inability to bring the outgoing states to heel despite accumulating sacrifices. If enough antiwar candidates won voters' support in 1864, the Confederacy would make good its bid for independence regardless of bluecoats' valor. In short, the inescapable necessity for voting in 1864 would more likely kill than continue the Union.

Commonly cited as proof of innate political-constitutional defects were the state secessions of 1860–61. Even before hostilities began, the rebel states had coerced out of Buchanan's lame-duck Congress an unamendable constitutional amendment, stipulating that slavery continue perpetually where it existed. Ratification was under way when the Fort Sumter resistance and the initiation of hostilities spurred northern unity beyond levels predictable before the attack, and made the proposed 13th amendment obsolete. In this sense Sumter was the first step in what became the 1864 election campaign. What followed the puny garrison's surrender in 1861 led to better alternatives three years later than the perpetuation of slavery or the abandonment of the Union.

Unity was desperately needed in the North. Despite the tenacious belief that the Confederates could not win, in many ways they could hardly avoid success. The Civil War's magnitude and longevity suggest the weight of southern assets. In statistical terms, of course, the Confederacy was the lighter contender. Yet enthusiasm for war was high among southern whites. Popular mythology insisted that long before 1860 the spirit of 1776 had been banished in the North, where allegedly inferior immigrants displaced Anglo-Saxon leaders with "boss" politicos. The northern society that had allowed the so-called "compromises" of 1820, 1850, and 1854 seemed unlikely to hold a militant course after 1861. Slavery allowed southern whites to maintain "purer" politics and values than materialistic northerners. Indeed, one southern justification for secession was the uncorrupted maintenance of these engaging, slave-based virtues. By this reasoning the Confederacy did not have to win its war against the United States; it had only to endure until anti-war candidates won elections in the North, and intervention by European friends and customers of the South resulted in independence with slavery.

In contrast, northern despondency was great not just because in 1861 there was little effective opposition to secession but because secession occurred at all. Although there had been earlier sectional confrontations, these had been worked through. By 1860 secession appeared to be a sophisticated political weapon designed to blackmail northern states into acquiescence to southern policies. When secession threats followed Lincoln's election, the common expectation was that a "compromise of 1860" was in the making. In short, secession was a gun that was not supposed to go off.

Nevertheless, the gun was fired. Once war came, logistical factors allowed the Confederacy to capitalize on its relative unanimity and on Union disunity. On the eastern coastal plain, the center of attention, the two sectional capitals were only one hundred miles apart. Yet it required four years and repetitive, bloody battles over the same territory for the Union's armies to complete the distance. An implicit issue of the 1864 election was whether bluecoats could ever cover the course.

Why was their progress so slow? Good Confederate use of the terrain was one answer. The dominating physical characteristic of this area was a complex river system whose waters descended eastward from Appalachian highlands, cutting valleys and ravines as they flowed. The Union Army, heading southward from the Potomac, had to use a few predictable roads, bridges, fords or ferries. Every river, run, stream, and creek, each forest and hill provided defenders with natural forts that advancing military technology and submissive slave labor could exploit.

Initial military moves beginning in midsummer, 1861, reflected these topographical and strategic factors. The amateur army that Lincoln's ninety-day call assembled in April moved toward Richmond only to meet a shocking repulse at Bull Run. The Union reverse resulted from shrewd Confederate employment of the Shenandoah Valley, a natural roadway which cut southwest through lush farming lands.

In contrast, Union soldiers using the valley as a bypass around the hazardous coastal plain had to travel the long leg of a triangle to Richmond's latitude, then turn eastward through a relatively few, easily-plugged mountain passes. Throughout the area a hostile population surrounded the bluecoats.

Each mile northeast through friendly communities up the valley's angled length brought the Confederates nearer to a dozen passes, undercutting Union defensive arrangements. Rebel commanders could then flank Union forces on the coastal plain as happened at Bull Run. They could threaten Washington, Baltimore, Philadelphia, New York, and Harrisburg, whose governors, mayors, and chambers of commerce were likely to pressure Washington for reinforcements for their cities, counties, and states. Election pressure was never far off. For example, opposition politicos, unfettered newsmen, and foreign diplomats saw how easily rebels penetrated the North and how difficult the Union's reverse trips were.

Even the Union's seaborne supremacy could not combat the atmosphere of defeatism because the Navy's power was oversold. It was thought that once the dispersed deep-water Navy assembled, the blockade of rebel ports which Lincoln proclaimed in April, 1861, would become a reality. But the configuration of the Atlantic and Gulf Coasts generally favored the Confederacy. South of Washington, 3,500 miles of estuarial indentations, peninsular extrusions, and insular obstacles formed a wrinkled maze impossible to dominate totally. The fragility of the Union's lead in naval combat terms was demonstrated in March, 1862. To threaten Union General George B. McClellan's peninsular attack on Richmond and indeed the entire blockading enterprise, the CSA *Virginia* (the ex-USS *Merrimac*), a lone, clumsy vessel, broke the line of Union battleships with impudent ease. The next day, the Union Navy's experimental ironclad *Monitor* arrived and challenged the *Virginia*, which withdrew up-river and never again threatened the blockade.

Amphibious expeditions landed McClellan's divisions near Richmond, and simultaneously, far to the south and west, another Union force occupied New Orleans. A thousand miles up-river, a third amphibious thrust trapped Confederate Forts Henry and Donelson. But these penetrations, organized only a year after Sumter, failed to force the Confederacy to give up, and the northern public, hoping to end the war cheaply, grew frustrated and depressed.

If the East was the graveyard for Union leaders' reputations and a hazard to the Union's prospects of survival, the trans-Appalachian West became the Union's school for success. Here topography aided the bluecoats. By midsummer, 1861, a western theatre linking Atlantic and midwestern sectors could be opened if Union strength won the Ohio-Mississippi River systems.

During the 1861–62 winter, an inland Navy adapted to shallow river channels came into existence. In the first days of February, 1862, in close collaboration with the Union's improvised river fleet, Ulysses S. Grant's troops occupied Confederate forts in the Ohio River's path, soon forcing the Confederates out of Kentucky and Nashville. The Union had won its first victories. Grant's "unconditional surrender" statement provided a combat hero to balance the growing McClellan cult in the East.

After Bull Run, McClellan, a young West Point graduate, only thirty-five years old in 1861, rebuilt the showpiece Army of the Potomac. In so doing, he swiftly became a political figure of considerable importance. His conservatism on race relationships attracted Democratic support and required Republicans in the White House and on Capitol Hill to treat him with caution and respect. But McClellan failed to return either. He never understood that he had to win battles in order to make himself and his racial and constitutional positions politically invulnerable. Disappointed at his inaction, Lincoln relieved him of his command. Nevertheless, in the spring of 1862, Lincoln had to call him back even without victories, and once again McClellan reshaped the major Union Army into a disciplined field force. It was just in time. Early in September, 1862, Lee moved northward in an effort to cut vital communications between Washington and the rest of the Union, and, in doing so, to display to Europe's diplomats and to northern voters—congressional, state, and local elections were close at hand—how weak the Union was. At Sharpsburg (Antietam), Maryland, bloody fighting forced Lee back to Virginia, but his Army remained intact because the cautious McClellan declined to exploit his initial success.

By contrast, substantial Union accomplishments in the West encouraged Unionists preparing for the 1862 elections. On April 26, 1862, an amphibious expedition occupied New Orleans, the South's largest urban and commercial center. Aiming to clear the northern reaches of the Mississippi River as well, Grant attacked a Confederate concentration at Shiloh early in April. The poorly planned assault stalled, but Grant's fault was too-hasty action not McClellan-style immobility. The Union's western armies were more combative against the enemy as well as more obedient to civilian direction.

Until Lee launched the Antietam campaign, Confederates could pose as the heirs of 1776, the defenders of home, state, and section. But the invasion of northern states contradicted this thesis (as did the 1863 Confederate thrust northward to Gettysburg). Many Europeans and northerners who had previously sympathized with the Confederates on the defense therefore lost their romantic outlook, and Antietam was enough of a Union victory for Lincoln to exploit a shifting tide in northern opinion and to alter the purpose of the war.

A great war has its own dynamics; its causes, aims, and results rarely coincide. As matters worked out, a year-and-a-half after Sumter self-interest had moved much of white America from the 1861 northern consensus in favor of reunion with the maintenance of slavery to a push for reunion with emancipation.

Ironically, the Confederacy's advantages and successes pushed the United States toward emancipation sentiment. Most northern whites were neither racial equalitarians nor civil libertarians. Few white men were concerned with these matters. Mid-nineteenth century white Americans lived almost unrestrained by any level of government and rarely encountered Negroes. Even opponents of the further extension of slavery—the common position among Republicans—wanted territories to be lily-white as well as slaveless. Therefore, without hypocrisy, Republicans in 1861 had supported the Crittenden resolution and the ultimately abortive 13th Amendment proposal. However, by 1862 the Republicans had moved to support emancipation, despite the Democratic party's contention that whites would support the war for the Union but would drop arms if asked to die in order to free southern blacks.

Support for emancipation resulted from the reluctant acceptance by most Republicans of the abolitionists' repeated claim that slaves were the Confederacy's basic resource; that the only way the Union could win was to raise its aims from victory to abolition. Such propositions could not alone have convinced many northern citizens, including perhaps Lincoln, if the awareness of ties between the Union's armies and the South's blacks had not grown.

Wherever bluecoats moved into slave states, Negroes served as guides, spies, and agents, and performed manual labor. Assuming that the flag brought freedom, increasing numbers of runaway slaves sought Union Army encampments. But the 1850 Fugitive Slave Law required all federal officers, including the military, to return fugitive slaves. McClellan adopted the public position that, even in a civil war, an army must respect all property rights of white civilians, slave ownership included. His men obeyed the Fugitive Slave Law, though other commands violated it openly. Privately, however, even McClellan's Democratic, conservative friends admitted that the Union Army could hardly escape the slavery issue. A New York *World* correspondent, assigned to "puff" the general into the White House in 1864, wrote candidly in December, 1861, to his anti-Lincoln publisher: "Every step taken [by the Army] in the rebel territory is complicating the necessity for some action to be taken by the Federal authority, as to the disposal of slaves belonging to the rebels found in arms. . . . I can see how the question will again and again force itself upon the public mind."

In public McClellan claimed that the Army had no influence on racial matters even within disloyal states. Privately he admitted the opposite. "Help me to dodge the nigger,—we want nothing to do with him," the general pleaded with the *World* publisher. But the black man could not be dodged. By the 1862 congressional elections, he was the measure of what the war had become and whether it should go on. Most Democratic party spokesmen stood firmly against emancipation and continuation.

Recovering swiftly from its 1860 rift and from the associative guilt of secession, the Democratic party in northern states appealed to and encouraged anti-emancipation, anti-Negro, and anti-war sentiments. These negative stands allowed Democrats to escape from the embarrassment of their party's implication in the secession process. Their conservative views were disguised in constitutional rhetoric distorted from the Jeffersonian heritage. A negative view of government and belief in the sanctity of property, including slaves, were compelling imperatives a century ago. This reverence for ownership combined easily with distaste for Negroes, and such attitudes made it at first enormously difficult for Republicans to decide on or defend emancipation.

For example, consider the pattern of anti-slavery congressional legislation. A Confiscation Act of August 6, 1861, provided that slaves in arms against the United States (a mythical corps) or providing anti-Union labor should be freed after proofs of such activities were placed before federal judges. But reconquest of seceded states was necessary before federal courts could resume operation. Elsewhere, federal judges, juries, and attorneys were unenergetic about confiscation proceedings. However, the pressures of war soon encouraged northerners to favor whatever weakened the Confederacy. In effect, the South's basic weapon against the Union—the war's longevity —produced in the North a backlash against slavery—a backlash that abolitionists encouraged but had not been able to create.

On April 16, 1862 Lincoln signed an act abolishing slavery in the District of Columbia (where the 1860 Crittenden proposal had said emancipation must never occur) with compensation to owners. On June 19, another statute stipulated that slavery could not exist in the federal territories, in effect reversing the Dred Scott decision and realizing the Republican platform positions of 1856 and 1860. Then on July 17, 1862, a second Confiscation Act freed slaves of persons convicted of treason (no one was) or who supported the rebellion (no test was specified for this). Whatever the limitations in these laws, congressmen gauged the North's attitude toward southern Negroes to be changing.

Lincoln sensed the winds of public opinion. Aware that Congress was unlikely to risk out-right emancipation, and feeling a need to act on behalf of men in uniform, the President reluctantly but decisively moved to change two centuries of race relations. On September 22, 1862, he issued the Emancipation Proclamation in the train of the Antietam "victory." The Proclamation, in which Lincoln declared that on January 1, 1863, slaves of persons still in rebellion "shall be then, thenceforward, and forever free," found its constitutional base in the Commander-in-chief's war power. Slaveowners had ninety days in which to abandon the Confederacy and, so doing, to keep this slave property.

Dreams of mass Confederate surrenders as result of the Proclamation, allowing reunion without major upset to pre-war race relations, dissipated during the three months after September, 1862. On January 1, 1863, Lincoln proclaimed further that emancipation in the specified rebel areas was in effect — which meant that it would go into practical effect when and if Union troops won those areas. A new element was introduced when the President added that Negroes would be enlisted in the Union's armies. Since the only large number of Negroes was behind Confederate lines, Lincoln was offering slaves a majestic reason to become runaways. Henceforward, the Union Army was to encourage not return fugitive slaves, and suitable Negro men would become uniformed, armed, free men.

In sum, Lincoln committed the nation and, as far as he was able, the still-rebel states to the abolitionist view that slavery had caused secession and nurtured the Confederacy, and that Negroes were men enough to be soldiers. Although executive emancipation was reversible by election results, judicial orders, or lack of enforcement, nevertheless the President and most of his countrymen had traveled an incredible distance in a short time. If the war could be won, the law of the land would be radically altered.

The biggest "ifs" centered on the Army and on the 1862 election results. Would voters return anti-emancipation congressmen? Would generals and privates accept black comrades-in-arms? From the West came word that Grant welcomed any source of recruits, and his stock rose higher in the White House. McClellan let his disgruntled troops and anti-war Democrats know that he opposed the Proclamation and wished Union military victory to lead only to a return to pre-secession conditions. In short, he wanted to halt history at the point of the familiar and comfortable, and he wanted to be elected President of the United States in 1864.

If he had cut Lee off after Antietam, McClellan might have been able to realize his ambitions. Failing in this, he lost the last vestiges of Lincoln's respect. On November 7, 1862, after the elections Lincoln removed him from all commands. But McClellan continued his ultimately successful efforts to win the Democratic party's 1864 presidential nomination.

The Emancipation Proclamation provided the Union with substantial assets despite deserved criticism that it ignored slavery in the loyal border states, leaving the nation speckled even if the rebellion collapsed. Henceforward bluecoats were invading Dixie not merely in order to restore the Union or to contain slavery where it existed in 1860. They were also liquidating a system of labor, an ordering of races, and a way of life that, unique among nineteenth-century slaveowning societies, had been expanding territorially in imperial fashion. For these reasons, in 1862 and 1864, election platforms and principles would be radically different from those of 1860.

The absence in the South of consistent two-party politics (as well as the provision in the Confederate Constitution establishing a six-year term for the President of the Confederacy) made changes difficult to arrange even when substantial numbers of white persons desired them. In the Confederate States politics rarely tested basic issues. Slavery, secession, and independence (or, in the Civil War's last phases, emancipation and reunion) never became Confederacy-wide or even state-wide questions. Although leading spokesmen at first claimed that this had advantages because it fostered unity, in the long run this may not have been so. Opposition politics could not develop serious alternatives to the official policies; parties could not blunt or absorb criticisms. Dissident southerners had to keep quiet or hide behind state sovereignty banners while criticizing or harassing obnoxious Confederate leaders or policies.

In the North two-party politics never ceased to offer opposition and alternatives. Proceeding as if no Civil War raged — indeed, proceeding at a vastly more vigorous pace *because* the war was being fought — election politics were both a hazard for the North and, retrospectively at least, an advantage.

An essential element in this advantage was the Union soldier's continuing involvements in politics as a citizen of his state. Politicians on every level of the federal system were keenly aware that several states allowed soldier-citizens to vote by direct or absentee ballots. Further, soldiers' relatives who were voters formed a substantial portion of the electorate. Numerous links tied the bluecoat to his homefront connections and with open politics. Literacy was so high that for the first time a military postal service was necessary. Unconstrained journalists and uncensored newspapers and periodicals, including many of anti-Administration views, fed the Union soldiers' astonishing hunger for information. Private health and morals associations helped even more to exchange opinions and attitudes between military men and civilians.

Despite fears that estrangement might occur the Union Army never became alienated from the civilian sector. By attending to soldiers' as well as to civilians' views, Lincoln was able to move as fast as general opinion allowed on such sensitive questions as emancipation. Disagreements were managed through party confrontations in elections instead of through clashes between national and state authorities.

Of course, the hazards were great. No matter what trivial local office was contested, every election could become an argument on emancipation, internal security, or reconstruction. Temptations must have been frequent and intense to suspend or delay elections despite the Constitution, or to corrupt them into prearranged spectacles of the sort Louis Napoleon was staging in France. The Democrats were especially successful in exploiting fears and irritations caused by mounting inflation, altering race relationships, abrasive internal security measures, and unfamiliar tariff, banking, taxation, and entrepreneurial subvention laws. The most potent Democratic charge of 1862 (and 1864) was that the war was hopeless: that the Union Army lost battles and Confederates persisted in rebellion because Republicans were elevating Negroes over whites and nation over states and individuals.

In response, Republicans in 1862 as in 1864 charged Democrats with disloyal copperheadism, and invited the so-called War Democrats into a patriotic "Union Party" coalition, at least for the war's duration. On issues such as emancipation, the War Democrat "Union" recruits were conservative, and a natural alliance grew between them and the Republican right.

The Republican spectrum did include a "radical" wing, whose members judged that success in the war was possible only by ending slavery in reconquered southern states at least, and, hopefully, in the loyal border states as well. Radical Republicans criticized Lincoln's patience with McClellan and chafed under the President's drift toward emancipation. Yet the Republican coalition successfully operated the congressional and state party mechanisms that produced tariff, banking, and railroad subvention laws, that coped with complex internal security, fiscal, and administrative responsibilities, and that maintained effective management of Congress. Lincoln nurtured cordial relationships with his party's congressional leaders, and together, they managed to keep civilian control over the military colossus the rebellion required them to build.

Nevertheless, in Allan Nevins' opinion, "The [Lincoln] Administration entered the [1862] political campaign under so many disadvantages that its supporters feared an ignominious defeat." The increasing war-weariness of many northerners invigorated the Democrats. More than a year and a half after the shameful Sumter surrender, the ninety-day militia muster implied by Lincoln in his April, 1861, call for troops, had become a great war requiring armed hordes in the field and basic reevaluations of race relationships. Many voters saw too little military progress or civilian purpose to justify the human or money costs and the racial shifts. Anti-war Democrats could hardly help regain strayed voters and repair their parties, especially along the high population eastern seaboard and in the Negro-fearing midwestern states.

In the 1862 elections Democrats cut from thirty-five to eighteen the Republicans' majority in the House of Representatives. Republicans lost control of Indiana, Illinois (Lincoln's own state), New Jersey, New York, Ohio, and Pennsylvania, five of which had gone their way in 1860. Pondering the election returns, discouraged Republicans increased efforts to broaden the party's patriotic appeal through "Union" coalitions with War Democrats. Over the opposition of conservative advisers, Lincoln determined forthrightly to acknowledge the racial factors tied in with the Union's death or salvation. He not only declared emancipation but greatly broadened its effects by recruiting Negro troops.

Democrats, especially those of the party's massive right-wing, peace-at-any-cost elements, were elated and looked ahead to future triumphs. The North's Democrats did not have to win in 1862 in order to expect triumph in 1864. They had only to make a fair showing, which they did. Thereafter, united in their stand-pat conservatism, they needed to endure as a party until Republican-Union factionalism, a northern backlash against Negroes, and general discouragements combined to oust emancipating Lincolnians.

Election results were barely counted when further Union setbacks increased the Republicans' loads. In November, 1862, General Ambrose Burnside replaced McClellan in command of the Army of the Potomac. Burnside blunted the Army in stubborn attacks on entrenched Confederate positions near Fredericksburg, Virginia, and once again the bruised Army of the Potomac returned to its camps. The soldiers' low morale was exceeded only by the drop in civilian sentiment. A week after the Fredericksburg frustration, the historian George Bancroft wrote to his son, an officer in the Army of the Potomac: "The outcry against the conduct of the war is deep and unanimous. All blame Lincoln: all, in all parties. I have not heard one who does not."

In 1863 Union spirits quickened with the arrival of spring and the appointment late in April of a picturesque new commander, "Fighting Joe" Hooker, for the Army of the Potomac. But, the Army seemed jinxed, and after bloody encounters near Chancellorsville, again retreated north of the Rappahannock River. Reports suggested that the Union was near the end of its rope as dissatisfaction increased with the quality of civilian and military leadership. Another Confederate invasion of the northern states would exacerbate these strains.

The Confederate commander decided to allow the North no rest. In early June, 1863, Lee launched a second Confederate expedition northward, up the Shenandoah Valley. All Pennsylvania, Maryland, and the District of Columbia lay before him. Hooker resigned from command despite the critical military situation, and Carlisle and York, Pennsylvania fell that day to Confederate soldiers. After Lincoln replaced Hooker with George G. Meade, both armies blundered into three days of combat near Gettysburg, Pennsylvania. On the Fourth of July, Lee gave up the field and escaped into Virginia.

Lee had been wrong. Gettysburg exhibited Union strengths rather than weaknesses. Even the mid-campaign change of top command from Hooker to Meade had not diminished the fighting capacity of the Army of the Potomac. Lincoln and his civil and military subordinates did not panic at Lee's approach. The outbreak, simultaneously with the Gettysburg battle, of anti-draft rioting and anti-Negro violence in northern cities failed to shake Lincoln's determination not to use Meade's troops until after the battle was decided. Then Meade's Gettysburg veterans quickly suppressed the rioters. To round out the catalog of Union strength news came in from the West, just as Lee lost his gamble in Pennsylvania, that after weeks of siege, Vicksburg, Mississippi had surrendered to Grant. The Mississippi River was again open. Combined with the news of Gettysburg, Vicksburg's capitulation made Independence Day, 1863, by far the brightest day of the war for Union patriots, marred only by the anti-draft vigilantism.

Soon after, William S. Rosecrans' Union Army of the Cumberland entered strategic Chattanooga. With eastern Confederate troops idle since Gettysburg, Lee rushed eleven thousand men westward by rail, and besieged the city. In mid-October, Grant, now chief general of the Union's western armies, moved two corps of veteran eastern troops to the West. By December 3, with Vicksburg won and Chattanooga secure, a way was open to the Atlantic. All that was needed was enough courage and steadfastness among soldiers and civilians to see the way, and to take it.

Despite the mid-1863 Union military upsurge, the Democratic political star seemed to be rising all that year. Dissatisfied persons responded to the anti-war, anti-Negro preachments which major Democratic spokesmen had made familiar during the 1862 elections. Inflation outdistanced workers' incomes and drove into Democratic ranks individuals who feared that freed Negroes would flock to northern cities and compete for jobs. Internal security measures, especially draft enforcement, irritated northern whites. Above all, the Confederacy's surprising resiliency nourished northern discontent.

Lincoln was heavily pressured to revoke emancipation in order to deflate the Democrats' chief weapon. Lincoln, however, held to his emancipation decision, encouraged by the fact that Negroes, once armed, did not indulge in vindictive bloodletting as racist folklore insisted would occur. But no one could foresee how long a decision for emancipation would stand or how long enlistments of Negroes into the Union's armies would continue. Meanwhile, blacks left Dixie in increasing numbers to join the northern forces; the Union's armies ate up ever-larger amounts of rebel real estate. Often aided by agents of sanitary, missionary, and welfare organizations interested in the slave's body, soul, and mind, the generals were rehearsing reconstructions.

As a result of persistent frustrations, Democrats scored a few more gains in local contests and in off-year state elections during 1863. But, where soldiers could vote, they voted heavily in favor of Republican-Union candidates.

The political lesson of 1863 for Democrats was to shift the bases of their appeals to voters. Despite the Democratic party's signal success in reviving itself after the secession winter, and in winning local contests in 1862, their anti-war and anti-Negro posture was not sweeping the Republicans aside. Nevertheless the Democrats' commitments against any changes resulted in a party apparatus incapable of making shifts. The Republicans were not so hindered. Their repeated association of Democrats with secession and copperheadism undercut those Democrats who wanted peace within the Union, but who resisted emancipation or other wartime innovations. Peace-at-any-price Democrats such as Ohio's Clement L. Vallandigham kept control of major party machineries, and their extreme statements provided Republicans with free campaign ammunition. The result, noticeable by the 1863 election, was that Democrats were unable to make breakthroughs beyond the 1862 level with a few local and temporary exceptions. The party had peaked; in Ohio's gubernatorial race in 1863, for example, Vallandigham's total was 11 per cent lower than in 1862. The political lesson of 1863 for Republicans was again to advance political discourse so as to keep in step with the "thinking bayonets" of the Union's armies and their numberless homefront connections. Lincoln, though he did not shoot ahead as swiftly as some men wished, exhibited the virtue of never receding. He had hit close to the heart of national sentiment.

The fact that Republicans generally, and Lincoln in particular, learned from all these events is evident in his December 8, 1863, proclamation granting amnesty or pardon for rebels who recanted their past disloyalty. Again employing his war powers as Commander-in-chief, Lincoln stipulated that if persons in each state equaled at least 10 per cent of the number who had voted in 1860 elections, and if they reestablished "loyal" state governments with new constitutions approving abolition and repudiating secession, then he would recognize the restored state. He warned that under the Constitution Congress, not he, controlled admission of states' representatives and senators, and that courts might abrogate this proclamation. Nevertheless he specified that his pardons protected all property rights of oath-takers "except as to slaves." In every other sense reconstruction would be conservative, for Lincoln stipulated that rebel states' boundaries, constitutions, and law codes, slavery excepted, "as before the rebellion be maintained." Last, the President noted that his proclamation was "a mode" not an unalterable blueprint, "and while the mode presented is the best the Executive can suggest with his present impressions, it must not be understood that no other possible mode would be acceptable."

The 1863 reconstruction proclamation soon exhibited itself as a useful way of restoring state government in reconquered areas. Each state so begun restricted voters and officeholders to whites. Many of the former were recent Confederates, and almost all indicated Democratic party preferences. Moreover, in those states, Unionist whites who had suffered exile, imprisonment, and confiscation as result of their patriotism, and Negro veterans of the Union Army who returned to their homes, protested vigorously against Lincoln's policy. An intra-Republican strain was in the making as the presidential election year opened, because, ironically, in military as well as political terms, the Union's survival prospects were improving.

Grant, now commander of all Union forces, determined to strike at major Confederate concentrations everywhere. Union conscription and recruiting apparatuses moved into high gear; Negro bluecoats were more welcome than ever. Fruitless Union attacks on Petersburg, twenty miles south of Richmond, indicated how tenaciously the Confederates intended to defend that vital satellite city, and, as at Vicksburg, Grant resorted to a full-scale siege. Weeks passed, then months, without apparent advance.

Meanwhile, the Confederates tried to exploit the strains of the election year. Unable to shake Grant in direct military clashes, Lee sent Confederate cavalry leader Jubal Early through Union concentrations in the Shenandoah. On July 11 Early was on Washington's outskirts, but again there was no panic. Grant detached field divisions to the District of Columbia in good time to push Early's troopers back to Virginia almost with contemptuous ease. The Union's armies were proving themselves to be proudly competent, confident in their civilian and military commanders, and unawed by Lee much less by his subordinate; the Lincoln Administration had proved it could not only find effective combat generals, but could also work well with those who fought vigorously and who obeyed direction.

How able was that civilian direction? By the end of 1863 Lincoln was no longer the unfamiliar rustic of the secession winter. The public knew him now, and opinion concerning the quality of his performance appeared to be very diverse and largely negative. Public confidence in the Administration's conduct of the war was draining swiftly because of Grant's costly, slow advances on Petersburg; "Tecumseh" Sherman's swift thrust toward Atlanta was still uncompleted. Even in highest Republican ranks there were gnawing fears of breakdowns in those major military pushes and of Democratic victories at the polls in 1864 undoing all gains. It was anything but clear that the Democrats were committing themselves to second place nationally as long as they were willing to accept Confederate survival as a war result. By 1864 the Republicans had brought into the Union coalition the War Democrats who might otherwise have made the Democratic party more responsive to the public temper about reunion. Still either Grant or Sherman could undo all the accrued improvements in the Union's political as well as military situations. And Democrats retained the sharp weapon of race prejudice.

Little wonder that worried, disgruntled Republicans were uncertain whether a new presidential candidate might not improve the party's chances for a second victory. President-guessing became a common sport. These lists reflect the aggressive, youthful, faction-ridden character of the party, and the desperation many of its leaders felt to win the White House and Congress at least once more. No matter what merely partisan or selfish purpose inspired individual efforts toward Republican successes in 1864, the basic impulse remained the reasonable conviction that a Democratic triumph would mean Confederate independence, the perpetuation of slavery, and the further fragmentation of the dis-United States. Early in August, 1864, Lincoln's Illinois friend David Davis summed up these hopes and fears when he wrote, confidentially, to an intimate, "Depend upon it, we must have [military] successes such as will satisfy the people, that the end [of the war] can be seen, or the election will be endangered. . . . If the South succeeds, then there is no common bond of union in the Northern States. The disintegration goes on and cannot stop. . . . Keep these views to yourself, and burn this letter."

To be sure, Lincoln badly wanted a second nomination. But since Andrew Jackson's time no President had won two terms. If Lincoln's ambition held, his renomination had to be won without over-straining his party's ties.

Fortunately, history and the Constitution allowed Republicans the longest permissible span of time in office after hostilities began before the 1864 test had to be faced. But that time came round at last. And competitors for the Republican-Union nomination surfaced almost as soon as 1864 began.

Would-be replacements for Lincoln spanned the Republican spectrum. Salmon Portland Chase's party supporters, convinced that a Lincoln renomination spelled disaster, puffed up a "boom" favoring the Treasury Secretary. But from behind the scenes the President arranged for pro-Lincoln endorsements to emerge from several state legislatures including Ohio, Chase's home. By early March, Chase withdrew his name from consideration as a presidential candidate; he was to campaign lustily for Lincoln. Benjamin F. Butler, the colorful and efficient Union military occupation commander of captured New Orleans and a former Democratic politican, appeared for a while a likely bridge to the War Democrats as well as to radical Republicans. But he lacked strength within the party's organizations, and he refused a possible vice-presidential spot. Even more colorful, John Charles Frémont, the original Republican presidential candidate in 1856 and a pro-emancipation Union general, enjoyed a brief play as a "Radical Republican" party candidate before the Republican-Union nominating convention made its

choice, and after it, as a substitute for Lincoln. Frémont had too many unfor-
giving enemies to displace Lincoln, however, and his champions never had an
inside track. Grant kept aloof from presidential lures.

Despite all differences and ambitions, the party's June nominating convention at Baltimore renominated Lincoln so smoothly in the initial balloting,
that, in the opinion of eminent scholars, "the ease with which this unanimity
was obtained becomes a matter of wonder." A partial reason for this unanticipated accord lay in Lincoln's adroit backstage maneuverings involved in the
construction of the platform and the choice of the Tennessee War Democrat
Andrew Johnson as his vice-presidential nominee. These agreements brought
concord rather than acrimony because, however reluctantly, most party leaders came to understand that Lincoln's candidacy was essential to victory.
Even William Cullen Bryant's *New York Evening Post*, often warmly critical
of Lincoln's ways and means, admitted just before the convention that "in the
first place he [Lincoln] is popular with the plain people, who believe him honest, with the rich people, who believe him safe, with the soldiers, who believe
him their friend, and with the religious people, who believe him to have been
specially raised up for this crisis." Continuing, the *Post*, which had earlier
suggested postponing the Republican nominating convention because no acceptable candidate was likely, commented on the party leaders' awareness of
Lincoln's popularity. They had "eagerly attached themselves to the car of his
success," Bryant editorialized.

Lincoln won unity less easily when the vice-presidential nomination was
in question. Party chieftains, unable to displace or dominate him, desired intensely to corral the next highest national office or to prevent it from coming
under control of another faction. The incumbent Vice-President, Hannibal
Hamlin of Maine, wanted a second term, but found that his state had too little weight to carry the convention. Massachusetts' Senator Charles Sumner
helped prevent party increments from going to New York whose Republican
leader, Lincoln's Secretary of State William Seward, supposedly exerted a
conservative influence over the President. But Lincoln had decided earlier
that the party had positive reasons to select Andrew Johnson, former United
States senator from Tennessee (1857–62) and Lincoln's military governor
in that state (1862–64), for the Vice-Presidency. As a War Democrat, Johnson symbolized the coalition character of the Union party. A stanch patriot from a seceded state, and the tough military governor there, he
exemplified the category of southern whites to whom Lincoln had addressed
the emancipation and reconstruction policy proclamations. Coming, like Lincoln, from the nation's central heartland, both men together appeared to offer
voters homely, relevant virtues. Middle-of-the-road Republicans had their
men.

The President swung the convention to this view so successfully that the
Johnson nomination did not require a second ballot and so adroitly that the
party's factions accepted the choices. Republican radicals were placated by
the platform which, with Lincoln's specific encouragement to the Republican
National Committee, called for continuing the war until the rebels' "uncondi-

tional surrender" was achieved. This meant that no military armistice was acceptable involving continuation of Confederate civil governments. Republicans adopted the old abolitionist position that slavery was incompatible with free labor and politics and was the cause of secession and war. This now became a national party platform plank. Emancipation was therefore necessary by means of an amendment to the Constitution. The platform supported the use of Negro troops, and insisted that laws of war apply equally to captured black bluecoats as to whites. Republican delegates approved immigration and homestead encouragements, the Pacific Railroad subsidy, and public debt policies. Last, the platform noted unhappily Napoleon III's adventure in Mexico, which had thrust a puppet emperor, Maximilian into uncertain power.

The Republican unity in the convention probably reflected the fact that they were never so divided as a tenacious scholarly tradition has suggested. Republicans' aspirations were bound up with the nation's survival and military victory; Democrats' conservative purposes depended upon defeat. The 1862 and 1863 elections had created a pattern of Republican factionalism but also of interdependence. By 1864 Lincoln and all Republicans agreed on victory, reunion, and emancipation as war aims, and the platform emerged as the proof of basic accords. Reconstruction was a focus of some difference, and the platform evaded details about this problem, but it did not become a fundamentally divisive issue.

Lincoln's convention triumph did not dissipate fears within the party that Republicans, from the President down, would be defeated in November and that emancipation and reconstruction policies, still pinned only to the President's proclamations, would thereafter be reversed. Therefore, a few weeks after the convention Maryland's Republican Representative Henry Winter Davis and Ohio's Senator Ben Wade decided to support the executive proclamations with statutes. The Wade-Davis bill of July, 1864, required 50 per cent of inhabitants in rebel states, not 10 per cent of the 1860 voters as in Lincoln's plan, to serve as a viable electorate, stipulated that the same criminal and civil laws embrace whites and Negroes, and specified that emancipation was perpetual and irreversible. Through habeas corpus appeals, United States courts were to hear cases in which Negroes alleged that they were held in involuntary servitude or enjoyed inadequate procedural remedies in states' courts. Slaveowning was to become a new federal crime.

Considerably risking the party unity won at the recent nominating convention, Lincoln pocket-vetoed the Wade-Davis bill. He feared that signing it would rile conservatives and disturb the state governments in Arkansas and Louisiana begun under his 1863 orders. Yet he had also to placate the numerous Republican congressmen and their constituents who supported the bill, and there were many features of it he found appealing. Therefore Lincoln issued a curious explanatory proclamation with his pocket veto, in which he specified the reasons for his extraordinary negative stand and invited southerners to come back into the Union under either plan.

In response, Wade and Davis published a "Manifesto" condemning Lin-

coln's fence-straddling. Pessimistic Republicans increased pressures to
"dump" Lincoln as the Republican-Union nominee, in favor of Butler, Chase,
or Frémont, among others, by means of another party convention. But this
move lacked broad support and collapsed utterly as news of military and naval successes came in, especially from Georgia and the Shenandoah Valley. By
November Lincoln had won back support of all shades of Republicans and War
Democrats. He rewon the politicos because he never lost popular support,
and because he gave evidence that he was moving toward the Wade-Davis
position. All party chieftains in Congress and in the states supported the Republican slate in November balloting; Lincoln was emerging as the most
effective party leader since Jackson. If he and his party won the 1864 election
his preeminence would be confirmed. But as the Democrats' convention time
neared, odds appeared very heavy against this. Six days before the Democratic
convention Lincoln secretly prepared this prediction: "This morning, as for
same days past, it seems exceedingly probable that the Administration will
not be reelected. Then it will be my duty to so cooperate with the President-
elect, as to save the Union between the election and the inauguration; as he
will have secured his election on such ground that he cannot possibly save it
afterwards."

The Democrats' platform and presidential nominee, selected at the party's
Chicago convention late in August, justified this gloomy prediction concerning the opposition "ground" and provided compelling reasons for Republicans to draw together behind Lincoln. Despite the advantages they enjoyed
of ceaselessly criticizing everything the Administration attempted or failed to
try, and of not having to create specific programs which Republicans could
attack, Democrats were seriously divided, perhaps more than their opposition. No clear leader had emerged to replace Stephen A. Douglas, who had
died in 1861, and even his memory was tarred by the party's troubles since
1854. In 1864 the most educable, Union-centered elements had abandoned
the party at least for the duration of the war, and perhaps permanently, to
enter Union party coalition with the Republicans. These moderate Democrats
were anxious for the states to reunite, but were willing for the war to go on
until reunification was won. Emancipation was by no means happily accepted
by these cross-over Democrats. The Union was their watchword, and, preferably, it would be as much like pre-Sumter society as possible.

Even such War Democrats contrasted sharply with the peace-at-any-cost
faction aligned with Vallandigham. To far right ideologues the war was a failure and emancipation a tragic error. Instead of elections, these pessimists
wished special referenda and conventions to opt for some form of armistice
with the Confederacy even if it resulted in recognition of southern independence, although they preferred a return to pre-Sumter conditions. Many Peace
Democrats were also members of secret anti-war societies, and Republicans
damned them all as disloyal copperheads. Retrospectively it appears that
1863 was the high water mark of the peace faction. Its excesses, and the failures of its front-runners to win local elections in 1863 gave relative moderates
the louder party voice at the 1864 convention.

Democratic "moderates" of 1864 deserved the label only by comparison with the Vallandigham type. Moderates also wished the Union to return to pre-war ways, considered the war to be a failure, and were willing to acknowledge Confederate independence by armistice. But these men judged that a popular appeal directed to these ends must fail. Therefore they wished to obscure the defeatism so prevalent among Democrats, by stressing the uneasiness many uncommitted northerners felt concerning irritating wartime restraints and unsettling changes. Even middle-of-the-road Democrats appealed to racial fears and economic self-interest. Democrats extolled the liberty to be won through new guarantees for slavery, and the stability to be gained through opposition to the Republicans' Emancipation Proclamation and abolition amendment. These were powerful appeals to a generation which had never before searched out the permissible limits of dissent and one which felt deep concerns about the desirability of biracial coexistence on terms other than master-slave. If the Democratic convention could somehow straddle the defeatist hurdle without estranging the deeply conservative middle or far right militants, a victory at the polls, a military armistice, and some form of slavery might yet emerge.

Considering also the well-publicized Republican factionalism, it is little wonder that the Democratic nominating convention assembled in Chicago late in August, 1864, expected democrats to win the election. The group nominated McClellan on the first ballot, with a scattering of votes for Governors T. H. Seymour of Connecticut and Horatio Seymour of New York. In effect, Lincoln's success in assembling and holding together the Republican-War Democratic (Union) coalition required the Democrats to shy away from their most conservative anti-war men. McClellan's theme since 1862 was not that a military victory was unobtainable but that Republican interferences had prevented him from winning the victory. Holding firmly to this thesis, he could be put forward as symbol of the patriotism of Democrats, whose basic position was that a Union military victory was impossible and undesirable.

In later years McClellan's admirers insisted that he was a reluctant candidate who never expected to win. Actually he and his supporters had worked hard to gain him the nomination and the evidence is impressive that he expected to win not only the nomination but the election.

To that end, the convention balanced his candidacy with that Congressman George H. Pendleton of Ohio for the Vice-Presidency. Pendleton trailed James O. Guthrie of Kentucky on the first ballot, but, after Guthrie's withdrawal, won unanimous nomination on the second. He was a conservative Democrat who had served in the House of Representatives since 1857. Pendleton leaned toward Vallandigham's views but had refrained from the rhetorical excesses which had resulted in the latter's loss of reelection, his arrest, and his banishment behind Confederate lines. Now back in the United States, Vallandigham, ignored by Lincoln's internal security officers, saw to it that the Democratic party's platform, if not the presidential nominee, spoke to the concerns of far-right peace men. Receiving enthusiastic support from the entire convention, the platform declared that the war was a failure, that states' rights and individual liberties were crushed under the Lincoln Administration's martial despotism, and that an immediate armistice with the South was necessary as this would be preliminary to the calling of a national convention to restore constitutional relationships as they existed in 1860. The Democratic platform carefully skirted the emancipation question; it was easier to let McClellan's glamour substitute for frankness or policy. Shrewdly touching the rawest sensibilities of the North, the Democrats protested not only altering pre-war racial relationships, but also the national government's disarming allegedly disloyal persons as a denial of the constitutional right to bear arms.

A week after the convention, McClellan, having become convinced that the party's "peace before reunion" plank could not attract adequate public support, disavowed that basic position. Instead he came out publicly for reunion as a condition of peace, but avoided the emancipation issue. Historians have said that the convention behaved foolishly by condemning the war, then nominating a general for President, and that the peace men, bitter at this choice, sat on their hands. But it was Vallandigham who moved that the convention make its choice of McClellan unanimous. Neither party let the election go by default, although some peace Democrats displayed a lack of enthusiastic campaigning for "Little Mac."

Realizing that the Democratic combination of a warrior-candidate with a peace platform was likely to exert wide appeal, Republicans closed ranks after their convention. Happy news of Sherman's occupation of Atlanta, of Grant's continuing progress at Petersburg, of Sheridan's triumphs in the Shenandoah, and of Farragut's Mobile Bay success helped to overshadow party divisions. Radicals won a concession from Lincoln in the form of the resignation from his Cabinet of the detested conservative Montgomery Blair, Postmaster General. Chase went on the stump in Lincoln's favor and then to the Chief Justiceship of the United States. Frémont withdrew from further presidential adventures and all efforts to drop Lincoln from the slate, by such visionaries as Horace Greeley, ceased. Thereafter almost every prominent Republican figure supported the party's candidates from the President down the line. The young Republican party had established itself as a national organization. It was capable of containing its differences and offering the voters a comprehensible and comprehensive program without splitting apart as the Democratic party had done in 1860.

The Democrats had also improved their party condition. Unlike the 1860 Buchanan-Douglas-Breckenridge split, in 1864 the party managed to hold together. An attempt by disgruntled peace men to build a splinter party fell apart, and the Democracy came forward, with a few reservations and grumblings, in favor of McClellan. This election was to be no runaway Republican triumph. Politics-watchers tested every straw the political winds blew in. Republican-Unionists won local early contests in Connecticut, New Hampshire, and Vermont, but these safe states were discounted. Kentucky was more significant. In August, 1864, that state held the first elections after the Republican convention, and a swing there in favor of Democratic local and judicial candidates was accounted a reaction against obnoxious emancipation and conscription policies.

It grew clear that, despite Republican conservatives' appeals that he do so, Lincoln would not back-track on emancipation. Therefore, Republican state leaders including the governors of Maine and Indiana, pressured him to placate popular opinion other ways, with lower draft quotas for their states and postponement of conscription until after the election. Although hated along with emancipation, the draft was the paramount symbol of firm national purpose. At the President's suggestion, Grant and Sherman testified publicly that the many thousands of Americans already in Union Army ranks and their families and friends would not support an Administration that was uncertain about continuing the draft.

Grant favored soldiers' voting in their states' elections in person or by absentee ballots, and allowed furloughs to thousands of bluecoats during the election so that they could vote in states which offered no absentee provisions. On election days there was the extraordinary spectacle not of expected military dominations of elections but of soldiers transforming themselves into citizens; of the sword sustaining rather than suppressing the ballot box. In a century when usurpers-on-horseback were common, the citizen-soldier voting was a measure of the strength the nation had amassed since the Sumter shame.

It was generally realized that having elections at all in 1864 and, especially, allowing bluecoats to ballot were hazardous and unique courses. Grant favored both courses and agreed with Lincoln that compared with all other nations "our circumstances are novel and exceptional." After the elections, Lincoln echoed commentators here and abroad, in marveling at "the extraordinary calmness and good order with which the millions of voters met and mingled at the polls." Whatever else voters decided—and it is important to remember that soldiers were voting—they opted to carry on the war until slaveless reunion resulted. No split occurred between civilians and soldiers. Democracy grew stronger because in 1864 it risked unmanaged choices and unmanageable hazards.

Aware of these implications, excited contemporaries likened the 1864 election to a battle by ballots equal in impact to Gettysburg and Vicksburg. Electioneering went on at an accelerated pace in every city, village, and country crossroad. Editorials, pamphlets, and broadsides issued by new associations such as the Loyal Publication Society, Union League, and Loyal League for the Republicans, and the Society for the Diffusion of Political Knowledge for the Democrats pleaded with readers; sermons or speeches lured the illiterate. Parades, barbecues, fairs, and picnics became forums for candidates and hecklers. College classrooms and debating societies transformed themselves into partisan associations. Convalescing Union soldiers and officers addressed crowds of sympathetic auditors; pageants and allegories produced by women's charitable auxiliaries, churches, labor unions, and farmers' societies, provided simplified tableaux to instruct the politically innocent. Patriotic organizations recruited runaway Negro slaves to hammer away on the theme of servile degradation; exiled southern Unionists disclosed the perils patriots faced in the Confederacy; bluecoats, home to vote, described the serious consideration they and their comrades devoted to the election's alternatives while in camp or hospital.

Evidence accumulated that the Republican-Union appeal was effective. Democratic stagemasters convinced McClellan that he must participate directly. Lincoln remained aloof from public campaigning, while he shrewdly played the patronage reins his position and experience provided, and allowed party heavyweights from the Congress, the Cabinet, and the state organizations to carry the Republican-Union message throughout the country. Secretary of State William Seward, speaking at Auburn, New York, early in September, ostensibly to celebrate the fall of Atlanta, typified the Republican strategy. Though detested by left of center Republicans, Seward knew that his New York party had managed a common front against the Democrats. Seward gained enthusiastic reception by linking the 1864 Democratic platform written at the Chicago convention to proposals of the secession winter and to the situation the Lincoln Administration faced when it assumed office in March, 1861. Then as in 1864 the Confederacy existed, proponents of an armistice or truce intrigued against effective military operations, and Democrats proposed "a languid debate with a view to an ultimate National Convention." Did Democrats suppose that Americans wished to return to "hopeless imbecility and rapid progress of national dissolution?"

All these electioneering techniques were familiar from pre-war times. What was different in 1864 was the intense interest of ordinary voters in issues and principles, men and measures, causes and aspirations. Violence at hustings and polls was almost non-existent despite dreary predictions of holocaust. In the midst of the western world's longest, most searching, and destructive war since Napoleon's surrender, the United States allowed ballots, many cast by soldiers, to determine basic civil and military policies and the destiny of millions of black people.

Tough young combat veteran William Grosvenor of Connecticut, a man of sharp insights into political realities, offered an uncynical evaluation. Since mid-1863 "the apprehensions of the wisest loyalists and the shrewdest rebels were alike turned to the political contests at the North, as affording to the rebellion a second chance of the victory which it could no longer hope to attain by triumphs in battle," he wrote immediately after the 1864 election returns were in. Continuing, Grosvenor noted that:

> The trial by ballot reached its crisis in the presidential election. In that most exciting canvass, conducted with the utmost license of speech and of the press even in the face of a great civil war, all the influences which could pervert the judgment, sap the loyalty, or shake the purpose of the people, culminated in a final appeal against the war and the administration. Ignorance of our system of government, of the duties of citizens and the rights of States; gross misrepresentations of fact as to the events and results of the struggle; attachment to a General [McClellan] who had been

the popular favorite in the days of our military babyhood; the conservative dryrot, hostility to all reform, and especially hatred of the negro and the abolitionist; prices, taxes, and pecuniary burdens already more grievous to sordid souls than any national dishonor or calamity; dread of the phantom of usurpation and of the prospect of another draft; influence of foreign agents, of rebel sympathizers, and of secret organizations, whose machinery was north but whose motive power was south of the border; the magic spell of a party name, and the yet mightier power of a church and a foreign-born clan; all threatened to bring about the abandonment of a struggle, the sufferings and sacrifices of which had been brought home to every household by the new-made graves in all our churchyards, and the little mounds of earth on a thousand fields of conflict. It would not have been strange if a few thousand votes had changed the result. But though, as at Gettysburg, the victory was won only when almost the last brigade of reserve had been called to the front of the battle, it was complete and overwhelming; and the nation was saved in the trial of patriotism on the 8th of November, 1864, as decisively as on the 4th of July, 1863, it was assured of final victory in the trial of arms.

By all contemporary standards the 1864 elections were free, and by contemporary standards fair as well. Some military interference occurred in the Border States, where legislatures and constitutional conventions had imposed numerous loyalty tests. Some vote-buying took place in Indiana's Union party state slate, and gang-voting was noted in some cities, but these were politics-as-usual. Certainly Lincoln's claim to a second term was untainted. Although some losers shouted contrary estimations about fraud and corruption, McClellan's private statement reflects the unmanaged nature of the contest: "For my country's sake I deplore the result—but the people have decided with their eyes wide open."

Seeing alternatives clearly, Americans in and out of uniform gave Lincoln 55 per cent of the popular vote, 15 per cent more than Republicans had won four years earlier, and a thumping Electoral College majority (212–21) reflecting a 2,206,938 to 1,803,787 popular tally. The results dissipated nightmare fears of a hung election and provided an astonishing reversal to confident anti-war men. Only Delaware, Kentucky, and New Jersey went for "Little Mac." Illustrating the uncontrolled character of the election, Delaware swung to McClellan because of the soldier vote; his majority was 612 statewide. Six cornerstone states, New York, Connecticut, Pennsylvania, Maryland, Indiana, and Illinois, totalling 101 electoral votes, probably went for Lincoln as result of soldiers' ballots. The five other states that one way or another provided for soldier-voting would have gone Republican in any case.

It is difficult to reconcile the weighty evidence about the sharp choices voters saw in 1864, with the Tweedledum samenesses that, subsequently, some scholars insisted characterized Lincoln, McClellan, and non-candidates such as Frémont. "The patent fact . . . is that all parties in the North were Union parties," states the most authoritative overview of the Civil War and Reconstruction. But such a judgment, harkening back to estimates offered by E. A. Pollard and Gideon Welles among contemporary commentators, ignores the Republicans' commitments to emancipation and for ordinary elections and constitutional amendment rather than extraordinary referenda. The Republican position against any conference or armistice with Confederates that could be considered as recognition of their government was very clear to voters as basically opposed to what Democrats offered. This awareness made the 1864 contests, in Lincoln's apt phrase, so "passion-exciting," because they asked these questions: What sort of Union did the parties' leaders and followers aim to rebuild or to build? What status in state laws should the freed blacks enter?

On this score it should be noted that the 1864 election presupposed at the least a Union in which two parties would continue to contest policies, places, and personalities in every state. This implicit commitment to continuity was a product of the fact that real contests occurred that year about the most basic public matters, and that Democrats performed so well. Overall, Democrats won 45 per cent of the national vote. The party's candidates ran surprisingly close races in states generally accounted as Republican strongholds. Connecticut's 86,958 voters provided a Union majority of only 2,388; New Hampshire's 69,441 went Union by 3,451; New York's 730,723 by 6,749; Oregon's 18,345 by 1,431; and Pennsylvania's 573,375 by only 18,849. Although Republicans took all the New England states the rate of Democratic increase over their 1860 total was twice the rate of the Republican increase, 66,995 to 32,661. Republicans totalled only 50.6 per cent in the populous Middle Atlantic States, the McClellan centers, and he took New Jersey and Delaware.

Democratic vigor there was more than accommodated by Republican increases in the midwestern heartland states. Except for Kentucky where border state resentment was so severe because of emancipation and internal security policies that it became the only soldier-voting state to go Democratic, every state in this vast section moved into the Republican column, and with large majorities. In addition to wartime factors, this heavy endorsement was a response to Republican support for homestead legislation and military aid against Confederate armies and pro-Confederate guerrillas. Totals favoring Republicans in Nevada, a new state, and in the Pacific Coast States, suggest the existence of gratitude for the transcontinental railroad subvention policies the Lincoln Administration favored. The former Democratic edge in the West was blunted. Taking the national totals of counties each party won over the 1860 pattern, Republicans gained 719 to the Democrats' 393. But 878 counties, located in the main in the seceded states, did not participate at all. Surely, in 1868, if the reentrance of those states to political participation occurred, their votes would reverse the 1864 results. No wonder that Democratic stage-masters of 1864 looked ahead to the next presidential contest. Careful scrutiny of these figures allowed the reasonable expectation that, in the words of the closest student of the 1864 returns, "throughout the country, the Democratic Party was still at least equal to the Republicans in popular, if not electoral, strength."

The upshot of 1864 was a consensus, not about the nature of a rewon Union, but about the validity of continuing two-party politics and regular elections in order to decide that nature. If nothing else, 1864 taught that no subject was too sensitive or fragile to include in parties' agendas or elections' alternatives. As a result, even the unanticipatable strains of post-Appomattox years, including a ballooning population, the abolition of slavery, Reconstruction, and the unique impeachment of Lincoln's successor failed to diminish the decision-making functions of election contests. Referring to these results of 1864, Walt Whitman offered this acute judgment:

> What we have seen here is not, towering above all talk and argument, the . . . last-needed proof of democracy. . . . That our national democratic experiment, principle, and machinery could triumphantly sustain such a shock, and that the Constitution could weather it, like a ship in a storm, and come out of it as sound and whole as before, is by far the most signal proof yet of the stability of that experiment — Democracy — and of those principles and that Constitution.

Of course, no one could peer into the post-Appomattox future. Delighted that as result of the 1864 balloting he and his party colleagues had until March, 1869, to shape the Union that bluecoats had not yet rewon, Lincoln heartily endorsed the new 13th Amendment emancipation proposal, long stalled in the House. It soon went out to the states for ratification. Meanwhile he exerted efforts, ultimately unavailing, to gain admission to the Thirty-eighth Congress' lame-duck session, for delegates from Louisiana, his show-piece product of military reconstruction. The point is that even in the immediate post-election honeymoon atmosphere, warmed by increasingly glorious military news, intraparty differences about a reconstruction were substantial, not to speak of interparty disagreements.

During the 1864–65 winter, final military success itself seemed uncertain. In a shipboard conference on Febrary 3, 1865, Jefferson Davis' orders bound Confederate emissaries meeting with Lincoln not to agree to any terms less than recognition of Confederate independence, a condition specifically forbidden by the 1864 Republican platform even if Lincoln had been disposed to consider it. By this time, however, Davis was deluding himself that the South could win essential points. By the end of March Sherman was preparing to link with Grant, and Lee, trying to break out of the trap closing around him and the Confederate capital, failed, at irreparable cost. On April 2, Lee evacuated Petersburg which meant also the abandonment of Richmond; on April 9, at Appomattox Court House, he surrendered the remnants of his Army to Grant. The simple capitulation by Grant's orders conformed to the 1864 Republican-Union party platform, for it carefully excluded from its terms any political matters such as civil government recognition by the victors.

In striking contrast, when on April 18, Johnston surrendered to Sherman the last major rebel armed force, "Tecumseh" blundered badly by allowing armistice-like terms and received a deserved disavowal by the White House. Meanwhile, in his Second Inaugural Address (April 4), Lincoln pleaded for a merciful reconstruction. Then on April 11, he advocated publicly that Negroes as well as whites enjoy public schooling in Louisiana and, by implication, in all the other defeated Confederate states. Further, he proposed that literate Negroes and black veterans of the Union armies vote as well.

Little wonder that the President and all but the most conservative Republicans and War Democrats were in accord. For by April 11, 1865, Lincoln had grown up to the vision expressed in the Wade-Davis bill in which the two-party system would extend political democracy into the South, and in which the two races would coexist equally under states' laws as voters and as students in tax-supported public schools. Like the nation as a whole, the President had traveled an astonishingly long distance in matters of race relationships since 1861. The 1864 election had underlined the vigorous condition of American political and constitutional institutions. As result of those elections and as the fruit of bluecoats' sacrifices, he could see to a reconstruction involving, initially at least, the employment of national military force in the South. This was aimed at reaching new shores of improved political democracy and more decent race relations.

On April 14 Booth's bullet cut Lincoln down, brought in Andrew Johnson as President, and reopened questions men had warred four years to adjust. Proved in war, could two-party politics manage to function after peace returned?

Election of 1876

by *Sidney I. Pomerantz*

On November 8, 1876, the Republican New York *Tribune*, in its page one lead story announced the election of Democrat Samuel J. Tilden to the Presidency of the United States, and followed this news up with a supporting editorial on the significance of the victory. Four tumultuous months of tension and dissension followed. On March 2, 1877, the Democratic New York *World* ran a headlined account of how, finally, Rutherford B. Hayes had been "elevated" to the office of President, and the next day carried a seering editorial on this Republican political "triumph." The circumstances surrounding this startling election reversal and the nature of the events that occurred in the period between the closing of the polls and the final adjudication of the contest make up one of the most striking episodes in the history of the American Republic and shed important light on the dynamics of the democratic process as it was tried and tested at a critical juncture in the post-Civil War era.

While the *Tribune* prematurely conceded Hayes' defeat, blaming Grantism, Butlerism, and Mortonism for the outcome, no such admission came from *The New York Times*, whose 6:30 a.m. "extra" that fateful Wednesday morning reported the election results as uncertain, with 181 electoral votes for Hayes and 184 for Tilden. Florida's 4 votes remained in doubt. But except for South Carolina, Louisiana and Florida, the South was solidly Democratic, along with New York, New Jersey, Connecticut, and Indiana. To Zach Chandler, Republican national chairman, and other like-minded strategists, the loss of these pivotal states pointed to almost certain defeat. The *Times* editors

168

thought otherwise, as did William E. Chandler, New Hampshire national committeeman, member of the National Executive Committee, and veteran party secretary in the Grant campaigns. With the three southern states in question still under military rule and the record of past national victories to go by, success might yet be theirs, but no time was to be lost and no vote remain uncounted. To the impartial and independent New York *Herald*, this "neck and neck" race, reminiscent of the contests of 1797, 1801, and 1824, fraught with possibilities of danger unparalleled since 1860, hinged on Florida's 4 electoral votes, which could go either way.

Democratic politicos were almost ready to concede these 4 votes and even South Carolina's 7 to Hayes, but were prepared to do battle for Louisiana's 8. Whatever the partisan calculations, the stage was set for the unfolding of a national drama of vast proportions, best understood in the light of the course of Reconstruction up to that time and against the background of the party struggles of an increasingly industrialized and urban America.

Soaring newspaper circulation figures after the election attested to the intensity of popular interest and concern. The *Herald*, widely acknowledged as one of the most venturesome and reliable of journals, ran up a sale of two hundred thousand copies on November 8. Commentators attributed the Democratic showing to the growing sophistication of the electorate, and the Republican managers were censured for relying on "politics as usual" to meet the challenge of a resurgent Democracy that had repeated its congressional victory of 1874. Clearly, the resolution of this unprecedented crisis on whatever level called for the highest statesmanship and revealed fissures in the political structure of the Republic of momentous historic significance.

On the surface, and on balance, the year 1876, marking as it did the centennial of national independence, seemed promising indeed as Americans gathered to take stock of their accomplishments at the International Exposition and World's Fair scheduled to open in the spring at Philadelphia's Fairmount Park. This was the sixth of the world's great fairs, and the first for the United States, and it served as the symbol, if not the concrete reality, of the new age, much as the politics of national reconciliation reflected the stresses and dilemmas of a modern state. A Gilded Age of individualism-run-riot, in politics, business, industry, and agriculture, was unprepared for the responsibilities and power now thrust upon men of little vision and less faith. America now emerged as a world power and influence in the arts and crafts increased as well as manufacturing. The products of soil and mine, factory and shop, produced a totality of exports which, for the first time that year, exceeded imports. The shift in the trade balance ushered in a new world outlook, and the Corliss Steam Engine exhibited at the fair's Machinery Hall supplied the power for the manufactured textiles, newsprint, wood products, leather goods, and numerous technological innovations contrived by mechanical ingenuity for mass production.

Walt Whitman and Mark Twain, John Greenleaf Whittier and Ralph Waldo Emerson, James Russell Lowell and William Dean Howells, Thomas Edison and Alexander Graham Bell lent distinction to the centennial year and underlined the sharp contrasts in cultural values, life styles, and diversity of interests to which America was heir. Custer's "Last Stand" that summer at the Battle of the Little Big Horn in the Black Hills of South Dakota signalized the climax of one phase of the westward movement, as it made way for another. Perhaps Thomas Henry Huxley's lecture tour of the United States in the summer and fall signified more than contemporaries imagined, for he set a people to thinking about its past along dynamic lines never before envisioned, and, in doing so, gave renewed vigor to the American democratic heritage.

The Republican party since its founding had played a crucial role in the making and testing of this tradition, a role that committed it to a broad program of national economic development and individual fulfillment. The spirit of enterprise as well as appeals to conscience motivated the formulation of policies designed to transform the central government into an agency for material progress and high moral purpose. The mandate of 1860 was translated into legislation to protect and nourish domestic manufactures, to promote internal improvements and a trans-continental railway network, to foster immigration, education, and western settlement, to make capital readily available by a national banking system and curb an elastic currency, and, through successful prosecution of the Civil War, to guarantee national survival and the equality of all men, black and white, before the law. The gains of a triumphant capitalism were spectacular, with benefits accruing to businessmen, workers, farmers, and all concerned. But a tragic war had been fought and its aftermath was bound to reflect the pressures and strains of radical change as well as all the congealed bitterness pent up in four years of conflict and retribution. Peace had come but so had crisis, and not all men are equal to the tasks before them or ready to exercise hard-won or newly-gained power in the public interest.

Partisan rivalries and intra-party conflicts, business calculations and sectional pressures, fiscal policy and banking practices, the "money power" and the silver interests, protectionist sentiment and a rising commerce—these were some of the underlying currents that sharpened the issues in the election of 1876. Over it all, like the sword of Damocles, hung the dark reality of Reconstruction, inextricably intertwined with the Grant regime. However much slavery may have been the root of sectional conflict, a burgeoning economy gave northerners the wherewithal to risk armed confrontation in espousing the cause of free men, free labor, and free land. The sequel to Appomattox witnessed the consolidation of wartime gains and entrenched the masters of capital in the seats of power, North and South. At first, geographical, occupational, and investment considerations divided the dominant leadership, but, by the early 1870's, the Republican high command, united as it was on the politics of Reconstruction and equality of suffrage for the Negro, took a traditionally conservative position on monetary management, inflation, and protection. Nor did economic exploitation of the South enter into Radical calculations, whatever may have been the plans, or schemes, of the northern business community. Yet in the end, mundane objectives, however diverse, intruded themselves where circumstances and opportunity warranted.

All along, signs of division in Republican party ranks were eagerly scanned by a rising Democratic opposition, local, state, and national. With more power, patronage, and plunder at stake than ever before in American history, cracks in Republican cohesiveness were bound to be exploited. With seven southern states returned to the Democratic fold by the end of 1874, the momentum of partisanship since 1870 had reached crescendo proportions, inspiring a strident confidence that Republican ascendency was over and that Radical Reconstruction was on the way out. Grant's every move was watched with jaundiced eye and congressional proceedings were marked by acrimonious debate and sharp parliamentary tactics. Even the Supreme Court was not immune from the swirling currents of party battle. Once Grant was in the Presidency, the Court's membership was raised from eight to nine, and William Strong, a former Pennsylvania supreme court justice, and Joseph P. Bradley, prominent New Jersey railroad attorney, were added to the bench. They supplied the needed votes in 1871 to reverse the decision of the Court a year before invalidating the Legal Tender Act of 1862 as it applied to contracts made prior to its passage. Independents and Democrats accused Grant of packing the Court, but, clearly, this was unfair to him and to those who held the $356 million greenbacks in circulation that year. Grant chose Bradley as the ninth Justice, and the appointment was to place the former attorney more than once in a crucial role of adjudication, especially so in the disputed election impasse.

With fiscal and monetary policy now firmly established as a congressional prerogative and the paper currency given a new lease on life, the Panic of 1873 served as a talking point for an increase in greenbacks and national bank note circulation. Despite terrific pressure from Senator O. P. Morton, of Indiana, and other inflationists, Grant took a stand for hard money, precipitating a party split of major proportions in Michigan, Indiana, Ohio, and Illinois, among other states. The net result was a divided party, Democratic capture in 1874 of the House of Representatives, and the election of Democratic governors in New York, New Jersey, Missouri, and Massachusetts. Efforts by such GOP regulars as James G. Blaine, James A. Garfield, and John Sherman to heal the monetary breach finally brought about the Act of 1875 for the resumption of specie payments by 1879, but not before strong criticism of its provisions by fiscall experts, Liberal Republicans, and sound money Democrats.

The chairman of the Senate Finance Committee, John Sherman of Ohio, carried great weight in and out of government, and yielded to no man in his commitment to fiscal integrity. In the interests of party harmony, he accepted the 1875 legislation as the best bill he could arrange. He was confident that once the greenbacks reached $300 million, funding would be adequate to meet redemption requirements in specie. This proved to be the case, thanks to a favorable trade balance, heavy European investment in government bonds and a mounting surplus in the Treasury. A collateral objective in backing this resumption bill was to take the issue out of the coming presidential election, but this was not to be. The Democrats in Congress voted against the bill, almost to a man, and in the Ohio gubernatorial contest that year it was a major issue, with Sherman backing Rutherford B. Hayes against the incumbent Democrat and fiat money champion, William Allen. Hayes, who had been in Congress and served two terms as governor, had impeccable Union qualifications, and mustered formidable Republican support. Party factionalism was forgotten as Sherman, Carl Schurz, and O. P. Morton joined in canvassing for Hayes, whose narrow victory catapulted him into national prominence. Sherman pressed this advantage, removing himself as a possible contender for the Republican presidential nomination, and urging instead a united Ohio delegation for Hayes.

More than just the year of panic, 1873 also marked the passage of the Coinage Act, a piece of legislation connected with plans for resumption of specie payments, stabilizing the currency, and promoting foreign trade by a single, gold standard. George S. Boutwell, then Secretary of the Treasury, his technical adviser, Henry Richard Linderman (later the first Director of the Bureau of the Mint) and John Sherman sought to head off an anticipated sharp rise in silver production and a corresponding fall in the price of silver by demonetizing the metal and seeking an outlet for excess bullion by a "trade dollar." This they achieved, but in so doing let loose in 1876 an avalanche of protest from the silver interests. Newspapers in Boston, New York, Chicago, and Cincinnati attributed the dropping of silver coinage to sinister if not conspiratorial forces. Congress joined in the hue and cry, demanding a return to bimetallism, and the next year gave widespread currency to its judgment of the law as the "Crime of '73." Whatever the later disclaimers of Boutwell and Sherman as to the full implications of the law in its impact on the silver market, the act, concludes historian Allen Weinstein in a closely reasoned analysis, "worked a silent revolution in American monetary policy," a view that is underscored by the research of other scholars.

And so, the economics of peace and Reconstruction loomed ever more ominously on the horizon of the centennial election, tempering the ambitions of ordinary men by the need for extraordinary statecraft, lest lack of expertise in the governing of an increasingly complex industrial society invite political reprisal, if not disaster. Legal tenders, specie payments, and silver coinage were matters sure to complicate the voting patterns of an electorate already strongly committed to panaceas and formulas for material well-being through political salvation.

High on the list was the protective tariff, which probably provided the decisive element in Pennsylvania and New Jersey in assuring the election of Lincoln, and which came to be identified with regular Republican policy during and after the war. The exodus of southern delegations from Congress in 1861 opened the way for the Morrill Act of that year and set in motion an upward revision of duties in 1862 and 1864 that reached all-time highs, benefiting cotton textile manufacturers, wool and woolens producers, and the iron and steel industry, among others. In 1870 rates were pushed up further, with specific duties adding to the tariff barriers. A 10 per cent reduction in 1872 was withdrawn three years later. Large-scale consumers, especially the railroads, were hard-pressed for capital to match the tariff-controlled price structure, and in many segments of industry the plea was heard for free raw materials, or, at most, a tariff for revenue only. Whether a reconstructed South and an expanding West would long remain in line under protectionist tutelage was problematical but in crucial states where coal, iron ore, steel, wool, and lumber dominated the economy, elections could and did turn on the tariff question.

The deepening depression of the 1870's proved fertile ground for the seductive claims of protection, but by the summer of the centennial year the prospects of the export trade for cotton, grain, and provisions were noticeably improved, despite uncertainties about prices at home and in America's best market, the United Kingdom. In consequence, the low tariff forces became increasingly vocal, sharpening the issues and prompting the pressure groups to their utmost exertions in this and related fields. Whatever the collateral issues, in the last analysis the election turned on Radical Reconstruction and the policies of the Grant Administration as they impinged upon the civic sensibilities of an aroused people. While 1874 marked the beginning of the end of Republican ascendancy in the South, by the close of the year the party still held on to four states and a vast army of officials — postmasters, court functionaries, United States marshals, and tax collectors. Radical Reconstruction was still very much in evidence, and the pall of the ever-threatening Enforcement Acts, with their sanction for the use of federal troops, hung over the South. Despite sweeping popular and electoral majorities, the Grant regime was unable to stem a rising tide of disapproval within the party ranks and in the nation at large, so much so that prospects for victory in 1876 seemed slim indeed even with the predictable Negro vote. The moral collapse shook the very foundations of the party structure and reverberated through the councils of government.

The Civil War had been devastating in men and in treasure. It was inevitable that those committed to high moral purpose, and there were many, should view with dismay and indignation the crumbling of ethical conduct in business and the startling erosion of civic integrity in public office. Idealism and sacrifice had given way in the post-bellum decade to materialism and greed. America could glory in its vastly expanding industrial plant, its engineering skill and mechanical ingenuity, its far-flung railroad trackage now spanning a continent, its increasingly intricate communications network, its conquest of the Great Plains by cattlemen and then wheat farmers, and its carving out of a mining empire on the far western frontier. A triumphant nationalism, bolstered by press and pulpit, by increasingly widespread schooling, and by the lavish generosity of a beneficent government seemed to carry all before it. Even the South, wracked by war and destruction though it had been, was enveloped in the new trends and was brought into the mainstream of the American economy, cotton culture and all, with an increasingly numerous farm yeomanry and small business class. Yet all was not well with America. Politics had become big business, and the rewards of partisanship, the stakes of power staggered the imagination of those in the seats of the mighty and led to temptation.

Workingmen and farmers, businessmen and politicians, clergymen and popular idols, all were caught up in the same acquisitive madness. Neither financial panic, deepening depression, widespread unemployment, agrarian unrest, nor general economic dislocation seemed to serve as steadying influences in a decade of unprecedent crises. Scandal followed upon scandal, and the ruthlessness of private competition spilled over to engulf the national Administration and the conduct of politics on every level. Daniel Drew, Jim Fisk, Jay Gould and other Wall Street speculators had their counterparts among officeholders, and even would-be statesmen. The "Salary Grab" of Congress in 1873, denounced by its critics as a "Back-Pay Steal," is a case in point, underscoring the callous disregard of the public in the very halls of the Capitol. Little wonder that the Credit Mobilier revelations should have reached right up to Vice-President Schuyler Colfax, and touched men like Representatives James A. Garfield and William D. Kelley, and Senator William B. Allison as well, not to mention such Union-Pacific officials as the road's vice-president, T. C. Durant and Oakes Ames, the financier and congressman who conceived of the construction company set-up in the first place and distributed its stock where it would "do the most good."

Even worse scandals were in store for Grant and the Republican regulars. By the election year an alert congressional opposition had ferreted out a widespread pattern of corruption in the executive departments. Added to these woes was the indictment of the President's private secretary, Orville E. Babcock by a St. Louis grand jury, the impeachment of Secretary of War William W. Belknap, and the resignation under fire of General Robert C. Schenck as minister to Great Britain. Babcock, a friend of John McDonald, central figure in the Whiskey Ring conspiracy, won acquittal on the charge of "defrauding the revenue," but his usefulness was over. Belknap, appointed by Grant in 1869, resigned in the spring of 1876 when charged with the sale of a post-tradership at Fort Sill in the Indian territory. Tried before the Senate, he nevertheless escaped conviction. General Schenck, who had lent his name to the promotion in England of the sale of stock in the Emma Silver Mine in Utah, was censured by a House committee, and returned home after five years abroad. So it went: an almost endless piling up of shocking scandals in the Administration. On top of it all, Grant had dropped key men, further disrupting the executive branch and dividing the party. The loss of David A. Wells, Commissioner of Internal Revenue, of Ebenezer R. Hoar, Attorney-General, of Jacob D. Cox, Secretary of the Interior, and of Benjamin Bristow, Secretary of the Treasury, dealt telling blows to party hopes and party harmony.

The exodus of key decision-makers from the Administration buoyed the spirits of the opposition as it lent fuel to the flames of partisan discord. David A. Wells, an original Lincoln appointee, had proposed a program to promote productivity, assure prosperity, and cushion the dislocations of technological unemployment. He pleaded for a fiscal policy and currency measures that would reduce the government debt, convert greenbacks into bonds, curtail the excise and subsidy system, and step up the export trade. His cogent prose in favor of tariff reductions and economy in government struck a responsive chord in Democratic ranks, North and South. Yet Grant dropped him in

1870, under protectionist pressures. Wells continued to wield much influence in his field and was consulted by Garfield and later by Cleveland. Also in 1870 the Attorney-General, E. R. Hoar, brother of the influential Massachusetts Congressman George Frisbie Hoar, withdrew from the Cabinet to accommodate Grant, who was maneuvering to push through the Santo Domingo annexation treaty and needed the office to line up votes for ratification by the Senate. Hoar, an old-time Massachusetts "Conscience Whig," and superior jurist, had been the President's confidant in the legal tender cases, but he was sacrificed. In 1876 he worked hard to win the Republican nomination for Benjamin Bristow, finally swinging to Hayes. Then there was General Cox, a former Ohio governor with close ties to the Garfield wing of the party there, who also tendered his resignation to Grant in 1870, and let it be known that merit in the civil service and the sanctity of the public lands stood above party loyalties. Cox was of presidential timber, joined the Liberal Republicans, and won election to Congress in 1876, helping the Hayes ticket in a critical state.

Lastly, Secretary Bristow, an experienced prosecuting attorney and partner of the eminent Louisville lawyer, John M. Harlan, played a major role in the unfolding drama of the oncoming election. With two years of service in the Union Army behind him, Bristow, as United States attorney for the Kentucky district, became the scourge of the Ku Klux Klan and the lawless distilling rings. Summoned to Washington by Grant, first as Solicitor-General, and then, in the summer of 1874, as Secretary of the Treasury, Bristow quickly exposed the western distillers' systematic evasion of internal revenue excises and brought the Whiskey Ring principals to trial in St. Louis, Chicago, and Milwaukee. For this master coup, Bristow won acclaim from party moderates, who gathered in the spring of 1876 at New York's Fifth Avenue Hotel to place his name before the national convention; but he also incurred the bitter hostility of Grant, who made him agree to resign from office right after the nominating proceedings.

As if these developments were not enough of a burden for the party in power to bear, there emerged a group of moderate and liberal northern Republicans, spokesmen for finance and industry, who were ready to make common cause with the rising conservative Democrats of the "redeemed" states of the South. As the possibility of these alignments crystallized in the mid-seventies, the hopes of the freedmen and the imperatives of Radical Reconstruction were lost sight of; even the Negro vote was no longer generally considered a vital element in the mapping of party strategy. Superficially, the national election returns in 1868 and 1872 might have led an ardent Republican to assume that his party was invincible and did not even need the vote of the freedmen in the South to assure victory, but, as historian W. Dean Burnham indicates, beneath the surface there were signs of critical weakness. Popular and electoral totals did not tell the whole story. Thin majorities in 1868 in a half dozen crucial states and the collapse of the Greeley campaign in 1872 clouded the true state of party vulnerability. In 1874 the cracks in Republican armor were revealed as well as the need to seek out southern support, Negro or white, if it could be had. With national elections and an extensive federal patronage in the South at stake, Stalwarts clashed with Mugwumps over the expedient course to follow.

The crumbling unity in Republican party ranks was matched by a corresponding fragmentation of support for congressional Reconstruction. By the early 1870's, the zeal of the older Radical leadership gave way to the opportunism of younger men. Promises to the freedmen were forgotten, and in place of the protective arm of the Freedmen's Bureau came a reassertion of domination by the planter class. Not only had death, defeat at the polls, disillusionment, and defection thinned the ranks of the Radicals, but with each passing year after 1870 the old southern leadership, rallying under the banner of "home rule" and the slogans of redemption and conservatism, reasserted itself, not hesitating to resort to a whole arsenal of intimidating tactics in state after state to regain power. Grant seemed to have neither the will nor desire to take a firm stand against the rising tide of Bourbonism despite the public displeasure of his circle of Stalwart advisers.

At first the cold steel of federal troops under sanction of the Enforcement Acts of 1870–1871 kept the Radical governments functioning in such states as South Carolina, Louisiana, Arkansas, and Mississippi; but this did not deter the opposition, whose numbers were swelled when the Amnesty Act of 1872 allowed most of the former Confederates back into politics. In Louisiana, for example, two contending "governments" sought control after the 1872 election, one headed by the conservative John McEnery, and the other by Governor William P. Kellogg, a Radical Republican backed by Grant through a four-year struggle. In Arkansas, Grant gave his aid to the Radicals, only to witness a Conservative victory in November, 1874. As for Mississippi, it was "redeemed" by the notorious "Mississippi Plan" of November, 1875, which set a pattern of strong-arm politics that was repeated a year later in South Carolina, Florida, and Louisiana under circumstances of grave national implication.

Democratic victory in 1874 had far-reaching consequences, for the North as well as the South, for the President as well as the Congress, and for the forthcoming national election. The Democratic triumph in the New York gubernatorial contest brought the widely heralded winner, Samuel J. Tilden, forward as a strong contender for his party's presidential nomination, and a fortuitous set of circumstances supplied the leverage for getting the Democratic campaign off to a head start. Republicans were compelled to reassess their commitments to Radical Reconstruction and Negro suffrage, as contrasted with the uncertainties of continued southern support. The burden of identification with the maladministration and scandals of the Grant regime posed additional grave problems. The Democrats, while not unscathed, were saved from these risky concerns and left in a strategic position to capitalize on the weaknesses of the party in power.

Tilden's New York sweep projected him into the national limelight at the opportune moment. The Tilden image seemed consonant with the mood of the country, subdued as it was by the deepening gloom of depression and the traumatic social experiences of post-war Reconstruction. Tilden had taken commendable initiative in the exposure and prosecution of the Tweed Ring. Feared by the spoilsmen, apparently respected by the electorate, and honored by his professional legal colleagues, Tilden's promise of "reform" was more than fulfilled as governor. Frugality in administration, strict fiscal accountability, and relentless prosecution of wrongdoers, particularly the Canal Ring conspirators, marked his term of office and thrust him into the presidential ring. More and more, he addressed himself to national issues, criticizing especially the excesses of Radical Reconstruction and championing "home rule" for the southern states. Henry Watterson, fiery editor of the Louisville *Courier-Journal*, hailed him as "the ideal statesman," and worked tirelessly for his nomination and election. Further, he enjoyed good relations with his party's chieftains and had served for eight years as chairman of the Democratic state committee.

Faced by the certainty of a revived Democracy, the Republicans frantically sought to salvage political treasure in the three month lame-duck session of the Forty-third Congress, which convened on December 7, 1874. It was this session that marked some of the sharpest confrontations between the opposing parties since the war crisis itself, and saw the emergence of a confident Democratic leadership. Representative Samuel J. Randall, powerful Pennsylvania protectionist and parliamentarian par excellence, raked over the appropriation bills and sponsored some nine resolutions directed at executive department expenditures. He was ably seconded by his Democratic colleague on the Rules Committee, S. S. Cox, of New York. Together, they carried the partisan struggle forward with unrelenting vigor. This was especially so in the heated debates over the Civil Rights Act and over a new Force Bill. These last two pieces of Radical legislation were pressed by the chairman of the Judiciary Committee, the ineffable demagogue, General Ben Butler of Massachusetts, whose sharp tongue and mordant wit were no legislative match for the delaying tactics of Randall and his fellow filibusterers.

On the Civil Rights measure, designed to implement the 14th Amendment by guaranteeing equality of treatment in places of public accommodation and on juries for all persons, the issue was drawn both inside and outside Republican ranks. The memory of Charles Sumner, who had labored in vain for years for such a law, was invoked in support of a strong statute, including a provision for equal educational opportunity. In the end, even the milder version met fierce Democratic opposition. Randall kept the House in continuous session for over forty-eight hours and secured an almost endless series of rollcalls before the watered-down measure finally passed on February 4, 1875.

The Force Bill ran an even stiffer gauntlet. Against the pleas for moderation of Speaker Blaine and like-minded Republicans, the Radicals won party caucus endorsement of a bill to empower the President "to suspend the privilege of the writ of habeas corpus in Louisiana, Arkansas, Mississippi, and Alabama for two years and from thence until the end of the next session of Congress." In its final form, this stringent Force Bill passed in the House on February 27, but only after three nights and two and a half days of dilatory motions, and too late for action by the Senate.

The dramatic nature of the controversy over the Force Bill served to enhance Randall's reputation among the rank and file of his party. He had now become a national figure, assuming an ever more important role in the councils of the Democracy as it prepared to take over the control of the House. The work of the Forty-third Congress was about finished. Tax and appropriations bills went through, as did a Mississippi Jetty Bill and a bill to admit Colorado as a state. This last was to be just in time to add three electoral votes to the Republican column. On March 3, Maine's noble son, James G. Blaine, delivered his valedictory address after six years as Speaker of the House. It was clear to his auditors where his ambitions lay.

Immediately after adjournment of Congress, the new Senate held an executive session at which Senator Morton of Indiana tried to gain the admission to that body of the Louisiana Senator-elect P. B. S. Pinchback. But this able politician of mixed racial lineage was never seated. The incident highlighted the uneasy peace in such states in the South as still remained under Radical rule. Against this background, Blaine prepared to make his bid for the Presidency.

As the Forty-fourth Congress was organized under the Democrats, party discipline was strained by the personal rivalries of the leading claimants for place and by the ideological conflicts that marked the efforts to commit the organization to policies deemed essential to national success. Randall, who controlled the party in Pennsylvania, hoped to enlist sufficient support to win the Speakership, despite his unpopularity among low-tariff men in both parties. He had clashed with one of their spokesmen, Michael C. Kerr of Indiana, back in the spring of 1872, when the protectionists were put on the defensive. Now he faced Kerr again, but this time he confidently expected backing from southern and western representatives impressed by his commanding role in the last session and by his consistent advocacy of economy in expenditures, integrity in government, and opposition to jobbery and subsidies for private enterprise. His part in demanding "a searching investigation" of the Credit Mobilier scandal, an explanation of the reasons for the increase in the annual subsidy to the Pacific Mail Steamship Company, and full disclosure of related matters, won him many friends.

Randall was nonetheless in an exposed position as a congressman. He represented the only Democratic district in Philadelphia and was constantly under pressure from the business barons. Gould and the *World*, Tom Scott and his Pennsylvania Railroad henchmen, Dana and the *Sun*—all sought commitments, but were uniformly rebuffed. The Democratic caucus, with L. Q. C. Lamar of Mississippi in the chair, selected Kerr, with the winning votes coming from the backers of "Sunset" Cox, while Randall's tally held to the end. The West and South, voting in concert, carried the day.

Graciously accepting the result, Randall moved that Kerr's nomination be made unanimous: "Let the wish of the majority be the voice of all. Our mission must be to restore the government to its Constitutional purpose, and to expose the corruption of the administration." Privately, he confided to his friend Chauncey Black that "the charge that Scott wanted me had its effect." It was clear, however, that the road to political preferment depended on his ability to attract and retain southern support. Here was the clue to his conduct in the oncoming presidential contest.

When the House convened on December 6, 1875, Kerr won the Speakership; Randall, "by common consent," was the choice for chairman of the Committee on Appropriations, a prized post; and Cox not only became chairman of the Banking and Currency Committee, but in mid-February, when Kerr took seriously ill, began serving as Speaker *pro tempore*, almost on a regular basis, throughout the remainder of that long and eventful session.

"Retrenchment and Reform" was now to become more than an election-year promise. As for retrenchment, Randall set out to reduce expenditures by $50 million and to win the Senate and the President over to his proposals. He conferred with Bristow at the Treasury, with Taylor, the First Comptroller, and other authorities on national finance; but, best of all, he enlisted the cooperation of William S. Holman of Indiana, who sponsored an amendment to the rules which permitted inclusion in an appropriation bill of any measure to change existing law, provided it was "germane to the subject matter" and reduced expenditures. Requiring only a majority vote, this new rule enabled the Appropriations Committee to recommend salary reductions, abolition of offices, and even recasting all legislation concerning the public service.

In Randall's hands, the Holman Amendment became a powerful instrument in the Democratic arsenal and a check on the President, particularly where army appropriations and the use of federal troops were at issue. From March 8 to the last days of the session, Randall occupied himself with his appointed task, and could finally report savings of well over $34 million. Charles Foster, congressman from Governor Hayes' home district, and a Republican member of the committee, tried to minimize the achievement, noting that perhaps two-thirds of the savings represented deferred payments. Actually, the reductions were substantial, and a decided tribute to Randall's leadership. But while he championed economy, Randall did not extend this goal to embrace tariff reforms; there was to be no curtailment of the Customs Service nor the revenues derived therefrom. Somehow, the ambitious plans for tariff reduction envisioned by William R. Morrison of Illinois, Kerr's appointee as chairman of Ways and Means, did not materialize.

The Democrats were building a record to which they could point with pride. As for reform, exposure of the all-pervading rottenness in the crumbling administrative edifice that Grant and his cohorts had set up seemed the first order of business. While House investigating committees were busy at work digging up the malodorous details of official transgression in a half dozen departments, the Cabinet itself was rocked by revelations of dereliction too shocking to be ignored. The list seemed bottomless: the trial of Grant's secretary, Babcock, in St. Louis, Belknap's impeachment proceedings, the Whiskey Ring prosecutions, the Pacific Mail Steamship exposures, the involvement of Grant's brother, Orville, in Indian post-tradership deals, the New Orleans custom house derelictions, and the ramifications of the Emma Mine swindle. All these, and more, came to a head on the very eve of the national election.

On May 25, 1876, Abram S. Hewitt, seeking to arouse the country to the "need for national reform," stood in the House and reported for the Committee on Foreign Affairs its unanimous findings in the Emma Mine scandal, noting former Minister to Great Britain Robert C. Schenck's complicity in the sale and distribution of stock in this Utah silver mining speculation, and implicating, among others, Jay Cooke, McCulloch & Co., the international banking house. The whole unsavory scheme, said Hewitt, symbolized "the general demoralization which seems to have crept into every other branch of the public service." He saw it all as an insidious undermining of the foundations of free government, and asked his colleagues to join in the universal centennial prayer, "God save the Republic!" The report and the speech were widely acclaimed and became telling documents in the Democratic appeal to the electorate.

Though the central figure in the quest for the Republican nomination, Blaine took little for granted. As Speaker from 1869 to 1875, he had finally allowed the victorious Democrats to play out their role in opposition to the Radical program. Now, as minority leader, he watched for opportunities, from whatever side they might come, to further his cause. One immediate concern was the heading off of the third term movement for President Grant. If backed by a vast army of federal appointees, a renomination for Grant was a real possibility. Late in May, 1875, the President intimated that if duty called, he would not decline. To forestall such an eventuality, the new House, on December 15, adopted a resolution, 233 to 18 with 38 abstentions (Blaine among them) reaffirming the two term tradition "as part of our republican system of government," and that any departure "from this time-honored custom would be unwise, unpatriotic, and fraught with peril to our free institutions."

That same day Samuel J. Randall sought a suspension of the rules to bring up a general amnesty bill covering some 750 ex-Confederates. After the Christmas recess, debate began in earnest, with Blaine offering an amendment to require an oath of allegiance as a condition of amnesty, with Jefferson Davis excluded altogether. On January 10, in a patent attempt to curry favor with the Grand Army of the Republic and to make up somewhat for lack of a war record of his own, Blaine "waved the bloody shirt" and put responsibility for "the crime of Andersonville" on Davis himself. "Sunset" Cox replied the same day, questioning the motives of "His Majesty of Maine!" On January 11, the former general, Benjamin M. Hill of Georgia, proclaimed: "The South is here, and here she intends to remain. We come to gratify no revenges, to retaliate no wrongs, to resent no past insults, to re-open no strife." Garfield defended Blaine; and on January 13, Proctor Knott of Kentucky, chairman of the Judiciary Committee, brought in a compromise bill, requiring a test oath, but omitting Davis from the list. The constitutionally prescribed two-thirds vote was not mustered, and amnesty was finally defeated. But Blaine came out of it all something of a hero; his state organization urged his candidacy on the party, and other states showed interest. Everything in Congress now was tinged with partisan relevance to the election.

If Blaine's star was in the ascendancy, the party itself had little cause for confidence. James A. Garfield sounded out Republican sentiment in New

England and found but scant hope for victory; he did notice the potency of the war issues, even at this late date. The southern question was to be the vital element in shaping a formula for success. From the opening day of the Forty-fourth Congress, the political strategists of both parties grappled with the problems raised by southern allegiance and southern defiance. Nor were the freedmen silent. Ex-Senator Hiram Revels of Mississippi, in an open letter to General Grant, noted that at the last election men of good will, irrespective of race, united against the incompetent and dishonest. The Republicans were put on notice to clean house if they wished to retain the Negro vote. Another black U.S. senator, Blanche K. Bruce of Mississippi, joined Senator P. B. S. Pinchback of Louisiana, in issuing a call for a national Negro convention at Nashville, Tennessee. This met April 6 and 7, and proceeded to lay down the specifications for a Republican presidential candidate acceptable to the Negro voters.

As attention focused on the Presidency, pet formulas and sound proposals were advanced to streamline the election machinery, to so modify it as to cancel out partisan advantage, and even to change the term of the office itself. Randall actually sponsored a constitutional amendment to limit the presidential term to six years. Referred to the House Judiciary Committee, it was reported out favorably in January, but failed to get the necessary two-thirds vote to pass. Of more immediate relevance, now that the Democrats controlled the House of Representatives, was the Republican Senate's efforts to extricate itself from the Twenty-second Joint Rule, which went back to 1865, and gave each House the power to reject the electoral vote of a state. Detailing the procedure for counting the vote, the rule provided that "no question shall be decided affirmatively, and no vote objected to shall be counted, except by the concurrent votes of the two Houses." This joint rule was dropped by the Senate in January, 1876, but the House took no action, thereby raising questions of some moment in resolving the disputed election of 1876. The rule had been invoked in 1868 and 1872 against the electoral votes of some of the southern states, but then the Republican party controlled the Congress; now, with the Houses divided, the balance of power had shifted.

Another scheme was advanced by Senator Morton of Indiana, whose advocacy of "thorough" Reconstruction and the 15th Amendment had won him the allegiance of the Negro leadership. Morton sponsored bills in the Forty-third Congress to overhaul the Electoral College system and amend the Twenty-second Joint Rule. As chairman of the Senate Committee on Privileges and Elections, Morton had a detailed plan for scrapping the "winner take all" electoral system in favor of a presidential district system of vote counting, but made little headway with the proposal, which needed a constitutional amendment. Nor did he fare much better with the joint rule, which he sought to modify by requiring the concurrent action of both Houses to reject an electoral vote, or to accept one of two conflicting returns. The bill passed the Senate but not before much debate on alternatives, including adjudication of disputes by a commission, the Chief Justice, the presiding officer of the Senate, or the Speaker of the House. Reintroduced in the Forty-fourth Congress, the bill never got beyond the Senate. Interestingly, neither the original Twenty-second Joint Rule nor the Morton bill would have been much comfort to the Hayes' candidacy when the votes were counted.

The final proposal on the Presidency deserves notice. Early in the campaign, a splinter group, the American National party, adopted at Pittsburgh a platform calling for the abolition of the Electoral College and a direct vote for President and Vice-President. It endorsed prohibition, the Bible in the schools, civil equality, justice for the Indian, sound money, and a return to specie payments "as soon as possible." Tinged with anti-Masonic and nativist ardor, the American Nationalist group never got off the ground, receiving only 2,600 votes at the election.

Brutal political infighting in Congress was only one dimension of the national political turmoil as the fall election approached. Another discordant element was the plethora of third parties, each of which advanced a bewildering array of recommendations and demands, ranging from moderate reforms to utopian panaceas. The National Prohibition Reform party, for example, gathered at Cleveland, Ohio on May 17, to name General Green Clay Smith of Kentucky for President and G. T. Stewart of Ohio for Vice-President; and adopted an impressive set of resolutions that reflected the high competence of its leadership and a dedication that ultimately bore results. While their vote on November 7, was only about 9,500, the cause of temperance was dramatized by the emergence of no less a champion than the President-elect's wife, whom history fondly remembers as "Lemonade Lucy," a characterization that the "wets" broadcast but the W.C.T.U. cherished. The Prohibitionists advocated equality of suffrage irrespective of race, creed, or sex; the suppression of gambling and lotteries; mandatory, free, public education; the complete separation of church and state; entire freedom of religious faith and worship; a humane system of punishment for crime; the direct election of the President and Vice-President and United States senators and of all civil officers "as far as practicable"; a liberal immigration policy; and a bimetallic standard.

More important was the convention of the Independent or National Greenback party, which met May 17 and 18 at Indianapolis. Nominated were the venerable philanthropist Peter Cooper of New York, and Senator Newton Booth of California, after which the convention endorsed an elaborate program for fiscal and financial reform. (Samuel F. Cary of Ohio, later replaced Booth). The Greenbackers' eventual total of some 81,700 votes not only influenced the outcome in such a critical state as Indiana, but in general reenforced the crucial appeal of the money question as a campaign issue.

However complicated the economics of currency manipulation, the subject had wide appeal in and out of Congress and kept alive the prospect of material gain as a function of governmental policy. Early in the Forty-fourth Congress, Holman of Indiana pressed for repeal of the Resumption Act of 1875, lining up a long list of Democrats for the purpose. But S. S. Cox, as Speaker pro tem., kept the lid on the movement until after the Democratic convention. Holman wanted the greenbacks to replace national bank notes, a proposal that fitted in neatly with the Independent platform demands and weakened the hard money position of the Democrats. Their ambivalent stand on resumption drew votes from the more consistent Republican candidates.

The Independent platform dealt exclusively with the meliorative promise of a greenback currency, interconvertible with United States bonds at 3.65 per cent interest. It demanded the immediate and unconditional repeal of the Resumption Act, including the provision for a new fractional silver currency. Later, the party agreed to back the old silver dollar as a legal tender, softening somewhat its opposition to silver purchase commitments. It also went on record against further issues of gold bonds for sale in foreign markets, proposing domestic sales at 3.65 per cent interest. This itself revealed the inadequacies of the greenback panacea for a nation as heavily involved and dependent on world trade as was the United States.

Cooper himself, at age eighty-five, had no illusions about his candidacy. He accepted the nomination conditionally, expressing the hope that the economic relief sought might come through one of the two major parties. His sponsors counted on his fame and fortune to lead them to victory, at which point he would be replaced by a younger man. California's former Governor Booth ruled himself out, however, and Cary's extreme fiat money views proved a bit too much even for the Greenbackers. There were others, however, like James B. Weaver of Iowa, who put muscle into the party in the congressional elections of 1878, and would become the presidential standard-bearer in 1880. Adlai E. Stevenson of Illinois, who was endlessly intrigued by Greenbackers, eventually remained in the Democratic fold, and joined Cleveland on the successful 1888 ticket. Another possible national political magnet for the Independents was the fiery Ignatius Donnelly of Minnesota, who became the People's party vice-presidential candidate in 1900.

The aged Cooper accepted the nomination because he was convinced that neither party would do much about the greenback question. One cannot discount the appeal of Peter Cooper's formula of bringing greenbacks to a par with gold. All that is required, he told an "immense mass meeting of working-men" at Cooper Institute on January 10, 1876, "is to so alter the law as to make Treasury notes receivable for *all* forms of taxes, duties and debts; and, at the same time, interchangeable, at holders' option, with bonds of the government, bearing a reasonable rate of interest." Despite a million pieces of greenback literature this single issue, however adroitly exploited, hardly held the secret of party victory. Greenbacker candidates would, however, disturb the normal political balance, sometimes with major consequences. In Illinois, for example, the Greenbackers won five senate seats in the state legislature, enough to hold the balance of power and to win Democratic support to elect Justice David Davis to the United States Senate on January 25, 1877. Davis, a Lincoln intimate, had been on the Supreme Court bench since 1862, and had courted the Liberal Republican presidential nomination in 1872. Slated for the Electoral Commission as the fifth Justice, and counted on by the Democrats to rise above party, he insisted he was no longer available, though remaining on the Court till March 3.

Sooner than the Independents expected, public attention shifted to watch the unfolding election drama in major party ranks. That April, fed up with over seven years of scandal, Republican party liberals and veterans of the Greeley campaign of 1872 issued a circular letter calling for a New York conference on May 15. The appeal of April 6 was signed by William Cullen Bryant, Theodore Dwight Woolsey, president of Yale, Alexander H. Bullock of Massachusetts, Horace White, erstwhile editor-in-chief of the Chicago *Tribune*, and Carl Schurz of Missouri. Henry Cabot Lodge was designated as secretary, and the stage was set for the Fifth Avenue meeting, where seventeen states were represented, and an "address to the American people" was approved on May 16, signed by an impressive list of political leaders, educators, journalists, businessmen, and other citizens. Not the aftermath of the Civil War, but the spoils system was singled out as the root cause of corruption. Needed were tried and trusted men of character, committed to good government, and capable of carrying through a thorough-going reform. The results were indecisive. With fine impartiality the conferees settled on no specific candidate, but showed special interest in Tilden, the Democrat, and Bristow, the Republican, with the latter preferred by Schurz, Bryant, and Woolsey, who headed the conference. Charles Francis Adams put Bristow first, but was ready to switch to Tilden if the Republicans failed to nominate the Treasury Secretary, who by now had accumulated strong newspaper support, including that of *The New York Times*.

Bristow's growing popularity affected adversely the candidacy of the leading Republican contender for the nomination, James G. Blaine, who was already under somewhat of a cloud in any case. Blaine had wrung all the variations on the "bloody shirt" theme as a device for partisan advantage; he went further, and following the recommendation of President Grant in his Seventh Annual Message of December 7, 1875, backed a constitutional amendment guaranteeing a state-supported public school system, free of sectarian influence, and barring the use of public funds for religious schools. This was designed to appeal to the strong anti-Catholic sentiment in the Middle West, aroused by fears of the Church militant as it gave expression to the pronouncements of Pope Pius IX. Blaine may have solidified his Republican following by this maneuver, but the Democrats were against him to a man, and this ploy came back to plague him eight years later in the last days of a campaign that almost won him the Presidency. What lost him that chance in 1876, however, was the Little Rock and Fort Smith Railroad entanglement, which, as Blaine himself noted, was rumored in February and speedily mushroomed into poisonous proportions.

In 1869, Blaine, as Speaker, presumably without ulterior motive, had ruled out of order a motion that would have voided renewal of a federal land grant to the state of Arkansas for the Little Rock and Fort Smith Railroad Company. Soon after, Warren Fisher, Jr. of Boston, made Blaine a proposition to participate in the marketing of the railroad's securities on a liberal commission and brokerage basis, and put him in touch with one of the company's promoters, Josiah Caldwell. Blaine made sales of bonds and stock to thirteen of his Maine acquaintances, and in four other instances, receiving

generous compensation in bonds and cash, but falling prices and other dissatis-
factions prompted him to reimburse his customers, so that by mid-April, 1872,
he was left holding a sizeable bundle of bonds, which he disposed of to several
railroads, including $75,000 worth to the Union Pacific. This railroad paid or
lent him $64,000 for the seventy-five land grant bonds in the deal, so it would
seem, but Tom Scott, then president of the Union Pacific, claimed the sale was
made by Caldwell to him, and he, in turn, sold out to the railroad.

Blaine took to the House floor on April 24 to defend himself, but though
he read letters of disavowal from the Union Pacific officials, and stated that
his "whole connection" with the Little Rock and Fort Smith road "has been
open as the day," the defense, for such it was, proved less than candid. The
charges were not refuted, and on May 2 the House Judiciary Committee had a
subcommittee, under Judge Eppa Hunton of Virginia, look into the allegations. Meanwhile, newspaper men close to Bristow and Hayes were alerted to
available evidence in the form of correspondence between Blaine and Fisher
preserved by James Mulligan, who kept the accounts of the Blaine transac-
tions for Fisher's firm. William Henry Smith, general agent of the Western
Associated Press at Chicago, a confidant of the Ohio governor and destined
for a critical role in the negotiations leading to the Compromise of 1877, was
among the first to learn of the "Mulligan letters," having been tipped off by
Senator Morton's brother-in-law. Through Smith, Joseph Medill, editor of the
Chicago *Tribune*, was apprised of the find. Since rumors were rife, many others also heard about the letters including General Henry Van Ness Boynton, Washington correspondent of the *Cincinnati Gazette*, the publisher of
that paper, Richard "the Deacon" Smith, and the editor of the *Cincinnati
Commercial*, Murat Halstead, all nominally in the Bristow camp. As Harry
Barnard tells the story in his biography of Hayes, Dana's *Sun* was allowed to
leak the facts so as to deflect Blaine's antagonism from either Hayes or Bristow, though, in fact, the Bristow forces were tagged with the disclosure, much
to the relief of the Hayes managers.

On May 9, the *Sun* needled Blaine, asking for more than "simple denials." The testimony before the Hunton subcommittee was writ large in the
headlines of the metropolitan dailies. By May 31, Mulligan was on the stand
and the whole country knew about the existence of incriminating letters, and
what the *Times* called Blaine's "deliberate attempts to deceive," adding a
reminder of another "dubious transaction" of Blaine's in Northern Pacific
stock. In a dramatic confrontation with Mulligan, Blaine retrieved the damaging correspondence, and used it adroitly in a speech on June 5 which characterized the Judiciary Committee as "rebel" oriented, and challenged the chairman, Proctor Knott of Virginia, to produce the London cable from Josiah
Caldwell, "completely and absolutely exonerating me." After several futile
meetings of the Hunton Committee, with Blaine adamant about retaining the
"Mulligan letters," the matter was dropped, as Blaine had a heat stroke of
some sort that Sunday, June 11, at church. When he recovered three days later
the Republican convention was under way. As he was shortly to be named
a senator from Maine to replace Morrill, who went to the Cabinet, Blaine
would no longer be under the jurisdiction of the House. His confidence re-

turned, his ambition soared, and he looked forward again to party preferment.

Amidst more than the ordinary excitement of a political gathering, the Republican national convention met at Cincinnati from June 14 to June 16. This was to be an open convention, the first since 1860. The net result of its deliberations was a fulfillment of the promise of its official call writ large in a platform that reaffirmed the constitutional rights, including suffrage, of every citizen, the obligations of public service, the sanctity of the country's credit, and the need for a common school system as "the nursery of American liberty," free from sectarian control. While the 756 delegates, their alternates, party workers, and a vast concourse of invited guests gathered at Exposition Hall for the proceedings, much that happened followed the classic pattern of behind-the-scenes bargaining for votes, particularly of the more populous states. This practice allowed Hayes, Ohio's favorite son, to slowly come from behind, gaining on each succeeding rollcall until the nomination was won on the seventh ballot.

Neither the reaffirmation of the goals of Reconstruction, the commitment to a protective tariff, the endorsement of homesteadism, or the formulation of principles designed to conserve public lands, to safeguard the status of immigrants, to guarantee equal rights for women, and to reward former servicemen, weighed too heavily with those whose quest for votes eschewed idealism in favor of promises of party patronage.

Blaine was the man to beat. The Grant regulars, remembering Hayes' loyalty in 1872 and his close ties in the Bristow camp, saw a place for the Ohio governor on a Grant, a Conkling, a Fish, even a Morton ticket. Under the right conditions, war veterans, Union Leaguers, Reformers, and Independents could be galvanized into vociferous acclaim for a winning combination. The same might be said of the Blaine strategists, who needed just such a bloc of votes as Ohio's 44 to carry the day. Then, again, there was the Bristow following, impressive enough not to be ignored by any serious rival, backed as it was by conservative business interests and an articulate press. Other hopefuls, like Governor Hartranft of Pennsylvania, and Grant men like Postmaster-General Marshall Jewell of Connecticut, and Elihu Washburne of Illinois, minister to France, could resolve or complicate changing alignments. In this category also was William A. Wheeler of New York, who had been president of that state's constitutional convention in 1867–1868, and then went on to Congress.

On May 9, the New York *Sun* had explained "why Hayes is likely to be nominated for President," noting the intense rivalry among the other candidates. This proved to be prophetic, especially since Hayes' manager, General Edward F. Noyes, had seen to it that Hayes was almost every faction's second choice. With G. A. R. support and the eloquent endorsement of William Dean Howells and other literary notables, confidence in the Hayes' camp was high, but by the time the nominating speeches had been made on June 15 and the convention was ready to ballot, the votes to win were still lacking. More than that, Robert G. Ingersoll's oratorical triumph nominating Blaine as "a man who has preserved in Congress what our soldiers won upon the field," suffused the hall that night with a glow of victory for "the plumed knight" that even New

York's Senator Roscoe Conkling's last-ditch holding action for a pro-Grant miracle could not dim; but the lateness of the time and the fact that the delegates had been in almost continuous session for nearly seven hours made an adjournment possible.

The Hayes managers then went into action. How they won over the Bristow men and maneuvered other dissident elements into a majority combination has been told in all its fascinating detail by historians E. Bruce Thompson and Herbert A. Eaton. Suffice it to note that the Bristow forces could hardly hope to break through the solid phalanx of party regulars arrayed against them; the prospects of a Blaine alliance had soured; and the inner circle behind the Treasury Secretary were ready to listen to men like ex-Governor Noyes of Ohio, and Stanley Matthews, who were very close to Hayes. The Morton men became parties to the agreement, which involved promise of high judicial office for John Harlan, sealed off Conkling, and Hartranft, and Blaine from any inkling of the deal, and even arranged for an initial display of the original nominees' strength before the shift to Hayes. The plan began to unfold on the fifth ballot that eventful June 16.

In all, seven ballots were taken, as follows:

NAMES	1.	2.	3.	4.	5.	6.	7.
Blaine	285	298	293	292	286	308	351
Bristow	113	114	121	126	111	111	21
Conkling	99	93	90	84	82	81	....
Hartranft	58	63	68	71	69	50	....
Hayes	61	64	67	68	104	113	384
Jewell	11	....	....	....	....	....	....
Morton	124	111	113	108	95	85	....
Washburne	....	1	1	3	3	4	....
Wheeler	3	3	2	2	3	2	....

With 378 votes needed for a choice and no unit rule in effect, Hayes' victory was exceedingly close. Blaine, clearly had been outmaneuvered. All that remained to complete the ticket was a strong candidate from a critical state for Vice-President. The choice fell on William A. Wheeler, a party regular, but not a Conkling man. *The Times* called it "an invincible combination."

Blaine, Morton, Bristow, Conkling, and Hartranft closed ranks and joined in the party's acclaim for the nominees. B. Gratz Brown of Missouri, spokesman for liberal Republicanism, predicted that forty thousand Germans would vote the straight ticket. Zach Chandler, Michigan party regular, currently Secretary of the Interior, and newly-chosen chairman of the Republican National Committee, moved quickly to plan strategy and set the campaign in motion. He, and the new National Committee secretary, Governor R. C. McCormick of Arizona, had much to do and to learn, especially from the former committee secretary and manager of the Grant campaigns,

William E. Chandler of New Hampshire. Fortunately for the party and for Hayes, Chandler, as New Hampshire's national committeeman, was named to the executive committee of the National Committee, in which capacity he had a hand in the conduct of the campaign and the last-minute determination to claim the election in the disputed southern states.

In accepting the nomination, Hayes reiterated his adherence to the convention's "Declaration of Principles," embracing civil service reform, resumption of specie payments, and a non-sectarian public school system, and pledged himself, if elected, to a single term, and to an enlightened southern policy, designed to attract labor, immigrants, and capital to the region. This mid-July commitment commended itself so strongly to the old Whig element in the South interested in federal encouragement of a vast system of internal improvements, including a Texas-Pacific railroad subsidy, that it made possible the successful negotiations leading to the Compromise of 1877.

By comparison with the Republican convention, the Democratic meeting at St. Louis, June 27 through June 29, was uneventful. This was the first Democratic convention west of the Mississippi and in the nation's largest inland city, St. Louis then only being exceeded in population by New York, Philadelphia, and Brooklyn, in that order. With 983 official delegates, many entitled only to half a vote, representation was well distributed. This augured well for the ticket, but there were signs of organizational weakness, too. There were no Negro delegates, and "Honest John" Kelly, Tammany leader, fished in troubled waters, much to Tilden's advantage on the convention floor, but disturbingly symptomatic of threats to party success in the pivotal states. The Tilden machine was in high gear, thanks to the candidate's widespread correspondence with party leaders, the press releases of his Literary Bureau and the systematic fence-building and fence-mending of Abram S. Hewitt, now the chairman of the National Committee.

It was a foregone conclusion that Tilden would win the nomination, though on the first ballot Thomas A. Hendricks, former senator and Indiana governor, ran up 140 1/2 votes and Governor Winfield Scott Hancock of Pennsylvania, 75. With a total delegate vote of 744, by the two-thirds rule prevailing at the convention, Tilden with 535, easily topped the 496 necessary for a choice, and the nomination was made unanimous on the second ballot. Hendricks was designated for second place, neatly balancing the ticket as a soft money candidate from a critical state, though when the convention adjourned on June 29, it was without any assurance that he would run.

Tilden had had his way, but it was not always easy. Two stormy days had been spent over the platform, first in the Resolutions Committee, and then on the floor itself. The document as a whole, drafted by Manton Marble, of the *World*, and presented by New York's Lieutenant-Governor William Dorsheimer, was impressive enough, but the paper money issue stirred the western delegates into action, and the Greenback forces, led by Congressman "Blue Jeans" Williams of Indiana, and ex-Governor William Allen of Ohio, backed General Thomas Ewing of Ohio, who sought to amend the plank on resumption of specie payments by demanding immediate and outright repeal of the law of 1875. The convention majority, after turbulent debate, stood fast by the original draft which stated: "We renounce the Resumption Act of 1875, and we here demand its repeal." The platform itself was approved, 651 ayes to 83 noes. Its theme was a call for reform on all levels of government, a reaffirmation of allegiance to the Union, the Constitution, and the Civil War amendments, a denunciation of the Reconstruction excesses in the South and the nation as a whole, and a reminder of the party's commitment to the supremacy of the civil over the military authority, and the separation of church and state. The tariff was condemned as "a masterpiece of injustice, inequality, and false pretence," and protection was repudiated in favor of a tariff for revenue only. Emphasis was placed on economy in government, conservation of the public lands, a qualified civil service, and public office as a public trust. Everything was in order now for a supreme party effort, and even John Kelly finally pledged his support.

One month later, following precedent and the example set by Governor Hayes, Tilden prepared and published his letter of acceptance, underlining his approval of the Democratic platform and sharpening the issues as they related to the restoration of purity in administration and the return of prosperity, goals that he felt his forty years in public affairs equipped him to attain. About the same time, the Republican press, in a bid for the very voters and interest groups to whom New York's governor appealed, featured William A. Wheeler's letter accepting the vice-presidential nomination on a platform of "good government, good-will, and good money." The campaign was now gathering momentum. In early August, the first serious salvos were fired in Congress.

Representative L. Q. C. Lamar of Mississippi, a moderate, respected son of Dixie, sounded what was meant to be a keynote of the Democratic appeal, noting the national character of his party, the South's chastened spirit in partisan councils, and the need to replace a corrupt Republican regime by a new Administration. The House had barely digested this address then General Garfield, head of the Republican Congressional Committee, seized the opportunity to set the Democrats on notice that the bloody memories of the War to save the Union were still fresh, and nothing that had transpired during Reconstruction would convince the country that the party of Tilden and Hendricks could be trusted with the reins of government. This speech of August 4 was a devastating rejoinder foreshadowing a bitterly developing contest. Governor Hayes thought the speech was "capital," and wrote Garfield that "the true issue in the minds of the masses is simply, Shall the late Rebels have the Government?"

Garfield had not only taken on the southern phalanx of the Democratic party, but he staunchly defended his record as chairman of the Appropriations Committee in the Forty-third Congress and challenged his Democratic critics, S. S. Cox and Samuel J. Randall to show where he had not been motivated by considerations of economy in federal spending. All this was by way of taking the sting out of the Democratic slogan of "Retrenchment and Reform," and to sow whatever dissension he could in Democratic ranks as its leaders jockeyed for the Speakership, since Kerr had died that August. But the Republicans were relying on more than high strategy and speechmaking to win the election. The party meant to enforce the 15th Amendment in the southern states under federal control, and to make sure there could be no fraud, intimidation, and violence at the polls. Orders to this effect were issued on August 15 by Secretary of War J. Donald Cameron to General W. T. Sherman, and on September 4 Attorney-General Alphonso Taft sent instructions to United States marshals to the same purpose.

While the Tilden-Hendricks ticket attracted some Liberal-Republicans like Charles Francis Adams, Parke Godwin, and Lyman Trumbull and wrapped itself in the mantle of reform, actual dependence was placed on the regular party workers, North and South, so much so that even a bid of support from the anti-Tammany New York County Democracy was rebuffed by the astute strategist Hewitt. He and his associates, Manton Marble and John Bigelow, New York's Secretary of State and Tilden confidant, relied on organization and detailed planning to defeat the Republican machine, with its hundred thousand federal placemen and an equal number of hopefuls. Out of Democratic headquarters at Gramercy Park in New York, managed by Tilden's nephew, Colonel William T. Pelton, a steady volume of campaign literature was issued. The most important single item, according to Hewitt, was the campaign textbook, which he and A. M. Gibson of the Washington office of the *Sun*, put together. Issued on September 1, it bolstered the arguments of the speechmakers, who were active in every state and city of importance. It has been estimated that the Democratic National Committee spent some $250,000 on the Literary Bureau and its attendant activities. Of this sum, Edward Cooper, party treasurer, accounted for $150,000, and the remainder was received directly by Tilden to meet party bills. How much he himself put into the campaign has never been made clear. Cooper, son of the Greenback candidate, and Hewitt's partner and brother-in-law, was highly competent. He had been one of the first to suspect Tweed of shady dealing and to alert Tilden, then chairman of the Democratic state committee, to that fact. A noted metallurgical engineer and business executive, he brought his leadership talents to bear in behalf of his party. In 1879 he was elected the fusion mayor of New York, a tribute to his political acumen. All this application to detail of Hewitt and company bore fruit, creating an image of Tilden that inspired country-wide confidence.

The "Boys in Blue" clubs whooped it up for Hayes, while Hewitt, Bigelow and others in Congress and on the hustings, challenged the calumnies of the whisperers, reaffirmed the loyalty of New York's sixty-two-year-old governor, and inspired an enthusiasm for victory that echoed and re-echoed across the continent, even embracing the perfervid speechmaking of a Henry George in California and the artful appeals of a "Sunset" Cox, a Thomas F. Bayard, an Allen G. Thurman, and a Henry Watterson in the pivotal states. Two Tilden campaign biographies, an illustrated song and joke book, and a veritable avalanche of printed matter blanketed the nation.

It was well that the Democrats pressed their cause, for Tilden was vulnerable on several counts. His wealth, his health—he had suffered a stroke the year before—his railroad connections, his relations with Tweed, his income tax returns, his views on the war and Reconstruction, even his stand on hard money had come under careful scrutiny. General John A. Dix denounced him as "a sham reformer." But the Democracy was not intimidated; and from its state and national headquarters at the Everett House the moves were made to saturate Indiana, Ohio, and Illinois with speakers, local and on circuit, to hold New York, take New Jersey, and fight for Connecticut. Louisiana, Florida, South Carolina were left severely alone, though Wade Hampton twice solicited Tilden's intervention in the latter state. All summer long the Republican rumor mills were busy, and by the fall, Hewitt was compelled to scotch one pernicious charge that Tilden planned to honor southern claims for wartime damages.

Harper's Weekly, especially cartoonists Thomas Nast and A. B. Frost, went after Tilden with bruising blows, irresponsibly linking him to Tweed, who was very much in the news that year, particularly after his flight to Spain, sensational apprehension, and return to Ludlow Street Jail late in November.

Though they were the party in power, the Republicans were running scared, as they had for two years now. In a surprising display of party unity almost all the big names, including Blaine himself, took the field for Hayes. Only Roscoe Conkling sulked. Carl Schurz went everywhere, bestirring the German voters and appealing to independents of all persuasions. Senator Edmunds, Morton, and Robert G. Ingersoll stumped Ohio and Indiana, as did Sherman, Garfield, and Jacob D. Cox. Bristow, George W. Curtis, Senator John A. Logan, and the New York reformer William M. Evarts, though a classmate of Tilden at Yale, spoke for Hayes to large audiences in the doubtful states. Even Mark Twain went on the hustings, lending color to the Hayes-Wheeler candidacy. And Zach Chandler saw to it that funds were available to press the party message home

Tradition decreed that Hayes could be seen but not heard. Kept from the lecture platform, the Ohio governor did not sit idly by but was in close touch with political developments and gave freely of his advice to the party wheelhorses, especially Garfield, Schurz, and Sherman. He was especially exercised about the use of public funds for sectarian schools, and thought a proposed 16th Amendment forbidding such practices could be made a winning issue. While the Republican press pictured Hayes, "every day and all day . . . quietly and steadily attending to his duties as Governor of Ohio," and three campaign biographies (one by William Dean Howells) portrayed him as a public servant of sense and sensibility, he became more and more the dedicated candidate, eager to win. Thus he cautioned Howells to be careful not to commit him "on religion, temperance, or free trade." Nor was he keen on publicizing his membership in the Sons of Temperance, being, in fact, a "liberal" on the subject.

In an age without polls, predictions of voter preferences were hard to rely on but in a presidential year, and this one in particular, some signs were unmistakable. September saw the state elections in Maine and Vermont go overwhelmingly Republican. On October 10 the electorate in Ohio, Indiana, and West Virginia voted, the Democrats taking Indiana and West Virginia, and the Republicans Ohio. The distribution of the vote, and the thin margins of victory in the crucial states of Indiana and Ohio foreshadowed a very close election, with the Democrats having something of an edge in the more populous centers and needing only one or two midwestern states to carry their ticket over the top.

Hayes, harassed though he was by partisan probing and prying into his tax returns, gave the situation in Indiana and his own state much serious attention before and after the October election, feeling especially that with Indiana "victory is assured," and alerting his party to the serious threat in the latter state from the "Greenback heresy." Funds were needed for a supreme effort, and this especially, since *The Times* in mid-August had reported "barrels of money already in the state," presumably on the Democratic side.

There was hope, too, that New York might be held in the Republican column, an expectation that Whitelaw Reid, of the *Tribune*, did not discourage. "Blue Jeans" Williams' narrow victory over General Benjamin Harrison for the Indiana governorship in October persuaded Hayes to confide to Schurz that this left New York to decide, but Hayes' preoccupation with what he considered a sectarian threat to the common schools led him to make an issue of Tilden's approval of the Gray Nuns Act, which permitted the order to prepare graduates to teach in New York's public schools. Though Tilden signed the bill repealing the law, Hayes would not let the matter rest, a circumstance that did him no good in the Empire State. At the same time efforts to link Tilden to the American Alliance, a nativist outfit, were sharply rebuffed. As Election Day neared, there were those who predicted a deadlocked electoral vote. Such was the view of Murat Halstead, who sought Republican votes at a Cooper Institute rally where the theme was "The War Claims of the South." Though roundly cheered at the Ohio Centennial Day exercises at the International Exposition on October 26, Hayes lost heart on the eve of the voting. "I shall find many things to console me if defeated," he wrote Schurz, listing the hard times, the desire for a change, and "the corrupt use of money" as militating against a Republican victory. But the *Nation* of November 2 was more sanguine, and reaffirmed Hayes' faith in "the permanency of the government and real prosperity of the country," no matter who won.

As for the Democrats, confidence was not allowed to become a pretext for inaction; even at the highest level details of strategy were scrupulously followed through. Late in September Randall was designated by Tilden to check on the organization in Indiana, and a month after, though facing a threat to defeat him in his own district, the next Speaker thoroughly canvassed the party situation in his state, coming away with an optimistic forecast, as well he might. For the tide was running strongly for the Democrats not only in the South and the Border States, but New York, New Jersey, Connecticut, Oregon, and even California looked doubtful for the Republicans. While Tilden assured Hewitt in an open letter on October 24 that he and the party would make certain that "no rebel debt will be assumed or paid," that the 14th Amendment will be upheld, and that "the questions settled by the war are never to be re-opened," the opposition, in seeming desperation, held that indemnifying the south for war claims was a distinct possibility, and said so repeatedly in the closing rallies of the campaign. The burden of the Republican argument was that one could not trust the Democratic party in the South, and, moreover, Tilden was not capable of controlling his party in any event, whatever his promises. While Attorney-General Alphonso Taft outlined to receptive audiences the measures taken to insure a free election in the South, the press ran lurid accounts of a Democratic reign of terror in Louisiana and Mississippi, and challenged Tilden to take a position "on the tactics of Wade Hampton in South Carolina."

The Republican National Committee may have written off Florida, Louisiana, and South Carolina, but Grant, good soldier that he was, readily responded to a plea from the Republican governor, Daniel Chamberlain, to send federal troops to South Carolina, where forces were already stationed under General Ruger. The situation was not much better in Florida and Louisiana, where both states were under military surveillance. Despite such precautionary measures, the vote was close, so much so as to permit easy manipulation, making possible the return of the Democrats to power in these states while at the same time the state-canvassing boards, riddled with intrigue, and Republican controlled, certified the electoral votes for Hayes by the narrowest of margins, thereby finally determining the election. But this came later. At first, as the returns poured in, it seemed to be Tilden by a landslide. The very night of the election, it was conceded that the Democrats had carried New York, New Jersey, Connecticut, and even Indiana. It was certain, too, that their popular plurality over Hayes would be impressive, perhaps reaching well over a quarter of a million votes. Democratic national headquarters at New York's Everett House had been a beehive of activity all through Election Day, with the party leaders increasingly confident of the result. By contrast, all was gloom at Republican headquarters, and when William E. Chandler arrived at the Fifth Avenue Hotel from Concord, New Hampshire, "a little before daylight," he found the committee rooms deserted, as they had been for some time since midnight when Zach Chandler, party chairman, had given up checking the returns and gone off to bed, persuaded that Tilden had won. A new day brought new hopes, but generally, informed opinion on November 8 interpreted the election figures as indicating a Democratic sweep. So most morning papers reported, and the later official count strongly bore this out in spite of all the manipulations of voting lists and tallies in the three disputed southern states. There it was decided that Hayes had carried Florida by some 922 votes, and Louisiana by 4,807. He won South Carolina by 964 plurality. But the total popular count gave Tilden 4,284,020 as against Hayes' 4,036,572, close indeed to the originally predicted 250,000 plurality.

Writing to his son Ruddy from Columbus on November 8, Hayes saw no reason then for doubting his own defeat, and recited the family reactions to it. He told his son, a student at Cornell, how he felt: "It would have been a great gratification to try to establish Civil Service reform, not to mention the good work for the South. But it is decreed otherwise and I bow cheerfully to the result. . . . We are all well. You will talk discreetly and exhibit no ill temper about adversaries." A day later, James A. Garfield, party leader in the House of Representatives and eager for the Speakership, wrote to his close friend C. E. Fuller in shockingly emotional temper: "It now appears we are defeated by the combined power of rebellion, Catholicism, and whiskey, a trinity very hard to conquer." The Presidency, the House, the Speakership, all have "gone down in the general wreck."

"But for the intervention of a single journal," wrote Allan Nevins, Tilden's "triumph might have been quietly conceded." While it is true that Abram S. Hewitt and D. A. Magone, chairman of the New York State Democratic committee, had blundered in making post-election inquiries of the staunchly Republican *New York Times*, and a particular mistake was made by Senator William Barnes of Connecticut, Democratic national committeeman whose query to the paper pinpointed the three southern states giving his party most concern, it is also true that *The Times* managing editor, John C. Reid, after an extended early morning conference at the paper, had rushed over to the Fifth Avenue Hotel, where he met and conferred with William E. Chandler, who then cleared plans with Zach Chandler, and sent out the telegrams to the state organizations involved to alert them to the need to hold their states for Hayes. But it must also be remembered that the Republican managers hoped from the start to win at least one of the southern states still under federal military support. To further this William Chandler left for Tallahassee, Florida that Wednesday evening some hours after the national chairman had sent out his provocative telegram: "Hayes has 185 electoral votes and is elected." But the Democrats thought otherwise. As the situation developed, the electoral vote actually stood at 184 for Tilden and 165 for Hayes, with twenty votes in dispute: Florida's 4, Louisiana's 8, South Carolina's 7, and one of Oregon's 3, where the Democrats claimed a Republican elector was disqualified. Tilden needed 1 vote for victory; Hayes needed 20. Following Chandler's example of an on-the-spot check of the state electoral count, Hewitt invited a representative group of "visiting statesmen" to go South to watch the count. Grant sent a Republican contingent to the disputed states for the same purpose.

Considering how the election was precipitating a battle of unprecedented proportions, Addison Oliver of Iowa, may have found some comfort in the fact that on January 6 of that year he had sponsored amendments to the Constitution for the direct election of the President and Vice-President and of the United States senators, joint resolutions that were referred to the Judiciary Committee of the House but which might very well have been a starting point for serious revision of the electoral process.

In an age without typewriters or telephones, reliance on personal consultation and the telegraph proved the speediest means of communication at so critical a juncture in national affairs, and as the leadership of the opposing parties faced each other, resort to the written record and spoken word resulted in an amazingly thorough documentation of actions taken, agreements arrived at, and roles played by the various parties to the dispute. And what the politicians and journalists knew or guessed at was shared, mid-way in Hayes' Administration, by the whole country as the Potter Committee on Alleged Frauds in the Late Presidential Election and the New York *Tribune* laid bare the "inner history" of the electoral count as revealed in detailed testimony, authenticated evidence, and deciphered telegrams. So complete was the record that a discerning reader could find spread upon the pages of the Washington, D. C., New York, and Ohio press in the four months preceding the completion of the count most of what occurred behind the scenes. Once it was all over, A. M. Gibson, W. E. Chandler, and Manton Marble added circumstantial, if strongly partisan, detail in published accounts.

By December 6, when the Electoral College vote was to be held at the respective state capitals, it was clear that the party battle was only beginning, and, whatever the count, the scene of the struggle would shift to the halls of Congress, convened but two days before for the short session. For some of the elder statesmen who rushed South, the task before them was extremely distasteful and they did not tarry long, leaving matters in expert legal hands under direction of discreet and adroit negotiators.

In Florida, within a week after Election Day, William E. Chandler marshalled a battery of lawyers to press the Republican claims: ex-Governor Edward F. Noyes of Ohio, and that state's Attorney-General John A. Little; Congressman John A. Kasson of Iowa; General Lew Wallace of Indiana; and importantly, General Francis C. Barlow of New York, who became convinced that Tilden had carried the state. The Democrats brought in thirteen "visiting statesmen," among them ex-Governor Joseph E. Brown of Georgia; C. W. Woolley, J. F. Coyle, and Manton Marble of the New York *World*. Marble took charge, confident of victory in a state predominantly white and where the Republican party was split between two rival candidates for governor. Another note of encouragement came from the fact that the Board of State Canvassers, unlike its counterparts in Louisiana and South Carolina, had Democratic representation. Of the three men who composed the state canvassers, William A. Cocke, Attorney-General, was a Democrat. The two Republicans were Samuel B. McLin, Secretary of State, and Dr. C. A. Cowgill, Comptroller. It was Cowgill whom Barlow sensed might be won over to the Tilden side, and it was McLin who, in a dramatic confession before the Potter Committee laid bare his misgivings about the conduct of the board in rejecting valid votes and retaining fraudulent ballots and tallies.

The immediate outcome favored the Hayes electors and Governor Stearns, but George F. Drew, the Democratic gubernatorial claimant won a state supreme court order defining the canvassing board's duties as ministerial and denying its power to reject votes. This put Drew in office, and made possible the proper certification of a belated return for the four Tilden electors, so that by the fourth week in January Congress had before it three returns, two correctly certified, those of Governor Stearns and Governor Drew, and one signed by Attorney-General Cocke in favor of the Democratic electors. Whatever McLin's public protestations in the spring of 1878, it was as nothing compared to the revelations in October of that year and the months that followed incriminating the Republican state canvassers in negotiations with Marble and Woolley in a scheme of vote purchasing that almost went through at an agreed upon price of $50,000 for one vote. Colonel William Tilden Pelton and Henry Havemeyer at Tilden's New York headquarters telegraphed to Tallahassee seeking to delay payment "until the vote of the elector was received." This halted negotiations, and on December 5, Marble advised Pelton that the proposition had failed, adding "Tell Tilden to saddle Blackstone."

At New Orleans in mid-November appeared an impressive representation of visiting statesmen, determined on a just count, if at all possible. Senator Sherman, Congressman Garfield, and attorney Stanley Matthews, all close to Hayes, headed the Ohio delegation; other prominent Republicans were William M. Evarts and John A. Dix of New York, John A. Logan of Illinois, John M. Harlan of Kentucky, Eugene Hale of Maine, and William D. Kelley and Matthew S. Quay of Pennsylvania. Hewitt matched this talent with an equally able Democratic group and left it to Henry Watterson, Kentucky's articulate editor and congressman to coordinate their efforts. Ex-Governor John M. Palmer and Lyman Trumbull of Illinois were there, as were former Senator Doolittle of Wisconsin, George W. Julian of Indiana, former Governor Bigler and Samuel J. Randall of Pennsylvania, L. Q. C. Lamar of Mississippi, Oswald Ottendorfer of New York, and Professor William G. Sumner of Yale.

All depended on the conduct of the State Returning Board, technically a five-man bipartisan body, but then strictly Radical Republican, with the fifth place unfilled since a Democratic resignation. The members of the board were ex-governor and port officer J. Madison Wells, president, Thomas C. Anderson, L. M. Kenner, and G. Casanave. These men came to be notoriously well known to those who followed the canvass, which was begun on November 20 and continued right down to December 6 when the designated electors voted. A dozen open sessions, to which the respective party delegations were invited, were devoted to a canvass of the parish vote, which was at best less than reliable and at worst revealed shocking discrepancies in population figures, voter registration, and ballots cast. The board had the power to reject ballots and did so with fine partisan calculation and cynical indifference to public opinion and the presence of expert counsel, especially so in the five "bull-dozed" parishes of East Baton Rouge, East and West Feliciana, Morehouse, and Ouachita, where the Democrats had piled up impressive majorities. On the face of the returns, the Democrats had a comfortable lead, but on December 4 the board went into executive session and came up two days later with a neat set of Republican pluralities, having thrown out the entire vote of East Feliciana and Grant parishes, along with thousands of other Democratic ballots.

"A majority of several thousand voters" for the Democratic electors was transformed into a Hayes and Wheeler victory that ran over 3,400 plurality for the lowest Republican elector to 4,800 for the highest. Added to this, the Republican candidate for governor, Stephen B. Packard, was credited with over 3,400 plurality, and the legislature also went Republican, according to the canvass. On the afternoon of December 6 the Electoral College formally cast 8 votes for the Republican ticket, which was duly certified by the incumbent Governor, William Pitt Kellogg, who was also an elector, a circumstance that raised questions about the legality of the vote under the Louisiana constitution. Board member T. C. Anderson then rushed the certificate to Washington, but, at Senate President Thomas W. Ferry's request, returned with it to New Orleans for correction of a faulty endorsement. When the second Republican certificate was finally deposited in Ferry's office, the signatures of two of the electors had been forged! Kellogg knew it then; Congress found out two years later during the Potter Committee hearings.

Meanwhile, a Democratic Committee on Returns canvassed the vote, declared the Tilden and Hendricks electors in by an average majority of over 7,800, and secured timely certification of this result by the *de jure* "Governor" John McEnery, one of the Democratic electors as well. This canvass also named General Francis T. Nicholls, a West Pointer who had lost an arm and a leg in the cause of the Confederacy, the governor-elect, with an 8,000 vote majority over his Republican rival, Packard, and in addition, designated a new Democratic legislature to meet in January.

Once again, Louisiana had two governors and two legislatures, with the *de facto* Republican regime dependent on federal recognition and soldiery for its survival. Grant maintained the *status quo* for the remainder of his term of office, with the Republican government gradually deteriorating under the economic and social pressures of the Nicholls supporters, who were bolstered by a continuation of the intimidating tactics which the White Leaguers and others had resorted to with such terrifying effect before the election. While rumors were widespread before December 6 that the State Returning Board could be influenced, and Senator Sherman became entangled in a web of alleged "guarantees" from which he could barely extricate himself, the fact is — as the Potter Committee hearings demonstrated — there were grave improprieties on both sides. One is inclined to accept the view of Tilden's biographer, A. C. Flick and others that a fair recording of the Negro vote would have given Hayes the state. But Democratic bitterness could not be assuaged as the leadership reviewed the "fraud, falsehood, and crime" resorted to by Republican agents. The majority report of the Potter Committee itemized the long list of patronage appointments that went to the Returning Board, all those connected with it, the Republican electors, parish and precinct supervisors, state officers, and even the "visiting statesmen".

South Carolina, with 7 electoral votes, was a prize that tempted resort to desperate tactics. Viewed in the light of the bloody Hamburg race riots that summer and the rhetorical and physical violence of the campaign itself, indications after the election pointed to much partisan impatience with the orderly processes of constituted authority. Anxiety on the part of the Republicans to get a new state government started quickly and safely under Radical auspices, was intensified by a pending state supreme court review of the canvass. Accordingly, on November 28 a new legislature was organized by a Republican-dominated House and willing senators, and on December 5 this body canvassed the vote for governor and lieutenant-governor and declared Daniel H. Chamberlain reelected over his Democratic opponent, the Confederate military hero, planter-aristocrat, Wade Hampton, by a majority of 3,433. The Democrats replied in kind, and at a joint session of the General Assembly the conservative legislators, now with victory almost in their grasp, made a somewhat irregular canvass on December 12, which included Edgefield and Laurens Counties (thrown out by the Republicans for "violence, intimidation, and fraud") in their count and found Hampton the winner by a majority of 1,134. Against this background of rival claims for control of the state and the functioning dual governments that it engendered, the canvass of the electoral votes assumed critical proportions.

While the final vote for governor was subject to legislative review, the electoral vote was checked by the Republican State Board of Canvassers and this year had the additional hurdle of passing scrutiny by the state supreme court under a legal ruling. The result, including all the counties, gave the highest Republican elector a majority of 964 over the highest Democratic claimant. Even the lowest Republican elector had 230 more votes than the highest Democrat. An independent tally by a United States House of Representatives committee, based on precinct returns rather than county figures, showed an average Republican majority of 666. Either canvass, and one was by a House Democratic majority, gave the state to Hayes. Wade Hampton may have promised reform, good government, public education, equality under law of both races, but that was not enough to carry the Tilden electors in, though the conservatives did have an edge in the legislature, the state offices, and the gubernatorial vote. Nor did the Democrats fare any better in extra-legal efforts to win or persuade defection among the seven-member Republican Board of Canvassers, though Smith M. Weed, a New York politico, in consultation with Manton Marble approached the canvassers eager for a bargain. After much haggling, beginning on November 14, a price was struck four days later for the votes of a majority of the Board in favor of the Democratic electors. As the Potter testimony showed, Weed was in communication with Henry Havemeyer, who, with Colonel Pelton, sought out Edward Cooper, party treasurer, to raise the $80,000 in cash needed at a Baltimore rendezvous. But Cooper alerted Tilden, and the scheme was promptly dropped. This did not deter Marble nor Pelton from a similar involvement in Florida some nine days later.

A foretaste of the intrigue that enveloped the southern disputed states had already occurred in the Oregon situation, where a dual officeholding elector gave the Democrats an opportunity they were quick to exploit. While the strategy was sound, an all-too-zealous agent named J. N. H. Patrick of Omaha, left a trail of incriminating telegrams behind him which ultimately not only gave the Republicans a chance for a diversionary rebuttal but served as prelude to the sensational exposures that came with the translation of the cipher dispatches two years later. Tilden and his advisers were quick to apprise the Democratic governor of Oregon, Lafayette F. Grover, of the party's

intense interest in the outcome of the electoral complication in his state resulting from the voters' choice of the Fayette postmaster, John W. Watts, as one
of three Republican electors. On the surface, the contest resolved itself into a
question of the power of the governor and secretary of state to serve as a
canvassing board to select three qualified electors. After an official inquiry,
the governor held Watts ineligible, though he had resigned as postmaster on
November 14, and designated C. A. Cronin, the Democrat with the next highest vote, to fill the vacancy.

At the Electoral College meeting at noon on December 6, with all the
electors present in the state capitol at Salem, the two Republican electors refused to sit with Cronin. They renamed the resigned Watts, then cast 3 votes
for Hayes and Wheeler. Cronin, on his own, filled two places, then reported a
vote of 2 for Hayes and 1 for Tilden. Only by going behind the two conflicting
returns could this impasse be resolved. This was Hewitt's hope when the
Electoral Commission began the count in February and a precedent was
needed to compel it to do more than accept formal certification by a state's
governor to validate a return. Unfortunately for the Democrats, Senator Morton's Committee on Privileges and Elections, having scooped up from Western Union the great mass of telegrams relating to Florida, South Carolina, and
Oregon that went to and from party headquarters, managed to break the cipher
system used in the Oregon dispatches and laid bare Patrick's vote-buying foray
to win a Republican elector to recognize Cronin's claim to a seat. Colonel
Pelton wired needed funds amounting to $8,000, some of it used for legal coun-
sel, "expenses" for Cronin, who insisted on it, and "just and legitimate" costs,
and nothing more. The Oregon telegrams had been easy to decode, based as
they were on the English Household Dictionary which was widely used by
business for the purpose. But the Florida and South Carolina dispatches
defied immediate translation, though their possibilities were not lost on William E. Chandler, who saw to it that abstracted copies finally reached Whitelaw Reid of the New York *Tribune*, with most going back to Western Union
and oblivion. At the moment, Oregon's indignant Republicans adopted a resolution the evening of December 6 challenging Lafayette Grover's qualifications not only as governor but as the new senator-elect from the state, and
held the Democrats "capable of as great frauds as their rebel confederates in
Louisiana or Florida."

As Congress got under way, Republican confidence in the ultimate outcome of the dispute was bolstered by the results of the Electoral College proceedings. It remained now to consolidate the gains achieved thus far, to claim
everything, concede nothing, and to hold the Democratic majority in the
House in check by divisive tactics played out in the halls of Congress and
behind-the-scenes. Alert, aggressive, resourceful, the seasoned veterans of the
party in power prepared to pursue the great game of politics with a grim determination and deadly earnestness that allowed for no retreat. The Democrats,
for their part, confident that right was on their side, trusted in the moral sense
of the people to insure an equitable solution of the dispute.

Hewitt was busily at work before the opening of Congress creating a favorable climate of opinion for the Democratic contention that the final deci-

sion as to the validity of the conflicting returns rested with the House and Senate in concurrent action. Even the properly Republican Chicago *Tribune* gave grudging support to this idea, comforted by the reflection that General Grant would preserve the national peace and see to it that the laws were faithfully executed. Hewitt thought so, too, for on December 3, just before Congress got under way, he saw the President, through the good offices of Secretary of State Hamilton Fish. He found Grant surprisingly objective about the contending forces in the disputed southern states, and ready to concede a Tilden majority in Louisiana or a situation not unlike that of 1872, when the state lost its electoral vote. This year, however, with no candidate having a majority, such a rejection of a state return would throw the election into the House. Hewitt, with the backing of David Dudley Field, soon to be Tilden's counsel before the Electoral Commission and August Belmont, the sometime national chairman, urged Tilden to dramatize the issues by an address to the nation claiming 185 votes on the face of the returns certified by the respective state governors and 203 votes if and when Congress finally went behind the returns. They even conceded the entire Oregon vote to Hayes but awarded the 19 disputed southern votes to Tilden. But Tilden demurred, preferring arbitration to the stirring up of partisan fervor, and reliance on legal precedent in the proper counting of the votes by Congress.

Tilden made sure to throw his support to Samuel J. Randall* in the speakership contest that ushered in the short session of the Forty-Fourth Congress as the House prepared to do battle with the Senate for control of the electoral count. Randall committed himself early to reliance on the Twenty-second Joint Rule as the surest guide to an acceptable settlement for all concerned, backed as it was by precedent. He was more than a match for Thomas W. Ferry of Michigan, president pro tem. of the Senate since Vice-President Henry Wilson's death. But Ferry, with the Republican party behind him, might well go beyond a mere opening of the certified returns, as the Constitution prescribed, and proceed to a count before the joint session of Congress. Here was the danger to avoid.

Randall saw the need for some agreement between Hayes and Tilden looking toward an amicable adjudication of the contested election. While in New Orleans as a visiting statesman, he had joined on November 14 with Watterson, Lamar, and Ottendorfer in a telegram to Governor Tilden urging him to take the initiative in approaching Hayes on the possibilities. His experience in Louisiana confirmed his conviction that waiting and delay would only encourage a hardening of claims and let loose sinister forces seeking to take advantage of a crisis situation. By November 19, Randall was anxious to get out of Louisiana and go back to Washington to do some political fence-mending before the speakership contest. He so informed New York headquarters in a coded telegram addressed to M. H. King, Colonel Pelton's deciphering clerk. Two years later the New York *Tribune* made much of this

---

*Special thanks are due Dr. Ira Leonard of Southern Connecticut State College for help in checking the Randall Papers in the University of Pennsylvania Library and in going through the newspapers.

incident, asking how Randall knew "the elaborate transposition cipher with its ten keys and private vocabularies—the most secret of all the ciphers used by Gramercy Park." Also, queried the *Tribune*, how did Randall know Woolley, who had left New Orleans for better prospects in Florida, by his secret name of "Fox". The Speaker denied complicity in any evil machinations at the time and explained that the telegrams had been handled for him by others.

On the eve of the Democratic caucus to select a candidate for Speaker of a predominantly Democratic House, the overshadowing question was that of the Presidency itself and the role that the Speaker could play in furthering Tilden's cause. A subsidiary issue revolved about Randall's high tariff commitments, but this was not sufficient to weaken his candidacy or make votes for S. S. Cox, the only other serious contender for the nomination. The East and West rallied to Randall's banner and overwhelmed an Ohio-southern alliance for Cox. Two days later, on December 4, Randall defeated Garfield for the office by a vote of 162 to 82. Randall, observed the *Nation*, is the Democracy's "most able man" for the crisis, "a skilled parliamentarian and a bitter partisan." In private, Randall could write: "All the party needs is nerve!" But on taking the chair after the vote, he cautioned the House: "by unceasing vigilance, let us prevent even the slightest departure from the Constitution and the laws, forgetting in a moment of difficulty that we are the adherents of party and only remembering that we are American citizens with a country to save." The next day, December 5, the House approved investigating committees to proceed to the three disputed southern states, but that line of action was not encouraging, having all the indications of a post-mortem, as were House efforts to revive the Twenty-second Joint Rule, despite its rejection by the Senate. While Tilden counseled patience, firmly believing that in the end the two houses of Congress would decide the issue, Henry Watterson, who kept close to the Democratic inner circle, urged, in the columns of the Louisville *Courier-Journal*, a march on Washington by one hundred thousand petitioners.

While Democratic hopes were lodged in the House of Representatives, the Republicans were in control of the executive branch of government, and in a majority in the Supreme Court, where Hayes' friend Morrison R. Waite of Ohio was Chief Justice. In the Senate, the Republican presiding officer, Ferry, had a vaguely prescribed Constitutional duty in the counting of the vote, but one sufficient to the purpose of recognizing the properly certified returns. At first Hayes placed his reliance on this procedure and the formidable agencies involved to assure his election; he was even willing, once President Ferry had announced the vote, to have a *quo warranto* proceeding take the matter to the Supreme Court for final adjudication. His acquiescence to the Electoral Commission plan, principally on the advice of Carl Schurz, seemed to Hayes a major concession, especially since he had earlier claimed as many as forty southern votes. In close touch with developments in the disputed states on the eve of the Electoral College vote, the Ohio governor cautioned Senator Sherman against fighting fire with fire. "There must be nothing crooked on our part," wrote Hayes. In this mood, he met privately on December 1 with Colonel William H. Roberts, editor of the New Orleans *Times*, an agent for Louisiana and other Democratic interests in the South. Despite denials on all sides, a deal, a bargain, an understanding was in the making, one involving recognition of Democratic claims in Louisiana and South Carolina in return for a new southern policy, perhaps even a Cabinet appointment. If voted in, Hayes would be guided by his letter of acceptance, which covered much ground on the southern questions and was subject to favorable interpretation.

Hard decisions were imperative. Time was of the essence. The political air was filled with wild schemes, pat formulas, enticing precedents, and intriguing suggestions. Only Tilden seemed unhurried and undecided. Hayes remained deep in conference, constantly assessing his alternatives. Grant, counselled by Senator Conkling, insisted on an equitable, peaceful solution. While he favored an electoral commission to adjudicate the count, for a time the President seemed interested in the idea of maneuvering for a third term through a vice-presidential election or as presiding officer of the Senate, should there be an impasse beyond March 4. Abram S. Hewitt, Democratic national chairman and member of the House, sounded out sentiment in and out of Congress, consulted with Ohio Senator Allen G. Thurman, and Delaware's Thomas F. Bayard, won over Tilden, and worked for compromise.

On December 7, at the start of the session, Iowa Republican Judge Mc-Crary introduced in the House a resolution calling for a committee to act with a like Senate committee to prepare a measure for the proper counting of the electoral vote "by a tribunal whose authority none can question and whose decision all will accept." Such a counting committee was approved on December 14 in the House and four days later in the Senate, and the membership was announced by Senator Ferry and Speaker Randall on December 21 and December 22, respectively, for Senate and House. The seven members of the House committee were Henry B. Payne, Ohio, chairman; Eppa Hunton, Virginia; Abram S. Hewitt, New York; and William M. Springer, Illinois, all Democrats; and George McCrary, Iowa; George F. Hoar, Massachusetts; and George Willard, Michigan, Republicans. The Senate committee consisted of four Republicans: George F. Edmunds, Vermont, chairman; Oliver P. Morton, Indiana; F. T. Frelinghuysen, New Jersey; Roscoe Conkling, New York (in place of John A. Logan, of Illinois); and three Democrats: Thurman, of Ohio; Bayard, of Delaware; and M. W. Ransom, North Carolina. These men were destined to play a major role in the deliberations that gave legislative sanction to Hayes' claim to the Presidency. Along with the counting committee, the Speaker on December 22 made J. Proctor Knott of Kentucky, head of a Committee on Privileges, Powers, and Duties of the House in Counting the Electoral Vote. Guided by Tilden, this committee denied any power rested in the President of the Senate to count the electoral vote and reaffirmed the principle of the Twenty-second Joint Rule, which invalidated votes rejected by either branch of Congress.

A joint meeting of the Senate and House counting committees was slow in getting under way and it was well into January before debate really began to indicate a workable agreement, with Judge McCrary again taking the initiative in pressing for a commission, preferably of Supreme Court membership and with a decision-making power that could not be overruled except by concurrent action of the two Houses. The deliberations of the committees, separately and jointly, seemed endless, punctuated by caucuses, conferences, and behind-the-scenes consultations of the principals. Congress was deluged with petitions from urban business interests to reach a speedy settlement; the independent press called on the members to "rise above party"; and even the pulpit pleaded for concessions on both sides. As finally decided, there was to be an electoral commission of fifteen, composed of five members from the House, five from the Senate, and five from the Court. This was, in essence, Senator Conkling's plan. Each house would elect its representation; the four justices, designated on a geographical basis from the First, Third, Eighth, and Ninth Circuits, would name a fifth justice, understood to be Judge David Davis, who was considered an independent. Implicit in the entire arrangement was the recognition that the right to count the vote, decide disputes, and name the President rested in the Congress. The choice of a commission simply implemented this right and laid down the ground rules for adjudication. The report accompanying the bill submitted to the House and Senate endorsed it as "a measure that will bring peace and prosperity to the country and show that our republican institutions are equal to any emergency." Only Senator Morton refused to sign the report.

Despite spirited opposition, the bill passed the Senate on January 25 and the House on January 26 by a strong Democratic vote. The vote in the Senate was 47 yeas to 17 nays, with 26 out of 28 Democrats in the affirmative. The vote in the House was 191 to 86, with 158 Democratic votes for the bill. The Democrats were for the bill, stated Paul L. Haworth in his classic study, partially because they were at a disadvantage; they also anticipated that David Davis would be the fifth judge. Blaine, Morton, and Sherman led the Republican opposition in the Senate; Garfield, Hale, and Kasson in the House. Morton and Garfield made the Commission; Davis bowed out after a surprise election on January 25 to the Senate by a Democratic-Greenback coalition in the Illinois legislature. Hewitt, who had led off debate for the bill in the House, was stunned, but he finally acquiesced in the choice of Joseph Bradley of New Jersey, a Grant Republican, as the fifth justice after reassurances of his neutrality from a mutual friend, John Stevens. Hewitt also recalled that it had been Bradley who had invalidated key provisions of the Enforcement Act of 1870 in *U.S. v. Cruikshank*, when it was initially before him on the southern circuit. When fully constituted, the Commission consisted of two Democratic justices, Nathan Clifford of Maine, the presiding officer, and Stephen J. Field of California, an erstwhile Republican; and three Republicans: William Strong of Pennsylvania, Samuel Miller of Iowa, and Bradley. The Senate elected three Republicans: Edmunds, Morton, and Frelinghuysen; and two Democrats: Bayard and Thurman, all previously on the counting committee. Thurman resigned on February 26 because of "physical disability," and was replaced by Senator Kernan of New York. The House chose three Democrats: Payne, Hunton, and Josiah G. Abbott of Massachusetts; and two Republicans: Hoar and James A. Garfield. Payne, Hunton, and Hoar had served on the counting committee.

While the vote for the Electoral Commission bill seemed to favor the Democrats, it was essentially, as its chief opponent Senator Morton pointed out, a compromise not unlike that in 1820 and in 1850. Sherman and Garfield had misgivings, too, but Hayes took it all in stride, and in correspondence with Carl Schurz hoped it would turn out well. Then, on January 29, the day Grant signed the bill, Hayes began drafting an inaugural address and listing Cabinet possibilities, soliciting Schurz's suggestions and expressing himself in favor of a single six-year presidential term, the pacification of the South, and "internal improvements of a national character," the last a euphemism for sympathy with the Texas and Pacific Railroad project. It was pressure for a subsidy for this enterprise that brought to the Hayes camp a formidable array of lobbying talent committed to lining up a congressional majority for the Republicans nationally and the restoration of home rule in the South under Democratic auspices. Tilden, for his part, also went to work early in January on a Cabinet slate, thinking of such men as Charles Francis Adams for State, Charles O'Conor as Attorney-General, and David A. Wells in the Treasury. He also considered places for Professor William Graham Sumner, Manton Marble, and Abram S. Hewitt.

While the Democracy put its faith in the Electoral Commission, the Hayes partisans began negotiations designed to crack the Solid South by capitalizing on economic and political pressures long in ferment. The very same group of journalist-politicians who had torpedoed Blaine's bid for the Republican nomination and had won over the Bristow following for Hayes at the national convention now welcomed support from the old Whig elements in the southern Democratic party. The Roberts interview set up by Hayes' old comrade-in-arms, General James M. Comly, editor of the *Ohio State Journal*, pointed the way; the Texas-Pacific Railroad proposals, advanced by such conservative leaders as Lucius Q. C. Lamar of Mississippi, Benjamin H. Hill and Alexander H. Stephens of Georgia, John C. Brown of Tennessee, and John Young Brown of Kentucky, added weight to the movement

Tilden and the northern regulars kept clear of involvement, since the Credit Mobilier scandal was still fresh in public memory. A Hayes administration seemed the last best hope for the trans-continental railroad interests in general and the Texas-Pacific scheme in particular, certainly so long as Holman of Indiana, and his like-minded colleagues in Congress watched over federal expenditures. Years in the planning but ever short on funds, the Texas and Pacific Railroad was an outgrowth of dreams for a southern route across the continent that had once interested men as diverse as John C. Calhoun and John Charles Fremont. Now under the guidance of Tom Scott, president of the Pennsylvania Railroad, General Grenville M. Dodge, formerly chief engineer of the Union Pacific, other industrial statesmen, freewheeling capitalists, and would-be empire builders, deliverance loomed. Blueprints called for a grand trunk line west from Fort Worth to San Diego, fed by five branch lines which tapped vast areas of the South. The plan would use a twenty-eight million acre land grant, and assume, in principal and interest on fifty-year bonds, some $200 million in fiscal obligations, to be guaranteed by the Federal Government. Scott had a rival in Collis P. Huntington, who controlled the passes across Colorado and was eager to push his Southern Pacific eastward, with or without subsidy. In common purpose, both roads pressed for national backing; in the end, Huntington went it alone, but not before the impact of the railroad lobby made itself felt on the alignments leading to the election compromise.

Henry Van Ness Boynton served as intermediary between the Scott lobby and Hayes' lieutenants. He outlined the "Scott Plan" to William Henry Smith in a letter on December 20 from the Washington office of the *Cincinnati Gazette*, and sought assurances all around for the pledge of decisive support for Hayes and Wheeler preferably at the Senate level. The arguments for the Texas and Pacific road were persuasive enough, and the *quid pro quo* seemed fair indeed to Smith, a key member of the Hayes strategy team. Smith also functioned as general agent of the Western Associated Press at Chicago, and coordinated the efforts of the newspaper fraternity in bringing together the railroad lobby, the Democratic representatives from the interested southern states, particularly West Tennessee, Arkansas, Kentucky, Louisiana, Texas, Misssissippi, and the Hayes high command. In *Reunion and Reaction*, C. Vann Woodward has done a masterly job of unraveling all the absorbing details that led from this joining of interests straight to the Compromise of 1877, which became a reality in mid-February and assured the peaceful inauguration of Hayes as the nineteenth President.

But the "Scott Plan," however promising initially, was only one aspect of a many-sided approach which ultimately gained firmer and more rewarding backing in understandings about purely political arrangements. These got under way early in December when Garfield and others of Hayes' inner council sensed confusion and conflict in Democratic policy. Overtures to Republican leaders came thick and fast from disenchanted southern Democrats. Casey Young, Tennessee congressman and Texas and Pacific champion, thought as many as fifty Democrats "would stand by Hayes" if there was an acceptable southern policy in consequence. And by mid-December, Montgomery Blair, who ran the Democratic Washington *Union*, complained to Tilden that "the Railroad men in Congress have sold you out," adding surprisingly accurate details of plans afoot in the opposite camp. He knew, for example, that on December 17 General Boynton, Congressman Charles Foster, and Garfield had a long midnight conference, and the next evening Boynton brought Colonel Andrew J. Kellar to see Garfield. Kellar, a director of the Western Associated Press and editor of the Memphis *Avalanche*, spoke for old-line Unionist-Whig elements in the South, and was promptly enlisted to seek out Democratic support, which he did with much success.

Hayes kept in close touch with developments. Smith sent him General Boynton's letter and other pertinent plans and proposals. On December 24, in response to the "Scott Plan," Hayes advised Smith that he would be "exceptionally liberal" about "education and internal improvements of a national character" as a means "to restore peace and prosperity to the South." Here was a guarded commitment that, for the first time, went beyond the letter of acceptance gambit. Tom Scott got the message, and by mid-January General Grenville Dodge had activated the railroad lobby. By then, too, a bill guaranteeing the bonds of both Scott and Huntington for building along the Texas and Pacific route had been pushed through the House Pacific Railway Committee by its chairman, L. Q. C. Lamar, who as head of the Democratic Advisory Committee presumably had weightier problems with which to grapple at the time. Garfield had grave misgivings about Texas and Pacific, but on the floor of the House his party gave it greater support than did the northern Democrats, who managed to keep it from making any headway, thanks to Holman, Cox, and Speaker Randall. The Democratic New York *Sun*, thundered against the bill as "the most nefarious railroad jobbery yet attempted in this country," thereby reinforcing the widely-held view that the Democracy could not be relied on in matters of "internal improvements." Interestingly, the Republican *New York Times* also characterized the measure as a "most audacious scheme of plunder," and repeatedly alerted the "friends of honest and economical legislation" to the dangers of its passing. In February, with the deliberations of the Electoral Commission under way, *The Times* thought it "almost incredible that the Texas-Pacific scheme should be pushed now."

At one in the afternoon on February 1, 1877, the senators filed into the Hall of the House of Representatives, and Senator Thomas W. Ferry, as presiding officer, called the joint meeting of the two branches of Congress to order to begin the electoral count, as prescribed by statute. The day before the Electoral Commission had met, adopted seven rules of procedure, designated the room of the Supreme Court for its deliberations, and drafted a notice to Congress that all was in readiness, as was the Commission the afternoon of the opening session, to count the vote, hear arguments, and decide disputes. The core of the Commission law made up for constitutional omissions in counting the vote by spelling out each step once the tellers, two from the Senate and two from the House, had opened the respective state certificates of election. Where there was only one return at issue, each House was to vote separately on the question in controversy; where there was more than one return, the matter went directly to the Electoral Commission, and its decision was final unless objections were filed by at least five senators and five representatives, when, as in the first instance, concurrent action of both Houses was necessary to invalidate the return in question. Provision was made for limited two hours debate at the separate sessions, no debate at the joint meetings, which were not to be dissolved until the count was completed, except for designated recesses and the hearings before the Commission itself. Finally, the act saved any right, if such existed, to question in the courts the title of any person to President or Vice-President.

While the public recognized the bipartisan character of the proceedings, and William E. Chandler and other Republican legalists emphasized the essentially ministerial capacity of the Commission, and Congress, in counting the electoral vote, actually it functioned as a quasi-judicial body. It kept a journal, and an authenticated record of proceedings, printed the "remarks" of members of the Commission in its consultations as later prepared by them, and published the full text of the election certificates and "objections" referred to it by the joint convention of the two Houses in the cases of Florida, Louisiana, Oregon, and South Carolina. Counsel of tremendous prestige and talent came before the Commission for both sides; for the Republicans, there were William M. Evarts and Stanley Matthews, E. W. Stoughton, J. A. Kasson, and Samuel Shellabarger, the latter Hayes' special designee. Charles O'Conor and David Dudley Field, brother of Commissioner Stephen J. Field, and such forensic giants as George Hoadly and Jeremiah S. Black, Lyman Trumbull and William C. Whitney, appeared for the Democrats. So impressive were Tilden's spokesmen that their insistence that the Commission go behind the state returns and examine the evidence as to the way the returning boards canvassed the votes sharpened the legal issue and dramatized the moral responsibility of the parties to the dispute.

In the presence of a notable assemblage, President Ferry, with Speaker Randall at his left, ordered the count to proceed. The sets of certificates were then formally opened and read in the alphabetical listing of the states, beginning with Alabama, then Arkansas, California, Colorado, Connecticut, Delaware, and so on. There being no objections, the vote was quickly counted. When Florida was reached, with a set of certificates for the Hayes electors and two sets for Tilden, objections were filed, and the papers referred to the Commission. The first day had passed quietly enough, but right from the opening of the Commission hearings in the Supreme Court room on February 2 the issue was joined, the party alignments crystallized, and attention was focused on Justice Bradley, whose role was to be crucial in deciding the way the count would go. The burning question, over which argument lasted for almost a week, was the readiness of the Commission to go beyond the formal certificates and inquire into the validity of the state electoral canvass itself, though, as Garfield warned, this would open a Pandora's box of problems and might prolong the count indefinitely. Republican counsel stood firmly by the contention that the choice of electors was a state function and Florida Governor Marcellus L. Stearns had made a proper and timely certification of the Hayes electoral slate. This contrasted with the Democratic certificate, signed by the new governor, George F. Drew, late in January, which Tilden insisted could be accepted, as of December 6, 1876.

The deliberations of the Commission reached a crisis point by February 7 with secret debate among the members all that day and evening. Indeed, there was precedent for congressional scrutiny and rejection of suspect electoral votes, as had been done most recently in 1872 in the case of Louisiana and of Arkansas. Bradley went home, pondering the issues, and that night John C. Stevens visited the Justice and heard his opinion favoring the Tilden electors. This was promptly reported to Hewitt. There were other visitors to Bradley as well, notably Senator Frelinghuysen and Navy Secretary Robeson who were even supported by Mrs. Bradley in a last minute appeal for Hayes. Pressure, too, came from subtler sources, including the railroad lobbyists, who remembered Bradley's handling of the receivership of the Memphis, El Paso, and Pacific Railway, whose properties were taken over by Texas and

Pacific. Nor were the Democrats reticent about using all the influence they
could bring to bear before the Florida count was finally announced. On February 8, the Commissioners balloted on the relevance of extrinsic evidence,
and Bradley joined the seven Republicans in holding that the governor's
certificate made out a *prima facie* case that the state canvassers had performed their duty. So, Bradley had changed his opinion; the vote was 8 to 7;
the die had been cast. Justice Clifford entered a vigorous dissent, as did
Commissioner Bayard, but to no avail. On February 10, after long, secret
debate, Florida's 4 electoral votes were awarded to Hayes, and it was so reported to the joint session of the two Houses, where objections were raised,
and the separate deliberations begun. The Senate sustained the decision
quickly enough, but the House recessed until Monday, February 12 in a delaying action that had wide Democratic backing. On that day the Commission
decision was rejected, 168 to 103, with 19 not voting. Since there was no
concurrence of the two Houses, there was no reversal of the Commission,
and the count went on.

The next week, February 13 through February 20, was critical on several
levels. Hewitt felt confident that all was not lost yet, and counted on exposure
of the so-called regular return signed by Governor Kellogg certifying the eight
Republican electors from Louisiana. This was riddled with fraud, though
embarrassingly enough congressional testimony at the time also pointed to
Democratic efforts to purchase the state's Returning Board. All else failing,
there was still the chance that Senator Roscoe Conkling, who was convinced
that Tilden had won, would rouse himself sufficiently to rally Republican support in the Senate for rejection of the Electoral Commission report, which, as
feared, favored Hayes. But on February 19, the appointed day for the Senate
vote, Conkling was absent, much to the mortification of his close friend Hewitt and other Democratic leaders. Senator John Sherman moved the resolution
to let the 8 to 7 decision of the Electoral Commission stand, mustering 41
votes against 28 and 6 abstentions. The next day, after much impassioned
oratory and heated debate, the House rejected the Commission report by an
overwhelming majority. As the Democrats saw it, the failure of the Commission majority to go behind the returns once again was a patent violation of the
letter and spirit of the Electoral Act.

Tilden's loss of Louisiana's electoral vote only served to accelerate
southern defection from the Democratic ranks, a movement initially precipitated by the Texas and Pacific dealings and which gained momentum after the
Florida decision. Hayes was in a conciliatory mood, and very early in February thought of John M. Harlan of the Bristow faction, and Senator James L.
Alcorn, Republican of Mississippi, a Texas-Pacific man, with strong connections among the southern Democrats, as Cabinet possibilities. But William
Henry Smith had better and bolder ideas. On February 17, word was carried to
Smith from Washington, where Alcorn had caucused with conservative leaders,
that David M. Key of Tennessee was their choice for the Cabinet, and the Post-
master-Generalship at that. To this was added agreement on a more realistic
federal patronage policy designed to strengthen a new party orientation of the

southern conservative Democracy as well as to accomplish the proposed liqui-
dation of the last Radical Republican governments by withdrawal of federal
troops from the beleaguered southern states, and internal improvements,
broadly conceived. For their part, Lamar, Hill, Stephens, and others, relying
on a congressional nucleus of forty-two ex-Confederates, agreed to stand
by the electoral count, to oppose filibustering tactics, and, for good measure,
to aid in organizing the Forty-fifth Congress by electing Garfield Speaker of
the House with the Conservatives' help. This sort of bargain commended itself
to the W. A. P. people, and, judging by subsequent events, won the approval
of Hayes and the Republican leadership. It was widely rumored and in fact
the New York *Herald's* Washington correspondent called the bargain "an
open secret," the details of which were writ large in the press of the day.
Its immediate consequences were to divide the Democracy, North and South,
and to raise doubts among the southerners themselves, particularly as to the
Speakership and Republican party restructuring. But it also meant a voice
in the councils of the next Administration no matter how the count turned
out. By the irony of history, the bargain came to be overshadowed by the better
publicized but infinitely less important Wormley agreements entered into near
the end of February.

The ranks of the filibusterers had been thinned significantly by the time
Oregon was reached in the count, but the legislative weapon of the dilatory
motion was still potent enough to delay proceedings beyond March 4, with
all that this implied. Major E. A. Burke, agent of the Nicholls government at
New Orleans, aided by Congressmen E. J. Ellis, William M. Levy, and R. L.
Gibson, of that state, and later by Henry Watterson, designated to speak for
South Carolina, pressed for special concessions. They made the rounds of the
Republican high command in Washington, consulting with Hewitt, dealing
with President Grant, and extracting pledges from Congressman Foster and
Stanley Matthews to assure recognition of the Nicholls government in Louisi-
ana and the Hampton administration in South Carolina. All this was formal-
ized at the Wormley Hotel conference the night of February 26 when Foster
and Matthews were joined by Senator Sherman, Garfield, and ex-Governor
Dennison, of Ohio. Into this highly charged situation, Congressman John
Young Brown of Kentucky, and Senator John B. Gordon of Georgia, injected
a further note of crisis by insisting on a signed statement, first from Foster
on February 26, and then a more precisely worded one from Foster and Matthews on February 27, committing Hayes to self-determination for the people
of South Carolina and Louisiana, "subject to the Constitution of the United
States and the laws made in pursuance thereof." This, in broad outline, was
the heart of the agreement, supplemented by Democratic promises to guarantee political and civil rights under the new dispensation, and to refrain from
partisan reprisals against the local Republicans. Details were publicized soon
after the conferences, and Stanley Matthews ordered release of the letters to
Brown and Gordon the end of March to quiet rumors designed to split this
conservative — Republican alliance, an alliance that seemed to be leading to
the choice of Garfield as Speaker of the new House and to other power plays
that would undermine the Democracy despite its popular mandate in 1876.

The Electoral Commission spent a few exacting sessions on the Oregon question, five more precious days, including joint meetings and separate House and Senate deliberations. The caucusing and filibustering at the Louisiana count were repeated once again, but a new sense of urgency pervaded the proceedings. Initially, Speaker Randall, whose responsibility was crucial to the faithful execution of the electoral count, was inclined to encourage the filibusterers. At a Democratic caucus on February 19 he advanced proposals that would lead to a new election, a strategy that did credit neither to his usual political acumen or parliamentary resourcefulness. He went so far as to advise a correspondent: "We intend to fight on the Electoral Commission inch by inch, and defeat the count at all hazards." But by February 20 there was a change, precipitated by the Louisiana decision, the pressures of the southern Democrats, and Hewitt's sympathy with business and industrial spokesmen of the North for a settlement. Then, too, as the Baltimore *Sun* pointedly remarked, the Electoral Commission was a patent of Democratic invention. Meeting the Democrats half-way, Congressman Foster spoke on the eve of the Oregon count. Conciliation was his theme; reassuring the South his purpose. Hayes will guide well: "The flag shall float over states, not provinces; over freemen and not subjects." But the Commission still had to decide, and the Oregon situation presented a new precedent-making issue, and a last opportunity for the Democrats.

George Hoadly, who had been before the Commission in the Florida case, carried the argument for the Tilden side, and insisted on the logic of consistency in pressing for the validity of Oregon Governor Grover's certification of Democratic elector Cronin in place of the allegedly disqualified Republican Watts. But Stanley Matthews, head of opposing counsel, made a fine distinction between going behind a governor's certificate and carefully scrutinizing the public record before the Commissioners. This showed that the proper canvassing authority in Oregon was the Secretary of State, who officially counted the vote in the presence of the governor. This had been done, and the three Hayes electors duly elected in consequence, Watts' eligibility having been legally established. The Electoral Commission, by now settled division of 8 to 7, accepted this reasoning, and so reported to the joint convention of the two Houses on February 23, much to the chagrin of the Democratic partisans.

"Once More Eight to Seven," screamed the New York *Sun*, dilating at length on "How the Job Was Done." Now the name-calling began, as Hayes' victory was almost certain, and he was made to bear the brunt of pent-up bitterness and disappointment. As the two Houses separated to pass on the Oregon decision, the rumblings of the filibusterers grew ominous. To put a brake on this movement, *The New York Times* featured Secretary of State Hamilton Fish's letter to General John A. Dix reaffirming the widely-held view that the President of the Senate had the constitutional right to open and count the electoral votes. This was by way of warning the Democratic leadership that should the House balk at an orderly completion of the count, Senator Ferry, President Grant, General Sherman, acting jointly or separately, would see to it that Hayes was installed as the Chief Executive. There were other possibilities to thwart deliberate delay, such as through the selection of a Vice-President. Speaker Randall, in a private conference held with Conkling, must have been alerted to some of these alternatives for the Republicans should an impasse develop. But there was no holding the irreconcilables in check. Their ranks were stiffened by the backing of southerners who knew of all the details of the recently concluded bargain and were now somewhat disillusioned, especially after a blundering *Ohio State Journal* piece on February 22 lambasted Louisiana and the Redeemers. All the while, down to the end of the congressional session, Senate and House committee hearings kept alive the Oregon vote-buying charge, thereby fanning the flames of partisanship.

Saturday, February 24, witnessed a major setback to filibustering efforts to prolong the count and the emergence of Speaker Randall as a determined and consistent champion of constituted authority. Clymer of Pennsylvania, Lane of Oregon, Springer of Illinois, Mills of Texas, Cox of New York, and O'Brien of Maryland, were no mean antagonists, but Randall proved a match for them, ruling out of order any motion to obstruct or impede the execution of the injunctions of the Constitution and the laws enacted thereunder to elect a President. Pandemonium broke loose in the House as the full import of the Speaker's position was realized, but cooler counsel prevailed. John Young Brown of Kentucky spoke up for a significant segment of southern opinion, promised that there would be no divided Democratic party, and urged his colleagues to stand by the execution of the electoral law. Hewitt, at once defiant and conciliatory, kept insisting that it was understood the Commission would go behind the returns, but went along with Tilden's request to Randall to complete the count. In the Senate Conkling finally took the floor to press for action to back the decision of the Electoral Commission on the Oregon vote, which was formally ratified that same day at the joint meeting of the Congress, concurrent action not being forthcoming to sustain the objections raised.

Despite delaying maneuvers, easily disposed of this time, Pennsylvania and Rhode Island were placed in the Republican column, and on Monday, February 26, South Carolina was reached in the call of the states. Once again, the pattern of an 8 to 7 Commission vote was set, and came almost as a matter of course, as the seven Republican electors had been officially certified by the incumbent governor, Chamberlain. The Democratic claimants lacked a gubernatorial stamp of approval, Wade Hampton having scrupulously refrained from injecting himself into his state's electoral dispute. Thus, by the end of the month, only six states were still to be accounted for, since the South Carolina case had proved small comfort to the diehard irreconcilables. Time was closing in on the electoral count now, with only three days left to the short session and inaugural day. By March 1, bargains, compromises, commitments, and promises on both sides seemed as firm as they ever could be. Grant would not recognize either of the rival governors in Louisiana or South Carolina; the days of Chamberlain in South Carolina and of Packard in Louisiana were clearly numbered; the federal troops would keep hands off civil affairs, and their removal was imminent. Should March 4 come and go without the choice of a President, the Senate had before it a bill passed by the

House establishing a line of succession listing first the President of the Senate, and then the Speaker of the House, and the Secretary of State.

But the filibusterers were not appeased nor quiescent, and on February 28 they took new heart when Abram S. Hewitt injected himself into the situation by coming up at the joint convention with a sealed Democratic certificate for Vermont, which President Ferry rejected as palpably belated. Again, as had happened so many times now, the two Houses separated; the Senate acted quickly enough in support of Ferry's ruling, and voted without dissent for the Hayes and Wheeler return; but the House held back, and on March 1, the filibusterers, with Earle Poppleton of Ohio, and Joseph C. S. Blackburn of Kentucky, in the foreground, went into action, aided by Proctor Knott of Kentucky, and other bitter-enders. Speaker Randall, with the help of Fernando Wood on the House floor, kept the prescribed rules for debate within bounds, despite deafening confusion, spontaneous and otherwise. He put down dilatory motions and insisted on a final and orderly vote after rejecting almost endless diversionary parliamentary stratagems. The exhausting day ground on until ten o'clock when the Vermont case was disposed of. That happened only because Representative William M. Levy reassured the House that once the count was completed the federal forces would be withdrawn from Louisiana and South Carolina, a pledge he felt a Hayes Administration would honor. Congressman William S. Haymond of Indiana, appealed to his fellow Democrats to see the count through, but when Wisconsin, the last state, was reached, Mills of Texas, made a desperate effort to turn an objection to a Republican elector's eligibility into a resolution to proceed at once to elect a President. Randall thwarted this, successfully put the original motion to disqualify the Republican elector to a vote, and then notified Senator Ferry to reconvene the joint meeting of the two Houses. He had in the meantime received word from Tilden to bring the count to a close.

It was now four o'clock in the morning of March 2; fully eighteen hours had elapsed since the legislative day had first gotten under way; at 4:10 a.m. Ferry formally announced that Hayes and Wheeler, with 185 electoral votes, had defeated Tilden and Hendricks, who had received 184 votes in the final tally. Randall and Hewitt had done their job well, the latter's Vermont gambit having held things up until Tilden's decision came through.

The early morning extras that fateful Friday reported Hayes and Wheeler in, with newpaper comment sharply divided and unmistakable evidence that, whatever the law, the dispute would linger on. The Boston *Post* concluded that the Republican claim to the Presidency rested on injustice and fraud. The Baltimore *Gazette* called the whole proceeding a confidence game. The southern press was surprisingly conciliatory. Characterizing the new President as a soldier-statesman, the Jacksonville (Florida) *Union* observed that the whole country would yet rejoice at Hayes' election. To the independent New York *Herald* the opening signs were auspicious, despite the outcries of a shocked Democracy. Hayes rode into Washington that March 2 in a private railroad car provided, ironically, by Tom Scott, of the Pennsylvania system. The trip had all the initial markings of a victory journey from the Ohio capital begun the day before, but, for the most part, it was subdued and dignified in tone, befitting the circumstances. On Saturday, March 3, President Grant held a state dinner for Hayes at the White House, and before it was underway, Chief Justice Waite, at Grant's request, administered the oath of office privately to Hayes in the Red Room, as March 4 fell on a Sunday, and the public inauguration was scheduled for Monday.

The count was over, but Congress still had business to complete before the session closed. There were appropriation bills to put through, and an army appropriation bill which precluded the use of troops to keep a state government in power unless it had been previously recognized by Congress. After several conferences, the Senate and House could not agree on this, and the bill was carried over to the next Congress, with the new fiscal year only a few months away and the implicit threat to the effective functioning of Hayes' Administration unmistakable. Other efforts to rid the South of continued military intervention, particularly in support of the governments of Chamberlain in South Carolina and Packard in Louisiana had been put forward earlier but with no success as such resolutions not only called for concurrent action of both Houses but required suspension of the rules by a two-thirds vote for passage. Nonetheless, the House, by large majorities, backed endorsement of the Nicholls government in Louisiana and Wade Hampton in South Carolina. The record also showed some last-minute maneuvers to win votes for a bill improving the Mississippi levees and a proposal for a Lake George, Florida, ship canal.

Speaker Randall may have pushed the electoral count through, but on the last day of the session, he did permit a vote on a resolution from J. Proctor Knott of the House Committee on the Privileges, Powers and Duties, holding that Tilden and Hendricks had won with 196 electoral votes, including the disputed states of Florida and Louisiana. Despite formidable Republican opposition, the resolution was adopted, 136 yeas to 88 nays, with 66 abstentions. Even Hewitt voted for it. To this was added another resolution, presented by David Dudley Field, declaring that in the counting of the electoral vote, Congress and the House have the right and duty to go behind the state returns. Then the House Democrats issued an "Address to the American People," reviewing the machinations that gave the Republicans the election, beginning with Zach Chandler's telegram and ending with J. Madison Wells, bargaining away his state's electoral vote. While there was much praise for Speaker Randall's handling of deliberations on both sides of the House, his valedictory to Congress that closing session made it crystal clear where he stood on the issues. It was a Democratic House that exposed fraud and corruption, introduced reforms, reduced expenditures, and reestablished peace. Victorious at the polls, the Democracy, to save the nation from civil commotion, "yielded temporary possession of the Administration," but the fact is indisputable that the Electoral Count Act was not carried out in the spirit of its creation nor according to the letter of its provisions. However, time will bring ultimate justice to the cause of the majority, concluded Randall.

Inauguration Day saw the sun break through overcast skies, heavy with snow-filled clouds, as Hayes, this time publicly, took the presidential oath on the central portico of the Capitol before a vast assemblage of spectators. The chill March winds lent a symbolic significance to the solemnity of the cere- monies. The day which witnessed the reaffirmation by the incoming President of the pledges of his letter of acceptance also saw the Senate convened in special session to confirm the nominations to the Cabinet and pass on its own membership, including Republican candidates from disputed southern states. The New York *Herald,* noting that the event signaled the beginning of the country's second century, predicted an era of progress and prosperity, long deferred but now, with the electoral crisis over, an attainable goal under a President committed to civil service reform, a sound currency, universal and nonsectarian education, simplicity and frugality in public and private affairs, and a southern policy of conciliation. Elaborating on this "new policy," the New York *Tribune* defined it as designed to appeal to the South's "most re- sponsible and influential classes," which would be encouraged to form "new political organizations." Hayes hoped thereby to unite the country, wipe out the color line, reduce partisanship, and promote national well-being. By way of reply to political pressures, the President enunciated the principle long to be remembered that "he serves his party best who serves the country best."

However numerous his political debts, Hayes managed to exercise a noteworthy leadership and independence that did credit to his Administration. His Cabinet choices, his withdrawal of troops from the South, his insistence, after vetoing a half dozen appropriation bills on the federal right to oversee congressional elections, his stand against the free silver interests and his suc- cessful support of the resumption of specie payments, all contributed to a shift in the balance of power from Congress to the Chief Executive. But the President was inclined to interpret the problems before him in narrowly politi- cal terms, and failed to come to grips with the complex social and economic forces generating the new issues of the day. His role in using troops to put down the nation-wide railroad strike and his mixed record on matters of civil service and the patronage limited his influence. The mounting pressures of a rapidly developing urban and industrial society eluded his statesmanship, remained unresolved, and became entangled in the bitterness, recrimination, and intense partisanship left in the wake of the disputed election. In the end, die-hard Democrats and some disgruntled Republicans, out to embarrass and destroy him, managed to keep the Administration on edge, particularly by the Potter Committee investigation of the past presidential election. Only the dramatic disclosures of the translated cipher dispatches served to redress the balance in favor of Hayes' title to office, and helped to rally his party behind him in the closing years of his term.

True to the understandings worked out by Boynton, William H. Smith, Kellar, Matthews, and Foster, President Hayes gave the southern Democrats good grounds for confidence as the new Administration got under way. Cabinet nominees not only included John Sherman, a confidant and strategist in the compromise maneuvers, William M. Evarts, reformer, liberal, and Hayes' counselor during the Electoral Commission deliberations, and Carl Schurz, now an eloquent champion of reconciliation with the South, but, as expected, the ex-Confederate, Senator David M. Key, who became Postmaster-General, and was entrusted with the disposal of vast patronage, hopefully to wean away enough conservative white Democrats to build a new Republican party in the South. Named also, as Secretary of War, was George W. McCrary, an appointment desired by the Scott-Gould railroad interests. With Evarts, Sherman, Schurz in State, Treasury, and Interior, respectively, Richard W. Thompson, a Morton man, in Navy, and Judge Charles Devens, Senator Hoar's nominee, as Attorney General, it was clear from the very first week in office in what direction the new Administration was headed and that Hayes would be his own master. Blaine, now in the Senate, and Stalwart Republicans like Conkling and Cameron were disposed, right from the start, to give battle and to question this leadership, but public opinion backed Hayes, the Cabinet choices were confirmed, and the way was cleared for the new dispensation.

Hayes had moved swiftly enough to show his good intentions toward the South in his Cabinet appointments, but on the crucial question of troop removals and backing for Hampton and Nicholls, he delayed action, seeking a satisfactory formula to redeem his pledges without unduly antagonizing the carpetbag regimes in South Carolina and Louisiana. While conservative Democratic pressures mounted and the Wormley letters of Matthews and Foster were released, with hints of more revelations to come, Hayes had Chamberlain and Hampton come to Washington and sent a five-man bipartisan commission under Wayne MacVeagh, as chairman to Louisiana to mediate between Nicholls and Packard. On April 10, 1877, the small federal contingent of troops protecting the Chamberlain government in the South Carolina state house at Columbia was withdrawn, and Wade Hampton took over. In Louisiana, the MacVeagh Commission, aided by Andrew J. Kellar, who had accompanied it to New Orleans, talked the Republican legislators backing Packard into joining the Democratic government of Nicholls, thereby making possible the necessary quorum for the conduct of state business. What material considerations prompted this change in allegiance only Kellar knew for certain, though rumors involving the Louisiana Lottery Company were rife. Hayes helped matters along by judicious federal and other appointments for the displaced Republican office-holders, including Packard. On April 24 the troops were recalled. Reconstruction was over in Louisiana and the South. The President had fulfilled a major promise, but the storm it aroused in Republican ranks was ominous. William E. Chandler, who had done so much to elevate Hayes to the Presidency, took a very dim view of it all, as did Republican Chairman Zach Chandler, former Massachusetts Senator George S. Boutwell, and other influentials of the Old Guard and Radical persuasion.

The test of how far the parties to the Compromise of 1877 would go in honoring the understandings came to a head in the contest over the Speakership of the new House. It was planned to put Garfield into office with southern votes. Hayes took this seriously enough, and dissuaded Garfield from seeking to replace Sherman as one of Ohio's senators, saving that post for his close associate, Stanley Matthews. The President convened the Forty-fifth

Congress in extra session on October 15. That same day, Samuel J. Randall won re-election as Speaker by a vote of 149 to 132. Democrats of all shades of opinion rallied to his support. Garfield, much to Hayes' discomfort, failed to muster the anticipated backing, even from his own party. In a hard and long canvass, lasting over seven months, Randall kept the Democrats in line, relying on party regularity, the hardening tradition of the "Solid South," and the good will resulting from his role in completing the electoral count. The Richmond *Dispatch* thought that if needed he might get some Republican votes, a not unlikely development as two years later Garfield himself got twenty Republican pledges to vote for Randall if disaffected low-tariff Democrats bolted their party's caucus nominee. Despite his stand against tariff revision, subsidies, and jobs, Randall was able to convince the South that as Speaker he would expedite legislation for internal improvements, reclamation of Mississippi River lands, and the construction of a Pacific Railroad. As a result, from Memphis to Galveston, southern papers rallied to his side. Meanwhile Hayes, appealing to the same interests, finally managed to disentangle himself from Tom Scott's Texas-Pacific scheme and to give Collis P. Huntington the go-ahead signal to build a Southern-Pacific line without federal aid.

Thus, by the opening of the special session of the new Congress, the Democratic South was in a strikingly strategic position to influence national affairs. With commitments from the President and the Speaker, with a major role on House committees, and with champions in the Senate from both parties, the southern Democracy had regained its old-time vigor in the councils of the government, perhaps enjoying as much power as would have resulted from a Tilden victory. On the other hand, the Republicans were a divided party, critically weakened by the reformist zeal of Secretaries Schurz, Sherman, and Evarts, and the President's inability to keep Congress in check, particularly after Democratic capture of the Senate in the elections of 1878. That year, too, marked a renewed effort to further becloud Hayes' title to office, a tactic designed to relieve pent-up frustrations in the opposition camp and to make political capital in anticipation of 1880. Against the background of the southern question, this threat to the President's right to office tended to put the entire election settlement in jeopardy, or so it was thought by Hayes and others, and the manner of its disposition added to the uncertainties and tensions of the Administration's "New Departure" politics.

The bitter disappointments that the President experienced at the hands of the Democrats in the special session of the Forty-fifth Congress only served as prelude to what was in store in overt partisanship once the regular session commenced on December 3, 1877. Gaining a party base in the white South may have intrigued the Hayes camp and its Liberal Republican following but Radicals, Stalwarts, and Half-Breeds were up in arms, certain that this new departure would do their party no good. Though the recipients of generous Administration patronage, southern Democrats generally sided with their northern colleagues in the political battles that ensued. Within a few months after inauguration, confessions and revelations of election irregularities in Louisiana and Florida set the stage for a sweeping investigation of the presidential count. In testimony, statements, and documents, Colonel T. C. Anderson, J. Madison Wells, J. E., "Scamp" Anderson, and D. A. Weber of Louisiana, and S. B. McLin and L. C. Dennis of Florida were involved in a sorry tale of fraud and chicanery in the canvassing of the election returns. All this was given wide press coverage, with the New York *Sun* hot on the scent from the very beginning.

That January, 1878, the Louisiana legislature debated the proper course to follow in the wake of the exposure of widespread corruption in the state's electoral canvass, finally seeking cover in an endorsement of Hayes and his southern policy of restoration, peace, and conciliation. Over in Maryland, Montgomery Blair, still bitter about the election outcome, moved successfully in the legislature to call on Congress to pave the way for state initiative in securing a Supreme Court review of the electoral decision. These developments spurred the Democratic high command, operating closely with Tilden, to press its advantage, such as it seemed at the time. The most likely tactic was a congressional investigation, and all through the spring there was mounting pressure in this direction, and a rising clamor that Hayes' election was the culmination of a plot engineered by his lieutenants Charles Foster and Stanley Matthews in collaboration with John Young Brown and other Democrats intent on a Texas-Pacific subsidy, no matter what the national cost. This was Montgomery Blair's theme and that of his close friend and business associate Republican Senator Roscoe Conkling, who, in a sensational interview widely circulated by the *World* and the *Sun*, hinted at a full-scale exposé of the Administration and its "Fraudulent President." Washington was in a ferment and demands piled up for a bill to authorize a *quo warranto* proceeding "to try the title of Mr. Hayes to the office he now occupies, but does not fill," as the New York *Sun* put it.

In the end, cooler heads prevailed and the Democrats fell back on a congressional inquiry, formally proposed by Clarkson N. Potter of New York, who, on May 13, sought to win the approval of the House by moving a vote on a question of privilege calling for an "investigation of alleged fraud in the late Presidential election in the states of Louisiana and Florida." The resolution recited the particulars of disclosures made and parties implicated, not excepting Secretary John Sherman and ex-Governor Edward F. Noyes, by then minister to France, whose role as visiting statesmen to Louisiana and Florida, respectively, was not above suspicion. Try as they might, the Republicans could not sidetrack the call for a select committee of eleven to investigate the alleged electoral frauds, nor could Speaker Randall, who had been briefed beforehand on the issues at stake, be dissuaded from ruling favorably on the question of privilege, taking into account the memorial of a sovereign state, Maryland, and the "the rightful occupancy of the chief executive chair of the Government." Disavowing any intention to impeach or unseat the President, nor, for that matter, "to disturb the peace and quiet of the country and that prosperity which is now beginning to revive," Potter finally managed on May 17 to round up the necessary majority for his resolution, which passed, 145 yeas, 2 nays, and 143 not voting. The Republicans to a man wanted no part in the proceeding. Three days later the committee selections were announced, with Potter chairman of the investigation, and both majority and minority membership clearly reflecting an anti-Hayes bias. Meanwhile, the Republican Congressional Committee issued an address to the country filled with dire forebodings about the future of the Republic, and called "on all who opposed the rebellion of 1861 to rally again to the support of law and order and stable government." Efforts to broaden the inquiry to include Oregon, South Carolina, and other states were thwarted, but a blanket authorization for the committee to investigate all fraud was forthcoming.

Postmaster General David M. Key of Tennessee and Congressman Alexander H. Stephens of Georgia rallied southern sentiment against the investigation, and despite disclaimers of evil intent by Potter, bipartisan concern to head off potential political mischief was sufficient to push through a suspension of the rules by a two-thirds vote of the House and the adoption of a resolution sponsored by H. C. Burchard, Republican of Illinois, to the effect that the Forty-fourth Congress had duly counted the votes for President and Vice-President, electing Hayes and Wheeler, and "that no subsequent Congress and neither House has jurisdiction to revise this action." This was on June 14, and hearings of the committee were already well under way in Washington and at Jacksonville, Florida. Significantly enough, of the 215 votes in favor of the resolution, there were three of the four Republicans on the committee, Jacob D. Cox of Ohio, Reed of Maine, and Hiscock of New York, and three committee Democrats, Eppa Hunton of Virginia, William R. Morrison of Illinois, and Stenger of Pennsylvania. Of the 21 negative votes 2 came from the hard-line committee Democrats, Blackburn of Kentucky, and Springer of Illinois. Among the fifty-five not voting were Chariman Potter and Democrat John A. McMahon of Ohio, and the nominal Republican Benjamin F. Butler of Massachusetts, a minority member of the committee but more than eager to embarrass the Hayes Administration and to make personal political capital out of the inquiry, as well he might, having espoused the Greenback cause while searching for Democratic favor in his own state. All the time Butler held a trump card in the form of a bundle of telegrams that came to him through William E. Chandler and were finally turned over to the Potter Committee in the wake of the sensational "Cipher Dispatches" revelations.

With hearings formally begun on June 1, the taking of testimony by the Potter Committee at the capital, in Florida, and at New Orleans and New York ran through the summer and into the fall, and was not concluded even as the last session of the Forty-fifth Congress got under way. These hearings at first were a devastatingly detailed exposure of electoral fraud and chicanery in the disputed states, with the onus resting squarely on the incumbent Republican-Carpetbag officialdom, aided and abetted by "visiting statesmen" and federal troops. In the end the inquiry turned out to be a débacle for the Democracy as the *Tribune's* decoding of the elaborate substitution and transposition cipher systems used in the telegrams of the opposition laid bare the full story of what Colonel Pelton and other Tilden men were up to in seeking a favorable canvass of the 1876 vote in the critical states. From June to October, it was all a Democratic show as the committee majority made headline copy in the testimony of Samuel B. McLin, among others and in the resounding chorus of confirmatory witnesses, who numbered over two-hundred before the evidence was all in, exposing the fascinating, if shocking, particulars of the behind-the-scenes maneuverings that won the election for the Republicans. But absorbing as the nearly three-thousand pages of finely printed testimony proved, the Democratic sense of high indignation engendered by the exposures gave way abruptly to a defensive and muted stance as the *Tribune* revelations revived sagging Administration morale and gave the committee minority its inning in a bid for renewed public confidence.

By the time the *Tribune* broke its story on October 7, 1878, enough had transpired at committee hearings to tarnish the reputations of the membership of the Louisiana Returning Board and Florida's Board of State Canvassers beyond redemption, and to trace the steps by which William H. Roberts, E. A. Burke, and Stanley Matthews, among others, engineered the bargain that gave Hayes the Presidency at the price of white conservative recognition in the disputed states. The results also encouraged an embittered Manton Marble to drive a wedge between Tilden and Abram S. Hewitt and to give impetus to an anti-Hayes Republican movement, pressed by William E. Chandler and the Grant camp. Whatever its original intention, the Potter Committee let loose a Pandora's box of damaging, if conflicting, evidence that only served to bring into disrepute the electoral process, and to put both parties on the defensive. With the cipher telegram disclosures, Republican derelictions were swiftly minimized, and the Democrats were denounced for frauds, violence, and intimidation, with Tilden himself compelled to answer before the bar of public opinion and the committee the charges of attempted vote-buying by his party managers.

The "Fraudulent Election" now was referred to as the "Crime of 1876." As the *Tribune* put it: "Instead of pinning 'fraud' on Hayes, the label has been turned on Samuel J. Tilden." On September 4, fully a month before the big exposé, that paper, in anticipation of coming events, retold the story of what deciphered telegrams had revealed about Democratic efforts to win over a Republican elector in Oregon, and considered this episode the retort perfect to Manton Marble's broadcast charge that the certificates of the three southern state returning boards had been for sale. They had been, of course, but only the *Tribune* knew the whole story by then, thanks to the cryptological skill of John R. G. Hassard and Colonel W. M. Grosvenor. Culpability in attempted bribery of the election officials rested on the Democrats, and the paper had some six hundred decoded telegrams to prove it. The telegrams originally were held by George E. Bullock, who had worked for Senator Morton's Committee on Privileges and Elections, where the cipher dispatches were initially abstracted from the great number turned over to it by Western Union. From Bullock, the telegrams passed to an Assistant Postmaster General, Thomas J. Brady and to William E. Chandler, Benjamin F. Butler, and other intermediaries, with copies and some originals finally reaching the *Tribune*.

The translated telegrams showed that Manton Marble and C. W. Woolley had been busily at work in Florida in a deal for electoral votes, and that Smith M. Weed was up to similar intrigue, first in Louisiana, and then, especially, in South Carolina, with Colonel Pelton directing negotiations from New York party headquarters. It was a sordid tale that compromised the Democratic managers and the National Committee beyond redemption, and gave the Republicans a fighting chance in the congressional elections of 1878, as the timing of the revelations was well calculated to do. Over a ten-day period the *Tribune*, with fine journalistic and partisan zeal, printed a full description of the cipher systems used and the keys to their interpretation, covering telegrams between New York headquarters and Democratic agents in California, Oregon, and the southern states. By October 16, when the last batch of incriminating dispatches had been spread upon the record, and Tilden had been baited mercilessly in the columns of the *Tribune* and other Republican papers, the Democratic standard-bearer, in a lengthy communication to the *Herald*, published October 18, took note of the disclosures of October 7 through the 16th, and denied any knowledge of or part in the Florida and South Carolina vote-buying allegations, but admitted that he had heard many rumors and called attention once again to the testimony of S. B. McLin and others before the Potter Committee as a surer clue to where the blame for corrupt dealings rested. This position was ably seconded by Montgomery Blair, who remained steadfast to Tilden as the party leader, and insisted on a sweeping condemnation of Hayes as the beneficiary of venal state canvassers, railroad and money interests, and a resurgent Whiggism, eager for internal improvements and other government favors.

But now the Democrats were on the spot, and the House Committee was a ready-made vehicle to pursue the cipher disclosures wherever they might lead. "Will they dare?" queried the *Tribune*. With the eyes of the country upon the committee, Potter had no choice, and after an agonizing delay of nearly two months, midway in the last session of the Forty-fifth Congress, a resolution was finally prepared and passed on January 21, 1879, calling on the committee to inquire into the cipher telegrams and to ascertain what, if any, illegal methods were employed to influence the electoral canvass in Florida, South Carolina, and Oregon. The very next day the committee went into executive session and requested one of its members, General Benjamin F. Butler, to turn over to it some six hundred telegrams in his possession. This he did, and Edward S. Holden, professor of mathematics at the United States Naval Academy was assigned the task of finding the keys to the cipher systems and verifying previous and preparing new translations. By February 21, Holden's report was submitted to the committee. Meanwhile, the majority proceeded to round up dispatches and to take testimony that might reveal Republican dereliction in the disputed states. Western Union officials were examined along with such luminaries as Whitelaw Reid, William E. Chandler, ex-Postmaster-General James N. Tyner, and Thomas J. Brady, but nothing especially derogatory developed to embarrass the Republicans. Some details came to light revealing Tyner's role in supplying subsidies for a Greenback journal and candidates in the 1876 October and November campaigns in Indiana, but that was not pursued, and, anyway, it had been disastrous for the Republicans.

Then a subcommittee opened hearings at the Fifth Avenue Hotel in New York. On February 6, Colonel William Tilden Pelton submitted to a nine-hour grilling. Adroit in shielding his uncle, he was forced to make admissions damaging to himself. Nevertheless, as he and Smith M. Weed and Manton Marble saw it, their party was not guilty but was being victimized by those who sought the bribes. It was merely recovering stolen goods from thieves, insisted Weed, and paying a sort of ransom, maintained Marble. Or, as the majority noted in its final report, the Democrats were being subjected to a form of blackmail. On February 7, Manton Marble was on the stand and he attempted to explain away the negotiations by insisting their pupose was to test the officials out. The relayed terms of the deals to purchase the Florida electoral votes he claimed were only "danger signals." Finally, on Saturday, February 8, Tilden, at his own request, appeared before the committee. His testimony was a reaffirmation of the position he had taken in his "card" to the *Herald* in October. The fiercely partisan *Tribune* not only raised doubts about Tilden's disavowals but painted a doleful picture of the witness as "a worn and haggard old man." Nor did the appearance that same day of his private secretary, George W. Smith, a coding expert, help the situation in any way. The committee hearings then shifted back to Washington and were continued until the very eve of congressional adjournment, at which time *Harper's Weekly* wrote off the Democratic pretensions to being the "party of reform," absolved Secretary Sherman and Minister to France Edward F. Noyes of any evil intent, praised Hayes as an authentic statesman, and downgraded Tilden to the level of "a shrewd politican." The Democracy felt otherwise, but, despite the ardor of his closest followers, who were determined on vindication in 1880, Tilden had, in fact, lost his hold on the party, and incurred the alienation of Hewitt, New York's Senator Francis Kernan, and the state's Lieutenant-Governor, William E. Dorsheimer.

The majority of the committee filed its report on March 3, reviewing testimony initially designed to humble the Administration; but the minority statement, drawn up by Jacob D. Cox of Ohio, was anything but defensive. Noting that the investigation into the cipher telegrams was still incomplete, the minority excoriated the Democrats for a systematic effort to corrupt the count in Florida, South Carolina, and Oregon. Castigating Weed, Marble, Pelton, and, by inference, Tilden, was only part of the indictment, for the overriding conclusion concerned itself with the condition of the freedman, victimized by the color line and now completely under the domination of his former master. What was needed was a change in the spirit and temper of the community and a respect for law and civil rights. Ben Butler made his own report, raising grave doubts about the constitutionality of the Electoral Commission, the involvement of the Supreme Court justices, and the count in Louisiana, which he maintained favored Packard and Tilden. Nor did he hesitate to question the propriety of the President in sending the MacVeagh Commission to Louisiana.

Hayes' term of office was now half over, but the burning issue of his "lawful title" to the Presidency was still very much in the public mind, and despite the ironic boomerang of the Potter Committee investigation, Democratic political ascendancy in Congress was undiminished. Pennsylvania and Ohio went Democratic in November, 1878, and the Republicans lost the Senate. The contest over the Speakership was almost a replay of 1877; Garfield spurned Greenback aid and allowed Randall to win without a fight; committee appointments favored conservative southern interests and a continuation of a tight budgetary policy. But there the truce ended. Hayes and Congress were still at odds over riders to the major appropriations for the Army and the civil establishment, and the Forty-sixth Congress had been convened in special session, March 18, 1879, to finally resolve this impasse. Developments in the South re-enforced Hayes' determination to eliminate the riders and thus assure funds for federal policing of congressional elections through available military personnel and United States supervisors and marshalls. By a succession of cogent vetoes and the able cooperation of Garfield in the House, Hayes convinced his party that the 15th Amendment guaranteeing Negro suffrage would be enforced, and thereby erased some of the apprehensions of Stalwart Republicans that the President had completely capitulated to the southern Democrats. This setback for the Democracy spurred Randall to enlist in Tilden's cause and to seek through his name, if not nomination, party Presidential victory in 1880. The Republicans, curiously were grooming Grant for a like role. Also, pointing to 1880, and with confirmation of his leadership in mind, Hayes went on a political fence-mending tour through the Middle West in the fall of 1879, stressing the indivisibility of the Union and the national obligation to protect the freedman in his constitutional rights. Nor was the President reticent about taking credit for the signs of business revival that were everywhere apparent.

However much Hayes and his party sought to get on with the business of government, it was clear that the Democratic leadership would not let the nation forget the circumstances of Tilden's defeat, nor would the northern Democracy and its allies in the West and South miss a single opportunity to take advantage of the developing political situation in their quest for ultimate victory and vindication. In the presidential election canvass of 1880 and again in 1884, the memory of 1876 was a spur to action, and the lessons of the Compromise of 1877 were interpreted for partisan ends. These were immediate repercussions, but their meaning was not lost on future generations, and as recently as the election of 1968 the results were recalled for guidance and as a warning in the choice of a President under our electoral system. The Union had been saved from disruption a second time but at a price that marked an all-time low in the functioning of popular government. Beyond this, materialism reigned triumphant and the idealism of the Liberal-Republican-Democratic coalition of 1872 gave way to capitalist ambition, industrial might, and sectional rigidity. Whatever Hayes' expectations for his party in the South, the "Lost Cause" was regained, the Democracy strengthened, and the Republicans left to seek greener political pastures in the West.

The Gilded Age was just about spent and the election of 1876 took its place in the mythology of America's historic past, along with such contemporaneous events as the Texas-Pacific Railway scheme, the escapades of Boss Tweed, the Beecher-Tilton scandal, Custer's last stand and the final surrender of Crazy Horse. Left unanswered was the question of how and when fundamental new problems posed by the new industrial era would arouse the political genius of the nation. The outcome of the War and the promise of the Reconstruction forged a new nationalism, with party and section vying for favor at the seat of government and in the councils of northern business interests committed to sound money, protective tariffs, state and federal subsidies, especially for internal improvements, and all this, paradoxically, in a *laissez-faire* political and economic environment. Under the pressures of a burgeoning industrial and technological society, the Presidency took on a new dimension and became a focal point of decision-making in the resolution of the conflicting issues that confronted the nation's lawmakers. Once again, accommodation or compromise was the order of the day, and executive leadership, in its reliance on an electoral system that was weighted in favor of just such solutions, promoted sectional harmony as it sought a sure formula for party survival. Southern backing of Hayes meant a respite from agitation of the War and Reconstruction, however much men like William E. Chandler, Roscoe Conkling, and James G. Blaine sought to wave the bloody shirt. While there was some talk of a Whig revival in the South, it seemed more likely, as the *Nation* observed early in May, 1877, "the true principles" that would decide the next presidential election were civil service reform, sound currency, reduction of taxation, stoppage of all grants and subsidies, and a tariff for revenue only. The Republican party made little headway in the South as the Conservative-Democratic alignment hardened. The blunt truth is, that whatever their original intentions, Hayes and his advisers had sacrificed the Negro in the South on the altar of political expediency.

The judiciary, despite its Republican orientation, joined with the executive and Congress in setting the pattern of the New Departure politics. The Supreme Court circumscribed the 14th Amendment, strictly limiting its application to actual state violations of due process and equal protection. This precedent was first set in 1876 in United States vs. Cruikshank, and then, in 1883, in the Civil Rights Cases, Justice Bradley, speaking for the Court, struck down the Civil Rights Act of 1875, turning back to the states responsibility for safeguarding civil liberties generally and, specifically, in places of public accommodation; and all this despite the constitutional mandate that Congress enforce the Reconstruction amendments by appropriate legislation. As Bradley put it, Congress cannot "create a code of municipal law for the regulation of private rights"; but Justice John M. Harlan, a Hayes appointee to the bench, in a vigorous dissent, made it unmistakably clear that "the substance and spirit of the recent amendments to the Constitution have been sacrificed by a subtle and ingenious verbal criticism." Three-quarters of a century were to elapse before that substance and spirit would gain national recognition once more, with the Warren Court playing a leading role in the renewed guarantee of civil rights and full equality for all.

As for electoral reform, it was all but forgotten as the South settled down to pursue its separate way. Party leaders on both sides showed little inclination to revise the Electoral College set-up for the choice of a President; and not until 1887 was there even any effort made to lay down the ground rules for an agreed-upon procedure in the electoral count. Had there been an apportionment of the electoral vote to parallel the popular vote, the Democrats would have won in 1888, and, as political scientist Neal Peirce shows, in 1880, and also in 1896; but the fifteen states of the Solid South saw more to be gained by the established electoral system, as did, of course, the Republicans, thanks to overwhelming strength in the North and the expanding western states. After 1892 Republican strategists felt little incentive to press for party favor, black or white, in the South, and the lessons of 1876 and 1888 had confirmed their faith in the general ticket or unit vote system for electing a President. By the Act of 1887 concurrent action of both Houses was needed to reject an electoral vote. This was nothing new, having been resorted to in the disputed election compromise on the count. More change was in prospect, however. Of the ten constitutional amendments adopted since 1870, five dealt with the Presidency, fixing the term of office (1933), setting a two-term limit (1951), allowing an electoral vote to the District of Columbia (1961), barring a poll or other qualifying tax in federal elections (1964), and tidying up presidential succession in case of death, disability, or disinclination to serve (1967). Each election brought home to the American people the inherent dangers to the democratic process in the winner-take-all Electoral College method of selecting the Chief Executive. But until the fears of those who see resort to popular election as a threat to the two-party system are set at rest, there is little hope of change. Half-way proposals, such as the proportional plan that won Senate approval in 1950, or the district plan for the choice of electors seem less appealing than the proposed direct popular vote amendment embodied in the Dirksen-Celler measure (1967), which sets a plurality of at least 40 per cent to win, and failing that, a run-off between the two highest candidates.

The transition from the ordeal of Reconstruction to politics as usual had put the nation to the severest test since the war itself. So much was at stake and so critical were the times that the very fate of Republican institutions and Democratic aspirations hung in the balance. In a mad scramble for political power and economic advantage honorable men were corrupted and party principles undermined. By the accident of history, it fell to Hayes and his Administration to embark on a program of political regeneration and high moral purpose on the crumbling foundations of a misguided southern policy. It became Tilden's sad lot to serve as the symbol and rallying point for an idealized version of what might have been, had the centennial of American independence witnessed the emergence of a triumphant Democracy. All contingencies considered, the only certainty, concluded the Nation on March 3, 1881, was that, whatever the tides of party battle, the great strides in population and industry would make a distinct change in the form and spirit of American government. Change there was, and democracy in practice proved itself equal to each succeeding challenge.

Election of 1896

by *Gilbert C. Fite*

The presidential campaign and election of 1896 took place in an atmosphere of national crisis. During the years preceding this important political contest, depression, political unrest, economic and class conflicts, and violence had tormented the country. In 1894 such events as the march of industrial armies on Washington and the Pullman strike had caused widespread alarm over the question of law and order. "Shall law and order prevail," asked one congressman at the time of the Pullman strike, "or shall mobocracy triumph." Indeed, many Americans in 1894 and 1895 expressed serious doubts about the nation's social stability and the viability of its democratic institutions. The fear, dissension, and unrest which intensified throughout the country after 1893 reached a climax in this hard-fought presidential election.

President Grover Cleveland's second term began on March 4, 1893, and proved to be a fateful period both for the nation and for the Democratic party. At the outset conditions appeared favorable enough. The President's popular mandate over Republican and Populist opponents in 1892 had been substantial, and the Democrats controlled both houses of Congress with good working majorities. However, the President had just settled in the White House when the Panic of 1893 spread throughout the country. Farm prices dropped to disastrous levels; thousands of businesses and banks closed their doors; unemployment reached staggering proportions. Retiring President Benjamin Harrison's claim, made in December, 1892, that "there has never been a time in our history when work was so abundant, or when wages were as high" soon became a mockery to the hundreds of thousands of workers looking for non-existent jobs. The nineties were anything but gay to the country's unemployed laborers and to farmers who struggled, often unsuccessfully, against bankruptcy and foreclosure.

Neither Cleveland nor the Democratic party was responsible for the Panic of 1893 and the subsequent depression, but because of the nature of American politics, many people placed the blame on the President and his Administration. In this situation, the key to future Democratic success would depend to a considerable extent on how Cleveland and his party responded to the problems facing the nation. His political philosophy and experience would dictate a conservative and traditional response to the country's problems, for firm and inflexible in his views, he did not believe in social and economic experimentation. The guidelines of his economic policy were careful and judicious public expenditures, maintenance of the gold standard, and reduction of the tariff. Cleveland viewed the Populist demand for free and unlimited coinage of silver, the suggestion of federally-financed work relief, government ownership of the railroads, or a graduated income tax as heresy. Social and economic reform was narrowly construed and mainly favored those representing established interests and power. It is not surprising then that Cleveland soon came into conflict with those in and outside of his party who were calling for seemingly radical measures designed primarily to benefit farmers and workers.

By 1893 and 1894, the most controversial issue before the nation was money. The depression intensified the demand for free silver and currency expansion which some groups had advocated for a decade or more. Inflationists argued that free silver would raise prices, lift the crushing burden of debt, and restore prosperity. Not only Populists and other agricultural spokesmen demanded inflation. An increasing number of Republicans and Democrats in the West and South joined them and the volume of literature favoring free silver continued to grow. One of the most popular publications was *Coin's Financial School*, a small, paperback volume by William H. Harvey. In this book Harvey presented the free silver arguments in dialogue form along with refutations of the gold standard position. He also included cartoons illustrating how the gold standard, supported by bankers and monopolists, exploited farmers and workers. One cartoon picturing the nation as a cow, showed western farmers feeding the cow, but an eastern banker enjoying the milk.

The money question was not the only cause of discontent. Many Americans believed that monopoly, concentration of wealth, and political and economic oppression threatened the very foundations of democracy in the United States. The editor of *Home, Field and Forum*, published at Guthrie, Oklahoma Territory, declared in 1894 that, "the United States today is completely under the control of the money power and bondholders. Wrong doing, extraordinary oppression, and monopoly are so firmly entrenched that they will not yield, even to the plain laws of the country." According to this writer, transportation as well as other necessities of life were controlled by the "hydra-headed monster," monopoly.

Many other citizens were rapidly coming to agree with this Populist position. The Grand Master of the Knights of Labor told a large group of unemployed workers in Baltimore that millions of men without work had been turned into felons, beggars, and tramps because a small, rich class had acquired nearly all of the nation's property. A poor woman in Arizona in 1893 wrote, "God only knows how the poor are oppressed, all over the United States and scarcely any one in power to help them." Two years later the Master of the Wisconsin State Grange declared that there was something "radically wrong in a system under which a few thousand people out of a population of about seventy million have been permitted to absorb more than one half of the entire wealth of the country." By the 1890's many Americans had concluded that the nation's economy was operating mainly for the benefit of the rich and the super-rich. The system itself was coming under attack.

Discussion, reconciliation, and compromise soon gave way to violent confrontations. The incidents at the Carnegie steel works at Homestead, Pennsylvania, and the mining community of Coeur d'Alene, Idaho, in 1892 were only a prelude to bigger and bloodier conflict. Throughout the spring of 1894 disagreement between labor and management erupted into violence. In western Pennsylvania coal miners stoned an engineer to death and threw his body in a coke oven. In Buffalo, New York, a thousand workers fought with police, and in Cleveland striking laborers rampaged through the industrial section of town throwing stones, breaking windows, and driving non-striking workers from the plants. Meanwhile, Jacob Coxey of Ohio, accompanied by a band of discontented and unemployed citizens, invaded Washington, D.C. to seek work relief and an inflationary monetary policy. Coxey engaged in a kind of civil disobedience and was arrested for carrying banners on the Capitol grounds and walking on the grass, but he had dramatized the difficulties and demands of many Americans.

Although these events caused widespread uneasiness, nothing raised such gnawing doubts and fears about the country's social stability as the Pullman strike of June and July, 1894. This strike led to a series of violent clashes between workers and law enforcement officials, including units of the Army. When Americans picked up their newspapers on July 9, they were faced with such frightening headlines as, "Troops Now Being Mobilized," in Chicago, "Mobs Ordered to Disperse," and "Law-Abiding Citizens Warned Not to Join in Riotous Demonstrations." Although most citizens approved of the police and troop action to quell the violence and stop the destruction of property, suppression was no permanent solution to the fundamental problems which had given rise to the disturbances. Cleveland had ordered sufficient force to restore law and order, but a more basic question remained: Why were men arming themselves and taking to the streets rather than solving their differences through the democratic process? From the vantage point of January, 1895, a writer in the *Forum* declared that "the social fabric seemed to be measurably near to dissolution, and the country was not far from the verge of anarchy." At the same time Albert B. Hart, the budding young Harvard historian, noted "the decline of the old-fashioned, good-tempered agreement to come to a decision and take the consequences if one is outvoted." There was, he added, a great impatience with "legal and constitutional methods of bringing about a change of laws."

The editor of the *Kansas Farmer* was only one of many who sought to explain this situation. He declared that the primary cause of the violence and bloodshed was a contest over the possession "of some of God's gifts to man." The writer continued by asking whether the United States was in the early phases of an internal struggle which would destroy the country or whether "organized society [government] shall be made the instrument for future advancement of the race and greater and more universal enjoyment." In other words, the distribution of economic and political power was at stake; would the established power structure extend a fair share of the benefits produced by all of society to those, mainly farmers and workers, who had so little? This same question was being raised by Populists, Socialists, intellectuals, and a host of social critics. President Cleveland, however, did not consider this fundamental problem.

As far as national issues were concerned, money continued to hold the center of popular attention. From the conservative viewpoint, a crisis developed in the summer of 1893, when abandonment of the gold standard became a genuine possibility. The main threat to so-called "sound money" was the Sherman Silver Purchase Act of 1890 which provided for the issuance of treasury notes to pay for the silver bullion purchased under the law. The notes could be redeemed legally in either gold or silver, but the Government had paid notes presented to it only in gold which placed a heavy drain on the Treasury. By April, 1893, the gold reserve had dropped to less than $100 million, the amount believed necessary to assure maintenance of the gold standard. Bankers, businessmen, chambers of commerce, and many political leaders frantically urged the President to call a special session of Congress to repeal the Sherman Silver Purchase Act as a means of saving the gold standard. No outside pressures, however, were needed. Already convinced that the gold standard must be preserved, Cleveland called Congress into special session on August 7.

The Administration controlled enough votes to repeal the controversial law on October 30, but the debate in and out of Congress demonstrated how politically divisive the money question had become. It not only produced splits within the Democratic party, but contributed to class and sectional conflicts as well. Millions of westerners and southerners bitterly opposed repeal because they believed that eastern business and financial interests were exploiting the agricultural sections by maintaining a depreciating currency. Gold was the symbol of that exploitation. During the debate in the House a young congressman from Nebraska, William Jennings Bryan, arose and declared that "on the one side stand the corporate interests of the United States, the moneyed interests, aggregated wealth and capital, imperious, arrogant, compassionless. . . . On the other side stand an unnumbered throng, those who gave to the Democratic party a name and for whom it has assumed to speak. Work-worn and dust begrimed, they make their mute appeal, and too often find their cry for help beat in vain against the outer walls, while others, less deserving, gain ready access to legislative halls."

Senator Henry M. Teller of Colorado, one of the nation's best known free silverites, warned the country to resist the economic royalists — "the men who own the money of the world, the bonds, and the interest-bearing securities" — or the country would sink into "a system of industrial slavery which will be the worst known of the human race."

Before the debate ended the President and his supporters were coming under bitter personal attack. Their opponents called them "cuckoos" and "pot-bellied 'hypocrites." Cleveland was greatly distressed by what he saw happening. "I am very much depressed," he wrote. "I find that I am looking full in the face a loss of popular faith in the Democratic party which means its relegation to the rear again for many years if not its destruction."

Controversy surrounding Cleveland's monetary policies were not confined to repeal of the Sherman Silver Purchase Act. Early in 1894 the gold reserve again fell to seemingly dangerous levels. In order to assure the maintenance of the gold standard, Cleveland instructed his Secretary of the Treasury, John G. Carlisle, to sell government bonds to private bankers in exchange for gold. This aroused bitter and widespread opposition among inflationists. To his free silver critics, the President had become a tool of Wall Street rather than a representative of the common people.

Meanwhile, the tariff, always a source of political dissension, created other problems. Cleveland's commitment to lower rates not only brought him into conflict with high tariff Republicans but with members of his own party who benefited from protection. In December, 1893, William L. Wilson of West Virginia introduced a bill which advocated extending the free list and lowering the duties on many other items. The Wilson bill passed the House rather easily early in 1894, but lack of support by eighteen southern and eastern Democratic congressmen foreshadowed future trouble for the Democrats. Spokesmen from Louisiana, for instance, adamantly favored a tariff on sugar and strenuously opposed placing it on the free list as provided in the House bill.

In the Senate, Democratic defections were even greater. Indeed, the Senate, with substantial support from Democrats, reversed much of what the House had done, by raising rates on many items and reducing the free list. Despite all that Cleveland and the Democratic House and Senate leadership could do, no tariff bill could pass which met Cleveland's desires or fulfilled Democratic platform pledges. The Wilson-Gorman tariff, adopted in August, 1894, lowered rates slightly, but did not come anywhere near meeting the demands of the President. Unhappy with the legislation, Cleveland allowed the bill to become law without his signature.

Controversy over tariff legislation had been long and bitter, extending from December, 1893, to August, 1894. During this time, debate over the issue had produced severe tensions within the Democratic party and throughout the country. Following the conflict over the conference committee report, the Springfield (Massachusetts) *Republican* declared: "It is a question whether the fight has not continued long enough as it is to cost the Democracy its place as a majority party, if not the very life of the organization."

A further threat to the Democratic party was President Cleveland's inability to hold the support of a number of prominent state Democratic leaders. One of these was Governor John Peter Altgeld of Illinois. Elected in 1892, Governor Altgeld was a man who had deep sympathy for the poor and underprivileged. He was flexible in his thinking and held more advanced views on social ánd economic matters than many of his contemporaries. Nevertheless, he was a true Democrat and hoped to work with Cleveland and other conservatives within the party. When the President ordered troops into Chicago over Altgeld's strong protest in July, 1894, the event produced irreparable conflict between the governor and the President. Moreover, Senator David B. Hill of New York, one of the most influential and active Democrats in the East, broke with Cleveland and criticized him as openly as some of the wildest free silverites. Irritating the situation was the growing disunity between eastern Democrats and those in the West and South.

The difficulties created for Cleveland and the Democrats by economic problems and political issues were greatly intensified by the worsening depression. By 1894 industrial conditions were stagnant and agriculture was at one of its lowest levels in the nation's history. Some fifty-six railroads with thirty thousand miles of track representing an investment of $2.5 billion had gone into the hands of receivers. Thousands of industrial plants had closed and construction had dropped drastically. Overall, there had been a great decline in investment which meant fewer jobs and less consumption; a heavy outflow of gold also forced bankers to tighten credit. The total effect of these conditions was the creation of extremely hard times. Unemployment affected at least 20 per cent of the total labor force, and more than two and a half million workers tramped the streets looking for non-existent jobs. Henry Adams recalled that "men died like flies under the strain, and Boston grew suddenly old, haggard and thin." Asking what would beçome of the unemployed, the New York *World* declared: "Starve—that's what. Without bread they will die. This is not talk; it's truth. Cut them open as they die and see." People in New York walked miles to try to get a loaf of free bread, only to find after standing in line that the supply was exhausted. "Yesterday morning when the last crumb was gone," continued the writer, "there was a line of men along Delancy Street clear to the Bowery, and a line of women along Chrystie Street up to the state entrance of the People's theater." Terence V. Powderly told a group of workingmen in August, 1894, that "charity has been strained as it was never strained before, but still the cry for bread from starving throats is heard all over the land."

Throughout the great expanses of rural America conditions were as bad as in the depressed industrial centers. By 1894 agricultural prices had dropped to the lowest point which any person could remember. Cotton brought only four and five cents a pound, wheat less than fifty cents a bushel, and corn was so cheap farmers burned it for fuel. The prices of cattle and hogs scarcely covered the cost of marketing. Farmers who were in debt found it impossible to meet their interest and principal payments, and thousands of them saw their farms taken through foreclosure. To make matters worse, severe drouth struck much of the Great Plains, forcing untold numbers of farmers to leave their homes and requiring others to rely on public and private charity.

Hard times, recent public disorder and violence, and bitterness over Cleveland's tariff and monetary policies worked against the Democrats as the midterm elections of 1894 approached. F. L. Stetson, Cleveland's former law partner, saw the situation clearly. Just before the election he wrote: "We are on the eve of a very dark night unless a return of commercial prosperity relieves popular discontent." However, there was no upswing in the economy. Indeed, Cleveland's statement calling for repeal of the Sherman Silver Purchase Act now seemed naive and silly. He had told Congress that the depression was the result of "financial distrust" and business fears resulting from unsound silver legislation. He implied that repeal of the act would restore prosperity by encouraging business confidence, but economic conditions had grown worse. Nothing the President said or did seemed to turn out right. The course of events, along with his own inflexibility, made it impossible for Cleveland to develop any kind of working consensus either within his party or across the nation.

The midterm elections of 1894 illustrated what had happened to the Democratic party. After a disastrous defeat the year before, the Republicans made a comeback in local and state elections in 1893 and then swept both houses of Congress. They turned their minority of 127 to 218 in the House and 38 to 44 in the Senate in the Fifty-third Congress, to a whopping majority of 244 to 105 and 43 to 39. The tremendous Republican victory in the House where candidates were directly elected was especially ominous for the Democrats in any future presidential contest. The Republicans made remarkable gains in the Northeast and Midwest, and did well in the Plains States; in the South some coalitions between Republicans and Populists threatened Democratic control. Not only did the Republicans win a majority in Congress in 1894, they won victory after victory in local and state elections as well. In the minds of millions of voters, the Democratic party had become the party of depression and hard times. Consequently, Democratic strength eroded away in both urban and rural areas. While the Populists success — 1,471,000 votes, 42 per cent above 1892 — represented growing dissatisfaction with both old parties, it was the Republican party which emerged as the country's strongest political force in 1894.

The Republican triumph in 1894 did not quiet the growing class and sectional divisions. Issues had become too deep and differences too strong to permit any basic consensus for, although the money question continued as the most important issue, much more was at stake. In 1895 the Supreme Court delivered three decisions which seemed to pit group against group and class against class. The E. C. Knight case, decided in January, 1895, acquitted the

American Sugar Refining Company of violating the Sherman Antitrust Act. Even though the company had a clear monopoly, the prosecution lost the case partly because of ineffective presentation before the Court. The decision convinced many citizens that the Federal Government was not really interested in curbing the power of giant enterprise. As William Howard Taft wrote, the decision's effect "was to discourage hope that the statute could be used to accomplish its manifest purpose, and curb the great industrial trusts."

In May the Court struck down the income tax which had been a part of the Wilson-Gorman Tariff Law. Conservatives, especially easterners, praised the judges for outlawing what they considered an unconstitutional and even communistic attack on property. But farmers and workers saw the decision as an additional victory for the rich and the powerful. Later in the same month the Supreme Court sustained the injunction against Eugene V. Debs issued the year before for his activities in the Pullman strike. Workers were as angered at this decision as farmers had been by the income tax case. These were not party but class issues, and the divisions were nearly as deep in the Republican party as they were in Democratic ranks.

By 1895 free silver had become the question of the day. No issue since the Civil War had aroused people's emotions so deeply or produced such bitter controversy. Despite efforts by supporters of the gold standard, free silver gained more and more adherents. Free silverites proclaimed that silver was the money of the masses while gold was the money of the classes; that silver coinage would help the great body of farmers and workers, while the gold standard oppressed the people and robbed them for the benefit of the rich. Senator John T. Morgan of Alabama wrote in the *Arena* in 1895: "Gold is the money of the speculator and the miser, while silver fructifies industry as the rains do the earth. . . . Silver is an incentive to trade and industry because it stimulates labor and gives to it, every day, the rewards of its daily earnings. Not so with gold; it waits for the more convenient season, when it can gather harvests where it has not sown." The American Bimetallic League and the National Bimetallic Union were among the organizations whose main purpose was to promote the cause of free silver. Indeed, free silverites flooded the country with articles, pamphlets, essays, and books, all of which advanced the economic arguments on behalf of free and unlimited coinage of silver. So rapid was the rise of silver sentiment throughout the West and South that Bryan predicted in February, 1895, "There is no question now that the campaign of 1896 will be fought on the money question . . . between the capitalists of the Northeast and the rest of the people of the country."

Although the Populist party had made free silver a major issue ever since 1890, a rapidly growing number of Republicans and Democrats were joining the free silver forces by 1894 and 1895. This created sharp internal dissensions within the old parties since both the Democratic and Republican leadership was committed to the gold standard. Richard P. "Silver Dick" Bland, a Democratic congressman from Missouri and one of the nation's most loyal silverites, told his colleagues in the House in January, 1895, that the Cleveland Administration was really not the Democratic party. Bland declared that he would appeal to the "vast yeomanry of this country, the great masses of the people, and I hope that there will be a sufficiency of the Democratic party to rally around the great principles of democracy . . . and organize the party on the principles of Jefferson and Jackson." To Bland such reorganization meant control by the party's supporters of free silver. Stories even circulated that Bland might bolt the Democratic party, but he spiked these rumors on March 23, insisting that he was a loyal Democrat and only hoped to bring the party back to "its old principles." At the same time, however, he emphasized that the Democrats could not gain any future victory "without utterly repudiating Cleveland's policy on the money question." Moreover, he could not personally support the Democratic party if it put up "a candidate on a platform in harmony with Mr. Cleveland's Administration." If this was not a threat to defect from the party, it certainly served notice that Bland would do everything within his power to wrest control of the party from the so-called "gold bugs."

About a month later, William Jennings Bryan, who was serving his last term in Congress, brought the question of silver and party loyalty into sharp focus. He declared that loyalty to the people and to the party was more important than loyalty to the President. "I want to suggest to my Democratic friends," he said, "that the party owes no great debt of gratitude to its President." Bryan ventured that the Democrats should have the same feelings toward Cleveland as "toward the trainman who has opened a switch and precipitated a wreck." The Nebraskan further charged that eastern Democrats and Republicans had locked arms to carry out financial policies inimical to the rest of the nation. If eastern interests continued to exploit the masses, Bryan predicted, "The rest of the people of the country will drop party lines, if necessary, and unite to preserve their homes and their welfare."

Bryan and Bland were articulating the deep spirit of unrest within Democratic ranks. Along with other colleagues, they decided that it was time for free silverites to try to gain control, and before Congress adjourned in March, 1895, Bryan attempted to organize these forces within the party. This movement resulted in a statement signed by thirty-one House members calling on Democrats to make their party the party of free silver. Following the adjournment of Congress, Bryan spoke widely throughout the Midwest and South where enthusiastic crowds applauded his attacks upon the money power and his call for new party leadership. In June a free silver convention in Memphis drew many prominent Democrats. Meanwhile, free silver literature flooded the mails. Alarmed at this publicity campaign, a leading Wisconsin Democrat wrote to the President's secretary in April, 1895, that he was amazed at the growing strength of the movement. "The difficulty in the nation is that the free silver advocates are active," he wrote, unlike those favoring Cleveland's position.

Following the Memphis convention in June, 1895, a group of free silver Democrats organized the National Democratic Bimetallic Committee. Among the leaders were Senators James K. Jones of Arkansas, David Turpie of Indiana, and Isham G. Harris of Tennessee, and their goal was to win control of the party before the presidential nominating convention in 1896. About two months later many movement leaders met in the District of Columbia to lay plans for their campaign. There a national committee was formed to recruit and organize free silver Democrats for the purpose of taking over the party organization.

Bryan was not at the Washington meeting, nor did he become a member of the Democratic National Bimetallic Committee. Rather, he worked alone, and hoped through his speaking and writing to bring not only Democrats but independents, Populists, and Republicans into a national movement for free silver. While Bryan hoped to rally all of the free silver forces in the Democratic party, he did not discount the possibility that free silverites might have to act independently if the gold forces controlled the Democratic convention. Thus, as Stanley L. Jones has pointed out: "While the Democratic National Bimetallic Committee shouldered the burden of reorganizing the party internally, Bryan individually took on the larger task of rallying the great multitude of free silver voters, who were not traditionally Democrats, into a silver Democratic party."

President Cleveland observed the growing free silver influence with deep dismay. While he was reluctant to take any action which would further divide the party, it became clear by the spring of 1895 that his wing of the party was in grave danger of losing control. In April the President vigorously defended his "sound" money policies in a letter to a group of Chicago businessmen, especially emphasizing how workers would be hurt by silver coinage and inflation. There could be no disguising the issue, Cleveland wrote, "the line of battle is drawn between the forces of safe currency and those of silver monometallism."

Cleveland also used patronage and powerful friends to help the gold standard supporters maintain control during intraparty disputes in some midwestern states, but as 1895 passed, he found it harder and harder to find reliable and influential supporters. Free silver sentiment in Illinois and Indiana, for example, was simply too strong to permit many Democratic leaders to back the President. In Ohio the liberal use of money and patronage allowed the gold standard Democrats to stay in power, but free silverites were winning more battles than the gold men in the Midwest and West.

The President also made a serious attempt to keep the South out of the hands of free silver Democrats. He argued that cotton growers benefited from the gold standard because they exported their cotton in exchange for gold, and he sent several members of his Cabinet into the South to speak for his monetary policy. Secretary of the Treasury Carlisle toured the Border States in May, speaking at the convention in Memphis among other places. In October the President himself visited Atlanta, but he could not hold the loyalty or support of many southern Democratic leaders. Attacking the President personally, Ben Tillman of South Carolina told the voters in his state: "Send me to Washington, and I'll tickle Cleveland's fat ribs with my pitchfork." Others joined him in heaping personal abuse on the President.

State and local elections in the fall of 1895 illustrated how internal division continued to hurt the Democrats; they suffered severe losses in Ohio, Illinois, and Kentucky. Senator Isham Harris of Tennessee wrote: "In the light of recent election results there is, in my opinion, no hope of Democratic success in 1896 unless we can succeed in so organizing the bimetallic Democrats as to secure in the national convention a plain, distinct, and unmistakable declaration in favor of the free and unlimited coinage of both silver and gold." Many Democrats agreed, including Bryan, who wrote Ignatius Donnelly, the Minnesota Populist, in November, 1895: "I am doing what I can to get the silver Democrats to capture the national convention. . . . I shall not support a gold bug for president."

The rapid rise of silver sentiment within Democratic ranks caused perplexing problems for the Populists. The People's party had supported free silver enthusiastically ever since 1890, but it had advocated a wide variety of other economic and political reforms as well. By 1895 the Populists faced the dilemma of fighting for broad reforms or concentrating mainly on the silver issue with which the party was so closely identified. Populists in the West and Midwest tended to support the narrower platform. Herman Taubeneck, Chairman of the National Executive Committee, wrote that "we shall, more than likely, confine ourselves to the money question in the future and make that the test of party fealty." Looking ahead to 1896, Senator Peffer said that he, too, was willing to "make free silver the single issue of the campaign."

Other Populists, however, objected to this course. They did not want to abandon their other principles, and especially feared that they would be swallowed up by the independent silver forces and the Democratic silverites if they concerned themselves almost exclusively with the silver issue. They believed any prospective fusion with the Democrats, particularly in the South, was dangerous. Davis H. Waite, former Populist Governor of Colorado, warned Ignatius Donnelly in the summer of 1895 against the trend which might result in a merging of Populists and Democrats. Waite accused James B. Weaver, Populist candidate for President in 1892, of being "in sympathy with Bland and Bryan" and advised against joining that "which is essentially a Democratic movement." By late 1895 the Populists found themselves in a difficult position and divided on future strategy. The silver Democrats and the National Silver party which was soon to be organized in Washington D.C. were claiming their most appealing issue and leaving them frustrated and confused.

The silver virus which spread so rapidly during 1894 and 1895 did not spare the Republican party. Hard times among western farmers and silver miners caused many Republicans in the Great Plains and Mountain States to be among the earliest proponents of free and unlimited coinage of silver. Indeed, by 1892 Republican congressmen and senators in most of the Far West had to support free silver in order to stay in office. But they were in a tough spot because their support of free silver alienated them from the main body of the party. Not many Republicans cared to lose their position in the national organization, although Senator John P. Jones of Nevada renounced his affiliation with the Republicans in late 1894 and joined the Populist party.

Senator Henry Moore Teller of Colorado was the recognized leader of the Republican free silver forces. A lawyer and former Secretary of the Interior, Senator Teller believed that adherence to the principle of free silver was more important than party loyalty. He announced early in 1896 that he did "not intend to support a candidate on a gold standard platform or a platform of doubtful construction." Some other free silver Republicans also indicated that they might bolt their party if it insisted on the gold standard. Meanwhile, party regulars were trying to straddle the money question in hopes of holding most of the free silver men. Their main proposal was to establish bimetallism through some form of international agreement. There was no chance to accomplish this, but it was a way of trying to avoid a party split over a divisive question.

Despite strong silver sentiment among some Republicans, most party leaders believed that the main issue in the campaign of 1896 would be the tariff. The great majority of Republicans, even western free silver supporters, generally favored protective tariffs, and if that could be made the major issue, the party would be in an unusually strong position. But whatever the question, prospects for Republican victory looked good because of the disunity within the Democratic party. The defections among Republicans over the money issue were minor compared to the basic split in the ranks of the Democrats.

Because of the strong probability of victory in 1896, several prominent Republicans eagerly sought the presidential nomination. Among the foremost contenders were William B. Allison of Iowa, Thomas B. Reed of Maine, and William McKinley of Ohio. Former President Harrison also had some backing, but he withdrew from consideration early in the year. Senator Allison hoped to draw his strength principally from the Midwest, although some eastern urban politicans also worked for his nomination. Reed, the heavy, sarcastic, and crusty Speaker of the House, believed that he could expand his power from a strong New England base. However, it was McKinley who clearly held the lead.

McKinley had emerged as one of the most successful politicians of his day. Born in Niles, Ohio, in 1843, he attended an academy and spent a few months in college before dropping out because of family financial difficulties. Following the attack on Fort Sumter, he enlisted in the Union Army and four years later was brevetted a major. He then studied law and began practice at Canton, Ohio, in 1866. He was less interested in law itself, however, than he was in using it as a base for a political career. In 1876 McKinley was elected to the House of Representatives where he became well known as one of the nation's most articulate spokesmen for the protective tariff. Although he was defeated for the House in 1890, the law of 1890 carried his name, and the following year Ohioans elected him governor. He served two successful terms at Columbus.

McKinley had most of the attributes of a successful politician. He was friendly, congenial, and sympathetic to the needs and desires of others; he inspired trust and confidence, and had the strong loyalty of his associates. His

personal life was spotless. He was deeply patriotic, had a strong vein of senti-
mentality, and was deeply religious. An excellent public speaker, McKinley
was especially successful in give and take situations. People saw him as an
honest, stable citizen and a dependable and capable public servant. He lacked
sophistication and was satisfied with the simple things of life. He had little interest in reading or the fine arts, but this only endeared him to the people he
served. Above all McKinley gave the appearance of a man of assurance,
strength, and stability.

During 1894 McKinley enhanced his position by scores of speeches. Not
a candidate himself, he was free to accept invitations which took him from
New England to Kansas, and even into the Deep South. In one day of speaking in Iowa and Minnesota he made twenty-three appearances dealing most
often with the tariff and the relation, as he saw it, between depression and
unemployment and Democratic tariff policies. On one occasion he told his
audience that the country was "tired of this tariff-tinkering, bond-issuing,
debt-increasing, treasury-depleting, queen-restoring Administration."

By 1895 McKinley had won a leading position in Republican ranks. He
had nationwide political support, a good personal reputation, and he came
from a key state which, after some maneuvering, gave him solid political
backing. Moreover, by concentrating on the tariff issue and emphasizing a
program of economic nationalism, McKinley had successfully identified himself as the "advance agent of prosperity." The editor of the *Nation* wrote in
January, 1895, that he believed McKinley was the man who could "show us
the way out of our troubles." How refreshing it was, continued the editor, after
listening to the fretting of congressmen and financiers, to hear McKinley
point the way to prosperity. The solution was to protect "our own markets for
our manufacturers and agricultural products," and develop "a foreign market
for our surplus products, which will not surrender our markets and which will
not degrade our labor to hold our markets." According to the editor, this was
a simple economic principle but one which reflected genius in its author.

On the other hand, McKinley skillfully avoided committing himself on free
silver, the most emotional and divisive public question before the country.
As one contemporary observed: "McKinley's whole point seemed to be to keep
the tariff question to the front and to ignore the financial question." On the
basis of his apparent strength, some political forecasters predicted over a year
before the convention that McKinley would win the Republican nomination.
John Hay wrote in 1895, "McKinley has a great diffused strength all over the
country, and is, in his own mind, almost certain of the nomination."

McKinley had the name, the reputation, support among rank and file
Republicans, and even an issue on which to base a campaign. What he needed
was an efficient organization. It was here that Mark Hanna, the wealthy
Cleveland industrialist, contributed so greatly to McKinley's pre-convention
campaign. Over the years Hanna and McKinley had developed a close personal friendship based on mutual respect and affection. Hanna understood
people and was a superb organizer, and though his talents had been devoted
to business, Hanna quickly and easily transferred this genius to politics. Be-

lieving that McKinley had the qualities needed in the White House, Hanna set out to manage a campaign which would win the nomination and election for his friend. He retired from business in 1895 and began devoting nearly all his time to development of an effective McKinley organization. One of the key men who joined the McKinley forces was Charles G. Dawes, a talented and ambitious young Chicago businessman.

At first Hanna seemed to believe that the best way of assuring McKinley's nomination was to gain the support of such eastern political bosses as Thomas Platt of New York and Matthew Quay of Pennsylvania in exchange for promises of patronage. McKinley, however, rejected the idea. "Mark," he was reported to have said, "some things come too high. If I were to accept the nomination on those terms, the place would be worth nothing to me and less to the people. If those are the terms, I am out of it." This did not mean, though, that McKinley was above making deals. It simply showed that he was convinced he could obtain the nomination without paying such a high price. Out of McKinley's repudiation of boss support came his popular pre-convention slogan, "The People Against the Bosses." Early in 1896 the editor of the New York *Tribune* speculated that if McKinley were nominated, he might well owe "his success to the underlying and deep-seated hostility of the mass of Republican voters to the dictation and domination of a Boss oligarchy."

McKinley appeared hypocritical to his opponents. Was not McKinley himself, they asked, under the control of one of the most crafty and ruthless political bosses in the country? Still, while it was true that Hanna influenced McKinley, he never dominated him. Indeed, the relationship between the two men was not the one pictured by the critics. Popular cartoons showed Hanna as a bloated capitalist marked conspicuously with dollar signs, holding a helpless and pliant McKinley in his pocket or under his arm. Such a portrayal was both inaccurate and misleading for in the political relationship between McKinley and Hanna, McKinley was always in control.

While McKinley stayed in the background during most of 1895 in order not to make the mistake of launching his campaign too early, Hanna proceeded to perfect a pre-convention organization. He rallied key politicians on McKinley's behalf, distributed large quantities of literature to important Republicans, spent money liberally, and sought friendly newspaper support. "McKinley has plastered the land with his literary bureau," wrote one opponent early in 1896. Senator Chandler of New Hampshire wrote that, "if Mr. Hanna has covered every district in the United States in the same manner that he did those in Alabama, McKinley will be nominated." No one felt the pressure of the McKinley steam roller any more than Senator Shelby B. Cullom of Illinois who also sought the Republican nomination. "The McKinley forces are organized all over my State," he wrote. "They have their agents tramping around, organizing McKinley clubs and doing anything in their power to make the State solid for McKinley. . . . There has been a large amount of money spent in Illinois by McKinley workers, and it is not easy to break up the schemes which have been set up for him."

By late 1895 and early 1896 it had become clear enough to most other Republican hopefuls that McKinley was the man to beat. His opponents attacked his relations with Hanna, cast doubts on his integrity by repeating gossip about his earlier financial dealings, worked to assure uninstructed delegations to the convention, and tried to combine against him as the front runner. Critics recalled 1893 when Hanna and several other wealthy businessmen saved McKinley from bankruptcy by raising more than $100,000 to pay debts which he had acquired by signing notes for a friend. The aim was to show how McKinley had been bought and paid for by bankers and industrialists, but these attempts to discredit McKinley failed completely.

He appeared equally invulnerable on certain issues. Asked whether he favored free silver, McKinley ignored the question, or simply pointed to his record in Congress. Some accused McKinley of hypocritically favoring the gold standard when speaking to conservatives and supporting silver when confronted by inflationists—a "prince of straddlers," they said. But McKinley held firm to a policy of bimetallism, saying only that he could not run on a free silver platform. This gave assurance to the East that he was sound on the money question without being explicit enough to alienate bimetallists. Determined to make his appeal on the tariff, McKinley treated the explosive silver issue as gingerly as possible. This may have indicated to some that he was weak on principle, but it demonstrated that he was shrewd in politics.

By the eve of the Republican national convention McKinley was virtually assured of his party's nomination. As H. Wayne Morgan has explained: "To a greater extent than any contemporary he captured the popular fancy. His record as an honest politician, his incessant drumming of the prosperity theme, his personality, his wide travels, the simplicity of his life and views, as well as his refusal to engage in calumny made him the most popular Republican of his day." Indeed, McKinley came closer to meeting the needs and hopes of the people than any fellow party member.

Shortly after noon on June 16, Republican delegates gathered in St. Louis for their eleventh national convention which the Hanna-McKinley forces had under firm control. Following the customary prayer, the convention named Charles W. Fairbanks of Indiana, a McKinley man, as its temporary chairman. Fairbanks set the tone of the approaching Republican campaign when he charged that the Cleveland Administration had been "three years of panic, of wasted energy, of anxiety and loss to the American people, without a parallel in our history." He credited Republican prosperity under Harrison to "honest tariff and honest money," while he associated Democratic depression with "free trade" and lack of confidence in Cleveland's financial policies. "The great questions for debate in the august forum of the United States," he concluded, "are free trade and free silver against a protective tariff and sound money."

The following morning Senator John M. Thurston of Nebraska, another McKinley supporter, was elected permanent chairman. In a short speech, he said that the American people had learned their lesson "and the doom of the

Democratic party is already pronounced." The afternoon session was devoted to inconsequential arguments over seating contesting delegations from Delaware and Texas.

The first order of business on June 18, the third and last day of the convention, was adoption of the platform. Presented by Joseph B. Foraker of Ohio, it was a damning indictment of Democratic policies and a ringing endorsement of Republican principles. Referring to the Cleveland Administration as "a record of unparalleled incapacity, dishonor, and disaster," the platform accused the Democrats and their policies of precipitating panic, blighting industry, closing factories, throwing men out of work, and prolonging the depression. On the positive side the Republicans promised to implement "the policy of protection" which was the "foundation of American development and prosperity." Altogether, the platform contained more discussion of the tariff than of any other issue.

There was never any serious doubt that the Republicans would favor "sound money" against silver. Party leaders and a great majority of the delegates were dedicated to this principle. Indeed, bankers and other gold standard advocates were so much in evidence that Mark Hanna was reported to have said: "You damn bankers will upset this whole thing if you keep on." A popular convention ditty emphasized the sentiment for gold:

> Gold, gold gold
> I love to hear it jingle
> Gold, gold, gold
> Its power is untold
> The women they adore it
> While the men try hard to store it
> There is not a better thing in life than
> Gold, gold, gold

Although planks on vital and controversial issues are characteristically vague in party platforms, the Republicans were clear and unequivocal on the money question. The platform read: "The Republican party is unreservedly for 'sound money'." So that there could be absolutely no doubt about what this meant, the money plank expressed unalterable opposition "to the free coinage of silver except by international agreement." Until that could be achieved, "the existing gold standard must be preserved." Although a number of prominent Republicans claimed to have been responsible for this plank, the heart of it had been written by McKinley himself and it was carried to St. Louis by Mark Hanna.

The platform also called for generous treatment of veterans, restrictions on immigration and complete exclusion of immigrants who could not read or write, honest enforcement of the civil service, early admission of remaining territories as states, and the expansion of women's rights. The planks on foreign policy recommended control over Hawaii, vigorous enforcement and extension of the Monroe Doctrine, and independence for Cuba.

By the time the clerk had completed reading the platform, the convention hall throbbed with tension and excitement. Delegates anticipated a sharp floor fight over the money plank, and they did not have long to wait for the drama to begin. Resolution Committee Chairman Foraker recognized Senator Teller to argue the case for free silver. At that moment his supporters went wild; they cheered and madly waved their hats, flags, and umbrellas. Teller had already lost the fight in the Platform Committee, but the free silverites were determined to present their case to the full convention and to the country. Teller's substitute plank read: "The Republican party authorizes the use of both gold and silver as equal standard money, and pledges its power to secure the free and unlimited coinage of gold and silver at our mints at the ratio of sixteen parts of silver to one of gold." Then, filled with emotion, Teller spoke for the cause of silver. He declared that by committing themselves to gold the Republicans were departing from their historic position of using both metals for money and insisted that it was foolish to expect any international agreement on bimetallism in light of England's opposition to such an arrangement. Teller claimed that the progress, happiness, prosperity, and morality of the country depended on free and unlimited coinage of silver. The single gold standard, he said, would "work great hardship" on the people. Convinced that the platform's gold plank meant disaster for his countrymen, Teller said that if it were adopted by the convention, "I must, as an honest man, sever my connection with the political organization that makes that one of the main articles of its faith." He could not, Teller concluded, "before my country and my God, agree to the provision that shall put upon this country a gold standard, and I will not." A writer for the St Louis *Republic* observed: "the magnificent old man bore a look of sorrow, but not of regret, at the step he was about to take." As Teller sat down there were tears in his eyes, and in the eyes of many who had listened to his plea.

Foraker then moved to lay the Teller substitute plank on the table, and by a rollcall of 818 1/2 to 105 1/2 the motion passed. Before accepting the entire platform, Senator Fred T. Dubois of Idaho demanded a vote on the financial plank only. This passed by a majority of 812 1/2 to 110 1/2, but now the dramatic climax was at hand. Senator Frank Cannon of Utah went forward and joined Senator Teller on the platform where he was introduced. Cannon was permitted to address the convention on a point of personal privilege and it was understood he would speak for the bolting silverites. As he proceeded he was frequently interrupted by shouts of "let him print it," "put him out," and "goodbye my lover goodbye." After declaring that the single gold standard would ruin the country, Cannon's statement, also signed by Teller and other free silver advocates, concluded: "we withdraw from this convention to return to our constituents." Teller and Cannon, followed by twenty-one other delegates, then walked down the aisle and out of the hall "amid the yells, hoots, cheers, and hisses of the audience." Mark Hanna was among those who shouted, "Go! Go! Go!" "Go to Chicago," and "Take the Democratic train with the rest." The loyal Republicans who remained inside yelled and waved their flags and handkerchiefs, and according to the official proceedings, the convention developed into "a general tumult such as was never paralleled in any other Republican national convention."

Many free silverites refused to bolt the convention, a fact which revealed how strong party loyalty and ties were. Senator Arthur Brown of Utah said that he and his fellow citizens "still remain true to the free coinage of silver," but only time, he added, could settle the issue. Brown appealed to the delegates to concentrate on the tariff question. The gold standard Republicans should have been encouraged at the small number of departing delegates.

It was about 1:30 p.m. when the silver supporters left the convention. As soon as order was restored the delegates proceeded to the nomination of candidates for President and Vice-President. Since McKinley's forces were in full command, it was only a matter of listening patiently to those who opposed him before making the decision. The names of Senator Allison, Speaker Reed, Governor Levi P. Morton of New York, and Pennsylvania's favorite son Matthew S. Quay were all placed in nomination, but every knowledgeable delegate knew that none of these hopefuls had the slightest chance. These nominations were only polite gestures, for the convention was only waiting to place its stamp of approval on the Republican of the hour, William McKinley.

When Foraker presented McKinley's name, the delegates staged a mighty demonstration. They shouted, sang, waved flags, and marched for nearly thirty minutes. After order was restored, Foraker said, "You seem to have heard the name of my candidate." Playing on the idea that McKinley had mass support, Foraker declared that "no other man so absolutely commands" the hearts of the people. In seconding the nomination, Senator Thurston pursued this theme further, emphasizing that McKinley was the candidate of "all the vast army of toilers."

Additional oratory was unnecessary. When the roll of states was called McKinley won on the first ballot, receiving 661 1/2 votes to a combined total of 239 1/2 for his four opponents. Reed had the second highest number, but he gained only a meager 84 1/2 votes. Moving on quickly to nominate a Vice-President, the convention ratified the choice already made by Hanna and McKinley—Garret A. Hobart. He was an inconspicuous politician and businessman from New Jersey, and his nomination gave the ticket good sectional balance.

The outcome of the Republican convention demonstrated how well Hanna and McKinley had organized their forces within the party. Hanna's task, however, had been made relatively easy because of the widespread enthusiasm which McKinley generated among rank and file Republicans. It had not been necessary for Hanna to manufacture sentiment for McKinley; he only had to unify and organize the broad support which already existed. Hanna did that with skill and imagination.

On June 19, the day following their walkout, the rebellious Republicans organized the Silver Republican party. They issued a public statement justifying their demand for free silver and suggested Senator Teller as the logical man to head the ticket. With Democrats and Populists in mind, leaders urged the parties which had not yet nominated a presidential candidate to back Teller. H. E. Taubeneck, chairman of the Populist National Committee, was in St. Louis at the time. He welcomed the invitation to all free silverites to back the Colorado senator. Events, however, worked out differently. Although some silverites continued to push for Teller's nomination right up to convention time, Democratic leaders had let it be known that their party would not nominate a man who had so recently been a Republican. Perhaps most Democrats felt like Senator F. M. Cockrell who said, "when we win a Democratic victory we want a Democrat. I have served long in the Senate with Mr. Teller and I respect him, but the next Democratic President will be a Democrat and fill the offices with Democrats."

While silver Republicans were fighting a losing battle in their party, free coinage supporters were gradually taking over Democratic control. Throughout the spring of 1896 free silver sentiment in the Democratic party grew like an avalanche. Criticism of Cleveland, his Administration, and the gold standard became frenzied. In April when Secretary Carlisle gave a strong "sound" money speech in Chicago, the Chicago *Record* declared that the Secretary of the Treasury had come "fresh from the banquet table of Wall Street to tell the idle and starving workingmen" that they should like being robbed by an unfair monetary standard. During April, May, and June the silver forces won control of one state delegation after another. Iowa Democrats voted 675 to 270 for silver, while Kentucky Senator Joseph Blackburn led the silver men to victory over Secretary Carlisle's opposition. Governor Altgeld of Illinois and the free silverites there overwhelmed Cleveland's friends, and free coinage men easily won control of the state convention in Indiana. The editor of the Kokomo (Indiana) *Daily Tribune* wrote: "The conservative, thinking, brainy men of the party were ruthlessly thrust aside to give place to the populistic agitators who have been preaching the heresy of the free and unlimited mintage of fifty cents worth of silver into a professed one hundred cent dollar." One critic wrote: "The God's truth is, the Democratic party in Indiana and Illinois is wildly insane on the subject of silver."

In the South the silver forces also ran roughshod over the gold men. Hoke Smith, Cleveland's Secretary of Interior, tried to rally the "sound" money forces in his home state of Georgia, but a close associate wrote: "All hell couldn't stop" the silver power in the state. Smith told William L. Wilson, his colleague in the Cabinet, as early as May 20 that the gold standard advocates had lost the Chicago convention. The tide of silver was running so strong in the Democratic party that life-long Democrats were wondering how they would react to a silver candidate. Wilson wrote in his diary on June 10: "The question constantly arises when gold standard men meet, 'What are you going to do when the party declares for free silver?'" According to Wilson, many answered that they would "vote for the Republican nominee, even if, as it appears sure to be, he is McKinley."

Frantic at the prospect of a silver victory at the forthcoming convention, supporters of "sound" money urged President Cleveland to more actively oppose the silver mania. In the middle of June Cleveland finally issued a statement declaring that in his judgment, the Democrats would never agree to the demand for free silver. The Democratic party, he said, was not so "unpatriotic nor foolish" as to injure the country and wreck the organization by such action. He predicted that the American people, upon "sober second thoughts," would not vote for a silver candidate, and that for the Democrats to nominate such a man would only be giving the Republicans an unnecessary political advantage.

During the last few days before the opening of the Democratic national convention, William C. Whitney, a former Secretary of the Navy and leading gold advocate from New York, agreed to head a last ditch stand against the onslaught of the silversites. Whitney and a number of associates arrived in Chicago on July 2, and any optimism which he and other gold standard supporters might have had was soon shattered. Trains filled with cheering free silver delegates were rolling into the city from the South and West. Touring the hotels to assess their prospects, Whitney's men found an uncontrollable sentiment for silver. One gold supporter declared: "These men are mad. We should get out a writ of *de lunatico inquirendo.*" Another associate felt that "for the first time I can understand the scenes of the French Revolution!" A national movement for the free and unlimited coinage of silver had crystallized; only a dynamic leader was lacking.

By the time of the Democratic national convention, no spokesman for free silver had emerged to a position of dominance. It was an open, fluid situation and no one could be certain of the outcome. One of the strongest Democratic candidates was Richard Parks Bland of Missouri. No man in the United States had better free silver credentials. Co-author of the Bland-Allison Silver Coinage Act of 1878, he was known throughout the entire United States. Among his principal handicaps, however, was his unpopularity among Populists who might otherwise support a free silver Democrat, and his wife's Catholicism. Another leading prospect for the nomination was Horace Boies of Iowa. A Republican who had turned to the Democratic party in the late 1880s, Boies had served successfully as governor and had helped carry his state for the free silver delegates during the pre-convention contests in 1896. Senator Joseph C. S. Blackburn of Kentucky also eagerly sought the nomination, and many Democrats considered Governor Claude Matthews of Indiana a worthy candidate. Two southerners who received prominent attention were John W. Daniel of Virginia and Benjamin Tillman of South Carolina. Of these possible candidates, Bland and Boies probably had the most general support. However, neither had an effective organization working in his behalf.

Still another possible candidate was William Jennings Bryan, but only in retrospect does it seem logical that Bryan could have been a serious contender for the nomination. At the time, he himself recognized that it would take an unusual combination of circumstances, including a generous amount of luck, for him to win. However, the fact that the convention was open, that a majority of the Democrats were uncommitted, and that the delegates were subject to persuasion actually made Bryan's chances better than they appeared. Despite his youth — he was only thirty-six — Bryan had excellent qualifications for leading the silver crusade.

Born in Illinois in 1860, Bryan attended an academy at Jacksonville and later was graduated from Illinois College. He then studied law for two years and began practicing in 1883. Four years later Bryan moved to Lincoln, Nebraska, where he gradually gave up law for politics. In 1890 he won the congressional seat in a strongly Republican district by a handsome majority, and was reelected by a narrow margin in 1892. In 1894 he unsuccessfully sought election to the United States Senate. By the time Bryan left Congress on March 4, 1895, he had become known for his strong and effective speeches against the protective tariff and in favor of free silver. His speech against the repeal of the Sherman Silver Purchase Act with its bitter denunciation of President Cleveland aroused praise from free silverites and added to his growing national stature among free coinage Democrats.

Bryan had many qualities and characteristics which nineteenth-century Americans sought in their leaders. He was deeply religious, a good family man and father—a person who inspired confidence and even affection among his associates. He appreciated the simple things of life and devoted himself unreservedly to what he considered worthy causes. His mind grasped things quickly, although he was not a deep or analytical thinker, and he tended to accept simplistic answers to difficult and complicated problems. An agrarian, he believed with Jefferson that a thriving agriculture was the basis for national prosperity and happiness. Perhaps his greatest asset as a political leader was his brilliant oratory. Few men in American history could match Bryan's effectiveness on the platform. His magnificent voice, his manner, his obvious sincerity, and his ability to articulate the feelings and thoughts of his audience combined to make Bryan an extremely persuasive man.

In the sixteen-month-period after Bryan left Congress and before the Democratic convention no one in the country did more to advance the cause of free silver. He wrote letters and articles, traveled widely, gave speeches, supported silver delegates, and promoted silver sentiment within the Democratic party. Moreover, Bryan worked with other groups supporting the same cause—Populists, silver Republicans, and the American Bimetallic Union —without becoming a part of any organization. Indeed, throughout all of his campaigning for silver he had been careful to maintain his independence and to avoid identification with any faction. Bryan stressed what he called "Principles First." He urged Democrats to unite on a silver plank in the platform, and then choose the best available candidate. Clearly, "the logic of the situation," as Bryan later phrased it, would more likely favor him if the convention were open and the delegates uninstructed.

A few months before the convention Bryan began actively, but quietly and cautiously, to seek support for his nomination. He sent out hundreds of letters, mailed his speeches to convention delegates, and gave out numerous newspaper interviews. In April he began to ask delegates to back him. Despite the fact that he came from an unimportant state and was barely past the minimum age required for the Presidency, a number of Democrats saw him as a logical candidate. John H. Atwood of Kansas wrote that Bryan alone had "every quality that goes to make up my ideal of a silver candidate." By convention time he had gained commitments from one or more individuals in most state delegations in the South and West. Thus, if Bryan should be nominated in an open, uncontrolled convention, he would have a group of eager and enthusiastic backers to promote his candidacy.

Moreover, several newspapers announced for Bryan. As early as April, the editor of the Little Rock (Arkansas) *Tribune* wrote: "Young, superb, coming from the geographical center of the nation, his record clear and unambiguous, William Jennings Bryan, stands today the embodiment of Young America in this great struggle for the emancipation of the common people and he is their idol." Josephus Daniels, the young editor of the Raleigh *News and Observer*, promised to support Bryan and advised his readers: "It is evident that the democracy of the West and South are in the mood to nominate the Honorable W. J. Bryan of Nebraska, for president."

By the time of the convention Bryan had become a formidable candidate, although he had been careful not to push himself too hard or too openly. There were, of course, prominent Democrats who scoffed at his youth and inexperience. Some party leaders sharply rebuffed his feelers of support. "Here was a young man barely thirty-six," wrote Senator C. S. Thomas of Colorado, "living in a comparatively unimportant Republican state west of the Mississippi River, audaciously announcing his probable candidacy for the presidential nomination. The very seriousness of the suggestion emphasized its absurdity." Governor Altgeld expressed admiration for Bryan but said he found "almost unanimous sentiment" among Democrats that the Nebraskan was "not available for president this time " Altgeld favored Bland. While Bryan was in no sense a "dark horse" candidate at convention time, there was nothing which seemed to indicate that he had any better chance, or even as good a chance, as two or three other leading free silverites. On July 5 polls which reported delegates' preferences for seven possible candidates showed Bryan at the bottom of the list.

The Democratic national convention opened in Chicago on Tuesday, July 7. Conflict within the convention expressed itself immediately over the election of a temporary chairman. The National Committee had voted by a slight majority for conservative David B. Hill of New York, but in open convention, the silverites threw their support to Senator John W. Daniel of Virginia, overturning the Committee's recommendation by a vote of 556 to 349. Silver sentiment was decisively in control of the convention. Once this fact was established, it would only be a matter of time until the contested silver delegates, of whom Bryan was one, would be seated, giving the silverites a two-thirds majority.

On July 8 the full convention ratified a decision of the Credentials Committee to seat the silver delegates from Nebraska, and Bryan marched down the aisle of the Coliseum leading his state's delegates to their chairs on the convention floor. Bryan then replaced a gold standard supporter on the Committee on Resolutions which was preparing the platform.

The money plank submitted by the silver majority of the Resolutions Committee remained as Bryan had written it several weeks earlier. It stated, "we demand the free and unlimited coinage of both silver and gold at the present legal ratio of sixteen to one, without waiting for the aid or consent of any other nation." The platform also took a slap at Cleveland by denouncing the issuance of bonds and trafficking with private bankers in order to maintain the gold standard. Furthermore, it demanded that national banks be denied the power to issue bank notes.

On the tariff, the platform recommended that "duties should be levied for purposes of revenue," and called Republican protection "a prolific breeder of trusts and monopolies." But the party opposed any changes in the tariff until "the money question is settled." The platform also tacitly criticized the Supreme Court for declaring the income tax unconstitutional, and demanded that Congress equalize the tax burdens. The Democrats promised to protect American workers by preventing "the importation of foreign pauper labor." On the problem of monopoly, the platform insisted on greater federal control over pools, trusts, and large-scale corporate enterprise; other planks included pensions for deserving Civil War veterans, admission of territories as new states, sympathy for Cuba's struggle for independence, and improvements in the nation's internal waterways. A plank which turned out to be highly controversial denounced arbitrary interference by federal authorities in local affairs "as a violation of the Constitution of the United States, and a crime against free institutions." It especially object "to government by injunctions as a new and highly dangerous form of oppression."

The minority report on the platform was submitted by gold standard members and referred to some planks in the majority document as "ill-considered and ambiguously phrased, while others are extreme and revolutionary." Attacking the free silver plank the gold men then declared that it would lead to a silver monetary basis which would "impair contracts, disturb business, diminish the purchasing power of the wages of labor, and inflict irreparable evils upon our nation's commerce and industry." The gold supporters also favored a resolution commending the Cleveland Administration.

The stage was now set for a debate on the platform. Senator James K. Jones, permanent chairman of the convention and free silverite, arranged for Senator Hill, Senator W. F. Vilas of Wisconsin, and Governor William F. Russell to speak for the minority report, while Benjamin Tillman and Bryan were scheduled to defend the majority position of the Resolutions Committee. On July 9 Senator Jones read the platform and the debate commenced. Tillman led off with an attack on Cleveland and gold in a bitter and vituperative speech. Next Hill defended the minority plank. Vilas and Russell then spoke, but stirred up little interest. The delegates and visitors in the galleries waited anxiously for Bryan, who, by careful planning and manipulation, had gotten to address the delegates last.

"Cheer after cheer went up as Bryan of Nebraska, tall, smooth-faced, youthful-looking, leaped up the platform steps, two at a time," wrote a reporter for the New York *Tribune*. Delegates waved banners, newspapers, hats, and fans in their enthusiasm, and their applause became deafening. Bryan now exhibited on the platform all the poise and finesse which had won him so much popular acclaim on the speaking circuit. Waiting for the crowd to quiet down, he began slowly and modestly: "I would be presumptuous, indeed," he said, "to present myself against the distinguished gentlemen to whom you have listened if this were a mere measuring of abilities; but this is not a contest between persons. The humblest citizen in all the land, when clad in the armor of a righteous cause, is stronger than all the hosts of error. I come to speak to you in defense of a cause as holy as the cause of liberty—the cause of humanity." Then Bryan reviewed the successful fight for free silver within the party and emphasized how the conflict was "a question of principle." Replying to the charge that the silver agitation disturbed business, Bryan declared that the definition of business must be expanded. To him workers, farmers, miners, and small-town merchants and lawyers were all as much businessmen as the great manufacturers and financial magnates. While he expressed no hostility toward the East, Bryan insisted that westerners deserved consideration by the party. These citizens, he said, wanted no war of conquest, but were fighting in the defense of their homes and their families. The downtrodden had petitioned, entreated, and begged for fair treatment, but Bryan shouted, "we beg no longer; we entreat no more; we petition no more. We defy them."

After answering specific criticisms of the platform, Bryan took up the money issue. He identified the gold standard with the exploiters of the poor and explained what he considered the two fundamental philosophies of government. One, he said, held that legislation should help only the wealthy with the idea that some of the prosperity would "leak through on those below." The other maintained that legislative action which assisted the masses would provide a base of prosperity for all. Then expressing his basic agrarianism, Bryan declared: "You come to us and tell us that the great cities are in favor of the gold standard; we reply that the great cities rest upon our broad and fertile prairies. Burn down your cities and leave our farms, and your cities will spring up again as if by magic; but destroy our farms and the grass will grow in the streets of every city in the country." Continuing his argument for the free and unlimited coinage of silver at a ratio of sixteen to one, Bryan reached a mighty oratorical climax. "Having behind us the producing masses of this nation and the world," he concluded, "supported by the commercial interests, the laboring interests, and the toilers everywhere, we will answer their demand for a gold standard by saying to them: You shall not press down upon the brow of labor this crown of thorns, you shall not crucify mankind upon a cross of gold."

For a moment the crowd set transfixed, but suddenly it burst into a thunderous roar. Men shouted, danced, cried, waved flags and banners, marched, and carried Bryan about the convention floor on their shoulders. Critics might ask what Bryan had said that had not been repeated hundreds of times before, but the delegates had little interest in analyzing the address. Bryan had captured their emotions and expressed their unspoken feelings in a matchless way. He had called for liberation of the masses from control and exploitation by special interests. Samuel Gompers, who was an observer at the convention, wrote later that, "Bryan spoke the language of humanity and he appeared as the proclaimed savior of the common people who would break the power of the gold standard scepter of Wall Street." Still committed to Bland,

Altgeld remarked during the demonstration: "That is the greatest speech I ever listened to, I don't know but its effect will be to nominate him." Although Bryan believed earlier that he had a good chance to win the candidacy, he now was sure of it. He told Senator Thomas that his nomination was "as certain as any human event can be."

Selection of a presidential candidate began the same evening. The names of Bland, Bryan, Senator Blackburn, Boies, Governor Matthews, and several lesser-known candidates were all placed in nomination. The following morning, July 10, the voting began. Bland led on the first ballot, but after that Bryan picked up strength much faster than Bland until on the fifth vote he went way beyond the necessary two-thirds majority to victory. Except for the gold standard men, the defeated candidates rallied around their popular hero and looked forward to "the battle of the standards." The next day the convention nominated Arthur Sewall for Vice-President. He was a banker and railroad and shipbuilding executive from Maine. He gave the ticket good geographical balance, and provided an appearance of respectability and stability which many easterners failed to associate with Bryan.

Bryan's nomination brought enthusiastic acclaim from other groups promoting free silver, and there was now a strong demand to unify all of the forces of monetary reform behind a single candidate. Senator Teller, who had earlier been mentioned as a possible nominee of the Democratic party, urged silver Republicans to back Bryan. James B. Weaver, William V. Allen, and other Populist leaders also urged their party to endorse the Democratic nominee. Both the National Silver party and the Populists had arranged to have their conventions in St. Louis on July 22, and it was a foregone conclusion that the disaffected Republicans would nominate Bryan and Sewall. On July 23 the National Silver party adopted a free silver platform and named the Democratic nominees as the party's standardbearers.

The Populists, however, were in a much more difficult position. Many party leaders wanted to fuse with the Democrats, but to do so would threaten the individuality and independence — and therefore the future — of the Populist party. It would also mean abandoning some of the basic Populist goals such as government ownership of the railroads. On the other hand, nomination of a separate candidate would split the free silver vote and assure victory for McKinley. There could be no misunderstanding: all of those favoring monetary reform must unite behind Bryan if free silver were to triumph.

In his keynote address opening the Populist convention, Senator Marion Butler of North Carolina frankly admitted that the Democrats had committed "petty and grand larceny by stealing the People's platform almost in its entirety," but he emphasized that the silver issue was greater than any party. Butler was careful not to take sides between those who favored all- out fusion with the Democrats and those who insisted on maintaining their Populist identity and supporting broad reforms. Butler ended his talk with a plea for unity.

Support for Bryan's nomination became clear when the convention elected Senator Allen, a fellow Nebraskan and Bryan man, as permanent chairman. The critical issue was how to nominate Bryan for President and yet gain the endorsement of those who bitterly opposed fusion. The Populists solved this problem by adopting their own platform which provided for much broader economic and political reform than that of the Democrats, and by nominating a separate vice-presidential candidate. Here was the compromise which permitted the Populists to join in a unified crusade for free silver and at the same time maintain their party organization. The convention nominated Thomas E. Watson, the fiery young Georgian, for Vice-President although he had opposed fusion. Watson declared that he would "accept the nomination in the interest of harmony and to prevent disruption of the Populist party."

James B. Weaver then placed Bryan's name in nomination for President, stressing that he could not "find a single good reason to justify. . . placing a third ticket in the field. The exigencies of the hour," he added, "imperatively demand that there shall be but one." Other leading Populists including Ignatius Donnelly, Jerry Simpson, Mary E. Lease, and H. E. Taubeneck seconded the nomination. S. F. Norton, editor of a Populist newspaper in Illinois, was also nominated, but Bryan received 1042 votes compared to only 321 for Norton. While the Populists left St. Louis somewhat divided, the great majority returned home dedicated to the election of Bryan and to the cause of free silver. Nevertheless, the nomination of Watson was an embarrassment to Bryan and the Populist platform, some of which he opposed, helped to give him a more radical image than he deserved. Although Bryan had stated publicly that he would not accept the Populist nomination unless the party also selected Sewall, he gladly accepted this additional support.

The issues in 1896 had created unprecedented political divisions, and produced new alignments in American politics. One of the most isolated groups included the conservative, gold standard Democrats. Although they did not bolt the Democratic convention, it was clear that they could not vote for Bryan. Nor was it easy for them to back McKinley because of his extreme protectionism. However, many eastern Democrats finally concluded that McKinley's election was necessary for the welfare and stability of the country, and they either openly or quietly supported the Republican ticket.

The conservative, "sound" money Democrats in the Midwest finally took the lead in forming a separate National Democratic party. Meeting in Indianapolis on September 2 and 3, the delegates nominated Senator John M. Palmer of Illinois for President and former Confederate General Simon B. Buckner of Kentucky for Vice-President. The convention adopted a platform which condemned the free silver Democrats, called for a "tariff for revenue only," and demanded maintenance of the gold standard. The New York *Tribune* recognized that the National Democratic party had no hope of electing Palmer and Buckner, but said that those who devoted themselves to defeating Bryan "are heartily welcomed by Republicans as allies in a struggle to uphold the honor of the nation and to maintain the integrity of free institutions." Two other minor parties also nominated candidates: the Prohibitionists and the Socialist Labor party.

Following the Democratic national convention in July, Bryan returned home to Lincoln. There he rested, made plans for the campaign, and prepared his acceptance speech. Bryan decided to schedule his official notification in New York City, and to launch his campaign from what he called the "enemy's country." Departing from Lincoln for New York on August 7, he addressed crowds at several cities along the way, emphasizing that he was proud to have the "support of those who call themselves the common people."

A packed and restless audience greeted "the boy orator of the Platte" at Madison Square Garden on the very hot night of August 12. Governor William J. Stone of Missouri, representing the Notification Committee, opened the meeting with a speech in which he sharply attacked Cleveland, denounced those who labeled Bryan's supporters anarchists, socialists, and cranks, and criticized the Republicans and the gold standard. After reading the formal letter of notification, Stone introduced Bryan to the cheering throng.

Bryan had prepared his address carefully. He decided to read it rather than to speak extemporaneously, so that he would be certain to state his views precisely, and also because he wanted to have copies for the press. Moreover, a calm, well-reasoned talk might help to dispel the idea, held by many easterners, that he was an irresponsible and dangerous radical. Trying to assure his audience that the Democratic platform was not a menace to private property or social stability, Bryan began by saying: "I assert that property rights, as well as the rights of persons, are safe in the hands of the common people." Without seeming to criticize the Supreme Court, he defended the principle of the income tax.

Then Bryan turned to the money question which he called the "paramount" issue of the campaign. He spent the next hour and a half arguing the cause of free silver and criticizing current monetary policy. Commenting on international bimetallism, he said that free silver advocates did not oppose such a course; they only refused "to await the pleasure of other governments when immediate relief is needed."

While Bryan's speech was fairly successful, it did not stir his audience as he had hoped. Many left the auditorium before he finished. Unfriendly newspapers eagerly interpreted this as a failure for Bryan and reported that his opening shot in the campaign had misfired. However, his supporters believed that he had shown eastern critics that he was a responsible statesman. Bryan stayed in New York State for nearly two weeks, speaking, resting, and preparing for the forthcoming campaign. On his way back to Lincoln he spoke to a huge Labor Day crowd in Chicago.

One of the main weaknesses of Bryan's campaign was the lack of proper organization. He himself had little interest in organizational matters and the Democratic National Committee under Senator James K. Jones was poorly staffed and inadequately financed. Jones set up the national headquarters in Chicago with another major office in Washington, D.C. The National Committee sent out literature about free silver, provided a speaker's bureau, and half-heartedly tried to raise campaign funds. Appeals to the common people for small contributions brought in some money, but not much. Republican charges that owners of silver mines were contributing large sums to the Bryan campaign were not true. The activities of the party frequently had to be curtailed because of a lack of funds and when the gold standard Democrats left the group, the party lost not only voters, but its best organizers and money raisers as well. Consequently, the main burden of the campaign rested on Bryan and on his personal ability to attract support to the free silver cause.

No man ever devoted himself more wholeheartedly or unselfishly to a presidential contest than did William Jennings Bryan in 1896. Completely committed to his objective, he spared nothing in his effort to save the nation from what he called the money power. During the ten weeks preceding the election, he traveled some eighteen thousand miles and delivered hundreds of speeches. People were deeply attracted to this "political evangelist." Even in the middle of the night they lined railroad tracks and crowded stations to catch a glimpse of their hero, or to hear him make a few informal remarks. No campaigner in American history had ever drawn such throngs of men and women. Crowds of twenty-five thousand to fifty thousand were common at his major addresses. People cried, prayed, hoped, and worked for his election as he became the popular idol of millions. "I want to say that no matter what may be the result," wrote his friend Charles M. Rosser of Texas, "you will be greater than any other man since Christ."

Bryan discussed all aspects of the Democratic platform, but he concentrated on the money question. Realizing that he could not expect any substantial support among the business and professional classes, Bryan directed his appeal toward what he called the great common people—farmers and workers. He explained repeatedly that industrial prosperity, and therefore jobs, rested on a prosperous agriculture. "Some of our opponents tell us that we should open the mills instead of the mints," he told a Kansas City audience, but "what use are the mills unless the people can buy what the mills produce?" Industries could not operate, he went on, unless "those who produce the wealth of the country, particularly the farmers" had a decent income. Then he added: "you gentlemen who live in this city, surrounded by an agricultural country, know that there is no way of bringing prosperity to Kansas City until you first bring prosperity to those toilers upon whose welfare Kansas City rests." He told a Minneapolis gathering that, "these cities rest upon your broad and fertile plains. If you make it impossible for the farmer to buy, I ask you how are the merchants of Minneapolis and St. Paul going to sell?"

Bryan explained hard times in terms of the quantity theory of money. He claimed farmers were poor because of low farm prices and heavy debts. Only the free and unlimited coinage of silver would raise farm prices, help farmers get out of debt, and restore prosperity to agriculture. The farmer wanted free silver, Bryan said, because "he suffers from falling prices" and believes the "only way to stop falling prices is to increase the volume of money."

He sought labor support by arguing that the gold standard had perpetuated depression and created widespread unemployment. Free silver, he insisted, would loosen the restrictions on industry and stimulate employment. Bryan also appealed to workers by criticizing the use of injunctions in labor disputes and endorsing the income tax. A number of labor leaders, including J. R. Sovereign, head of the Knights of Labor, supported Bryan, and workingmen greeted him enthusiastically in many cities; in Indianapolis laborers cheered him for sixteen minutes. Samuel Gompers made speeches for free silver and endorsed the personal candidacy of Bryan, but he maintained his policy of keeping the American Federation of Labor out of party politics by not supporting the Democratic party. Bryan avoided the tariff issue because he did not think it was of pressing importance. When a prominent Minnesotan asked him about that subject, Bryan replied, "There is a question before the American people of far greater importance. The tariff question can be settled at any time, but there is one question which must be settled now." Bryan's speeches tended to be general and often ignored hard economic realities. That free silver would solve many of the nation's problems was taken for granted—accepted on faith—rather than demonstrated by facts and reason.

Questions even more fundamental than free silver ran through Bryan's campaign speeches: who should control the Government and who should be the chief beneficiaries of government policies. Admitting that free silver would not solve all of the country's problems, Bryan said it would help "to restore the heritage which has been bartered away; it will help each man to secure a more reasonable share of the fruits of his own toil. When the Government has been taken out of the hands of the syndicates, the stock exchanges, and the 'combinations of money grabbers in this country and Europe,' the door will be open for a progress which will carry civilization up to higher ground." In his second Chicago address, Bryan said that he was willing to "trust to the intelligence of the American people to decide whether this Government is safer in the hands of those who believe in the ability of the people to govern themselves, or in the hands of the trusts and syndicates which have been bleeding the people." Bryan articulated this theme most clearly in a speech at Ottumwa, Iowa, late in the campaign. He described how abuses sprang up in every generation and how those who "have great interests at stake gather around legislative halls and secure legislation that grants them special privileges, and then entrench themselves behind the privileges granted." Behind the money question lay the question of power and "behind the money power," according to Bryan, "stand all those combinations which have been using the Government for public plunder."

The fundamental question, as Bryan saw it, was one of power. He drew on the traditions of Jefferson and Jackson to show how democratic forces had earlier curbed the influence and privilege of great wealth. He considered silver much more than a metal or a system of coinage; it was a symbol—a symbol of the hopes, aspirations, and future welfare of the great mass of common people resisting exploitation by a government which framed policies favorable chiefly to special interests. Silver was the symbol for those who were demanding a redistribution of the nation's economic and political power.

While Bryan was traveling thousands of miles exhorting his audiences to elect him and destroy the influence of concentrated wealth, McKinley conducted a front porch campaign from his home in Canton. Republicans initially scoffed at the idea that Bryan might be a formidable candidate. How could a young man from such an unimportant state, barely old enough to meet the constitutional age requirement for President, and with so little support from the "respectable" classes, even hope to be elected? At first failing to realize that the money question had become the paramount issue, McKinley intended to center his campaign around the tariff. In July he told a group of friends: "I am a tariff man standing on a tariff platform. This money matter is unduly prominent. In thirty days you won't hear anything about it." Judge William R. Day countered with the remark: "in thirty days you won't hear anything else." Any thought that McKinley could give secondary attention to the money issue soon vanished. Republicans watched with alarm as the coalition of silver Republicans, Populists, and Democrats rallied behind Bryan.

By late July and early August Republican leaders recognized the inadequacy of old campaign tactics and methods. Popular response to Bryan's appeals clearly indicated that the GOP faced a challenge which few had anticipated. Senator Eugene Hale, expressing a widespread feeling, observed, "The political situation was entirely changed by the Chicago performance. We could have beaten an old-fashioned democratic nomination and ticket without half trying, but the new movement has stolen our thunder." Hanna became so frightened at Bryan's large and enthusiastic crowds that he urged McKinley to take to the campaign trail. McKinley, however, refused. "I might just as well put up a trapeze on my front lawn and compete with some professional athelete," he said, "as go out speaking against Bryan. I have to think when I speak." Moreover, McKinley considered such tactics beneath the dignity of a person seeking the office of President.

The Republicans placed their faith in organization. Mark Hanna, who had already demonstrated his managerial genius in the pre-convention campaign, developed the most extensive and successful political organization known up to that time. He established two headquarters, one in Chicago and the other in New York. These offices worked closely with the state Republican parties and provided money for state efforts. The National Committee raised huge sums of money, organized speakers' bureaus, and distributed tons of literature for Hanna believed that people must be educated on the heresies of free silver, and told about the virtues of the protective tariff. This could be accomplished, he believed, by flooding voters with the printed word. During August, September, and October the Republican campaign organization distributed millions of pamphlets and other documents. At times material favorable to McKinley reached five million homes weekly. The Committee supplied country newspapers with prepared stories, "boiler plate," and ready prints. Republican campaign materials left Chicago by the carloads. On the eve of the election hundreds of speakers blanketed doubtful communities to speak on behalf of McKinley and "sound" money.

The Republican campaign in Iowa was typical of that conducted in other midwestern states. H. G. McMillan, Chairman of the Republican State Committee, wrote that in the middle of August the "situation . . . really looked threatening." It seemed, he said, as though "in many counties the free silver craze had taken the form of an epidemic. Entire townships that had heretofore been strongly Republican deserted us almost en masse." But then the Republicans began a "very vigorous and thorough education campaign." They collected names and addresses of all farmers inclined toward free silver and started flooding them with literature on the financial question. McMillan wrote that it was more effective to mail out material which appeared to be nonpartisan, yet giving "trustworthy information." One of the best ways to reach Iowa farmers, McMillan revealed, was to get articles "setting forth our side of the case" in the agricultural journals. After some three weeks of this kind of intensive effort McMillan reported his belief that Iowa was safe for McKinley.

Both parties recognized that the Midwest was the key to victory. Bryan would probably carry the West and the South, while McKinley felt sure of the Northeast. Consequently, Republicans and Democrats alike concentrated on the states between Ohio and Iowa.

The Republicans, however, did not rely on political persuasion alone. Wherever possible, party supporters exerted the severest kind of economic pressure. Employers threatened their workers with dismissal if they did not vote for McKinley; bankers told farmers that they would extend mortgages if McKinley were elected, but require immediate payment if Bryan won; businessmen inserted so-called "Bryan clauses" in purchase contracts which declared that they would buy certain goods at specified prices "unless Bryan is elected." Bryan openly criticized these tactics, but they continued right up to the election.

Such an extensive and highly organized political effort required tremendous sums of money. The Republicans, fortunately, experienced no shortage of funds. Not only did wealthy party members contribute, but rich Democrats as well poured thousands of dollars into McKinley's campaign. Moreover, Charles G. Dawes who managed the Republican finances did a superior job. Money literally poured into the two national headquarters. Dawes recorded in his diary on September 9 that he had drawn on Cornelius N. Bliss for $50,000 and had received another $15,000 from the representative of a prominent railroad. At lunch on September 11, Hanna handed Dawes $50,000 in cash, the contribution of another railroad company. Standard Oil gave $250,000 and the four big meat packers $100,000 each. Dawes' records show that the Republicans raised about $3.5 million in campaign funds, but money was flowing out as fast as it was being received. By October the Republicans were spending about $60,000 a day.

While Mark Hanna directed the Republican national organization, McKinley was busy at his home in Canton greeting thousands of visitors who trekked to his front yard. The small town became a kind of Mecca for loyal Republicans, and delegations came and went in a steady procession. McKinley would greet the people, thank them for coming, answer questions, and usually make a short talk. These meetings in front of the McKinley house were not so much spontaneous demonstrations of grass roots support as carefully organized gatherings in which every detail had been worked out ahead of time. Briefed in advance, McKinley knew what questions would be raised and he had time to give close attention to his replies. Moreover, McKinley had a folksy manner and often made personal asides. This caused his visitors to think that he was very much like one of them or their neighbors—which he was. When a group of wool growers from Harrison County, Ohio, called on McKinley, he expressed his regret that John A. Bingham could not be with them. He then asked that his best wishes and "earnest prayers" be taken back to Bingham. Between June and November some 750,000 people—farmers, workers, women, and church groups—beat a path to McKinley's door.

Although the Democrats forced McKinley to deal with the money question, as the campaign advanced he gave increasing attention to the tariff. In his acceptance speech on August 26, he sought to expose the fallacies of free silver and suggested that the mere mention of such a policy by the Democrats had created "universal alarm" among the financial and industrial interests. But it was not just bankers and business men who opposed free silver. "No one," McKinley argued, "suffered so much from cheap money as the farmers and laborers." He insisted that when men parted from their labor, their products, or their property, they should "receive in return money which is as stable and unchanging as the ingenuity of honest men can make it." To debase the currency, he said, would destroy values and hurt everyone. McKinley also warned workingmen that inflation would mean increased food costs. What workers needed, he said, were jobs, and McKinley promised that employment would follow restoration of protective duties.

McKinley argued vigorously against what he called the silver menace, but he was equally if not more concerned with the other issue of supreme importance—protection. On this question McKinley felt absolutely secure and confident. Throughout the campaign he contrasted the happy condition of the country before Cleveland and the Democrats began tinkering with the tariff with the present situation. According to McKinley, Cleveland had aroused fears and financial distrust which brought general economic decline. Then he explained how the Republican policies for the gold standard and protection would assure prosperity. "It is not more money we want," he said in his acceptance address; "what we want is to put the money we already have to work. When money is employed, men are employed. Both have always been steadily and remuneratively engaged during all the years of protective tariff legislation. When those who have money lack confidence in the stability of values and investments, they will not part with their money. Business is stagnated—the life-blood of trade is checked and congested."

The Democrats sought to associate hard times with depreciated currency and the gold standard. The Republicans, on the other hand, explained the depression in terms of the Democratic tariff and the attack on gold, both of which, they said, had destroyed business confidence. By October, McKinley was concentrating heavily on the tariff question. His principal theme had become protection and prosperity. Workers and farmers both, he insisted, would benefit from the protective tariff. Advancing the home market argument, McKinley said that agricultural prices were low because unemployed laborers and closed factories could not buy the products of the farm; on the other hand, industries were bankrupt and workers were without jobs because farm purchasing power was so low. McKinley claimed that protective tariffs would break this log jam and restore prosperity to both sectors of the economy. While Bryan declared in true Jeffersonian fashion that industrial prosperity depended on good times among farmers, McKinley reversed the argument. He held that the basis for prosperity in rural America was a thriving and expanding industry. As a protectionist, McKinley became the "advance agent of prosperity"—the man who would bring "the full dinner pail" to America. A popular campaign song which bound together McKinley, protection, and prosperity went as follows:

Get down the empty dinner pail,
　Let's polish it once more.
Ah, good old friend, come off the nail,
　For work will reach our door
As soon as we get Grover out
　And Bill McKinley in.
Then give a long, loud Yankee shout
　For Bill McKinley's tin.

'The Tariff is a tax,' they said,
　With brazen free trade lie.
Give us more 'tariff tax' and bread,
　Or else we starve and die.
'The tariff is a tax' it's true
　When of the free trade brand
It taxes every man of you
　And palsies labor's hand.

Give us McKinley's bill again,
　Give us his good protection,
Give us this friend of James G. Blaine,
　Who bears our heart's affection,
Let fact'ry whistles shriek once more,
　To labor's friend all hail.
And shout the cry from door to door—
　'McKinley's dinner pail.'

Republicans constantly accused Bryan and the Democrats of being free traders. *The American Economist*, published by the American Protective League, falsely charged that Bryan favored "absolute free-trade" and was "a rank apostle of Cobden." To McKinley and his supporters protection represented patriotism and nationalism. In a story headed, "Our National Honor," the Champaign (Illinois) *Daily News* referred to "protection and reciprocity" as the twin measures of "a true American policy." Other protectionists declared that foreigners were the principal beneficiaries of low tariff rates. The flag of protection, said the editor of *The American Economist*, was the stars and stripes. That was McKinley's banner; Bryan's standard was the English flag of free trade.

The Democratic argument that farm prices were low because of monetary deflation won widespread acceptance among debt-ridden farmers. Republican campaigners, however, advanced arguments which destroyed the plausibility of this proposition. Denying that there was any relationship between a depressed agriculture and the gold standard, Republicans explained low farm prices in terms of overproduction and limited demand. McKinley told a visiting labor delegation that "the price of wheat is fixed by the law of supply and demand, which is eternal. Gold has not opened up the wheat fields of Russia, India, or the Argentine Republic, nor will free silver in the United States destroy them." In McKinley's view surplus production at home and expanded output abroad were the chief obstacles to prosperity on the farm. This explanation for low prices was much easier to understand than one based on monetary policy, and thousands of farmers accepted it as sound. Moreover, Republicans kept repeating that farm prices were going up in anticipation of McKinley's election and enactment of higher tariff duties. Some very slight price rises for wheat and other agricultural products in the months before the election seemed to confirm this propaganda. Actually, however, farmers were influenced more by what they *thought* was going to happen than what was *really* taking place.

Besides stressing that free silver would harm the great majority of citizens and that a Republican tariff would restore national prosperity, McKinley had a third theme in his campaign. He called for a spirit of unity and nationalism among all of the people and in particular denounced sectionalism and Bryan's talk of class conflict—labor against capital, farmers against bankers and manufacturers, the poor against rich. He deplored the idea of class distinctions which, he said, were "repugnant to our form of government," and which, besides, did not truly exist. To discuss conflict of interest in the United States was, according to McKinley, "in the highest degree reprehensible." As H. Wayne Morgan has written: "This sense of nationalism shrewdly capitalized on the average man's unwillingness to believe in classes in a land that stressed individual opportunity."

One aspect of Republican campaign strategy had nothing to do with issues: Republican writers and speakers exerted every effort to portray Bryan as a wild-eyed radical whose election on what they charged was a socialistic Democratic platform would destroy the American system. Dubbing the youthful Nebraskan a Popocrat, critics insisted that he favored the entire Populist program, including government ownership of the railroads and telephone and telegraph lines. Many writers presented Bryan as nothing more than a Populist in disguise and accused him of being a demagogue, a socialist, an anarchist, and even a communist. He was called a liar, a traitor, and a thief. Henry Watterson, the conservative Democratic editor of the Louisville *Courier-Journal* charged that Bryan was a "dishonest dodger," a "daring adventurer," and "a political faker." Editorializing on Bryan's talk to labor groups in Chicago, the New York *Tribune* said: "He is simply a demagogue, who tries to play upon the passions and prejudices of workingmen, in order to steal their votes." When Eugene V. Debs announced his support of the Democratic ticket, the Kokomo (Indiana) *Daily Tribune* declared that Debs, "who has done time for anarchy" truly belonged among the Bryan backers. The writer added that "the friends of liberty and law, should take (themselves) straight into McKinley's camp." Some voters pretended to see a threat of revolution in Bryan's election. One conservative Democrat wrote that if Bryan won, the United States could not "escape the terror of the mob." Another correspondent observed: "I like Bryan, always have liked him, he is as honest as daylight, but being honest, he will pay his debts to Altgeld, Tillman, Stone, Peffer, Cyclone Davis, and that crowd, and that will bankrupt him and the country." The Republican tactics were clear: identify Bryan's Populist, free silver, and other nonconformist supporters as being dangerously radical, and then apply the principle of guilt by association.

Despite Bryan's deep religious commitment and devout personal life, ministers and priests attacked him as though he were the Antichrist. One New York cleric denounced Bryan from his pulpit as "a mouthing, slobbering demagogue whose patriotism is all in his jaw-bone." An editor of the Chicago *Daily Tribune* reported on September 29 that at least ten good sermons had been preached in Chicago the previous Sunday "against the attempt to plunder the people by a change of standards." But, he added, there should have been ten times more. John P. Newman, a Methodist bishop, criticized Bryan's "Cross of Gold" speech as being inappropriate and irreligious. The cross was a symbol of atonement, he said, and was "never intended to be the emblem of a political party or to be used to teach anarchistic doctrines. The crown of thorns was for the Savior's brow, and not for those who would overthrow the best government on earth."

The Republican campaign also benefited from lack of full political unity among the silver forces. The Democratic-Populist fusion did not work out as free silverites had hoped. Many Populists were unhappy with Sewall and urged him to withdraw from the ticket in favor of Watson. When neither Bryan nor Sewall would approve such a move, Watson became angry and vituperative. He campaigned as far west as the Rocky Mountains, but his crowds were small and he was often confronted with Bryan-Sewall signs. There was little coordination between Watson and Senator Marion Butler who headed the Populist organization, and, to make matters worse, the Populists scarcely had enough money to keep a national campaign office open in Washington. On the other hand, the National Silver party closely coordinated its efforts with Bryan and the Democrats, and ran a well-organized campaign with adequate financing.

As the campaign progressed, the Republicans grew more confident. Their smooth-working organization, support by a great majority of the country's newspapers and magazines, divisions among Bryan's backers, and help from the gold standard Democrats all increased the prospects of a Republican victory. Palmer and Buckner, the National Democratic candidates, went through the motions of conducting a campaign, but Palmer finally admitted to a Missouri audience a few days before the election: "I will not consider it any very great fault if you decide next Tuesday to cast your ballot for William McKinley."

On November 3 more Americans trudged to the polls than in any previous presidential election. The total vote was nearly fourteen million, about two million more than were cast in 1892, reflecting the deep interest in the candidates and issues. The outcome showed McKinley with 7,102,246 votes (51 per cent) compared to 6,492,559 (46 per cent) for Bryan, or a majority of 609,687. The minor candidates received 3 per cent of the vote. Palmer, the gold Democrat, polled only 133,000 votes, while the Prohibition candidate, Joshua Levering, won nearly as many—132,000. In the Electoral College McKinley triumphed 271 to 176. Although his victory was not overwhelming, it was very decisive. Indeed, his majority over Bryan was greater than that of any victor since Grant in 1872. Despite his loss Bryan got nearly one million more votes than Cleveland had polled in 1892.

Although McKinley carried only one more state than Bryan—23 to 22 —McKinley's strength lay in the centers of population and economic power. He carried New England, and the Middle Atlantic States and that sharply contested battleground—Ohio, Indiana, Illinois, Michigan, and Wisconsin. Out of those five states the vote was close only in Indiana and there McKinley's margin was nearly 20,000. The eight states of New York, New Jersey, Pennsylvania, Ohio, Illinois, Indiana, Michigan, and Wisconsin cast about half of the total votes and McKinley carried them all. His strength lay in the leading industrial states and the older, more prosperous commerical farming areas between Iowa and Pennsylvania. Here was the basis of the nation's economic power structure, whose spokesmen favored McKinley, "sound" money, and the protective tariff. Moreover, McKinley carried the four Border States of Maryland, Delaware, West Virginia, and Kentucky. Bryan's chief strength was in the South and west of the Mississippi River, but in the broad reaches of the West he lost Iowa, Minnesota, North Dakota, Oregon, and California.

The reasons for McKinley's victory are clear enough. The Republican organization was unequaled in the annals of American political campaigns up to that time. Supported by almost unlimited funds, the Republicans carried on an unprecedented educational effort to discredit Bryan and free silver and to present McKinley and his program in a favorable way. McKinley's forces had an easier political task because the Republicans had emerged as the dominant party after 1894. By 1896 there was already a strong Republican trend and for Bryan to win would have meant reversing the nation's political direction. In other words, Bryan had to change voters' minds; McKinley had only to play on the sympathies and prejudices already present. So strong was Republican party loyalty that it was difficult, indeed impossible, for Bryan to wean enough faithful Republicans into Democratic ranks. Such key states as Ohio, Indiana, and Illinois had gone Republican in nearly every presidential election since 1860. Moreover, Bryan labored under the handicap of an unpopular, depression-ridden, divided Democratic Administration. "I have," Bryan declared, "borne the sins of Grover Cleveland." That statement contained much truth. Lack of Democratic unity was a severe blow to Bryan—not so much because of the number of Democrats who voted for McKinley or Palmer, but because the disaffected party members had most of the money and organizational ability which Bryan needed so badly if he were to win.

Bryan's failure to gain greater farm and labor support was an additional handicap. Farmers and workers supposedly suffered the most from monopoly, concentration of wealth, unequal distribution of income, and the other economic ills against which Bryan campaigned. Many urban workers did support him, but a majority of voters in the industrial centers tended to back McKinley. They were not attracted by Bryan's argument for cheap money. They feared a rising cost of living if farm prices rose, and besides, they were drawn to McKinley's claim that the protective tariff would stimulate industry, open up the factories, and provide jobs. Of course, it cannot be overlooked that economic pressure on workers probably kept Bryan from getting more labor support.

A majority of the traditionally Republican farmers in the Middle West did not respond to Bryan's appeal for free silver. More diversified and prosperous, and carrying less debt in relation to the value of their property, farmers in the crucial area from Iowa to Ohio stayed with McKinley and the Republican party. Bryan's greatest success among farmers outside of the South was in the Western Prairies and Great Plains where frequent droughts and crop failures, along with low prices and heavy debts, had created bitter political discontent. Bryan claimed that he spoke for the great agricultural sector of the nation against the powerful control of business and industry, but this was only partially true. He not only failed to get enough of the farm vote, he was unable to win it in such key states as Indiana, Illinois, and Iowa. Farmers, like many workers, believed McKinley's protectionist argument. In emphasizing the tariff issue, McKinley demonstrated his remarkable ability to identify a popular and meaningful political question. Undoubtedly, the tariff was more important than monetary reform to a great many voters.

McKinley's victory was also based on his and Mark Hanna's ability to translate economic power into political backing. The economy had undergone fundamental changes in the previous generation, and by 1890 industry was rapidly surpassing farming as a producer of wealth. McKinley drew support from most of the bankers, industrialists, and leaders of transportation who made up the backbone of the new industrialism. By articulating their needs and desires, and making other groups in America's pluralistic society feel that their welfare depended on a prosperous industrial base, McKinley drew on the basic source of power. Bryan appealed to the agrarian tradition, part of which held that farmers were exploited by the nonproductive interests, but the day had passed when a candidate could be elected by appealing chiefly to the country's agricultural classes. Economic change had forced new political realities upon presidential candidates.

Perhaps more than anything else Bryan was defeated because of the image of radicalism which the Republicans so successfully pinned on him. Republican propagandists appealed strongly to the conservative tradition in American society, and McKinley seemed to be the protector—indeed, the personification—of that tradition. A vote for Bryan was pictured as an attack upon property, law, and order, and as a step toward control of the country by riffraff and criminals. To be for McKinley, on the other hand, was to be on the side of American institutions and social stability.

McKinley dealt with the important law and order issue in his acceptance speech. He assured the country that the Republicans would "meet the sudden, dangerous, and revolutionary assault upon law and order . . . with the same courage that we have faced every emergency since our organization as a party. . . . Government by law must first be assured; everything else can wait. The spirit of lawlessness must be extinguished by the fires of an unselfish and lofty patriotism." Everyone who believed in his country and national honor, McKinley concluded, must resist the Democratic attack on "the public faith."

Law and order became a popular theme. Commentators recalled the unrest, violence, and bloodshed of 1894 and claimed that representatives of those disruptive forces were now supporting Bryan. The Democratic attack on the use of federal injunctions in labor disputes was interpreted as opening the way for lawlessness and anarchy. Early in the campaign the Galveston *Daily News* admitted that the money and tariff questions were of great importance, but, the editor said, they were not the most fundamental issues at stake. "The first thing to be decided," he concluded, "is whether this is to be a land of law and order." A writer in the *Commercial and Financial Chronicle* insisted that all of the worst elements in American society were backing Bryan because they believed that, if he were elected, they could take advantage of industrial disorder and anarchy. In the *North American Review* for August, Senator Chandler wrote that the issue "is between security to property and personal rights, and peaceful prosperity maintained by the friends of law and order," and "Anarchy and Socialism, promoted by the advocates of public disorder and riotous violence." Chandler said that the main issue in the campaign was the difference between "the mass of the careful, conservative, and prudent people of the country" who were for McKinley, and the "Anarchists, Socialists, and destructives in society" who rushed to Bryan's banner. "The real enemies of society," he further explained, "the men who arouse the mobs in our cities, and in order to remedy evils. . . would resist the officers of the law, destroy property, burn buildings, and commit homicides, will rush naturally to the support of the candidates nominated at Chicago."

With deep emotion Republican writers and speakers declared that the nation faced a crisis which was as serious as that of 1861. Indeed, they pretended that the Republicans were saving civilization from permanent destruction. "The present task," wrote a McKinley supporter in the *Atlantic Monthly*, "is to save it [government] as an instrument of civilization." Archbishop Ireland of St. Paul said on October 12 that he had to speak up "for the integrity of the nation, for social order, . . . for the honor of America and the permanency of free institutions." McKinley and the gold standard became symbols of patriotism, nationalism, Americanism, and social stability, and Bryan was powerless to overcome the image of a radical rabble-rouser which Republicans forced on him. Consequently, many people believed that he was not quite dependable or trustworthy. As Senator Peter Norbeck of South Dakota wrote more than thirty years later: "People liked him but did not have confidence in his judgment; they felt his heart might be right, but that his leadership was not safe." In contrast, McKinley reflected the image of a man who was solid, trustworthy, stable, and committed to social order.

Bryan conducted one of the most valiant presidential campaigns in American history. Almost alone he challenged the forces of corporate wealth, and appealed to the masses to throw the money changers out of the national temple. He was the strongest candidate the Democrats could have put in the race, and, although he lost, no Democrat could have won the Presidency in 1896.

This was the most important presidential contest between the Civil War and World War I. What was its significance? In the first place, the campaign helped to destroy free silver as a powerful political issue. At the same time, however, the widespread discussion of monetary questions brought a growing demand for basic reforms in the country's monetary and banking policies. Moreover, the election effectively doomed the Populist party. Although the campaign was not strictly an agrarian-industrial conflict, this election came closer to a contest between classes, economic interests, and sections than any other campaign in the late nineteenth century. It was a triumph for the business and industrial groups over the agrarian forces, and for a while settled the question of who would control the Federal Government and who would benefit the most.

Finally, the campaign, perhaps inadvertently, gave indirect support to the movement for broad economic and social reforms. On the surface the election seemed like nothing more than a victory for conservatives who successfully resisted demands for basic changes. But the emphasis on monetary policy, the income tax, labor legislation, and control of monopoly helped to educate the people to the need for fundamental change and reform. Free silver was only the symbol of broader reforms and even though the symbol faded away, the real issues continued to demand attention. In a democracy agreement often comes slowly, but within a few years many of the objectives Bryan and the Populists advocated had been achieved. The power structures did respond to change, and out of the divisions and conflicts of 1896 Americans moved on to find a workable degree of political consensus.

Election of 1912

by *George E. Mowry*

During the late winter and early spring before the 1912 political conventions, President William Howard Taft should in theory have looked forward with confidence to renomination and reelection. The Republican party had not denied an incumbent President a renomination for over thirty years, and, except for the 1910 off-year election, had been consistently victorious at the polls since 1894. Taft's accomplishments over the previous three years gave him an impressive record. His Administration had dissolved more trusts, added more acres of land to the national parks and forest reserves, and enacted more social legislation in three years than Theodore Roosevelt had accomplished in seven years. Although the so-called "high cost of living" irritated some voters in 1912, the nation was prosperous: agricultural prices were high and climbing, unemployment was negligible, and the stock market was buoyant. Except for trouble with revolutionary Mexico, more irritating than menacing, no major international threat appeared to endanger the continuation of prosperity.

Yet, the President was in such deep trouble by the late winter of 1911-12 that his renomination was not at all certain, and his chances of reelection were even more dubious. Contending with him for the nomination were two active challengers, Senator Robert M. La Follette of Wisconsin and the more formidable ex-President, Theodore Roosevelt, Taft's predecessor, political benefactor, and former personal friend. Many discerning politicians were not at all sure that Taft could withstand the Roosevelt challenge. Even if he did, more were inclined to think the nomination virtually worthless in view of the bitterness nurtured by the two contestants and the apparent rising strength of the Democratic party.

It is not easy to explain Taft's predicament in the spring of 1912. Part of the reason for the political turbulence was, of course, the approaching presidential contest in which personal ambition and rivalry unleashed, as it does every quadrennium, some of the less gracious aspects of political life. But behind these human constants, and perhaps more fundamental to 1912 than to most other presidential elections, was a sharp and divisive struggle over impending major changes in the Constitution which would determine not only how, but also, and more importantly, in whose interest, the nation was to be governed.

Until the twentieth century the general structure of American government remained close to the form and spirit imparted to it by the Constitutional Fathers. True, the Presidency, as well as a good many state and local offices, had responded to an ever increasing democratizing process; the powers of the states had been somewhat limited, and those of the national government augmented by the Civil War and by subsequent judicial interpretation. Nevertheless, in 1911 the nation was still essentially a federal republic in which the powers of the central government were strictly limited and the reserve powers of the states substantial. It was still a representative republic, since in only a very few local communities did the people have direct legislative power. And in both theory and practice the Republic was still the "balanced" one for which John Adams had contended, since both the United States Senate and the Federal Courts remained sheltered from direct popular control. Both institutions had so consistently favored wealth and property that the Senate was widely acknowledged as the best "rich man's club" in the nation and the Court was called the "sword and buckler" against regulatory, social welfare, and leveling legislation. At the end of the nineteenth century the Populists had sharply challenged this happy state for the "wise, the good and the wealthy" — a movement carried forward by the progressives in the twentieth century. By 1911 several western states had adopted the Swiss-inspired devices of the initiative and the referendum, thus permitting the voters to initiate, pass, and nullify state legislation. The year before, Oregon had extended the democratic principle to record the people's preference for presidential nominees. Over thirty states had adopted either a compulsory or advisory popular vote in the selection of United States senators. After the 1906 publication of David Graham Phillips' articles on "The Treason of the Senate," it seemed certain that this American House of Lords, created by the Constitutional Fathers to represent wealth and high caste, would soon be democratized.

More alarming to conservatives than the democratization of the Senate was the growing demand that the recall be applied to judges as well as administrative officials. If this popular weapon were to be extended to federal judges, in particular to the Supreme Court — a proposal already made by some radical Democrats — the original constitutional checks on the masses would, according to many conservatives, vanish, taking the old Republic along with them.

Much of the political tension in 1911 was inspired by the emergence in

Congress of these democratizing principles. The issue of recalling judges was raised by the petition of the Teritory of Arizona for statehood. The Arizona Enabling Act passed in both Houses was defeated by Taft's veto, a veto which forced the state temporarily to delete a recall measure from its constitution. But after a two-year struggle the resolution for amending the Federal Constitution to require the direct election of senators was finally passed.

These proposed structural changes would not in themselves have taken one dollar of property away from the nation's wealthy, nor have lightened by one ounce the burdens of the poor, the sick, and the hopeless, nor would they have opened by one inch the door to opportunity for millions of the would-be prosperous. But behind these procedural innovations — and brought to the surface by the same swelling democratic tide — was a host of substantive Populist and Progressive legislative proposals for the federal control of corporations and trusts, the protection of labor, women, and children in industry, the freeing of trade unions from legal disabilities, and even for changing the classical laws of the market place to protect farmers, small businessmen, wage earners, consumers, and even investors, from the overly greedy. The intimate relationship between governmental form and substance was brought into sharper focus in 1911 and 1912 by a determined liberal drive for a federal income tax.

The income tax, which was to supply most of the finance for the social service state of the future, had been declared unconstitutional by the Supreme Court in 1895. Subsequent measures to assure its constitutionality had been repeatedly passed by the House and just as often defeated in the Senate. By 1911, however, twenty-three western and southern states had approved a constitutional amendment validating the tax. At this juncture the New York State legislature ambiguously defeated the income tax and yet approved the direct election of United States senators. Lest the obvious paradox in this vote be concealed from the public, *The New York Times* lamented that Arkansas would soon benefit from the wealth of New York, and the Bowery from that of Fifth Avenue, since "the bars to the pillage of the rich" were falling. Giving point to the *Times'* remark was the action of the House of Representatives on March 19, 1912. Attempting to compensate for the loss of revenue by the new sugar tariff, by a vote of 252-40 the body approved a 1 per cent tax on the yearly net incomes of all firms and on individual incomes exceeding five thousand dollars. Despite the turgid rhetoric and the conflicting promises of the 1912 campaign, millions of voters grasped the basic issue: what classes were to control the national legislature and the courts and to what ends?

Sharply increasing the disunity already existing in each of the major political parties were the 1911-12 proposals for the direct election of senators, the recall of judges, and an income tax. The 40 negative votes in the House on the income tax measure were all Republican, indicating the rigid conservative bent of one faction of that party. But more than double that number of Republicans voted with the majority Democrats, thus displaying a serious schism in the once well-disciplined organization that had dominated the elections before 1910.

Partially responsible for the Republican rift was the developing quarrel between the supporters of President Taft and those of ex-President Theodore Roosevelt. But more basic to the development was the inherent difficulty of maintaining a political structure dedicated to conservative policies while resting for support upon a rapidly urbanizing East and an agrarian-minded West. In each section the insurgent spirit had grown against the once dominant conservative leadership. In the West the Populist tradition, stripped of its more radical overtones, had been gaining strength in Republican ranks, aided in good part by Roosevelt's trust busting and his efforts at railroad regulation, but perhaps more by his endless sermonizing on the old morality which in essence expressed the attitudes of small town America. The ex-President had also been responsible for nurturing in eastern Republican ranks major disaffection with the party's traditional doctrines. His emphasis upon protection of the consumer, a square deal for labor, and the protection of women and children appealed to the lower class urban mind just as his conservation doctrines, his desire to substitute the regulation of corporations for trust busting, and his broad hints at a new partnership between government and big business, attracted the attention of the technically educated and the more adventurous businessmen. For the new technocrat, whether engineer, social worker, economist, or scientist, as well as the new breed of businessmen, the nineteenth-century Republican doctrines were as archaic and irresponsive to the rapidly rising urban world as the agrarian-centered policies of William Jennings Bryan.

By adroit political maneuvering Theodore Roosevelt had, in the seven years of his Presidency, managed to submerge most of the growing dissidence in the party. But the sharp Democratic gains in the 1908 elections prefigured that party's congressional victory in the canvass of 1910, the same election that witnessed the emergence of the insurgent or progressive Republicans as a self-conscious group.

The insurgent or progressive faction of Republicans emerged in Roosevelt's last years. Its real crystallization occurred, however, during the first two years of the Taft Administration. Amidst the struggles over the limitation of Speaker Cannon's powers in the House, and over the Payne-Aldrich Tariff and the Mann-Elkins Act to further regulate interstate carriers, a group of middle and far western senators and congressmen coalesced in their opposition to the existing Republican congressional leadership, and eventually to President Taft who attempted for a time, à la Roosevelt, to run with both the progressive hares and the conservative hounds, but whose lack of nimbleness as well as conservative temper impelled him almost inevitably to the "old guard" side of the agrument. Taft's attempt to purge the insurgents in the primaries of 1910 almost guaranteed their opposition during the succeeding congressional session as well as in the presidential race of 1912. Leading these congressional opponents of Taft were Senators Robert M. La Follette of Wisconsin, Jonathan Dolliver and Albert B. Cummins of Iowa, Albert J. Beveridge of Indiana, Moses Clapp of Minnesota, Joseph L. Bristow of Kansas, William E. Borah of Idaho, Jonathan Bourne of Oregon, and Congressman George Norris of Nebraska.

Taft had also inherited more than the normal quota of personal ill feelings which usually attend the succession of the Presidency within the same political party. The President's wife, a sickly, proud, and ambitious woman, was hardly as gracious as she might have been in easing the transition for Roosevelt's immediate family. A misunderstanding of greater political importance occurred between the retiring and incoming Presidents as to just who was to be kept of the Roosevelt Cabinet. Among the most important of these was James R. Garfield, the incumbent Secretary of the Interior, among whose administrative responsibilities were the conservation of natural resources, which Roosevelt ranked as one of his dearest concerns and most important achievements. Garfield's replacement excited the suspicions of Gifford Pinchot, Chief Forester, and a close personal friend of Roosevelt. The quarrel over the public land policy between Pinchot and Taft's newly appointed Secretary of the Interior, Richard Achilles Ballinger, resulted in Pinchot's dismissal and subsequently a heated national debate on conservation policy. Since the western insurgents almost unanimously supported Pinchot and Garfield, the incident tended to build a personal as well as policy bridge between them and Theodore Roosevelt.

Meanwhile Roosevelt, who had been absent from the country for over a year in Africa and Europe, received long and scathing accounts from both factions of the warring Republicans. He had also held a confidential talk with Gifford Pinchot in Portugal. Although he insisted publicly that he would not take sides in the quarrel, probably for as many personal as political reasons, his sympathies lay with the rebels and he was inclined to be critical of Taft for permitting the quarrel to become public and divide the party. Once home he made the mistaken assumption that he could materially help to reunite the party on "a sanely progressive basis" by simultaneously supporting the progressives and the moderates to produce a new center of gravity within the party. He attempted as much during the 1910 election by supporting Taft's moderate candidates in New York against the choices of the local Republican machine and at the same time supporting many of the western progressives.

Throughout his last year as President, Roosevelt had become increasingly convinced that public opinion was rapidly veering toward social reform. This opinion, further supported by the insurgent movement in the West, was mainly responsible for his celebrated speech, "The New Nationalism", given in Ossawatomie, Kansas. Based in part on Herbert Croly's recent book, *The Promise of American Life*, but more on his own developing political philosophy, "The New Nationalism" was a truly radical charter of political and social reform. It underwrote practically all of the democratic devices, including the popular recall of judicial decisions, that had been proposed by reform forces for the past twenty years. In blunt words the speech demanded that property rights be held secondary to human rights and proposed a long series of basic economic and social reforms which, if implemented, would have taxed the wealthy to protect the poor and the unfortunate. Roosevelt's "New Nationalism" also included expanded federal regulation of corporations, a sharp reduction in the rights of states, and an inverse increase in the power of the national government. In short, it looked forward to a welfare state; it left the great mass of Republican conservatives, including President Taft, in a state of shock.

Despite his intensive efforts to reunite the Republican Party on a pivot considerably left of where it had been, Roosevelt's plans in 1910 met disastrous defeat almost everywhere. He was bitterly criticised by both insurgent left and conservative right. His relations with Taft during the period grew much more difficult and candidates he personally supported, including Albert Beveridge in Indiana and Henry Stimson in New York, were soundly defeated. The only marked victors in the contests of 1910 were the Democrats and the western insurgent Republicans.

Unquestionably cheered by the 1910 elections and by the prospect of holding the balance of power in the Senate, the insurgents were also strengthened by the steady erosion of Republican conservative leadership in both houses of Congress. By the end of 1910, through death or resignation, all four of the powerful standpat senators—Nelson W. Aldrich, John C. Spooner, Orville H. Platt, and William B. Allison—who had dominated the body during most of the Roosevelt years were gone. Fifteen more stalwart Republican senators were to leave the body in the next twelve months. And since "Uncle Joe" Cannon had been replaced as Speaker of the House as a result of the 1910 elections, the regular Republican leadership in Congress lacked both experience and prestige. By comparison, insurgent leaders like Robert La Follette, William E. Borah, and George Norris were national figures. Their plans, announced late in December, 1910, to organize a National Progressive Republican League were thus taken as a serious bid for the control of the congressional party as well as a real challenge to President Taft and his hopes for renomination in 1912.

The first national organizing meeting of the League in Chicago, January 23, 1911, was attended by every insurgent Republican senator except Borah, by thirteen members of the House, and by six middle western Republican governors. The League's announced principles included all the democratic devices for the direct election of government officials including the delegates to the national nominating conventions, and the incorporation in state constitutions of the initiative, the recall, and the referendum. One of its stated purposes was to capture the Republican party for progressive Republicanism; a corollary as yet unstated was the defeat of Taft and the nomination of a Progressive Republican, widely understood at the time to mean Senator La Follette of Wisconsin.

An obvious weakness of the Progressive League in the spring of 1911 was its decidedly western character. By April, six state organizations had been constructed, all in the Middle West except for one in Seattle, Washington. All of the League's leading members had assiduously wooed the nation's leading eastern Republican exponent of progressivism, Theodore Roosevelt. Although the ex-President had been complimentary and had even promised to praise the League and its leading man, La Follette, he neither joined the League nor endorsed La Follette for the 1912 nomination. Progressive Republicans in the spring of 1911 had to content themselves with the enrolling of a few, but certainly not a majority, of Roosevelt's close political and personal friends.

While handicapped by its lack of strength in the East this "new Salvation Army," as Taft called it, continued to thrive throughout the spring and summer of 1911. At the start of the special session of Congress in March it requested and obtained from the regular Republican organization in the Senate one-quarter of the Republican seats on all important Senate committees. And, though it failed to gain its demand to make its own choices for the committee posts, it constituted an organized congressional group which held the balance of power between the Republicans and Democrats. Throughout 1911, however, the seriousness of the Progressive threat to Taft's control of the party depended largely on Theodore Roosevelt. Had he publicly supported La Follette and his western Progressives, the President's future would have been extremely precarious. But instead of speaking out, the ex-President continued the rather obscure policy he had pursued since his return from Africa in June, 1910. As he had promised, he wrote a few articles in the *Outlook* praising La Follette's accomplishments as governor of Wisconsin. At various other times he wrote in support of direct primaries, the referendum and the recall, and especially in advocacy of his solution to the industrial problem by regulatory measures instead of by the Administration's trust busting activities. In New York City and at his home in Oyster Bay he conferred with a stream of moderate and progressive Republicans, including most of the leading members of the Progressive Republican League. Except for letters to Lodge and Root, and an occasional one to the President in answer to a direct request for advice, his communication with the conservative wing of the party was practically nonexistent.

Inevitably it was suggested that Roosevelt himself would be an active candidate. But when pressed by a reporter he unequivocally stated that he was not, had not, and would not for months take any position on the candidacies of others. Privately, however, he was extremely critical and dissatisfied with both Taft and La Follette—Taft for his "lawyer's insensitivity" to the rising demand for change and for his inability to keep the party unified, La Follette and the westerners for their advocacy of a "kind of rural toryism" which would have returned the nation's economic institutions to those existing sixty years previously. This retrogressive fear of big business and of increased governmental power separated them, he thought, from "real progressives" of his own kind and made unified action of the liberal wing of the party impossible. Moreover, in a direct reference to La Follette, he felt that, though the westerners had developed several able state leaders, they had failed to produce anyone "big enough to size up to the nation scale." On balance he felt that the party would renominate Taft, and that he would have to support the ticket although he was under no illusions about the chances for victory. That would not be possible until 1916.

Although losing the 1908 presidential election, the Democratic party, especially in the Middle West, had reversed the ten-year trend toward the Republicans. In the 1910 off-year election this Democratic upswing invaded the East with startling results. For the first time since the early 1890's the older party won a majority in the House, elected three New England governors and the first senator from that section since the Civil War. More importantly, among the six new Democratic governors were two, Judson Harmon of Ohio and Woodrow Wilson of New Jersey, who were soon to be considered as potential presidential candidates for 1912.

Confronted with the rise of insurgency and progressivism in the Republican ranks, conservatives were not entirely displeased with the 1910 Democratic successes. In analysing the surprising results they came to the cheering conclusion that the party so long dominated by Bryanism had finally swung toward the conservative side of the spectrum. The party, they agreed, having escaped both the "terror of Tammany and the bedlam of Bryanism," was returning to the best and soundest doctrines of its greatest days: "to a reverence for the Constitution, a warm attachment to states rights and a hatred of Federal interference and power." Even some Democratic liberals agreed. The political wit, Mr. Dooley, remarked that he had been a Democrat throughout the long dreary years when to be one and to be caught in a bank was to be shot on sight. But 1910 had changed all that. For the first time in his life Mr. Dooley found himself in the same party with "ivry man who's richer the day befure pay day than he is the day afther."

On the surface the 1910 and early 1911 developments in the Democratic party held out little hope for the liberals. In both the Nebraska and Ohio Democratic state conventions of 1910, in which Bryan had made himself an issue, the Commoner was soundly defeated. Subsequently the intra-party fight over the congressional leadership resulted in more conservative victories in both the Senate and the House. Meanwhile, almost every suggested Democratic candidate for the Presidency, save for Champ Clark, came from the conservative sector of the political quadrant. Oscar Underwood, Democratic floor leader of the House, was supported by the so-called southern Bourbons; Governor Judson Harmon of Ohio was a well known Cleveland Democrat; and Woodrow Wilson of New Jersey was by his early record and his chief supporters associated with traditional party views. By mid-1911 the old alliance between ante-Populist southerners and the northern urban machines appeared to be in control of the Democratic party.

Actually, however, a progressive yeast was fermenting in the Democratic organization, activated in part by developments in the opposition and also stimulated by most of the newly elected Democrats in 1910. In New Jersey the newly elected Governor Woodrow Wilson turned against the machine that had just nominated him to support a liberal Democrat, James A. Martine, for the United States Senate. Following the same pattern, twenty-one insurgent Democrats, under the leadership of the young Franklin D. Roosevelt, walked out of the New York legislative caucus and refused to support Tammany's candidate for the Senate. In Washington, at the end of the old Congress, a rebellious group of Democratic senators so disgusted their party leader, Joseph Bailey of Texas, with their "Populist tendencies" that he resigned.

Some recognition of the new spirit in the party was given by the selection

of Champ Clark of Missouri as the new Speaker of the House. Clark was a
Bryan supporter but he was neither rejected by the southern conservatives
nor by the northern political machines. The selection of Clark as Speaker,
however, did not appease the growing liberal faction. Within a short time,
opposition to the floor leadership of Underwood also became pointed at
Clark, as the Speaker naturally sought to support his party's formal organization. By 1912, the Democratic insurgents were able to defeat an Underwood-
Clark scheme for limiting what became known as the Pujo investigation into
the "money trust." Significantly two of the three rebel leaders were from the
newly elected northern Democrats, while most of the support for a limited
investigation came from "old line" southern Democrats.

Simultaneously the existing breach in the Senatorial party had also widened. In the South a new breed of Senators like Hoke Smith of Georgia and
Luke Lea of Tennessee were more inclined to vote with the newly elected
northern and western Democrats than with the old group of so-called Bourbons. The pattern was evident during the spring of 1912 on the voting for a
workman's compensation bill. Among the opposition were fifteen "old style"
southern Democrats, while Senators Chamberlain of Oregon, Newlands of
Nevada, Pomerene of Ohio and Lea of Tennessee led the majority of the senatorial party in support. Significantly, three of the four had been elected in
1909–10. With the growing liberal strength in both major parties the press
by 1911 regularly spoke of a four-party Congress, which in a sense was true.
Although the 1910 elections had greatly depreciated Bryan's personal
strength within the Democratic party, they had nevertheless increased the
support for many of the Commoner's principles.

Had Taft been more of a politician, he might have recouped his position
even as late as 1911 and conceivably have won the election of 1912. But his
actions during the twelve months before the elections were anything but
politically judicious. Having alienated the insurgent faction of his party he lost
the confidence of conservatives and the farmers by pursuing an anti-trust campaign and supporting Canadian reciprocity. The suits against the tobacco, steel,
and harvester companies were just as bitterly condemned in Wall Street as
Canadian reciprocity was in the corn and wheat belt. By the end of 1911 most
conservative politicians were admitting that they might have to support the
President for reelection, but only as a less repugnant choice between bad
alternatives.

Of the many political mistakes Taft made in 1911, his decision on October 23, 1911, to initiate the anit-trust suit against the United States Steel Corporation was the worst. As its major reason for the action the government's
brief cited the corporation's 1907 acquisition of the Tennessee Coal and Iron
Company, a transaction to which Theodore Roosevelt as President had given
tacit consent in a White House meeting with the company's executives. The
close political and personal friendship between Roosevelt and Taft had already disappeared. But after the filing of the steel suit Roosevelt's coolness
turned into blazing indignation. Until the suit he had been adamantly opposed
to taking any personal part in the coming elections. Within a few days after its
filing he set in motion the long process which led him first to announce his

candidacy for the Republican nomination and subsequently to found an independent party. His often expressed opinion that the Republican party would be defeated in 1912 and his reiterated statement that he would not play an active part in the election allow no other conclusion than that he was motivated by anger and a burning desire to strike back at the unhappy President.

Even in his anger against Taft, however, Roosevelt made no precipitate announcement of his candidacy. By the end of November he had told only a few close personal friends that they could "sound out the possibilities for his nomination." A month later, still without committing himself, he was supplying names to these friends for the purpose of building trial organizations. Even after these organizations showed the expected possibilities, Roosevelt insisted that if he were to run for a third term the process be given the appearance of answering a widespread popular demand. Accordingly, eight Republican governors and ex-governors formally requested him to seek the nomination, the petition having been carefully phrased by Roosevelt and his intimates in Oyster Bay. Only then did the Colonel give a direct commitment. "My hat is in the ring," he announced while on a speaking trip to the Ohio constitutional convention, and shortly thereafter he gave his formal acquiescence to the beseeching governors.

Roosevelt's Ohio announcement immediately set in motion a train of related events. One was the collapse of the La Follette candidacy. Two months prior to the announcement many of La Follette's friends had been covertly transferring their allegiance to Roosevelt. But, since they were not sure that Roosevelt would take an unequivocal position, they remained members of La Follette's organization and thus opened themselves to a charge of treachery. The bitter Wisconsin senator charged Roosevelt with duplicity and blamed him for destroying progressive unity. La Follette was to repay Roosevelt later in like coin by refusing to support him in the presidential race while most of his remaining loyal followers worked for Wilson. But, from the moment of Roosevelt's announcement, the La Follette candidacy was no longer meaningful except in Wisconsin, Minnesota, and the Dakotas.

The possibility and then the certainty of Roosevelt's candidacy also strongly affected the strategy of Taft's renomination campaign. During the first two months of 1912 in states without presidential preferential primaries, the local Republican organizations attempted to accelerate the process of selecting delegates for the national convention. In the South, where the local Republican organization and federal officeholders were almost identical, no effort was spared to insure loyalty to the President. Although Taft had not planned actively to campaign, speaking tours were now arranged in the states where the primaries would decide the character of the delegation to the national convention.

Roosevelt's own campaign strategy helped the President to maintain his control of the Republican state organizations. From the first Roosevelt realized that his only hope for the nomination was to win what presidential primaries existed in such a sweeping fashion that it would convince most organization-minded Republicans that the President had no chance of victory in

November. The need for popular support, his intuition that the country had shifted steadily toward the liberal side of the political spectrum, and his desire to distinguish his principles from those of Taft moved him further toward radicalism than his customary caution had permitted in the past. In his "Charter for Democracy" speech before the Ohio constitutional convention, he not only advocated a "pure democracy" in which human rights would be supreme over all others including those of property and wealth, but also specifically endorsed the initiative, the referendum, and the recall, including the recall of judicial decisions "subject only to action by the Supreme Court of the United States." This frightened conservatives enough to make them ardent supporters of Taft. Many of Roosevelt's more traditionalist personal friends such as Lodge, Root, and Stimson shifted from a neutral to a Taft position after the Columbus speech. In the heavily conservative Republican organization and among the ranks of its wealthy supporters, thousands decided that possible victory was not worth the risk of Roosevelt's principles.

Who, then, in the Republican ranks supported the ex-President? All of the eight governors who had asked him to enter the race remained after Columbus. Most of the former La Follette suporters did likewise. Many of his old associates of presidential days stood fast, including, of course, people like Pinchot and Garfield who had incurred Taft's displeasure, others out of friendship, and a few on the grounds of principle. Some hard-bitten bosses like Walter Brown of Ohio, William Ward of New York, and William Flinn of Pittsburgh, judged that their personal fortunes were more likely to be enhanced by following Roosevelt rather than Taft. Some such realistic calculation also affected the incumbent Republican state chairmen in Louisiana and Texas. But on the whole most of the professionals remained with Taft, while Roosevelt had to depend on amateurs.

The Roosevelt-Taft contest for delegates was rough and riotous. In early April the two former friends set the pattern by publicly disparaging each other in Massachusetts. By the time the Ohio primary was held in late May the exchange of personal invective often obscured major issues. Fist fights, lockouts, and contested results punctuated most local and state conventions. This was particularly true in the South where the Roosevelt minority, attempting to counter Taft's federal machine, repeatedly selected contesting delegates whose credentials were almost entirely without status of either legal or customary variety. Elsewhere, however, the disputed results were based upon more substance and presented the Credentials Committee of the national convention with difficult decisions.

At one level the Taft-Roosevelt fight for delegates was a personality contest; on a more theoretical plane it was a dispute to determine whether the party would officially espouse liberal or conservative doctrines; and a further issue was plainly one between the official party and the voters who called themselves Republicans. Of the three categories only the latter was firmly settled by the pre-convention contests. As expected, Taft won in most of the states not having a primary for the selection of delegates. But in this first national election when the direct primary was extensively used, the total votes were Roosevelt 1,157,397, Taft 761,716 and La Follette 351,043. Roosevelt won primaries in Illinois, Pennsylvania, California, Minnesota, Nebraska, Maryland, South Dakota, Ohio, and New Jersey. He lost Massachusetts to the President by a slight margin and Wisconsin and North Dakota to La Follette. Of particular significance was the Roosevelt victory in Taft's home state of Ohio, where he won by an almost 2 to 1 margin. Of the two men Roosevelt was unquestionably the choice of the Republican voters.

By the end of the pre-convention contests the role of delegates, as well as it could be tabulated, stood at 326 uncontested delegates for Taft, 432 for Roosevelt, 41 for La Follette, and 254 contested, of which the great proportion rightfully belonged to Taft.

Such contests were decided traditionally by the National Committee, which, of course, was controlled by the President's friends. In a series of stormy sessions held before the convention, with continual charges of fraud, occasional threats of violence and the creation of a third Roosevelt party, the Committee allotted 235 of the contested delegates to the President and only 19 to Roosevelt. This action brought forth daily charges of theft from Roosevelt and eventually his presence in Chicago "to protect his own rights against the naked robbery being undertaken by the Taft forces." Among the welter of charges and counter charges it is extremely difficult for an investigator to decide what the outcome might have been had justice been the determining factor in the deliberations. Possibly, the Roosevelt delegates added to La Follette's might have been numerous enough to have stopped Taft's nomination on the first ballot. In that contingency there is little question that Roosevelt would have been eventually nominated. But the National Committee, supported by past precedents, was determined to allocate enough delegates to the President to assure his renomination. Once that objective was realized, the Taft men quickly organized the convention, selected the temporary chairman, Elihu Root, wrote the platform, and renominated Taft and his Vice-President, James Sherman, by a vote of 561 to 107 for Roosevelt and 41 for La Follette. Many Roosevelt delegates (344) refused to participate, thereby characterizing the proceedings as fraudulent and raising the question of their future relations with the party.

Although at vital points a conservative document, the Republican platform was not entirely without progressive features. It promised to enact legislation to limit the labor of women and children, to protect workmen in dangerous occupations, and to establish a system of workmen's compensation. It proposed a parcel post scheme and the expansion of existing programs of reclamation and conservation. Although affirming the traditional Republican view on the tariff it advocated a federal trade commission to regulate interstate industries and to police the market place. However, it retained a remarkable silence on two major national issues: labor and the proposed central bank.

No part of the platform was less ambiguous than its stand on the courts. While favoring improvements in the process whereby a derelict judge might be removed from office, it labelled the recall of judges "unnecessary and un-

wise." Its song of praise for the part "independent Courts of Justice" had
played in defending even the humblest individual's rights, including that of
"justly acquired property" left no doubt as to the official party's stand on the
judicial issue and its determination to protect property.

A bare recital of the results of the convention gives no indication of how
turbulent it really was. Long before the National Committee had even decided
on the contesting delegates, Roosevelt had come to Chicago and repeatedly
threatened that he would not abide by the decisions if they were not justly
reached. After the primary votes, justice to Roosevelt meant his own nomination. As if to underline the threat, the Roosevelt men both in the National
Committee and later in the Credentials Committees walked out on the proceedings. As early as the night of June 19–20 Roosevelt made his decision to
establish a new party, despite the fact that many of the Republican officeholders supporting him, including seven of the eight governors who had originally called for his nomination, were opposed to the move. That decision
dictated many others during the convention. It made the proposals for a possible compromise candidate, which at various times included the names of
Charles Evans Hughes, Senator Cummins of Iowa, and more often Governor
Hadley of Missouri, a futile exercise. It led to the silence of 344 Roosevelt
delegates in the final vote and, most important, to the call for a Saturday evening meeting of Roosevelt supporters in Orchestra Hall to found a new party
"dedicated to progressive principles." There, the bolting Republican delegates
listened to both Governor Hiram Johnson of California and Theodore Roosevelt and agreed to hold a national convention of a new Progressive party during the first week in August.

Much ink has been expended in attempting to explain why Roosevelt, an
uncommonly good politician in the past, should have made a snap judgment to
form a new party and accept its nomination in face of an almost inevitable
autumn defeat. Probably his personal anger at Taft bulked largest in his real
reasons for entering the contest, plus the fact that by the end of convention
week he had publicly expressed such moral indignation that silence and inac-
tivity were an impossibility for one of Roosevelt's temperament. One other
possible factor—the chance of victory—has not been much discussed by
commentators on the election. In letters to friends during the summer of 1912
Roosevelt predicted his own defeat. But he had also been gloomy about his
chances in 1904. Until the Democratic convention had made its choice, it was
not at all certain that the popular ex-President could be counted out before
the ballots were cast. Given a conservative Democratic opponent, the complexion of the contest would have been changed radically. The shadow of
Theodore Roosevelt was to hang ominously over the Democratic convention
as it had over Chicago.

Just after the Democratic congressional victory in November, 1910, William Jennings Bryan suggested four names in preferential order as possible
1912 Democratic candidates for President: Governor Folk of Missouri, Mayor
William Jay Gaynor of New York, and the just-elected Governors Harmon of Ohio and Wilson of New Jersey. Among his leading candidates, Bryan

explained, Folk and Gaynor were liberals, Harmon and Wilson the conservatives. But the list of Democratic possibilities changed so rapidly that within fifteen months both Folk and Gaynor had been dropped, and the conservative floor leader of the House, Oscar Underwood—the first southern aspirant since 1860—added. Underwood's rise in party esteem was largely accounted for by his fending off Bryan's attempt to dominate the congressional policy of the party during the 1911 session. At the same time the Speaker, Champ Clark, and surprisingly enough Woodrow Wilson, both in the more liberal end of the party, were increasing favorites. Clark, baptized James Beauchamp, but universally known as Champ, had by far the most impressive liberal credentials. A Kentuckian by birth, an ex-editor and college president, Clark, until he became Speaker, had consistently supported Bryan and his radical agrarian policies. In 1911–12, as a liberal, he managed to win the support of his home state delegation in Missouri against Folk and rapidly became a favorite of the westerners. Supported by William Randolph Hearst and many of the northern machine politicians, Clark went to the Baltimore convention with the largest number of delegates and was the favorite-on-odds to be nominated.

Few careers in American politics have been as paradoxical as that of Woodrow Wilson. Outside professional politics until 1910 as a college professor and university president he had nevertheless often made clear his conservative preferences. As an eminent conservative he had been selected by George Harvey, president of Harper and Brothers and editor of *Harper's Weekly*, as a possible presidential candidate through whom Harvey and his wealthy backers might eliminate William Jennings Bryan's influence from the dominant councils of the party. And in 1910, as a conservative, he was offered the Democratic gubernatorial nomination of New Jersey by a coterie of state bosses in dire need of a respectable candidate.

Governor of a state long dominated by an easy alliance between political machines and corporate wealth, Wilson surprised both his supporters and liberal opponents by half persuading and half coercing a balky legislature into passing a reform program which struck at both machine and corporate power in the commonwealth. During the 1911 legislative session, primary and corrupt practices acts were passed, a measure for workingmen's compensation was enacted, and a state commission was created with power to regulate railroads and municipal utilities.

Wilson's New Jersey legislative successes were terminated in the autumn of 1911 when a state election returned a Republican majority to the House and continued the power of the Smith-Nugent machine in Essex County—the organization that was largely responsible for his original nomination. By that time, however, Wilson was in command of the statewide Democratic organization and, just as important to his ambitions, he had acquired a national reputation as a liberal and anti-machine governor. As at Princeton in 1909, when his career was threatened by powerful opponents, he turned to another field for success, this time to national politics.

In the fall of 1911 Wilson was introduced into Democratic national politics, as he had been in New Jersey, by George Harvey, and was supported by the contributions of two very wealthy New York capitalists, August Belmont and Thomas Fortune Ryan. As his campaign expanded, so did the liberalism of his speeches and his inclination to separate himself from the group of conservative editors and corporate magnates who had originally fired his political ambitions. Wilson's separation, but not divorce, from the New York group was managed rather clumsily and left him with both political debits and credits. His request to Colonel Harvey to diminish his public support because it was hurting him in the West gave further evidence to the professional politicians in the Democratic party that here was a man who would not obey the first law of the game: repay all debts and favors. On the other hand, it helped convince many doubting liberal Democrats that Wilson was one of their own, especially after Bryan had commented that somewhere, somehow, along the road Wilson was traveling, "Saul had become Paul."

Whether Wilson had seen the light of conviction or whether it was expediency, the affinity between him and the more liberal elements of the party by the spring of 1912 was widely accepted. Generally, then, Wilson was the liberal candidate, Clark the choice of the moderates and the northern professionals, and Underwood and Harmon, the hope of the conservatives, even though during Harmon's Ohio administration as much progressive legislation had been passed as Wilson had achieved in New Jersey. Measured along another dimension, Wilson was largely the candidate cf the non-professionals and non-officeholders and he was also the most national candidate in the sense that his support came from practically every section of the country.

When the Democratic convention met in Baltimore on June 25, Clark clearly had the largest number of pledged delegates, followed by Wilson, Harmon, and Underwood in that order. It was also clear that no condidate had a majority, to say nothing of the two-thirds vote necessary for victory. The way was then open for much under-the-counter bargaining among the leading candidates and factions of a party long noted for both the variety and number of its contesting groups. By far the freest and most skilled in this art of convention manipulation were the state bosses of northern political machines whose power rested mainly on automatic majorities rolled up in large urban and industrial centers. Charles P. Murphy, the boss of Tammany Hall, Roger Sullivan of Illinois, and Thomas Taggart of Indiana were all certain to play major roles in the proceedings and to place their bets behind a potentially successful candidate and one friendly to their own local interests.

Another individual force was apparent to every delegate in almost every session of the convention. William Jennings Bryan, chairman of the Nebraska delegation, which was pledged to Clark, obtained only 1 vote for the presidential nomination on the first ballot. But his influence was as pervasive as his ends ambiguous. Throughout the pre-convention period he declared he was not a candidate and he refused formally to enter his name in the contests. Moreover, despite the fact that as a Nebraska delegate he was pledged to Clark, he had also refused to endorse personally any other contestant and to state that he would not run if nominated. His opposition to the conservatives Harmon and Underwood was long a matter of record and in the first vote of the convention he came in direct conflict with the Clark forces over the choice of a temporary chairman. A Clark-Tammany combine was victorious in the National Committee and proposed Alton B. Parker, the conservative 1904 Democratic nominee, for the post. In a direct challenge from the floor Bryan protested against "predatory wealth" dominating the party, implying that Clark was a party to the corrupt bargain. And though the Commoner obtained from the Convention an anti-Wall Street resolution, he personally met defeat as a candidate for the chairmanship when the Clark managers delivered enough votes to insure a narrow victory for Parker.

Bryan's unsuccessful challenge cemented the Clark-Murphy alliance at the cost of casting a conservative shadow over the Speaker—a shadow that was to haunt him later. It also convinced many astute observers that Bryan was attempting to deadlock the convention by killing off the leading candidate in the hope of winning the nomination himself. Both the floor managers for Wilson and Clark felt that Bryan was contriving his own selection, and the Wall Street betting odds on Bryan went from even-stephen to 3 to 1.

If Bryan hoped for a deadlocked convention he got his wish, for during the first 9 ballots the margins between the leading candidates varied little from the pattern of the first, when Clark, the leader, got 440 1/2 votes, Wilson 324, Harmon 148 and Underwood 117 1/2. On the tenth ballot, however, the Tammany-led New York delegation shifted its vote from Harmon to Clark, giving the Speaker 556 votes, more than a majority of the convention. And, since for over seventy years no Democratic aspirant with a majority had failed to win the nomination, it appeared that Clark's support of Tammany on the chairmanship issue had paid off, particularly since Wilson, a previous opponent of the two-thirds rule, sent a private message to his convention manager releasing his delegates to vote for whom they would.

Whatever logic impells the wider movements of history, the decisions revolving around individuals often fall on the knife edge of chance. During the remainder of the tenth ballot the New York shift to Clark did not cause the expected break among the Harmon and Underwood delegates to the Speaker's cause. The Wilson release message, never made public, was countermanded, and the convention continued through its fifth day of balloting.

During the Saturday session an event occured which has been cited by some historians as throwing the victory to Wilson. On the fourteenth ballot Bryan addressed the convention again to explain the shift of his and other Nebraska votes from Clark to Wilson. Although Nebraska had pledged its votes to Clark, Bryan asserted that the state was also progressive and supported the previously adopted resolution that it would oppose all candidates obligated to Tammany Hall and Wall Street. Bryan continued that he considered Clark now under such obligation and he would accordingly withhold his vote from the Speaker and cast it for Wilson. Since Wilson won the nomination, the easy assumption is sometimes made that Bryan's speech was the turning point of the convention and that the Commoner was thus responsible for Wilson's nomination.

Actually Bryan had not declared for Wilson. He had simply withdrawn his vote from Clark and that only as long as New York continued to support the Speaker. Bryan's action did help to maintain the deadlock in the convention for over 30 more ballots. The decision for Wilson finally came not over the Tammany and Wall Street issue, but through a series of intricate negotiations made by the Wilson managers, William F. McCombs and William G. McAdoo, with a number of state delegations including those of Illinois and Indiana led by the so-called bosses, Roger Sullivan and Thomas Taggert. The agreement with Sullivan has never been fully explained, but Taggert was won by a promise of support for Indiana's vice-presidential candidate, Thomas R. Marshall. In the final swing of many Underwood delegates to Wilson, conservatism was obviously forgotten by the southerners, aided no doubt by the consoling thought that Wilson after all had been born and raised in the South. In summary, Wilson's nomination was achieved by a traditional bundle of bargains and compromises that defied ideology.

Although the Democratic platform has generally been called progressive, it was of the Populist-Progressive tradition rather than progressivism's more urban strains. It won labor's applause by promising an exemption from the Sherman Law as well as jury trials for contempt cases growing out of labor disputes, support for the income tax, and the direct election of senators. Nevertheless, its dominant notes were Bryanesque strictures against monopoly and big business in favor of economic freedom for the small man.

Wilson's nomination greatly diminished any hope Roosevelt may have had for a November victory. For with the Republican pary split, all the Democratic candidate need do to win was to hold most of the loyal Democrats, a task which seemed relatively easy since the nominee's past could be interpreted as both conservative in principle and progressive and anti-boss in action. Wilson's convention victory also left its mark on Progressive party policy. With Taft taking the conservative position and Wilson the moderate one, there was little unoccupied political area remaining except toward the left.

The Progressive party's movement toward radicalism was further accelerated by the defection of many of the Republican officeholders previously supporting Roosevelt. Most of them, including seven of the eight governors originally asking for Roosevelt's nomination as a Republican, decided to remain with the old party. As a result the August Progressive convention at Chicago was composed of as varied and dedicated a group of reformers as had met in the country since the Omaha gathering of the Populists two decades before. Suffragettes, social workers, urban planners, conservationists, political reformers, and idealists of all strains and colors were represented. Neither the candidate nor the platform let them down. For Roosevelt's "Confession of Faith" speech and the platform itself contained plans for a democratic social service state that was not to materialize in the country for another quarter century. The more democratic state was to be achieved by an easier method of amending the Constitution, by the universal use of the direct primary, by the initiative and referendum, by equal suffrage of the sexes, by a popular referendum on laws declared unconstitutional by the state courts, by the curbing of judicial power in issuing labor injunctions and in contempt

cases, and by strict regulation of electoral procedures. More social justice was
to be attained by national prohibition of child labor and the convict contract
system, by the regulation of minimum wages and maximum hours for women,
by a workmen's compensation act, and by a system of social insurance against
sickness, unemployment, and old age. The small businessman was to be protected by "a strong national regulation" of interstate corporations, the inves-
tor by governmental supervision of the issuance of securities, the farmer by
the reestablishment of a country life commission, and the public in general by
the consolidation of all existing health agencies into a "single national health
service." The wherewithal to pay for such a regulatory state was to come
from an income and graduated inheritance taxes.

Roosevelt so dominated the Progressive convention that real debate
broke out on only two points: the Negro question in the South and the party's
official position on the trust problem. A Progressive dilemma was occasioned
by the fact that the Taft Republicans had very early in the primary race won
the allegiance of most of the anti-Democratic Negro leadership in the South,
leaving the rebellious Progressive Roosevelt Republicans largely a "lily-
white" faction. Nevertheless, southern Negroes, attracted by the social message of the new reform party, came to Chicago as contesting delegations.
Roosevelt attempted to solve the color problem by accepting lily-white organizations in the South and mixed delegations from the Border States of Maryland and West Virginia. He defended the paradoxical position of a reform party
opting for southern segregation as best he could, first in a long published
letter to Julian Harris and later in his "Confession of Faith" speech, concluding the latter with the hope that in the future the Progressives would welcome
colored delegates from the Deep South just as they were then receiving those
from the Border States.

The second and more serious dispute occurred over the famous "missing
anti-trust plank" in the platform. The issue arose because of the conflict between Roosevelt's strong views favoring government regulation of large industry and those of Progressives, whom he had once referred to as "rural tories," favoring dissolution through the Sherman Act. Supporting Roosevelt
were most of the eastern Progressives, including the two financial angels of the
party, George W. Perkins and Frank Munsey. In opposition were most of the
westerners and the two Pinchot brothers, Amos and Gifford. Two separate
paragraphs, the first approving of Rooseveltian regulation and the second
strengthening the Sherman Law, were adopted by the Resolutions Committee. But apparently the Sherman provision was later deleted by Roosevelt and
Perkins, only to be reinstated without the knowledge of the candidate and his
financial backer. Subsequent to the convention, Roosevelt ordered the Sherman provision to be deleted, exciting the question further and widening the
split between the contending factions, a split which eventually moved the Pin-
chots publically to challenge Perkins' "House of Morgan" control over the
destinies of the party. The document was most often printed as the Resolutions Committee approved it, with both regulatory and the Sherman planks
included.

The proprietary control that Roosevelt exerted over the Progressive party was as obvious over the remainder of the convention's proceedings as it had been during the minority and trust debates. No other candidate for the party's chief nomination was even suggested. The selection of Hiram Johnson, then Governor of California, as vice-presidential candidate, the final shape of the platform, and most of the other important actions all bore the stamp "made in Oyster Bay." Despite such control, as apparent as it was real, the exuberant enthusiasm of the meeting for its leader has rarely been approached in the history of American politics. Even tough, irreverent newspaper reporters testified that they had seen nothing like it. Roosevelt's appearance before the convention excited a spontaneous, standing ovation of fifty-two minutes, and his closing peroration, "We stand at Armageddon and we battle for the Lord" brought the body to an emotional state that could only be released by the reverential singing of the Battle Hymn of the Republic.

Even further left than the Progressives was the Socialist party, so confident of its increasing strength that its 1908 candidate Eugene V. Debs entitled one of his main pre-election addresses "This Is Our Year." The Socialists had good reason for optimism. Between 1910 and 1912 Socialists had elected over twelve hundred of their candidates to public office. Five daily Socialist newspapers flourished in 1912 and a Socialist candidate managed to poll one-third of the total vote for the presidency of the A.F. of L. meeting in Indianapolis. In May, however, the party split as usual between the advocates of violence on the left and the gradualists. By over a 2 to 1 vote the moderate political actionists adopted a resolution expelling the advocates of sabotage. But the meeting then proceeded to ignore the split by nominating the candidate of the radicals, Eugene Debs, on a typical revisionist platform.

By their total neglect of foreign affairs, the Socialists agreed with the general tone of most of the party platforms of 1912, including those of the Prohibitionists and the small splinter Socialist Labor party. The Democratic, Republican, and Progressive documents all advocated the building of a stronger navy, but aside from the usual praise for arbitration of international disputes and a condemnation of Russian treatment of American Jews, all the platforms were silent on the menacing developments abroad. Americans were so secure in 1912 and so engrossed in domestic problems that foreign affairs were not discussed at any length in either the conventions or the campaign.

With the conventions over, the voters as usual ignored the various party platforms or at most gave them a cursory reading before turning their attention to the candidates. Three of the nominees had long been familiar to most Americans. Beloved by all who knew him and admired by many people who opposed all of his policies, the long, lean, and friendly figure of Eugene V. Debs had been a fixture of American politics for two decades. Born in Terre Haute, Indiana, of immigrant Alsatian parents, Debs had worked his way up from a railroad shop to a position of power in his union and then to being a perennial candidate of the Socialist party. Debs was always two persons, one the across-the-fence American small town neighbor, generous and friendly, tolerant of human foibles and yet possessed of a character which might have served as a model for middle class morality and integrity. The other Debs, however, was everything the middle class anathematized—a labor agitator rejected equally by capitalists and traditional labor leaders, and a firebrand Socialist orator whose eloquent denunciation of existing society was only equalled by his appeals for the revolution. Eugene Debs was a gentle man who approved of the violence of others when employed for the cause. His popular appeal to the faithful was as great as his knowledge of socialist theory was scant. His contradictions, perhaps as much as any other factor, explain the failure of the American Socialist party to rival in number and power those of Europe. Debs was so much of an American that he could not be a good Socialist in the prime tradition.

The personality of the incumbent President, William Howard Taft, was almost an open book to Americans in 1912. He had been in public life for almost thirty years and his was a figure hard to miss—his weight, despite strenuous bouts of dieting, varied between 250 and 350 pounds. The four-year Presidency proved the most irritating period in the life of this large, kindly, often placid, and usually jovial man. Taft was never meant to be a politician and never succeeded in being a good one. His character was too open, his sense of what was fair and honest too rigid, and his first rate if not original mind too inflexible to meet the ever shifting requirements of democratic politics. The physical demands and the pressure for decisions inherent in the office were too intense for a person inclined to procrastinate and who loved a leisured, orderly, low-keyed life. Taft was never happier than when he was on the bench, never more successful than when he was an administrator, whether in the Philippines or in Washington expertly carrying out the policy of other men, and never more troubled than when he had to seek a compromise between the jostling, always demanding, and often self-seeking realistic politicians, a compromise that often had to reflect not only what he considered legal but also what was politic.

Taft had other troubles between the years 1909 and 1913. By taste and intellect he was essentially a conservative heading a nation in some of its most progressive years. Moreover, he was intensely loyal to his principles, to his friends, and to the promises he had made. During his Administration he attempted to be loyal to Theodore Roosevelt, who had made him President, to the pledge he had made to carry out his predecessor's policies, to the Republican party which had supported him, and to his own firmly held political philosophy. It was an impossible task. For as popular opinion veered rapidly toward more reform, Theodore Roosevelt was facilely changing his policies. Both in Congress and the nation the Republican party had become divided between a radical and a conservative faction, and the country's rising expectations were far exceeding what Taft's conservative mentality found permissible. Taft was indeed a very unhappy man in 1912. For the first time in his Administration he was supporting the conservative principles that agreed with his deepest convictions. But he was also warring with old friends, and he was among the first to realize that his reelection was almost impossible.

By 1912, after the Spanish War, few facets of Roosevelt's personality had not been publicly discussed *ad nauseam*—the term as governor of New York, the seven bully presidential years, and the big game hunt among the lions of Africa. Roosevelt had become heavier over the years, and with his own recognition that he was no longer young, rather more solemn. All the old crowd-exciting mannerisms were still there, the earnest and indignant high pitched voice, the clenched fist, the thrusting jaw. He could still make a political speech sound as if he were leading a cataclysmic struggle between good and evil. Although the love of battle remained in his platform manner, one commentator noted that the Colonel's responses were a little slower, his personal zest for the oft-repeated ritual seemed to be slightly muted. But if something of his youthful spirit was lacking in Roosevelt's 1912 manner, his almost unequivocal stand for radical action inspirited his followers to a pitch of devotion seldom seen in a political campaign. The testimony Roosevelt received from his followers also seemed to work a change in him. At the very end of the contest several journalists remarked that they detected a Roosevelt different in both word and spirit. The pronoun, "I", which had peppered his former speeches, was now replaced by the more seductive and modest "we;" the old sarcasm and belligerence by sincerity and conviction. After his last major speech at Madison Square Garden one commentator noted that apparently Roosevelt had finally persuaded himself of the justice and inevitability of the program he espoused.

Compared to the usual presidential candidate, Woodrow Wilson was something of a maverick. For one thing he was the first candidate since the Civil War to be born and raised in the South. For another, an immigrant background lay not too far in his past. On his mother's Scottish side of the family he was just one generation away from the Old World, on his father's Scottish-Irish side, two. He was also atypical in that he was the first Ph. D. to run for the Presidency and had been a professor and a college president rather than the usual politician or military figure. Neither commanding nor impressive physically, he was not even a crowd pleaser in the usual sense, and far from a rabble rouser. In the campaign, as during the Presidency, there was between him and his countrymen something of the air of the classroom—something of the distance between a teacher and his pupils. Wilson was also a devout Presbyterian, a "Presbyterian priest" one of his close associates remarked, and his appeal was largely to the moral and ethical fibre of man. He talked of visions, purposes, responsibilities, and ideals. Even when discussing more mundane things such as tariffs, trusts, and trade, his language was often reminiscent of the pulpit. And though some of his audience might have difficulty understanding the exact meaning of his precise and polished sentences, there was no mistaking their moral tone and the conviction of the man who uttered them. Wilson was easy to respect, but difficult to love. Had the times not been what they were—a product of progressivism's decade-long emphasis upon moral duty and righteousness—Wilson might never have been nominated. Democracy usually likes its heroes of uncommon size but with a few visible human imperfections, if for no other reason than to stress the quality of the remainder.

Given the bitter personal character of the nomination battles, the ensuing election campaign was something of an anti-climax. President Taft contributed principally to the moderating tone of the contest by refusing to campaign and confining his activities to writing a few dignified letters for publication. Although in private he described the Progressive party as "a religious cult with a fakir at the head of it," not once in his statements did he descend to personal acrimony against either of his opponents.

Wilson also sought to soothe the irritated feelings in his own party. With alacrity he accepted Bryan's offer of help and went out of his way to be cordial to the defeated Champ Clark. Moreover, he refused to indulge in personalities with either Taft or Roosevelt and kept his side of the debate on a dignified and intellectual level. On learning that the President was in the same hotel he was using at Boston, the Democratic candidate asked to pay his respects, and the two contestants chatted with each other in a meeting reporters characterized as courteous and full of good humor.

Both Wilson's temperament and his campaign strategy also kept him from indulging in sharp personal conflict with Roosevelt. He repeatedly refused, for example, to discuss the manifold specific reform issues presented by the Progressive candidate and the Progressive platform. Never once did he mention the third-term issue or the radical propositions of the Progressive party except to label them collectively as well-intentioned but impossible of achievement. Heckled at one meeting by an ardent feminist who demanded that he take a position on women's suffrage, he kept answering that the question belonged to the realm of state politics, until at last the objector was escorted from the hall by guards.

Wilson also limited the geographical area of his campaign as sharply as the issues he was willing to discuss. Compared with Roosevelt's long journeys that took him to the Pacific Coast and into the Deep South, Wilson traveled neither west of Denver nor south of Delaware and Missouri. Obviously he felt the South would support him willy-nilly, and the West he left to Bryan, who covered as many miles as the nominee did. Almost everywhere Roosevelt went west of the Mississippi he was trailed by the Commoner whose western appeal by now was almost legendary. As the election figures proved, it was effective strategy. If Wilson owed his election to any other man save himself it was to Bryan, whom a few years before he had wished to "knock into a cocked hat."

As the tenor of the campaign was set by his competitors, Roosevelt was deprived of using those skillful cutting phrases that had formerly struck down many an opponent. The most he could come up with was rather gentle comments upon Wilson's professorial mind and mien, and a description of Taft as "a dead cock in a pit." Roosevelt was further disarmed by Wilson's refusal to debate with him except on a very few issues. The Colonel's marked skill at such oratorical mayhem was thus blunted, and at the end of the campaign he commented that at times it seemed he was attacking an opponent "who wasn't there."

However dignified the debate between the principal actors, both Roosevelt's character and program excited violent remarks from supporters of his

two adversaries. In the speech notifying Vice-President Sherman of his renomination, Senator Sutherland set a tone that was almost immediately
followed by the New York press. The Bull Moose platform, the Senator remarked, was compounded of vicious vagaries and impractical political nos-
trums such as had never before been collected "outside of the violent wards
of a madhouse." The New York *World* called it a change from "English law
to the Roman law which has been the inspiration of a thousand tyrants." The
Times predicted that such a program would lead to a fourth term, then to dictatorship, and then to monarchy. On a more personal note the New York *Sun*
did not doubt that if the mad Mahdi of Oyster Bay broke into the White
House again it would be his, permanently. "As the Emperor Sigismund was
above grammar, so is Theodorus Rex above recall, except that of his promises
and his principles." The *North American Review* stated that Roosevelt "was
the first President whose chief personal characteristic was mendacity, the first
to glory in duplicity, the first braggart, the first bully, the first betrayer of a
friend who ever occupied the White House."

Perhaps such wild talk, reminiscent of the campaign of 1896, was in part
responsible for what happened in Milwaukee on October 14. There another
chapter in the nation's long tale of violence unfolded when Roosevelt was
shot by a madman while on his way to make a speech. Fired at close range,
the bullet fortunately was deflected by a spectacle case and inflicted only a
deep flesh wound. Against medical advice the Colonel insisted on going
through with the speech, waving as he did so a bloody handkerchief to the
horror of the crowd and to the subsequent delight of the nation when it was
learned that the accident would only incapacitate him for a few weeks.

The canvass was further enlivened by a public debate over Roosevelt's
past campaign expenditures. Seeking to counteract the ex-President's charges
that the Republican nomination had been won by the liberal use of money
supplied by large corporations, Senator Penrose charged Roosevelt with accepting $150,000 from the Standard Oil Company in 1904 and asking for
more. Whereupon, in the middle of a campaign trip, Roosevelt, as *The New
York Times* pointed out, miraculously produced a letter written to the treasurer
of the Republican party in 1904, requesting him not to seek or receive large
contributions from big business. The subsequent exchange between Roosevelt
and the senator was as lively as it was inconclusive, the whole affair petering
out into a congressional investigation of campaign funds since 1900.

Roosevelt's real or fancied past financial dealings with large corporations
was a particularly sensitive subject to the Progressive high command because
of the internal objection within the party to the dominant role played by
George W. Perkins, whose intimate relations with the House of Morgan and
the U.S. Steel and the Harvester corporations was well known to friend and
foe. The suspicion against Perkins, first aroused by the missing trust plank in
the platform, was kept alive by the two Pinchot brothers and other radical
Progressives. As they trenchantly pointed out, Roosevelt was in a poor position to contend for the government regulation of industry when his own party
treasurer represented some of the most dominant industrial and financial in-

terests in the nation. Faced with the threat that the contention would become public, Roosevelt at first cajoled and then virtually ordered the dissidents to keep the peace, at least until the election was over.

Trouble also visited both the Taft and Wilson organizations. Taft's difficulties were largely financial, since many of the traditional contributors of large sums to Republican coffers were so pessimistic about the chances for a victory that they preferred to place their money on sounder speculations. Whereas, Taft wrote, the national party usually had more than $2 million in the past, the treasurer had managed to collect less than half that sum. The Taft campaign was further weakened by the death of the vice-presidential nominee during the week preceding the election. As a replacement the National Committee selected Nicholas Murray Butler, president of Columbia University.

In the Wilson organization the trouble was largely of a personal nature centering around the difficult character of William F. McCombs, the nominal campaign manager. Closely associated with Wilson since the latter's first political activities in New Jersey, McCombs was intensely loyal to his chief, but he was also relatively inexperienced in national politics and in none too good health. During the Baltimore convention the rivalry between McCombs and William G. McAdoo was already apparent. And as Wilson increasingly leaned on the advice of McAdoo, McCombs' possessive spirit became more tense. Eventually McCombs suffered a nervous breakdown, after which the old relationship with Wilson was never restored.

"I have no part to play but that of a conservative," William Howard Taft wrote to a friend at the beginning of the campaign. And from his acceptance speech up to the elections the President seldom varied from that ideological stance. Following the pattern set by the official Republican campaign book, he never once mentioned Roosevelt by name, but throughout the contest stressed the danger to the Constitution inherent in Roosevelt's views and those of his party. Both Roosevelt and the Progressives, he contended in the acceptance address, would subject the country to radical schemes "involving dangerous changes in our present constitutional form of representative government and our independent judiciary." At one point he did agree that a national incorporation of the trusts was desirable provided the rights of the states were not interfered with, and he supported a plan devised by Myron T. Herrick to support loans to farmers' cooperatives. But otherwise the President's emphasis was all on safeguarding present institutions and laws, including the Sherman Act.

Against Wilson, whom the President believed to be his chief antagonist, Taft seized upon the tariff as the main issue. Fortunately prosperity was increasing in the country and Taft chose to interpret the benevolent economic tide as a direct result of the high protective tariff, which, he stressed, had been a Republican instrument since the Civil War. The election of Wilson and the Democrats, he wrote in one of his campaign letters, would introduce free trade and thus imperil the home market upon which the farmer and the laborer as well as the merchant and the manufacturer depended. In one of his last campaign documents he boldly claimed that the prosperous times were Republican-induced. His last remarks before departing to vote in Cincinnati again warned the country against the constitutional peril from the Progressives and the threat to the economy from the Democrats.

Realistic as he often was about his own future, Taft had no real hope for victory. In fact, shortly after his nomination he wrote to a personal friend that he interpreted his part of the election as one of saving the Republican party so that after "the discipline of defeat" it could be made again a conservative force with which to confront their "old line enemies, the Democrats."

Aside from his own failure to win the Republican nomination, Roosevelt's greatest disappointment in the campaign of 1912 was the failure of most of the incumbent Republican politicians who had supported him before Chicago to follow him into the Progressive party. Of the eight governors who had originally asked him to run for the nomination, only one, Hiram Johnson of California, officially declared himself a Progressive. The defections among the senators and congressmen were as great. True, most of these former friends refused to follow La Follette's example in opposing Roosevelt, many of them writing that they would support him unofficially and quietly, but as Republicans. The failure of the progressive Republican officeholders officially to join the Progressive party unquestionably cost Roosevelt many votes. It also tended, perhaps in an oblique way, to shove him further toward a radical campaign. Officeholding has a way of inducing caution in politicians; and most of Roosevelt's advisers were consequently untainted with this customary source of restraint.

"I've been growing more radical instead of less radical, I'm even going further than the platform," Roosevelt assured the crowds during his first campaign speeches in Rhode Island. And with that prelude Roosevelt continued to play variations on the ideological themes he had stressed in his fight with Taft for the nomination. To separate himself from the Republicans he constantly stressed the events before the Chicago convention as indicative of how the party was controlled by its officeholders, corporate lawyers, and their financial masters—a control which made it impossible for the party to react to the conditions of the day to assure social justice. In one of his last efforts in his own New York county he called Elihu Root "a counsel against the people" standing for "that substitution of legalism for justice against which we protest."

The Democratic party and its candidate Wilson were, if anything, more tied to the unjust past by their antiquated doctrines. Wilson he described as an "ultra-conservative" groomed for the Presidency by George Harvey and other Wall Street interests precisely because his confused and doctrinaire stand on industrial regulation meant freedom for corporations to do as they would. Roosevelt continued throughout the campaign to score debating points off Wilson's conservative past. He cited Professor Wilson's pre-1908 opinions of William Jennings Bryan and his attitude toward the function of trade unions as expressed in a Princeton Commencement address—to produce as little as possible for the wages paid—as typical and fully consistent with his statement during the campaign of 1912 that "the history of liberty is the limitation of government powers, not the increase of it." If that piece of "professorial rhetoric means anything," Roosevelt added, "it means that every law for the promotion of social and industrial justice which has been put upon the statute books ought to be repealed, and every law proposed should be abandoned." He subsequently asked the Democratic candidate whether he favored destruction of the Interstate Commerce Commission.

In a less personal vein Roosevelt supported his own newly found political and economic philsophy. Throughout the campaign, he continued to insist upon the democratization of the governmental structure. "The American people," he wrote in August, "and not the courts, are to determine their fundamental policies. The people should have the power to deal with the effects of acts of all of their governmental agencies. This must be extended to include the effects of the judicial acts as well as of the executive and legislative representatives of the people." On the regulation of industry, Roosevelt sharply separated his position from that of both Taft and Wilson, by attacking the Sherman Law and proposing a regulatory commission to supervise all interstate commerce. Pointing to the example of Standard Oil, he emphasized that the price of the corporation's stock had risen after the so-called dissolution, and quoted Pierpont Morgan to the effect that once eggs were in an omelet they could not be unscrambled. The proper approach to the industrial problem was to assure such "administrative control by the Government as will prevent the eggs from ever being scrambled."

Roosevelt's approach to the tariff was to maintain its high protective quality. But he insisted that the prosperity derived from a protected market should be distributed more equitably among the farmers and the workers. He wanted to increase "the prize" accruing from enterprise and hard work, "but we stand for a more equitable division of the prize money." Continuing the theme of social justice before the first all-feminine audience in American campaign history, he told five thousand women in Seattle that the Progressive party alone stood for increase in governmental powers sufficient to protect women, cripples, and children not only against industrial hazards but against poverty, disease, and the other ravages of urban life. Summing up his campaign at Madison Square Garden he argued that neither states rights nor a constitutional fetish should prevent the national government from eradicating "fossilized wrong" from the nation: the Progressives were for liberty, but "for the liberty of the oppressed and not for the liberty of the oppressor to oppress the weak and to bind burdens on the shoulders of the heavy laden. It is idle to ask us not to exercise the power of the government when only by that power . . . can we curb the greed that sits in high places, when only by the exercise of the government can we exalt the lowly and give heart to the humble and down trodden."

In summary, Roosevelt's 1912 campaign was one of the most radical campaigns ever made by a major American political figure and deserves to rank along with Franklin Roosevelt's in 1936 and Harry Truman's in 1948. Its content of political reform outweighed those proposed by either the later

Roosevelt or Truman and, given the time the New Nationalism was conceived, its social doctrines were not entirely negligible by comparison. For the Roosevelt vision of 1912 looked forward to an industrial and urban social service state, centralized, powerful, and inspired by a humane and protective outlook toward its citizens. If the campaign was a losing one, so were the efforts of Roosevelt and Truman if measured by the immediate enactment of their promises into statutes. Over the course of the years and judged by eventual results, the New Nationalism remains one of America's principle charters of reform.

Why historians usually depict the Wilson campaign of 1912 as unusually progressive is something of a mystery. Perhaps it is because of the liberal character of the Democratic platform, or because such writers are reading their history backward — inferring the progressive character of Wilson's campaign pronouncements from his later legislative achievements, or because in attempting to impart a logic to history they have tried to identify the New Freedom with the New Deal. As a matter of record most of Wilson's campaign ignored most of the suggested reforms in the platform, looked backward instead of forward, and was essentially conservative instead of progressive.

The backward looking and conservative tone of Wilson's efforts was struck in his acceptance address on August 7, 1912. Almost one-half of the speech was devoted to an analysis of the protective tariff as a breeder of special privileges and special favors. There followed a major section on big business, which, the candidate explained, was not bad because it was big but because its bigness was "an unwholesome inflation" created by "privileges and exemptions" and by the ineffectiveness of the existing anti-trust law. On the other hand, Wilson assured his audience that he was "not seeking destruction of any kind nor the destruction of any sound or honest thing." The Democratic candidate did argue that legislation providing care of the working people "where they cannot protect themselves" was not class legislation. But he did not mention the unions then or later in his campaign, he referred to none of the proposals for the democratization of the governmental structure then being debated, nor did he mention the income tax. On the whole the speech was cast in such moderate and general phrases that even the most conservative newspaper in New York could refer to the "reasonable and sober program" of the Democratic candidate.

Throughout the remainder of the campaign Wilson maintained this air of reasonableness and sobriety. Until October his canvass consisted mainly of attacks on "the excessive tariffs and the intolerable monopolies" that had grown up under successive Republican Administrations, including those of Roosevelt. He professed to see little difference between the Progressive and the Republican stand on the trusts except that Roosevelt's program would legalize them, in which case he was sure the monopolies would regulate the government instead of vice-versa. As for the rest of the Progressive program, it was at best a clutch "of impossible pledges;" at worst one that would install bureaucrats and experts in the government who would in the end become masters of the people. "What I fear therefore," he exclaimed, "is a government by experts instead of one of full and open discussion." The Democratic candidate throughout his campaign even belittled the efficiency of the expert in government. Thus, alluding to Roosevelt's proposed tariff board, he suggested that the "experts would advocate the same sort of narrow approach as the chemistry experts had on the pure food issue." And although Wilson did assert to an assemblage of Pennsylvania steel workers that "America is not now, and cannot be in the future, a place for unrestricted individual enterprise," just a week later he was full of praise for individualism and individual enterprise that had made places like Kokomo, Indiana, "great." That needed spirit, he concluded, was being submerged in the country not by free competition that had sired it, but rather by "illicit competition."

Wilson's approach to the whole industrial question was, in fact, very confused until he held a long conference with Louis Brandeis in September. Afterward he began to make the distinction between the regulated monopoly he professed to see issuing from Roosevelt's program and the regulated competition which he asserted would be the result of his own. In speeches at Indianapolis and St. Louis he emphasized a New Freedom, a phrase that was later applied by historians to his campaign to distinguish it from Roosevelt's New Nationalism. But in continuing to talk of freedom, Wilson reiterated his distrust of governmental power. Thus at a Labor Day speech he was opposed, he said, to the Progressives' minimum wage proposal because it would automatically bring most wages down to that minimum level. Additionally he cautioned labor against being taken care of by government, because at that moment they would become "wards, not independent men."

Unquestionably the conversations with Brandeis and other liberals also spurred Wilson into a more tolerant view of social questions. Although he still insisted on rejecting "paternalism," he admitted that since property was only an instrument of humanity government should be more concerned with human than with property rights. Still, by the end of his campaign Wilson had made very few explicit reform promises other than those of lowering the tariff and of amending the anti-trust laws so as to restore the equality of competition for all businessmen. These proposals had been made in such a manner, moreover, as not to frighten conservatives of almost any variety. It was instructive to note that not one conservative journal depicted Wilson as a danger to the existing institutions and that, apart from those of the Progressives, most of the criticisms of his campaign came from the liberals and the radicals of his own party, from men like Louis Brandeis, Franklin K. Lane, and Senator Chamberlain of Oklahoma. In fact, if one bases one's judgement solely on the campaign, Wilson was scarcely entitled to be called a liberal except in the British classical definition of that word. If either the content or the spirit of his campaign words meant anything, he was closer to Cleveland than to Bryan, more akin to Herbert Hoover than to Franklin Roosevelt.

The campaigns of the minor candidates were conducted along the predetermined lines of their platforms. The Prohibitionist, Eugene W. Chapin, concentrated on the liquor traffic and Arthur Reimer of the Socialist Labor party on revolution. Reimer did introduce a novel note by calling Taft the twentieth-century Constantine of "an ultra montane theocracy," Roosevelt the Cromwell of "absolute militarism," and Wilson the present day Hamlet who only saw events "after they had happened."

The Socialist Debs opened his campaign by a salute to Karl Marx, a call for total revolution and an uncompromising attack against the Progressives. Roosevelt's party, he declared, was at least progressive as compared with the other two. It was also "lavishly financed and shrewdly advertised." But it remained a capitalist party which would never emancipate the working class. That objective would have to be achieved by the workers themselves through total revolution. After a transcontinental speaking tour Debs ended his campaign in the same manner with bitter criticism of the Progressives and a call for revolution.

The results of the election of 1912 amazed few observers since most knowledgeable people had long since predicted a sizeable Wilson victory. From the viewpoint of electoral votes it was all of that: Wilson won 435 to Roosevelt's 88 and Taft's 8. But the election figures in popular votes told another story. There the figures for Wilson totalled 6,293,120 to Roosevelt's 4,119,582, Taft's 3,485,082, and Debs' surprising 900,672. Obviously Wilson was not the choice of the majority; he was not even as popular in his own party as Bryan had been. In each of his three elections Bryan, in fact, had polled more popular votes than Wilson. Obviously thousands of voters who had preferred Bryan in 1896, 1900 and 1908, had now voted either for Roosevelt or for Debs.

Among the minor parties only the 900,672 votes cast for Debs was significant. Eugene W. Chafin, the Prohibitionist candidate, won 206,275 votes, a figure that had not changed materially over the past elections; the total for Arthur E. Reimer, of the radical Socialist Labor party was 28,750. Even though Debs had raised the total Socialist strength by over a third from that of the previous election, his votes did not materially affect the results. Approximately one-half of the total Socialist votes were cast in Ohio, Illinois, Pennsylvania, California and New York, states in which Roosevelt also ran well. But if the total Socialist votes were added to those of Roosevelt, the end result would have been the same. A similar addition in the nation would have changed the results in only two small states, Kansas and Montana.

As important to Wilson as his winning electoral votes were the election results for Congress. There, because of the Republican split, the Democrats held solid majorities in both the Senate and the House for the first time since the Civil War. Cleveland had enjoyed nominal majorities for a few months, but the waxing Populist strength soon made a mockery of Democratic control. By the 1912 elections the count in the Senate stood at fifty-one Democrats, forty-four Republicans and one Progressive; in the House, 291 Democrats, 127 Republicans, fourteen Progressives. Given no serious divisions within its ranks, the long time opposition party was presented for the first time since the Civil War with the opportunity of passing a comprehensive legislative program patterned to their own wishes.

In the inter-party fight between Roosevelt and Taft, Roosevelt was the victor but certainly not by a decisive lead. Of the combined Republican-Progressive vote Roosevelt received approximately 53 per cent of the total, Taft 47. The Taft quotient indicated two things: the strength of conservatism, or of traditional voting habits, within the party, and the surprising weakness of the conservative position in the country compared with the total number of popular votes cast for more moderate or radical candidates. Is it possible that the lack of conservative strength in the country persuaded Woodrow Wilson to be more of a liberal as a President than he had been as a candidate? There is no hint of that in his papers, but such results have been known to have persuaded other prominent politicians to alter their views on public questions.

Roosevelt's win over Taft indicated, on the surface at least, that the new party had got off to a significant start. No new political organization had been able to displace either of the two major parties since the Republican party had been organized. Immediately after the victory over Taft, Roosevelt felt that it was a "sizeable achievement." But there was one major flaw in the semi-victory, as Roosevelt soon recognized. His victory, if one can call it that, was a personal one, even though, as in the case of New York State, the Progressive candidate for governor outpolled the Colonel. Throughout the nation, except for Roosevelt, the Progressive party suffered a devastating defeat in the gubernatorial as well as in the congressional and lower state contests. Only one quasi-Progressive governor was elected, no senators, and only a handful of representatives. Including the incumbent Republicans turned Progressives not standing for elections, the Progressive total of major officeholders after the canvass of 1912 amounted to one governor, two senators and sixteen members of the House of Representatives. The party's plight in the lower state offices was even worse and almost nonexistent at the local level. The Progressives, for example, elected only one of the total fifty-one members of the New York State senate, only four of 150 representatives. Even this meager total was better than that coming from most states.

Part of the difficulty came from a lack of time in which to organize. For example, the party had managed a full slate of candidates for the national House of Representatives in only fifteen of the forty-eight states. More serious, perhaps, was the lack of well known political names even in the spots where their organization was relatively thorough. Only in California, where Hiram Johnson had moved his Progressives into the new party in such numbers that the Republicans were even deprived of an official place on the ballot, were the Progressives able to nominate clusters of well-known officeholders. The result was that the party was deprived of most federal patronage as well as local officeholders. And as Roosevelt was keenly aware, the glue that held a political party together was jobs. As he later ruefully wrote in analyzing the causes of the radical Progressive decline, "there were no loaves and fishes."

One of the other Roosevelt regrets was that the 1912 bolt had actually hurt the opportunity for liberal political action in the future. As he wrote immediately after the election, in New Hampshire, Kansas, Nebraska, and Iowa, where two years before the progressive-insurgent Republicans had been dominant, the Progressives now found themselves "in a minority, and not even with a plurality in our favor." Among former progressive Republicans who fell to opposition challengers were Senators Dixon, Bourne, and Beveridge of Montana, Oregon, and Indiana respectively. And though the main corps of insurgent-progressive Republicans, led by senators La Follette, Borah, and Cummings, survived the election, there was little question but that the Roosevelt bolt had hurt future progressive action within the Republican Party.

Since polls based upon scientific sampling were still far in the future, any detailed attempt to analyze voting blocks in the election of 1912 is more an exercise of fancy than fact. But something can be rendered from the gross figures of the returns. As could be expected, Wilson's main strength was in the Solid South and the Border States. But surprisingly the Democratic candidate failed to secure a majority in any state outside the old Confederacy. His second greatest cluster of strength lay in Bryan country running from Iowa to Nevada. And that configuration plus wins in states like New York, Massachusetts, New Jersey, and Ohio, which were unquestionably due to the Republican split, meant victory. Roosevelt's main center of strength lay along the Pacific Coast, and in the tier of northern middlewestern states lying from Michigan through the Dakotas, but exclusive of Wisconsin, which, due to La Follette's "silent endorsement" of Wilson, voted for the Democrats.

Seen through another focus of geography, the city voter clearly favored Roosevelt's vision of a social democracy over the programs of the other two candidates. The Progressive leader polled the largest vote in the first three, and in eight of the ten largest cities of the country. If one can extrapolate from those figures, Wilson's vote in the North came largely from the small towns, the villages, and from the countryside. And to that extent again Wilson inherited the Bryan tradition. One would like to know how the one million women who voted in the election of 1912 for the first time cast their ballots, and equally how organized labor responded. Because of Roosevelt's outright endorsement of women's suffrage and Wilson's refusal to take a stand on the question, it is probable, though not certain, that the Progressive candidate won a large share of the new feminine vote. Since the American Federationist recommended both Roosevelt's and Wilson's stand on labor, it is anyone's guess, until a detailed study of ward and precinct voting is made, how organized labor cast its vote. But considering Roosevelt's blast at labor after the Los Angeles *Times* bombing episode, it is probable, though again not certain, that the Roosevelt majorities in the large cities came more from the educated middle classes than from the laboring wards. It probably took an imagination fired either by education or by ideology to comprehend and sympathize with Roosevelt's proposed industrial and social service state.

One of the most erroneous of the immediate post election analyses came from *The New York Times*. Persuading itself that the people had voted against "radicalism and agitation," the *Times* predicted that Wilson would make a "conservative President." On the basis of the campaign the prediction was not unreasonable, though an analysis of the gross voting patterns in the election may help explain why the conservative candidate became the liberal President of the years 1913–17.

Wilson's victory in the Solid South and even in the Border States did not much change the existing character of the congressional Democratic party. But the Democratic congressional victories in the wheat belt, the silver country, and in the large northern cities added materially to the number of liberal Democrats who had already badgered the Democratic leadership in both the Senate and the House. It was this band of northern and western rebel Democrats who in 1911 had led in the passing of an income tax measure, and then had forced the Underwood-Clark establishment to broaden the enquiry into the money trust. Wilson had been the candidate of the liberal Democrats for the nomination. Most of his close campaign advisers were liberals. And he would have been a poor politician indeed if he had not recognized the importance of the newly elected western and northern Democrats to the ideological balance of the party. He would have been an even poorer politician had he not also been aware of William Jennings Bryan's contributions to his victory. Wilson's subsequent appointment of Bryan as Secretary of State was probably as much an ideological token of his future course as President as it was a gracious receipt for past services.

Election of 1916

by *Arthur S. Link*
and *William M. Leary, Jr.*

Throughout the greater part of American history, presidential elections have rarely had implications beyond the shores of the New World. The rise of the United States to a position of international power, however, brought a change. Today, the character of the President of the United States affects not only his own countrymen but people all over the world. It is clear in retrospect that the first presidential election to have world wide implications occurred in 1916. In that year, the citizens of the United States chose a man destined to influence the course of human events in a more profound way than any of his predecessors.

It would be comforting to believe that Americans selected this leader in a dispassionate and sober manner, weighing carefully the implications of their action. But the democratic process rarely functions in this manner. Political parties in the United States are loose coalitions of diverse factions held together for the most part by the spoils of office. Although a good deal of latitude for opposing political views is permitted within the party structure, the desertion of one's party is among the most heinous of political crimes. The Republican party in 1912 had experienced such apostasy. Theodore Roosevelt, longing to exercise political power once again and convinced that the GOP, now controlled by the reactionary Old Guard, was incapable of responding to the problems facing the nation, had raised the banner of revolt by leading a new third party, the Progressive, or Bull Moose, party. The result had been a political disaster of the first magnitude for both Republicans and

Progressives, as the Democrats went on to capture the Presidency for the first time since 1892. If the Republican party was to stand any chance at all in the election of 1916, the deep wounds of 1912 somehow would have to be healed.

This would be no easy task. When the Progressives split off from the GOP, many Republicans who remained loyal to the party nevertheless shared Roosevelt's ideals. This was evident throughout the Sixty-third Congress of 1913–14. Republican legislators, despite pleas from their leaders to stand firm against Woodrow Wilson, proved unable to agree on the iniquity of such Wilsonian measures as the Federal Reserve Act, Federal Trade Commission Act, and the Clayton Anti-Trust Act. Only opposition to the tariff policies of the Democratic Administration evoked a modicum of unity. The problem of the Republican leaders was, therefore, twofold:. Progressives had to be brought back to the fold, and dissension within the ranks of the party had to be stilled.

The congressional and state elections of 1914 offered a good indication of political trends. Roosevelt's Bull Moose was out in force, determined to demonstrate the vitality and permanence of his party. The Democrats pointed to their impressive legislative record of the past two years and sought a vote of confidence. The GOP, focusing on the recent emergency revenue legislation, accused the Democrats of fiscal irresponsibility.

After a rather dull campaign, the Republicans emerged victorious in the three-cornered contest. They not only reduced the Democratic majority in the House of Representatives from 73 to 25, but also swept New York, Illinois, Pennsylvania, Ohio, Kansas, New Jersey, Connecticut, and Wisconsin. In fact, the party doubled its congressional strength in the East, made substantial gains in the Middle West, and held its own in the western and Border States.

The Democrats could console themselves with the knowledge that midterm elections invariably bring losses to the party in power, but there was no brighter side for the Progressive party. With the exception of Governor Hiram Johnson's victory in California, Progressive candidates were defeated all across the country. Theodore Roosevelt, for one, knew what this meant. "East of Indiana," he observed, "there is not a state in which the Progressive party remains in condition even to affect the balance of power between the two old parties. . . . The people as a whole are heartily tired of me and of my views."

With the Bull Moose relegated to "innocuous desuetude," to use former President Taft's phrase, Republicans began to look with renewed confidence toward 1916. Woodrow Wilson, Republican spokesmen liked to point out, had won in 1912 because the GOP had been divided. Polling only 42 per cent of the popular vote, Wilson had failed to establish the Democracy as the majority party in the nation. Only in the eleven former Confederate states had the President received more votes than the combined totals of Roosevelt and Taft. Wilson's election, GOP leaders emphasized, had been a political accident. The Democrats would stand little chance of victory in 1916 against a reunited Republican party.

This public optimism, it should be added, was tempered by a good deal of private caution. The Bull Moose might be dead, but large numbers of Progressive sympathizers remained, both within and outside of the GOP. The party's nominee in 1916 would have to be acceptable to them as well as to party regulars. As Medill McCormick of Illinois, a leader in the search for unity, explained to Senator William E. Borah of Idaho in the summer of 1915: "Wilson will be reelected, unless there can be an agreement on a candidate and a platform, which together will command the energetic and genuine support of the elements which were divided in 1912."

Certainly it would be no easy matter to find a candidate capable of bridging the gulf which separated the two contending factions. The absence of such a figure was reflected in a poll taken of some 750 Republican editors, senators, and representatives in late 1915. The leading choices of these leaders for the party's nomination in 1916 included Senator Elihu Root of New York, Associate Justice Charles Evans Hughes, also of New York, Senator Lawrence Y. Sherman of Illinois, and former Senator Theodore E. Burton of Ohio, None of these individuals, however, emerged as a clear favorite. The one significant aspect of this poll was the absence of any support for the former Republican Presidents, William Howard Taft and Theodore Roosevelt. Everyone, it seemed, agreed that the debacle of 1912 would not be repeated. That this was true was confirmed when Roosevelt made a strenuous campaign for the Republican nomination in the spring of 1916 and failed utterly to win support.

Taft and Roosevelt may have been out of contention for the nomination, but they would certainly exert a powerful influence on the choice of the Republican standard bearer. Taft, aware that his own candidacy was "resting in a tomb," was determined that the nominee should be a regular Republican. Either Hughes or Root would be acceptable to him. Roosevelt had always thought highly of Root. Indeed, the senator from New York had been the most influential member of Roosevelt's Cabinet, serving successively as Secretary of War and Secretary of State. On the other hand, Roosevelt recalled that his former friend had played a prominent role in securing Taft's renomination in 1912. Roosevelt, never inclined to take a broad view on such matters, considered this a case of personal disloyalty. Root, therefore, was not acceptable to him. Root, moreover, would be seventy-one years old in 1916. "As for Hughes," Roosevelt commented, "I thoroughly dislike him." The former Rough Rider favored the nomination of "the type of Hiram Johnson." However, Roosevelt himself wrote, "I don't suppose there is any chance of this." Consequently, Roosevelt remained undecided about a candidate, but one thing was abundantly clear. As the *World's Work* put it, Roosevelt's "supreme ambition is the political destruction of Woodrow Wilson. The President has taken Mr. Taft's place as the pet abomination of Oyster Bay."

By early 1916, Charles Evans Hughes had emerged as the leading contender for the nomination. Root's chances had suffered a blow when the voters of New York rejected a new constitution that the senator had helped to shape. On the other hand, as Roosevelt reported, Progressive politicians were "tending toward Hughes." This was confirmed when a poll of fifteen hundred Republican and Progressive state legislators indicated a clear preference for the Supreme Court Justice. Despite his generally progressive record as governor of New York, Hughes also found support among conservative elements in the GOP. Taft, for example, thought highly of Hughes, commenting, "I think he [has] learned a great deal since he was governor."

Except to say that it was unseemly for a member of the Court to engage in politics, Hughes maintained a discreet silence on his candidacy. This attitude produced consternation in some quarters. *World's Work* said that if Hughes were at all serious about the nomination, he should resign from the Bench. "It would be madness," this journal continued, "to nominate a man for President and find out afterward what he thinks about the conduct of the Nation and of national affairs." Yet this was precisely why Hughes appealed to the diverse elements in the GOP: no one knew where he stood on the issues. A forthright stand on any public question undoubtedly would have alienated either the Progressives or the Old Guard. Hughes' silence may have been somewhat disconcerting, but it made him few enemies.

Meanwhile, a good deal of work was being done to prepare the way for Hughes' nomination. Eugene Meyer and Frank H. Hitchcock, close associates of President Taft, quietly put together the nucleus of a campaign organization and began to round up delegates. Although Hughes repudiated this effort on his behalf, Meyer and Hitchcock refused to be discouraged.

Of course, there was the possibility that Hughes in fact was not interested in the Presidency. Although largely discounting this line of thought, Taft took the initiative in pointing out the path of duty to Hughes. The country's greatest need at the present time, Taft wrote on April 11, 1916, was "the restoration of the Republican party to power to do the constructive work needed in carrying out a policy of reasonable preparedness which involves financial and economic preparedness." Taft went on to consider the men available to lead the party to victory in 1916. Root, although "admirably qualified to be President," would not be a strong candidate and could not unite the party. Roosevelt would only divide it. Senator Burton was "not a leader of magnetic qualities, either personal or on the stump." There were no other serious active contenders for the nomination. Taft then predicted that unless Hughes announced his decision not to accept the nomination under any circumstances, he would be the party's choice for President.

"You will certainly be elected if you accept the nomination," Taft continued,

> and you will reunite the only party from which constructive progress can be expected at a most critical time in the country's history. Your opportunity as President to guide the country through the trials bound to come after the war will be as great as Washington's or Lincoln's. And you are equal to it. Strong men will respond to your call because you are yourself so satisfying in strength and in your political courage and patriotism.
>
> In view of all this, my dear Justice Hughes, I appeal to you not to decide the question until the Convention acts. Then approach its decision, as you will, with a solemn sense of the responsibility on you and with the willingness to make the sacrifice if your duty to accept appears clear.

Taft did not wish a reply to this letter, nor is there any evidence that he ever received one. By his very silence, Hughes indicated his availability for the nomination, should it be offered.

The Republican convention convened in Chicago at the huge fortress-like Coliseum on June 7. Warren G. Harding, the distinguished-looking senator from Ohio, opened the gathering with an appeal for unity. "We did not divide over fundamental principles," Harding said, doubtless to the consternation of the battle-scarred veterans of 1912; "we did not disagree over a national policy. We split over methods of party procedure and preferred personalities. Let us forget the differences, and find new inspiration and new compensation in a united endeavor to restore the country." Upon the completion of Harding's remarks, the secretary of the convention announced that the mayor's entertainment committee had made one thousand automobiles available to the delegates for the purpose of viewing the city. The convention thereupon adjourned.

June 8 brought reports from the various committees of the convention. In contrast to 1912, everything went smoothly. The delegates were seated without debate, and the rules of the convention were adopted unanimously. Senator Henry Cabot Lodge of Massachusetts then strode to the podium and read the draft of the party's platform. This, too, was an exercise in decorum. The document attacked the foreign policy of the Wilson Administration, supported peace, favored the firm maintenance of international rights, and advocated a program of limited military preparedness. Regarding domestic affairs, the platform called for economy and efficiency in government, tariff protection for American industry, and a limited program of social justice, including a child labor law, workmen's compensation for federal employees, and rural credit legislation. All in all, this mildly progressive document contained little that was new or controversial. Nor was it intended to. It was progressive enough not to alienate the advanced elements in the party and conservative enough for the Old Guard; it was adopted without significant debate.

Thus the Republican national convention, in the words of one observer, "proceeded steadily and stolidly upon its appointed course. Everything had been done in the stereotyped way on the stereotyped time table in the stereotyped language. No impropriety or infelicity had been permitted to mar the smooth texture of its surface." Harmony was the keynote. The mistakes of 1912 would not be repeated.

On June 9 the delegates were ready for the main business of the convention, the nomination of a presidential candidate. Alabama passed when the rollcall began. Arizona, the next state to be called, yielded to New York. Governor Charles S. Whitman of the Empire State rose and offered Charles Evans Hughes, "the man of action, the champion, the idol of the electorate, the faithful public servant, the profound thinker on national affairs . . . the American spirit incarnate." Shouts, cheers, and applause echoed through the Coliseum, while members of the New York, Michigan, Maine, Vermont, and Mississippi delegations marched around the hall with their state banners. Finally, one member of the Maine delegation "carried a toy elephant of about two feet in height on his head to the platform."

After the demonstration subsided, the rollcall proceeded. Nicholas Murray Butler of New York nominated Elihu Root. Less prominent candidates then received their brief moment of adulation. Everything went according to plan until the roll reached New Mexico and Senator Albert B. Fall began to walk toward the stage. A great demonstration broke out, and there were cries of "Teddy! Teddy! Teddy!" Fall spoke briefly. There was no need to say much about this man, Fall said. "To refer to his birth place, to his early life, to what he has said and what he has done would be absolutely futile because he is known to every one of you. I name for your consideration and for your votes Theodore Roosevelt of New York."

The hall exploded with an enthusiasm that had been absent during the preceding nominations. The noise was deafening, but observers noted that most of it was coming from the galleries. Some delegates joined in the demonstration, but most looked angry. Their anger increased as the shouting continued. After thirty-five minutes of tumult, some of the delegates called upon the chairman to restore order. This was accomplished several minutes later. The galleries might want Roosevelt, but the delegates had other plans.

Evening had fallen before all the nominating and seconding speeches and demonstrations came to an end and the serious business of balloting could begin. The first ballot was indecisive. Hughes led with 253 1/2 votes. His nearest rivals were Root, 103 votes, and Senator John W. Weeks of Massachusetts, 105 votes. The remaining 535 1/2 votes were scattered among fourteen other presidential hopefuls. Although Hughes lacked 240 1/2 votes of the majority required to nominate, the broad basis of his strength—only thirteen states had passed him by—put him in a commanding position.

Hughes picked up additional support on the second ballot, polling 328 1/2 votes. Root and Weeks lost ground, and no favorite son emerged as a serious contender. With rumors sweeping the floor that Illinois would leave its favorite son on the next ballot and go to Hughes, it began to look as if the rush to the New Yorker had begun. But there would be no third ballot that evening. At 9:48 p.m., the convention voted to adjourn.

The decision to adjourn was not an attempt to stop Hughes. The party leaders were now certain that the Justice would receive the nomination on the next ballot. Before this happened, they wanted one more opportunity to reach an understanding with the followers of Theodore Roosevelt.

The Progressive party had opened its national convention coincident with the Republican gathering, meeting one mile away at the Chicago Auditorium Theater. Whereas the Bull Moose had been united in 1912, this time it was rife with faction. On one side stood a small number of professional politicians, headed by Walter Brown of Ohio and William Flinn of Pennsylvania. They had had enough of the battle for righteousness and wanted to rejoin the Republican party under any conditions. The great majority of delegates, however, wished to continue the fight. This group, led by Governor Hiram Johnson, was prepared to nominate its own candidate. In the middle stood George W. Perkins, chairman of the party's National Executive Committee and Theodore Roosevelt's spokesman in Chicago.

Most delegates at the Progressive convention did not want to bargain with the hated Republicans, but few were prepared to defy Roosevelt's wishes. Perkins' announcement that the party would not ballot until after the Republicans had nominated their candidate brought few cheers. Reluctantly, the delegates approved a platform closely resembling the GOP's. But they rebelled when Perkins sought approval for the appointment of a special committee to meet with a Republican delegation. Only after a letter from Roosevelt, advocating cooperation with the Republican convention, had been read did the Bull Moosers give their grudging approval.

The Progressive and Republican Conference Committees met at the Chicago Club on Thursday on June 8. The Progressive group, led by Perkins and Hiram Johnson, made their case for Roosevelt's nomination. The Republicans, after flatly rejecting this argument, asked the Progressives for an alternative. The Bull Moosers countered by asking the Republicans to suggest a name. This would be inappropriate, the GOP spokesmen said, because the convention had not yet acted. Having settled very little, and with few prospects of doing any better until the GOP had settled on a nominee, the meeting broke up at 3 a.m. on Friday morning.

The last chance to reach some sort of understanding came when the two groups met again later in the morning. The Progressives reaffirmed their previous position: they wanted Roosevelt. The Republicans dismissed this idea as preposterous. With some reluctance, they suggested Hughes. The Bull Moosers rejected this proposal. Again the conferees parted without having made any progress. Although another meeting would be held on Saturday morning, the die had been cast. The parties would go their separate ways.

Roosevelt, who had been keeping in close touch with developments by means of a private telephone connection between Chicago and Oyster Bay, had the final word. The former Rough Rider, who obviously had been using the Progressive convention for trading purposes, knew by this time that his own chances of gaining the GOP's nomination were nil. In what can only be described as a fit of perversity, the former President on Saturday morning recommended to both conventions the name of his old friend, the arch conservative Henry Cabot Lodge. The Republicans were bemused, the Progressives, incredulous. The Bull Moosers, finally throwing off the restraints of the party leadership, proceeded to nominate Roosevelt. He refused to accept the nomination.

While the Progressives were making their futile gesture, the GOP was selecting its standard bearer. The Hughes bandwagon began to roll on Saturday morning, June 10, when Senator Weeks withdrew his own name. Then Congressman William A. Rodenberg, Illinois' favorite son, released his delegation. The end came when Medill McCormick, a former Progressive, announced that he was shifting his personal support from his good friend, Theodore Roosevelt, to Charles Evans Hughes. The Supreme Court Justice swept the field on the third ballot, gaining 949 1/2 votes. After making Hughes' nomination unanimous and selecting Charles W. Fairbanks as his running mate, the convention adjourned.

Although a few individuals claimed knowledge of Hughes' availability for the nomination, the Justice had made no commitment, either public or private, on this matter. However, any lingering doubts concerning his intentions were dispelled when, upon receiving official notice of his nomination, Hughes wrote the following letter:

> To the President: I hereby resign the office of Associate Justice of the Supreme Court of the United States.
> I am, sir, respectfully yours,

> *Charles Evans Hughes*

Wilson's response was equally curt:

> Dear Mr. Justice Hughes: I am in receipt of your letter of resignation and feel constrained to yield to your desire.
> I, therefore, accept your resignation as Justice of the Supreme Court of the United States to take effect at once.
> Sincerely yours,

> *Woodrow Wilson*

Hughes next sent a message to the convention saying that he had not wanted to leave the Bench but could not neglect the call of duty. He continued: "You speak at a time of national exigency, transcending merely partisan considerations. You voice the demand for a dominant, thoroughgoing Americanism with firm protective upbuilding policies, essential to our peace and security; and to that call, in this crisis, I cannot fail to answer with the pledge of all that is in me to the service of our country. Therefore I accept the nomination."

President Wilson was so preoccupied with pressing foreign and domestic problems that he had little time for partisan politics during the early months of 1916. Wilson's first political concern was finding a way to ease William F. McCombs out of the chairmanship of the Democratic National Committee. The President had no intention of going into the campaign with the party machinery controlled by a man he no longer trusted. On the other hand, McCombs could not be dismissed summarily without damaging the party's image. Wilson entrusted this delicate and unpleasant task to his chief adviser, Colonel Edward M. House. With the assistance of Bernard M. Baruch, a friend of McCombs, House secured the chairman's resignation in late April.

As the mid-June date for the opening of the Democratic national convention approached, Wilson began to devote more attention to party matters. The President selected former Governor Martin H. Glynn of New York to deliver the keynote address, and he asked his old friend, Judge John W. Westcott of New Jersey, who had nominated him in 1912, to make the nominating speech again. After Speaker Champ Clark declined an invitation to become permanent chairman of the convention, Wilson secured the services of Senator Ollie M. James of Kentucky.

With these details out of the way, the President turned to the party's platform. After consulting the Democratic leaders in Congress, Wilson drew up a preliminary draft of the document, which he read to the Cabinet on June 9. By the time the Democrats gathered in the Coliseum in St. Louis on June 14, the platform, having undergone a number of revisions, was ready to be considered by the Resolutions Committee. There was a considerable amount of controversy during the Committee's deliberations, but Wilson had his way for the most part.

The Democratic platform of 1916, largely the President's own creation, stands as one of the most significant documents in the history of modern American democracy. Its adoption put the Democratic party, for the first time, squarely behind a policy of internationalism in the conduct of foreign affairs and the bold use of federal power to achieve economic progress and social justice at home.

"The circumstances of the last two years," the plank on foreign policy read, "have revealed necessities of international action which no former generation can have foreseen. We hold that it is the duty of the United States to use its power, not only to make itself safe at home, but also to make secure its just interests throughout the world, and, both for this end and in the interest of humanity, to assist the world in securing settled peace and justice." The document went on to reaffirm such international ideals as the right of every nation to live in peace and security and a condemnation of all forms of aggression. "We believe," the platform continued, "that the time has come when it is the duty of the United States to join the other nations of the world in any feasible association that will effectively serve those principles, to maintain inviolate the complete security of the highway of the seas for the common and unhindered use of all nations."

At home, the platform called upon the Federal Government to revitalize the American merchant marine, provide a system of rural credit, and assist the states in highway construction. Additional planks pledged national action to provide a living wage and workmen's compensation for federal employees. New social justice measures were called for, including a federal child labor law.

"Americanism" was the keynote when the Democratic convention opened on June 14. Flags draped the Coliseum; the sounds of "The Star-Spangled Banner," "America," and "The Red, White, and Blue" filled the hall; cheers rang out, on cue, when America or the flag was mentioned. Governor Glynn sounded the same theme in his keynote address, alluding to "the Americanism of the Fathers," "the mystic influence of the Stars and Stripes," and "the magic spell of citizenship." But the delegates responded with a notable lack of enthusiasm until Glynn began a rather prosaic recital of past instances when the United States had refused to be provoked into a war. Shouts of "Hit him Again, Hit him Again" rose from the floor. Glynn was so flustered that it took him a few minutes to realize that he had struck a responsive chord. Departing from his prepared text, the keynoter began a long account of American neutrality. At the end of each example, the delegates cried: "What did we do? What did we do?" Glynn shouted back: "We didn't go to war."

"This policy," Glynn continued with mounting ardor,

does not satisfy those, who revel in destruction and find pleasure in despair. It may not satisfy the fire-eater or the swashbuckler. But it does satisfy those who worship at the altar of the God of Peace. It does satisfy the mothers of the land . . . at whose hearth and fireside no jingoistic war has placed an empty chair. It does satisfy the daughters of this land, from whom brag and bluster have sent no husband, no sweetheart and no brother to the mouldering dissolution of the grave. It does satisfy the fathers of this land, and the sons of this land, who will fight for our flag, and die for our flag, when Reason primes the rifle . . . when Honor draws the sword, when Justice breathes a blessing on the standards they uphold.

The delegates, who had punctuated Glynn's remarks with shouts and cheers, thundered their approval. William Jennings Bryan, sitting in the press box, wept.

The second day of the convention saw a repetition of this tumultuous eruption when Senator James, "the genial giant from Kentucky," delivered his address as permanent chairman. He began with a review of the party's accomplishments under Wilson. The mention of neutrality brought the delegates to their feet. But James, not yet ready for the climactic moment, deftly turned to other matters. Finally, he was ready. Raising his voice, the permanent chairman begain to detail Wilson's diplomatic achievements. James, by now almost shouting, went on: "Without orphaning a single child, without widowing a single American mother, without firing a single gun, without the shedding of a single drop of blood, he wrung from the most militant spirit that ever brooded above a battlefield an acknowledgement of American rights and an agreement to American demands." The delegates leaped from their seats with a roar, stood on their chairs, marched in the aisles, and waved banners for twenty minutes. James went on to finish his speech, but the delegates were exhausted, both emotionally and physically. Everyone welcomed adjournment when it came at 1:28 p.m.

The convention reassembled at nine o'clock that evening for the purpose of nominating Wilson. However, the gathering was no sooner called to order than shouts of "Bryan! Bryan!" were heard throughout the hall. The party's three-time nominee had fallen on unhappy days. Scorned by the public and by many of his own followers since his resignation as Secretary of State over the President's handling of the *Lusitania* crisis, Bryan had not even been able to win election as a delegate from Nebraska. He had had to attend the convention as a newspaper correspondent. But now all the bitterness was forgotten as the rules of the convention were suspended to enable Bryan to address the delegates. The Commoner, speaking in subdued tones, lauded the domestic achievements of the Administration. He saved his warmest praise for Wilson's search for peace. "My friends," he said, "I have differed with our President on some of the methods employed, but I join with the American people in thanking God that we have a President who does not want this nation plunged into war."

The call for nominations then went out. Alabama yielded to New Jersey, and Judge Westcott offered Woodrow Wilson's name. Following demonstrations and seconding speeches, the President was nominated by acclamation. It took the convention only two minutes to decide that Vice-President Thomas R. Marshall would again occupy the second position on the party's ticket.

The Democratic party was now ready to do battle in the fall. It was a united party, proud of its past accomplishments and confident of victory. And it was a party with a slogan—"He kept us out of war"—which had been inserted into the final draft of the Democratic platform, by whom and whether with Wilson's approval, we do not know.

Wilson turned to certain pressing affairs of state following the convention while Charles Evans Hughes concentrated on preparations for the campaign.

Hughes may have been the compromise candidate of a badly split party, but he had much to recommend him to the nation. Now fifty-four years old, a graduate of Brown University and Columbia University Law School, Hughes had had a distinguished legal career, both as a corporation lawyer and professor of Jurisprudence at Cornell University. He had first come to the public's attention in 1905, when he directed an inquiry by the New York legislature into the corrupt practices of certain insurance companies. Elected governor of the state in 1906, and reelected in 1908, Hughes had proved an efficient administrator and even something of a reformer. Various progressive laws were enacted during his term in office, including measures for control of public service corporations, election reform, the prohibition of child labor, and workmen's compensation. He had been appointed an associate justice of the Supreme Court in 1910 by President Taft.

Temperamentally, Hughes seemed more fitted for the Bench than for the hurly-burly of politics. For one thing, he distrusted politicians. He enjoyed life on the Court, and he had accepted the Republican nomination with reluctance. Hughes best personal qualities—his warmth and wit—were evident only in small gatherings of friends. Publicly, he appeared aloof and austere, as Theodore Roosevelt put it, as "a bearded iceberg."

Hughes, in preparing for the campaign, blundered in selecting a campaign manager. Given his own lack of political expertise, the candidate might have been well-advised to choose a professional politician. Instead, he named William R. Willcox, an old friend and associate. Willcox had many sterling qualities, but he lacked political experience. Hughes, apparently, sought a manager who would reflect his own high standards of politics. But this appointment, in the words of his biographer, "was to prove Candidate Hughes' first major mistake."

Formally opening his campaign at Carnegie Hall in New York City on July 31, the Republican candidate attacked the Wilson Administration on a broad front. He lashed out, in particular, at Wilson's Mexican policy. "Decrying interference," he said, "we interfered most exasperatingly." American policy, characterized by inconsistency and vacillation, had succeeded only in alienating the Mexican people. Turning to European affairs, Hughes accused the Administration of substituting empty gestures for vigorous action in protecting American maritime rights. He called for "the unflinching maintenance of all American rights on land and sea," and he advocated an expanded preparedness program, terming this "the essential assurance of security." Domestically, the New Yorker viewed Americans as "living in a fool's paradise." The existing prosperity, he predicted, would only be temporary; only a protective tariff would assure prosperity after the war. Hughes voiced his support for rural credits, a national budget, efficient administration, the merit system in the civil service, the proper regulation of transportation and industry, and the just interests of labor.

"Americanism," however, was the main theme of the speech. By "Americanism," Hughes told his audience,

> I mean America conscious of power, awake to obligation, erect in self-respect, prepared for every emergency, devoted to the ideals of peace, instinct with the spirit of human brotherhood, safeguarding both individual opportunity and the public interest, maintaining a well-ordered constitutional system adapted to local self-government without the sacrifice of essential national authority, appreciating the necessity of stability, expert knowledge, and thorough organization as the indispensable conditions of security and progress; a country loved by its citizens with a patriotic fervor permitting no division in their allegiance and no rivals in their affection — I mean America first and America efficient.

Hughes' debut proved disappointing, even to his admirers. His speech, running more than an hour and a half, was much too long. His language lacked fire and seemed more appropriate for a legal argument than for campaign oratory. Worse still, he failed to set forth a positive program of his own. "The impression one receives from Mr. Hughes' notification speech," summarized the Springfield *Republican*, a not unfriendly critic,

> is one of solidity, and perhaps heaviness, rather than brilliancy. It is likely to appeal to many of the Republican candidate's more conservative supporters as a careful and strong indictment of the present Administration, with no display of flightiness or instability in the discussion of constructive policies. . . . There is scant attention given to the policies of social and industrial justice which were the backbone of the Progressive movement, while there is little to suggest Rooseveltian fervor and conviction in the discussion of the later issues of preparedness and Americanism.

Hughes prepared for a speaking tour that would carry him across the country with two objectives uppermost in mind. First, he intended to dispel the "iceberg" myth. Second, he planned to develop the issues outlined in his acceptance speech.

The Republican candidate was able to establish a "folksy" image, at least of sorts. Not only did he attend a baseball game in Detroit, but he even jumped over a railing to shake hands with the players and to chat with Ty Cobb. During the course of the western swing, Hughes descended to the bottom of a copper mine in Butte, Montana, climbed to Bear Lake in the Rockies, and kissed every baby and shook every hand in sight. "In fact," noted the St. Joseph, Missouri *News Press*, "he is liked better than his speeches."

The *News Press*, unwittingly, pointed to the major problem in Hughes' campaign: his inability to define an effective issue. The Republican candidate first tried foreign affairs. When this failed to excite his listeners, he turned to the Administration's appointment policy, particularly the placing of "deserving Democrats" in the foreign service. Hughes certainly was on solid ground with this issue, but his attacks roused little interest. Above all, the New Yorker seemed incapable of developing his own program. "It is not enough to demonstrate President Wilson's sins of omission and commission," commented the *Independent*. "The American people know them already. It is not enough to promise to instil efficiency into the government service and eliminate graft. Everybody knows Mr. Hughes will endeavor to do this. The American people want to know what constructive program Mr. Hughes has to offer them."

Any benefits that Hughes derived from his first western tour were more than offset by his alienation of Governor Hiram Johnson of California. Johnson was running for the United States Senate on the Progressive ticket, and he was engaged in a bitter fight with the regular California Republican organization. Although he had announced his support for the Republican presidential nominee on June 27, Johnson had little love for "the mysterious, stuffed prophet Hughes." Hughes, therefore, would have had to walk a very thin line to avoid antagonizing either Johnson or the party regulars. This would have been difficult with the best of political advice, but Willcox had no great political acumen.

Although a great deal has been made of an incident that occurred during Hughes' visit to California—his associates neglected to tell him that Governor Johnson was staying at a hotel where he was stopping in Long Beach—the trouble between Johnson and Hughes stemmed from more than personal pique. Willcox, disregarding the advice of wiser politicians, allowed the regular Republicans to gain control of Hughes' campaign in the state. This, in effect, aligned the GOP nominee squarely against Johnson. Willcox misjudged both Johnson's strength and the vitality of the Progressive party in California. As it turned out, the Progressives gained control of the Republican state committee in the primary election. And the state committee was responsible for running the presidential campaign in the state. Johnson continued to back Hughes publicly, but the party organization failed to mobilize grass roots support for the New Yorker. Hughes went on to lose California by some 4,000 votes.

"If the election were held in the next fortnight," Medill McCormick wrote to Hughes as the western tour drew to a close, "Wilson would win." Many Republican leaders, believing that most of Hughes' difficulties were due to Willcox's bungling, were convinced that the national chairman had to go. A delegation of Republican senators got in touch with Harvey D. Hinman, a close friend of Hughes, and urged him to persuade the candidate of the urgent need for professional assistance. Hinman met the campaign train when it pulled into Buffalo. Hughes admitted that his campaign was in trouble, and he agreed that a more experienced manager was needed. But Hughes could not bring himself to dismiss Willcox. Instead, he asked Hinman to visit Willcox and stress the need for a more effective campaign. Willcox, according to one account of the meeting, "laughed and said that Hughes was a great candidate, the campaign was going well, and he had no question about the outcome." This ended the matter.

Woodrow Wilson was not impressed with Hughes' campaign. Certainly he felt no need to respond to the Republican candidate's attacks on his Administration. "I am inclined to follow the course suggested by a friend of mine," Wilson wrote in mid-August, "who says that he has always followed the rule never to murder a man who is committing suicide, and clearly this misdirected gentleman is committing suicide slowly but surely." The President, reported one of his managers, "believes he is making better progress by attending to his duties than he could hope to make in a political tour."

The burdens of office pressed heavily upon Woodrow Wilson during that hot summer of 1916. The United States and Mexico stood on the brink of war; relations with Great Britain were strained nearly to the breaking point; a nationwide railroad strike threatened; decisions had to be made on important legislative matters. His handling of all these vital issues, Wilson knew well, would affect not only the destinies of his country but also his own political fortunes.

The most dangerous problem by far was Mexico. In March, Wilson had dispatched across the border a punitive expedition, led by General John J. Pershing, to apprehend the bandit, Pancho Villa, who had raided Columbus, New Mexico. The Mexican government had sanctioned this attempt to catch the elusive Villa, but only with great reluctance. As General Pershing penetrated deeper into Mexico, this reluctance turned to fear and anger. The Mexican authorities now demanded the immediate withdrawal of all American troops. Wilson refused this demand while Villa was still at large.

The incident that could have meant war came on June 21, when a detachment of American troops clashed with units of the Mexican army near Carrizal, in northern Mexico. The President, upon hearing of this incident, prepared a message to Congress that very likely would have plunged the two countries into war. But Wilson's good sense prevailed. Instead of seeking a military solution, he made a passionate plea for peace. "Do you think," he asked in New York on June 28, "the glory of America would be enhanced by a war of conquest in Mexico?" The voice of reason was also heard from Mexico City, when the Mexican authorities suggested negotiations to end the crisis. As a result, a joint high commission was appointed to investigate the situation and recommend a solution. Although many difficulties remained, at least the two sides had agreed to talk instead of fight. Wilson, by refusing to be provoked into hasty action, had managed to avoid what would have been a tragedy for both the Mexican and American peoples. At the same time, the President had succeeded in neutralizing the Mexican problem as an effective campaign issue.

Just as the Mexican crisis began to abate, the Administration was caught up in a bitter controversy with Great Britain over certain British war measures.

The British government, well aware of its dependence upon the United

States for all manner of supplies, had been careful not to permit a major quarrel over American rights at sea to break out. But as the war entered its third bitter year, Great Britain decided to risk a possible confrontation with Washington in order to tighten its economic warfare against the Central Powers. The Administration, in May, 1916, had reacted sharply to the British seizure of American mails. The publication on July 19 of a "blacklist" of eighty-seven American firms, with whom British subjects were forbidden to deal because of their suspected trade with the Central Powers, caused a veritable explosion in Washington.

"I am, I must admit," Wilson wrote to Colonel House on July 23, "about at the end of my patience with Great Britain and the Allies. This black list business is the last straw." The State Department dispatched a sharp note, largely written by the President himself, protesting against the blacklist. When the British failed to reply promptly to this communication, the President moved to secure authority from Congress for possible retaliatory action. The legislators moved with unusual speed to meet the President's request. An amendment to the Shipping Act of September 7 empowered the Administration to refuse clearance to any vessel unwilling to carry the cargo of a blacklisted American citizen. Amendments to the Revenue Act, adopted the following day, went even further. These authorized the President to deny clearance and port facilities to ships of any nation that discriminated unfairly against American commerce, and, if necessary, to use the armed forces of the United States to enforce these provisions.

The British authorities, misled by information received from Secretary of State Robert Lansing, discounted the possibility that Wilson would ever exercise the authority he had received. Therefore, they reaffirmed their right to seize American mails and blacklist American firms. This failure to appraise Wilson's intentions accurately might have proved a fatal miscalculation had not Germany resorted to a campaign of unlimited submarine warfare in January, 1917.

Although Wilson's response to the violation of American rights was not prompted by domestic considerations, as the British believed, there is little doubt that his forthright actions served to blunt Hughes' criticism of alleged weakness in dealing with the European belligerents. The President, therefore, did reap political advantage, if unintended, from this episode.

The summer of 1916 also marked Wilson's final transition from the New Freedom to the New Nationalism, that is, from the philosophy of the Federal Government as an impartial mediator in the nation's affairs to the concept of the Government as an active promoter of social justice.

The nomination of Louis D. Brandeis, the leading progressive jurist, to the Supreme Court in January 1916 had forecast this change in policy, as had the Administration's support for federal underwriting of a rural credits system. The Democratic platform had revealed Wilson's new attitude even more clearly, but few observers could have predicted the remarkable legislative accomplishments that were soon to come.

There were two major pieces of legislation before Congress in the summer of 1916: a model workmen's compensation measure for federal employees and the Keating-Owen child labor bill. The President hitherto had demonstrated little interest in these measures. He had not opposed them, but neither had he supported them. Both bills had passed the House of Representatives by mid-July and had gone to the Senate. There was little prospect that the upper House would take action before the end of the session.

It was at this point that the President intervened. Accompanied only by two Secret Service men, Wilson went unannounced to the President's room in the Capitol on July 18 and summoned Democratic senatorial leaders. He proceeded to place the full power and prestige of the Presidency behind the two progressive measures. The fortunes of the Democratic party, Wilson warned, depended upon prompt and favorable action on these two bills.

Wilson's personal intervention proved decisive. The child labor bill passed the Senate on August 8. The workmen's compensation measure won approval eleven days later.

Historians will continue to debate the reasons for Wilson's shift to advanced progressivism. There is little doubt that he had jumped on the progressive bandwagon because he was convinced that a Democratic victory in the fall might well depend on the votes of social justice advocates. But this is not to say that Wilson was motivated solely by political expediency. The President was deeply committed to the creation of a more just society; however, he was unsure of the means by which this goal might be achieved. Political considerations might govern the means, but Wilson's end remained constant.

The President had to face one more crisis, a threatened nationwide railroad strike, before the hectic summer of 1916 drew to a close. The four railroad brotherhoods were demanding an eight-hour day, with no reduction in wages, and time-and-a-half for overtime work. The railroad managers considered these demands excessive. After mediation failed, and a general strike appeared imminent, Wilson decided that the time had come to step into the controversy.

The President invited the contending parties to the White House on August 13 and appealed for a compromise solution in the national interest. When neither side would yield, Wilson offered his own proposal: an eight-hour day for the workers, without punitive overtime pay, and the appointment of a federal commission to study the entire railroad labor problem.

The unions promptly accepted the President's offer but the railroad managers turned it down. Despite attempts to bring public pressure to bear on the managers during the following weeks, they refused to budge. Wilson had no choice but to impose a solution if a strike was to be avoided.

The President appeared before Congress on August 29 and outlined a comprehensive program, designed not only to solve this particular dispute but also to guarantee that the nation would never again be threatened with such a catastrophe. Congress, however, was not likely to pass such sweeping legislation before September 4, the date set for the walk-out. Chairman William C. Adamson of the House Interstate Commerce Committee as an alternative drew up a bill imposing an eight-hour day, to become effective on January 1, 1917, and providing for a commission to study the railroad problem. Realizing that this was the only measure that could be passed in time to prevent the strike, Wilson supported it, and the Adamson bill quickly received congressional approval. On September 3, the President signed it into law.

Wilson had not only averted a potentially disastrous railroad strike but had also brought the power of the Federal Government to bear on labor-management relations in a way never before known in American history. This bold exercise of national authority delighted advanced progressives. The labor unions were even more pleased. The Brotherhood of Railroad Trainmen, for example, later advised its members that the union "owes the eight-hour work-day law to President Wilson and his party in Congress; it has suggested that the support of its members should be given to the President for the reason that the Administration that enacted the law should be returned to enforce it."

While Wilson was busy with affairs of state, Democratic leaders were building a campaign organization. Vance McCormick, a newspaper publisher and a leader in the progressive faction of the party in Pennsylvania, who had replaced McCombs as chairman of the Democratic National Committee, established two regional offices to coordinate and direct campaign activities. The larger office, headed by former First Assistant Postmaster-General Daniel C. Roper, was in New York. It contained various departments or bureaus to deal with foreign-born voters, labor, women, and other interest groups. Robert W. Wolley, Director of the Mint, was in charge of the important Publicity Bureau, which prepared and distributed a wide variety of campaign literature covering every issue in the election and appealing to every conceivable segment of the population. Senator Thomas J. Walsh of Montana headed a comparable if smaller western headquarters in Chicago.

The important and difficult task of raising money for the campaign fell to Wilbur W. Marsh and Henry Morgenthau, members of the Democratic National Committee's Finance Committee. Contributions came in at an encouraging rate until adoption of the Adamson Act. Businessmen, antagonized by this measure, turned en masse to Hughes. Although Marsh and Morgenthau sought to raise funds through appeals to smaller contributors, the financial problems of the Democratic organization remained in a precarious state throughout the campaign.

Wilson launched his bid for reelection on September 2, when he formally accepted the party's nomination. A crowd of some fifteen to twenty thousand Democratic faithful gathered at the President's new summer home, "Shadow Lawn," in Long Branch on the New Jersey shore, to hear what was to be the first of many "front porch" addresses. Wilson, speaking in a conversational tone, reviewed the Administration's achievements during the past four years. All segments of American society had benefited from Democratic rule, he said, including business, farmers, labor, and children. Not only had the Democracy redeemed all the promises made in the party's platform of 1912, Wilson continued, but "we have in four years come very near to carrying out the platform of the Progressive party, as well as our own." And this had been accomplished in the face of stubborn resistance "by the interests which the Republican party had catered to and fostered."

The President went on to defend his record on foreign affairs. Neutrality, he said, was the wisest course for the United States during the present conflagration in Europe. He noted that the rights of American citizens frequently had become involved in dealing with the belligerents. "Where they did," he said, "this was our guiding principle: that property rights can be vindicated by claims for damages when the war is over, and no modern nation can decline to arbitrate such claims, but the fundamental rights of humanity cannot be."

Relations with Mexico, Wilson went on, had been trying and difficult. American troops had been sent to protect American lives along the border, but a great deal of restraint was needed. The Mexican Revolution, Wilson emphasized, was inevitable and right, and he would do nothing to impair the Mexican people's struggle for freedom. "I am more interested," Wilson observed, "in the fortunes of oppressed men and pitiful women and children than in any property rights whatever. Mistakes I have no doubt made in this perplexing business, but not in purpose or object."

The nation was passing through difficult times, the President concluded, and there would be even more trying days ahead. America had to be strong and vital at home in order to lead in the postwar search for a lasting peace. "We are Americans for Big America," he said, "and rejoice to look forward to the days in which America shall strive to stir the world without irritating it or drawing it on to new antagonisms, when the nations with which we deal shall at last come to see upon what deep foundations of humanity and justice our passion for peace rests. . . . Upon this record and in the faith of this purpose we go to the country."

It was a fighting speech; but, instead of answering Hughes' criticism, Wilson had emphasized the solid accomplishments of his Administration. This aggressive stance forecast the President's posture in the campaign. The Democrats, for the first time in more than twenty years, had a record to stand on. Wilson was determined to capitalize on this fact.

Just as the Democratic drive got under way, Hughes' campaign seemed to take on new life. In what was undoubtedly the best speech of his campaign to date, Hughes lashed out at Wilson's handling of the railroad dispute in a Labor Day address at Nashville on September 4. "I am opposed," he declared, "to being dictated to, either in the executive department or in Congress, by any power on earth before the facts are known, and in the absence of the facts." This was a new Hughes, a more vigorous and decisive Hughes. His performance at Nashville, one journalist commented, "may well prove to be the turning point of his campaign."

Republican prospects received a further boost the next week when election returns from Maine showed a clean sweep for the GOP. Maine, the only state to hold gubernatorial and congressional elections before the November election, usually served as a political barometer. In 1912, the state had gone to Wilson due to the split in the Republican ranks. This time, however, the Maine voters returned a Republican governor, two Republican senators, and four Republican representatives. "It looks good," Hughes said when he learned of the results. "I don't see how we can lose now." The New York *Evening Post* agreed: "If the Progressives of 1912 throughout the Union were to act like those of Maine, Wilson would certainly be defeated."

There were other straws in the confusing political wind that blew during September, and not all of them favored the Republicans. One explosive issue concerned the "hyphenate" voters, that is, American citizens of foreign birth or descent who were deemed to place the interests of their mother country above those of their adopted land. Both candidates were on record as opposing this particular form of disloyalty. Hughes, however, appeared to lack conviction in his condemnation of these individuals. Theodore Roosevelt, at one point during the campaign, received reports from various quarters that Hughes was "pro-German." Roosevelt denied these allegations, but he believed that the accusation was sufficiently important to call it to Hughes' attention.

Wilson had an opportunity to dramatize the hyphenate issue in late September, when he received an insulting telegram from Jeremiah A. O'Leary, president of the German-financed American Truth Society. "Again we greet you with popular disapproval of your pro-British policies," O'Leary wired following the victory of Senator James E. Martine, a frequent opponent of the President, in the Democratic primary elections in New Jersey. "Senator Martine won because the voters of New Jersey do not want any truckling to the British Empire nor do they approve of dictatorship over Congress. . . .When, Sir, will you respond to these evidences of popular disapproval of your policies by actions?" Wilson immediately shot back: "Your telegram received. I would feel deeply mortified to have you or anybody like you vote for me. Since you have access to many disloyal Americans and I have not, I will ask you to convey this message to them."

The President's forthright action drew nearly unanimous approval from the press. "The American people," one journal commented, "have a great fondness for strong words that are said at exactly the right time and have exactly the right ring." *The New York Times* asked: "At what time will Charles E. Hughes send such a message to the disloyal Americans who cheer him when he utters his careful platitudes?" The New York *Nation* accurately summed up the episode as follows: "Self-respect alone demanded just such an answer, and the scathing effectiveness of the message plainly springs from the intense indignation which inspired it. But what self-respect dictated, political calculation would equally approve."

The pace of the campaign accelerated during October, as the candidates attempted to define the major issues for the voters. Hughes continued to emphasize the need for a strong and efficient government, high tariffs, and the protection of American property and personal rights in Mexico and on the high seas. But the paramount issue in the campaign, Hughes stressed throughout October, was the Adamson Act. "The Adamson bill," Hughes emphasized, "is a force bill. It was legislation without inquiry, without knowledge. The demand by the Administration for such legislation as the price of peace was a humiliating spectacle. It was not only a serious misuse of official power, but a deplorable abdication of moral authority." Hughes stated that he did not object to the eight-hour day as such; but there was more at issue than fixing the hours of labor. The government was now seeking to fix wages. Hughes viewed the Administration's action as a capitulation to organized labor. Where would it all end, he asked. Reason, not power, should determine the actions of the government. "The issue thus presented is fundamental," Hughes argued. "The multiplying activities of the government would be intolerable if we did not proceed in accordance with judgment based on an examination of the facts. These processes of reason are the only alternative to tyranny."

Whatever the justice of Hughes' attacks on the Democrats, one thing is clear: his campaign was proving to be one of the most lackluster in the history of modern American politics. "On all sides," summarized the New York *Nation*, "you discover the depression which Mr. Hughes' speeches have caused. On every side dejected Hughes men are to be encountered. They are going to vote for him, most of them, but they will do it without a particle of enthusiasm. They have not been stirred or thrilled. More than that, their intellectual expectation and craving have not been met. They looked up eagerly, but they have not been fed."

Hughes' failure was in large part a personal one. To begin with, he was temperamentally unsuited for political leadership. "The icy Mr. Hughes," one reader of the *Nation* commented, "has tried manfully to reveal himself a man of fire—a man of what the age worships under the name of 'punch' and 'pep.' It has not been a convincing exhibition. The hand might be the hand of Esau, but the voice was that of Jacob." But an even more important reason for Hughes' failure was the intellectual bankruptcy of the Republican party. The GOP had no solutions for the pressing problems of modern industrialized America. In 1912, the party leadership had voted for the past when it repudiated the ideas of Theodore Roosevelt. The opportunity to point the way to the future had been lost. And Charles Evans Hughes, of all people, did not have the ability or the vision to breathe new life into the corpse.

Woodrow Wilson, on the other hand, succeeded in putting together a new coalition of advanced progressives during that fateful October of 1916. Independent progressives—social workers, sociologists, and intellectuals—moved en masse into the Wilson column. The men and women who had followed Roosevelt in 1912 would continue the fight for social justice, but now under the Democratic banner. They included virtually the entire leadership of the advanced wing of the Progressive movement in the United States: Lincoln Steffens, George Creel, Jane Addams, John Dewey, Amos Pinchot, Norman Thomas, Lillian D. Wald, Washington Gladden, Ben B. Lindsey, Herbert Croly, and many others. Walter Lippmann doubtless spoke for many of these people when he gave his reasons for supporting the President: "Not Mr. Wilson's eloquence, but his extraordinary growth has made the case for him. I

shall vote not for the Wilson who has uttered a few too many noble sentiments, but for the Wilson who is evolving under experience and is remaking
his philosophy in the light of it, for the Wilson who is temporarily at least creating, out of the reactionary, parochial fragments of the Democracy, the only
party which at this moment is national in scope, liberal in purpose, and
effective in action."

Labor, as might be expected after passage of the Adamson Act, came out
strongly for Wilson. "Never at any time within the last fifty years," read a
message from the Executive Committee of the American Federation of Labor
to all officers of the union, "have the workers had more at stake in any political campaign than in the one that is to be decided in the election November
7th. . . . The issue is represented in the campaign by the conflicting interests
represented by Labor and Wall Street." The Committee urged the union's
members to get to the polls and support Wilson. In fact most surveys taken at
the time showed that Wilson was the overwhelming choice of labor.

Farm leaders and voters, impressed by such Democratic measures as the
Rural Credits Act, also indicated strong support for the President. The newly
organized Non-Partisan League, for example, swung its full weight behind
Wilson's candidacy. "I feel sure," wrote Herbert Quick, influential farm editor, "that Wisconsin, Minnesota, and North Dakota will cast their votes for
the President this fall. So many men have said in our meetings: We are Republicans but we think the present Administration had done more for the
farmers than all past Administrations combined." Quick's estimate seemed
confirmed when a poll taken by *Farm Journal* indicated that farmers were
backing the President by a margin of 2 to 1.

Finally, the accession to the Democratic ranks of practically all independent newspapers and periodicals completed the great progressive coalition
and added powerful support to Wilson's candidacy. *The New York Times*, the
New York *Evening Post*, the *Nation*, the *New Republic*, *Pearson's Magazine*, the Scripps newspapers, and other leaders of independent opinion came
out, some of them reluctantly, for Wilson. As Herbert Croly of the *New Republic* put it:

> I shall vote for him chiefly because he has succeeded, at least for the time
> being, in transforming the Democracy into the more promising of the
> two major party organizations. . . . The party program no longer seeks the
> restoration of a régime of incoherent, indiscriminate, competitive, localistic
> individualism. It foreshadows rather a continuing process of purposive
> national reorganization determined in method by the realities of the task but
> dedicated to the ultimate enhancement of individual and associated life
> within and without the American commonwealth. For the first time in
> several generations the party has the chance of becoming the embodiment
> of a genuinely national democracy.

Progressivism was one theme that emerged during Wilson's campaign.
Another theme, and one that undoubtedly has a profound impact on most voters, was peace. The President was impressed by mounting manifestations of
the deep longings for peace by the American people. The reaction to "He
Kept Us Out of War" in St. Louis had pointed the way. And Wilson was

aware that most Progressives were pacifists, or at least opposed to participation in the European War, unless there was an overwhelming assault upon American rights. Furthermore, anti-war sentiment was particularly strong in the Middle West and Far West, the very regions that the Democrats had to carry if they were to win. Should the President forget these factors, the party's leaders had no hesitation in reminding him of the political facts of life.

As it turned out, Wilson was prepared, even eager, to capitalize on the peace sentiment. By September his efforts to cooperate with the Allies in ending the war had failed. He was growing suspicious of British motives and was persuaded that neither side should win. The war, he said in one speech, had degenerated into a drunken brawl without any worthy ends or purposes. Thus the President easily slipped into the role of champion of non-intervention. Conscience could approve the policy that expediency strongly recommended.

The President first sounded this new note on September 30 in one of his "front porch" speeches at "Shadow Lawn." Some three thousand people, mostly members of the Young Men's Democratic League, listened while Wilson came out foursquare for progressivism. At the end of his speech, however, the President departed from his prepared text and turned to Republican criticism of his foreign policy:

> All our present foreign policy is wrong, they say, and if it is wrong and they are men of conscience, they must change it; and if they are going to change it in what direction are they going to change it?
> There is one choice as against peace, and that is war. Some of the supporters of that party, a very great body of the supporters of that party, outspokenly declare that they want war; so that the certain prospect of the success of the Republican Party is that we shall be drawn in one form or other into the embroilments of the European war, and that to the south of us the force of the United States will be used to produce in Mexico the kind of law and order which some American investors in Mexico consider most to their advantage. . . . The only thing I want to lay emphasis upon in this connection is this—that a great, fundamental, final choice with regard to our foreign relationsships [sic] is to be made on the 7th of November. Some young men ought to be interested in that.

Democratic campaign managers and speakers all over the country now rushed to play upon the peace theme. Senator Walsh dispatched an army of orators to Illinois, Iowa, Nebraska, the Dakotas, Missouri, Kansas, and Colorado, with instructions to highlight the peace issue. William Jennings Bryan was in the forefront of this army, sounding the call of peace up and down the prairies and plains of the Middle West. "I cannot refrain," Wilson wrote to the Commoner, "from dropping you at least a line to express my admiration of the admirable campaign you are conducting. It is, of course, nothing novel to see you show your strength in this way, but I feel so sincerely appreciative of your efforts in the interest of what we all feel to be the people's cause that I must let you know with what deep interest I am looking on." Bryan replied: "I believe I am making a more convincing speech in your behalf than I have ever been able to make in support of my own candidacy, history being more conclusive than promise or prophecy."

Pamphlets and newspaper advertisements poured from Democratic head-

quarters highlighting the peace issue. New York distributed five million copies of Glynn's speech at the St. Louis convention and six million copies of
Wilson's speech against war with Mexico before the New York Press Club on
June 30. Nearly every piece of campaign literature, no matter what the topic,
contained some reference to the peace issue. For example, the pamphlet,
Children's Emancipation Day, reminded mothers that Wilson had saved their
children from sweatshops just as he had "saved their sons and their husbands
from unrighteous battlefields!"

The President continued to pound home this theme. "I am not expecting
this country to get into war," he declared at "Shadow Lawn" on October 21.
"I know that the way in which we have preserved peace is objected to, and
that certain gentlemen say that they would have taken some other way that
would inevitably have resulted in war, but I am not expecting those gentlemen
to have a chance to make a mess of it." Ten days later the President wrote for
publication in western newspapers: "Thank you warmly for your letter of
October twenty-third. The reason you give for supporting me touches me
very deeply, that you should feel when you see 'the boys and mother' together
in your home circle that I have preserved the peace and happiness of the
home. Such a feeling on the part of my fellow-citizens is a sufficient reward
for everything that I have done."

The climax of this particular aspect of the campaign came with the publication of a full-page advertisement in leading newspapers on November 4 by
the Wilson Business Men's National League:

You Are Working—*Not Fighting!*
Alive and Happy;—*Not Cannon Fodder!*
Wilson and Peace with Honor?

or

Hughes with Roosevelt and War?

Roosevelt says we should hang our heads in shame because we are
    not at *war* with Germany in behalf of Belgium!
Roosevelt says that following the sinking of the *Lusitania* he would
    have foregone diplomacy and seized every ship in our ports flying
    the German Flag. That would have meant *war*!
Hughes Says He and Roosevelt are in Complete Accord!

The Lesson is Plain:
If You want WAR, vote for HUGHES!
If You Want Peace with Honor
VOTE FOR WILSON!
And Continued Prosperity

Wilson's campaign was certainly going well, in brilliant contrast to Hughes'
efforts. Yet the country still had a normal Republican majority. Many people

would vote for the GOP no matter who the candidates were and what they said. A Democratic victory, therefore, was far from assured. Wilson summed up his own views on the progress of the campaign in a candid letter to his brother in mid-October:

> It is hard to answer your question as to how the campaign is going. I hear all sorts of reports, most of them encouraging (except about Maryland), but I never allow myself to form confident expectations of any kind. I believe that the independent vote, the vote of the people who aren't talking and aren't telling politicians how they are going to vote, is going to play a bigger part in this election than it ever played in any previous election, and that makes the result truly incalculable. It is evident, of course, that Mr. Hughes is making very little headway, because he has done so many stupid and so many insincere things, but other influences are at work in his behalf which are undoubtedly very powerful, chiefly the influence of organized business. I can only conjecture and hope.

The presidential campaign reached its climax as October drew to a close. Both candidates went all out in last minute appeals to sway voters. Hughes maintained his attacks on the Administration, hammering especially at the Adamson Act. Wilson continued to emphasize the themes of progressivism and peace. In early November, Hughes and Wilson capped their respective campaigns with massive rallies in Madison Square Garden in New York City. Hughes appeared confident in these final days, Wilson, a bit out of sorts. On election day Hughes took his family to see a performance of *The Music Master* and returned to his suite for a brief nap, followed by a quiet dinner. Wilson motored from "Shadow Lawn" to Princeton on the morning of November 7, cast his ballot at the firehouse on Chambers Street, then returned to Long Branch for a day of work and a dinner with family and friends. Both candidates had done their best. It was now up to the voters.

The early returns from the East indicated a tidal wave for Hughes. By evening it was clear that the Republican candidate had carried most of the big eastern and midwestern states and had an almost certain 247 electoral votes, only 19 short of the number required for election. *The New York Times* conceded the election to Hughes shortly after 10 p.m., the New York *World*, soon afterward. Congratulations began to pour into Hughes' suite at the Astor Hotel. Reporters demanded a victory statement, but Hughes, awaiting Wilson's concession, held back.

Wilson, although he appeared resigned to the inevitable, did not believe that the time had come yet to concede defeat. The President, of course, had considered the possibility of a Republican victory. In fact he had drawn up a plan in such an event by which Hughes would be appointed Secretary of State, then become President upon the resignation of Wilson and the Vice-President. This would avoid the problem of a lame-duck President during a time of international crisis. For the moment, however, Wilson decided to go to bed and see what the new day would bring.

Returns from the West began to filter in about 2 o'clock in the morning. Although they were fragmentary at first, the trend toward Wilson was clear.

Joseph P. Tumulty, the President's secretary, called Wilson before breakfast with the cheering news that the election was now in doubt. Wilson went out to play golf and had lunch with a few close friends. He spent the afternoon in his study following the returns. All day long the results continued to show a trend toward the Democracy. By midnight Wilson had 251 electoral votes to Hughes' 247. California's 13 electoral votes, Minnesota's 12, North Dakota's 3, and New Mexico's 5 were still in doubt. These votes would decide the election.

It was not until eleven o'clock in the evening of November 9 that Wilson's reelection became certain. New Mexico had gone for Wilson, as had North Dakota. Most important, the President managed to offset an early Republican lead in California and gain that state's 13 crucial votes. A Democrat would serve a second consecutive term as President for the first time since Andrew Jackson.

The victory was a narrow one. The final tabulation showed Wilson with 9,129,606 popular and 277 electoral votes, Hughes with 8,538,221 popular and 254 electoral votes. Still it was a smashing personal triumph for Wilson. Hughes had not done badly. In fact he had polled some 850,000 more votes in 1916 than Taft had polled in 1908. But Wilson had done even better, polling some 2,700,000 more votes in 1916 than Bryan had in 1908, and some 2,830,000 more votes in 1916 than he, Wilson, had polled in 1912.

The configuration of the election map clearly demonstrated that Wilson had consummated the union of the South and West which Bryan had failed to accomplish in 1896. The President had carried every state west of the Mississippi and south of the Mason-Dixon line, except for Minnesota, Iowa, South Dakota, Oregon, and West Virginia. Hughes had swept the East and Middle West, except for New Hampshire and Ohio. Here was the basis for a new political coalition—a combination of agricultural interests, organized labor, and the social justice element. Only the future could show whether this coalition would be transformed into a new party.

Analysts and politicians noted other portents for the future of American politics. First of all, the highly touted German-American bloc had been so riddled by the Democratic peace appeal that it was not a decisive factor in the outcome. The same was even more true of Irish-American voters. Not only did the peace issue prevent any defections from the normal Democratic allegiance of this group, but Irish-Americans voted for Wilson in larger numbers than they had for any previous candidate. Analysts could not find any pronounced alignment among Roman Catholic voters on purely religious grounds. Roman Catholic bishops and priests, opposed to the President's Mexican policy, played a significant role in the outcome apparently only in Oregon. The labor vote, as expected, went largely to Wilson and helped him to carry at least New Hampshire, Ohio, California, Washington, Idaho, and New Mexico, although it was apparently decisive only in the latter three states. The women's vote in the middle and far western states, local observers all agreed, went disproportionately to Wilson on account of the peace issue.

Together with the peace issue, the most decisive factor in the outcome of the election was Wilson's success in winning former Progressives. Generally speaking, he carried those states in which he did well among former Bull Moosers. Statisticians estimated that he received, all told, about 20 per cent of the former Progressive vote, but it varied importantly from state to state, as the following table reveals:

WILSON'S GAINS IN 1916 OVER 1912 AS PERCENTAGES OF THE PROGRESSIVE VOTE IN 1912

Utah	109%	New Hampshire	45%
Wyoming	72	North Dakota	40
Idaho	68	New Mexico	39
Montana	59	Nebraska	34
Colorado	53	Ohio	34
Washington	47	Kansas	30

Finally, approximately 300,000 Socialists and independents in the left wing of the Progressive movement who had voted for the Socialist candidate in 1912 swung to Wilson in 1916. Their support was also decisive in states like California, Ohio, and Washington.

Virtually all observers agreed that Democratic success had come on account of Wilson's and his party's promises of continued peace, prosperity, and progressivism. "The President," Senator Robert M. La Follette of Wisconsin said, "must accept the outcome of this election as a clear mandate from the American people to hold steadfastly to his course against war." Bryan added: "The peace argument evidently had more weight than arguments based upon economic progress . . . the country is against war. It is opposed to intervention in Mexico, and it protests against being drawn into the war in Europe." The British Ambassador in Washington, a more impartial observer, agreed in a post-election report: "The United States does not want to go to war, and the elections have clearly shown that the great mass of the Americans desire nothing so much as to keep out of the war. It is undoubtedly the cause of the President's reelection."

It is ironic that Wilson should have won mainly on the peace issue only to lead the nation into war six months later. Yet the President did not betray his mandate. It is doubtful that the American people were for "peace at any price." Rather, they expected the President to do all within his power to prevent the United States from being drawn into the conflagration raging in Europe. In this sense, Wilson was faithful to his trust. The decision for war was forced upon him; he could see no honorable alternative.

The war prevented Wilson from cementing the coalition of 1916 into a new political party. However, he had pointed the way. The Democratic party would remain the party of movement. The new leadership necessary to revitalize the Wilsonian coalition would be found in 1932 in the person of Franklin D. Roosevelt. New groups would be added and new policies would be developed, but the Democracy would remain very Wilsonian.

Election of 1932

by *Frank Freidel*

The election of 1932, coming in the third year of the Great Depression, focused upon the responsibility of the Government for the economic welfare of the American people. The debates of the campaign were less momentous than the aftermath of the election—the establishment by President Franklin D. Roosevelt of a new relationship between the Government and American society. Thereafter the Federal Government took active, vigorous steps to promote and preserve prosperity, going far beyond the limited, tentative measures of President Herbert Hoover and his predecessors. The election also marked the beginning of a long period in which the Democratic party, since 1892 the minority party, was the majority party among the electorate.

It would have taken a bold prophet indeed to have forecast in the afterglow of President Herbert Hoover's landslide victory in 1928 that only four years later he would be the victim of a comparable landslide victory for his Democratic opponent. The collapse of the boom of the 1920's, for which the Republicans had, understandably, taken credit, brought upon Hoover the blame for the Depression. It was the prime factor in his defeat.

Even during its heyday in the New Era of the 1920's, the Republican party was not so strong as the topheavy victories in three successive presidential elections seemed to indicate. Democratic candidates had made impressive showings in the congressional elections of 1922 and 1926, and in 1930, before the Depression had become catastrophic, already had won control of the House of Representatives, and almost obtained a majority in the Senate. The appeal of Democrat Alfred E. Smith to urban voters was so great that in 1928 the results in several major cities had, for the first time, countered the Republican landslide and given Smith majorities. In New York, where Smith lost heavily despite his formidable margin in New York City, the Democratic candidate for governor, Franklin D. Roosevelt, won by a very narrow margin. Had prosperity continued, President Hoover could perhaps have looked to victory in 1932, but the Republican party was far from invulnerable.

For its part, the Democratic party had acute internal weaknesses which had to be overcome if it were to achieve victory even in a depression year like 1932. In both 1924 and 1928 it was seriously split over the issues of Catholicism and prohibition between its northern, urban wing—the ardent supporters of the Catholic, wet Smith—and its southern and western rural wings —predominantly Protestant and prohibitionist. The party had dead-locked between the two wings for three weeks in the 1924 convention before nominating a compromise candidate, John W. Davis, whose defeat was a foregone conclusion. In 1928, the party avoided deadlock, quickly nominating Smith, whose candidacy led to widespread defections in the South and West. The defeat of Smith in the 1928 election eliminated the urban wing from party control, as the defeat of William Gibbs McAdoo in the 1924 convention had ended southern and western domination. The defeats had prepared the way for the compromise essential to bridge over the gulf, and the Depression brought a new, transcendent issue which could relegate to the past the bitterness within the party over the wet-dry and religious controversies.

In the immediate aftermath of the 1928 election, when a vista of almost endless prosperity seemed to loom ahead, the newly elected governor of New York, Roosevelt, seemed the leading contender for the 1932 Democratic nomination. His had been the most significant Democratic victory in the year of the Hoover landslide. A country squire with urban connections and experience, he was the most influential party leader working through the 1920's among both urban and rural Democrats to restore party unity. As yet the prospect of winning the 1932 Democratic nomination seemed little more than an empty honor, scarcely worth a stubborn battle. Less than a year later, in October, 1929, the great crash of the stock market triggered the Depression, and gave an entirely different appearance to the forthcoming presidential election. A Democratic party moving toward unity and strength would have what was almost certainly a winning issue—unless, of course, a strong and obvious economic recovery were to take place before November, 1932.

President Hoover's positive appeal to the electorate in the campaign of 1928 had been his identification with prosperity; he seemed to be taking responsibility for the continued economic well-being of the nation. "Given a chance to go forward with the policies of the last eight years," he had declared in his acceptance speech, "we shall soon with the help of God be in sight of the day when poverty will be banished from this nation." And in his Inaugural Address, he had asserted: "Our first object must be to provide security from poverty and want. . . . We want to see a nation built of home owners and farm owners. We want to see their savings protected. We want to see them in steady jobs. We want to see more and more of them insured against death and accident, unemployment and old age. We want them all secure."

When the privation and hardships of the Depression hit the American people they turned to the President, whose reiterated first concern had been their security, looking to him for succor. Nor did Hoover try to avoid his responsibilities as a deflationary sag after the Wall Street crash slowly carried the economy into ever deepening depression. He took immediate steps of a minor nature, and, as the crisis became serious, resorted to increasingly strong measures. Within most of these there was a critical limitation — President Hoover's belief that the Federal Government should do no more than provide encouragement to business, which would voluntarily undertake the task of securing recovery. Through the prosperous years of the 1920's, he had emphasized, as he continued to insist during the Depression, that the only way to obtain national well-being was through private enterprise rather than federal legislation. That, he held, was the only proper means to attain the lofty end he had proposed in his acceptance speech and Inaugural Address. At one point during the Depression, in response to suggestions that the United States (like the Soviet Union) should issue a plan for its future, he sketched a glowing picture of abundance. It would be attained, he said, by the American people through their own efforts.

Even while Hoover continued to stress self-reliance, or what he had termed earlier "rugged individualism," the deepening Depression pushed him toward increasingly significant government intervention. Even before the stock market crash, several sectors of the American economy, such as bituminous coal mining in the Appalachians and textile manufacturing in New England, had been depressed. In the late 1920's, building construction had declined, and the sale of automobiles had started to sag. Above all, agriculture had suffered since the ending of government price supports on the great staples in 1920. By latter-day standards, the industrial worker had not fared well during the 1920's; his average pay of $1,500 in 1929 was only a third the real wages of workers forty years later, but the average cash income of farmers (with which to purchase manufactured goods and make payments on mortgages and taxes) was only $548 per year. Farm organizations throughout the 1920's sought some sort of government price-fixing scheme such as they had enjoyed during the First World War, but twice President Coolidge vetoed measures passed by the congressional farm bloc. Even before the Depression hit, President Hoover sought to redress the complaints of the farmers. He called Congress into special session in the spring of 1929 to pass the Agricultural Marketing Act, a device to try to raise farm prices. It created a Federal Farm Board with a half-billion dollar revolving fund with which to buy surpluses. Congress in 1930 also passed the Hawley-Smoot Tariff, which placed prohibitively high barriers against farm imports as well as some manufactured goods (and provoked retaliation from other countries). It raised tariffs on farm products 30 per cent, and on manufactured goods 12 per cent. As late as the winter of 1930–31, the Farm Board was able to maintain the price of wheat within the United States at twenty-five to thirty cents per bushel above that in European markets, but by 1932 it had run out of funds, warehouses were overflowing, and prices within the United States had dropped to the world level. The funds of the Farm Board were too limited, and it possessed no power or enticement to persuade farmers to plant less.

At the time that Hoover took office, the great bull market of the 1920's had long since given him alarm. He blamed the Depression in part upon the speculation during the Coolidge Administration. Twice he had tried to persuade President Coolidge to insist that the Federal Reserve Board raise interest rates, but Coolidge refused to interfere. Soon after he became President, Hoover did get the Federal Reserve Board to raise the rates, but this did little to quell speculation in the few remaining weeks before the crash.

At the beginning of September, 1929, the stock market soared to a height that it would not again reach until the 1950's then sagged for several weeks and finally crashed spectacularly in late October. When it was temporarily stabilized in mid-November, stock prices were only half what they had been at the peak of the boom, yet far above the depths to which they intermittently declined during the next three years. *The New York Times* average for twenty-five industrial stocks was 452 at the peak in 1929, and only fifty-eight at the lowest point, in 1932. The stock collapse led to a drop in real estate and other values, leading to deflation, and gradually declining employment.

In the first months after the stock market crash, the Depression developed slowly, seeming to require only limited government action. President Hoover obtained pledges from business and labor leaders that they would continue as before, without seeking changes in wages and hours. Significantly, Hoover also took mild steps to counter the deflationary cycle: a substantial tax cut, a lowering of Federal Reserve interest requirements, and a record breaking appropriation for public works, $423 million. Together with the Farm Board's agricultural aid, these expedients counteracted to some extent the slow decline in production and employment through 1930. Businessmen became pessimistic, but thus far the Depression was not unusually severe.

European repercussions gave a sharp downturn to the American economy in the spring of 1931. The failure of the central bank in Austria threatened the financial systems of Germany and other nations. Desperate Europeans began to withdraw their gold holdings from American banks. President Hoover tried to stem the European crisis by agreeing to a moratorium for one year on German reparations payments and the payments of war debts to the United States by former allies. The Federal Reserve Board raised interest rates to try to stop the withdrawal of gold. But the moratorium was of scant help to European countries, and the increase in interest rates speeded deflation within the United States.

By the summer of 1931, the Depression was becoming acute in the United States, and it continued to worsen for a year. President Hoover reluctantly turned toward more drastic government action. He proposed a comprehensive program, but the Democrats, in the ascendancy in Congress after the election of 1930, were slow to enact it. Hoover charged then and subsequently that they were hampering him in order to profit politically in the election of 1932. An examination of the views then and later of Democratic leaders in Congress would suggest rather that most of them did not approve of the Hoover program. The suggestions they made after Hoover was defeated and Roosevelt elected were for the most part more conservative, except on relief spending.

Congress did create in January, 1932 a large-scale loan agency patterned somewhat after a first World War predecessor. This was the Reconstruction Finance Corporation, which in 1932 loaned $1.5 billion, a sum almost half the size of the previous national budget, but far from adequate to stop bank and business failures. Congress also debated the appropriation of large sums to provide relief for the millions of destitute being kept alive on pittances from private charity, and local and state governments. Since city and state governments were with few exceptions running out of funds and unable to borrow further, the pressure upon the Federal Government became acute. Sympathetic congressmen tacked amendments providing for direct relief onto a bill appropriating money to make seed-loans to farmers in drought areas. Hoover, feeling that the Democratic congressmen were seeking to make him appear heartless, in February, 1931, issued a public statement:

> This is not an issue as to whether people shall go hungry or cold in the United States. It is solely a question of the best method by which hunger and cold shall be prevented. It is a question as to whether the American people, on one hand, will maintain the spirit of charity and mutual self-help through voluntary giving and responsibility of local government as distinguished, on the other hand, from appropriations out of the Federal Treasury. . . . If we start appropriations of this character we have not only impaired something infinitely valuable in the life of the American people but have struck at the roots of self-government. . . . I am willing to pledge myself that if the time should ever come that the voluntary agencies of the country together with the local and state governments are unable to find resources with which to prevent hunger and suffering in my country, I will ask the aid of every resource of the Federal government because I would no more see starvation amongst our countrymen than would any Senator or Congressman.

By the summer of 1932 the point of desperation had clearly been reached. Hoover did recommend and sign a bill—but only after protesting against what he condemned as Democratic efforts to turn it into a pork-barrel measure with something for every congressional district. This bill appropriated what for the time seemed staggering sums for relief and recovery; it authorized the Reconstruction Finance Corporation to loan state and local governments $300 million for relief, and $1.5 billion for self-liquidating public works.

Although Hoover had gone much further than any preceding President in taking positive steps to combat the Depression, he had made little political headway for himself or his party. His measures, while significant innovations, were far below the scale economists would now consider minimal to counter the deflationary spiral. If he seemed cold and remote, it was in part because Democratic politicians maneuvered him into making statements that seemed

to echo Grover Cleveland: "We cannot squander ourselves into prosperity."
He became even more unpopular because the extent and degree of suffering
in 1931–32 was far worse than the calm appraisals from the White House
indicated. By the time the election came, according to the cautious estimates
of Hoover himself, one worker out of five was unemployed. One out of three
was unemployed in big cities such as Chicago. A large part of those still working were receiving such low wages or working so few hours that they barely
survived. A quarter of the women employed in Chicago were earning less
than ten cents an hour. Relief payments outside of a few relatively rich states
like New York were usually a starvation level pittance; in Detroit payments
were five cents a day per person. Hoover's Secretary of War, Patrick J. Hurley, proposed that restaurants help by saving the table leavings of their pa-
trons for hungry people. It was an unnecessary suggestion. Few restaurant
scraps went unsalvaged; few garbage piles were without scavengers. Edmund Wilson reported that in Chicago he saw a woman take off her glasses
while hunting scraps for her son so that she would not see the maggots in the
meat. Several hundred thousand unemployed, including many teenage boys
and some girls, drifted about the country on freight cars, or camped in shanty-
towns along the tracks, under bridges, or in dumps—towns always known as
"Hoovervilles."

Farmers fared little better, although most of them did have something to
eat, as long as they could hold on to their farms. A quarter of them had lost
their holdings before Hoover left office. In some areas cotton remained un-
picked, farmers could pay so little to the pickers—not enough to keep the
pickers fed. Mountains of produce went to waste. Corn held over from the
previous year cost much less than the cheapest soft coal, so that many Iowa
farmers kept themselves warm burning corn. Some sheep raisers found when
they marketed their lambs that each brought no more than the cost of a pair of
lamb chops in a railroad dining car. Evicted tenant farmers and migrant farm
workers, traveling along the highways, shared the national hunger. They too
made bitter jokes about the Hoover Administration. An Oklahoma editor,
Oscar Ameringer, gave a ride to a family of these tenant farmers in Arkansas.
The wife was clutching a chicken she had found killed on the highway, remarking, "They promised me a chicken in the pot, and now I got mine."

Amid the suffering and the fright, there was surprisingly little violence.
There was not even much radicalism. One Republican senator created a flurry
in the newspapers in May, 1932, when he declared that the nation needed a
Mussolini to rescue it from its difficulties. His was almost a lone voice, and
his statement was not to be taken seriously. Rather the electorate was waiting
for the election of 1932 to bring a change. That was probably what was
worrying the Republican senator.

The Republicans, despite the growing unpopularity of their party and the
overwhelming unpopularity of their President, had no real choice in 1932 but
to renominate him. Although Hoover had not been notable for his political
skill, he did have firm enough control over the party machinery to prevent any
serious challenge to his nomination. Nor was the nomination worth a serious

fight had there been a strong contender. R. V. Peel and T. C. Donnelly in their contemporary study of the 1932 campaign remarked, "After 1929 no stock depreciated in value more than that of the GOP."

There were only a few tentative efforts to obtain another candidate. The most serious, from the standpoint of the Democratic opposition, were the feelers among one-time Theodore Roosevelt Progressives, the Bull Moosers of 1912, on behalf of either Senator Hiram Johnson of California or Governor Gifford Pinchot of Pennsylvania. Johnson refused to become involved. Senator William E. Borah, another Republican progressive, declined even to allow the Idaho delegation to the convention to pledge itself to him as a favorite son. Indeed, Borah would not serve on the delegation. On the other hand, Pinchot did not stop Harold L. Ickes of Chicago from making a canvass upon his behalf. It showed so little support that Pinchot refused to be a candidate. But, had the Democrats not nominated Roosevelt or some like-minded figure, the progressives within the Republican party might have formed a third party. Mrs. Pinchot reported to Borah after the Republican convention that she had been to Washington and seen Hiram Johnson, who felt as they did, and would "be delighted to come into a small group to talk things over next week — after we see what happens in the Democratic Convention."

A few Republicans seeking a more popular candidate tried to start a "draft Coolidge" movement in the fall of 1931. Coolidge, in such ill health that he could hardly participate in the 1932 campaign, firmly squelched proposals "that a former president should use his prestige to attempt to secure a nomination against a President of his own party." Senator Dwight Morrow of New Jersey, renowned for his skilful restoration of amicable relations with Mexico, and as the father-in-law of the aviator Charles Lindbergh, would have been a likely Republican choice had Hoover decided not to run a second time, but Morrow died in October, 1931. As it was, the only open challenger to the President was a conservative former senator from Maryland, Dr. Joseph I. France. He entered presidential preferential primaries where, unopposed, he won empty victories; Republican conventions in these states chose Hoover delegates. At the national convention France received 4 votes.

The Republican convention, opening at Chicago on June 14, 1932, was a dull, dispirited gathering. There was little illusion among most of the delegates. Many of them were federal officeholders facing the loss of their positions in the almost inevitable overturn of the Republicans. Meanwhile, with the convention machinery being firmly run from the White House, the delegates had little to do but ratify its decisions. The only modification that the convention made in the platform draft that Secretary of the Treasury Ogden Mills brought from Washington was in the fabrication of the prohibition plank. Indeed, the delegates seemed to take little interest in the acute economic problems the depression had created, and preferred to focus upon the question whether or not the 18th (prohibition) Amendment to the Constitution should be retained. Mauritz Hallgren asserted in *The Nation*: "The sight of some hundreds of representatives, even of Republican officeholders, bawling for beer, while all about them is misery in the extreme, has virtually crushed what little faith

I have left in American society. The wet circus might at least have been partly excused had the convention in any substantial way recognized the need for action to meet the unemployment problem. But not a single voice was raised in behalf of the hungry millions."

On the second evening of the convention, when James R. Garfield of Ohio, chairman of the Resolutions Committee, read through the eighty-five hundred-word platform, the delegates paid little attention to any of the thirty-seven planks except the one on prohibition. It was a compromise that Hoover's supporters had worked out at the convention. On the one hand, it defended prohibition, and, on the other, it asserted that if the people of the states wished to modify it through a new amendment they should have the right to do so:

> We . . . believe that the people should have an opportunity to pass upon a proposed amendment the provision of which, while retaining in the Federal Government power to preserve the gains already made in dealing with the evils inherent in the liquor traffic, shall allow states to deal with the problem as their citizens may determine, but subject always to the power of the Federal Government to protect those states where prohibition may exist and safeguard our citizens everywhere from the return of the saloon and attendant abuses.

The Republican platform was a comprehensive defense of the Hoover program, ranging from its economic policies to pledges to stamp out racketeering and illicit narcotic traffic. It promised "equal opportunity and rights for our Negro citizens"—a plank which was to have no counterpart in the Democratic platform. The fundamentally conservative nature of the platform was most evident in its conclusion, a damning of the Democratic record in Congress:

> In contrast with the Republican policies and record, we contrast those of the Democratic as evidenced by the action of the House of Representatives under Democratic leadership and control, which includes:
> "1.   The issuance of fiat currency;
> "2.   Instructions to the Federal Reserve Board and the Secretary of the Treasury to attempt to manipulate commodity prices;
> "3.   The guarantee of bank deposits;
> "4.   The squandering of the public resources and the unbalancing of the budget through pork-barrel appropriations which bear little relation to distress and would tend through delayed business revival to decrease rather than increase employment.
> "Generally on economic matters we pledge the Republican Party—
> "1.   To maintain unimpaired the national credit.
> "2.   To defend and preserve a sound currency and an honest dollar.
> "3.   To stand steadfastly by the principle of a balanced budget."

These economic matters led to no debate. Rather, the convention argued for hours whether to accept the prohibition plank or vote for outright repeal. Senator Hiram Bingham of Connecticut, who introduced a minority report of the Platform Committee and President Nicholas Murray Butler of Columbia University denounced the prohibition plank as an insincere compromise. Ultimately they were voted down, 681 to 472.

The Republican platform, the keynote address of Senator L. J. Dickinson of Iowa, and the address nominating Hoover by Representative Joseph L. Scott of California, all had much in common. They defended the Hoover Administration and spread out with pride the Republican record of the 1920's. With equal vigor they attacked the Democratic opposition. But the program they recommended for the future was nothing more than a continuation of the present policies of the Administration. In the preamble to the platform was the formula for overcoming the Depression, set forth in words that sounded as if they might be Hoover's own: "The people themselves, by their own courage, their own patient and resolute effort in the readjustments of their own affairs can and will work out the cure. It is our task as a party, by leadership and a wise determination of policy to assist that recovery." Senator Dickinson, excoriating the proposals of "zealots and demagogues, socialists and communists" for ending the Depression, suggested that the only sound solution was the re-election of the President. "Through all this shouting and turmoil, while our self-appointed saviors strutted in the lime-light of publicity," he declared, "the man in the White House continued patiently and persistently the great task of restoring our normal economic balance." Representative Scott, in his nominating speech hinted that any more positive governmental program than Hoover's would mean dictatorship. "We deny the right of our political adversaries to arrogate to themselves the credit of placing human rights before property rights," he declaimed. Reminding the delegates that Lincoln had asserted (with reference to slavery), "God never made a man good enough to keep his fellow man in subjection," Scott addressed himself to Hoover and the Depression: "So, in these days of stark communism and ill-starred militarism, we had better renew our course. . . . [President Hoover] has taught us to strain our individual selves to the limit rather than cowardly to lie down under a paternal government because he knows that rewards come to those who bear the burden of the heat of the day."

There was scant indication in the convention oratory that any course other than that already fixed was essential to redress the acute national distress. The Administration leaders seemed to be confining the convention to a defense of the President's policies even though at that very time, June, 1932, the country had slipped into the lowest depths of the Depression. There was no sign that these policies would suffice, and ample evidence throughout the country indicated that Hoover and the Republican party were being held responsible for the national plight. Perhaps it made no difference that the convention did not put forth a strong set of proposals, since only an economic upswing far more positive than the meager improvement beginning soon after the convention, could save the Hoover Administration in November.

In any event, the delegates reacted enthusiastically to Representative Scott's nominating speech, parading up and down the aisles for a half-hour while the organ blared and balloons bearing Hoover's name drifted down upon them from nets hung under the rafters. The Republican managers were careful that there was no opportunity for the national radio audience to hear any dissent. When Senator France was being nominated, something went wrong with the public address system. When France tried to obtain the rostrum to withdraw (and place the name of the popular Coolidge in nomination), police dragged him from the hall, ostensibly because his credentials were not in order. The convention managers were being overcautious; there was not the slightest likelihood of a stampede for Coolidge. The first ballot was:

Herbert Hoover	1,126 1/2
Senator John J. Blaine of Wisconsin	13
Calvin Coolidge	4 1/2
Joseph I. France	4
James J. Wadsworth, Jr.	1
	1,149

Three delegates did not vote; one was absent.

Hoover's running mate, Vice-President Charles Curtis of Kansas, evoked little enthusiasm even among the delegates. He was notable only because he was partly of Indian ancestry and had spent much of his boyhood on a reservation. He was elderly, conservative, and dull. Republican publicists listing "Curtis epigrams" had to content themselves with words like these: "Expenses of Government should be reduced wherever and whenever it is possible to do so." The delegates would have liked to bolt to Coolidge's dynamic Vice-President, General Charles G. Dawes. When Dawes refused to permit his name to be placed in nomination, opposition to Curtis deteriorated. Five other candidates were nominated, but Curtis received the Republican nomination. When, at the end of the first ballot, he was only 19 1/4 ballots short of a majority, Pennsylvania switched its 75 votes to him. Curtis was a weak candidate, but that seemed to make little difference. The delegates left in the hands of the President, who had so successfully dominated the convention from its opening to its close, the task of rescuing himself and the party from impending disaster.

The Democrats for their part approached the campaign of 1932 with jubilant anticipation. The presidential nomination became a prize worth the most strenuous efforts, since almost any candidate they might choose seemed certain to be elected. Only a willful course of self-destruction such as the three-week deadlock at the 1924 convention could prevent victory in 1932. Yet the debacle of 1924 could conceivably be repeated, since the convention rules, inserted to protect the southern minority in the Jackson Administration, still required a two-thirds majority of the delegates to nominate a candidate. A repetition of the 1928 fiasco when the Solid South in the general election deserted the wet, Catholic candidate could also threaten defeat. These two recent disasters led to a certain wariness among most Democratic leaders, who by 1932 were ready to prefer national electoral victory to internecine triumph. Still, the prize was so desirable that the conflict, within bounds, was keen, and the result at the convention by no means certain until the last minute. The battle for the nomination was sharper and more dramatic than the national campaign that followed.

From the outset almost four years earlier, Governor Franklin D. Roosevelt was the front runner. His task was to preserve his candidacy against all combinations among his opponents, and somehow to continue in front. Early candidacies often suffered political blight long before the presidential year. Roosevelt was aware of his peril, and having no choice but to be an early candidate, sought to put himself so far ahead of other contenders that they could not conceivably catch up with him.

Roosevelt was unusually well prepared to be a presidential contender. Unlike President Hoover, Roosevelt's absorbing interest, since he had left a New York law clerkship in 1910 to run for the state senate, had been political craftsmanship. In a number of campaigns and offices he had gradually perfected it.

Franklin D. Roosevelt was proud of his name, in itself a considerable asset during the Depression years. (He was also firm about how he wanted it pronounced, and sent word to the radio networks in 1931 that it was: "Ro-se-velt. With the accent on the first of the three syllables. And the *o* pronounced as if there were only one instead of two.") For some years he had followed in the footsteps of Theodore Roosevelt, his own remote cousin, and his wife's uncle. He too had served in the New York state legislature, had been Assistant Secretary of the Navy, and, after a considerable hiatus, became governor of New York. Much of the Roosevelt aura had rubbed off onto him, giving the impression that his election as President would bring a return to spectacular action. "There was never a more *true red blooded* fighting American than dear old Teddy Roosevelt" an admirer wrote in 1931. "To my mind I think that you would be a chip off the old block."

Within the Democratic party, Roosevelt had sought as early as 1920 to establish himself as the young heir to Wilsonian progressivism. In that year, although only thirty-eight, he had received the Democratic nomination for Vice-President, perhaps in part because of his name, but even more because of his outstanding record as an effective Assistant Secretary of the Navy during the First World War. Although the Democratic cause was hopeless that year, he had campaigned energetically both as a progressive and an advocate of the League of Nations, obtaining a national network of friends among Democratic party workers.

In 1921, a severe polio attack deprived Roosevelt of the use of his legs and seemed to remove him as a contender for high office. He continued actively in politics, even through months of acute pain as he convalesced. Since he was not an officeseeker, he was able to avoid much of the factionalism, and to seek throughout the 1920's to close the gap between the Democrats of the northeastern cities and those in the rest of the country. It was these qualifications that led Governor Alfred E. Smith of New York to choose Roosevelt in 1924 to lead his pre-convention campaign and place his name in nomination. Roosevelt was one of the few Democrats who came out of the 1924 convention with his reputation enhanced. In subsequent years, as Roosevelt developed Warm Springs, Georgia, as a treatment center for polio, he also strengthened his alliance with southern Democratic leaders. In 1928 he again nominated Smith, then was edged almost completely out of any voice in the Smith campaign. Yet Smith persuaded the reluctant Roosevelt a few weeks later to run for governor of New York in order to strengthen the ticket in that key state. (Roosevelt had reiterated that he did not want to seek office until he had regained the use of his legs. Moreover, he had not wanted to run in as bad a year as 1928). After a slow start, his campaign gained momentum. Smith himself effectively squashed suggestions that Roosevelt was physically unable to hold office, saying, "A Governor does not have to be an acrobat."

Roosevelt quickly demonstrated his strength as governor of New York. In so doing, a coolness developed between him and Smith. As a renowned governor who had brilliantly reorganized the New York State administration, Smith had never taken Roosevelt very seriously, and may even have thought that he could continue behind-the-scenes to influence state affairs. He was stunned by both his national defeat and Roosevelt's failure to depend upon him and his lieutenants for counsel. Roosevelt became very decidedly governor in his own right, which was vital if he were to be a serious contender for the presidential nomination. It also led to a bitter struggle in 1932 with Smith and his followers.

Roosevelt undertook the governorship of New York amidst unusual public attention, already the leading possibility for the 1932 presidential nomination. Even the sober *New York Times* pointed out editorially as early as November, 1928, that Roosevelt was "within reach of the elements of party leadership." He continued his correspondence and occasional meeting with Democratic party leaders from throughout the country, and undertook a mildly progressive course within the state of New York. He demonstrated himself to be a capable administrator and a brilliant political master over the Republican legislature from which he wrested considerable legislation. He won a substantial following among the upstate electorate by courting farmers and struggling to obtain cheaper electric power. He spoke to voters in person during frequent tours of the state and appealed to them effectively through informal radio talks, the forerunners of the presidential "fireside chats." James A. Farley, who became state chairman of the Democratic party, began building an effective statewide organization. Louis McHenry Howe, who had been Roosevelt's alter ego since 1912, conducted from an office in New York City a swelling national correspondence—in effect a Roosevelt letter-writing factory. Both men were ready at the proper time to launch a carefully planned and coordinated national campaign.

By the late fall of 1929, in the aftermath of the stock market crash, Roosevelt's strategy was becoming apparent. He wrote the powerful Nevada senator, Key Pittman on November 18, 1929:

Do you remember my telling you of my meeting with Jim Cox after the 1920 election? I told him that we Democrats would not elect a President until some fairly serious industrial or economic depression had occurred under a Republican administration. The great question now is whether we are headed for this period of depression or not. . . . I think that you people in the Senate are doing an excellent piece of work. The fact that we Democrats are not doing much talking and are letting the Republicans fight it out very publicly among themselves, is causing just the right situation. . . .

Meanwhile, up here in Albany things are going along smoothly enough. I am preparing my program for the legislature and am stressing social welfare, judicial reform, reorganization and reform of town and county government, and, last but not least, electricity in the home through the development of the St. Lawrence water power.

I hope much that I can see you some day soon.

The Republicans, determined to prevent Roosevelt from growing into a national challenger of President Hoover, had also worked out their basic strategy by the fall of 1929. They were attacking Governor Roosevelt for failing to intervene against corruption in Mayor Jimmy Walker's New York City, where two-thirds of the state's Democratic votes were to be found. Roosevelt side-stepped in 1929 and continued to dodge as pressure, directed by reform leaders like the Socialist Norman Thomas and a Democratic judge, Samuel Seabury, intensified in subsequent years. Roosevelt repeatedly protested that he would not act where to do so would exceed his legal power or deny a fair hearing to the accused. In February, 1932, when he was under particularly strong pressure, Colonel E. M. House pointed out to him, "You could get the nomination and be elected by taking an unjust stand against Tammany, but you could not be nominated and elected if you were considered a wholehearted supporter of that organization." Roosevelt did not act, and in reply to a prominent Episcopalian clergyman who had also been a Harvard classmate, he protested, "I wonder if you remember the action of a certain magistrate by the name of Pontius Pilate, who acted upon public clamor after first washing his hands?" Roosevelt may have been sincere, but his refusal to intervene in New York City caused many liberals to overlook his notable achievements as an administrator and to write him off as an amiable but ineffectual governor. Walter Lippmann, who preferred Newton D. Baker, felt that Roosevelt was straddling on all the important issues, and early in 1932 published the most widely quoted criticism against him: "Franklin D. Roosevelt is no crusader. He is no tribune of the people. He is no enemy of entrenched privilege. He is a pleasant man who, without any important qualifications for the office, would very much like to be President."

By the time these words appeared in 1932, Roosevelt was by far the most formidable contender for the Democratic presidential nomination. As the Depression had gradually become worse, he had become one of the most resourceful of the governors in dealing with it, although in a limited way. Not until 1931 did he become more daring than President Hoover was at the national level. He urged local communities to spend as much as they could for public works, and began to advocate state unemployment insurance and old-age benefits, to be financed by joint contributions from the employers, the employees, and the state.

Even before Roosevelt began his campaign for reelection as governor in 1930, he was all but an announced candidate for the 1932 Democratic nomination. In April, when he addressed the Jefferson Day dinner in New York City, he slipped out early so that the succeeding speaker, the influential progressive senator from Montana, Burton K. Wheeler, could propose Roosevelt as a presidential candidate who would stand for lower tariffs and public utility regulation. The first Democrat of national standing to come out for Roosevelt, Wheeler was trying to head off a new Smith movement. At the 1930 Governors' Conference in Salt Lake City, Roosevelt, despite his own protestations to the contrary, added to the impression that he was seeking the nomination. On the one hand he aired his progressive proposals for ameliorating the Depression, and on the other he emphasized states rights, and attacked Hoover and the Republicans for having accepted a "wholly new economic theory that high wages and high pressure selling could guarantee prosperity at all times regardless of supply and demand." Roosevelt was cutting both to the left and the right of the President.

On the troublesome prohibition issue, Roosevelt straddled successfully until the fall of 1930 when it became apparent that New York voters heavily favored repeal. At that time he took a public stand similar to what the Republicans put in their 1932 platform which favored repeal of the 18th Amendment, but protected state and local options where people felt otherwise. Already Roosevelt was emphasizing that economic problems were far more important than prohibition. He entered the gubernatorial campaign of 1930, with the slogan "Bread not booze."

In the campaign of 1930, Roosevelt won reelection over a dull Republican candidate by an unprecedented plurality of 725,000 votes. He even carried the Republican upstate area by 167,000 votes, although only because a Prohibition party candidate pulled 181,000 votes away from the "wringing-wet" Republican contender. Nevertheless, the campaign had demonstrated that Roosevelt was right in stressing depression issues, and that he was a phenomenal vote-getter.

From this point on, Roosevelt was the presidential aspirant that not only the Republicans but rival Democrats as well were determined to stop. Since, by encouraging "favorite son" candidates, the Democratic candidates might well muster the one-third of the delegates needed to block Roosevelt, the threat was serious. Roosevelt was far in front in the aftermath of the 1930 election but it was essential for him to engage in the most adroit political maneuvering to stay ahead. He had no choice but to be the front runner, so his managers made the most of it. On the day after the election, James Farley and Louis Howe drafted a statement which Farley, without consulting Roosevelt, gave to the press:

I fully expect that the call will come to Governor Roosevelt when the first presidential primary is held, which will be late next year. The Democrats in the Nation naturally want as their candidate for President the man who has shown himself capable of carrying the most important state in the country by a record-breaking majority.

Out of respect for political conventionalities, Roosevelt for more than a year continued to pretend that he was not a candidate while Farley and others worked indefatigably to keep him in front of other contenders. What he said in response to Farley's initial statement was to come from him repeatedly, with variations. In November 1931 his words were:

I am giving no consideration or thought or time to anything except the duties of the Governorship. I repeat that now, and to be clearly understood, you can add that this applies to any candidacy national or otherwise, in 1932.

While Roosevelt pretended not to be a candidate, his close associate of many years, Louis McHenry Howe, in January, 1931, opened "Friends of Roosevelt" headquarters in New York City to carry on an accelerated national correspondence and seek funds. Howe, asthmatic and unprepossessing, had all he could do to run this operation. Someone else was needed to solicit convention delegates in person throughout the nation. This task fell upon Farley, who brought to it unusual qualifications. He was of Irish ancestry, and Catholic, which made him personally attractive to innumerable urban Democratic politicians, yet he was himself from a small town, and personally dry. He quickly established for himself a reputation for absolute reliability, loyalty to Roosevelt supporters whose names he knew by the thousands, together with a friendliness that made him an incomparable political organizer. Howe and Farley, together with the Bronx leader Edward J. Flynn, began to build support and to obtain substantial contributions from a handful of wealthy supporters. Their most difficult task was in trying to discourage, or at least avoid involvement, with unscrupulous organizers of Roosevelt clubs in several southern states, who, as in earlier organizing for the Ku Klux Klan, seemed interested primarily in collecting membership fees. In the end these organizers proved more a nuisance than a serious embarrassment.

The first great challenge that Roosevelt faced was from the conservative Democrats who, after Smith's 1928 candidacy, remained in control of the party machinery. John Raskob, chairman of the Democratic National Committee, earlier had been friendly toward Roosevelt, providing heavy loans and substantial donations for Roosevelt's Warm Springs Foundation. Politically his views were decidedly to the right of Roosevelt's, and a struggle for national leadership of the Democratic party was inevitable. Raskob seemed to win the first skirmish after the 1930 election when he obtained the signatures of the three previous Democratic candidates for President and the two southern Democratic leaders respectively of the House and the Senate, John Nance Garner and Joseph Robinson, to an open letter pledging President Hoover their support in his recovery program. They omitted any mention of progressive issues, and to the dismay of most southerners, even accepted the highly protectionist Hawley-Smoot Tariff. Most southern and western Democrats disliked the letter.

Roosevelt had little difficulty in assuming leadership among the southern and western opposition to Raskob and among the eastern conservatives when they held a special meeting of the Democratic National Committee in the early spring of 1931. Raskob announced that the meeting would discuss plans for the 1932 campaign; his intention was to pass resolutions committing the party to a high tariff and prohibition repeal in 1932. He hoped through the repeal issue to separate Roosevelt, who had been reelected in New York on a repeal plank, from the dry South and West. It was an impossible strategy, since Roosevelt along with repeal had advocated states rights-local option—the right of each state or area within a state to decide whether or not it wished to retain prohibition. At once Roosevelt enlisted the support of a leading southerner, Representative Cordell Hull of Tennessee, who had just been elected to the Senate. The Roosevelt-Hull alliance (which Farley represented in Washington) so completely controlled the meeting of the National Committee that Raskob did not even submit resolutions to be brought to a vote. Not only had Roosevelt won the first important battle, but he had also convinced Hull and his southern associates that Roosevelt was a trustworthy ally, irrevocably at odds with Smith and Raskob. From this point on the Roosevelt candidacy began to take on serious dimensions in the South and West. Hull noted in his memoirs that southern Democratic leaders began to look to Roosevelt as the only alternative to Smith-Raskob domination of the party.

In contrast to the Democratic conservatives, Roosevelt as governor of New York was increasingly demonstrating in 1931 and 1932 that he was dynamic and positive, ready to experiment vigorously in his search for programs to combat the Depression. In these programs he was not only establishing himself as a most resourceful governor, but was also directly challenging President Hoover. At first he was cautious in seeking stronger legislation to protect small depositors in wobbly banks; after the spectacular failure of the Bank of the United States, he sharply criticized the cautious banking community and firmly demanded reform. He was more impressive in his study of means to spread work to avoid seasonal unemployment and in his advocacy of unemployment insurance. While he did not obtain a law, at least he persuaded the legislature to establish a commission to study the problem. He was the first major political leader in the country to advocate unemployment insurance. At a conference with eastern governors, Roosevelt sought agreements to deal with unemployment problems through interstate compacts. These did not materialize. As private and local resources became exhausted in the summer of 1931, Roosevelt called the legislature into special session to establish a state relief agency (which became the model for the subsequent New Deal relief system), the Temporary Emergency Relief Administration. At the yearly governors' conferences, Roosevelt repeatedly took the lead in advocating immediate massive action against the depression. In June, 1931, he told the governors:

> More and more, those who are the victims of dislocations and defects of our social and economic life are beginning to ask respectfully, but insistently of us who are in positions of public responsibility why government can not and should not act to protect its citizens from disaster. I believe the

question demands an answer and that the ultimate answer is that government, both state and national, must accept the responsibility of doing what
it can do—soundly with considered forethought, and along definitely constructive, not passive lines.

It was this viewpoint, politically unexceptionable as it would seem to later
generations, that aroused increasing anger and antagonism among Democratic conservatives even as it kindled hope among the dispossessed. By the
summer of 1931, economic conditions were so serious that Democratic politicians were ready to rally behind Roosevelt rather than the conservative alternatives. One of Roosevelt's supporters, Jesse I. Straus, president of the R. H.
Macy and Company department stores, in the spring of 1931 quietly conducted
a poll of the delegates and alternates to the 1928 convention, and announced
that Roosevelt led in thirty-nine out of forty-four states. A poll of Democratic
business and professional men (except in New York) showed Roosevelt leading Smith by a margin of 5 to 1, and the businessmen's favorite, Owen D.
Young, chairman of the board of General Electric Company, by 2 to 1. When
Farley in the summer of 1931 traveled through the Middle West and West,
ostensibly to attend an Elks' convention in Seattle, he sent exuberant reports
from eighteen states. At this point Roosevelt was far in front of any possible
contender. The question was whether a combined conservative movement
could stop him.

The conservatives, under the leadership of Smith, Raskob, and Jouett
Shouse, secretary of the Democratic National Committee, spent the fall of
1931 not in promoting Smith, but in encouraging favorite sons. They also
tried to develop a new national leader. When neither Owen Young nor Newton D. Baker, who had been Wilson's Secretary of War, gave them encouragement, they turned toward Melvin Traylor, the wealthy president of the
First National Bank of Chicago, whose appeal lay in his poverty-stricken rural
origins. They also tried to stir interest in the handsome, right-wing, wringing-
wet governor of Maryland, Albert C. Ritchie, a titan in the eyes of H. L.
Mencken. Since none of these men, all cautious on economic questions, had
nearly the popular appeal of Smith, the pressure was increasingly upon Smith
to become the open challenger to Roosevelt.

It was Roosevelt who first formally announced his candidacy, on January
22, 1932, in order to meet legal requirements for entering the North Dakota
primary. A few days later, Smith declared his availability for the nomination.
The struggle was out in the open. A number of opinion polls, something of a
novelty at the time, showed Roosevelt a clear favorite both for the nomination
and for election over Hoover in November. Nevertheless, since Roosevelt
had to obtain two-thirds of the votes in the convention, it was clear that the
opposition had an excellent fighting chance to deadlock the convention and
nominate a dark horse candidate.

Favorite sons and potential dark horses began to emerge. Some of these were like the lanky, entertaining governor of Oklahoma, William H. "Alfalfa Bill" Murry, who with his slogan, "Bread, Butter, Bacon, and Beans" captured innumerable headlines but few votes. Another potential challenger, Speaker of the House John Nance Garner of Texas, was quite a different matter. Garner, a West Texas banker who through long service and party regularity had risen to be Speaker, became the candidate of the powerful newspaper publisher, William Randolph Hearst. He chose Garner because of his opposition to American participation in the League of Nations, but it was Garner's western background that won him enthusiastic support throughout the Southwest. He became the leader of those who did not wish to join Roosevelt yet opposed Smith and the urban and conservative eastern Democratic leaders. Garner and his followers were far more opposed to Smith than they were to Roosevelt, who accordingly was careful not to antagonize them. Nor did Roosevelt dare risk the implacable opposition of Hearst, the foe of the internationalists. To the horror of devotees of Wilson and the League, Roosevelt in February, 1932, declared in a speech that, because of the fashion in which the League had developed during the years since its founding, he did not favor American participation in it. He probably was expressing his genuine views at the time, but, in leaving the way open for nomination, he was also exposing himself to charges of opportunism.

During the fight for convention delegates during the spring of 1932, Roosevelt succeeded in amassing a substantial majority, but suffered sufficient setbacks to fall ominously below the required two-thirds. Through the Democratic organizations of southern and Border States he obtained the delegations of twelve of the sixteen states. One other delegation from the region was friendly. Initial victories in other parts of the country, combined with this southern sweep, made the Roosevelt organization overconfident. Stinging defeats followed. Tammany managed to grab for Smith a large block of delegates in Roosevelt's own New York; Smith won every delegate in Massachusetts, Rhode Island, and Connecticut. Whatever remaining chance there was for a first-ballot victory was shattered when Garner won the forty-four delegates of California. After all the contests for delegates were over Roosevelt was still eighty short of the requisite two-thirds majority.

This was the preconvention lineup of delegates: Garner claimed ninety delegates in California and Texas; Senator J. Hamilton Lewis, a favorite son personally favorable to Roosevelt, held the fifty-eight delegates of Illinois; Governor George White of Ohio held the state's delegation of fifty-two; Senator James M. Reed of Missouri was the state's favorite son, with thirty-six delegates; Murray had twenty-three delegates from Oklahoma and North Dakota; Governor Harry Byrd of Virginia held the state's twenty-four delegates, and Governor Ritchie the sixteen from Maryland. There were six uncertain delegates from Indiana. The claims of Smith to 209 delegates, and of Roosevelt to 690, were at a few points overlapping:

Smith — Instructed or Favorable

Connecticut	16	Pennsylvania	34 (claimed)
Massachusetts	36	Rhode Island	10
New Jersey	32	Canal Zone	6 (claimed)
New York	65 (claimed)	Philippines	6 (claimed)

Puerto Rico   4 (claimed)

Roosevelt — Instructed or Favorable

Alabama	24	New Mexico	6
Arizona	6	New York	45 (claimed)
Arkansas	18	North Carolina	26
Colorado	12	North Dakota	9
Delaware	6	Oregon	10
Florida	14	Pennsylvania	60 (claimed)
Georgia	28	South Carolina	18
Idaho	8	South Dakota	10
Indiana	24 (claimed)	Tennessee	24
Iowa	26	Utah	8
Kansas	20	Vermont	8
Kentucky	26	Washington	16
Louisiana	20	West Virginia	16
Maine	12	Wisconsin	26
Michigan	38	Wyoming	6
Minnesota	24	Alaska	6
Mississippi	20	District of Columbia	6
Montana	8	Hawaii	6
Nebraska	16	Canal Zone	6
Nevada	6	Philippines	6 (claimed)
New Hampshire	8	Puerto Rico	6

Virgin Islands   2

The strategy of Smith and the conservatives, the "Allies" as they came to call themselves at the convention, was, through the machinery of the Democratic National Committee, to maintain control over the chairing of the convention and then, through standing firm, to deadlock it. Out of the deadlock, the Allies hoped to nominate a compromise candidate.

The strategy of Roosevelt and his supporters was, through their strong membership on the Democratic National Committee to wrest control over the chairing of the convention away from Raskob and Shouse. With the convention machinery in their control they might then try to rescind the two-thirds rule (which would take only a simple majority of delegates' votes) and then proceed to nominate Roosevelt. Or, alternatively, they could stand firm and make sufficient attractive offers to favorite sons to win them over after the first complimentary ballots. If that did not suffice, then it would be essential to obtain the Garner votes, which, as Roosevelt privately commented in advance "would clinch the matter." Operating for the Allies was the force of tradition—it would not be easy to wrest power from Raskob and Shouse, and even more difficult to persuade southerners to give up the two-thirds rule which in effect gave them a veto over unpalatable nominations. On the other hand, Roosevelt could benefit from the southerners dislike for Smith and most of his cohorts, and their fear that a deadlocked convention as in 1924 could lead to a donnybrook ruining the party and guaranteeing a Republican victory. Roosevelt made an asset of this fear. He wrote his Kentucky supporter, Robert W. Bingham of the Louisville *Courier-Journal*, "The drive against me seems to be on. All I can hope is that it will not develop into the kind of a row which will mean the re-election of Brother Hoover."

In the contest for convention machinery, Roosevelt had to accept a compromise which subjected him to later charges of deceitfulness. Some of Roosevelt's advocates, not realizing how disastrous it would be for Raskob to be temporary chairman, had pledged their support for what they thought a meaningless honor. They had forgotten that Raskob could hand down unfavorable rulings on vital matters. Consequently, when the Arrangements Committee met, Roosevelt had to agree that in exchange for obtaining Alben Barkley of Kentucky as temporary chairman, his men would "commend" (not recommend) Shouse for permanent chairman. Roosevelt regarded this as an empty gesture of goodwill, since he controlled a majority of the delegates at the convention and with them could then elect a friendly permanent chairman. The Roosevelt men later claimed that they had explained to Shouse what Roosevelt meant; Shouse ever afterwards interpreted "commend" as a binding promise to vote for him, and accused Roosevelt of bad faith.

As the delegates assembled at the Democratic national convention in Chicago late in June, both sides freely claimed victory. Farley was continuing his first-ballot predictions. Smith labeled these "Farley's Fairy Stories," and Shouse told reporters, "We have Roosevelt licked now." The Allies distributed to the delegates reprints of an attack columnist Heywood Broun made upon Roosevelt, whom he labeled a "Feather Duster," the "cork-screw candidate." With the cooperation of the Chicago machine they packed the galleries with raucous supporters of Smith who hissed Roosevelt and howled for prohibition repeal—tactics that would not help hold Garner supporters in the coalition. Meanwhile as delegations arrived they were ushered into Roosevelt headquarters where they were given the opportunity to talk by direct telephone wire with Roosevelt who remained at the Governor's Mansion in Albany.

The first skirmish at the convention came before it opened—over the two-thirds rule. A gathering of Roosevelt leaders under the influence of Senator Huey Long of Louisiana, fearful of a Smith deadlock, voted to fight the rule. Other southern leaders supporting Roosevelt strongly objected. Southern objections to changing the rule had time to solidify and it became apparent that the convention might vote down the change. Rather than risk defeat, Roosevelt announced that the rule would not be challenged. (Four years later he quietly had it abolished.)

On June 27, the Democratic convention began its sessions in the Chicago Stadium. After Senator Barkley had delivered a two-hour keynote address, the testing of strength could begin. When the Credentials Committee brought forth its recommendation that Roosevelt delegates be seated from Louisiana and Minnesota, the Roosevelt forces won by a margin of more than 100 votes. Then came a close fight over the seating of Roosevelt's choice as permanent chairman, Senator Thomas J. Walsh of Montana, rather than Shouse. Roosevelt won by 626 to 528 — a crucial victory, since Walsh, as an excellent parliamentarian, kept the convention from being turned at tight moments into an anti-Roosevelt machine.

The platform won easy acceptance. It had been drafted in previous months, under Roosevelt's supervision, primarily by the former Attorney General in Wilson's Cabinet, A. Mitchell Palmer. In it, Palmer had incorporated the consensus of several important senators favorable to Roosevelt. It emphasized economic problems rather than prohibition. The prohibition plank called for no more than the resubmitting of the question to the American people. Among many of the delegates there was strong sentiment for outright repeal. Farley did not care how the delegates voted, since, if they inserted the wringing-wet plank that Smith and Ritchie wished, they would eliminate a major reason for nominating one of them. With Roosevelt delegates free to vote as they wished, the repeal plank was inserted 934 3/4 to 213 3/4.

With both sides retaining their confidence, and in private seeking to make deals to switch delegates, nominating began on the afternoon of June 30. For hour after hour, the perspiring delegates were subjected to florid oratory and endless demonstrations that went on until dawn. Roosevelt sent word to Farley to proceed immediately to the balloting in spite of the exhaustion of the delegates; to do otherwise might seem an indication of weakness.

The first ballot began at 4:28 a.m. on the morning of July 1, and, since several of the delegations had to be polled man by man, it lasted an hour and a half. Roosevelt came out with almost as many votes as Farley had predicted in his more careful pre-convention estimates, 666 1/4 — only 104 short of two-thirds, and 464 1/2 more than the nearest rival. But the hoped-for bandwagon switch did not materialize. A second ballot followed; Roosevelt received a few additional votes that Farley was keeping in reserve (since it was necessary that Roosevelt go a bit upward each time). But the Allies held their lines firm; Senator William Gibbs McAdoo kept California for Garner, and Mayor Anton Cermak of Chicago refused to switch the Illinois delegation. Roosevelt's floor leader, Arthur Mullen of Nebraska tried to adjourn after the second ballot, but the Allies, striving for deadlock, insisted upon a third ballot. It was nip and tuck, since several of the Mississippi delegates were eager to abandon Roosevelt. Mississippi was kept in line; Farley managed to muster a handful of additional votes, but brought the Roosevelt total up to only 682. Finally at

9:15 a.m. the convention adjourned until evening. The jubilant Allies were predicting that Roosevelt would crack on the fourth ballot, and there were whispers that Newton D. Baker would be the candidate.

This was the vote on the first 3 ballots:

	First	Second	Third
Roosevelt	666 1/4	677 3/4	682.79
Smith	201 3/4	194 1/4	190 1/4
Garner	90 1/4	90 1/4	101 1/4
Byrd	25	24	24.96
Traylor	42 1/2	40 1/4	40 1/4
Ritchie	21	23 1/2	23 1/2
Reed	24	18	27 1/2
White	52	50 1/2	52 1/2
Murray	23	–	–
Baker	8 1/2	8 1/2	8 1/2
Will Rogers	–	22	–

The presidential nomination depended upon whether or not the Roosevelt forces could quickly gain spectacular delegate strength. So it was that despite their exhaustion, numerous of the delegates probed and negotiated in many directions. In subsequent years there have been many accounts by those engaged in some of these negotiations, more than one of whom was convinced that he was responsible for the dramatic outcome. The probing turned out to be of consequence only in the negotiation for Garner delegates, where undoubtedly several efforts helped bring about the result for which Roosevelt was striving. At the heart was the work of Farley, who agreed with Howe that everything must be staked upon trying to win Texas. Farley conferred with Garner's manager, Representative Sam Rayburn, who promised to see what he could do. The Vice-Presidency was not mentioned.

Simultaneously a number of people had been trying to persuade McAdoo to switch the California Garner delegates, but Hearst rather than McAdoo was the real controlling power over the delegation. Some people argued with Hearst, who became amenable – but in the final analysis only Garner could release the California delegates, or persuade the Texans to switch. In this respect, the final responsibility rested with Garner.

In Washington, Garner had no intention of being party to a potentially disastrous stalemate. He had not thought past compromise choices to be men likely to win. For that matter on policies, Garner and his supporters were much closer to Roosevelt than to Smith-Raskob forces. Garner had been ready to wait for 3 ballots. On the afternoon of July 1, he refused to accept a telephone message from Smith, but did receive Hearst's message recommending that the Garner delegates be released to Roosevelt. Garner called Rayburn telling him the nomination should come on the next ballot. Rayburn reported that the California delegation would switch to Roosevelt if released, but that the Texans would not do so unless Garner agreed to become candidate for Vice-President. Garner was reluctant to leave his powerful position as Speaker, but years later reminisced: "So I said to Sam, 'All right, release my delegates and see what you can do. Hell, I'll do anything to see the Democrats win one more national election."

On the evening of July 1 when the convention reconvened, the morale of the Allies was still high since they had obtained Mississippi. McAdoo quickly exploded it when California was reached on the fourth ballot. He declared, "California came here to nominate a President; she did not come here to deadlock this convention or to engage in another disastrous contest like that of 1924." California's 44 votes thus went to Roosevelt. Illinois switched when it was reached on the rollcall, Indiana followed, and Governor Ritchie cast Maryland's votes for Roosevelt. With a total of 945 votes, Roosevelt was nominated on the fourth ballot. (Smith refused to release his delegates, and thus kept the nomination from being unanimous.)

Some opposition leaders remained bitter. Their failure had in some degree been caused by Smith's lack of resilience. He sought renomination as a vindication, and was not interested in maneuvering toward another candidate. As Mencken noted, "The failure of the opposition was the failure of Al Smith. From the moment he arrived on the ground it was apparent that he had no plan, and was animated only by his fierce hatred of Roosevelt, the cuckoo who had seized his nest. That hatred may have had logic in it, but it was impotent to organize allies." Shouse wrote Newton D. Baker a few days after the convention, "If McAdoo had not broken the pledges he made, Roosevelt would not have been nominated. On the fourth ballot there would have been serious defections from his ranks with the result that some other nominee would have been certain. That nominee would have been either you or Ritchie. I don't know which."

Nevertheless, there was no serious rift within the party. Unusually united, almost all of the delegates met the next day to nominate Garner for Vice-President, and to await the unprecedented arrival of Roosevelt to deliver his acceptance address before they adjourned. After a flight that was hours late because of buffeting headwinds, Roosevelt arrived at the Chicago Stadium. He brought with him an acceptance speech that had been fabricated in Albany, but Howe, meeting him at the airport, thrust into his hands a different one. He glanced through the new speech while en route to the convention. When Roosevelt rose to speak, he delivered the first page of Howe's draft but then switched to his familiar prepared text. It was a statement in generalities of what Roosevelt had earlier been advocating, and what the platform had spelled out: the domestic (i.e., Republican) causes of the Depression, and suggestions of the means to remedy it—rigid economy in the Government, a crop reduction program and rediscounting of mortgages for farmers, a lower tariff for businessmen, relief and mortgage refinancing for those in desperate straits, construction of self-sustaining public works, regulation of securities sales, and repeal of prohibition. All this was couched in the idealistic moral phraseology of the earlier progressive moment. "Today we shall have come through a period of loose thinking, descending morals, an era of selfishness, among individual men and women and among Nations," he declared. "To return to higher standards we must abandon false prophets and seek new leaders of our own choosing." In conclusion he declared:

> On the farms, in the large metropolitan areas, in the smaller cities and in the villages, millions of our citizens cherish the hope that their old standards of living and of thought have not gone forever. Those millions cannot and shall not hope in vain.
> I pledge you, I pledge myself, to a new deal for the American people. Let us all here assembled constitute ourselves prophets of a new order of competence and of courage. This is more than a political campaign; it is a call to arms. Give me your help, not to win votes alone, but to win in this crusade to restore America to its own people.

Out of the speech came the label "New Deal" for the Roosevelt program. The words were picked up by the political cartoonist Rollin Kirby, who drew a farmer gazing upward at an airplane with New Deal written on its wings. Within a few days the term was generally accepted.

The nomination of Roosevelt and the setting forth of a New Deal program established the lines of the Democratic contest against the incumbent President Hoover. On the ballots of various states there were nineteen other party names. The more significant of these were the Socialist, Communist, Prohibition, Farmer-Labor, Socialist-Labor, Liberty, and Jobless. All of these were insignificant side-shows attracting little attention and fewer votes. The very failure of third parties, even revolving around such crucial issues as the Depression and prohibition repeal, during this crisis period, warrants examination of the three most prominent ones.

Numerous intellectuals during the campaign, damning both Hoover and Roosevelt, insisted that the only candidate offering them an opportunity to vote honestly for significant change was Norman Thomas, the candidate of the Socialist party. Some of these intellectuals, including Paul Douglas, at that time a University of Chicago economist, offered disillusioned Republican and Democratic voters the opportunity to pair their votes so they could cast their ballots for Thomas without hurting the chances of whichever major candidate they thought a lesser evil. Thomas in later years claimed that the New Deal swallowed up his party and enacted his platform of 1932. The Socialist platform called for much that did become part of the New Deal: heavy appropriations for relief and public works, free public employment agencies, unemployment insurance, old-age pensions, improved workmen's compensation programs, abolition of child labor, aid for homeowners and farmers facing difficulties with their mortgages, adequate minimum wages, heavier income taxes, and some aids to farmers. Some of these already were pledged in the Democratic platform. On the other hand, the greater part of the platform called for socialization of basic sectors of the American economy including banks, several constitutional changes in the frame of Government (such as proportional representation), and strong planks supporting Negro rights and American entrance into the League. Altogether, the Socialist platform was far from a blueprint for the New Deal, although some of its proposals such as health insurance and civil rights did become parts of Democratic programs after the Second World War.

The Socialists hoped to poll a strong vote, as large as two million. Thomas campaigned in thirty-eight states, attracting polite attention wherever he went, but received only 885,000 votes.

The Communist party, also hoping to profit from the crisis, met in Chicago in May, 1932. It nominated for President William Z. Foster, best known for his leadership in the Steel Strike of 1919, and for Vice-President a thirty-nine-year-old Negro from Alabama, James W. Ford. They issued a forthrightly revolutionary platform: "Fight for the workers' way—for the revolutionary way out of the crisis—for the United States of Soviet America!" During the summer, Foster and Ford made a number of speeches, although they were several times put into jail. In mid-September, Foster became ill and cancelled further speaking engagements. The Communists received little attention in newspapers or over the radio, though a number of writers and intellectuals endorsed the Foster-Ford ticket. They polled 103,000 votes.

The Prohibition party, which since 1872 had offered candidates for the Presidency, hoped to benefit from the wet planks in both major party platforms. It had always urged other reform issues, and in its 1932 platform, as two contemporary observers, Roy V. Peel and Thomas C. Donnelly pointed out, proposed a nine-point recovery program "practically identical with that later urged by Governor Roosevelt." What made their platform distinctive was a plank proposing federal censorship of motion pictures. The Prohibition candidate for President was William D. Upshaw, who had long been a Democratic member of Congress from Georgia. He received 80,000 votes.

Both the Republicans and Democrats as they prepared for the campaign ignored the third parties; to most voters the only possible choice seemed to be between President Hoover and Roosevelt.

In the days immediately after the nomination of Roosevelt, President Hoover and most Republican leaders had few illusions that they had much chance to win. They were correct, and indeed in retrospect the most serious contest during the campaign was that between Roosevelt and his Democratic opponents over the Democratic nomination. The struggle between President Hoover and Roosevelt seemed reminiscent to some of the 1896 campaign between William McKinley and his agrarian challenger, William Jennings Bryan—but this time the agrarian revolt in the depressed West was being lead by a polished easterner. After visiting Hoover, Secretary of State Henry L. Stimson wrote in his diary on July 5:

> I found the President rather blue on the subject of Roosevelt. The people around him evidently had been rather overconfident . . . and are now awake to the full power which Roosevelt will produce in the field to the radical elements of the West and the South. Roosevelt is not a strong character himself and our hope is that the four months' campaign will develop and prove that he has pretty well lost the confidence of the business elements in the East. But he is making his appeal to the West, and in hard times it is very easy. An inflation campaign and soft money campaign make it look like some of the elements of 1896. But the difficulty is that then it

was the Democrats who were in power during the hard times and now it is the Republicans who are in power. That gives us an uphill fight. Also there is no split yet in the Democratic party as there was in 1896, and there is no Mark Hanna in the Republican party to organize a very big educational campaign.

Only monumental folly on the part of the Democrats—of which there was no sign—or spectacular economic improvement—of which there were only slight signs, could rescue the Republicans. Between August, 1932, and January, 1933, *The New York Times* "Weekly Index of Business Activity" rose from two-thirds of normal (66.2 per cent) to nearly three-fourths (73.8 per cent). Hoover and some of his followers asserted in later years that this marked the beginning of total recovery, destroyed, first, by lack of business confidence in Roosevelt, and secondly, after Roosevelt took office, by the New Deal policies. Whatever the sources of the moderate business upturn in the weeks before the election, it was not reflected in better living conditions for many Americans. Unemployment remained staggeringly high, and commodity prices remained so low that they were forcing farmers into bankruptcy. Poverty was visible everywhere in the United States, nowhere more so than in Washington, D. C., where eleven thousand veterans of the First World War were encamped trying to persuade Congress to pay them immediately a bonus for their wartime services—a bonus not due them for several years. President Hoover had no intention of thus adding to the serious federal deficit (nor did his opponent Roosevelt). Congress voted them their rail fare home, but half the veterans lingered on. President Hoover ordered the army to drive the men from the Washington streets back to their camps. Chief of Staff Douglas MacArthur did more. Looking upon the veterans as "a bad looking mob. . . . animated by the essence of revolution," he used soldiers wearing gas masks and carrying fixed bayonets to evict them from their hovels while news reel cameras recorded the grim scenes. The eviction of the "bonus army" underscored the prevalent poverty, and added further to Hoover's unpopularity.

In theory at least the Republicans had in operation the full party machinery with which to mount a massive effort to reelect Hoover. The President chose Everett Sanders to be the Republican chairman. Sanders had served three terms in the House of Representatives, and had served President Coolidge as a secretary and political adviser. Hoover also selected an executive committee for the party, which was to perform the duties of the Republican National Committee during the campaign. As these appointments indicated, Hoover was personally assuming responsibility for and direction of the campaign. He was bitter toward his many Republican critics in Congress who either deserted him or gave no more than token support, not wishing to associate themselves with an unpopular national candidate. State organizations were scarcely more useful. Even some of the members of Hoover's Cabinet seemed less than enthusiastic.

The Republicans had difficulty in raising money, but thanks to large contributions from a wealthy few, faced defeat with a more substantial treasury

than their opponents, about $2. million, which enabled them to buy more ra-
dio time than the Democrats—seventy hours at a cost of $437,000. As usual
they gave away or sold quantities of posters, pamphlets, buttons, and other
souvenirs, including poster-type covers to place on the spare tire that custom-
arily rode on the side or rear of automobiles.

Hoover may well have thought of himself during the campaign as the in-
trepid, high-principled captain, standing alone on the quarter-deck while the
ship sank slowly beneath him. Scorning the new campaign techniques that
were coming into use, Hoover himself wrote every single word of his speeches.
There were nine of these major speeches, each of the "omnibus" variety
touching upon wide arrays of issues. Each sounded like a state paper, a manifesto warning of the greater disasters that would befall the American people if
they discarded Hoover's wise and careful leadership for the radicalism of
Roosevelt and his advisers. Hoover in addition to his own efforts assigned
one or two Cabinet members to answer specific Democratic attacks. It was not
a successful technique in the eyes of Stimson, who wrote in his diary, "Every
time Roosevelt makes a speech, Mr. Hoover has [Secretary of the Treasury
Ogden] Mills or [Secretary of War Pat] Hurley answer it, and the result is that
it is rather wearing out the popularity of the two men."

In contrast, Roosevelt ran what in most respects was the first truly modern, well-organized presidential campaign. He took over the national party
machinery immediately after his nomination, obtaining the election of James
A. Farley as chairman of the Democratic National Committee. Throughout
the campaign Farley was in charge of campaign tactics (but not ideology),
working through the National Committee members and the regular Democratic
organizations in all of the states (even though these organizations might
have opposed Roosevelt before the election). There was some bitterness
among Democrats at outs with these organizations who had fought for Roosevelt before the convention, but Farley felt his policy would bring the best
results. Roosevelt was ready to reward these loyal early supporters after election day, but not before. The women's division was also carefully organized
and vigorous. The letter writing from New York continued at a stepped-up
pace. Numerous special committees came into existence, arranging speeches,
turning out pamphlets, and obtaining pledges of support. Altogether it was a
large and energetic organization in which Farley did his best to make his
influence felt down to the level of the precinct workers. "The fellow out in
Kokoma, Indiana, who is pulling doorbells night after night," Farley once
wrote, "gets a real thrill if he receives a letter on campaigning postmarked
Washington or New York."

The exploration of campaign issues and the presentation of them in
speech drafts was the work of Roosevelt's "brain trust" working under the
general supervision of Professor Raymond Moley of Columbia University.
For politicians to make use of academic specialists was nothing new, but
Roosevelt recruited and utilized them on a larger scale and more systematically
than ever before. His main speechwriter, beginning with the New York
gubernatorial campaign of 1928, had been Samuel I. Rosenman, an expert on

state issues. In the spring of 1932, as Roosevelt began to concern himself more completely with national problems, he added Moley (who had previously worked for him on crime prevention problems), and had Moley recruit a number of additional academic experts, mostly from Columbia University. The most conspicuous and important among these was Rexford G. Tugwell, an economist, whose thinking was well to the left of Roosevelt's and Moley's, and who in later years wrote in detail of his unsuccessful efforts to win Roosevelt over to his views. Roosevelt was receptive to ideas of almost any sort, as long as they were humane and democratic, but always weighed them in terms of their political feasibility. Neither Tugwell, nor Moley, nor Adolph A. Berle, Jr., the other important academic braintruster, was often completely satisfied with Roosevelt's decisions, but all did have an opportunity to expose him to fresh ideas, some of which in modified form became part of new programs. After the convention, Bernard Baruch (who had opposed Roosevelt's nomination) contributed a colorful conservative speechwriter to the group, General Hugh S. Johnson. Various politicians also came and went. It was, altogether, under the skilful management of Moley, an effective organization which could assemble speeches in keeping with Roosevelt's strategy.

From the beginning of the campaign to the end, Roosevelt kept the initiative, harrying and attacking President Hoover from both the right and the left. His speeches were relatively brief, interesting and dramatic to millions of radio listeners. Ordinarily each dealt with only a single subject. In addition to making speeches, Roosevelt engaged in innumerable meetings with politicians, winning over to at least nominal support even the reluctant Smith. And there were countless motor cavalcades and whistle-stop gatherings where crowds roared their pleasure at seeing a smiling, confident Roosevelt.

Despite the warnings of political advisers that he might do himself more harm than good, Roosevelt decided to take his campaign directly to the people, first through a grand swing by train to the Pacific Coast and back. This displaying himself directly to the nation had a significant effect in those pretelevision days. It demonstrated that Roosevelt's polio attack had not deprived him of the physical vigor essential to a President. Far from it, he appeared overflowing with good health and high spirits, and since he loved campaigning, the longer he campaigned the more buoyant he appeared. The contrast in personal appearance and in radio voice with the tired, dreary, depressed Hoover was an intangible difficult to measure, yet was an important factor in the campaign.

By October all the public opinion polls then in operation, crude and uncertain though they were, indicated a sweeping Roosevelt victory. Consequently in October, Roosevelt coasted at the very time when he might have been expected to make his greatest effort. He campaigned in the South even though he could not possibly lose a single southern state. There was no apparent reason. Perhaps he loved being in the South. Perhaps he was thinking ahead to his legislative program and wished to establish a strong rapport directly with the southern people so that he could later better pressure southern congressional leaders.

It was not until October that Hoover, except for his formal acceptance speech, focused his attention upon campaigning. It was too late to do anything but try to speak to a loyal minority for the historical record. Roosevelt could not be pressed hard enough to be forced to answer the contradictions that Hoover saw in some of his statements. Hoover was deadly serious in this campaigning, even though he had no illusions about the outcome. Years later he devoted a hundred pages in his *Memoirs* to an effort to set right for all time his campaign positions compared with those of his opponent.

President Hoover in his speeches again and again enumerated the many measures he had undertaken in order to combat the Depression. He pointed out what he deemed the errors of Roosevelt, and warned that, if the Democrats came in, the result would be far greater economic difficulties if not indeed the breakdown of the Republic. On the one hand he accused Roosevelt of equivocating on the issue of a high protective tariff, as indeed Roosevelt was. Roosevelt's statements, said Hoover, were like "the dreadful position of the chameleon on the Scotch plaid." Yet Hoover on another occasion charged that Roosevelt would so drastically lower the tariff that the "grass will grow in streets of a hundred cities, a thousand towns." But the tariff issue was minor. More important in Hoover's mind was his insistence that Roosevelt and the New Dealers represented an alien governmental philosophy which would destroy the traditional American system. He declared on November 5 concerning certain unspecified groups: "Indeed this is the same philosophy of government which has poisoned all Europe. They have been the fumes of the witch's cauldron which boiled in Russia and in its attenuated flavor spread over the whole of Europe, and would by many be introduced into the United States in an attempt to secure votes through protest of discontent against emergency conditions."

Nevertheless, Roosevelt, like Hoover, basically believed in laissez-faire economics. He was as orthodox as Hoover in his belief in a balanced budget. He was less orthodox in feeling that there could be beneficial modifications in monetary policy. Unlike Hoover, who believed that the Depression was of international origin, Roosevelt ascribed American roots to it. On foreign policy there was so little difference between the two men that Roosevelt did not mention it during the campaign. He remarked to Moley that Hoover was correct on the subject. Neither Hoover nor Roosevelt seemed to concern themselves particularly with the Negro votes, and did not direct remarks toward Negroes.

Professor Moley remarked after the campaign that in Roosevelt's speeches were to be found forecasts of almost all of the early New Deal policies. This was true. Yet the speeches so often veered either right or left and contained so many generalities that to contemporaries it would have been hard to have predicted from them what the New Deal might be. However, enough did grow out of them that affected the New Deal to make worthwhile a brief examination of some of the major themes.

Few Democrats, either to the right or left, failed to cheer when Roosevelt opened his campaign by lambasting the Republican economic policies of the

1920's. He did so in an address at Columbus, Ohio, on August 20. At the heart of the speech was an example of the way in which Roosevelt could make a dreary subject entertaining:

> A puzzled, somewhat skeptical Alice asked the Republican leadership some simple questions:
> "Will not the printing and selling of more stocks and bonds, the building of new plants and the increase of efficiency produce more goods than we buy?"
> "No," shouted Humpty Dumpty. "The more we produce the more we can buy."
> "What if we produce a surplus"
> "Oh, we can sell it to foreign consumers."
> "How can the foreigners pay for it"
> "Why, we will lend them the money."
> "I see," said little Alice, "they will buy our surplus with our money. Of course, these foreigners will pay us back by selling us their goods?"
> "Oh, not at all," said Humpty Dumpty. "We set up a high wall called the tariff."
> "And," said Alice at last, "how will the foreigners pay off these loans?"
> "That is easy," said Humpty Dumpty, "did you ever hear of moratorium?"

Politically more important was Roosevelt's major farm speech at Topeka, Kansas in September. Weeks of work and the touches of at least twenty-five advisors had gone into it. At its heart, where the principal farm group, the Farm Bureau Federation, could see it, were specifications which would permit the domestic allotment system upon which Roosevelt had already decided. But the specifications were drawn so broadly that those favoring inflation or other farm programs such as McNary-Haugenism were not specifically excluded. And all the possible farm legislation was talked about in such technical language that it would not frighten off easterners who did not wish the Federal Government to be generous to farmers. The speech would not completely satisfy many people; Henry A. Wallace had preferred Al Smith's more forthright McNary-Haugenite stand in 1928. On the other hand, the talk drove few people away, and Roosevelt's main task was to reap the anti-Hoover farm vote rather than to draw positive lists of specifics. The success of the speech, which drew a crowd of no less than eighteen thousand people, was to be found in its inoffensive ambiguities.

On the other hand, when Roosevelt spoke in Portland, Oregon, on September 21, he was crisply specific in outlining his power program. He insisted that regulatory commissions should be protectors of the peoples' interest and set rates on a prudent-investment basis. He advocated full regulation of utility securities and holding companies. While he did not wish complete public ownership, he proposed certain government owned and operated services to act as a yardstick to measure private rates. It was, in total, a firm statement of the views of Senator George Norris and the public power advocates. It was also, as Roosevelt pointed out, basically the power policy he had followed as governor of New York. The talk strengthened Roosevelt in the West and brought him additional support from Republican progressives.

Intellectuals at the time, and since, have been most interested in the speech that Roosevelt delivered at the Commonwealth Club in San Francisco several days later—a speech making a strong positive affirmation of political liberalism. It was based on a memorandum Berle had prepared for Roosevelt. In the speech, Roosevelt hypothesized a mature American economy in which it was the task of the Government to police irresponsible power in order to guarantee every citizen a comfortable living. Government should act as a guarantor of the common good within the existing economic system. This was to become the basic philosophy of the New Deal.

On the tariff, Roosevelt, as Hoover pointed out, fared not so well. He had learned that farmers would not favor a low tariff, yet it was an integral part of the southern Democratic tradition. Roosevelt ordered Moley to weave together in a single speech both low and high tariff ideas. The despairing Moley later commented, "One might as well weave glass fibers with cobwebs." The Republicans attacked delightedly, but Roosevelt was done no basic harm, and indeed may have saved himself from damage.

There were other inconsistencies. On October 13, speaking over the radio from Albany, Roosevelt answered queries of social workers and outlined an advanced program for social welfare and unemployment relief. On the other hand, at Pittsburgh only six days later, he delivered a diatribe Hugh Johnson had drafted, denouncing the reckless deficit financing of the Hoover Administration. How Roosevelt would reconcile the heavy expenditures his social welfare program would entail with a balanced federal budget was a question he had not yet faced. (As President he was to "balance" the regular federal budget and run a deficit far larger than Hoover's in an emergency budget.) Yet Roosevelt was sincere both in his humanitarianism and his fiscal conservatism. The only loophole he left at Pittsburgh was his pledge, "If starvation and dire need on the part of any of our citizens make necessary the appropriation of additional funds which would keep the budget out of balance, I shall not hesitate to tell the American people the full truth and ask them to authorize the expenditure of that additional amount."

In the final weeks of the campaign, charges and counter-charges between the two contending parties became more heated. President Hoover set his theme during the month in his address at Des Moines, October 4, when he declared: "Thousands of our people in their bitter distress and losses today are saying that 'things could not be worse.' No person who has any remote understanding of the forces which confronted this country during these last eighteen months ever utters that remark. Had it not been for the immediate and unprecedented actions of our government things would be infinitely worse today." When Roosevelt, speaking at Baltimore on October 25, ad libbed into an attack upon "the 'Four Horsemen' of the present Republican leadership: the Horsemen of Destruction, Delay, Deceit, Despair," his comment that the Republicans controlled the Congress, the Presidency, and the Supreme Court, aroused Hoover's indignation:

Aside from the fact that the charge that the Supreme Court has been controlled by any political party is an atrocious one, there is a deeper implication in that statement. Does it disclose the Democratic candidate's conception of the functions of the Supreme Court? Does he expect the Supreme Court to be subservient to him and his party? . . . .

My countrymen, I repeat to you, the fundamental issue in this campaign, the decision that will fix the national direction for a hundred years to come, is whether we shall go on in fidelity to the American traditions or whether we shall turn to innovations, the spirit of which is disclosed to us by many sinister revelations and veiled promises.

Roosevelt, listening on the radio, was furious and told his advisors he would not let anyone so impeach his patriotism. They persuaded him not to make any rebuttal, but rather to keep his own speeches above personal attacks. In his own final major appearance at Madison Square Garden on November 5, he declared:

From the time that my airplane touched ground at Chicago up to the present, I have consistently set forth the doctrine of the present-day democracy. It is the program of a party dedicated to the conviction that every one of our people is entitled to the opportunity to earn a living, and to develop himself to the fullest measure consistent with the rights of man.

It was up to the voters to choose, and to the surprise of few, Roosevelt was elected by a wide margin. He carried forty-two states compared with six for Hoover, with a total of 472 electoral votes to 59. The popular vote was equally decisive—22,800,000 to 15,750,000 (57.4 per cent to 39.7 per cent). All the minor parties combined had received only 1,160,000 (2.9 per cent) of the vote. It had been a national victory, although Roosevelt was strongest in the South and the West. The percentage of the vote by sections was:

	Roosevelt	Hoover
New England	49.1%	48.4%
Middle Atlantic	50.5	45.4
East North Central	54.2	42.7
West North Central	60.6	37.2
South Atlantic	67.0	31.9
West South Central	83.4	16.2
Mountain	58.4	38.4
Pacific	58.2	36.7

While these are not the careful class analyses of the vote later made possible by scientific public opinion research, there are indications from some Chicago studies made at the time that the same groups that voted for Smith in 1928 voted for Roosevelt (but in 12 per cent greater numbers) in 1932, and that the division in status between those who voted for and against Roosevelt was (with the exception of Negroes) approximately the same in 1932 as it was to be in 1936. Those of higher social and economic status consistently tended to vote more heavily Republican.

On the other hand, Roosevelt had campaigned more as a one-time progressive than as a future New Dealer, and as he planned the New Deal in the

three months before he took office he thought of himself as the future President of all the American people. He had received a strong popular mandate
and was to make vigorous use of it, but just what that use was to be, beyond
the assumption by government of larger responsibilities for the economic welfare of the nation, only the future disclosed..

Election of 1940

by *Robert E. Burke*

Franklin Roosevelt's second Administration was chiefly a troubled time. Ironically, his political prestige had never been higher than in November, 1936, when he won all but two states in his reelection campaign against the liberal but hapless Republican candidate, Governor Alfred M. Landon of Kansas. In this same election the Democrats increased their already swollen majorities in Congress and improved their commanding positions in state capitals throughout the country. Yet less than a month after his second Inaugural Address Roosevelt was in serious political difficulty. He proposed an enlargement of the United States Supreme Court, which had declared key parts of his program to be unconstitutional, and his "bombshell message" to Congress was received by all but the most devoted New Dealers with a distinct chilliness. Enemies of the New Deal, frustrated through much of his first term, at last had a popular issue with which to belabor FDR. By the summer of 1937, thanks to a startling series of pro-New Deal Supreme Court decisions and to exceedingly astute leadership on the part of his opponents (headed in public by members of his own party), Roosevelt was humiliated by the Senate's open burial of his "court packing" scheme.

His legislative accomplishments in 1937-38 were by no means insignificant—a public housing law, the second Agricultural Adjustment Administration Act, and the Fair Labor Standards (or "wages and hours") Act. When seen in perspective these major attainments appear to constitute a rounding out of the New Deal program and are even more impressive because

355

they were achieved in the President's second (and presumably last) term, when political analysts contend that little can be accomplished.

While it is uncertain if President Roosevelt's prestige with the American people at large suffered appreciably from his defeat on the Court Plan, there can be no doubt that he lost much popular confidence because of the "Roosevelt Recession." This brief but jolting depression began in the fall of 1937 with a sharp drop-off in the New York Stock Exchange. Within weeks many businesses were in trouble and unemployment grew rapidly. While several New Deal economists had foreseen this recession and attributed it to the Administration's newly instituted and essentially conservative budget-balancing policies, they were unable at first to affect decision-making. For months the President stuck by his policies, abetted by such economically conservative advisors as Secretary of the Treasury Henry Morgenthau, Jr. and Secretary of Agriculture Henry A. Wallace. By the early spring of 1938, when the recession showed no signs of letting up, Roosevelt suddenly decided to take the advice of the more committed New Deal spenders such as Secretary of the Interior Harold L. Ickes and Relief Administrator Harry Hopkins. The President asked Congress for a huge relief and public works appropriation and both houses obliged by quickly passing the Administration's bill. This sudden resumption of "pump-priming" had a distinctly favorable effect on the economy. While the experience probably cured FDR of the last vestiges of his economic orthodoxy, it gave his enemies a new weapon—evidence that Roosevelt's much-touted recovery was exceedingly insecure.

The legislative battles over the Court and reorganization proposals and the wages-and-hours law, added to the loss of face suffered by the President over the "Roosevelt Recession," resulted in a division in the Democratic party leadership both in the Congress and in the states. The conservative coalition of Republicans and disaffected Democrats in Congress seemed a very formidable block in the way of any further reforms Roosevelt and his New Deal stalwarts may have had in mind. Indeed, it was not certain by the spring of 1938 that liberal elements would be able to retain control of the party and nominate a 1940 ticket which would uphold the accomplishments of the Administration and pledge to carry them further.

It was in this atmosphere that President Roosevelt embarked upon his celebrated "purge" campaign with one of his radio "fireside chats" on June 24, 1938. In his speech he identified himself as leader of the Democratic party, charged with the responsibility of seeing that its candidates remained faithful to their liberal platform pledges. This pronouncement put Democratic candidates, the incumbent members of Congress and aspirants for the presidential nomination in 1940, on notice that Roosevelt would not support them if their overall record was not in accord with the principles of the New Deal. The highly publicized purge campaign which followed was hastily thrown together and severely limited in its scope, but it had great symbolic importance. Roosevelt's endorsement of several faithful New Deal senators may have helped them to win renomination. His opposition, in their own home states, was too little and too late to bring about the defeat of anti-Administration conservative

Democratic senators in Georgia, South Carolina, and Maryland, but it did warn Democratic officeholders that the President was unwilling to support those party members he felt had betrayed their trust. The purge had one major success, the defeat for renomination of the conservative, obstructionist chairman of the House Rules Committee, Representative John J. O'Connor of New York City. In this race, unlike the senatorial contests in the South, careful preparation and professional management of the Administration's campaign led to success.

The November, 1938, "off-year" elections were held in the ominous atmosphere of the tense weeks which followed the Munich crisis. Roosevelt played no open role in these elections, except for a single radio broadcast in which he endorsed the Democratic ticket in his home state and spoke fondly of a few embattled liberals in other states. Significantly, he did not refer to himself as the leader of the Democratic party, nor did he ask the voters to return a Democratic Congress to power. The elections resulted in the first important Republican gains in a decade, with very strong showings for the GOP in the Northeast and Midwest. Republicans won eight new Senate seats (for a total of twenty-three in the new Congress), eighty-one new House posts (where their total would now be 169), and a net gain of thirteen governorships (making eighteen in all).

While the Democratic party was still dominant, predictions of a Republican demise after the disastrous 1936 election were clearly premature. Republican success in winning control of state governments in Connecticut, Michigan, Ohio, and Pennsylvania (from the Democrats), Wisconsin (from the Progressives), and Minnesota (from the Farmer-Labor party) was particularly significant. Furthermore, the GOP had some badly needed new faces: Robert A. Taft and John W. Bricker, newly elected Ohio senator and governor; Governor Harold E. Stassen of Minnesota; and Thomas E. Dewey, the "racket-busting" district attorney who almost won the governorship of New York from the popular incumbent, Herbert H. Lehman.

President Roosevelt, even though he was increasingly preoccupied with urgent problems of defense and foreign policy, gave no sign that he was going to abandon either his domestic program or his control over the Democratic party. In his annual message of January 4, 1939, he warned of international dangers and stressed his Administration's foresight: "Never have there been six years of such far-flung internal preparedness in our history." In a much-quoted passage he seemed to herald the end of experimentation: "We have now passed the period of internal conflict in the launching of our program of social reform. Our full energies may now be released to invigorate the processes of recovery in order to preserve our reforms, and to give every man and woman who wants to work a real job at a living wage." Three nights later FDR warned his fellow Democrats at the annual Jackson Day dinner that they could expect to retain power for their party "only so long as it can, as a party, get those things done which non-Democrats, as well as Democrats, put it in power to do." The President professed to be pleased at the prospect that the Republicans would now have some strength of their own. "The first effect of the gains made by the Republican Party in the recent election should be to restore it to the open allegiance of those who entered our primaries and party councils with deliberate intent to destroy our party's unity and effectiveness." His message was a simple one: the Democratic party deserved power only if it remained liberal and (as he saw it) responsive to the needs of the people. The implications of FDR's Jackson Day address were clear enough for anyone to see.

The year 1939 brought the Roosevelt Administration a series of domestic set-backs at the hands of a Congress now dominated by a southern Democratic-Republican coalition, especially powerful in the House. The new Republican minority leader of the House, Representative Joseph W. Martin, Jr. of Massachusetts, proved to be highly adept at marshaling his forces behind proposals of anti-New Deal Democrats, often led by his friend Representative Eugene Cox of Georgia. Relief spending was cut drastically and certain programs, notably the Federal Theater Project, were eliminated. The Administration resisted a series of efforts to modify its pro-organized labor policies. The only major piece of domestic legislation passed in 1939 was the Administrative Reorganization Act, a modified version of the rejected 1937-38 bill, important chiefly for its provision permitting the establishment of the Executive Office of the President. Even this measure was not passed without heroic efforts by Administration leaders, indicating how far Congress had gone in its willingness to stifle every proposal coming from the White House.

It was to be foreign policy which would be Franklin Roosevelt's principal concern in 1939. In his January 4 State of the Union Message he warned: "There are many methods short of war, but stronger and more effective than mere words, of bringing home to aggressor governments the aggregate sentiments of our own people." He hinted broadly that he would ask Congress to alter the Neutrality Act of 1937, with its mandatory arms embargo: "At the very least, we can and should avoid any action, or any lack of action, which will encourage, assist, or build up an aggressor. We have learned that when we deliberately try to legislate neutrality, our neutrality laws may operate unevenly and unfairly—may actually give aid to an aggressor and deny it to the victim. The instinct of self-preservation should warn us that we ought not to let that happen any more." Unfortunately for his cause, Roosevelt decided to leave the initiative up to the Democratic leadership of Congress, perhaps sensing that his own growing unpopularity in both houses might imperil his program. The seniority rule, however, was unkind to the Administration. Neither the chairman of the Senate Committee on Foreign Relations, the erratic and bibulous Key Pittman of Nevada, nor the clownish chairman of the House Committee on Foreign Affairs, Sol Bloom of New York, was a competent leader. Leaders of the Senate "peace bloc," such as Arthur H. Vandenberg of Michigan and William E. Borah of Idaho, both Republicans, were more than a match for Pittman. Faced by divided counsels and inadequate aid from the State Department and White House, Pittman allowed matters to drift through the early months of 1939, even after the Nazi take-over of the remains of Czechoslovakia in March made the coming of war to Europe seem closer than ever before. Late in May, at the belated request of Secretary of

State Cordell Hull, Sol Bloom introduced an Administration measure for the modification of the Neutrality Act. Bloom's bill would have repealed the arms embargo and given the President extensive discretionary powers, including the right to designate combat zones off-limits to American vessels. His measure also provided that title to goods exported to belligerents would pass to them before the materials left the United States ("cash-and-carry," as it was dubbed). The committee, by a strict party line vote of twelve Democrats in favor and eight Republicans against, reported the Bloom bill on June 13. With the House Democratic leadership expecting early passage, and trouble in the Senate, the House instead adopted an amendment by John M. Vorys (Republican, Ohio) which retained the embargo on arms and ammunition while lifting it on "implements of war" (things which might be used for peaceful purposes). It was Hamilton Fish, Jr. of New York, who forced the vote on the Vorys amendment; the rollcall on April 30 found the Republicans solidly opposed, 150 in favor to 7 against, while the Democrats were badly divided.

With the adoption of the Vorys amendment, which destroyed the heart of the Administration's bill, attention turned back to the Senate where Pittman was still dragging his feet. The showdown came in a meeting of the Foreign Relations Committee on July 12, when a motion was carried by one vote to postpone any further consideration of neutrality legislation until the next session of Congress (January, 1940, unless summoned earlier by the President). The deciding vote against the Administration was cast by Walter F. George, an old Wilsonian internationalist known to favor repeal of the embargo, but also one of the would-be victims of Roosevelt's 1938 purge. The President tried for one more week to get his bill passed. Finally he summoned a small bipartisan meeting of Senate leaders to see if something could be done. Borah told the gathering that war was not about to break out, regardless of what the President contended: "I have my own sources of information which I have provided for myself, and on several occasions I've found them more reliable than the State Department." Although Borah's words were to attain a sort of immortality of their own, it was what Vice-President John Nance Garner told Roosevelt that mattered, "You haven't got the votes, and that's all there is to it."

When the Nazis invaded Poland on September 1, 1939, and declarations of war by Britain and France followed, President Roosevelt told his people by radio, "This nation must remain a neutral nation, but I cannot ask that every American remain neutral in thought as well." His own dislike of the Nazis and his determination to aid the western Allies was, of course, very widely known. On September 5 he issued two neutrality proclamations, one of the traditional sort, warning Americans against committing unneutral acts, the other in conformity with the Neutrality Act of 1937. This second placed an embargo on the sale of arms, ammunition, and implements of war to belligerents. Roosevelt now had to face the nightmare he had so long worried about, a situation in which Allied control of the seas would be rendered meaningless. Neutrality would favor the aggressor, Germany, since it would deny American war materials to those resisting the Nazis.

Roosevelt decided to call Congress into special session to secure repeal (or at least modification) of the embargo act. This time he prepared his campaign with care, knowing that the matter was far too serious to be left up to people like Pittman and Bloom. First, he cultivated dissident southern Democrats, either directly or through neutral politicians. Second, he sought and found support among the leaders of the business community, long since disaffected as a consequence of the New Deal. Finally, he decided to stress bipartisanship, inviting the defeated 1936 Republican candidates, Landon and Colonel Frank Knox, to attend a White House conference with leaders of both parties in Congress. On September 21, the day after the conference, a grim-faced President made a powerful address to a joint session of Congress. He called for "a greater consistency through the repeal of the embargo provisions, and a return to international law," for the protection of the western hemisphere. He insisted, however, that the Government had the obligation to keep American ships and citizens out of combat zones and he flatly opposed the extension of loans and credits to belligerents. The international lawyer might have had trouble locating precedents for such things, but Franklin Roosevelt was selling a policy and not practicing law, and he knew well that he would have to win votes away from the powerful "peace bloc." Furthermore, the President favored "requiring the foreign buyer to take transfer of title in this country to commodities purchased by belligerents." This requirement and the ban on credits insured that purchases would "be made in cash, and all cargoes . . . be carried in the purchasers' own ships, at the purchasers' own risk."

The isolationists — or "peace bloc" as they liked to call themselves — went into action at once. A group of twenty-four gathered in Senator Hiram Johnson's office and vowed to fight the Administration's efforts. Both Johnson and Borah were now long past their prime, but they had strong supporters among the younger men, including Vandenberg, Gerald P. Nye (Republican, North Dakota), Robert M. La Follette, Jr. (Progressive, Wisconsin), Burton K. Wheeler (Democrat, Montana) and Bennett C. Clark (Democrat, Missouri). It was a skilled, formidable group, but the Administration did not lack able supporters of its own. These included Landon and Knox, former Secretary of State Henry L. Stimson, publisher Henry Luce, and editor William Allen White. The Pittman Bill passed the Senate after prolonged and bitter debate on October 27, by a vote of 63 to 30. Only twelve Democrats voted no, while fifteen Republicans were opposed. The crucial vote in the House came on November 2 over a measure which would have required the House members of the Conference Committee to insist on the retention of the arms embargo. This resolution went down to defeat, supported by only thirty-seven Democrats and opposed by 217; Republicans, however, favored the measure, 142-24. On the final rollcall on the conference committee report, only six Republican senators and nineteen Republican congressmen favored the Pittman embargo repeal bill. The Republican party in both houses of Congress had an almost completely isolationist voting record as 1940 opened. Would this have an effect on the party's chances at winning the election?

Early in 1940 Republican prospects for the presidential campaign were clouded by two puzzling phenomena—the Second World War and Franklin D. Roosevelt. The war was then in what was popularly if inelegantly called its "phoney" stage in western Europe; it was not yet certain whether it would develop into major, bloody strife. Poland had been conquered and Russia was in the process of overwhelming Finland, but Germany and its major western opponents, Britain and France, were holding back. Would a kind of stalemate continue indefinitely and the war never really materialize? Military experts disputed among themselves on this point and many others. Meanwhile, the American Administration pursued its policy of neutrality-in-favor-of-the-Allies and continued to build up its own military strength.

The Roosevelt phenomenon puzzled Democrats and independents as well as Republicans. Indeed, the President kept his intentions about a possible third term a secret from his own intimates; his remarks were either cryptic or evasive, both in public and (apparently) in private. Surviving friends continue to argue about Roosevelt's intentions thirty years later and historians have no really firm evidence about when he decided to do what. All that is certain is that until well into the spring, no one knew for sure what FDR would do in 1940. By that time the phenomenon of the war had also been clarified. Whether there was a cause-and-effect relationship here is not entirely clear, but in the practical politics of the time this scarcely made any difference.

In the early months of 1940 there appeared to be three serious candidates for the Republican presidential nomination: District Attorney Thomas E. Dewey, and Senators Robert A. Taft and Arthur H. Vandenberg. A Gallup poll of Republicans published on March 25 indicated that Dewey was the choice of 43 per cent, Vandenberg of 22 per cent and Taft of 17 per cent; no other potential candidate secured as much as 10 per cent of the sample. Another poll published the same day indicated the Republican nomination prediction of a segment of the voting public at large. A majority (51 per cent) expected Dewey to be the candidate, with 24 per cent picking Vandenberg and 17 per cent Taft. While these and other polls seemed conclusive enough there existed a certain amount of doubt about the strength of each of the three. This doubt would be intensified if the international situation deteriorated—and if President Roosevelt decided to be a candidate again. An assessment of the attributes of the Republican contenders shows clearly enough that the party, resurrected though it was, was still far from robust.

Dewey had two serious shortcomings—his youth and his lack of an important political office. At thirty-seven he was only two years over the constitutional minimum age for the Presidency. When he announced his candidacy in December, 1939, the terrible-tempered Secretary of the Interior, Harold L. Ickes, chortled that Dewey had "thrown his diaper into the ring." This rather nasty jibe, destined to go into the annals of political wisecracks, was quoted frequently and served to remind people of Dewey's youth in a time of crisis. While he was one of the country's most important prosecutors, with a long list of important criminal convictions to his credit, he had lost his bid for the governorship of New York in 1938. Apparently recognizing that he would have to demonstrate his energy and competence before the public if he were to have any chance at the nomination, he entered the presidential preference primaries, and won most of them. With the bulk of his own New York delegation pledged to him plus the convention votes he picked up in the primaries and the popular strength he was shown to have by the opinion polls, Dewey was a formidable candidate by early spring. His brand of Republicanism was a moderate one, as befitted the former running mate of Mayor Fiorello La Guardia, and his foreign policy was one well-suited to the holder of the office of District Attorney of New York County. In essence Dewey was a personality in search of policy as well as power.

Taft, the son of former President William Howard Taft, was a conservative fifty-year-old freshman U. S. Senator from Ohio. Joining the small and not very hardy band of Republicans in the Senate he had soon drawn attention to himself as a relentless, articulate opponent of the New Deal domestic policies and Roosevelt's foreign program. He worked closely with the southern Democrats to become one of the leaders of the Senate's conservative coalition. While it is true that he became a rather tardy convert to the arms embargo repeal in the fall of 1939, this was almost the only blotch on his otherwise-perfect isolationist voting record. Taft's strength lay with the Old Guard Republican organization men and women, the people who still remembered his father with affection and who saw in the son a hope for a restoration of the "good old days" before the First World War. These people may have been naive but they were devoted and hard-working; their strength was concentrated in the Midwest and South. By arrangement with his fellow leader, Governor John W. Bricker, Taft had the powerful Ohio delegation as the core of his convention support. Taft's recent entry into national politics was not the liability it might have been in other times simply because of the previous weakness of his party. He did, however, have one serious shortcoming as a politician, an aloof, almost icy, public personality (quite unlike his affable father's). Taft seemed quite unhappy in the role of political campaigner and indulged in it as little as he could manage. Thus he avoided the primaries and cultivated his fellow professional politicians.

Vandenberg was a veteran senator, a member of the upper house since 1928. Although he was only in his mid-fifties he somehow appeared to be older. A journalist before he entered Congress, Vandenberg seemed to be almost a caricature of the pompous, old-fashioned, spread-eagle orator in manner and appearance; he was a cartoonist's delight. His voting record was slightly more liberal than Taft's, as well as a decade longer, but in foreign policy matters his isolationism was perfectly consistent. It is not clear that Vandenberg was really serious about his candidacy in 1940, although it is possible that he thought that he would win out on the basis of his political experience. It is certain that he did not campaign widely, either out of inertia or over-confidence. When Dewey went to Wisconsin for a whirlwind campaign and displayed his stamina as well as a new-found fondness for isolationism, Vandenberg stayed in Washington. On April 2 Dewey swept the Wisconsin primary, seriously damaging Vandenberg's hopes. When Dewey repeated the feat in Nebraska a week later Vandenberg was typed as a loser even in his own Midwest. Vandenberg's Michigan delegation was his power base but he seemed to be the hero only of the stern, unbending isolationists of the West, still mourning the recent demise of their ancient hero, Borah of Idaho.

In retrospect it can be seen that Dewey, Taft, and Vandenberg were essentially fair-weather candidates. It is quite possible that any one of them might have been nominated and elected President of the United States if the war in western Europe had remained "phoney" and if Roosevelt had decided not to seek reelection. But on April 9, the day of the Nebraska primary, Nazi forces invaded Denmark and Norway; Denmark fell at once, Norway was occupied after three weeks of resistance. On May 10 the Germans launched their *blitzkrieg* against the Low Countries and France. By June 22 the Battle of France was over and an armistice had been signed. German power seemed to many to be invincible; some expected Britain to be bombed into submission or conquered by invasion. Thus by the time the Republican national convention met at Philadelphia on June 24 the world crisis had increased the probability that Roosevelt would run again. It had also emphasized the weaknesses of the three major Republican aspirants.

Fortunately for the Republican party in 1940 there was an alternative (albeit an unlikely one) to the three major candidates for the nomination. Wendell L. Willkie, head of the great Commonwealth and Southern utilities corporation, had been brought to the attention of the American public and especially to the convention delegates by an energetic and well-financed publicity campaign. His emergence as a serious contender for the nomination coincided with the very world crisis which brought trouble to the three apparent front-runners and can only be explained in terms of that crisis. The current edition of *Who's Who in America* listed him as a Democrat. When Willkie arrived in Philadelphia seeking the Republican nomination for President he was told semi-publicly by Old Guard former Senator Jim Watson, "Well, Wendell, you know that back home in Indiana it's all right if the town whore joins the church, but they don't let her lead the choir the first night."

Had the times been "normal" Willkie's nomination by the Republican national convention would have been inconceivable. Forty-eight years old, Indiana-born and educated, Willkie was the son of two active attorneys, themselves the children of German immigrants. He was both a Wall Street lawyer and the head of a privately owned utility and thus he simultaneously held two of the least popular positions a candidate for the Presidency could have had. Furthermore, he had never once run for office and had never even held an appointive post in government at any level.

Wendell Willkie began his own law practice in Akron, Ohio in 1919 and remained there until 1929, when he moved to New York City to join a law firm which represented Commonwealth and Southern. Less than four years later Willkie had risen to the presidency of the corporation at a difficult time, the worst of the Great Depression. Between 1933 and 1939 he became the very symbol of beleagured private enterprise as he sought to defend his private utility in the losing struggle against the Tennessee Valley Authority. Willkie was both a hard fighter and a highly attractive personality, a tousled, rumpled figure, informal and folksy with his Hoosier twang, enthusiastic and very nearly indefatigable. Not until he had been convinced by Supreme Court decisions that his was a losing cause—and until he got the Roosevelt Administration and Congress to agree to limit the area of T.V.A. operations —did he finally quit. He drove a hard bargain when he finally sold his company's properties in its region to the T.V.A. in 1939.

In spite of the Wall Street-utilities connection which made many western progressives permanently suspicious of him, Willkie was no reactionary. Indeed, he was far more of a liberal than a conservative. He was openly sympathetic with much New Deal social legislation and with the labor movement. Unlike most Republicans, he strongly supported the reciprocal trade agreements program. Finally, he was quite convinced that healthy economic growth was attainable with an enlightened policy on the part of the Federal Government. He loved to debate with those who considered the economy "mature" and the unemployment problem permanent.

Nor was Willkie an isolationist. In Ohio he had been an associate and strong partisan of Newton D. Baker, Woodrow Wilson's second Secretary of War and the recognized upholder of the Wilsonian faith. In 1924 Willkie had been a delegate from Ohio to the Democratic national convention at Madison Square Garden, where he had voted (in vain) for an explicit endorsement of American membership in the League of Nations. After this time Willkie's interest in world affairs seems to have diminished for a while, especially after he moved to New York and became deeply involved in the intricate affairs of Commonwealth and Southern. But by the late 1930's Willkie was again identifying himself with his old Wilsonian persuasion in a form now commonly known as "collective security against aggression." He condemned Hitler's Third Reich as the Nazis expanded into central Europe and as they continued their persecution of the Jewish people. Moreover, he advocated the lifting of the arms embargo and other measures to assist Britain and France. By the time the Republican convention met in late June, 1940, Willkie alone among the possible nominees for President had a clear, consistent anti-isolationist position on foreign policy.

It is not at all surprising that among Willkie's ever widening circle of friends and admirers he should have won growing respect as the epitome of the businessman-statesman—and a potentially superb, if highly unorthodox, candidate for the Republican nomination. Contrary to widespread popular belief at the time and to political folklore in the years since 1940, the "Draft Willkie" movement was not an overnight affair which suddenly swept the convention off its feet. Arthur Krock, in his influential *New York Times* column, named him as the "darkest horse" but the one to watch, as early as August, 1939 (when Willkie had at last made his well-publicized peace with the T.V.A.).

By this time a secret Willkie campaign force was already in existence. The prime mover was the youthful and energetic Russell Davenport, managing editor of Henry R. Luce's business magazine, *Fortune*. Davenport's chief early associates were Charlton MacVeagh, a young Wall Street financier with experience in publishing and extensive Republican party contacts, and Frank Altschul, wealthy New York banker, a masterful fund-raiser with impeccable Republican credentials. These three complemented one another; Davenport was expert at publicity; MacVeagh was adept at getting along with party politicians, and Altschul was a near-genius at raising money from the business community. Other important members of the original Willkie team were his close friend and advisor Irita Van Doren, editor of the *New York Herald Tribune* book review section, and Congressmen Bruce Barton of New York, who had entered politics after one of the most brilliant careers in the history of the advertising business.

The Willkie publicity mounted rapidly in the early spring of 1940. But even before then his name had been kept before the public by a widely noticed series of personal and radio appearances and by the publication of a large number of articles by and about him in newspapers and magazines. The mass-circulation *Reader's Digest* ran a piece by him in December, 1939. The liberal weekly *The New Republic* ran another article by Willkie in its March 18, 1940 issue.

But the Willkie campaign really broke into the open with the publication of a piece entitled "We the People" in the April issue of *Fortune*. This article appeared under Willkie's name, although it was largely the work of Russell Davenport, who also contributed an editorial underlining its importance. The main article was a vigorous liberal critique of the New Deal, which it said had "acquired a vested interest in depression." Willkie-Davenport charged that the Administration was defeatist and had retarded economic recovery because of its anti-business bias. Although there were conservative overtones in "We the People," Willkie's essential liberalism came through clearly:

> Some of the recent reforms must be modified in order to protect our power; other, new reforms may have to be introduced. For instance, there has grown up a new concept of public welfare. Our new outlook must include this. Government, either state or federal, must be responsible not only for the destitute and the unemployed, but for elementary guarantees of public health, the rehabilitation of farmers, rebuilding of the soil, preservation of the national forests, clearance and elimination of city slums and so forth.

He particularly stressed the need for increased productivity and left no doubt that he sincerely believed that it could be attained if the Federal Government would only adopt policies "*primarily* for the sake of generating opportunities for private enterprise." Willkie attacked the New Deal for its inability to conquer the Depression; these points appealed strongly to conservatives who might otherwise have been put off by his approval of the Administration's social welfare program. "We the People" took a firm anti-isolationist position in foreign policy, condemning "aggressive countries" and calling for freer world trade and improved standards of living in other parts of the world. Willkie-Davenport concluded, "We do not want a New Deal any more. We want a New World."

One of the many interested readers of the *Fortune* piece was Oren Root, Jr., twenty-eight year old New York lawyer and grand-nephew of former Secretary of State Elihu Root. Oren Root had not yet met Willkie but he had been attracted to him while watching him deliver one of his vigorous speeches. Root was especially impressed with the "petition" accompanying the Willkie article, a brief hard-hitting summary of the people's alleged grievances against Franklin D. Roosevelt. Root decided to have copies of the petition printed for wide circulation and he placed an advertisement in the *Herald Tribune* asking for aid in the distribution of the document. Davenport and his associates had already secured the establishment of about two thousand Willkie "mailing clubs," with the assistance of private utility companies throughout the country. These clubs were alerted by telegram to Root's appeal, and Root and his friends were almost inundated by responses. Davenport was apparently alarmed at what he felt was a premature campaign, but after all it was Davenport who had brought Willkie's candidacy into the open and he could scarcely deny Root the chance to do his own part. This episode indicates that the Willkie campaign was still an amateurish affair, in spite of its strong financial support and of the really talented people involved.

Between April 9, when Root began to mail out his petitions, and June 24, when the Republican national convention met, the Willkie bandwagon picked up speed as well as eminent passengers. The Luce magazines — *Time*, *Life*, and *Fortune* — the Scripps-Howard newspapers (ardent supporters of Roosevelt in 1932 and 1936), the Cowles newspapers in Minneapolis and Des Moines (as well as the Cowles magazine *Look*), and the *New York Herald Tribune* were all enlisted in the cause, although the latter held back its front-page endorsement until June 27. Important supporters were gathered in the business-financial world by Altschul and his associates: Lammont DuPont, Ernest T. Weir, Thomas W. Lamont, Edgar Monsato Queeny, and Joseph N. Pew, Jr. This group was bitterly anti-New Deal and (with the possible exception of Lamont) basically conservative, but they felt drawn to Willkie as one of their own — and as a possible winner. Even the conservative Republican national chairman John D. M. Hamilton was a secret member of the Willkie camp, as was Governor Harold E. Stassen of Minnesota, the convention keynoter. Joseph W. Martin of Massachusetts, Republican minority leader of the House and permanent chairman of the convention, was also a secret Willkie man. Indeed, the convention machinery was completely, if surreptitiously, controlled by the Willkie forces.

Willkie arrived in Philadelphia two days before the convention opened to take charge of his own campaign, a most unorthodox step. Willkie clubs deluged the delegates with thousands of telegrams and uncounted numbers of letters and phone calls. Hundreds of "Willkie amateurs" showed up in person to buttonhole delegates, circulate petitions and in various other ways throw their energies into the fight. The Willkie crusade had an almost religious fervor about it at this stage; it drew its strength from middle-class business and professional people who did not normally engage in political activity and who were generally suspicious of those who did so. The forces of the regular candidates — Dewey, Taft and Vandenberg, as well as the usual favorite sons — hardly knew how to cope with the Willkie drive; one delegate said that his campaign was "unfair to organized politics."

The convention began on Monday, June 24, just four days after President Roosevelt had dramatically appointed important Republicans to the chief defense positions in his cabinet. The new Secretary of War was Henry L. Stimson of New York, who had held the same position under President William Howard Taft and had been Hoover's Secretary of State. The publisher of the *Chicago Daily News*, Colonel Frank Knox, 1936 vice-presidential candidate with Landon, was named Secretary of the Navy. These appointments were intended to give a bipartisan flavor to the Administration, to bring able men into leadership of the defense effort, and (no doubt) to take some of the sting out of the anticipated criticism by Republican orators of alleged negligence in the defense build-up. Needless to say, many Republicans were infuriated by what they considered the apostasy of Stimson and Knox; National Chairman John D. M. Hamilton sought to banish them from the party.

The keynote speaker, Harold Stassen, liberal "boy governor" of Minnesota, did not mention Stimson and Knox, however; his remarks were mostly on domestic matters and his criticisms of Democratic foreign and defense policies were exceedingly general. Congressman Martin, the permanent chairman, a secret Willkie supporter with a consistent isolationist voting record, avoided the war issue in his address to the convention on its second day; he confined his remarks to patriotic pronouncements designed to appeal to his audience. Former President Hoover spoke to the convention that night, blistering the New Deal's record, foreign as well as domestic; if he was trying to stampede the convention into nominating himself he failed, for he roused little enthusiasm among the delegates. The platform plank on foreign policy, finally revised and polished for acceptance on Wednesday, was in line with Hoover's position. It favored "the extension to all peoples fighting for liberty, or whose liberty is threatened, of such aid as shall not be in violation of international law or inconsistent with the requirements of our own defense." This was eminently satisfactory even to such last-ditch isolationists as Congressman Hamilton Fish. At the same time, the vagueness of the plank made it seem flexible to the Willkie people, who decided not to contest it while they were still seeking to win the nomination for their candidate.

A simple majority of the one thousand delegates was necessary. Dewey, the apparent leader, decided that his best chance lay in getting the largest possible vote on the first ballot; if he could get four hundred or so he might be able to count on the bandwagon spirit to bring him the rest. Taft, with his fifty-two Ohio delegates, one hundred more from the South and about one hundred from scattered areas, decided to move cautiously, building up his count from ballot to ballot. Vandenberg had the 38 votes of Michigan and about the same number from various places; his only hope was to win after the leaders became deadlocked. While there were several favorite son candidates, it was evident by the second day that only Willkie was a serious rival for the leaders. That night a secret meeting of emissaries from Dewey and Taft was held, in an effort to settle things on the first ballot. But the Taft people would not step aside for Dewey and the Dewey people would not step aside for Taft. And thus passed the only real opportunity to stop Willkie on the first ballot.

The Willkie strategy was similar to Taft's: begin with a small but respectable vote and add to it from ballot to ballot, as the delegates were freed of their obligations to favorite sons and other faltering candidates. The Willkie managers hoped that this would have the added benefit of not arousing a "stop Willkie" coalition until it was too late. It was well known that many of the delegates in the Dewey camp were tied to their man by only the most fragile of threads. In view of his youth and his rather minor position as a county prosecutor, Dewey did not inspire confidence among those who wanted a man who could win in November. On Wednesday, before the rollcall for nominations began, Governor Stassen officially assumed the role of Willkie's floor manager. Willkie's name was placed in the running as Indiana's favorite son by Congressman Charles Halleck. He replied to those who had stressed their own candidates' long records as party workers by asking, "Is the Republican party a closed corporation? Do you have to be born in it?" After Halleck's speech, Martin recessed the convention until the following morning, allowing time for Halleck's remarks to be widely publicized and for the delegates to ponder the implications of his questions.

The balloting began late Thursday afternoon. Two votes were taken before a dinner recess was called. The totals for the chief candidates were:

	First ballot	Second ballot
Dewey	360	338
Taft	189	203
Willkie	105	171
Vandenberg	76	73

These ballots clearly illustrated Dewey's vulnerability and Vandenberg's continued weakness. They also showed that both Taft and Willkie had reserve strength and that the contest would be between them. After the recess Dewey went steadily downhill: 315 on the third ballot; 250 on the fourth; a mere 57 on the fifth. The corresponding figures for Vandenberg were 72, 61, 42; he, too, was fading fast. On the third ballot Willkie took the lead over Taft and never lost it. Their vote was 259 to 212 on the third; 306 to 254 on the fourth; and 429 to 377 on the fifth. The sixth ballot was the last. As the galleries kept up their chant, "We Want Willkie," delegates began to abandon their favorite sons (including Vandenberg). By the time Virginia cast its vote, Willkie had his majority. As others began to switch, a motion by Governor Bricker of Ohio to make the vote unanimous was carried with a roar.

Wendell Willkie won the Republican nomination for President in the early hours of Friday, June 28. There remained only the problem of choosing a running mate. Congressman Martin, well aware of the way in which the Democrats would put the "Power Trust" label on Willkie, strongly recommended Senator Charles L. NcNary of Oregon, a strong advocate of public power and reclamation projects. McNary's high tariff views and his consistent isolationism were in striking contrast with Willkie's positions, but the veteran western senator would give what the professionals call "balance" to the ticket.

McNary agreed to run with great reluctance and only out of loyalty to the party whose Senate Leader he had long been. When the choice of McNary had been ratified, Willkie appeared briefly before the convention to state that he had made no pledges except to advance "your cause" and to preserve democracy; he promised them a "crusading, vigorous, fighting campaign." With characteristic tactlessness he concluded, "And so, you Republicans, I call upon you to join me." It was a proper climax for a most untypical presidential candidate.

By the time of Willkie's victory at Philadelphia the Democratic party appeared to be destined to nominate Franklin D. Roosevelt for a third term. The President had not yet spoken out about his intentions but he had not eliminated himself from the race. Nor had he disavowed the endorsements he had received from such New Deal stalwarts as Senator Joseph Guffey of Pennsylvania and Governor Culbert L. Olson of California and from certain members of the Cabinet (Ickes, Wallace, Hopkins, and Attorney General Frank Murphy). He flatly refused to discuss his political future at press conferences.

It is noteworthy that those who endorsed FDR for a third term frequently contended that he was the only Democrat who could win in 1940. And, especially after the outbreak of the Second World War, his supporters began to stress his experience in foreign affairs and to do variations on that old political adage, "Don't change horses in the middle of the stream." Roosevelt's own attitude (something always difficult to pin down) was perhaps best expressed in a letter he sent to Colonel Frank Knox at the end of 1939, when he was already trying to get Knox to take a seat in the Cabinet:

> If things continue as they are today and there is a stalemate or what might be called a normal course of war in Europe, I take it that we shall have an old fashioned hot and bitter campaign this Summer and Autumn. Such campaigns — viewing with alarm and pointing with pride — are a little stupid and a little out of date, and their appeal to prejudice does little to encourage a more intelligent electorate. . . .
>
> On the other hand, if there should develop a real crisis such as you suggest — a German-Russian victory — it would be necessary to put aside in large part strictly old fashioned party government, and the people would understand such a situation. If this develops, I want you to know that I would still want you as a part of such an Administration.

While Roosevelt was being cautious, his implication seemed to be that he had little taste for running again unless "a real crisis" developed in Europe; if this were to happen he clearly expected to run and to win. It is notable, however, that FDR did not flatly declare himself out of the race if the European war continued to run "a normal course," even in this private letter to one of the most eminent Republican supporters of his foreign policy.

Meanwhile, several other Democratic candidacies had been at least tentatively considered by the White House. Indeed, the list of people who had been led to believe that they were under consideration, or had convinced themselves that they had been so led, was a very long one. Roosevelt himself certainly encouraged Harry Hopkins, well before the second term was half over. Hopkins was made Secretary of Commerce early in 1939, as part of an obvious build-up but drastic surgery and continued illness put an end to his presidential aspirations.

Others who were encouraged by the White House were Paul V. McNutt and Cordell Hull. McNutt, former governor of Indiana and High Commissioner to the Phillipines, was named as the first head of the new Federal Security Agency in the summer of 1939. McNutt clubs began to appear about the country but his candidacy flickered and died when his campaign failed to win any significant support outside Hoosier circles. On various occasions Roosevelt told Secretary of State Hull that he hoped Hull would be the next President. It is doubtful that Roosevelt was being more than polite to his sixty-eight-year-old Cabinet officer and it is certain that the presidential candidacy of Hull failed to excite many Democratic politicians outside the South.

More important than any of these possibilities for the presidential nomination were two "self-starters," Vice-President John Nance Garner of Texas and Postmaster-General (and Democratic national chairman) James A. Farley of New York. Relations between Roosevelt and his running-mate of 1932 and 1936 had deteriorated since the beginning of the Great Court Fight in February, 1937; by now they scarcely existed. Garner openly opposed much of the later New Deal program and he made no secret of his long-lived isolationism. He was not willing to run again with FDR even if Roosevelt *had* wanted him to do so. In December, 1939, "Cactus Jack" Garner announced that he was willing to accept the presidential nomination. He was not, however, willing to campaign for it since he seemed to find public speaking a great bore. New Dealers, as well as most "regulars" were determined to stop the seventy-one-year-old Garner and they did so in one primary after another, culminating in his utter humiliation in the California election in May. Even in Texas Garner was reduced to the status of a mere favorite son, since Congressmen Sam Rayburn and Lyndon B. Johnson were able to arrange for the delegation to switch to Roosevelt after casting a complimentary vote for Garner.

The candidacy of Farley was a far more difficult matter for the President. FDR had asked his veteran campaign manager to run for governor of New York in 1938, impressing upon Farley that this would be part of a build-up for higher office. But Farley refused to run, preferring to seek the Presidency (or perhaps the Vice-Presidency) in 1940. Early that year he announced that a slate pledged to him had been entered in the Massachusetts primary. The Roosevelt forces, still attempting to placate the valuable Farley, did not oppose his delegation in this primary, the only one Farley contested. In New York, the President vainly sought to secure a favorite-son vote for Governor Herbert H. Lehman; in time a compromise was worked out, giving Farley a sizeable minority of the delegation. The Postmaster General was embittered when he read frequent press reports that he was considered ineligible for the Presidency by many people (including FDR) because of his Roman Catholic faith. Farley was further disappointed by the great party bosses who ran the city and state machines and who had often proclaimed their complete loyalty to him (in exchange, of course, for his many favors to them). They were now quite unwilling to support him because they were convinced that only Roosevelt could carry many of the Democratic state tickets to victory.

Roosevelt summoned Farley to Hyde Park early in July, a week before the Democratic national convention was scheduled to meet in Chicago. The President informed a not-too-surprised Farley what he intended to tell the convention: that he did not seek renomination but was willing to run again if drafted. Farley replied that he would not stand aside, since he disapproved of the third-term candidacy; he also announced that he would soon resign from the Cabinet and from the national chairmanship. Thus the 1940 campaign would have to be managed by someone else. This meeting, which must have been highly unpleasant for both men, terminated a long and mutually profitable friendship.

The Democratic national convention met in Chicago on Monday, July 15, under the watchful eye of Mayor Edward J. Kelly. The mayor, one of the most powerful city bosses of his time, had visited with the President and a group of intimate White House advisors just a week before and was fully aware of FDR's political plans. Kelly, as host to the convention, violated political etiquette when, in his opening greetings, he came out with an endorsement of Roosevelt:

> The salvation of the nation rests in one man, because of his experience and great humanitarian thinking. I think I know that the President has no wish to labor longer under the burden of this office. He has discouraged every advance I have made toward his becoming a candidate. He is not a candidate.
> But this convention faces a world condition that surmounts any man's convenience. We must overrule his comfort and convenience and draft Roosevelt.

That night Farley, as national chairman, addressed the delegates in what many knew would probably be his swan song. He warmly endorsed the record of the Democratic Administration (without mentioning Roosevelt's name) and asserted, "The choice still lies between a party unable to cope with the conditions and problems of the 20th Century and a party which has made this nation the last stronghold of genuine democracy in a world of violence and ruthless force." He pledged his support to the nominees of the convention and to "our successors" in the party organization. Speaker of the House William B. Bankhead of Alabama came next, delivering a lengthy keynote address in which he lauded the Administration's domestic accomplishments in great detail and praised its foreign policy and defense achievements. Like Farley, Bankhead was careful not to mention the President by name.

Even before the convention opened, Secretary of Commerce Harry L. Hopkins, fresh from nearly continuous conferences with FDR and his trusted political associates, had moved into a suite in the Blackstone Hotel to act as the President's personal emissary. A direct telephone line to the White House symbolized his authority. The rumpled, restless, rough-spoken Hopkins, never before involved in any way with a national party convention, had the task of coordinating the communications between Roosevelt and his convention forces. One of his goals was to make the President's renomination as painless and as much like a draft as possible. The other was to see to it that the convention ratified FDR's own choice for his running-mate.

Before Hopkins left Washington he knew that Roosevelt was leaning toward Henry A. Wallace for the vice-presidential nomination; this did not please Hopkins, who had never been one of Wallace's admirers, but he was utterly loyal to the President. Roosevelt's reasons for preferring Wallace are not entirely clear. The Secretary of Agriculture had recently overcome his worries about deficit spending and become a thorough-going New Dealer. Furthermore, he was an ardent, outspoken supporter of Roosevelt's foreign policy. Finally, the President seemed to believe that Wallace, although he had never run for elective office and was only a recent convert to the Democratic party, would have considerable strength in the midwestern farm states where disillusionment with the Roosevelt regime had long been evident.

FDR apparently gave serious consideration to only two other possible running mates, Secretary Hull and Senator James F. Byrnes of South Carolina. Hull was probably passed over because of his age and his lack of enthusiasm for certain New Deal domestic programs. Brynes, a powerful supporter of the Administration as well as a personal friend of the President, had two serious liabilities: he was an ex-Catholic and he was a southerner. His presence on the ticket with Roosevelt would not have strengthened it, and might have brought danger in the North and West, where many voters disliked the racial attitudes of the white South.

Hopkins carried with him to Chicago a longhand letter from the President for delivery to Speaker Bankhead, in which Roosevelt said that he had no wish to remain in office after January, 1941, and asked Bankhead to tell the convention this fact in the course of his keynote address. Roosevelt also toyed with the idea of sending a similar letter to Senator George W. Norris (Independent, Nebraska), long a symbol of nonpartisanship in American public life. But neither letter was delivered, since FDR and his associates concluded that they might not produce the desired effect, a "draft" of Roosevelt by the convention. Bankhead was not very friendly and Norris was not even a Democrat. Instead, on the second day of the convention the President told his press conference that he had sent a message to the delegates. This message was delivered that night at the conclusion of his characteristically rambling speech by the convention's permanent chairman, Alben Barkley of Kentucky, Senate majority leader and faithful New Dealer. Barkley read what Roosevelt had written out for him:

> I and other close friends of the President have long known that he has no wish to be a candidate again. We know, too, that in no way whatsoever has he exerted any influence in the selection of delegates or upon the opinions of delegates.
>
> Tonight, at the specific request and authorization of the President, I am making this simple fact clear to the Convention.
>
> The President has never had, and has not today, any desire or purpose

to continue in the office of President, to be a candidate for that office, or to be nominated by the Convention for that office.

He wishes in all earnestness and sincerity to make it clear that all the delegates to this Convention are free to vote for any candidate. . .

At the conclusion of Barkley's speech the giant amplifying system of the Coliseum blared forth with shouts of "Illinois wants Roosevelt," "America wants Roosevelt," and even "The world wants Roosevelt." These shouts, which stirred up some floor demonstrations, went on for over an hour. Meanwhile, all the microphones in the hall had been cut off, except that reserved for the chairman. Warren Moscow, an enterprising reporter for *The New York Times*, traced the voice to the electrician's office in the basement and found that it belonged to Chicago's Superintendent of Sewers. Moscow discovered that city officer, on special assignment by Mayor Kelly, hard at work on the job of stirring up a demonstration via the loud speaker system. Barkley finally restored order and recessed the convention after midnight. Moscow's discovery was reported in the *Times* and elsewhere and "the voice from the sewer" has ever since been accorded a somewhat inglorious place in the annals of American politics.

On the following afternoon (July 17) the platform, a draft of which Hopkins had brought with him from Washington, was adopted. The President himself had resolved the committee's knottiest problem by advising it to add the words "except in case of attack" to the plank disavowing any intention to "participate in foreign wars" or to send Americans "to fight in lands across the sea." The only excitement over the platform on the convention floor came when a Minnesota congressman sought to amend in an anti-third term pledge; the delegates shouted down his motion.

Roosevelt's renomination was accomplished swiftly that night, but not without some bitterness. Senator Lister Hill, Alabama New Dealer, placed the President's name before the convention in a short but rousing speech; most states, as the rollcall proceeded, seconded the nomination. Three other candidates were formally placed in nomination: Garner, Farley, and Senator Millard Tydings, Maryland conservative and enemy of FDR and one of the targets of the 1938 purge. Farley's nominating speech was made by the aged, bitter anti-New Dealer, Senator Carter Glass of Virginia. But only one ballot was needed. The vote (omitting fractions) was:

Roosevelt	946
Farley	72
Garner	61
Tydings	9
Hull	5

Roosevelt's nomination was made unanimous upon the motion of Farley.

There still remained the problem of a running-mate for the President, since Vice-President Garner was both unwilling and unwanted. Soon after the convention recessed for the night, Mayor Kelly phoned FDR and learned to his dismay that Wallace was still the President's choice. Hopkins phoned Sam Rosenman in the White House to check with FDR's chief speech drafter on the matter. When Rosenman confirmed that Wallace was the one, Hopkins replied: "There's going to be a hell of a lot of opposition. So far there must be at least ten candidates who have more votes than Wallace. It'll be a cat-and-dog fight, but I think that the Boss has enough friends here to put it over." Hopkins was right in every respect.

Delegates who had gone along with the third-term nomination because they felt it was necessary were appalled at the prospect of Wallace as Vice-President. If Roosevelt had not been adamant it is certain that the convention would not have agreed to the Wallace nomination. Wallace was scarcely a Democrat and he had the general reputation of being an aloof, mystical, and impractical person (although his detractors had to admit that he was both an able agricultural scientist and an effective administrator). Few delegates knew Wallace or saw any advantage in his nomination. Eight names were placed in nomination for Vice-President and in the course of the convention deliberations many harsh words were said, both about Wallace and about the dictatorial methods that were allegedly being employed to nominate him. The galleries frequently booed and hissed Wallace's name. Although half of those named withdrew from the contest some did so with ill-concealed bitterness.

Before the actual balloting began, Eleanor Roosevelt spoke to the convention to appeal for unity behind her husband. She had come to Chicago to try to heal the party's wounds and hopefully to secure the acceptance of Wallace by acclamation. Her calm, dignified address—plus the hard practical work done on the floor of the convention by the loyal if somewhat disappointed Senator Byrnes—aided the Agriculture Secretary's cause in the time of crisis. It took only a single ballot, in which Wallace received 626 votes and Speaker Bankhead (his only serious rival) got 329, chiefly from southern and Border States. Roosevelt, in the meanwhile, had been angered by the convention's attitude toward Wallace and had Rosenman prepare drafts of a withdrawal message in case the delegates had refused to ratify his choice of running-mate.

With the nomination of Wallace by the convention, however, Roosevelt was ready to accept renomination. He did so by means of a radio address beginning at 12:25 a.m. on Friday, July 19. In this message he spoke of his "mixed feelings," his "desire for retirement on the one hand, and that quiet, invisible thing called 'conscience' on the other." He said that he had fully intended to retire after his second term but that a public statement to that effect would have tied his hands in the world crisis. He thanked the convention for its endorsement and made it clear that he would not run as a mere Democrat: "But I know you will understand the spirit in which I say that no call of Party alone would prevail upon me to accept reelection to the Presidency." He referred to the many people he had summoned to serve in the country's defense and questioned whether he had the right to "decline to serve my country in my own personal capacity, if I am called upon to do so by the people of my country." He promised to serve if drafted in the election, thanked the convention for the nomination of Wallace ("his practical idealism will be of great service to me individually and to the nation as a whole"), and paid a graceful tribute to Jim Farley.

Roosevelt, in his acceptance broadcast, emphasized that he would be almost completely absorbed by foreign policy and defense matters. He warned, however, that he would campaign under certain circumstances: "I shall not have the time or the inclination to engage in purely political debate. But I shall never be loath to call the attention of the nation to deliberate or unwitting falsifications of fact, which are sometimes made by political candidates." Toward the end of his speech he gave, in a single sentence, a clue to his basic strategy: "If our Government should pass to other hands next January—untried hands, inexperienced hands—we can merely hope and pray that they will not substitute appeasement and compromise with those who seek to destroy all democracies everywhere, including here." It was a somber message, one in which he reiterated his determination to aid victims of aggression and to preserve democracy and freedom. After the unpleasantries and tensions of the convention the clear, dignified address must have been reassuring to many previously disgruntled delegates.

Wendell Willkie, meanwhile, was preparing his campaign against the man he liked to call "the Champ." He resigned his position at Commonwealth and Southern and began to busy himself with the problems of putting together his political team. He had won the nomination with the aid of certain professional politicians, but the impetus behind his drive had come from important parts of the business community and from an intensive propaganda campaign. His personal magnetism was probably his greatest single asset but how could he make it widely felt, in the course of his indictment of the New Deal and his promise of an even newer one? And how could he run as the true liberal he felt himself to be (and to a very considerable extent surely was), while running as the candidate of an essentially conservative party? How could he overcome the suspicions of the professional Republican leaders in many parts of the country who viewed him as an interloper, in order to win their energetic support in the campaign? Finally, how could he compete for attention with the Commander-in-chief at a time when the Administration's defense program was moving swiftly ahead?

These were among the more difficult problems Willkie had to face and they proved to be ones that he never could resolve satisfactorily. While the "Willkie amateurs," symbolized by the almost ever-present Russell Davenport, continued to play a vigorous part in the campaign, the candidate felt that he had to have the fullest assistance of the "pros" who were in close touch with the faithful party workers. Early in July, just before he departed for a three-weeks vacation in Colorado, Willkie appointed Govenor Stassen as the head of an advisory campaign committee of professionals of widely varying ideological persuasions. He also replaced Republican national chairman John D. M. Hamilton with the somewhat reluctant House minority leader, Congressman Martin. Hamilton, a man with more than his share of enemies and

with the reputation of having been the 1936 "architect of defeat," remained as
the well-paid executive director. The affable Martin seemed to Willkie to be
the very epitome of the best type of professional politician, in spite of the fact
that Martin's conservative-isolationist record was a striking contrast with
Willkie's own policy professions. It is very doubtful if Martin had much real
influence outside the House of Representatives Republican membership, a
group with a record like his own. His political acquaintanceship outside the
state of Massachusetts was limited. Willkie's own lack of political experience
was shown by the approach he made to campaign management. Some analysts believed that he relied too much on his "amateurs," often offending the
established leadership by so doing. Others felt that he tried too hard to appease the professionals, of whom he was still in some awe. In retrospect, it
seems clear enough that Willkie did both of these things simultaneously, thus
compounding the already-existing confusion in his campaign.

Willkie publicly asserted that he would be his own speech-writer with the
wisecrack, "I roll my own." This was the remark of a supremely confident
orator, well aware that his articulateness was a large part of his charm but
thoroughly oblivious to the demands of actual, sustained campaigning. He
obviously had no intention of following the fatherly advice of his running-mate,
Senator McNary, who told him at their first encounter, "Don't forget, young
fellow, in politics you'll never be in trouble by not saying too much." Willkie
was inexperienced at reading set speeches in front of the fixed microphones
employed in 1940; he had trouble with his emphases and did not always remember to speak directly into the mike. Furthermore, he had an almost irre-
sistible tendency to ad lib, varying his speeches until newspapermen found
that their advance texts were often of little use. Finally, Willkie never learned
the art of pacing himself—his voice was often rasping and hoarse from over-
use as well as from unnecessary shouting and he himself was often haggard
with fatigue as the campaign wore on.

Willkie began his campaign against FDR with his acceptance speech, delivered to a huge throng at his old home town of Elwood, Indiana, on August
17. It was carefully written but far too long; Willkie doggedly read it through
in the intense heat. The speech was a disappointment to those looking forward to old-fashioned political oratory. While there was a good bit of fire in
the speech, its line of reasoning was scarcely one that would appeal to a mob
of about two hundred thousand crammed into a town of eleven thousand
normal population in the middle of summer. Willkie's shortcomings as an orator speaking before a crowd were evident to all who listened over the radio.

The main argument in the acceptance speech came early, when Willkie
frankly identified himself as "a liberal Democrat who changed his party
affiliation because he found democracy in the Republican party rather than the
New Deal party." He was making an appeal to Democrats as well as independents for support in a crusade to preserve "American liberty." He contended that the Republican leadership, in and out of Congress, had already
joined this crusade. His chief attack on the New Deal was aimed at its alleged
defeatism: "What we need in America is a new leadership that believes in

America. I represent here today the forces that will bring that leadership to you." Willkie insisted that the country was quite unable to live in isolation and expressed his sympathy with the countries which had recently lost their freedoms. "In the foreign policy of the United States . . . I would do everything to defend American democracy and I would refrain from doing anything that injured it." He endorsed the Administration's defense program, generally, and specifically pledged his support to "some form of selective service," as well as to the fullest possible aid to beleaguered Britain. While offering his overall approval to the Administration's expressed aims in foreign policy, he expressed serious doubts about Roosevelt's management of that policy: "There have been occasions when many of us have wondered if he is deliberately inciting us to war." He said that he considered that "it is the first duty of a President to try to maintain peace." He moved on to an endorsement of a long list of New Deal reform measures but argued that these were not enough: "I say that we must substitute for the philosophy of distributed scarcity the philosophy of unlimited productivity." Toward the end he challenged the President to meet him in a series of debates in different parts of the country, to thrash out the "fundamental issues." The Elwood speech put forward the most advanced independent positions Willkie was to put forth during the campaign. Significantly, it was the only campaign speech not composed under stress of time and the only one which Willkie was to read verbatim.

President Roosevelt did not rise to Willkie's challenge to debate. He preferred, as always, to ignore his challengers in public, to choose his own weapons and to follow his own timetable. In his own radio acceptance speech to the Democratic convention a month before, he had announced the circumstances under which he would be willing to speak out on political matters. Roosevelt, although preoccupied with defense and foreign affairs, did not neglect to attend to his political fences. With the resignation of James A. Farley it was necessary to choose a new national chairman. Roosevelt picked his old friend Edward J. Flynn of New York, "Boss of The Bronx," an expert political technician. Flynn, who preferred to keep out of the limelight and did not want to live in Washington, did not succeed to Farley's other job, Postmaster General; another close political associate of the President, Frank C. Walker, was named to this position. Harry Hopkins also withdrew from the Cabinet, partly on health grounds and partly because, after the Chicago convention, he had become a political liability. He was kept out of the subsequent campaign by Boss Flynn, who had a completely free hand in political management and who silenced or exiled several other New Dealers. Secretary Ickes, however, with his marvelous gift for invective and his widespread popularity as "Honest Harold," was highly welcome. Ickes made the Administration's informal reply to the Elwood address with his usual vitriol. His description of the Republican nominee, who had taken such pains in his acceptance address to identify himself as a Hoosier, as "a simple barefoot Wall Street lawyer" was to become another of the 1940 campaign's contributions to the permanent annals of American politics.

Most of the President's time in the summer of 1940 was consumed by matters of defense and foreign policy. He sought and secured from Congress huge defense appropriations; he signed a $4 billion bill on July 20 and another for $5.25 billion on September 6. On August 18, while the Battle of Britain raged on into its tenth consecutive day, he conferred on mutual defense matters with the Canadian Prime Minister, W. L. Mackenzie King, at Ogdensburg, New York. Roosevelt toured defense installations, as he was to continue to do throughout the campaign; while he made no political utterances on these occasions he did command public attention as Commander-in-chief. For one of his most important defense measures, selective service (or "the draft," as it was commonly called), the President sought advance support from Willkie. He did not get it, and he had to content himself with Willkie's endorsement of the principle of selective service in the Elwood address. Passage of the draft act was bitterly opposed by isolationists of both parties, as well as by some who felt that the measure was a dangerous thing to pass in a "peacetime" election year. Significantly, Senator McNary voted in favor of the bill, while Taft, Vandenberg, and most other Senate Republicans voted "no." National Chairman Martin was one of fifty-two House Republicans to vote for selective service; 112 voted against it. With strong Democratic majorities in both houses, and Willkie's moral support, the Administration won passage of the Selective Service Act, which FDR signed on September 16.

In the meanwhile, Roosevelt had sought his opponent's aid on another vital matter, a plan to provide fifty American destroyers of World War I vintage to the British, in exchange for the transfer of a chain of British bases in the western hemisphere. The "destroyer-bases deal" had been under negotiation between the President and Prime Minister Winston Churchill for some time, but it became highly urgent as the British found their position more and more precarious. Early in August FDR phoned the liberal Kansas editor-publisher, William Allen White, to seek his aid in winning the advance endorsement of their mutual friend, Willkie, as well as Willkie's assistance in lining up Republican congressional support. Willkie, finding himself in a very difficult position with his fellow Republicans, declined to commit himself. When Roosevelt secured an opinion from his Attorney General that he could transfer the ships and accept the bases without the authority of Congress, the President again sought Willkie's public support. Once more Willkie declined to join forces with his opponent. The President then went ahead on his own, making a public announcement on September 3. Willkie at once announced that, while he approved of the scheme, he regretted that FDR "did not deem it necessary in connection with this proposal to secure the approval of Congress or permit public discussion prior to adoption." Three days later, after conferring with Senator Vandenberg, Willkie shifted his position. He called the deal "the most arbitrary and dictatorial action ever taken by any President in the history of the United States." Clearly bipartisan foreign policy was going to be out of the question during the two months remaining in the 1940 campaign.

Ten days after the destroyer-bases deal was announced, Willkie began his long campaign-train trips. His journeys took him to Chicago, the Southwest and the Pacific Coast and back, up to New England and the Middle Atlantic states, back to the Midwest, and finally to Madison Square Garden, where he gave his wind-up speech on November 2. The August Gallup polls looked very promising for Willkie, but by the middle of September they indicated that he was running behind in New York, New Jersey, and Pennsylvania and was headed for almost certain defeat. But by mid-October Gallup's interviewers found that the decline in his popularity had been arrested. Illinois, Indiana, and Michigan were reported as switched to Willkie and the campaign now looked like "a horse race." Soon after this, President Franklin Roosevelt announced that he would make a series of five frankly political addresses to reply to those he considered guilty of "systematic and deliberate falsification of the facts." The Roosevelt forces, having felt at the outset that Willkie was a very strong candidate, had been heartened by his popularity slump. Now the President's managers were alarmed at the sudden rise in Willkie's political fortunes.

How was it that Willkie's prestige varied so greatly during the campaign? At the time of his nomination he seemed to be a fresh, attractive personality who might be capable of providing the country with vigorous new leadership —the very kind of leadership which most of the country had felt Franklin Roosevelt had given during his first term. However, during August and September (critical months in the Battle of Britain), the President took some decisive steps in his role as Commander-in-chief. His huge defense program and his firm commitment to aid to Britain were never more prominently displayed —and the polls showed that they were welcomed by most Americans. Two of Willkie's basic arguments—that FDR was not rearming the country quickly enough and that he was holding back prosperity—were seriously weakened, for many people who could see the achievements of the rapidly developing defense boom. While Willkie had long professed his concern for the safety of the British, he had declined to associate himself with the destroyer-bases deal and, after it was announced, had criticized the President's handling of it. Fortunately for Roosevelt, the general public reaction to the ships-bases arrange-, ment was highly favorable; even the bitterly anti-New Deal *Chicago Tribune* approved, although for curious reasons.

Willkie, as he set out on his first campaign swing, was thus already in a difficult position. His weaknesses as a campaigner were soon evident. His first two days were so jammed with speeches, many of them both casual and unprepared, that he badly strained his voice. He showed signs of resentment over the attacks which labelled him an "appeaser" and as the candidate of pro-Nazi elements. At Joliet, Illinois, on September 14, the second day of his trip, he made the flat charge that Roosevelt "telephoned Mussolini and Hitler and urged them to sell Czechoslovakia down the river at Munich." His press secretary had to admit that Willkie had "misspoken." At Peoria the candidate modified his position, although he continued to identify FDR with the Munich appeasement. Willkie frequently coupled this charge with the more tenable contention that Roosevelt's policies had often been isolationist during his first term. Unfortunately for the Willkie cause, the American people seemed much less interested in his rather strained historical interpretations than in the here-and-now problems of national defense and security.

On his western swing Willkie developed his several campaign themes, sometimes in impromptu remarks. At Coffeyville, Kansas, where Willkie had once taught school, he indicted the Administration for being power-grasping and incompetent in its economic programs. In a much-noticed passage he proclaimed that if "you return this Administration to office, you will be serving under an American totalitarian government before the long third term is up." At San Diego the Republican nominee endorsed the aged one-time progressive Senator Hiram Johnson, the very symbol of rigid isolationism, as a "true liberal." At Hollywood Bowl Willkie reminded a crowd of seventy-five thousand of Roosevelt's 1932 promise to cut Government costs by a quarter and of the 1940 Democratic platform pledge that the United States would not participate in a European war. "I hope and pray," said Willkie, "that he remembers the pledge of the 1940 platform better than he did the one of 1932. If he does not, you better get ready to get on the transports." This note was to be repeated again and again, more and more stridently as Willkie began to treat Roosevelt as a warmonger.

At Portland, in the home state of his rather unenergetic running-mate Senator McNary, Willkie sought to remove his "power trust" onus. He denied that he was opposed to federal hydroelectric development projects, although he did say that he was in favor of allowing the people of a region to decide whether the distribution of power should be over publicly or privately owned facilities. At Seattle on September 23 he delivered his last major speech before turning back toward the East. In it he made a vigorous plea for labor support, saying, "Some time back the New Dealers gave up talking about jobs and just talked about unemployment." He reiterated his endorsement of "every one of the social gains that labor has made," including the right of collective bargaining and social security, even promising to expand the latter program. He asserted, in another of his attacks on the Administration's spirit, "The New Deal candidate does not believe there are any more jobs, whereas I know there are." While these remarks must have seemed incongruous when delivered in a city beginning to show all the signs of a defense boom town, they unquestionably represented Willkie's most fundamental thinking on domestic economic policy.

As his campaign train moved east from Seattle it was already evident that it was Willkie's increasingly bitter attacks on Roosevelt's management of foreign policy that were making the strongest impression on the public. He soon discovered, as he toured Michigan industrial cities at the end of September, that he had not won over the workingmen. He found himself booed and jeered, bombarded with fruit and eggs, in scenes of tumult and near-violence. Even his pledge at Pittsburgh to appoint his Secretary of Labor from the leadership of the labor movement — a statement which he must have thought would be helpful to his cause — was marred by his *faux pas*, "And it won't be a woman, either." This was, of couse, a slap at Secretary Frances Perkins, but it was also a slap at the whole feminine sex and the Democrats were able to make the most of it.

During the first half of October Willkie's speeches were increasingly critical of Roosevelt's defense program and of FDR's conduct of foreign relations.
At Philadelphia he charged that the Administration "lacked the ability to get
things done." In a radio speech he contended, "We are being edged toward
war by an administration that is alike careless in speech and action." At Boston on October 11 he promised a huge crowd in a ball park: "We shall not
undertake to fight anybody else's war. Our boys shall stay out of European
wars." Willkie's campaign seemed to be moving ahead at last—the polls were
suddenly more favorable and the Republican leaders began to show confidence in their candidate. It is ironic that it took Willkie's strident charges
that the New Deal had totalitarian leanings, that it was mismanaging national
defense, and that it was blundering into war, to put real life into his campaign.
It had been a long time since Elwood.

The Democratic campaign had been under way all the while the President was being non-political in public. Under the general direction of Chairman Flynn, pro-Roosevelt speakers blistered the Republican congressional
voting record on both domestic and foreign issues and repeatedly reminded
the public of the desperate straits in which FDR had found the country in
1933 and of what the New Deal had accomplished. They tagged the Republican party as the vehicle of isolationism and appeasement; many insisted that
the aggressor nations hoped for the defeat of Franklin Roosevelt. Among the
major spokesman for the Democratic cause were Governor Herbert H. Lehman of New York, Secretary Ickes, Mayor Fiorello La Guardia of New York
City (who said that he favored "Roosevelt with his known faults to Willkie
with his unknown virtues"), Senator Norris of Nebraska (who was perhaps
the foremost spokesman for public power and who did yeoman work in parts
of the country where federal reclamation and power projects were popular),
and the vice-presidential nominee, Henry A. Wallace. Wallace proved to be a
more effective campaigner than most had expected, especially in the areas of
foreign and agricultural policies. One of Wallace's tours lasted from September 22 to October 7; he delivered ten or more speeches a day in twenty-three
states from coast to coast. Indeed, Wallace's energy added much to the Democratic effort to keep up the attack on Willkie.

Roosevelt delivered a rousing defense of his labor record to the Team-
sters Union convention in Washington on September 11, but he began it by
saying that he wasn't able to tell whether he was delivering a political speech
or not. On several other occasions in the next few weeks he gave ostensibly
"non-political" speeches, but they contained political overtones which could
scarcely be missed. At Philadelphia on October 23 he openly entered the
campaign, with the first of a brilliant series of five addresses. These speeches
were drafted by Samuel Rosenman and the playright Robert E. Sherwood,
with some suggestions from the newspaper columnist Dorothy Thompson (a
former enemy of FDR) and the vigorous criticism of Harry Hopkins. As usual,
the President retouched them in his own highly effective style. As set political speeches the five were among the most devastating Roosevelt ever made.
As a group they managed both to reply to Willkie's many charges and simultaneously to put the Republicans on the defensive.

In the Philadelphia address, while referring to many "falsifications," Roosevelt replied in detail to two of them. The first was the charge that he had made secret treaties or agreements to involve the nation in war: "I give to you and to the people of this country this most solemn assurance: There is no secret treaty, no secret obligation, no secret commitment, no secret understanding in any shape or form, direct or indirect, with any other Government, or any other nation in any part of the world, to involve this nation in any war or for any other purpose." Most of the rest of the speech contained Roosevelt's refutation, in great detail, of Willkie's charge that the New Deal had failed to bring about economic recovery. He pointed out that a story in the financial section of *The New York Times* (which was supporting Willkie) said that, "Dreams of business 'flat on its back' must come from smoking campaign cigars or else the speakers are talking about some other country." The President jibed, "Wouldn't it be nice if the editorial writers of The New York Times could get acquainted with their own business experts?" He concluded with a brief statement that the Administration was not arming for a foreign war, but for self-protection. His last sentence was, "It is for peace that I have labored; and it is for peace that I shall labor all the days of my life."

At Madison Square Garden on October 28 FDR gave the second of his five admittedly political speeches, a blistering attack upon the Republican party record in defense and foreign policies. He quoted Representative Fish, former President Herbert Hoover, Senators Vandenberg and Taft, with savage effect. For example, Taft in February, 1940, had asserted that, "The increase of the Army and Navy over the tremendous appropriations of the current year seems to be unnecessary if we are concerned solely with defense." FDR was not going to let the people forget in October what Taft had said in February. He charged that the Republican leadership had been "playing politics with defense" and that they were "playing politics with the national security of America today." He called the roll of the opponents of the repeal of the arms embargo, ending with "a perfectly beautiful rhythm—Congressmen Martin, Barton and Fish." This refrain, which he soon repeated, was received with howls of laughter; it, too, went into the permanent annals of politics.

Two nights later, in Boston, President Roosevelt delivered the third in his series of political speeches. He expanded on his Administration's defense accomplishments, and, contending that he was refuting rumors, assured "the mothers and fathers of America that each and every one of their boys in training will be well housed and well fed." In what was destined to be the most frequently quoted of his campaign remarks of 1940, Roosevelt said flatly: "I have said this before, but I shall say it again and again and again: Your boys are not going to be sent into any foreign wars." Rosenman recalled later that he had suggested that Roosevelt qualify this statement with the phrase, "except in case of attack," as he had done in the past and would do again, but Roosevelt refused with the remark, "If we're attacked it's no longer a foreign war." In the Boston speech Roosevelt dwelt at length on the conservative-isolationist record of the Republican national chairman, Congressman Martin of Massachusetts. And he did not neglect to point out that he was one of "that great historic trio. . . Martin, Barton and Fish." The Boston audience, many of whom must have heard the last speech, joined in the refrain.

Two more Roosevelt political addresses remained, one in Brooklyn on November 1, and the wind-up speech in Cleveland the next night. At Brooklyn Roosevelt referred to "the very strange assortment of political bedfellows who have been brought together in the Republican political dormitory." Although he did not say so, FDR was replying to John L. Lewis, head of the Congress of Industrial Organizations and of the United Mine Workers, whose increasing bitterness toward the President had culminated in his endorsement of Willkie. Roosevelt noted that there had grown up an alliance "forming within the Republican Party between the extreme reactionary and the extreme radical elements of this country." He noted a recent pro-Republican paid advertisement in the Communist organ, the *Daily Worker*. He spoke fondly of his Administration's economic and social accomplishments, achieved in spite of the opposition of Republican leaders, and charged these leaders with hypocrisy in their present professions of support for New Deal reforms.

In the Cleveland speech, which Rosenman considered to be the greatest of all Roosevelt's addresses, the President stuck a positive, idealistic note, giving to his campaign an unusually vigorous and effective conclusion. He spoke of his vision of an America without poverty or monopoly, with economic, cultural, and educational opportunities for all, and a beneficent government guaranteeing to those who work "a fair share in the national income." He spoke of "a great storm raging now, a storm which makes things harder for the world," saying that it was "the true reason that I would like to stick by these people of ours until we reach the clear, sure footing ahead." He concluded: "The spirit of the common man is the spirit of peace and good will. It is the spirit of God. And in His faith is the strength of all America." Although Willkie continued to campaign during the last two weeks before the election, Roosevelt managed to capture public attention. Willkie's speeches, now beginning to show signs of his growing fatigue, were no match for the superlative ones delivered by FDR in what one historian has aptly termed "The Two-Weeks Blitz." Willkie's wind-up address at Madison Square Garden on November 2, delivered after he had listened over the radio to FDR's Cleveland address, was essentially a rather tired summary of his oft-repeated charges against the New Deal and "the third-term candidate."

Suddenly, the bitter, sometimes vicious, frequently confused campaign of 1940 was over. The final Gallup poll gave Roosevelt 52 per cent of the popular vote and Willkie 48 per cent, but indicated a "strong trend" toward Willkie with nineteen states with 274 electoral votes in doubt. For a while, early on election night, the returns from the East looked dangerous for Roosevelt; the President grimly shut himself up with his radio at Hyde Park. But in the end Roosevelt was reelected quite decisively. He won 449 electoral votes to Willkie's 82, with a popular vote margin of nearly five million. Still, Willkie made a considerably better showing against Roosevelt than either Hoover in 1932 or Landon in 1936. He carried a total of 1,147 counties throughout the country; Landon had won only 459. Significantly, Roosevelt was victorious in

every city with a population of more than four hundred thousand, except
Cincinnati. Republicans made a net gain of five national senators and two
governors, although they lost ground slightly in the House.

It is important to note where Willkie's voting strength lay. He carried ten
states — the ever-faithful Maine and Vermont (although by unimpressive margins); politically important Michigan and Indiana (by very close votes); and a
tier of six western farm states — North Dakota, South Dakota, Nebraska,
Kansas, Colorado, and (alas, for Henry Wallace) Iowa. Farm belt disaffection
was a certainty of life in 1940. Close observers noted that Roosevelt had done
poorly, as might have been expected, in areas where there were significant
numbers of voters of Italian, German, or Irish birth or extraction. New York
gave Roosevelt an uncomfortably close margin, approximately 225,000 votes.
Indeed, the New York Democratic vote for the President (45 per cent) was
less than that cast for Willkie (48 per cent); the 417,418 votes FDR secured
as the candidate of the American Labor party, however, more than made up
the difference.

The bitterness between Roosevelt and Willkie was short-lived. They had
been rather friendly enemies during Willkie's Commonwealth and Southern
days. They became political allies soon after the election, when Willkie conceded his defeat with extraordinary graciousness and took to the radio to
plead for an end to internal differences. "We must constitute ourselves a vigorous, loyal and public-spirited opposition," he proclaimed. Soon Willkie was
giving full support to the Administration's foreign policy, including the vital
Lend-Lease Act of 1941, and was even acting as a wartime emissary for his
recent political enemy. In time Roosevelt came to have the highest regard for
Willkie, even to the extent of suggesting that they constitute a coalition ticket
in 1944. Truly the 1940 election has no parallel in American history.

Election of 1952

by *Barton J. Bernstein*

On March 29, 1952, President Harry S. Truman greatly improved the political fortunes of his party by declaring that he would not be a candidate for re-election. His own popularity was near its nadir and his Administration had become a major liability to the Democrats. Many voters blamed the President for our Korean involvement, corruption, Chinese aggression, and communism, as well as high taxes and inflation. A large number of voters had grave doubts about the party that had occupied the White House for almost a generation.

In the normal course of events, the Truman Administration would have been voted out of the office in 1948, but somehow Thomas E. Dewey, the Republican standard-bearer, managed to extract "defeat from the jaws of victory." While Dewey waited for the voters to ratify the judgments of the experts, who predicted a Republican landslide, Truman, fighting vigorously for his political life, pulled together a dispirited party in his "give 'em hell" campaign. He also benefited from the Progressive party, which absorbed much of the taint of communism from the Administration, and from the Dixiecrats, whose bolt placed many white liberals and northern Negroes behind Truman. For his part, the President was successful in patching together the tattered New Deal coalition of urban workers, western farmers, northern Negroes, and southern whites. Furthermore, by concentrating his attack on the GOP right wing (Robert A. Taft, in particular), Truman was able to exploit the fears of a depression and to blame the Republican Eightieth Congress for its anti-labor legislation, its failure to restrain prices, and its "soak the poor" tax cut.

Soon after its victory, however, the unstable Democratic coalition crumbled. Within a year of the election, China fell to the Communists and the Truman Administration was blamed for the defeat of Chiang-Kai-shek. Conveniently forgetting that few in the Republican party had shown much interest in China until late in 1947, the Republicans attacked the Administration. How, asked the GOP, could the Administration commit itself to stopping Communism in Europe and yet propose that Chiang ally with Communists in China? Although few Republicans had been willing to commit American troops to Chiang's aid before the collapse of China, they still saw no contradiction in condemning Truman for not acting to "save" China. Unfortunately for Truman, he had not extended the bipartisan foreign policy to the Far East, and the GOP was not about to share responsibility for the loss of China.

Because the Administration left the American people unprepared for victorious revolutions, and particularly for the fall of China, many troubled citizens defined the problem in unrealistic terms: Why had America "allowed" a Communist triumph? ·Unwilling to acknowledge the limitation of American power, and promised success in the long run by the Administration, they concluded that only bumbling or betrayal could explain the seemingly unexpected Communist victory, and such interpretations were not the monopoly of the Republicans and the right-wing of the Democratic party. In the House, for example, a young Democrat, John F. Kennedy, in discussing China, declared, "What our young men had saved [in World War II] our diplomats and our President have frittered away."

Unfortunately for the Administration, its failure in China coincided with apparent evidence of espionage and subversion—by Alger Hiss, Judith Coplon, and Julius and Ethel Rosenberg. The result was an indictment of the New Deal-Fair Deal government's handling of communism at home. In the view of some, the Democrats had willingly harbored communists, even placed them in positions of power, and thereby betrayed the nation. In 1948, and even earlier, the GOP had tried unsuccessfully to exploit these themes for significant partisan advantage, but the evidence had seemed less impressive and the Progressive party had drawn off the charges of red taint. The apparent failures of the loyalty program, as well as the fall of China, made the Administration even more vulnerable.

The GOP's assaults upon the loyalty and judgment of the Administration were also encouraged by the Administration's fluctuating, and seemingly contradictory, policies in Korea: first, the effort to push North Korean armies back to the thirty-eighth parallel and restore the *status quo ante bellum*; then, the attempt to conquer North Korea and unify the nation; and finally, after the intervention by the Chinese Communists in the autumn of 1950, the acceptance of stalemate, proclamation of limited war, and a shift to more limited objectives. (It was not a "pointless and inconclusive struggle" declared Dean Acheson, in 1951, for the United States had achieved "a powerful victory" by defeating "Communist imperialist aims in Asia" and stopping the communist conquest of Korea.) This final redefinition of aims baffled and angered many citizens who found stalemate an unwise and cowardly policy. "It all fits into a pattern," declared Senator George Malone, Republican of Nevada, "we deliberately lose Manchuria, China, Korea, and Berlin. We follow the pattern of sometimes apparently unrelated events—but it all adds up to losing strategic areas throughout the world."

Some were also suspicious of the Administration's contention that bombing China, particularly the area near Manchuria, would lead to war with Russia. Certainly the Administration's contention was neither self-evident nor necessarily realistic, and it did seem incompatible with earlier assurances that encircling Russia with bases would not lead to war. How, many asked, could bombing China mean war with the Soviet Union when the Administration promised that arming Western Europe and planting U.S. bases around the Soviet Union would not provoke Soviet antagonism? Truman's critics were not denying the Sino-Soviet defense pact; they were simply questioning whether the Soviets would honor it if, as it seemed, the pact meant the sacrifice of Soviet interests and welfare. "The whole Atlantic Pact, certainly the arming of Germany," asserted Taft, "is an incentive for Russia to enter the war before the army is built up. I cannot see that any bombing of China without invasion can be regarded in any way by Russia as an aggressive move against Russia itself, or a reason for war, unless they have made up their minds to start a third world war anyway."

The Administration was also victimized by its own tactical mistakes. In June, 1950, when Truman had committed United States forces to Korea, he had not asked for a declaration of war and thereby he left the GOP free later to criticize his decision. In June, most congressmen endorsed his decision and only a few, like Senator Robert A. Taft, criticized him for acting without congressional authorization. But by the winter of 1950-51, as the Chinese forces overran United Nations positions and American casualties multiplied, many Republicans blamed Truman for entering the war, for refusing to extend the war to China, and for continuing in a war he would not seek to win. For Truman, the price of seeking victory was too high; he feared all-out war, antagonizing suspicious European allies with a "go it alone policy," and the possibility that the United States might lose Europe by becoming bogged down in Asia. For many Republicans a policy of stalemate was less attractive than withdrawal or expansion.

Republicans had long been agitating for the employment of Chiang's troops to open what Minority Leader Joseph Martin, Republican from Massachusetts, ambitiously entitled "a second front in Asia." Looking forward to nearly 800,000 Nationalist soldiers (150,000 was more realistic), he contrasted that number with the 200,000 soldiers in the United States and emphasized that the addition would be "the cheapest operation" possible in Asia. But "if we are not in Korea to win, then this administration should be indicted for the murder of thousands of American boys." Persuaded that the Nationalists had been sold out earlier by the Administration, he warned, "If we want a strategy that will save Europe and Asia at the same time . . ., we must clear out the State Department from top to bottom, starting with Dean Acheson." Though most Democrats opposed the use of Chiang's troops as foolhardy and dangerous, few Democratic congressmen would defend Truman's embattled Secretary of State who, despite his avowed anti-communism and his strategy for building American strength, had become the symbol of appeasement, sometimes even of betrayal.

Many in the GOP were obviously seeking to exploit the issue of the war for partisan advantage, but their analyses were also often sincere and flowed from deep convictions about the use of American power and the nature of American policy. When in April, 1951, Truman fired General Douglas MacArthur, the supreme allied commander in the Pacific, Truman provided an outlet for the nation's pent-up emotions. Expressing the sentiments of many Americans, Senator Joe McCarthy of Wisconsin declared, "The son of a bitch ought to be impeached." All parts of the GOP, stretching from the so-called "internationalist" wing, represented by Dewey and Harold Stassen, to the so-called "isolationist" wing, represented by Taft and Senator Kenneth Wherry, criticized Truman. But it was primarily the latter group who accused Truman of dismissing MacArthur because the United Nations commander wanted to win the war.

MacArthur, justifiably removed after numerous acts of insolence and insubordination, had wanted to take the war to China—by blockading the coast and bombing her industrial capacity—and to use Chiang's troops in Korea, while also allowing Chiang to engage in "diversionary action (possibly leading to counter-invasion) against vulnerable areas of the China mainland." It was MacArthur, himself, who called those who wished to limit the military the "new isolationists"—a term later applied by liberals to MacArthur and his supporters. Challenging the wisdom of the Administration policy, the General concluded that the "only way to prevent World War III is to end the Korean conflict rapidly and decisively." MacArthur, usually more concerned about Asia than Europe, had expanded the Administration's argument that aggression in Asia must be blocked in order to save Europe, thus reaching the dubious conclusion that Europe would remain safe only if communist aggression was defeated in Asia.

Though liberals called such demands irrational, many others found them no less rational than what the Administration was offering—limited war, limited aims, continued bloodshed. If the Administration was right in saying late in 1950 and afterward that Russia might enter the war if China was bombed, then the Administration was probably wrong earlier in the year when Secretary Acheson emphasized that China and Russia were not reasonable allies and that China had good reason to fear Russia. (At the same time, he called the Soviet attempt to control Outer and Inner Mongolia, Manchuria, and Sinkiang "the single most . . . important fact" in Asian developments. He had concluded that the United States, not Russia, could prove to be the friend of China and was obliquely suggesting an ultimate Sino-American rapprochement and the abandonment of Formosa—which angered many Republicans.) Neither estimate was self-evidently valid, but they did seem incompatible. Those Republicans who concluded that the Soviet Union was exploiting China —that nation was a victim of "Russian imperialism," according to Acheson —and was therefore unwilling to go to war to protect her were actually following some of the lines of the Administration's own analysis. These Republicans, however, were unsympathetic to the Administration's argument that an expanded war would destroy the American alliance with Western Europe. Angry that Europe contributed so little to the war, and persuaded that European nations depended upon the American alliance for protection, they were antagonized by Truman's declaration that "We cannot go it alone in Asia and go it with company in Europe."

The GOP blamed the Truman Administration for the war. In fact, members of both parties charged that Secretary of State Dean Acheson had invited red aggression when, in January, 1950, he had defined Korea outside the American defense perimeter in the Far East. The GOP conveniently overlooked General MacArthur's similar statements a few months earlier. Republicans also charged that the Administration had not given South Korea adequate equipment to resist aggression. The GOP conveniently neglected to point out substantial earlier Republican opposition to financial aid for Korea, and the Administration was unwilling to explain publicly that it had not provided heavy armored tanks and other material because the Korean dictator, Syngman Rhee, could not be trusted. ("Some appeaser in the State Department," sneered Taft in 1951, "was afraid that with real arms they might have attacked . . . North Korea.") In the years before the Korean War, American advisers had warned periodically that Rhee might invade the North in an attempt to unify the divided nation, and he had made the most recent of his public threats on this theme only a few weeks before the war started.

Some in the GOP raised another vexing question about foreign policy: If Acheson was wise in January, 1950, when he declared Korea outside the American defense perimeter, why was Korea so vital in June, 1950 or in 1952 and worth defending? The Administration replied obliquely that Acheson had indicated the possibility of the United States, under United Nations auspices, assisting South Korea if she was attacked. The Administration also responded that Korea was the test case of communist aggression, that a communist victory there would unleash the forces of revolution and expansion elsewhere, and that the United Nation's resistance would halt the communist surge. "This is the Greece of the Far East," declared Truman. For many Americans, as the war dragged on and sapped the nations' patience and resources, the Administration's self-defense seemed highly questionable.

Savoring victory in 1952, the Republicans were sure that the voters would repudiate the party of Truman and rectify the "mistake" of 1948. For many in the GOP, the first—ultimately the most—significant battle was the struggle within the party between the liberal and conservative wings. The liberal eastern wing, financed by some of the nation's major financial and industrial firms, had captured the presidential nomination in the past three elections. Led by Dewey, this wing included such prominent men as Senators Henry Cabot Lodge and Leverett Saltonstall of Massachusetts, Ralph Flanders and George Aiken of Vermont, Irving Ives of New York, and James Duff of Pennsylvania; ex-governor Harold Stassen of Minnesota and Governor

Sherman Adams of New Hampshire; it included bankers like Winthrop Aldrich of the Chase National Bank and John H. Whitney of J. H. Whitney Co. and industrialists such as Paul Hoffmann of Studebaker and Thomas Watson of IBM. In foreign policy, this wing, led by Senator Arthur Vandenberg until his death, had endorsed the basic approach of the Roosevelt-Truman foreign policy.

The conservative wing, rooted primarily in the Midwest and financed largely by midwestern interests, was led by Senator Robert Taft of Ohio. It included Senators John Bricker of Ohio, Everett Dirksen of Illinois, Karl Mundt of South Dakota, Homer Capehart and William Jenner of Indiana, Kenneth Wherry of Nebraska, and Joseph McCarthy of Wisconsin. It drew heavy financial support from men like General Robert E. Wood of the Sears, Roebuck Co., and Henry Timken, Jr., of Timken Roller Bearings, and press support from Robert R. McCormick's Chicago *Tribune*. It received advice on foreign policy from men like Arthur Bliss Lane, Truman's former ambassador to Poland, William C. Bullitt, Roosevelt's former ambassador to the Soviet Union, and Generals MacArthur and Albert C. Wedemeyer. Both had served in the Pacific during World War II and were long embittered by the Truman-Roosevelt emphasis on Europe first.

The leading candidate of the conservative forces was Taft, the brilliant "Mr. Republican" who had announced his candidacy in October, 1951. The slightly paunchy figure, with his thinning hair, round face and glasses, was a familiar figure in American politics. The son of William Howard Taft, a graduate of Yale University and Harvard Law School, he was a midwestern patrician. He was also a self-proclaimed foe of the New Deal and Fair Deal at home and abroad. Denied the GOP presidential nomination in 1948, Taft, unlike Wendell Willkie and Dewey, wanted a clear cut departure from Democratic foreign and domestic policies. He was the candidate of the rock-ribbed Republicans who resented the quadrennial dominance of the internationalist, more liberal eastern-wing of the party.

Taft's strictures and attacks were often extreme; for example, he warned that the New Deal, excessive federal spending, and economic planning meant socialism—for him, the end of American liberties. Yet he had actually supported aid to agriculture, public housing, higher minimum wages, expanded social security, and federal grants to education and hospitals. And although he vigorously emphasized economy in government and opposed the welfare state, he was legitimately concerned about unfortunate Americans—estimated by Taft as no less than a fifth of the nation—whom he was prepared to offer what he openly called federal "charity." He opposed price and wage controls immediately after World War II, but he was not a doctrinaire advocate of laissez-faire; he usually put his faith in the free market and distrusted government red tape and bureaucracy. Despite his concern for a balanced budget, he did not believe that the budget had to be balanced annually and, as a result, endorsed the major tax cut in 1945, even though it clearly meant a deficit in 1946.

Fearing bureaucracy and viewing the state as a threat to liberty, he preferred local government, which he assumed was close to the people, to centralized government. He was also generally unconcerned about business power and private restraints on competition, except for labor unions. He also emphasized in the case of labor unions the dangers of leaders misusing funds or of coercing their members. His solution—the Taft-Hartley law—was poorly constructed, though it was not a "slave labor" bill, as labor leaders and the Administration had charged.

So great was his concern with liberty and his fear of the Federal Government that he had opposed the draft in 1940. Along with many congressmen in the early Cold War years, he again was a proponent of voluntarism until reluctantly retreating from this position in 1948 so that America could meet its increased foreign commitments. In combatting communism at home he had shown similar concerns about protecting individual liberty. He was unwilling to outlaw the party and opposed government interference in colleges to root out reds. Taft could on occasion appear foolish, as when he opposed the nomination of David Lilienthal to the chairmanship of the Atomic Energy Commission because the former New Dealer was "soft on Communism." As the election approached, Taft's concern for political liberties seemed to wane and he even supported Joseph McCarthy. First regarding him as reckless, Taft, repudiating his own values, was later quoted as saying that the Senator from Wisconsin "should keep talking and if one case doesn't work out, he should proceed with another." "It was the pro-Communist policies of the State Department which fully justified . . . McCarthy in his demand for an investigation," Taft declared. He also played loosely with the truth when he declared that McCarthy's investigation had been "fully justified by repeated dismissals of employees of doubtful loyalty."

It was in foreign policy, more than in domestic policy, that Taft's position differed from that of the Administration and the eastern wing of the GOP. Taft was more critical of national objectives and more wary of the ways in which American influence was being expanded. Unlike the eastern leaders, he denied that America had a mission to extend democracy abroad, and he warned against trying to impose American democratic institutions in foreign lands. It was not, as was so often charged, that Taft was an isolationist and they were internationalists, but rather that he was usually more conscious of the limitations of American power and less willing to extend American commitments abroad. A supporter of America First before Pearl Harbor, he had denied that Germany constituted an imminent threat to the United States, and therefore he had been considered an isolationist. During the war years, when Soviet-American friendship was a popular theme and American policymakers publicly praised the Soviet Union and its democracy, he warned that the alliance was grounded in common need and common enemies, not common values. In the late war years, Taft, like many Republicans, was a supporter of the U.N., though unlike Vandenberg, then a celebrated internationalist, Taft foresaw more of the world organization's shortcomings and problems, concluding that it would not solve many of the basic problems in international relations. Each wanted the world organization to be an instrument of American foreign policy, but Taft, always more interested in law, despaired that the U.N. could not develop or enforce international law.

Differing with the early Truman foreign policy, as well as the similar policies of the eastern wing of his own party, Taft repeatedly questioned efforts to extend American influence abroad and to establish international peace and prosperity. He challenged their firm belief that the American economy depended significantly on foreign trade, and he doubted whether expanding foreign trade and investment were necessary in order to increase domestic employment or produce prosperity. He did not believe that America was in danger of economic stagnation. Like other critics of earlier American economic expansion abroad, he believed that the domestic market, not the foreign market, was the key to American prosperity and he supported tariffs to reduce foreign competition in the home market. He also feared that greatly increased investments abroad would "build up hostility," not friendship. As a critic of economic multilateralism, Taft, unlike the Administration or the eastern wing, did not have the same faith that the reduction of trade barriers and the expansion of world trade would necessarily reduce world tension and promote peace.

In 1947, Taft objected to Truman's request for military and economic aid to Greece and Turkey and emphasized that America's action was dangerous and provocative. "I do not want war with Russia," he said. Moreover, the Truman Doctrine could mean "domination over the affairs of those countries [which is] similar to Russia's demands for domination in her sphere of influence." Unlike many Americans, he pointed to the dangers of a double standard: "If we assume a special position in Greece and Turkey, we can hardly . . . reasonably object to the Russians asserting their domination in Poland, Yugoslavia, Rumania, and Bulgaria." Reluctantly he acceded to the President's request, lamely explaining that the Senate should not rebuff the Chief Executive on such an important matter and thereby damage his prestige. Taft also supported the Marshall Plan, though he tried often to reduce appropriations and he emphasized the dangers to the domestic economy, contending that exports would contribute to inflationary conditions. Taft drew strong support from the limited number who *shared* his sophisticated analysis, but much of his support on foreign policy came from the larger number who simply mistrusted aspects of America's new role in the world. And it was the latter position which prominent GOP House leaders like John Taber, Joseph Martin and Harold Knutson seemed to represent.

In 1949, when the Administration presented the North Atlantic Treaty to the Senate, Taft led the opposition and tried to break the bipartisan consensus on foreign policy. He denied that Russia was committed to military expansion or that she constituted a military threat to western Europe or the United States. A military alliance with nations on the border of Russia, he stressed, was dangerous and might well provoke Russia into war. In addition, he posed some major legal objections: that the treaty violated the U.N. charter; and that it obligated the United States to send troops and arms to Europe. He was not opposed, however, to the concept of American involvement in Europe and he recommended, in lieu of the pact, that Congress pledge that the United States would retaliate militarily if the Russians attacked western Europe. In effect he was contending that the United States should make explicit its reliance on the nuclear deterrent and extend that protection to western Europe. Because he feared weakening the domestic economy through excessive expenditures for defense and he was reluctant to commit more troops abroad, he emphasized an American defense based on air and sea power. It was not "isolationism" or a "Fortress America" that he was proposing but, rather, a different strategy for defending America and the areas he regarded as useful, though not essential, to her security. Unlike the Administration and the Dewey wing, he did not regard Western Europe (outside Britain) as essential to American security. To defend this area, he was not proposing massive retaliation, but he was offering policies "to deter Russia from military aggression [without being] so provocative as to give Russia a sound reason for such aggression."

Taft was defeated by the bipartisan coalition on foreign policy. They swept away his arguments and stressed that the alliance was essential to stop Russian military expansion into western Europe. (Administration spokesmen, under probing questioning, admitted a different case: the treaty was essential, not to block Soviet expansion, but to bind the European nations together, to restrain impulses for "appeasement," and to strengthen American influence in Europe.)

In. 1951, facing the same bipartisan coalition in the so-called "Great Debate" on foreign policy, Taft, Herbert Hoover, and other conservative Republicans were blocked in their efforts to trim the defense budget, redesign American strategy, and cut American commitments abroad. Like many Americans, Taft and his cohorts were angry that America's European allies had not created large armies for their own defense, and for this reason, having little sympathy for Europe's economic problems, the Republicans favored avoiding what they judged an unnecessary, costly, and dangerous troop commitment to Europe. Europe's paltry armies, even when supplemented by American ground troops, could neither deter nor defeat a Soviet attack, these men concluded.

Hoover, warning of the danger of land war in Europe and fearful of weakening the American economy, recommended that the United States concentrate on the defense of the Western Hemisphere (a "Fortress Gibraltar") and rely upon building up the navy and air force, not the army. Taft, advancing the same concern about the economy, also raised fundamental, strategic objections to building up American forces in Europe: a great increase by the United States might at first provoke an arms race, but if the Soviets feared that they would ultimately lose ground, they might be provoked into attacking first. Put bluntly, if the American build-up was designed to offset the Soviets, and if it would not be completed for about three years, why should the Soviets delay? "If they have no intention to attack," as Taft concluded, "then we don't need the armed forces."

The Administration relied on General Dwight Eisenhower who returned from Europe to testify on behalf of the program. His testimony, however, supported portions of the Taft-Hoover analysis. He did not argue that the addition of American troops would deter or defeat the Russians; he claimed only that American troops would improve the morale of Europeans and make them more likely to expand their own armies and improve their own defense.

In substance, he was agreeing with Taft and Hoover that Europe was primarily responsible for its own ground defense, but he was disagreeing on the *means* of inspiring Europeans to construct that defense. Eisenhower, unlike Hoover and Taft, however, did assert that Europe was essential—not just useful, as Taft purported, or unnecessary, as seen by Hoover—to American security.

When Secretary of Defense George Marshall indicated that the United States intended to send no more than four more divisions to Europe, the debate dwindled to narrow, but important, disputes over presidential power and secrecy. The latter, probably the more important in the long run, received the least attention. Taft and a few others complained that the Administration concealed so much strategic information on the grounds of military security that the Senate could not properly exercise its authority. The Administration and its supporters avoided a direct confrontation on this issue. Instead, they focused upon defending their contention that the President, without explicit authority from the Senate, had the power to commit troops to the NATO defense. The fundamental question was partially resolved by passage of a Senate resolution that "it is the sense of the Senate that no troops in addition to such four divisions should be sent to Western Europe in implementation of the North Atlantic Treaty without further Senatorial approval." On this vote, thirty-eight Republicans and eleven Democrats triumphed over a coalition of thirty-five Democrats and eight Republicans. It was this minority of Republicans, all members of the eastern liberal wing of the party, who sought to protect the GOP and the nation from Taft and his followers by blocking his presidential candidacy.

To stop Taft, the liberal, "internationalist" wing of the Republican party sought a candidate who could win and would maintain the European orientation of the bipartisan coalition on foreign policy. As early as the autumn of 1950, Governor Thomas Dewey had removed himself from the campaign and proposed Dwight D. Eisenhower, "a very great world figure, the president of Columbia University, one of the greatest soldiers of history, a fine educator, a man who really understands the problems of the world."

The popular commander of the allied forces in Europe during World War II, Eisenhower had been coveted by the politicians of both parties since the defeat of Germany. So enamored of him was President Truman in 1945 that he had told him (but later denied), "There is nothing that you may want that I won't try to help you get. That definitely and specifically includes the Presidency in 1948." Though the General's political affiliation was unknown, liberal Republicans had tried to enter him in presidential primaries in 1948 and that year the Americans for Democratic Action had sought to dump Truman in favor of Eisenhower. Although he rebuffed both parties, Eisenhower still remained the favorite hope of many in both parties.

"Nothing in the international or domestic situation especially fits for the most important office in the world a man whose adult years have been spent in the country's military forces," he explained in 1948. "My decision to remove myself completely from the political scene is definite and positive." When he completed his term as Chief of Staff in 1948, he told reporters that he had no presidential ambitions: "I don't believe a man should even try to pass his historical peak. I think I pretty well hit my peak in history when I accepted the German surrender in 1945. Now why should I want to get into a completely foreign field and try to top that? Why should I go out and deliberately risk that historical peak by trying to push a bit higher."

His refusals deterred few. His claims of inadequacy were interpreted as modesty, thereby contributing to his greatness. To politicians and pundits, the amiable General seemed an embodiment of virtue and a potentially powerful political leader. Unlike the arrogant, austere MacArthur who could command respect but seldom affection, Eisenhower was the GI's general—understanding, knowledgeable, sympathetic; in short, a wise father. Born into a Texas family in modest circumstances, reared in Kansas, he became in his own lifetime a legend. With his magnetic grin and personality he was a candidate worthy of a P.R. man's invention. Even his failure as president of Columbia was little known beyond the university, and few politicians or other citizens would begrudge him his interest in football and his lack of interest in education.

Fortunately for Eisenhower, he was quickly lifted out of Columbia when President Truman asked him in late 1950 to become the Supreme Allied Commander in Europe, where he would struggle to create a strong NATO force. Symbolizing collective security and a Europe-first orientation, the General rendered himself an even more attractive candidate. By the spring of 1951, a Gallup poll indicated that 40 per cent of the Democrats favored him for the Presidency while only 20 per cent wanted Truman. Among GOP voters Eisenhower was also the front-runner: Eisenhower, 30 per cent, Taft, 22 per cent, Dewey, 16 per cent, and Earl Warren, governor of California, 13 per cent.

By late summer, 1951, a Draft Eisenhower organization was taking form. Its sponsors were Dewey, Herbert Brownell (Dewey's former campaign manager), Senators James Duff of Pennsylvania, Henry Cabot Lodge and Leverett Saltonstall of Massachusetts, Frank Carlson of Kansas, and Irving Ives of New York; and Governors Sherman Adams of New Hampshire, Val Peterson of Nebraska, Edward Arn of Kansas, Arthur Langlie of Washington, Walter Kohler of Wisconsin, and Dan Thornton of Colorado. At the same time, a group of Eisenhower's friends, including Philip Reed, chairman of the board of General Electric, and General Lucius Clay, then a Wall Street financier-industrialist, were independently organizing to promote Eisenhower. In October, the prestigious *New York Herald-Tribune*, a major Republican paper, endorsed the General, and Lodge, selected by the Draft Eisenhower group, became the campaign manager of the uncommitted candidate.

In 1951 politicians of both parties scurried to SHAPE headquarters to enlist Eisenhower in the presidential race. While the General refused to commit himself and still seemed unwilling to seek the nomination, there is evidence that men on his staff, presumably with his knowledge, were working for his nomination. In November, when he returned to Washington for military talks with Truman, Eisenhower, according to Washington reporter Marquis Childs, seemed to be leaning toward becoming a candidate. The General "held a press conference at which the 'no' was so faint as to become the equivalent of 'yes.'" When reporters asked whether he had authorized Senator

Duff to work on his behalf, he replied evasively, "If I have friends that have been my friends so long they know how I would act and react under given circumstances, that's their own business and I have never attempted to interfere with any man exercising his own privileges as an American citizen." This ambivalence persuaded many that the General was indeed in the running.

Looking back upon this period in later years, Eisenhower stressed the importance of the September visit by Lodge, who implored the General to become a candidate. More than a year before, in June, 1950, Lodge also had discussed the subject with Eisenhower and told him that he might have to run in order to preserve the two party system and avoid permanent Democratic hegemony, the death of the GOP, and what Lodge's biographer, William Miller, calls "the inevitable drift into a third-rate socialism." Eisenhower admitted that if those were the threatening possibilities that his election could forestall, he would run, though "it would be the bitterest moment of my life." In their 1951 meeting, Lodge, emphasizing the need of the GOP and the dangers of deficit spending, inflation and centralization of power, found Eisenhower (as the senator later reported) "in substantial agreement." The party, they concurred, needed someone who would reverse the trend at home but avoid the Old Guard's "fatal errors of isolation." (Eisenhower told a publisher privately: "Taft is no more an isolationist than I am. In fact, he goes farther in some things than I do, not as far as I do in other things, but he certainly is not an isolationist.") "For the first time," Eisenhower later wrote, "I had allowed the smallest break in a regular practice of returning a flat refusal to any kind of proposal that I become an active participant . . . I began to look anew — perhaps subconsciously — at myself and politics." When Truman queried him in December about his political intentions, Eisenhower responded that there had been no change in his "personal desires and aspirations," but he also noted that "fervent desire may sometimes have to give way to a conviction of duty."

What the liberal internationalists had was a prospective candidate willing to be drafted but unwilling to plan a draft or struggle for the nomination. On January 4, 1952, Lodge, acting without Eisenhower's express approval, declared that the General was a Republican and entered his name in the New Hampshire primary. "I will not be repudiated," he told reporters. "Go and ask the General." A day later, Eisenhower confirmed Lodge's statement that he was a Republican but still emphasized that he would not "seek nomination to political office." Stressing the importance of his duties at NATO, he said, "In the absence of a clearcut call to political duty, I shall continue . . . [at this] vital task." Alongside the statement of obligation and duty was an assumption of some arrogance, for Eisenhower was suggesting that the politicians and the party might bestow the nomination on him without even knowing his position on many issues. His supporters put together reprints of his earlier remarks and from these often vague statements the staff tried to piece together his policies.

It was difficult for Eisenhower's opponents to run against the "phantom candidate," as some of Taft's supporters unwisely described the General.

But it was equally difficult for the professional politicians backing him, for they feared that his chief rival would secure delegates while the General presided over NATO. To demonstrate Eisenhower's popularity to politicians and to Eisenhower himself, his backers arranged a late-night rally (*after* a prize fight) at Madison Square Garden in February. Fifteen thousand enthusiastic supporters attended, and the jamboree was put on film, which was immediately flown to Paris for Eisenhower's viewing. To emphasize the growing support, nineteen Republican Congressmen urged him to return and campaign actively for the nomination.

On March 11, in the New Hampshire primary, the first in the nation, the Taft and Eisenhower candidacies met. Actually it was a three-cornered race, with the irrepressibly ambitious Harold Stassen, the youthful ex-governor of Minnesota then on leave from the presidency of the University of Pennsylvania, also an announced candidate and staking out roughly the same terrain on foreign policy that Eisenhower would occupy. Stassen toured the state, and Taft, who had been campaigning in Colorado, moved into New Hampshire. The senator attacked the General for his absence and warned the voters not to support a man without knowing his position. Taft expected defeat but hoped for a close race, feeling he could not afford to let Eisenhower win by default. Against Taft, the Eisenhower forces massed a powerful array of supporters: Governor Sherman Adams, several former New Hampshire governors, and Lodge, who helped win for the General an even greater victory than Taft had feared. The Dewey group had even advertised in New York that New Hampshire voters living in the city could get a free ride home for the primary. Not even MacArthur's telegram to a backer "Suggest you support Taft," could reverse the tide. Eisenhower received 46,661 votes, Taft, 35,838, and Stassen, 6,574. "The way is clear and victory stands at the end for all to see," declared the powerful Washington *Post* in support of the General. From Paris Eisenhower announced his gratitude in characteristically wooden prose. "Any American who would have that many Americans pay him that compliment would be proud or he would not be an American. '

Eight days later his candidacy received an unexpected boost in Minnesota, the home state of favorite son Harold Stassen. A local attempt to put Eisenhower on the ballot, despite the protests of the national organization which wanted to avoid a clash with Stassen, had been rejected because of defective petitions, but the General's supporters in the state decided just five days before the election to launch a write-in campaign. When the votes were counted Eisenhower had been edged by Stassen by only about 20,000 votes (129,076 to 108,692), with Taft, without an organized write-in campaign, a distant third, receiving 24,093 votes. In response to the so-called "Minnesota Miracle," Eisenhower told reporters that he was "astonished." "The mounting number of my fellow citizens who are voting . . . [for] me . . . are forcing me to reexamine my present position and past decision."

During these victories, the Taft organization was working effectively to secure delegates and stressing the Ohio senator's popularity with the people and with GOP rank-and-filers. Repeatedly cast on the defensive by charges that Taft could not win the Presidency and that labor would oppose him, his backers stressed his landslide victory, by the greatest margin in Ohio history, over his Democratic opponent for the Senate in 1950. They neglected to mention that the opponent was a nonentity and that Ohio's popular Democratic governor had backed Taft. The Taft organization also worked feverishly to circulate the results of favorable polls and to conduct their own. In a poll of Republicans shortly before the primaries, Taft received 34 per cent, Eisenhower 33 per cent, and MacArthur, Stassen, and Earl Warren, each 14 per cent. In a poll of House Republicans in February, 81 of 144 responding favored the senator and only 37 preferred the General. By late March, after the selection of delegates was completed in four states (Florida, New Hampshire, Oklahoma, and North Carolina) and almost completed in five others (Minnesota, Tennessee, Pennsylvania, Kansas, and Arkansas), the Associated Press gave Taft 50 delegates, Eisenhower 32, Stassen 22, MacArthur 2, with 18 uncommitted.

During the spring, the Taft forces continued to lead in lining up delegations, though the results in the primaries and state conventions suggested a near stand-off. Eisenhower clearly was more popular on the East and West Coasts, and Taft was stronger in the Midwest. In the Wisconsin primary which the Eisenhower forces did not enter, Taft won a plurality over Warren and Stassen but lost in three congressional districts in and around Milwaukee and Madison, thereby encouraging renewed fears that labor and city voters would oppose him. In Nebraska, where both Eisenhower and Taft were write-in candidates, the Senator won 36 per cent (79, 357) of the votes while Eisenhower received 30 per cent (66, 078), and Stassen, who was on the ballot, got 24 per cent (53,238). It was a bitter campaign in which the Taft organization charged that "Eisenhower . . . is the candidate of those who would have American boys die as conscript cannon fodder thousands of miles across the ocean."

On April 11 Eisenhower asked to be relieved of his duties by June 1, and his campaign organization, then receiving able guidance from Herbert Brownell of the Dewey machine, became more optimistic with the prospect that their man would return in time to meet and court the convention delegates.

Four days after Ike's announcement, the General won the New Jersey primary by almost 160,000 votes over Taft, who had tried unsuccessfully to withdraw after Governor Alfred Driscoll broke his pledge of impartiality and backed Eisenhower. In Massachusetts, all but one member of the Taft slate was defeated by the "unpledged" delegation that represented Eisenhower. Taft, as expected, won in the uncontested primary in his home state, as well as all but one delegate in West Virginia. In the Oregon primary, however, the Eisenhower forces triumphed, as they did at the state conventions in Washington and Connecticut. Both major candidates stayed out of the California primary on June 3, won by Governor Earl Warren—a favorite son, liberal Republican, and dark horse candidate who was hoping for a convention deadlock. The same day, in South Dakota, Taft won a narrow victory over Eisenhower, 64,695 to 63,879.

On June 2, Eisenhower retired from the army and returned to Abilene,

Kansas, his boyhood home, where he enjoyed his second homecoming in seven years. At the celebration he offered the townspeople his counsel: "In spite of the difficulties of the problems we have, I ask you this one question: If each of us in his own mind would dwell more upon those simple virtues—integrity, courage, self-confidence, an unshakeable belief in the Bible—would not some of these problems tend to simplify themselves? . . . I think it is possible that a contemplation, a study, a belief in those simple virtues would help us mightily." That evening the General offered a nationwide audience the same simple thoughts. He was calling for the regeneration of American life. He looked for responsible citizenship and promised that neither "international difficulties nor internal problems . . . [could] defeat the real America." He warned of four threats to American life—disunity at home, inflation and swollen federal spending, the federal bureaucracy, and communism abroad. He proclaimed his faith in "peace with honor" and "reasonable security with national solvency," and concluded that he believed "in the future of the United States."

In the next few weeks Eisenhower actively campaigned for the nomination. Glad-handing delegates as far east as New York, he also made speeches throughout the Midwest and Texas. He opposed socialized medicine, called for the end of price and wage controls "as rapidly as possible," endorsed state ownership of off-shore oil, promised not to send an ambassador to the Vatican, favored reducing the voting age to eighteen, warned of the worldwide communist threat, and urged "sound fiscal practices and integrity in government." In an attack on the Taft-Hoover wing, he warned against those "who preach that we need do nothing except maintain a destructive retaliatory force for use in the event the Russian army should march." He urged support for the UN and, in a clear challenge to Taft, called for support of NATO. He also broke publicly with the Taft-MacArthur Far Eastern strategy by opposing a military victory in Korea because it could lead to a general war. Chiang's troops were needed in Formosa, he further maintained, and could not be deployed in Korea or encouraged in assaults on the mainland.

By July 6, when the Republican convention opened in Chicago, Taft, according to *The New York Times*, led in the number of delegates, with 530 (including 72 contested), needing only 74 for the nomination. Eisenhower had 427 (including 21 contested), with Warren having 76, Stassen 25, 20 scattered, and the other 118 uncommitted. A Gallup poll predicted that in a race against Adlai Stevenson, the General would receive 59 per cent of the vote; against Kefauver, 55 per cent. In contrast, both Democrats received more support than Taft: Stevenson, 45 to the senator's 44 percent; and Kefauver, 55 to 41 percent.

Despite the polls, however, the Taft forces had reason for confidence that the Ohio senator would win the nomination. After all, they controlled the National Committee and therefore were able to dominate the convention machinery, an important asset to a strong candidate. They named General MacArthur, who himself still hoped for a popular draft, as the keynoter, made a Taft supporter the temporary chairman, and loaded the list of speakers with such right-wing senators as McCarthy, James Kem of Missouri, and Harry Cain of Washington. In control of the convention, the Taft forces expected to be able to settle in their own favor the disputes over the sixty-eight delegate seats of Texas, Georgia, and Louisiana. Of the three, the one involving the Texas delegation became a cause célèbre and its resolution shaped the decision on the other two and forecast the outcome of the convention.

The National Committee met in Chicago the week before the convention to settle the disputed delegate issue. The committee promptly refused the request of the Eisenhower camp for telecasts and broadcasts of its deliberations. "Let the people see and hear the evidence," declared Dewey. Guy Gabrielson, chairman of the GOP and a Taft supporter, presented Taft's compromise on the Texas delegation: twenty-two delegates for the senator and sixteen for the General, probably the fairest resolution of the complex problem. Lodge, rejecting the proposal, declared: "General Eisenhower is a no deal man." Undoubtedly Lodge realized that the National Committee, after Taft's offer, had to endorse the compromise, and he saw no advantage in burying an emotional issue that could still be exploited. Planning to appeal to the convention, Lodge believed that the Eisenhower forces might also gain some of the seventeen Georgia and eleven Louisiana delegates that the National Committee had awarded to Taft.

At the convention, the delegates, despite the objections of many Taft supporters, passed the so-called "fair play" amendment named and proposed by the Eisenhower forces—that contested delegates who had failed to receive at least a two-thirds vote by the National Committee could not vote on the credentials of others. Actually, just a few minutes before the opening session, Taft's managers had agreed to the substance of this proposal, but Lodge, who wanted a public victory, rejected the offer and urged support of the "fair play" amendment, which, to his delight, the Taft group refused to endorse on the floor. The wisdom of this strategy was confirmed when Eisenhower won, 658 to 548, on this first test. Truman, recognizing the significance of the vote, remarked with a smile, "I am afraid that my favorite candidate is going to be beaten."

On the convention floor, the court of last appeal, the Taft forces lost on the Georgia delegation, as had been expected, and then they decided to yield on the Texas delegation. Apparently they were unwilling to risk another loss on a rollcall count. Not only had Taft lost some delegates to whom he was probably entitled, but he had also lost moral prestige and his movement had lost momentum. The embittered Taft group tried to regain the initiative by concentrating their attack upon Dewey, who, they charged, was the mastermind of the Eisenhower crusade. They attacked him as "the most cold-blooded, ruthless, selfish political boss in the United States today." During the debate on seating the contested delegation, Senator Everett Dirksen, the Taft representative, contributed to one of the ugly incidents at the conventions, as television viewers watched him point accusingly at Dewey and remark that the GOP "had a habit of winning conventions and losing elections." When Dirksen charged Dewey with taking "us down the path to defeat," and warned, "don't take us down that road again," the Taft delegates began booing the New York governor and then Dewey's supporters assailed Dirksen with boos. Dewey, contributing to the division in the party earlier, had given orders that the New York delegation should absent itself from Mac-Arthur's keynote address.

Taft, not Eisenhower, probably better represented the politics and hopes of the delegates. But many were convinced that he could not win. Echoing this judgment, Clare Booth Luce, delegate from Connecticut and wife of the powerful *Time-Life* publisher, a political enemy of the senator, also argued that Eisenhower's defeat "would be taken by European Communists as the signal that America was going home. It would give Stalin the only real political victory he has had in Europe since the formation of SHAPE." Committed to the same theme, the prestigious *New York Times* ran three editorials entitled "Mr. Taft Can't Win." Reporting from the convention, James Reston wrote, "It is difficult to overestimate the bitterness of the men, now in their fifties and sixties, who have devoted all their mature lives to this political struggle."

According to the estimates of *The New York Times* on the eve of the convention, Taft needed about 75 votes beyond those pledged to secure the nomination. When he lost the three disputed delegations, he needed 120, and his chances waned. Of the delegates either uncommitted or committed to dark horses and favorite sons, Taft could not make sufficient inroads. The 24 Maryland votes, initially pledged on the first ballot to the favorite son, Governor Theodore McKeldin, were released, with Eisenhower getting 16, when the governor was selected to nominate the General. The Minnesota delegation, pledged to Stassen, a longtime adversary of Taft, could not have been lured onto the Taft camp. Nor could Taft have secured Warren's support and the votes of his delegation, for Warren's hopes rested on a deadlock and his Republican politics were antithetical to Taft's. During the second and third days of the convention, when the Eisenhower forces secured majorities in the previously uncommitted delegations from Michigan and Pennsylvania, it was becoming clear that Eisenhower would triumph. In Michigan, powerful Arthur Summerfield entered his camp, and in Pennsylvania, Governor John Fine, after a patronage deal, also joined the Eisenhower camp. Taft also lost thirteen delegates from New York when Dewey, reminding them that he had "a long memory," intimated a loss of patronage should they stay with the Ohioan.

On July 10, the first rollcall confirmed the predictions of observers and the fears of the Taft forces. Before states began switching, Eisenhower secured 595 votes, Taft, 500, Warren, 81, Stassen, 20, and MacArthur, 10. In the South and Far West the candidates were about even, but Eisenhower had run 230 votes ahead (301 to 71) in the Northeast, easily offsetting the senator's lead of 120 votes (232 – 112) in the Middle West. When Minnesota shifted and cast 19 votes for Eisenhower, he officially became the party's nominee. Even then, 280 delegates, 212 from the Middle West, refused to turn their backs on Taft until there was a move by his campaign manager, John Bricker, to make the nomination unanimous.

In looking back upon the race, Taft attributed his defeat to several powerful forces: (1) the New York financial community and interests subject to New York influence, which, despite exceptions like banker Lewis Strauss, strongly backed Eisenhower; (2) many of the influential GOP newspapers, which outside the McCormick, Hearst and Knight chains, "continuously and vociferously" objected to Taft, with many "turning themselves into propaganda sheets for my opponent"; and (3) the opposition of most GOP governors. Taft regretted not having put on a "real primary campaign" in Pennsylvania, New York, Michigan , and Oregon, states whose delegates voted 198-28 for Eisenhower. "The difficulty," the senator noted, "was the tremendous expense involved and the lack of time to make an adequate campaign against newspaper influences."

For Warren and Stassen the convention was the expected disappointment, for MacArthur a source of bitterness. Hoping to be drafted, the vain General, recently second in public esteem behind Eisenhower, was now only a grand old man to the Grand Old Party, to be revered but not fully trusted. Hoover, privately explaining part of MacArthur's weakness, said the General "has an approach to all great questions in the spirit of the St. James version of the Bible . . . He had a Napoleonic bent to put through the ideas which he holds very strongly." Rejected by the GOP, the General ultimately became an unwilling candidate, along with eager Jack Tenney, California's local version of Joe McCarthy, on Gerald L. K. Smith's Christian Nationalist party. The party, gaining a place on the ballot in nine states, affirmed the importance of Christianity, decried traitors in government, and called for MacArthur's "victory" strategy in Asia. It drew support from the extreme right wing of the GOP and underlined the alienation of some of the disgruntled General's loyal supporters but at no time did the split seriously trouble GOP leaders.

In selecting a vice-presidential candidate, the Eisenhower camp had an opportunity to heal party divisions by offering the position either to Robert Taft or to Taft's own candidate, Everett Dirksen. They were unwilling to make that concession. Instead, Eisenhower's advisers chose Richard Nixon. Nixon, a thirty-nine-year-old junior senator from California, had long flirted with the nomination. He offered the party fine geographical balance, an appeal to youth, a record of opposition to corruption, and impressive credentials as a crusading anti-communist. He was also the bête noire of many liberal Democrats because of his red-baiting campaigns in California. "A vote for Nixon is a vote against the Communist-dominated PAC," he had declared in 1946. In 1950, Nixon assailed liberal Congresswoman Helen Gahagan Douglas, who had first been unfairly red-baited by her opponent in the Democratic primary as "a member of a small clique which joins the notorious partyliner, Vito Marcantonio of New York, in voting time after time against measures that are for the security of his country." Nixon had already received recognition and acclaim for his tenacious pursuit of Alger Hiss, a probe that ended with a jury finding that the former New Dealer had committed perjury and with the widely-held conclusion that he committed espionage.

Regarded by many Republicans as a responsible investigator of communism, Nixon also evoked strong sympathy from such anti-communist crusaders in the Taft wing as Senators Jenner, Cain, Kem. His record was eminently acceptable to the Dewey wing. He had supported the Truman Doctrine, the Marshall Plan, NATO, and troops for Europe, though he had voted for some cuts in foreign aid. Like many Republicans, he was fond of blaming Truman for the Korean War and castigating him for the removal of MacArthur. On domestic economic issues he was more willing to use government power than were such staunch conservatives as Martin or Charles Halleck of Indiana but less willing than, say, Jacob Javits of New York. In the Eighty-second Congress, for example, Nixon had generally supported price and wage controls and favored federal support for school construction, but opposed tax reform, expanded public housing, aid to medical schools, and liberalization of the immigration laws.

Described by one journalist as a "Republican meld of Paul Revere and Billy Sunday," Nixon in the preceding two years had become one of his party's more sought-after speakers. The year before in an address, "The Challenge of 1952," he had urged the party to conduct a "fighting, rocking, socking campaign." He attacked the administration for "the whining, whimpering, groveling attitude of our diplomatic representatives who talk of America's fear rather than of America's strength and of America's courage." Sharply critical of Truman's government, he charged that "top administration officials have refused time and time again to recognize the existence of this fifth column . . . and to take effective action to clear subversives out . . . of our government."

The GOP platform represented an uneasy compromise between the Taft and Eisenhower factions and managed by its ambiguities and vagueness to avoid antagonizing either faction. Beginning with a catalog of sins, the Republicans charged the Democrats with depriving citizens of rights, fostering class strife for political purposes, debauching the money system, striving to establish socialism, allowing corruption in high places, shielding traitors, appeasing communism at home and abroad, and plunging the nation into war without the approval of Congress or the "will to victory." They assailed the Administration for past mistakes, affirmed the danger of excessive spending for defense, promised greater preparedness at a lower price, and endorsed the value of collective security. Following Taft and his cohorts, they repudiated "secret understandings such as those at Yalta which aid Communist enslavements," condemned the Administration for losing the peace in Europe and allowing Mao to win in China, and proclaimed the end of containment.

The foreign policy section, drafted by Senator Eugene Millikin of Colorado and Clarence Buddington Kelland, two Taft men, and by John Foster Dulles, a former member of the bipartisan coalition of foreign affairs and a representative of Eisenhower, was prepared without bitter disputes. As early as May, Taft had told Dulles confidentially that his speeches indicated "a large area of possible agreement," suggesting that the two camps could write a mutually acceptable plank. Early in the convention, Dulles confided that he had been instructed by the General's political advisers not to reveal that there would be agreement "for they thought it useful to keep the issues alive." The foreign policy plank followed much of Dulles' recent article ("A Policy of Boldness") in *Life*. There he had called for "liberation" of the captive peoples of Eastern Europe and implied that American opposition to their enslavement and the inspiration of the Voice of America would lead them to revolt against their oppressors. In the platform this theme was more muted: "The policies . . . will inevitably set up strains and stresses within the captive world which will make the rulers impotent to continue . . . and [will] mark the beginning of their end." In short, the GOP was promising "liberation" without much American expense or the use of American troops.

The platform, while pledging the United States to some undefined "aid" to Europe, also contained a subtle rebuke to the European allies who had failed so far to provide the military forces they had promised. Such criticism was certainly compatible with Eisenhower's position as well as with Taft's analysis. Seeking to chart a course between the "China-first" and the Europe-first wings of the party, the platform tried to solve the problem by condemning the Administration for an "Asia-last" policy and implied that both Asia and Europe could be first. Conveniently the party neglected that Eisenhower's own efforts had contributed to the emphasis on Europe and, therefore, to the comparative neglect of Asia.

The party assailed the Administration for past mistakes in Korea: the withdrawal of occupation troops "in the face of the aggressive, primed-for-action Communist military strength"; the announcement that "Korea was no concern of ours"; the commitment of the U.S. to fight "under the most unfortunate conditions." The platform also complained that the Administration did not seek victory: "by their hampering orders they produced stalemates and ignominious bartering with our enemies, and no hope of victory." The GOP, however, was not prepared to endorse MacArthur's strategy of bombing Red China and left unclear what strategy would achieve victory or what victory would mean.

The section on civil rights, particularly when contrasted with the anti-communist crusade, was pitifully weak. The party, aside from condemning bigotry, affirmed the federal government's responsibility to "take action toward the elimination of lynching . . ., the poll tax . . . [and] segregation in the District of Columbia." Retreating from the 1948 platform which implied compulsory FEPC, the 1952 platform emphasized the obligation of states "to order and control [their] . . . domestic institutions" and lamely suggested that the "Federal Government should take supplemental action to further just . . . employment practices." The party, torn between hopes of bringing Negroes back into the GOP fold, on the one hand, and fears of federal power and expectations of making inroads into the South on the other, wrote off the Negro.

Appraising the platform, *The New York Times* concluded that it was "broad enough to cover the diverse elements of the party, vague enough not to offend minority or special interests, and denunciatory enough to provide phrases for the campaign ahead." Its meaning, of course, would be defined in the campaign and later by the man in the White House.

No Democratic candidate could fully escape from the liability of the Administration, but men distant from Truman at least had a chance of asserting their independence. Such a man was Estes Kefauver, the forty-eight-year-old junior senator from Tennessee. Catapulted to fame by the daily national television coverage of his special Senate Crime Investigating Committee, Kefauver had become a familiar household figure as a result of his crusade against crime. An outsider, a foe of conservative Senator Kenneth McKellar, and conqueror of the corrupt Crump machine in Memphis, Kefauver entered the Senate in 1948 after ten years in the House. In Congress he had followed the New Deal-Fair Deal domestic and foreign policies. Troubled by the stalemate in Korea, however, he did differ with the Administration on strategy. He wanted the UN to set terms for a truce, give the Communists a deadline for agreement, and then carry the war to Manchuria if the Communists did not agree.

Emphasizing his independence, he rebuked the Administration for failing to root out corruption. Unfortunately, for him, his expertise seemed unduly restricted, and his war against crime lacked heroic proportions. Also, as a result of his bold investigations, he had uncovered links between organized crime and big city Democratic bosses, which rendered him unacceptable to powerful men in the party. Indeed, Scott Lucas, former Senate majority leader from Illinois who lost his seat in 1950, blamed his defeat on the exposés of the Kefauver committee. In addition, Kefauver's opposition to the filibuster and his support for home rule in the District of Columbia, which southerners saw as an assault upon segregation, made him unacceptable to the South.

A few weeks after Kefauver's declaration and before Truman's withdrawal from the race, two other senators entered the contest—Robert Kerr of Oklahoma and Richard Russell of Georgia. Kerr, however, promised to withdraw if Truman decided to become a candidate, while Russell, who had polled 263 votes in the 1948 convention, asserted that he would remain a candidate regardless. Kerr, the respected junior senator from Oklahoma with only two years experience in the upper house, was near the inner circle of the Senate and had already exercised power in the upper house. Previously a governor of his state and keynote speaker at the 1944 presidential convention, he was a millionaire partner of the powerful oil firm of Kerr-McGee. Because he wore a company button in his lapel, and had used the Congress to advance the interests of his company and the industry, he was sometimes called the "Senator from Kerr-McGee." He generally supported Truman's foreign and domestic policies.

In contrast, Richard Russell was an arch-enemy of the Fair Deal. As head of the southern caucus and chairman of the Armed Services Committee, he was one of the most powerful men in the Senate. He had blocked much of Truman's reform legislation and had maintained an effective alliance with the GOP in opposing the Administration's domestic program. Loyal to the Democrats in 1948, when the Dixiecrats bolted, Russell was clearly a sectional candidate in 1952. His chances were slim, and probably his candidacy was designed primarily to gain leverage within the party for the southern interests. Probably to strengthen his position, he hinted that he might accept a third-party nomination if he failed within his own party.

In the first scheduled primary, in New Hampshire in early March, Kerr and Russell stayed on the sidelines, while Kefauver confronted Truman. To the surprise of the nation, Kefauver defeated the President, 19,800 to 15,927, thereby possibly pushing Truman to announce his withdrawal from the race. In Key West, in 1951, the President had confided to close associates that he would not seek another term, and there is no evidence that he wavered in that decision, but there is also none that he had planned before this defeat to make such an early announcement of his plans. Probably the primary did not shape his decision to withdraw, for he knew that he could have the nomination if he wanted it. But the primary did confirm evidence of mass disaffection for the man and his Administration, and thereby emphasized that he probably could not be reelected.

With Truman's announced withdrawal, the party bosses needed a man who could stop Kefauver. Neither Kerr nor Russell could rally national support, and in the absence of popular rivals the senator from Tennessee was winning primaries. Securing twenty-eight delegates in the Wisconsin primary, in which he was unopposed by Kerr and Russell, Kefauver also won in Nebraska, receiving 64,531 votes to Kerr's 42,467. He continued to win the preferential vote primaries—in Illinois, New Jersey, Massachusetts, and Maryland—but in the first three states the delegates by law remained unpledged. Not until May in Florida, against Russell, did Kefauver suffer defeat in a preferential poll, 368,000 to 285,000, thereby losing nineteen of the twenty-four delegates. That defeat seemed to confirm predictions that Kefauver would not receive any southern votes aside from Tennessee's at the convention and that Russell would carry the South.

The candidate many party leaders wanted was Adlai Stevenson, the scholarly and reflective governor of Illinois. Urged by Truman in January to become a candidate and promised support by the President, Stevenson claimed to prefer to run again for the governorship. Admired for his ability and eloquence, the fifty-two-year-old Stevenson, a midwestern patrician, had established an enviable record: he had cleared up the Republican corruption in Illinois, established a reputation as a reformer, and yet demonstrated that he could work effectively with Jacob Arvey, the Democratic boss of Cook County. Moreover, as a former member of the Roosevelt Administration, Stevenson could claim a portion of the New Deal mantle; and his service as Assistant Secretary of the Navy and Assistant Secretary of State offered the promise of expertise in foreign and military affairs. His chief liability, aside from his comparative obscurity, was that he was a divorced man.

Reluctant to become a candidate despite Truman's offer of support, Stevenson seemed to be favoring W. Averell Harriman, Mutual Security Administrator and former Secretary of Commerce. "If Presidents are chosen for their vision, their courage, and conviction, for their depth of understanding of the meaning of this revolutionary era and the mission of America, you will find them all in [Harriman]," Stevenson declared in late May at a testimonial dinner. As a former ambassador to the Soviet Union for Roosevelt and Truman, Harriman, of all the candidates, was most closely allied with the Roosevelt-Truman Administrations. Even though his experience was largely in foreign affairs, and despite the fact that he was a multi-millionaire, he was acceptable to labor. Within the party, he appealed to the liberal wing and sought to reconstruct the New Deal coalition, but he lacked the organization and support to extend his candidacy much beyond his native state of New York.

On the eve of the Chicago convention, which opened on July 20, the delegates were widely split: Kefauver, 257 1/2; Russell, 161 1/2; Harriman, 112 1/2 Kerr, 45 1/2, and Stevenson, 41 1/2. Stevenson seemed the favorite among party leaders, Kefauver the leader among Democratic voters, and Russell the southern choice.

Truman, opposed to Russell, Kerr, and Kefauver, had given up on Stevenson and recognized that Harriman could not win. In the days before the convention, the President leaned toward Alben Barkley, the popular Vice-President who could, Truman believed, unify his party. A Kentuckian, remembered fondly as the majority leader during the New Deal years, Barkley, was likely to be acceptable to both the northern and southern wings of the troubled party. But labor bosses blocked him, ostensibly because he was too old, but also because they feared that the Kerr-Russell forces might unite behind his candidacy and exercise disproportionate control in the party.

With Barkley rebuffed by labor and forced to withdraw from the race, the convention became a battleground for sectional forces. There were disputes over civil rights and party loyalty, the latter issue emerging in a fight over credentials. It started as a seating contest over the seventy delegates from Texas and Mississippi. The loyalists, representing groups who had backed the national ticket in 1948 and who had promised to do so in 1952, challenged the elected delegates of the states' rights group who some feared would bolt or refuse to support the convention's nominee if a strong civil rights plank was included. The Kefauver and Harriman forces, looking for support (and opposed to the states' rights groups), backed the loyalists. This liberal coalition sponsored a loyalty pledge, approved by the convention over the bitter opposition of the South, that no delegate could be seated unless he assured the Credentials Committee "that he would exert every honorable means . . . in [his] official capacity . . . to provide that the nominees of this Convention . . . or . . . electors pledged to them, appear on the election ballot under the . . . Democratic party." Upon the urging of the President and party officials, the southern coalition finally agreed to a weak pledge: "That for the convention only, such assurance shall not be in contravention of the existing law of the state, nor of the instruction of the state Democratic governing bodies." This compromise allowed the seating of the Texas and Mississippi delegations.

Even under the relaxed rule, however, Louisiana, South Carolina, and Virginia refused to file the required statements. Senator Harry Byrd, the dominant power in Virginia politics, explained, "We're just going to sit here and maybe they'll have to throw us out." When the votes of Virginia were challenged publicly, the convention, on the first reading of the roll, opposed seating the delegates. At first it appeared that the efforts at compromise by Frank McKinney, chairman of the party, and Speaker Sam Rayburn, permanent chairman of the convention, had failed; but the Illinois delegation, presumably under the guidance of Arvey, shifted its votes and led a turnabout. In explaining the shift a year later, Arvey said that he realized suddenly that "the strategy of the Kefauver supporters and the northern liberal bloc was to make impossible demands on the Southern delegates so that they would walk out of the convention" and thereby reduce the opposition to the senator from Tennessee. Completing the defeat of this liberal coalition, the convention also voted to seat the other two states.

On the disruptive civil rights issue, the early position of the liberals was weakened through defection and compromise. From the beginning, it was clear that not even moderate southerners, like Senator John Sparkman of Alabama and Representative Brooks Hays of Arkansas, would accept a platform that included the formation of a compulsory fair employment practices commission. Nor would they accept repeal of the Senate rule on cloture. When some liberals on the twenty-four member Platform Committee agreed to retreat on these issues, a compromise solution engineered by Sparkman and Dawson was hit upon. There was no specific mention of changing the rules of cloture or of establishing a compulsory fair employment practices commission. The final civil rights plank, retreating from the position of 1948, remained wonderfully vague and was, in substance, a surrender to the southern wing of the party.

The nature and politics of this compromise, as well as the hostility of the convention management and the bosses to Kefauver, made it clear that Stevenson was the likely candidate. Long the choice of party officials and considered the man most likely to consolidate sectional factions, Stevenson disclaimed interest in the nomination without, however, asserting unequivocally that he would not run.

Prior to the nomination Stevenson emerges as a man of self-doubt, uneasy modesty, indecision, ambivalence: he would not seek the office nor would he refuse it. He sought power, prestige, and responsibility, but he also felt unworthy, inadequate, unsure. By late June he acknowledged that he would accept a genuine draft, yet he pleaded not to be drafted. Appearing at the caucus of the Pennsylvania delegation, he denied "indecision, . . . coyness and . . . uncertainty." "I couldn't, wouldn't, did not wish to be a candidate for President," he told the group. "I ask you therefore in the spirit of our cause . . . to abide by my views and do not nominate me." Wrote columnist Doris Fleeson, who was close to high-ranking Democrats, "It looks as though . . . Stevenson will be dragged to the Presidential altar, his shrieks are growing fainter, his suitors more importunate."

For many party leaders, Stevenson was an alternative to Barkley, who was too old and rejected by labor; to Russell, who was too clearly identified with the South and segregation; to Kerr, a marginal candidate who represented the oil and gas industries; to Kefauver, who had antagonized party leaders; and to Harriman, who was too liberal and without lustre.

By the fourth day of the convention, July 24, Stevenson, having slowly resolved his ambivalence, decided to become a candidate. The rest of the drama unfolded in roughly predictable form. Although the Kefauver camp tried to launch a "stop Stevenson" movement, other liberals, viewing Stevenson's nomination as inevitable, chose to jump on the band wagon and hoped thereby to move Stevenson away from the southern camp and toward their own political orbit. Truman, without an alternative candidate and once more wanting Stevenson, backed the governor.

The first ballot was highly inconclusive: Kefauver, 340; Stevenson, 273; Russell, 268; Harriman, 123 1/2; Kerr 65; and Barkley, 48 1/2. On the second ballot, Kerr released his votes, Stevenson's vote increased by 50, Russell's and Kefauver's each by 20, and Barkley's by 30. The Vice-President, who had allowed his name to be placed in nomination, had a brief flurry of hope that his candidacy might emerge from a deadlocked convention. His hopes were dashed even before the third-ballot voting had begun. Harriman, as he had earlier promised Stevenson, announced his withdrawal in favor of the Illinois governor. Governor Paul Dever of Massachusetts, a favorite son, followed suit. Shortly thereafter Kefauver tried to announce his withdrawal, but Rayburn, the presiding chairman, apparently eager to rebuke him publicly, denied him this privilege and unwisely refused to let him interrupt the rollcall. At the end of the rollcall but before the results were announced, Stevenson was 2 1/2 votes short of the necessary majority. Kefauver was then recognized and withdrew, followed immediately by Russell. The delegates then made the nomination unanimous. A man largely unknown to the nation or even to party members — except for the eloquent welcoming address he had given the convention as Governor of Illinois — had been chosen by the Democrats in a convention that had so far avoided the schism of 1948.

The next day, in what is usually an anticlimactic decision, the party moved formally to consider a vice-presidential candidate. The leaders were unwilling to risk antagonizing the South with Kefauver, and they could not risk estranging the North with Russell. The ideal candidate would have been one who would placate many in one section and delight those in the other; a suitable candidate, however, need only please one section and not antagonize the other. In order to soften the blow to the defeated candidates, a meeting of leaders, including Stevenson, Rayburn, Truman, and McKinney, decided to exclude from candidacy all who had been contenders for the presidential nomination. Apparently concerned with conciliating the South, they decided to endorse Senator John Sparkman of Alabama, Russell's floor manager at the convention.

Regarded as a liberal on economic matters, he had voted against granting tidelands oil to the states, for price controls and increased public housing, and against the McCarran Act. On foreign policy, he had backed the Administration on the important issues: the Marshall Plan, NATO, arms and troops to Europe, and Point IV. His record on civil rights, however, was unsatisfactory to liberal Democrats. While not succumbing to open racism, he had demonstrated that he would struggle within the party to defend segregation and racial inequality. "If the nomination of Sparkman was a slap in the face of the Negro voters," declared the *Nation*, "it was given a special sting by the dishonest attempt to induce Negroes to accept him as something he is not and to justify his record on the grounds that, after all, a Southern liberal must hedge on civil rights measures."

Sparkman was one of the architects of the compromise on civil rights engineered to bring the South into the fold. So disgruntled were fifty of the black delegates, including Congressman Adam Clayton Powell of New York, that they bolted the convention. "They cram a candidate down our throat," declared Powell, "but they cannot make us vote for him."

On most domestic matters, the platform adhered to the New Deal-Fair Deal liberalism: extension of social security and unemployment assistance, implementation of the public housing program, maintenance of maximum production, repeal of Taft-Hartley and the McCarran-Walter Immigration Act, and continuation of a strong farm program. The party congratulated itself for its loyalty program, which "has served effectively to prevent infiltration by subversive elements and to protect honest and loyal public servants against unfounded malicious attacks." In addition, the platform promised to continue the fight against inflation and, in a clear attempt to run once more against Herbert Hoover, to maintain prosperity.

Undoubtedly the most important section of the platform was the portion devoted to foreign policy. Under the theme of "peace with honor," the party endorsed intervention in Korea, asserted that such action established that the UN would resist aggression, declared that communist aggression had been halted, and promised that the United States would welcome "a fair and effective" peace. In a direct rebuke to the GOP, the Democrats affirmed their commitment to balanced military forces (and not reliance upon the air force) and declared that the economy could support the expenditures that security required. Endorsing collective security, including the Truman Doctrine, the Marshall Plan, NATO, and the Japanese-U.S. military alliance of 1951, the party pledged that it would "not abandon the once-free peoples of Central and Eastern Europe who now suffer under Kremlin tyranny in violation of the Soviet Union's most solemn pledges at Teheran, Yalta, and Potsdam."

The party, proclaiming the accomplishments of the past twenty years, had written a platform defending its past and promising a continuation on most issues of the Fair Deal policies at home and abroad.

For the Eisenhower campaign the initial strategy for victory was well-defined. A "Campaign Plan," prepared by a former advertising man and revised by Eisenhower's advisers, called for the General to court the normal GOP support that was often still attached to Taft and to seek significant inroads among the approximately forty-five million "stay at homes." They, not the four million independent voters courted by Dewey, were deemed the pivotal voters. Recognizing that the GOP was a minority party and assuming that the "stay at homes" would vote if sufficiently agitated, the recommended strategy was to launch a wholesale offensive. The GOP candidate, by attacking, could define the issues. "The whole spirit of a campaign conducted on this level," explained the plan, "would be one which could inspire a crusading zeal that is impossible to engender by the 'me too' approach, or anything which promises only to better what the administration is doing." Eisenhower, conceiving of himself as a candidate who could unify the country left badly divided by Truman's bungling at home and abroad, had been offered a strategy that corresponded with his hopes for a "Great Crusade." He did not then clearly foresee what others would come to lament: the candidate and the program were being merchandised.

In line with the general strategy, Eisenhower consulted with party leaders, consolidated his control of the party, and journeyed to the Midwest to meet with Taft supporters who feared his position on international affairs and who resented his victory over the Ohio senator. In August he also developed the outlines of his tactics; his early speeches criticized the Administration for corruption, stressed its failures in foreign policy, and warned against communism in government and in the nation.

On August 25, appearing before the American Legion in Madison Square Garden, Eisenhower presented his first statement on foreign policy since his acceptance speech. He echoed the themes of "liberation," declaring that the American "conscience" could never rest until the people behind the iron curtain were free, but he carefully avoided specifying the means of freeing them. Like the GOP platform, his declaration offered promises without responsibility, a pledge without tactics. Yet, in words that did frighten some Europeans, he did assert that peace with the Soviet Union was impossible as long as there were captive peoples. He offered an analysis of Soviet goals and strategy — "economic containment and gradual strangulation of America." He explained that the Soviets were aiming to destroy America's productive power and economic strength by slowly gaining control of the many areas (through "infiltration" or "seizure") upon which the American economy depended for critical materials. Stalin, Eisenhower declared, would never attack until the Soviet Union had gathered the materials and men that would guarantee victory. He concluded that America had time, that war was not near, and that a strong military with "great retaliatory power" (the phrase he had earlier deleted from the platform) would deter attack.

He had avoided the slam-bang assault on the Administration that his supporters were counselling. The closest he came to harshness was the complaint that the Administration had allowed the "disintegration" of America's military strength and prestige, and lost China "through . . . false starts, fractional measures, loud politics and faint deeds." He also congratulated the Legion for its efforts in ferreting out communists at home without "recklessly injuring the reputations of innocent people." His critics rightly concluded that he was insensitive to the need to protect civil liberties, while most supporters applauded his acknowledgment of the internal communist menace and the need of private groups to take action. It remained for admirers, following *Time* Magazine, to interpret this statement as a subtle rebuke to Senator Joe McCarthy.

So disappointed were Eisenhower's admirers in the lackluster performance of their candidate, so dismayed were they that he refused to slug the Administration, that sour jokes at his expense soon circulated. One reporter, after a speech by the General, remarked, "He just crossed the thirty-eighth platitude." "Ike is running like a dry creek," declared the front-page editorial of the Scripps-Howard papers. On the public rostrum he continued to be a disappointment; he was vague and lifeless, often poorly informed, frequently indefinite and floundering. Aside from Eisenhower's personal weaknesses, the problem as *Newsweek* explained, was "how to make such a moderate position dramatic and exciting enough to the millions of independent and Democratic voters the Republicans must enlist if they are to win."

For the next few weeks the campaign pepped up somewhat as Eisenhower continued to dwell upon the themes of bungling in Korea and communism and corruption in government — what Karl Mundt, in outlining GOP strategy, called "K_1C_2." On September 4, for example, he lashed out at the Administration: "This Washington mess is not a one-agency mess or a one-bureau mess . . . it is a top-to-bottom mess . . . Washington waste and extravagance and inefficiency; of incompetence in high places and low places; of corruption . . .; of bungling in our affairs at home; of fumbling in the life and death matter of war and peace."

Throughout September, however, the chief concern in the Eisenhower camp was not the General's speeches but two other developments: the rapprochement with Taft and the Nixon Fund. On September 12, Taft, accepting Eisenhower's invitation, journeyed to the presidential candidate's home at Morningside Heights to confer on the campaign. What resulted, labeled by Democrats as "the surrender of Morningside Heights," was a retreat by Eisenhower on domestic policy and the endorsement of many of Taft's positions.

Taft, knowing well the value of his support, had an advance guarantee that the General would meet his demands. The senator brought to the meeting a prepared statement which Eisenhower slightly revised before Taft issued it. Taft declared that they agreed "100 per cent" on domestic policy and "to a large extent" on foreign policy. They agreed also that the issue between the Republicans and Democrats was "liberty against creeping socialism," that the nation needed a "drastic reduction in federal spending" (to $70 billion, not $78.5 billion later proposed by Truman for fiscal 1954, and to $60 billion in fiscal 1955), and that Taft-Hartley was basically right. The statement on domestic policy was a retreat from the position that Lodge and Dewey had earlier staked out for the General, but it was a necessary concession by the victorious forces in the party. On foreign policy, however, despite Democratic charges of "surrender", there was nothing more than a vague phrasing that might be taken as retreat: their differences were simply of "degree." It was a matter largely of symbols, not of substance. Eisenhower's greatest concession was not on matters of policy but on party spoils: he promised, if and when elected, not to discriminate against the Taft wing in making appointments. In return, Taft promised to urge his supporters to work for Eisenhower and the senator agreed to campaign vigorously in thirteen states for the GOP ticket. The "great crusade," quipped Stevenson, had become the "great surrender." He said that the General had sat in the love seat with Taft, "matching pennies against principles." In short, Eisenhower, who had claimed originally to be seeking the GOP nomination to save the nation from Taft, was now embracing him and minimizing differences in order to win the Presidency.

On September 18, Eisenhower's "Great Crusade" stumbled on an unexpected embarrassment: the charges that Richard Nixon had received a private "slush fund" of about $16,000 from California businessmen. Declaring the "existence of a 'millionaire's club' devoted exclusively to the financial comfort of Senator Nixon," the New Deal-Fair Deal *New York Post* broke the story that afternoon under the headline "Secret Rich Men's Trust Fund Keeps Nixon in Style Far Beyond his Salary," and it was promptly picked up by the nation's press and splashed on front pages. For the Eisenhower campaign, which condemned corruption in Truman's government, the charges meant scandal, the besmirching of Eisenhower's case, maybe even the dumping of his running mate. How could Eisenhower promise a clean sweep when his hand-picked vice-presidential candidate, charging the Democrats with a "scandal a day," was taking money under the table?

At first few in the party realized the explosive nature of the charges. Nixon issued a prompt statement: the money, collected by some supporters in the 1950 campaign, had been used to defray the political expenses — for travel, postage, and secretaries — which he felt could not be charged to the Federal Government. Soon the Eisenhower group recognized the danger. The short-run strategy was to delay until the issues could be assessed, until there was more time for public reactions, until advisers could confer. Keeping Nixon could be a liability. But his dismissal might be even more costly. Sherman Adams later reported that Eisenhower had told him privately, "If Nixon has to go, we cannot win." The evening after the *Post*'s story, Eisenhower announced that Nixon would provide a full accounting of the fund. Departing from his prepared text on corruption in government, Eisenhower told a Kansas City audience: "Knowing Nixon as I do, I believe that when the facts are known to all of us, they will show that Dick Nixon would not compromise with what is right. Both he and I believe in a single standard of morality in public life."

The Washington Post and *The New York Herald-Tribune*, which were supporting the GOP ticket, called for Nixon's resignation. Volunteers for Eisenhower across the country joined the chorus. In the New York office of the Eisenhower headquarters most of the nonprofessionals, like Emmet Hughes, the speech writer, favored dumping Nixon. His support came chiefly from the professional politicians. Robert Taft, for example, declared that there was no impropriety in accepting financial assistance as long as there were no favors in return. Adlai Stevenson avoided condemnation and offered a similar standard. (Years later, when Nixon looked back upon what he had first considered Stevenson's charity, he saw it as an effort to avoid disclosure of the governor's own political fund, which was used to assist underpaid officials.)

Two days after the *Post* story, the chief trustee of the fund made public the details of the fund (actually $18,235) and confirmed Nixon's statement that the money was for political expenses. There were seventy-six contributors (the average was $250 and the largest was $1,000) whom *Time* called a "Who's Who of Southern California business" — oilmen, department store owners, bankers, and industrialists. Denying any wrongdoing or any attempt to win influence, he explained that the fund was established "because Dick Nixon is the best salesman against socialism and government control of everything in this country." Allen Haywood, CIO executive vice-president, charged that the businessmen had "earned handsome dividends," and he cited Nixon's support for the oil depletion allowance, his vote against raising the capital gains tax, and his opposition to public housing and rent control.

Nixon, cast on the defensive, lashed out at his attackers. He blamed the "smear" on the "Communists and the crooks in the Government," who were trying to stop his attacks on them. Senator Karl Mundt of South Dakota, co-chairman of the Republican Speakers Bureau, called the assault on Nixon a "filthy" tactic devised by "left-wingers, fellow-travelers," and a "self-admitted three-year member of the Young Communist League," James Wechsler, the anti-communist editor of *The New York Post*.

To regain support Nixon had to take his case to the people; to remain pure but to avoid condemning Nixon, Eisenhower had to let the people decide whether the senator should remain on the ticket. Nixon, partly on the advice of Dewey, presented his case on national television. Appearing on September 23, just five days after the story first broke, Nixon addressed the largest television audience ever assembled to that date. His speech, described variously as a "masterpiece" and a "soap opera," detailed the argument he had made earlier, disclosed information about his debts and the disbursement of funds, jibed at Democrats ("Pat doesn't have a mink coat"), scolded Democratic Senator John Sparkman for having his wife on the payroll, and included a tear jerker: He was putting his future in the hands of the people, but there was one present he would not return, "Checkers", the young cocker spaniel given to his daughters. They loved him too much, and he would not hurt his children. Declaring that his record was unblemished, that he was no "quitter," that he was dedicated to Eisenhower and to driving "the Communists and those that defend them out of Washington," he asked the American people to determine his future by wiring or writing to the GOP National Committee.

In the Cleveland auditorium where Eisenhower was scheduled to speak, nearly fifteen thousand had watched Nixon's performance. "Many women were weeping," reported *The New York Times*. Eisenhower tossed away his prepared speech and discussed the Nixon case: "Tonight I saw an example of courage." Before making a final decision, however, he concluded that he should speak privately with Nixon. The vice-presidential candidate, feeling rebuffed and believing that the General should have immediately offered his public blessing, briefly considered resigning. The deluge of telegrams—nearly 200,000—to the National Committee, as well as the unanimous support of all national committeemen who could be reached, made Eisenhower's decision inevitable and politically safe. At the airport, he met Nixon, announced "You're my boy," and in fatherly fashion put his arm around the shoulder of the man whom some still regarded as the wayward son.

In his speech, Nixon had jabbed at Stevenson, who, it had been revealed, also had a private, secret political fund. The Illinois governor had explained a few days before that he used his fund ($18,700 from his 1948 gubernatorial campaign, and later supplemented by $2,900) "to make gifts, usually around

Christmas time, to a small number of key executives who were making sacrifices to stay in State Government." The real question, in both cases, was not whether the monies swelled the wealth of the candidate but whether the donors received special benefits, though unkind rumors continued to linger around Nixon.

Eisenhower, having made peace with Taft and having weathered the storm over Nixon, still had to maintain unity in the party, particularly in the right wing. After the convention, when asked whether he would back red-hunters like Senators Jenner and McCarthy, the General had declared that he would endorse all GOP candidates but would not support "anything that looks . . . like unjust damaging of reputation." The first major test of this policy occurred in mid-September in Indiana, where the General appeared on the same platform with Jenner, who had called General George Marshall, Eisenhower's former superior, a "front man for traitors," and received from the senator two or three public embraces. "I felt dirty from the touch of the man," Eisenhower later told an associate. When the "Great Crusade" rolled toward Wisconsin, McCarthy joined the campaign train, met with Eisenhower for an hour's conference which the senator told reporters had been "very, very pleasant," and then introduced Eisenhower at one of the stops in Wisconsin. Earlier, among Eisenhower's staff, there had been considerable confusion about whether McCarthy would introduce the presidential candidate. Eisenhower, himself, in one address, when McCarthy was on the campaign train, said: "The differences between me and Senator McCarthy . . . have nothing to do with the end result we are seeking . . . of ridding this government of the incompetents, the dishonest, and above all the subversives and the disloyal. The differences apply to method."

On October 3, in Milwaukee, the General was scheduled to deliver a major address, which included a strong rebuke of McCarthy and a staunch defense of Marshall, whom the senator had called a "traitor." "I know that charges of disloyalty have . . . been leveled against . . . Marshall. I have been privileged for thirty-five years to know . . . [him] personally. I know him, as a man and as a soldier, to be dedicated with singular selflessness and the profoundest patriotism to the service of America." That statement, originally drafted at Eisenhower's request, was also deleted at his request. Apparently when the paragraph was shown to Governor Walter Kohler of Wisconsin, he pleaded, Sherman Adams later recalled, that "it should be omitted since it was out of context and a too obvious and clumsy way to take a slap at a Senator." Under pressure from other state GOP leaders, and his advisers, particularly "Jerry" Persons, Eisenhower concluded that the offending section should be stricken. (Commenting later on the event, Emmet Hughes, author of the offending passage, remarked, this incident "gave warning that certain qualities of the man, even virtues in themself, could be wrenched in the play of politics . . . Clearly, there was in him a profound humility—a refusal to use the full force of his personal authority or political position against a critical consensus.") Pained by the deletion, Arthur Hays Sulzberger, publisher of the powerful, pro-Eisenhower *New York Times*, cabled the General, "Do I need to tell you that I am sick at heart?" Stevenson, who was chided by Eisenhower

for his humor, remarked, "My opponent has been worrying about my fun-
nybone. I'm worrying about his backbone." There was little comment from
Democratic critics when Eisenhower, two weeks later in Cleveland, called
Marshall one of the "great American patriots."

As the Eisenhower campaign seemed in its practices and politics to be
moving toward the right, the General received further assistance from his
running mate and from McCarthy. Nixon, a master of tasteless invective,
called Stevenson "Adlai the appeaser" and a "Ph.D. graduate of Dean Acheson's cowardly College of Communist Containment." He assailed Stevenson
for his "satisfaction with the appeasing, disaster-bent policy of 'containing'
global communism" and for his "soft attitude toward the Communist conspiracy at home." By the middle of October, as the campaign heated up, Nixon
charged that Stevenson had been "duped by Communist Alger Hiss," and he
condemned the Democratic nominee for having testified on behalf of Hiss.
"Can such a man as Stevenson," Nixon asked on a nationwide broadcast, "be
trusted to lead our crusade against Communism?"

Stevenson had been asked in 1949 to testify on the basis of "the speech
of . . . persons [who have known Hiss] what was his reputation" for integrity,
loyalty and veracity. To which the Illinois governor had responded, "Good."
Manipulating that evidence, Nixon challenged Stevenson's judgment and cast
doubts on his loyalty. In response, Stevenson explained that he had had a
responsibility to answer the deposition and that he could not lie: "Hiss' reputation—so far as I had heard from others—was good. [That was] the simple,
exact, whole truth." Stevenson also pointed out that Dulles, in 1946, before
Hiss was installed as president of the Carnegie Endowment, of which the
Republican foreign policy expert was president of the Board of Trustees, had
been told that Hiss had a "Communist record" and was offered evidence to
support the charge. Dulles rebuffed the informer and affirmed his confidence
in Hiss' "complete loyalty." Moreover, the Board, including Dulles and Eisenhower, later rejected Hiss' resignation after he was indicted, and instead
granted him a leave of absence. Despite Stevenson's efforts in his own defense, and even his charges against Dulles and Eisenhower, Nixon's attacks
helped to blame the Democrats for subversion at home and communist victories abroad. Eisenhower, while not dwelling on the theme, was willing to exploit the same charges. The Administration, he declared, had "allowed the
godless Red tide to . . . engulf millions [and had] failed to see the Red stain
seeping into the most vital offices of our Government."

McCarthy, in his campaigning, hit on the same themes. On October 28,
just eight days before the election, McCarthy delivered a nationwide address
devoted to establishing that Stevenson aided the communist cause. Twice
during the speech McCarthy called Adlai "Alger." Inventing falsehoods, fab-
ricating quotes, and misusing evidence, he charged Stevenson with "conniving" with communists in 1943 and surrounding himself with such allegedly
pro-communist advisers as Arthur Schlesinger, jr., Wilson Wyatt, James
Wechsler, and Archibald MacLeish. He conveniently overlooked the anti-
communism of these notable liberals and of the ADA, which he found red-

tainted, and he stated falsely that the Communist party was supporting Stevenson in 1952. Governor Sherman Adams, offended by McCarthy's vicious onslaught, dissociated himself from the senator and hoped that the speech would not cost Eisenhower votes. The General remained silent. The Democratic party promptly rebutted McCarthy's charges, stressed Stevenson's anticommunism and that of his advisers, and emphasized that the *Daily Worker* was not supporting the Democratic nominee.

Earlier, when Arthur Summerfield, Eisenhower's appointee as GOP chairman, had charged that Stevenson's selection of Wilson Wyatt as campaign manager "clearly demonstrates that the ultra-left wingers—not the Democratic Party—will have complete charge of the campaign," the ADA responded that Wyatt had always been in the "conservative faction of the body." Adding to the innuendoes from the right, Dirksen, already known for his mellifluous, purple prose, asked: "Just how well does [Stevenson] think his associates look—Alger Hiss, Dean Acheson, Wilson Wyatt, ADA, and the 'lavender lads' of the State Department?"

Eisenhower, having made concessions to the right wing of the GOP, which cost him the support of Senator Wayne Morse, was also pursuing his southern strategy. He spent more time in the South than had any other Republican presidential candidate. His caution on civil rights, as well as his endorsement of state ownership of the valuable tidelands oil, was winning defectors from the Stevenson ticket. Introduced in New Orleans by the mayor of the city and the governor of the state before a huge crowd, he called the Democratic platform "un-American" and spoke, in reference to tidelands oil, of "the policy of the Washington power mongers as a policy of grab." In Dixie, he did affirm the need for equal rights for black men, but he would not support any mechanism to accomplish this reform, and even his muted calls for a revision of spiritual values did not threaten racial prejudice or estrange the southerners he sought to woo. Earlier he had warned that compulsory FEPC, then much hated in the South, would only increase racial antagonisms. Even in the North, where his voice on civil rights was stronger, he was usually vague. He claimed credit for the GOP for the gradual advancement of civil rights under Republican governors, and he affirmed the value of a voluntary FEPC over the compulsory agency which Truman had requested. He also attacked Truman's civil rights record as senator, and charged (with some accuracy) that the President had exaggerated his friendship for the Negro. "Would a true friend advocate on an all-or-nothing basis measures to improve race relations that were so extreme as to be certain of uncompromising opposition?" Eisenhower asked. In Harlem, he avoided civil rights, aside from claiming falsely that he had worked in the army to eliminate military segregation and promising as President to complete the task (which actually was not even started in Europe until 1952). In this election, unlike 1948, civil rights was not a popular issue, and the GOP would not invest much capital in a cause that did not enlist their sympathy or concern.

Eisenhower, by accepting the New Deal, removed from the campaign the dispute over welfare so dear to the hearts of many right-wing Republicans.

"Social security, housing, workman's compensation, unemployment insurance, and the preservation of the value of savings—these are the things that must be kept above and beyond politics and campaigns," he concluded. "They are rights, not issues." When explaining the GOP farm plank at the United Plowing Contest in Kasoon, Iowa, he ended by backing away from it and endorsing the Democratic program of federal restrictions and subsidy payments at a high level of parity.

To many observers within and outside the campaign, Eisenhower seemed to be losing control of his own "crusade." At an early briefing when advisers and advertising men were talking about how best to merchandise his candidacy, he felt neglected, disgusted. "All they talked about was how to win on my popularity," he complained to an associate. "Nobody said I had a brain in my head." The "great crusade" was carefully planned: advance men, crowd builders, telephone campaigns to get out the masses, recruited cheerleaders to toss confetti. So detailed was the planning that there was a thirty-nine-page blueprint for his appearance at Philadelphia's Convention Hall. It called for "fresh cut roses (25,000) . . . noisemakers (3,000) . . . flags (5,000) . . . programs (25,000)." The final touch was that Eisenhower should stand so as to be photographed with his right hand on the Liberty Bell.

The merchandising reached its climax with the plan for a $1.5 million campaign of radio and television "spots" in forty-nine key counties in twelve states in an "all-out saturation blitz" during the last three weeks. In New York City alone, there were 130 "spots" in one day. The emphasis, selected by Gallup, was on the Korean War, corruption, taxes, and the cost of living. The dialogue of "Eisenhower Answers the Nation" went like this: Man-in-the-Street—"Mr. Eisenhower, what about the high cost of living?" Eisenhower—"My wife, Mamie, worries about the same thing. I tell her it's our job to change that on November 4." To a similar question another time, he replied —"Why, there is only one answer. Get that high price crowd out of Washington." Man-in-the-Street—"General, the Democrats are telling me I never had it so good." Eisenhower—"Can that be true when America is billions in debt, when prices have doubled, when taxes break our backs and we are still fighting in Korea? It is tragic. It is time for a change."

As the campaign unfolded, it became clear how often the major domestic issues were related to the war and to the fight against communism. High prices, high taxes, and the high budget, the products of rearmament and war, were important issues to consumers. Eisenhower, by promising to cut expenditures for defense was able to offer military security at a lower price. In substance, his message was prosperity without war, high incomes without high taxes and high prices. Challenging the Democrats' claims that they had established prosperity, Eisenhower charged that war and the threat of war had created good times. Moreover, he pointed out that the average real family income had failed to rise appreciably since World War II, and that the sense of greater prosperity was largely illusory. Not only had the New Deal failed to lift the nation out of the Depression, but the Fair Deal, he charged, was plunging the nation into a recession, averted only by the Korean War and the rearmament program. The slogan "you never had it so good," he warned, "is a slick Fair Deal paraphrase for, 'you'll never have it any better under us – unless military expenditures keep the economy steamed up.' The Democrats could purchase full employment only at the price of dead and mangled bodies of young Americans."

As the campaign progressed, Eisenhower was slowly making the main issue foreign policy, particularly the war. The General, unwilling to remove this issue from politics as Truman had requested, charged the Administration with squandering American prestige and power. Midway through the campaign, on October 2, he spoke for the first time on the peace negotiations that had been dragging on for nearly fifteen months. Like many others, particularly those in the right wing of his party, he concluded that the negotiations were a "swindle," a "Soviet trap" designed to allow the North Koreans to repair their weaknesses. Turning from direct criticism of the Truman Administration, he offered his own "plan" for conducting the war: prepare the South Koreans to defend their own front lines. "If there must be a war [in Korea], let it be Asians against Asians, with our support on the side of freedom." He was counselling what the Administration was *seeking* to accomplish: train the South Koreans to bear a greater burden. But his thought was so loose, so ambiguous, that he could also be interpreted as proposing total withdrawal of American troops and letting the South Koreans alone continue the battle. In bitter responses, Truman and Stevenson, backed up by General James Van Fleet, United States Commander in Korea, pointed out that the South Korean troops could not take over more of the fighting. This "proposal of a quick and easy way out of Korea . . . is false," Stevenson declared.

In early October, Eisenhower reversing his position of June, announced that "I have always stood behind General MacArthur in bombing those bases on the Yalu from which fighter planes are coming." He also found it a "useless war," though in July and August he had defended Truman's decision. He still continued to stress that all-out war in Korea had to be avoided, and he admitted that he had no solution to the war. "I am not going to be put in a position that I am personally a messiah," he explained. While the General was unwilling to claim the mantle of "messiah," others in the GOP were willing to make bold claims for Eisenhower. Stalin is most afraid of Eisenhower, certainly not Stevenson, declared Dewey. The road to peace, both major parties agreed, was to force the Soviets to yield, and Dewey and Dulles, along with their cohorts, were promising peace through the election of Eisenhower.

On October 24 in Detroit, Eisenhower moved beyond his earlier caution. He promised that, if elected, his Administration would "concentrate on the job of ending the Korean war – until that job is honorably done." "That job," he continued, "requires a personal trip to Korea . . . I shall go to Korea." That promise, apparently introduced at the recommendation of Emmet Hughes, galvanized many voters who sought relief from the war. (The speech greatly angered Truman, who sharply asked the General, "Are you sure that you are much better than your old colleagues – Generals Bradley, Ridgeway, and Van Fleet?") The great impact of the speech rested upon the military prestige of the General, a man whom many believed could end the war. Stevenson, also contemplating a similar gesture, had rejected it as an unworthy gimmick, and undoubtedly it would have been unsuccessful for him. The Illinois governor, despite his experience in the State Department, did not command the same respect for his prowess as a guardian of American freedom and a resolver of problems in foreign policy. "We can trust *the man who won the peace*," House Minority Leader Joseph Martin and Senate Minority Leader Styles Bridges announced. In the last eleven days before the election, Eisenhower's speeches were dotted with promises to end the war. How? What did he mean by "honorable terms"? The terms on which he would end the war remained unstated. History would define them.

Stevenson's style and strategy, unlike much of his program, contrasted sharply with Eisenhower's. While the General attacked Truman, the Illinois governor, saddled with the poor record of the Administration, was seeking desperately to establish his independence of the President. Stevenson, quickly capturing the fancy of intellectuals, promised in his campaign to "talk sense to the American people," which evoked cheers from many who disregarded his dubious assertion that the Democratic platform "neither equivocates, contradicts, nor evades." The intellectuals were also pleased by his eloquence, realism, and nationalism. He warned of the need for "sacrifice, patience, understanding and implacable purpose"—words that were to bridge the rhetoric of the Roosevelt and Kennedy years.

The nominee, hoping to reweave the tattered New Deal coalition, sought to regain the South, keep the Negro and labor vote, and make substantial inroads in the Far West and Midwest. In short, he aimed to win the support that had returned Truman to the White House, but he hoped at the same time to escape from the liabilities of that Administration. It was a campaign that Stevenson, until recently unknown to many Americans, did not seem to believe he could win. The Democratic nominee, by necessity a defender of the recent past, was by conviction a celebrator of American life and an enthusiastic protector of the Administration on the important issues—not Truman, but the New Deal-Fair Deal state and the bipartisan Cold War policy.

Assisting him in his venture were talented speech writers who also offered style and wit. Unlike Eisenhower, Stevenson drew upon a distinguished group of liberal intellectuals: Arthur Schlesinger, jr., the young, brilliant, Pulitzer Prize-winning Harvard historian; David Bell, a Truman assistant, former Budget Bureau official and later John F. Kennedy's Budget chief; John Kenneth Galbraith, the tall, Harvard economist and former *Fortune* editor; Bernard De Voto, Pulitzer Prize winner, literary critic and essayist; John Fischer, an editor of *Harper's*; Carl McGowan and W. Willard Wirtz, able Illinois attorneys; Herbert Agar, a popular author; and John Bartlow Martin, a skilled journalist. The campaign manager was Wilson Wyatt, ADA'er and briefly Truman's housing expert, who was assisted by George Ball, law partner and close friend of the candidate. Only Bell and Clayton Fritchey, Pulitzer Prize-winning southern editor, were closely identified with Truman. The team had a clear ADA flavor, and Stevenson counted heavily upon them to assist him in explaining the issues to the people. The candidate, unlike Eisenhower, remained throughout in control of the content and the style of his speeches. He decided what he wanted to say, and they helped him say it. No advertising men, perhaps unfortunately for Stevenson, shaped the campaign or merchandised the man.

To Truman's displeasure, in mid-August Stevenson had announced that he could clean up the "mess in Washington." Wounded by this admission that corruption was an acute problem, the President warned that such attacks upon him would only injure the party and its presidential ticket. "I am the key of the campaign," he asserted. Stevenson, after Truman's successful Labor Day tour, invited the enthusiastic President to join the campaign. In early September and again in October, Truman sought to assist the ticket, but, as he complained later, there was little coordination between his Washington headquarters and Stevenson's office in Springfield. "How Stevenson hoped he could persuade the American voters to maintain the Democrats in power while seeming to disown powerful elements of it, I do not know," Truman later wrote.

Whether the President's efforts proved a liability or asset is difficult to determine. He did draw crowds and arouse enthusiasm. In the early stages of the campaign, he patronized Eisenhower: a good man duped by the GOP "right-wing." Truman's message was that Eisenhower and the nation had to beware of the isolationists: they would cut foreign aid, slash the defense budget, and embark upon a reckless policy of "liberation." But as Eisenhower's attacks upon the Administration sharpened, and when he failed to repudiate McCarthy, the General became the butt of Truman's scorn. The President, loving the combat of the campaign, even charged that Eisenhower was "willing to accept the very practices . . . [of] the master race."

Stevenson, though trying to distance himself from the Administration, did not depart from Truman on such matters as federal responsibility for the economy or the farm issue. He continued the New Deal-Fair Deal line in appealing to farmers and workers, and in warning against a GOP-created depression. He periodically conducted the campaign against Hoover, not Eisenhower. It was not "time for a change," he declared, countering the GOP propaganda. On labor, he deviated slightly from Truman's policy and denied that Taft-Hartley was a "slave-labor act" but he did assert that it was "biased and politically inspired," concluding that it should be revised. He wished to restore the closed shop, which Taft-Hartley outlawed; to remove the anti-strike injunction, which Taft-Hartley authorized; and to establish flexible, but ill-defined, measures to deal with critical strikes. While these proposals won the support of labor's leaders, who still regarded Taft-Hartley as a vital political issue, he also offered two revisions that won less favor: the need to maintain prohibitions similar to those in Taft-Hartley against unfair labor practices (such as jurisdictional strikes); and a rule barring unions from restricting Negroes and other minorities from union membership because of race.

Of all the domestic issues, it was on civil rights that Stevenson departed most from Truman. The President, initially a wary advocate of rights for the

Negro, had moved during his years in the White House to assaults upon Jim Crow in American life and to efforts to advance the welfare of the black man. Though Truman's rhetoric was usually bolder than his actions, he had become by 1952 a conscience for his party on civil rights. He had wanted a stronger plank in the platform, and had reluctantly acceded to political necessity and accepted the retreat from a commitment to compulsory FEPC. Stevenson, moving slowly and under pressure from blacks, finally went beyond the platform: he supported restrictions on filibusters and endorsed establishment of a modified compulsory FEPC (with judicial, not executive, enforcement) in cases where states did not have commissions. By these decisions, Stevenson, despite Sparkman's record on civil right, was able to woo Adam Clayton Powell and other black Democratic defectors back into the fold.

Stevenson's success in courting the Negro vote, assisted by the Democratic record and Truman's efforts on behalf of the ticket, contrasted sharply with his failure in the South. His statements on civil rights, according to *The New York Times*, "did not make much of a stir in the South," where party officials knew that the filibuster could block any legislative effort to change race relations. Many southerners, long estranged by the New Deal-Fair Deal reforms, regarded Stevenson's shift on civil rights as additional evidence that the "presidential party" would sell out the South to northern liberals, big city bosses, and blacks. Some southerners were also angered by his position on tidelands oil. Stevenson, approving Truman's veto of a bill bestowing the multi-billion resource on the states, declared that the Federal Government should retain title to the land. As a result, the Texas Democratic party, after fulfilling its pledge to place Stevenson and Sparkman on the official ticket, endorsed the Eisenhower-Nixon slate. "Every Democrat in Texas," they declared, should "vote and work for the election of Dwight D. Eisenhower." They were not bolting the party, only the ticket. In Louisiana, Governor Robert Kennon and his machine also moved to Eisenhower. In South Carolina, James F. Byrnes, Truman's former Secretary of State, declared that Stevenson had succumbed to "Trumanism" in domestic policy and announced his support for Eisenhower. Virginia's Senator Harry Byrd, long an opponent of the New Deal and Fair Deal, also backed the General. Elsewhere, conservative Democrats, attracted by Eisenhower and his program, and estranged from the northern wing of the party, were moving towards the GOP, thereby promising it the first success in Dixie since Hoover cracked the South in 1928. The South's powerful Richard Russell, despite promises that he would campaign for the ticket, offered one perfunctory testimonial and then retreated into silence. Speaker Sam Rayburn, Senator Lyndon Johnson, and Sparkman struggled to halt the defections.

Throughout the campaign the voters received many examples of the Stevenson wit. After a platform on which Eisenhower had been standing collapsed, Stevenson quipped, "I'm glad the General wasn't hurt. But I wasn't surprised that it happened—I've been telling him for two months that nobody could stand on that platform." On another occasion, the Democrat nominee remarked, "If the Republicans will stop telling lies about us, we will stop telling the truth about them." In Phoenix, he complained that the GOP was a "two-headed elephant." "One head agrees with everything I say and the other head fumes and curses at everything I say." When Eisenhower sharply scolded Stevenson for taking the issues lightly, for regarding it as "amusing that we stumbled into a war [and] . . . that there are Communists in government," Stevenson responded that GOP stood for "Grouchy Old Pessimists."

Stevenson's humor delighted the intellectuals but may have offended other Americans who regarded him sometimes as undignified. His strong support for civil liberties, his firm anti-communism, and his clear dedication to patriotism won support from liberals. He called for patriotism, which he defined — in what then seemed platitudinous terms — as "putting country before self." Fingering McCarthy amid the senator's supporters at the American Legion convention, Stevenson bravely condemned those self-styled patriots who "for political or personal reasons" attacked the loyalty of men like General Marshall. Stevenson was not soft on communism, he was quick to add, in what had become a reflex action for McCarthy's opponents; he just did not want to "burn down the barn to kill the rats." Communism, he knew, meant "the strangulation of the individual . . ., death for the soul. Americans who have surrendered to this malignant ideal have surrendered their right to our trust." By opposing vigilantism before the American Legion, Stevenson was faithful to his ideals and won the praise and respect of liberals.

In foreign policy, where Stevenson was willing to run on the substance of the Truman record, his views were straightforward. He accepted the Cold War, attributed it to Soviet malevolence and expansion, and viewed the United States as the protector of freedom in the world. Looking at Europe, he defended NATO as the necessary bulwark against Soviet aggression, but never adequately explained how the understaffed armies could stop Russia, how the Europeans could realistically rely on anything but the nuclear deterrent, or why the deterrent would be credible. Affirming collective security in Europe and warning the nation that Eisenhower was a captive of Taft and his fellow isolationists, Stevenson counselled that American policy must acknowledge limited means and therefore restrict itself to limited goals: victory was not always possible. By increasing American military strength, he hoped to achieve an eventual settlement in the Cold War. "I think the Soviet Union," he explained, "will be influenced only by the steady, serious, undeviating determination to build up the strength of the free world — not with a view toward war but with a view toward preventing war and negotiating the conditions of peace."

Along with Truman, he warned against MacArthur's strategy for victory — an attack on China across the Yalu — as well as against proposals for American withdrawal from Europe and Asia. "I am . . . proud," he asserted, "that we have had the fortitude to refuse to risk extension of the war despite extreme Communist provocations and reckless Republican criticisms." The military budget, he concluded, could not be cut significantly without impairing America's international obligations and endangering her security. His message was the "lesson of Munich": strength and will would restrain aggression. In turn, he deplored the Republican policy "which proposes to reduce our contribution to free world strength . . . while it steps up its verbal threats against the enemy."

Confronted by Eisenhower's charges that the Administration had made "a mess of foreign affairs," "lost" China, abandoned millions to Soviet tyranny in Europe, and "bungled" the nation into Korea, Stevenson admitted that the Administration had made minor "mistakes" but stressed that China could not have been saved, nor the Iron Curtain rolled back without war. He decried "liberation" as either reckless or meaningless. The Korean War, he implied, could have been averted if America had not allowed rapid postwar demobilization, underestimated Soviet strength, and withdrawn troops from Korea. Stevenson declared that the GOP had to share responsibility for these mistakes: Dewey had criticized the government for delaying demobilization; Eisenhower had supported demobilization; and the General had badly estimated Soviet intentions when, for example, he had told a congressional committee in November, 1945, "Nothing guides Russian policy so much as a desire for friendship with the United States." Moreover, the General, as Chief of Staff of the Army, had joined in the recommendation of the Joint Chiefs of Staff that South Korea was of little strategic value to the United States and that American troops should be withdrawn from the peninsula.

In defending American participation in the war, Stevenson declared that Korea "was the testing point for freedom throughout the world. . . Every one of us knows in his heart why we had to stand up and fight in Korea." Had the United States not intervened, the price would have been great: the communists "could have picked away at the free world and engulfed more millions, piece by piece . . . [until] we would have had to fight"; the free world would also have lost Japan and East Asia, with her valuable manpower, rubber, tin and oil. He lashed out at those GOP congressmen who had originally greeted the war with enthusiasm and now "attempt to make you believe that it was almost an act of treason." "We are not," he declared, "a race of whimpering adolescents who can't face the truth, but a race of men and women, proud, courageous and unafraid." To the question: "How long can we keep up the fight against this monster tyranny?" he answered, "As long as we have to." The high budget, high taxes, inflation, even deaths in Korea, in his view, were the price America must pay to maintain freedom—for itself and the world. The battle was against "the anti-Christ."

Opposing any extension of the war into China, agreeing with General Omar Bradley that war with China would be "the wrong war, at the wrong place, at the wrong time, and with the wrong enemy," Stevenson promised "by perseverance [to] win the military decision in Korea": an honorable peace which would halt the Communists at the Thirty-eighth Parallel. When Eisenhower electrified the nation with his promise "I will go to Korea," Stevenson sharply criticized the General for not having a program. The truce negotiations, the Democratic nominee rightly explained, were stalled because the United States refused to accede to Communist demands for forced repatriation of all prisoners. What would Eisenhower do with these 50,000 prisoners, many of whom had reputedly declared that they preferred death to repatriation? Would Eisenhower, like Senator Homer Capehart, the Indiana Republican, force the prisoners to return? Not only was this position "identical with that of the Communists," emphasized Stevenson, but "if we give up on this point . . . we will no longer lead the coalitions of the free world." America, he explained, symbolized freedom. That was her greatest asset in the Cold War, and it would be lost if the United States acceded to forced repatriation.

In 1952, the Cold War consensus was challenged only by the fringe parties of the left. The most interesting was the Progressive party, which in 1948 had briefly threatened to ruin Truman's chances by snaring enough disaffected Democrats to throw the election to Dewey. By 1952, however, Henry Wallace, its standard-bearer, and many other non-communist stalwarts had departed, leaving only a fragmented shell. Some left because they felt that communists were dominating the party, while others, like Wallace, perhaps tired of being embattled, seceded when the party's executive council opposed American intervention in the Korean War. "The Russians could have prevented the attack by the North Koreans and undoubtedly they could now stop the attack if they wish," Wallace declared three weeks after the war erupted. "When my country is at war and the United Nations sanctions that war, I am on the side of my country and the United Nations."

Behind Wallace's bolt was a long-standing dispute on whether the Soviets shared some responsibility for the Cold War or whether America was solely to blame. In 1948, Wallace had acknowledged that the Soviets were sometimes culpable, and the platform had hinted that the Soviets shared responsibility for the Cold War. After 1950, despite many defections, the disagreement on Soviet responsibility continued, and the 1952 platform suggested that the Soviet Union had contributed in some minor, unstated way to the Cold War.

Unlike the major parties, the Progressives had steadfastly opposed the Truman Doctrine, the Marshall Plan, NATO, the arms and troops programs for Europe, rearmament of Germany and Japan, the alliances with Franco and Chiang, and the support of colonialism. As the Truman Administration had forged military alliances abroad and begun establishing what Acheson called "situations of strength," the Progressives castigated the government for "war mongering." However, because they believed they were preserving the heritage of Roosevelt, the Progressives were unable ideologically to challenge the New Deal tradition in foreign policy. As a result, like many postwar liberal critics, they argued, simply, that Truman and the bipartisan coalition had reversed Roosevelt's foreign policy of accommodation with the Soviet Union.

The Progressives called for the halt of stockpiling nuclear weapons, an international agreement outlawing these weapons, and repeal of the draft. How America would be protected they did not need to explain, for, in their view, there was no Soviet threat, no aggressive impulse to be thwarted. For evidence, they emphasized that Administration officials had admitted that they did not expect the Soviet Union "to start a war now or at any time." To suspicious Americans, who had come to believe that their nation's safety depended upon a nuclear arsenal and a large military establishment, the Progressives simply offered negotiations and "peaceful understanding and peaceful relations" with the Soviet Union; that is, peaceful coexistence. To settle the German "problem" they proposed a neutral, disarmed, united Germany. To assist the underdeveloped nations, the party recommended a fund of $50 billion, to be distributed by the UN. In addition, the Progressives wanted the elimination of trade barriers between the United States and communist nations, and endorsed the recognition of Red China and withdrawal of recognition from Chiang's government.

In 1952 the party's nominees were Vincent Hallinan, a prominent California attorney who was serving a sentence for contempt of court, and Mrs. Charlotta Bass, a black and former editor of the California *Eagle*. During the campaign Mrs. Bass proudly declared, "Win or lose, we win by raising the issues." Whether or not the Progressives found consolation in such analysis is difficult to say, but certainly it contained an element of truth. In many respects the Progressives saw more deeply the defects, and also the possibilities, of American life. In condemning the "tweedle-dum, tweedle-dee" approach of the major parties, they were heirs to a part of the nation's radical tradition. "Both old parties," asserted Hallinan, "are sold to a program of war against labor, against the Negro. . . . They are both captive parties and both parties are captive to the same interests." Although his analysis may have been overwrought, distorted, and too simple, he did focus upon three major problems in American political life: the Cold War, poverty, and race relations.

For the Socialist party, already torn by doubts about its own relevance and possessing less support than the Progressives, the campaign of 1952 was again ritualistic. Norman Thomas, the party's perennial presidential candidate, had announced in 1950 that he would not run again, arguing that the party should no longer support a national ticket but channel its energies into educational efforts and the election of liberals. Others in the party, particularly outside New York, the stronghold for Thomas' position, were reluctant to withdraw for the electoral success of liberals and wanted a national campaign in order to maintain the party and promote socialism. In 1952, the party nominated Darlington Hoopes, a Reading attorney, for the Presidency, and Samuel Friedman, a New York labor leader, as his running mate. Correctly anticipating an even smaller vote than in 1948, they spoke before small enclaves and appeared on the ballot in only sixteen states. The ticket received the formal support of Thomas and his cohorts, though he asserted that he hoped that Stevenson would win and thereby hinted that Socialists should not "waste" their ballots on Hoopes.

The Socialist platform, technically to the left of the Progressives on domestic issues, once more proclaimed the value of democratic socialism and called for nationalization of major industries. Like the Progressives, the Socialists urged abolition of segregation in all public and public-supported institutions, including housing and the armed forces. They called for anti-lynching legislation and protection of the right to vote. They also demanded enforcement of the 14th Amendment and the reduction of congressional representation in cases where citizens were deprived of the right to vote. Unlike the Progressives, the Socialists, who were having doubts about centralization of power, openly and perceptively recognized the need for action on the community level to abolish segregation that could not be eliminated by legislation.

Like the Progressives, however, they were unable to devise effective tactics for challenging America's racism.

On foreign policy, the parties on the left differed significantly. The Socialists, despite serious divisions on other matters, were stridently anti-Stalinist. Whereas the Progressives agreed that America was primarily responsible for the Cold War and argued about the amount of Soviet guilt, the Socialists stressed Soviet guilt and argued about American responsibility. Norman Thomas, for example, zealously attacked Soviet foreign policy while remaining a sympathetic critic of recent American policy. Pledging himself "to do everything possible" to defend socialism, he labored to block efforts within the party to condemn American imperialism and to treat the United States and the Soviet Union as equally culpable in the Cold War. Privately he explained his fears of a platform "couched in one or another of the numerous doctrinaire Marxist sets of formulas or which would backtrack [on our support for Truman's intervention in Korea] in favor of a curious blend of pacifism and near-Trotskyism." In order to prevent problems at the convention, he prepared an advance draft of the platform which he hoped would establish "approximate agreement" among party leaders. It did not.

Hoopes, Thomas' running mate in 1944 and the representative of the party's left wing on foreign policy, rejected Thomas' analysis. The party, he declared, should not go along with "distasteful features" of American policy —for example, NATO, and support of dictators and European colonialism. He denied that these policies were simple "mistakes." They were "inherent in the nature of our capitalistic government, and until we make a clean break with these policies we cannot fight Communism."

At the party convention in Cleveland, the delegates hammered out a compromise. Peace, they explained, was blocked by "four tremendous obstacles": first and most important, "the aggressive imperialism of the [totalitarian] Soviet Union"; second, the militarization in the West that developed in response; third, unfair dealings with underdeveloped nations; and fourth, capitalism.

On election eve both major parties made their final appeal on national radio and television. Truman, Barkley, Stevenson, and Sparkman spoke for the Democrats. Truman, attacking the GOP's "campaign of fear and deception," declared that the choice was between prosperity or depression, between extending civil rights and liberties or succumbing to "smear and fear," between stopping Communism and retreating before the red menace or plunging the world into atomic warfare. Stevenson summed up the themes of his campaign: prosperity could not be entrusted to the GOP; "we are winning the worldwide struggle with communism"; and the times were difficult and demanded Democratic leadership.

Following this performance, the GOP had an hour-long telecast emphasizing the people's dedication to the "Great Crusade." Opening with Eisenhower, his family and friends, the camera moved to sequences of Alger Hiss, of "five-percenters," of men in battle in Korea, of Eisenhower with Churchill and the GI's, and of the General at home in Abilene with his grandson. The camera then flashed to supporters. A veteran, asked why he was backing Eisenhower, said, "Well, all the guys I know out in Korea figure there's only one man for the job," the General. There was also a San Francisco typist "crusading" for Eisenhower, a Nisei physician in Seattle, a youngster who had organized "Tykes for Ike," a Gary steelmaker, and a suburban housewife and mother, and a Los Angeles "Coffee-with-Eisenhower" meeting that ended with a prayer. Throughout, the theme was the same: the nation needed Eisenhower to end the "mess" at home and abroad. At the end of the program, the General and Mrs. Eisenhower cut a victory cake.

The campaign had been long, expensive, and fatiguing. Eisenhower had travelled 33,000 miles, two-thirds by air, visited the South twice, gone to forty-four states, skipping only Nevada, Maine, Vermont, and Mississippi, and delivered 228 speeches, of which forty were major and nationally televised. Nixon, making 375 speeches, had journeyed 42,000 miles. Stevenson had travelled 32,500 miles, appearing in thirty-two states and delivering 203 speeches, of which twenty-one were on national television. Sparkman, going to thirty-eight states, had delivered more than 450 speeches. The two major parties, it was estimated, had spent nearly $80 million on the campaign, the first which relied heavily upon television to reach American voters.

So close did the forthcoming election seem that most pollsters, still wary after their mistakes in 1948, would not predict a victor. They painfully recalled the late shift of the "undecided" vote in 1948. *The New York Times*, in its final election survey, concluded that the outcome was "highly uncertain." Louis Bean, who had been correct in 1948, begged off, asserting this time that there were "too many factors involved for which there were no statistical analyses." Samuel Lubell foresaw substantial defections from the Democratic ranks but also warned of other likely developments that could offset this shift, George Gallup of the American Institute of Public Opinion, while finding substantial Eisenhower strength, warned that a continuation of the late-developing trend to Stevenson would give him a majority: he needed the same 3 to 1 ratio that Truman had received from the undecided or uncommitted voters, who were about 13 per cent (about seven million voters) of the expected total vote of fifty-five million.

"Ike in a landslide," declared election-day headlines. In retrospect, to many it all seemed inevitable. The General, in gathering 33,936,234 votes, 55.4 per cent of the two party vote, had won by the largest popular vote of any presidential candidate to that date. Stevenson, with the second largest Democratic vote in history, had received 27,314,992 votes, 44.4 per cent of the vote, from the greatest turnout of voters in American history. Eisenhower carried thirty-nine states for 442 electoral votes, while Stevenson had triumphed in only nine states — in West Virginia and eight in the South — with 89 electoral votes.

So great was the support for the GOP ticket that 670 counties outside the South that had supported Democratic presidential candidates since 1932 broke and backed the General. Eighteen states that had always cast their elec-

toral votes for Roosevelt and Truman went Republican. There was no denying the landslide victory, though it should be remembered that Harding in
1920, Coolidge in 1924, and Roosevelt in 1932 and 1936 exceeded Eisenhower's plurality.

Eisenhower easily captured the key states of New York, California,
Illinois, Ohio, Michigan, and Pennsylvania by pluralities ranging between
269,000 and 848,000. In 1948, in contrast, Truman had narrowly lost the last
four but won Michigan and New York by small pluralities. In the West, Eisenhower won all eleven states by a margin of 57.3 per cent. In New England he
was the first Republican since Coolidge to sweep all six states. In the Midwest,
a comparative stronghold of GOP sentiment, the General easily moved to victory with Minnesota recording his lowest percentage (55.6). Even in the
South, the traditional Democratic stronghold, the General polled the largest
vote ever received by a Republican, as he won four states: Florida (55 per
cent), Virginia (56.3 per cent), Tennessee (50 per cent), and Texas (53.2 per
cent).

Across the country there had been substantial defections from the Democratic coalition—among white urban and some black belt southerners, among
Irish, Poles, and Germans, among Catholics, among low-income families,
among skilled and semi-skilled workers, and among the members of labor union families. All income classes, reversing the normal patterns, had given Eisenhower a majority of the votes cast. In addition, sources of traditional GOP
strength, particularly the suburbs, turned out unusually high votes for Eisenhower, and new voters, both young and old, had also favored the General.
The farmers, an unexpected source of support in Truman's surprising victory,
also returned in large numbers to the GOP column.

Nearly 25 per cent of the final vote for Eisenhower, concluded Angus
Campbell and his associates at the Michigan Survey Center, came from those
who had voted for Truman in 1948. In 1952, unlike 1948, the issues and the
candidates broke down party affiliations in many cases. This shift alone was
almost sufficient to create an Eisenhower victory. Added to that was the fact
that almost thirteen million "new" voters—one-third were too young in 1948
and the rest had not voted then—provided significant support for the General.
The young supported him 57-43 per cent, and the almost nine million older
citizens, the GOP's "stay at homes", endorsed him by a 53-47 per cent margin. (In contrast, Louis Harris, depending upon Roper polls, contended that
these young voters, troubled by Eisenhower's concessions to Senators Jenner,
McCarthy, and Taft, backed Stevenson 56-44 per cent.) Not only had the
turnout of voters (63.3 per cent) been the highest since 1908, but the GOP
strategy of seeking votes among this group had been successful. These "new"
voters did not make a decisive difference, however, because they supported
both candidates at about the same rate as did the rest of the electorate. Had
they split the way the uncommitted had gone in 1948, and had they been
evenly distributed throughout the nation, however, the result in 1952 would
have been a Stevenson victory. The difference, primarily, was that those who
switched each increased the Eisenhower plurality by two.

Unlike 1948, when domestic issues dominated the campaign and shaped the votes, the dominant issue in 1952, according to most surveys, was the Korean War. "It was probably our most emotional election" since Bryan and McKinley in 1896, concluded Lubell, who found widespread frustration and anger about the war, the stalemate, and the growing battlefield death toll. Apparently the campaign helped convert the war into a major issue. In January, according to a Roper survey, 25 per cent of those asked to indicate the most important problem facing the nation mentioned the war; in June the figure had reached 30 per cent, in September 33 per cent, in mid-October 39 per cent, and in late October 52 per cent. The Roper poll also found in June that there was no agreement on what should be done to end the stalemate. Thirty per cent had faith in negotiations; slightly more than 30 per cent wanted to step up the war and try to drive the Communists out of Korea; less than 20 per cent favored a "pull-out" About 75 per cent of the voters most concerned about the war believed that Eisenhower could bring it to an end more quickly. The war issue, concluded Louis Harris, "was easily the Achilles heel of the Democratic campaign."

The Survey Research Center, in contrast to Harris' and Lubell's analysis, found foreign policy to be slightly less important than domestic issues for the voters in 1952. Thirty-two per cent cited foreign policy as their reason—some gave more than one—for voting for the GOP, while 36 per cent mentioned domestic policies. Only 13 per cent of those who endorsed the GOP thought the party would solve the war. It is clear on the basis of this study, as well as those by Lubell, Gallup, and Harris, that many who selected the GOP because of their concern about the war did so because of their favorable view of Eisenhower. Indeed, 47 per cent of the sample that voted for Eisenhower mentioned his personal qualities, his experience, or his being "the best man" as an important reason for their vote. Very few cited party allegiance.

The issue of communists in government, according to Harris, was less significant than many feared. Never in 1952 did more than 11 per cent of the people volunteer it as a major issue. Only when they were offered it as a possible issue did substantial numbers select it as important. As additional, but indirect, evidence of its small influence is the fact that McCarthy and Jenner, who had closely identified themselves with the issue, ran well behind the national ticket and their party's gubernatorial candidate, and three GOP senators who exploited the communism-in-government issue were defeated.

Corruption was another major issue, with nearly one-third of the electorate citing it. But it did not significantly aid the General and the GOP, despite their efforts at "marketing" the issue. About half thought it would continue if Stevenson was elected, and about half thought he would end it. By the end of the campaign, after Truman's vigorous activity, about five out of every eight concerned about corruption believed it would continue under Stevenson. Harris concluded that, in the last stages of the campaign, most citizens "who were disturbed and upset about Korea and Communism in government also tended to be more upset about corruption." In turn, those least distressed by the war were less concerned about corruption. Consequently, the importance of corruption as an influence on the vote declined as election day approached, but the issue was "another significant nail Eisenhower was able to drive in the Democratic coffin."

Economic issues in 1952 were a mixed bag. Concern with high taxes and government spending, despite the widespread complaints, apparently did not have much effect on the election. Two-thirds of those who cited these as major problems revealed, when questioned, that they did not believe that the Republicans would improve the situation. The problem of high prices, however, was a more significant issue; like communism, it was a "trailer" issue, Harris found. "It's bad enough to have so many fine young men slaughtered in Korea," explained one housewife in a typical comment, "but to make it worse we have to have the terribly high cost of everything you buy these days. And it's all because of that war over there." Some charged the Administration and the Democratic-controlled Congress with failing to restrain prices, an issue that Eisenhower ably exploited and on which Stevenson did not adequately defend himself. Of the many who cited high prices as a major problem, 60 per cent concluded that the GOP would do a better job in restraining inflation.

Both Harris and Lubell concluded that the fears of depression were responsible for a "great deal" (Harris' words) of Stevenson's 44 per cent. For many, particularly those in the working class, economic security was still associated with the Democrats. Hoover's depression, Hoovervilles, and breadlines had not been forgotten by a generation of Americans, many of whom incorrectly lauded the New Deal, rather than World War II, for restoring prosperity. "No working man can vote Republican," many workers told the pollsters. "The Democrats are the friend of the working man." "The pocketbook argument," Harris concluded, "was a formidable one. It turned out to be nearly the only appeal the Democrats had on a mass basis." Economic security and the war, with its associated problems, were the two opposite poles tugging at Democratic voters in 1952. Many who broke with the Truman-Stevenson party let the war overpower them. In some cases they even saw prosperity as war-inspired ("stop trading blood for money," one said) and chose to vote *against* the war, not *for* security.

Of professional men and managers, nearly 60 per cent (up from 57 per cent in 1948) voted Republican, while 27 per cent (up from 15 per cent) voted Democratic. While Stevenson ran behind among all white collar groups, only among the managers and professionals did he improve on Truman's percentage. Among most other groups, Eisenhower gained substantially over Dewey, while Stevenson generally fell behind Truman: other white collar—Eisenhower, 52 per cent (Dewey, 39); Stevenson, 28 (Truman, 38); skilled and semiskilled workers—Eisenhower, 34 (Dewey, 15); Stevenson, 40 (Truman, 52); unskilled workers—Eisenhower, 19 (Dewey, 12); Stevenson, 40 (Truman, 33). Only among manual workers did Eisenhower run behind the Democratic nominee. But when the voting is analyzed in terms of income classes, the General triumphed in all three. Among the low-income (to $1,999), he won 34 per cent to Stevenson's 22 per cent, though Truman had topped Dewey 28 to 16. In the middle-income group ($2,000–$4,999), Eisenhower gained 40 per

cent and Stevenson 36 per cent, while Truman had topped Dewey, 36–24.
Among the high-income group, Eisenhower received 57 per cent and Stevenson less than half of that with 28 per cent, though Dewey had beaten Truman
only 46 to 28.

Among farmers, of all major occupational groups, there was the greatest
defection from Truman to Eisenhower. In 1948, when only 42 per cent had
voted, nearly two-thirds had supported Truman. In 1952, however, when two-
thirds of all farmers voted, 63 per cent of them supported the General. The
figures for rural areas, which include farm families and farm-related enter-
prises, are almost identical. Outside the South, farmers had returned to their
normal GOP anchorage. In 1948, Truman, aided by a late downturn in prices,
had carried Minnesota, Iowa, and Wisconsin, but in 1952 the last two states
reverted to their GOP pattern of 1944, and Minnesota also went Republican.
In Kansas, Nebraska, South Dakota, and North Dakota, states where Truman had received between 45 and 48 per cent of the two-party vote, Stevenson fell to between 28 and 31 per cent. Eisenhower, by promising a continuation of farm prosperity, had removed the major reason for rural support for
Stevenson and Sparkman outside the South.

In the cities in 1952, the GOP candidate weakened the New Deal coalition, cutting into the normal Democratic margins. Chicago, which had given
Truman about 55 per cent, gave Stevenson only 50.3 per cent; in Cleveland,
which Truman had taken with 54.6, Stevenson received 46.3; Boston, which
gave Truman 69 per cent, gave Stevenson 60 per cent; and in New York
City, Stevenson won only 55 per cent, not Truman's 59 per cent. In Pittsburgh, where Truman had a plurality of 73,000 votes, Stevenson slipped to
13,800. In Los Angeles and San Francisco, the General swept to victory. In
the suburbs, Eisenhower rolled up great margins, wiping away the Democratic
plurality in five of the eight largest cities that had gone Democratic. As
Jacob Arvey, Cook County boss, put it, "the suburbs are murder."

German-Americans, Irish-Americans, and Polish-Americans, but not
Italian-Americans, contributed significantly to the defection from the Democratic party. German-Americans, constituting about 14 per cent of the electorate, heavily backed Eisenhower. Harris concluded that nearly 79 per cent
of the German Protestants, and 73 per cent of the German Catholics, endorsed the General. Between September and October, many shifted to the
GOP candidate as they concluded that a Democratic victory was not essential
to their well-being. Unhappiness with the war, linked to concern about communism in government, was of particular concern to this group, especially the
Catholics. In the case of the Irish (nearly all Catholics), there was an even
split on McCarthy but there was wider concern among the group about communism in government. Again issues of the war, joined with the secondary
issue of communism, cut into the normally strong Democratic ranks and significantly reduced their support for the Democratic Party and thereby helped
to produce the General's victory. Like the Germans, the Irish had been torn
between economic security (identified with the Democratic party) and the war
and Communism, but by October they resolved this dilemma and a substan-

tial number bolted to Eisenhower. Poles, too, worried about communism in America, as well as in their homeland, which many thought Roosevelt had sold out. They defected in great numbers to the GOP ticket. Their usual 70 per cent Democratic vote dropped all the way to 50 per cent. Italians (nearly all Catholics), however, were more impressed by the Administration's foreign policy, especially its aid to Italy, and believed also that their economic security depended upon the continuation of the Democratic party in power. As a result, they stayed with the New Deal-Fair Deal party, with between 55 and 60 per cent of their votes going to Stevenson.

In terms of religion, the sharpest break occurred among Catholics, long the backbone of the big-city machines. In 1948, two-thirds of all Catholic voters had supported Truman, but in 1952 that percentage had been sliced to 51.2. Labor union membership seemed, however, to place a brake on defections. Less than one out of every ten voting Catholic union members bolted to the GOP. Among Catholics without union members in the family, nearly 62 per cent backed Eisenhower, a dramatic reversal of the pattern of 1948. In general, the evidence shows that the union member vote held for the Democratic party. Yet, it is dubious that the political efforts of the unions had much effect. Most likely, union members, like their leaders, preferred the Democrats for the same reasons: the preservation of economic security and the rights of labor. Ironically, while the union man was voting for Stevenson (60 to 40 per cent), his family was defecting to Eisenhower by a 55 to 45 per cent margin.

The role of women in the voting is less clear. Gallup and Harris both estimated that about 17.6 million women voted for Eisenhower and about 12.7 million for Stevenson. The Michigan Survey however, found there was little difference—a conclusion that Samual Lubell also supported. Whatever the precise answer, all agreed that a majority of the voters of each sex cast ballots for Eisenhower.

For many the most interesting question about 1952 was: what happened in Dixie? Ike, securing 48.9 per cent of the two party vote in the South, had been more successful than any GOP candidate since Hoover (49.7), whose strength was sometimes in similar sectors, particularly in Tennessee, Virginia, Arkansas, Georgia, and North Carolina. There was also a loose relationship between the Democratic defections to the Dixiecrats in 1948 and those to Eisenhower in 1952. Eisenhower lost in the four states that went Dixiecrat in 1948—Alabama, 35.2; Louisiana, 47.3; Mississippi, 40.1; and South Carolina, 48.3. In three, however, Eisenhower made deep inroads into the Black Belt area, the source of Dixiecrat strength, but in other states, like North Carolina, Tennessee, Texas, and Virginia, his major support lay elsewhere. Most significantly, middle- and upper-income white areas in cities and suburbs went for Eisenhower, while the low-income areas, sometimes the residences of minorities, went for Stevenson.

In the South, as well as in the North, Stevenson was most successful, and Eisenhower least successful, with black voters, whose ballots carried South Carolina and Louisiana for Stevenson. Overall, they were the only ethnic group to give the Illinois governor substantially greater support than Truman had received. The Survey Research Center concluded that Stevenson received 81 per cent of the black vote, while Truman had won about 64 per cent. Civil rights, the Roper pollsters found, dominated the voting decisions of northern blacks. They were also concerned about the cost-of-living (which they thought Democrats were most likely to restrain) and a depression (which they felt the Democrats would be most likely to avert). They bought the Democratic slogan, "You've never had it so good." On foreign policy, however, they differed with the Democrats and wanted to withdraw from Korea and cut aid to Europe. For them, civil rights and foreign policy coalesced: Dollars sent abroad could be used instead to assist the underprivileged at home. Another minority, the Jews, Harris found, backed Stevenson by 74 to 26 per cent, or roughly a margin of a million votes. They were also the strongest supporters of Truman's foreign policy in Korea and Europe, and they admired the Administration's record on civil rights.

Looking at the landslide victory, students of politics might wonder whether there had been a fundamental shift in the party loyalties of voters. Was there a Republican majority? Despite the hopeful estimates of some GOP analysts at the time, the answer was no. True, in the South, the defections suggested the *possibility* of building a Republican party – among the new rich, the urban middle-classes, and some black belt whites – but most were still loyal to the Democrats on the local level. Their protest, despite the GOP victory in four contests for the House, was primarily against Washington, against the national or presidential party. Often the contest within the state was a struggle for power within the party. Symptomatic of their concern for the state Democratic party was the demand by Governor Kennon of Louisiana, who was supporting the Eisenhower ticket, that the GOP withdraw two candidates from congressional races. Throughout most of the country it was clear that the General's popularity had helped carry other GOP candidates to victory. Local and congressional candidates, who usually run slightly behind the national ticket, had on the average run far behind Eisenhower (nearly 19 percentage points). In the face of the greatest GOP landslide since Coolidge and Hoover, the party had barely captured the Congress. In the House they gained only twenty-one seats for a majority of nine. In the Senate, they captured twenty-three of thirty-five races, gaining three over their previous number and thereby securing just forty-eight seats. In ten states – six outside the south – the voters had endorsed Eisenhower but split enough ballots to return Democrats to the Senate. Among the governors, the Republicans won twenty of the thirty races, for a gain of five. Alfred DeGrazia concludes that Eisenhower's strength among Democrats and independents (including the GOP's "stay-at-homes") was so great that his presence on the ballot increased the GOP congressional and local vote by nearly 5 per cent of his own total. If that percentage was spread evenly throughout the country, it would have accounted for Republican victories in thirty-nine congressional, thirteen senate, and seven gubernatorial contests. Thus, he finds the Eighty-third Congress owed "its Republican majorities to Dwight D. Eisenhower's candidacy."

The Democrats, it appeared, had lost an election, but they had lost it to Eisenhower, not to the GOP. Many candidates had run on the General's coattails. "If the voters liked the Republicans the way they liked Ike," cracked one Democrat, "the two-party system would be in bad shape." The Michigan Survey Study found that 47 per cent of the voters considered themselves Democrats while only 27 per cent thought of themselves as Republicans. In 1952 the GOP remained a minority party, though its members' hopes for the future were strong. Perhaps with Eisenhower's assistance, they could be transformed into the majority party. The new moderate Republicans like Senators Jacob Javits and Irving Ives of New York, John Sherman Cooper of Kentucky, and Ralph Flanders of Vermont, if aided by Eisenhower, might offer an attractive alternative to the Old Guard and the Democrats. Perhaps Eisenhower could transfer much of his popularity and the Administration's successes would aid the GOP. Only later would the break in 1952 and 1956 clearly become what V. O. Key has called a brief "Republican interlude."

In 1952, other aspects of the voting pattern attracted less attention. The Progressives, as expected, ran poorly, receiving 140,023 votes, far behind 1948 when they received slightly more than a million votes. Lacking a well-known candidate and subjected to red-baiting, they tallied more than half of their votes in two states: California, 24,106; and New York, 64,211. If the pattern of 1948 obtained, they probably did disproportionately well among Negroes and Jews, two minorities with elements most likely to be disaffected from the two party system. The Socialist party, placing its national ticket on the ballot for the last time, received only 19,685 votes, with two-thirds from three eastern states: Pennsylvania, the home of Hoopes, 8,771; New Jersey, 8,593 (almost the same vote as in 1948), and New York, 2,664. In 1952 they even fell, for the first time, behind the DeLeon Socialist-Labor party and climbed only slightly ahead of various MacArthur tickets. The results dramatically confirmed what most citizens knew: the American "left" was dead. In New York, the American Labor party, the strength of the Progressives, soon collapsed. Elsewhere, many on the "left" went into political retreat: many who had devoted years of their lives to reforming America gave up politics and devoted themselves to participating in other parts of American culture. Their children in a later generation would often rediscover politics beyond the two party, even the electoral, system and demand of their parents and the nation what the "left" was groping toward in 1952. In that year, perhaps the deathknell of the "left" was best symbolized by the *Partisan Review* symposium among intellectuals on "Our Country and Our Culture." Rejecting their own past, many asserted new values in rediscovering the value of American culture, in announcing the uniqueness of America, and in affirming the success of American democracy in extending benefits to its citizens.

The results of the 1952 election also contributed to a growing faith that class was of marginal importance in American society. The two party system, in the Eisenhower landslide, had contributed to the blunting of the class orientation of American politics, a process under way since the election of 1940 had revealed that the sharp class cleavage of 1936 had been softened. Put bluntly, the poor, the middle- and upper-income groups in 1952 all favored the GOP ticket. In turn, among the wealthy, Stevenson had done slightly better (28–22) than among the poor who had *voted.* What many neglected, however, was that, of all the economic groups, the poor were also the most likely *not* to vote. Their rate of non-participation is striking: 47 per cent of the poor did not vote, as compared to 24 per cent of middle-income adults and 14 per cent of high income. Amid the great celebration that characterized the 1950's, this fact should have suggested disaffection or alienation of an important, sizable, neglected portion of the citizenry—to be known later as "the other America."

Election of 1960

by *Theodore C. Sorensen*

The 1960 presidential election was a watershed in American political history. The oldest man ever to serve in the Presidency was succeeded by the youngest man ever elected to it. It was the first time that the nation had elected a Catholic President; the first time that a major party had nominated two incumbent senators for President and Vice-President; and the first time that the Democrats had sent a sitting senator to the White House. He was in addition the first Democratic presidential nominee from New England in over a hundred years.

Other entrenched assumptions were cast aside—including those that proclaimed the necessity of a winning candidate's possessing a large state electoral base, executive experience as governor or general, and the backing of his party's elder statesmen and best-known political leaders in the pre-convention struggle. The medium of television and the mechanics of public opinion polling played far greater roles in 1960 than ever before. The suburbs surrounding the nation's great cities became a hotly-contested key to the outcome for the first time. The professional politicians and party organizations played a lesser role than ever before. For both parties it was at that time the most expensive campaign in history. Not surprisingly it produced the largest vote in history and the closest popular vote in seventy-six years.

Eight years under President Eisenhower had produced no war, no depression, not even a single clear-cut issue to seize the electorate or rouse the Democratic opposition. Eisenhower had been an enormously popular

President, presiding over a relatively united Republican party that had far more support from the nation's newspaper editors and political donors than any Democratic contender in 1960 could hope to muster. He had been re-elected in 1956 with an overwhelming margin from a comfortable, contented, complacent electorate. Had the Constitution not been amended after Franklin Roosevelt's death to prohibit a third presidential term, he could have easily been reelected again. For the divided opposition party to switch enough votes in such states as New York, New Jersey, Michigan, and Pennsylvania —not one of which had been won by a Democratic presidential nominee since 1944—to turn the Republicans out of the executive branch seemed contrary to all historical precedent. For a youthful, controversial Roman Catholic senator with no executive experience to do it seemed impossible.

To some the presidential campaign of 1960 seems in retrospect a romantic chapter in the often sordid history of American politics. A young idealist surrounded by amateurs and intellectuals emerged from his battles with death and racketeering to overcome the forces of bigotry and bossism and narrowly win the nation's greatest prize after a grueling contest with a widely distrusted opponent, only to be killed one thousand breath-taking days later. Other more cynical observers regarded the 1960 election essentially as a contest between two ruthlessly ambitious young men, both smoothly skilled in politics and public relations, and both possessing more cool reserve than deep emotional convictions. Neither of these two pictures conveys the whole truth, but only time will shake the tenacity of those still convinced that either one is correct.

Others at the time emphasized the extent to which the election of 1960 passed the torch to a new generation of leaders. Richard Nixon and Hubert Humphrey were defeated. Lyndon Johnson, losing his bid for the presidential nomination, settled for the Vice-Presidency. Nelson Rockefeller found he could not even enter the arena. All of these men, it was widely said, were permanently out of the presidential picture which the Kennedy brothers might well dominate for many years to come. These prophecies turned out to be badly mistaken.

All presidential campaigns in modern times necessarily begin well before election year. Few begin a full four years earlier as completely as did the 1960 contest. In 1956 both Richard M. Nixon, Vice-President of the United States, and John F. Kennedy, United States senator from Massachusetts, fixed their courses on respective routes from which they would not swerve for four years.

Despite the distinguished precedent set by Adams and Jefferson, no American Vice-President since Van Buren had been elevated into the Presidency by election. Frequently placed in the second spot on a campaign ticket for reasons other than their ability to lead the nation, the occupants of this somewhat peculiar and amorphous office were destined to reach the White House only upon the death of the President they served. Vice-President Nixon conducted himself with widely admired discretion and delicacy in late 1955 when President Eisenhower suffered a serious heart attack and much of the world wondered whether Nixon was about to succeed him or act for him.

That episode helped persuade Eisenhower and the Republican party to disregard an attempt more publicized than powerful by White House advisor Harold Stassen and others to prevent Nixon's renomination as Vice-President at
the 1956 convention. Solidifying himself with party leaders as he criss-
crossed the country supporting their local candidates and raising money for
them, and standing out as the only *political* star on the Eisenhower team so
long as Chief Justice Earl Warren remained on the Bench, Nixon from 1956
on was the heir apparent.

The Democratic national convention of 1956 also produced a new star
for that party, though it could hardly be said to have guaranteed the 1960
presidential nomination for anyone. Troubled by the conflicting claims on his
friendship and presidential prospects that were made on behalf of various
vice-presidential aspirants, and seeking a public contrast with the Republican
convention's pre-ordained selection of Nixon, Democratic presidential nominee Adlai Stevenson took the unprecedented step of asking an open convention to select his vice-presidential running mate. In the scramble that followed, the name of Senator John F. Kennedy rose surprisingly rapidly to the
top. He was backed by urban delegations who hoped his Irish Catholic credentials would help the ticket in their areas, by southern delegations who
found him more acceptable than his chief rival, Senator Estes Kefauver of
Tennessee (whose brand of liberalism was largely indistinguishable from
Kennedy's but struck his fellow southerners as traitorous), and by others impressed with his World War II heroism as a PT boat skipper as well as his
personality, writings, and speeches. A cliff-hanging, see-saw, roll-call contest
between Kennedy and Kefauver captured the imagination of the delegates
and television audience; and despite the Tennesseean's emergence as the
nominee, the young Massachusetts senator's graceful concession speech
made him an instant nationwide attraction. Speaking invitations poured into
his Senate office, and the Presidency became his unspoken goal.

But Kennedy was not alone on that trail. As the American economy fal-
tered in 1957–58 and the Russian Sputnik shocked the nation into a debate
over the adequacy of our education, space, and missile programs, the creaking
Democratic coalition slowly began to recover from its 1952 and 1956 trounc-
ings at the hands of General Eisenhower. To the dismay of Nixon and others,
Eisenhower had made little effort to translate his enormous personal popularity
into a solid top-to-bottom Republican political organization. As a result the
Democrats had with one brief exception in 1952 maintained their position as
the majority party in the Congress and country, and in the congressional elections of 1958 won a tremendous victory. Thus it was natural that several
Democrats began to edge toward a presidential race, convinced that a Democrat had a better chance to win than in 1956, that Nixon was beatable in an
election on his own, and that Kennedy's youth and religion made him an unlikely nominee despite his high standing in the Gallup Poll.

To an extent unprecedented since the days of Webster, Clay, and Calhoun, the presidential spotlight between 1956 and 1960 turned on the United
States Senate. Both parties in the past had more often looked for presidential

candidates among the governors of large states with their executive experience. But national and international problems with which governors had little
contact—on which senators, however, spoke every day—increasingly dominated public affairs after the Great Depression and the Second World War.
Governors, beset by rising state government costs and taxes, had little opportunity to become known in the nationwide media that focused on Washington
and New York. As the Republican governor of New York itself, Nelson
Rockefeller—elected to that post in 1958—was an obvious exception. But
Democratic Governors Edmund Brown of California, Robert Meyner of New
Jersey, J. Leroy Collins of Florida, and G. Mennen Williams of Michigan
found their own ambitions for the Presidency overshadowed by the struggle
on the Democratic side of the Senate. At least eight Democratic senators
were prominently mentioned as 1960 presidential possibilities, and four of
them—Lyndon Johnson, Hubert Humphrey, Stuart Symington, and John
Kennedy—became active candidates.

Lyndon Johnson, a tall, complex Texan, was not only the leader of the
Democratic majority in the Senate but dominated that body as had no one
else—not even Robert Taft or Alben Barkley—in many years. Working
closely with his fellow Texas Democrat, Speaker of the House Sam Rayburn,
Johnson's influence in Washington was second only to that of the Republican
President in the White House. Some Democratic partisans complained that
the Johnson-Rayburn team compromised with the Administration too often on
issues that might otherwise have been valuable campaign ammunition. But
Johnson was a shrewd head-counter as well as a remarkably persuasive arm-
twister. Valuing the respect he had earned from the nation's press as well as
the President for refusing to take his party down a straight obstructionist path,
he carefully employed his slender Senate majority to build a record of congressional legislation passed rather than presidential vetoes provoked, challenging the President only on those few economic and social issues on which
all wings of the Democratic party could unite.

By judicious use of his influence on committee assignments, bill advance-
ments, and other legislative favors, Johnson won the gratitude and loyalty of
virtually every Democratic senator, including all of the other leading presidential contenders. Not surprisingly, a poll of Senate Democrats showed him
to be their favorite for the Presidency. But senators rarely control, and in most
cases barely influence, their home state national convention delegations, and
reliance on their support may have temporarily misled Johnson, who was
comparatively inexperienced and untraveled in national politics outside of
Texas and Washington.

Close to Johnson personally but far more outspoken on liberal issues,
Minnesota Senator Hubert H. Humphrey was one of that body's most tireless
and agile debaters. He had campaigned more openly than the others for the
vice-presidential nomination under Stevenson in 1956 and had been painfully
rebuffed by the convention; but he remained a hero to the Stevenson forces,
who saw him as their logical champion if the 1952 and 1956 nominee stepped
aside in 1960. Humphrey's ability to speak forcibly and interestingly, if

lengthily, on every issue had earned him scorn in less liberal quarters but endeared him to the farm, labor, civil rights, disarmament, education, social welfare, housing, and countless other groups whose causes he had so eloquently and energetically championed.

Minnesota and other businessmen were in this category, for Humphrey worked hard on behalf of all his constituents and had earned the respect of many moderates by gradually toning down his rhetoric in the decade following his 1948 election to the Senate. A boundless campaigner for other liberals around the country, he possessed, more than most, a keen knowledge of those individuals outside of Washington—particularly in the Midwest and West—who were key to the presidential nomination. Late in 1958, an extraordinary eight-hour interview with Soviet leader Nikita Khrushchev gave him the kind of enormous publicity splash of which all candidates dream.

The following year Khrushchev again played a major role in America's presidential picture—not only by a tour of this country as President Eisenhower's guest but also by engaging in a highly publicized, widely photographed "debate" with Vice-President Nixon at an American exhibition in Moscow. Khrushchev—who in 1960 would again have an impact on American politics when he denounced Eisenhower at an abortive Paris summit conference in the spring, and still again when he attended the United Nations General Assembly in the fall—was increasingly important in American politics as well as American foreign policy because he symbolized the issue to which would-be candidates were more and more addressing themselves: namely the growing Soviet military, economic, and political strength that offered a challenge if not a threat to the United States. Foreign policy questions, such as the alleged "missile gap" between American and Russian total war capacities, were rapidly coming to the forefront of political debate in the latter years of the Eisenhower Presidency.

Missouri Senator Stuart Symington's prospects for the Democratic presidential nomination rested largely on that single issue of military preparedness. A handsome, wealthy, former Air Force Secretary under Truman with a business background, he had pursued that subject with single-minded determination since even before his election to the Senate in 1952. Hoping to emulate his hero Winston Churchill by sounding the alarm before others recognized the need, he followed a soft-spoken moderate approach on other issues that befitted a border state senator. He lacked the nationally-renowned stature, intellectual depth, and platform zest of the other major contenders; but he had the right location both ideologically and geographically to become the compromise choice that could hold the party together. As the handicaps of the other candidates were weighed in practical political circles, Symington's name emerged as either the favorite choice or the most predictable winner in various polls of congressmen and political leaders.

It was indeed a strange political season as 1960 neared and the talk in Democratic ranks centered more on the candidates' liabilities than on their assets, as though the nomination would be made by a process of elimination rather than elevation. Lyndon Johnson was a southerner, and not since the

Civil War had one so identified been nominated or elected President. Johnson insisted that he was a westerner and a national Democrat in the Franklin Roosevelt tradition. He skillfully guided two civil rights bills through the Senate over Deep South opposition. But the more southern Democrats of all stripes united on his candidacy, the more doubts northern Democrats expressed as to whether he was acceptable in their cities among black and labor union voters.

Hubert Humphrey in turn was regarded as unacceptable to the South and to other old-line or small-state Democrats who feared his controversial reputation as an outspoken liberal. Adlai Stevenson, who had not yet decided on his 1960 role, was dismissed by many of the professionals as a two-time loser whose reluctance to plunge into the ordeal of a presidential campaign once again was matched by their reluctance to campaign with him once again. Jack Kennedy was not only too young and inexperienced, said the professionals, but his membership in the Catholic Church made him in the eyes of all who remembered the party's debacle in 1928 non-electable as President and a popular choice for Vice-President. Symington, according to his supporters, was everyone's second choice, but his detractors made exactly the same point.

All of these candidates had considerable assets as well. Kennedy's included a Pulitzer Prize for his *Profiles in Courage*, a study of senators risking their careers for what they regarded to be right; a campaign team and technique well-honed in Massachusetts, which reelected him to the Senate in 1958 by a record margin; a beautiful wife; and both the physical and intellectual attributes necessary to communicate clearly and appealingly on the television tube as well as the public platform. He also possessed some mixed blessings: a famous father who had good judgment and connections but a mean reputation as a conservative isolationist; an impassioned investigator brother Robert, along with whom he had incurred the wrath of politically powerful labor leaders as well as the praise of millions of TV viewers for doing battle against corruption in the union movement; and a family fortune that stirred resentment and presumably set the young senator apart from the average American but also enabled him to organize in advance a fully-staffed campaign with all the necessary trimmings.

The Kennedys were wealthy, very wealthy. But their riches paled in comparison with those of the only serious Republican threat to Nixon's nomination, New York's Governor Nelson A. Rockefeller. Charming, hard-driving, and well-connected by family fame and fortune as well as his government experience, the handsome governor appeared at first to be a formidable contender. His popularity among Republicans had been at a peak immediately after the 1958 elections. His sweeping victory over Averell Harriman contrasted sharply with the resounding setbacks suffered by Republican candidates across the nation, despite Vice-President Nixon's back-breaking campaign on their behalf. Speaking out strongly on such national issues as defense, medical care, and economic growth, his stands did not differ sharply from those of the Democratic contenders. Nor did his office require him to defend the

Eisenhower Administration. Recruiting a vast and talented team of aides, advisors, researchers, political scouts, and publicity men, he sought to position himself to moderate and liberal Republican President-makers as a fresh, exciting alternative to Nixon (whom he disliked), an alternative who would be less vulnerable to Democratic attack and more appealing to that majority of voters outside the regular Republican tent.

But the Vice-President, with far more political experience and know-how, could not be dislodged from the inside track. He alone was identified among Republican leaders with their popular President. He alone had gained the necessary contacts and political IOU's in his trips across the country. The New York governor's advocacy of state tax increases caused adverse reactions far beyond the boundaries of Rockefeller's own state. His increasing preoccupation with state issues largely confined him to Albany. His only real chance of defeating Nixon for the nomination lay in a sweep or near-sweep of the presidential primaries; and his scouting reports and poorly-received personal trips into other states persuaded him that his prospects of winning over the regular Republican vote in those primary states was clearly too slim to justify the time away from his Albany duties that such a campaign would entail.

Thus in late December, 1959, the Republican contest for the presidential nomination virtually ended before it had formally begun. A public statement issued by Governor Rockefeller concluded: "I am not, and shall not be, a candidate for the nomination for the Presidency. This decision is definite and final." While this guaranteed Nixon's nomination, the Vice-President had already felt assured of that prize and was genuinely disappointed at being denied the opportunity to gain more exposure for himself and experience for his organization in a series of contested primaries that he was confident he could win. He had reason to believe, moreover, that Rockefeller would remain waiting in the wings for a Nixon slip.

His judgment was correct. While the Vice-President entered all Republican primaries in order to rally his followers, these were largely uneventful non-contests that could not compete with the Democratic primaries in the same states for headlines and voter interest. Rockefeller, meanwhile, publicly rejected suggestions that he serve as Nixon's runningmate or as convention chairman, stating that he would not even attend the national convention in Chicago. After an American U-2 "spy plane" had been downed over Russia at a time destined to wreck the Paris summit conference and cast a shadow over the Eisenhower Administration's handling of foreign policy, Rockefeller called for an open national debate on that subject. Immediately thereafter he indicated his availability to be drafted for President. In June he issued a challenge to the Republican party and its platform-drafters to repudiate in effect the Eisenhower Administration policies on a whole host of national security, civil rights, and other issues.

A successful and spontaneous draft of an unwilling presidential candidate is a rarity, if not an impossibility, in modern American politics. Nelson Rockefeller in 1960 was not unwilling, the large Draft Rockefeller movement with all its bands and banners was not spontaneous, and it had no chance of being successful. Nixon nevertheless, in order to avoid a bitter platform fight and in order to build a united party for the November elections, flew to New York for a long, secret meeting with the governor that produced a compromise statement on the disputed issues. Conservative Republicans were furious at what appeared to be Nixon's surrender, and for a brief moment they threatened to put forward their champion, the articulate and personable Senator Barry Goldwater from Arizona, as a serious presidential candidate. Eisenhower also was reported unhappy with the wording that implied his Administration's inadequacies.

But a smooth Nixon operation eventually quieted all storms. His swift nomination by the convention, his selection of the popular United Nations Ambassador Henry Cabot Lodge as his runningmate, his excellent acceptance speech that rang all the right notes for Republicans everywhere, all left the Grand Old Party united and prepared for the November election. "I believe in the American dream," Nixon told an enthusiastic convention, "because I have seen it come true in my own life. . . . When Mr. Khrushchev says our grandchildren will live under Communism, let us say his grandchildren will live in freedom."

This show of Republican harmony was in sharp contrast with the Democratic picture. The number and diversity of Democratic candidates contending for the presidential nomination in 1960 had enlivened the political year but increased the scars in the party. Not all of these contenders entered the primaries. Adlai Stevenson remained undecided about a third try for the nomination, though rejecting the pleas of other candidates for his endorsement and acquiescing without commitment in the efforts of many of his long-time supporters and financial backers to organize a Draft Stevenson movement. Stuart Symington, continuing on the course of caution he hoped would result in his emergence as a compromise candidate after the other candidates damaged each other, decided to stay out of all primaries. Lyndon Johnson, with no desire to tackle Kennedy and Humphrey in primary contests that appeared to be unfertile territory for a Texan, felt his route to the nomination lay through his Senate Majority Leader's office. These may well have been crucial decisions. Johnson would later encounter skepticism on his claim that he could carry northern states, because he had no primary victories to prove it. Had Symington entered and won in Indiana, or Stevenson in Oregon, or Johnson in West Virginia, the convention decision in July would probably have been different.

For Kennedy and Humphrey the primaries were not a matter of free choice. Neither had a chance of being nominated without entering and winning these pre-convention contests to disprove their critics, and both knew it. Neither one had the support of the party's powerbrokers, who would select a safer candidate if the decision were left to them in a "managed" convention. Both had to prove their acceptability to a cross-section of rank-and-file voters beyond the borders of their home states, Kennedy because of his age and religion, Humphrey because of his reputation for extreme liberalism. Nor did either one have any hope of obtaining the necessary convention majority so long as the other was in the race. Thus while neither could wrap up the nomination in the primaries, either or both could lose it on those battlefields and each hoped to knock the other out of the contest.

Thus early in 1960 the battle was joined in a series of primary contests from the coast of New Hampshire to the coast of Oregon. Senator Wayne Morse made a dark-horse entry into a handful of those fights but Symington, Johnson, and Stevenson stayed away. Their supporters hoped for a double knock-out or, failing that, at least the elimination from the contest of Kennedy, who was the front runner in the public opinion polls. Kennedy at one point charged that the others were "ganging up" on him, but it would have been a difficult charge to document, other than the existence of some fund-raising for Humphrey by Stevensonians.

This was natural. Although both Kennedy and Humphrey had been warm Stevenson supporters in 1952 and 1956, the Minnesotan had a closer relationship with the former standard-bearer and his principal adherents, as well as a better-known record of support for the various liberal causes dearest to their hearts. Many of them were suspicious of Kennedy's religion, wealth, father or brother, and regarded the Massachusetts senator as a young opportunist who had equivocated on civil liberties and civil rights. His record in the Senate was not as noteworthy as that of Humphrey, who had been elected to that body in 1948, four years before young Congressman Kennedy had upset the incumbent Massachusetts Senator Henry Cabot Lodge.

But Kennedy was not lacking in assets in this battle between two inexhaustible campaigners. In the three and one-half years following his sudden arrival on the national scene at the 1956 national Democratic convention, he had fulfilled speaking invitations in every one of the fifty states and appeared on dozens of national television shows. The delivery of hundreds of speeches — consistently crammed with statistics and literary or historical allusions, and inevitably beginning with humor and ending with a dramatic quotation — had considerably improved his style and increased his inventory of subjects. Despite warnings from the experts that he was starting too early and attracting too much attention too soon, he had been either author or subject of several dozen prominent magazine articles, and had collected his best speeches and writings in another book. He had maintained through mailings, telephone calls, Christmas cards, and visits frequent and friendly communication with important Democrats — not merely the nationally-known names who were largely hostile or skeptical regarding his candidacy but also those lesser known leaders at the state, county, and city level who were more likely to be, to choose, or to influence delegates to the 1960 national convention. He had built a small, efficient, devoted staff which had almost no national political experience but matched the candidate's determined and confident zeal.

Finally, and of considerable importance, the Kennedy family had ample funds and Humphrey did not. Both men had to raise money to finance a nationwide campaign; but the inherent advantage of a wealthy candidate — symbolized by the Kennedy family plane and his retention of a private pollster — was understandably resented by the Humphrey team. Despite round after round of criticism on this subject, it appeared to influence few voters.

The two key primaries were in Wisconsin and West Virginia. Humphrey had not contested Kennedy in the latter's neighboring state of New Hampshire, and Kennedy for the same reason had been fearful of accepting Humphrey's challenge to contest with him in Wisconsin. But knowing that his own political handicaps required him to risk all in order to gain all, and encouraged by his private polls, Kennedy literally moved himself, his family, and his campaign team into Wisconsin for the month of March, 1960. He shook hands outside meat factories at 5:30 in the morning with the temperature at 10° and visited dairy farms deep in mud. He talked about Wisconsin issues —milk, timber, waterways—as did Humphrey, whose record on agriculture was far more appealing in a farm state than that of the Bostonian.

The press, however, emphasized another issue, the religious issue, despite Humphrey's prompt repudiation of all bigoted attacks on Kennedy in the state. When Kennedy won the primary on April 5, his victory was tarnished by the prominence given in most news analyses to the religious identity of those voters and districts supporting and opposing him. While geography appeared to some to be a more decisive factor than religion—Humphrey having run best particularly among farm voters in the areas bordering Minnesota —undoubtedly the Massachusetts senator's religion was at least one reason many voters preferred him and others opposed him. The press (which had predicted he would sweep all ten Wisconsin districts, not merely the six that he carried) refused to grant him the verdict he sought: namely, that defeating Hubert Humphrey next door to Minnesota demonstrated Kennedy's electability and Humphrey's non-viability as a candidate.

One result was to encourage Humphrey to abandon his plans for withdrawal and to carry the battle into the next contested primary state, West Virginia. Another result was to make the entire country, including 95 per cent Protestant West Virginia, acutely aware of the religious issue; and the same private pollster, whose earlier survey showing a 70–30 margin for Kennedy over Humphrey had helped induce the Bay State senator to enter West Virginia's primary, now predicted a 60–40 victory for Humphrey in that state on the basis of a new poll. The Kennedy family and team moved in, aided by Franklin D. Roosevelt, Jr., but vigorously opposed by a coalition of unions and other candidates' supporters. The open manifestations of anti-Catholic sentiment were overwhelming. In a Washington speech before the American Society of Newspaper Editors and thereafter throughout the hills and hollows of West Virginia, Senator Kennedy met the religious issue head on, emphasizing his record on separation of church and state, on independence from ecclesiastical authority, and against public aid to parochial schools.

> I am not the Catholic candidate for President. I do not speak for the Catholic Church on issues of public policy, and no one in that Chruch speaks for me. . . . Are we to say that a Jew can be elected Mayor of Dublin, a Protestant can be named Foreign Minister of France, a Moslem can sit in the Israeli Parliament but a Catholic cannot be President of the United States?

Despite a tide of anti-Catholic sermons and pamphlets in West Virginia, responsible Protestant clergymen there and across the nation began to deplore the issue. Humphrey again made it clear he wanted no votes on that basis. Both candidates—despite some acrimonious personal exchanges inspired by Humphrey's bitterness at Kennedy's far greater spending and Kennedy's bitterness at Humphrey staying in the race when he no longer had a chance to be nominated—stressed the importance of other issues in that hungry and impoverished state. The wealthy young Bostonian, visibly moved by the human misery he saw as never before among the unemployed coal miners and their families, came away from West Virginia in May with a far deeper feeling about poverty in America.

He came away also with an upset victory by a 61–39 per cent margin. Humphrey made a tearfully stirring statement of withdrawal from the presidential race and returned to Minnesota to seek reelection to the Senate. Kennedy continued on to the Maryland and Oregon primaries, having also won unopposed in Indiana and Nebraska. The results were no longer in doubt or even very close. But he knew that the votes of the primary states were not enough. Even during the primaries, he had continued his quest of delegates in other states, flying to various state Democratic dinners, conventions and committee meetings, soliciting endorsements, recruiting delegates, neutralizing opponents. His remarkable knowledge of the delegate selection process, and his inexhaustible energy in pursuing it, outmaneuvered the other candidates in much the same way as Senator Goldwater would in his party four years later.

Humphrey's withdrawal did not leave Kennedy alone in the 1960 field. Stuart Symington, backed by former President Harry Truman, had formally announced in March; but his search for delegates as a compromise second choice candidate had lost much of its force among northern leaders unable to deny the impact in their states of Kennedy's primary victories. Symington had to hope for a deadlocked convention. Lyndon Johnson also hoped for a stalemated convention—one in which the votes cast for favorite sons and other candidates would make a Kennedy majority impossible, causing the convention to turn eventually to the party leader in the Senate with his genius for accommodation and his ties to nearly every state. That prospect strongly depended on a sizable vote among northern delegations for Adlai Stevenson; and the former nominee's resistance to seeking renomination openly had not deterred his supporters from stepping up their efforts for him and increasing his schedule of speeches.

The growing prominence of foreign policy issues (on which Stevenson was a recognized leader) following the collapse of the Paris summit conference, combined with Stevenson's repeated refusal to take his name out of the race or back any other candidate, spurred on the Draft Stevenson volunteers. They too counted on a convention deadlock, on Kennedy being unable to obtain a majority on an early ballot. Much as Symington and Johnson and their respective supporters were doing, the Stevenson leaders criss-crossed the country seeking delegate votes or alternatively urging them to stay uncommitted or stick with favorite sons. The movement toward Kennedy after the West Virginia Primary made their task difficult. But all estimated headcounts made clear that every delegate vote was crucial. If Johnson could add to his southern bloc enough votes in the West and Midwest—where he now openly campaigned against Kennedy as a boyish appeaser of the Soviets—and if Stevenson could pick up enough votes in the big states, then the convention deadlock of which three presidential camps dreamed was a certainty.

But there was no deadlock. Kennedy's sixty-five thousand miles of air travel in two dozen states during 1960 prevented the "Stop Kennedy" coalition from obtaining impressive support outside the South. Nor was it ever a real coalition. Had Johnson and Symington united their forces behind Stevenson, or had the Stevenson liberals and Johnson southerners compromised on Symington, the Kennedy surge might have been stopped. Instead a nationally televised attack on Kennedy's age (and, some felt, implicitly on his religion) by former President Truman virtually on the eve of the convention served only as an excuse for a masterful Kennedy reply that helped demolish the whole youth and inexperience argument. A shabby attempt by Johnson's managers in a press conference to cast doubt on Kennedy's physical fitness enabled the young senator to refute the rumors that had long circulated because of an old adrenal condition. Stevenson supporters in large numbers picketed the outside of Convention Hall in Los Angeles, and cheered wildly on the inside for both their leader who made a brief address and for Senator Eugene McCarthy's brilliant nominating speech; but Stevenson's home state of Illinois stood firm for Kennedy. Johnson challenged Kennedy to debate before their two delegations, but Kennedy's graceful and gently humorous response to the Majority Leader's charges solidified the front runner's standing.

Many of the experts still predicted a Stevenson-Kennedy ticket. The widow of former President Franklin Roosevelt, a long-time Stevenson admirer, was among those urging Kennedy to take second spot where he would have an "opportunity to grow and learn." Humphrey endorsed Stevenson; but his long-time ally, Minnesota Governor Orville Freeman, made the nominating speech for Kennedy. Privately, Kennedy was nervous. If he did not win a majority on the first roll call, he felt, defections could lead to a deadlock and a compromise choice.

Aided in the last hours by the withdrawal of a favorite-son candidate in Iowa, and by narrow majorities deciding to give him all their states' delegates in two other states, Kennedy received his majority as the first alphabetical roll call reached Wyoming, the last state to be called. Unanimous support from New England, victory in every primary entered, the backing of all the big northern states and half the votes from the western states comprised his majority. He received only 13 votes in the entire South compared to the 307 cast for Johnson, who finished second with 409 votes behind Kennedy's 806.

It was logical, therefore, for Kennedy in his immediate quest for a runningmate to turn first to Johnson—the runner-up in the convention, the candidate of the one area most opposed to Kennedy, the leader of the Democratic party in the Senate, and a man who had not only the suitably Protestant, rural, and big-state background, but also the kind of genuine ability which Kennedy respected. The new presidential nominee could not have known, however, that Johnson would accept the second spot, for the Majority Leader had been publicly scornful of this possibility for months. But, in a decision that would help shape American presidential politics not only in 1960 but in 1964 and 1968, Johnson did accept. Outraged protests from labor and liberal delegates were quieted. An exhausted Kennedy delivered his acceptance address on "The New Frontier"—"not what I intend to offer the American people but what I intend to ask of them." And the race was on.

Both candidates expressed confidence, yet both recognized that a close, difficult contest lay ahead. The Democratic primaries and convention battles had given Senator Kennedy more recent nationwide publicity than Vice-President Nixon had been able to garner from his relatively smooth track to the nomination. But Nixon had been nominated by a more united party and a less tumultuous convention. He was better known nationally as the result of eight years of almost constant compaigning in the Vice-Presidency. Nixon's runningmate, although he would prove to be a far less industrious and effective campaigner, was also better known nationally than Kennedy's as a result of television coverage of UN debates. The Democratic party was still regarded as the majority party in the country; but this was largely due to Democratic strongholds in the South which Nixon expected to crack. A Gallup Poll taken immediately after both conventions gave Nixon a 50–44 lead with only 6 per cent undecided.

In truth there were many more undecided, and many of those voters saw only the superficial similarities between the two major party nominees. Both were comparatively young and earnest men first elected to Congress in 1946 but still shy and nervous in many circumstances that political veterans instinctively enjoyed. Both were widely traveled abroad and preferred foreign policy as a specialty over domestic policy. Both were proud to be professional politicians and were more expert in their knowledge of that profession than any of their advisors. Both possessed an understanding of the unique importance of the office of the Presidency, a genuine dedication to advancing the national interest, and a sense of dignity and self-confidence as presidential candidates. Both had an uneasy time trying to please the disparate regional and other factions of their respective political parties, although in the end it was the Republican nominee who pursued this balancing act longest and suffered the most for it. Both had on at least one notable occasion won the scorn of the nation's intellectual liberals, Nixon for his zealous role on the House Un-American Activities Committee and his famous "Checkers" speech of 1952 defending his use of private funds in Washington, and Kennedy for going unrecorded even by "pairing" in 1954 when illness caused him to be absent on the Senate roll-call vote censuring Senator Joseph R. McCarthy.

But the grueling campaign would in time reveal to these undecided voters substantial differences based on party, personality, and philosophy. In his speeches the Democratic challenger looked to the future—to the fate of new generations and new nations, the conquest of space and disease, the realization of the American dream for all. President Eisenhower's deputy was required to look more often than his opponent to the past—to the preceding

eight years in which the American people had on the whole been more prosperous and contented than ever before. The younger candidate spoke in idealistic terms about what the nation could do; the incumbent Vice-President
spoke in proud terms about what his Administration had done. To many Nixon
had shown a tendency toward flexibility and expediency over the years that
raised doubts in their minds whether he had any deep convictions to which he
was committed, other than a narrow anti-communist militance.

The first phase of the campaign saw setbacks for both candidates. A serious infection from a knee bump suffered on a successful tour of the South
confined Nixon to a hospital for nearly two weeks, thereby diminishing both
his visibility and his vitality at a crucial time. Kennedy had felt equally frustrated by his earlier confinement to a late August session of Congress to
which Johnson and Rayburn had committed their respective houses before
the convention recess. At the time it had been regarded by many as a ploy in
Johnson's campaign, designed to give him increased stature and leverage with
reluctant liberal and labor delegates who desired specific bills passed and give
him as well post-convention exposure in a setting he could turn to his own advantage as presidential nominee. Whatever the original motive, the session
was a disaster for the Democrats. It revealed the deep split in their party over
civil rights, gave them an appearance of impotence in their inability to enact
any of the items in their new liberal platform, and kept Kennedy on the Senate floor, where he was least effective politically, and away from the campaign
circuit, where he was most effective.

But once they were released from their frustrating confinements, both
candidates spent nearly every waking hour of every remaining day and night
in action. Kennedy concentrated on the large industrial states and hoped, with
Johnson's help, to pick up enough southern and other states to achieve the
necessary electoral college majority. Nixon, aware of Kennedy's big-state
strategy but unable to write off those states, pledged to campaign in every one
of the fifty states, a pledge that he maintained despite pleas from his advisors—particularly after his loss of time in the hospital—that he focus his efforts
on the most crucial states. Both men relied on enormous national organizations, with advance men to drum up crowds, organizers to register and solicit
the faithful, fund-raisers and speechwriters, press agents, pollsters, transportation and communications aides, researchers, advisers and all the rest.

Both men on the stump deviated constantly from the mimeographed texts
given to the press, to the latter's dismay. But Kennedy was more accessible to
the press than Nixon, gave them more variety in his extemporaneous remarks,
and was generally regarded by many of the veteran reporters covering both
campaigns as being more considerate and relaxed in his relations with them.
Such differences in reaction were bound to be reflected in the dispatches filed
by these correspondents to their newspapers back home. The atmosphere of
rapport and geniality on the Kennedy campaign caravan also added to the
sense of confidence that continued to emanate from the candidate and his
staff, and this affected press predictions as well.

But by 1960 television had replaced the newspaper as the most influential medium affecting voter opinion, and Nixon had planned from the outset to make the most of his shrewd and intimate knowledge of this means of communication. A devout believer in timing the pace of a campaign so that it "peaked" exactly on Election Day, he planned a saturation television effort for the weeks leading up to that day topped off by a four-hour telethon on the final day. The Kennedy campaign—which began cutting back expenditures as his party went deeply into debt—could not match the Nixon investment in television or his expertise on its use. Nevertheless the senator's ability to communicate effectively on this medium was rated higher than the Vice-President's. He was natural, relaxed, extremely handsome, and spoke in cool tones and language more suited to the living room audience than was the political hall oratory of most candidates. He too made extensive use of television, preferring five-minute televised segments of his campaign in action to thirty-minute nationwide addresses, and seeking all the free time possible on panel interview and other public events programs.

For both candidates the crucial use of television came in their series of four nationally-televised debates over all major TV and radio networks at prime viewing time in late September and October. These were made possible by a generous network offer and a congressional suspension of the equal time rule that would have required inclusion of numerous fringe party candidates. To the surprise of both his advisors and his adversaries, a confident Nixon accepted Kennedy's challenge. Thus the largest campaign audience in American history—estimated at seventy million adults—watched the candidates confront each other face-to-face on September 26.

All agree that the first debate was a turning point in the campaign. Kennedy, well-rested and well-briefed, appeared forceful yet at ease in answering questions posed by a panel of newsmen to the two candidates. Nixon appeared to be tired, uneasy, and defensive, and holding in check his customary aggressive debater's style for fear of undermining his new image as statesman. It is doubtful that either of them scored any decisive points in formal debate terms. Both men were well-informed and articulate, both appeared nervous in their opening statements, both used lines previously tried out on campaign audiences. But if Kennedy did not win the first debate, Nixon lost it. He was still underweight from his hospital stay; and his make-up and grey suit under the studio floodlights made him look pale beside the always tan Kennedy. Nixon's sometimes hesitant and weary manner contrasted sharply with Kennedy's more confident and vigorous style.

Kennedy, moreover, had gained merely by showing up. If the first debate resulted in a draw, as the pundits of the press all declared, Kennedy had still become better and favorably known to millions who had previously heard only that he was a rich, young Catholic. Nixon's basic argument that as Vice-President he was more experienced and had "stood up" to Khrushchev in their debate now had less appeal to those who had watched him debate with the more decisive and determined Kennedy.

If—as some said—only a tiny fraction of the voters moved from Nixon to Kennedy as a result of the debate, that was enough in a close election. The widespread assumption that the experienced Nixon would trample Kennedy made even a draw helpful to the Democrat. Most importantly, the debate solidified Kennedy's strength in his own party, where Nixon had counted on major defections. Stevenson Democrats, suspicious of their party nominee's runningmate and his refusal to commit himself on their hero as Secretary of State, now rallied to the party banner. Previously cool Protestant Democrats and conservative Democrats were also among those moving from the ranks of undecided into the Kennedy column.

The remaining three debates were less important but preserved the gains Kennedy made through the first one. Nixon returned to a more aggressive style and appearance, and was at his best in the third round when he was not required to be present in the same studio as Kennedy. These three debates were judged to have aided both candidates about equally; but the private pollsters for both Kennedy and Nixon as well as subsequent in-depth surveys concluded that the four debates as a whole had on balance aided the Democratic nominee.

The issues raised in these four confrontations, like most of the issues raised in the campaign generally, had less effect than the general impressions left by the candidates. The Peace Corps was the only important new proposal to come out of the campaign, and even that had been suggested in various forms for several years. Kennedy's basic theme was the necessity "to get this country moving again," to confront the challenges of the sixties instead of complacently drifting as in the 1950's, and thereby to increase America's prestige abroad, economic progress at home, and national security standing. Nixon's basic theme was the continuation of the peace and prosperity achieved under Eisenhower. He accused Kennedy of unpatriotically running down the nation, of lacking the necessary experience, and of advocating radical programs that would bankrupt the Treasury and inflate the cost of living. Kennedy urged his audiences to cast off inertia and indifference and meet their responsibilities as Americans to maintain freedom. Nixon warned his audiences not to tamper with the strength of America's leadership and economy with a naive young President who did not know what it was like either to be poor or to deal with the communists. Kennedy stressed the historical negativism of the Republican party and, never criticizing Eisenhower by name, deplored the greater Russian progress in space, the decline in U.S. prestige abroad, and the lag in America's appeal to the developing world. Nixon, always mentioning Eisenhower by name but rarely the Republican party, proposed a variety of peace missions and conferences as well as domestic programs that went well beyond those of the Eisenhower Administration. He gibed at Kennedy's wealth, youth, and allegedly left-wing advisors and supporters. Kennedy accused Nixon of lacking credibility and consistency.

The unusual place occupied by President Eisenhower in the American political scene posed a delicate problem for both candidates. Kennedy privately held Eisenhower responsible for the national drift and disarray that constituted the premise of his campaign attack, and he also regarded the President as more conservative on most domestic issues than his Vice-President.

But Eisenhower's continuing popularity made it impossible to campaign against him by name. Nixon recognized the value of his identification with Eisenhower and the need for the President's direct intervention in the campaign. But he disliked being forced to defend another man's record and decisions and was sensitive about his having merely served Eisenhower in a secondary role—a sensitivity increased by Eisenhower's presumably but not clearly facetious remark at a press conference that he would need a week to think of some Nixon contribution to Administration policy. The Vice-President did not feel he could pressure the older man, who was not only his Chief but had a recent history of ailments and a well-known disdain for political combat, into an earlier and more intensive role in the campaign. Nor did he want his own independence in the campaign overshadowed by presidential speeches that stressed their minority party and some of their Administration's less popular policies. As a result, the all-out participation of President Eisenhower in Nixon's effort that fall was delayed. When it began, the President drew tremendous crowds and responses. But the shape of the campaign was by that time fairly well set, and Kennedy continued to press the same issues he had raised all along.

The three most solidly identifiable foreign policy issues in the campaign turned out to have very little real substantive content. Kennedy, along with Symington, Johnson, and others in both parties, voiced alarm about the possible dangers of a future USSR–US "missile gap." This helped illustrate his generalized complaint about America making a second-best effort during the contented 1950's. In fact aerial photographic intelligence collected early in 1960 by the Central Intelligence Agency indicated that the Russians had not converted their head start in rocketry and engine thrust into a massive military superiority based on intercontinental ballistic missiles. The Democrats, however, were given no hard information on this intelligence and were suspicious of Republican efforts to dampen the issue in a campaign year. Many of the Administration's own experts in previous years had warned that the Soviets possessed the industrial and technological capacity to seek a dangerous first-strike advantage. Nixon was not at liberty to reveal the contents of these secret intelligence reports and was forced to reply to his opponent's charges with general reassurances.

Nixon was similarly unable to reveal the Administration's plan to assist an army of Cuban exiles seeking the overthrow of Fidel Castro. Thus he could not respond directly to a loosely-worded call for action along these lines released by Kennedy, a call from which Kennedy later retreated. He continuing, however, to cite the Castro-communist take-over of Cuba only ninety miles from American shores as an example of the drift and decline under the Republicans that he had been stressing. A sharp divergence on a minor issue arose when Kennedy told a questioner that two little islands off the coast of communist China, Quemoy and Matsu, should be evacuated by the Nationalist Chinese as indefensible. Nixon responded that not one inch of "free soil" should be yielded to the communists. Eventually both candidates buried the issue by agreeing on America's commitment to defend Formosa, Kennedy insisting that Quemoy and Matsu should not be defended unless that was essential to protect Formosa, and Nixon insisting that they should be defended as essential to the protection of Formosa.

Even the more generalized foreign policy issues, though central to Kennedy's theme of "getting the country moving" and to Nixon's theme of "experience," were not decisive. Domestic problems played a far more important role in the final outcome. Here fate conspired against Nixon, as an economic slowdown of sizable proportions began to affect American industry across the country. It was the third recession in Eisenhower's eight years, undoubtedly related to his tight budget and interest rate policies; and while it was not visible at the start of the campaign to those untrained in economics, its impact was felt by hundreds of thousands who lost their jobs or their overtime pay at the very time that Kennedy was calling for greater economic growth and job development. Nixon had been warned of this prospect early in the year; but Administration actions to correct it were too little and too late to curb voter dissatisfaction in the major industrial centers. The Vice-President had little choice but to deny the existence of the recession and to defend the Eisenhower Administration record, while Kennedy was presented with grim evidence of his basic theme.

Black Americans as always were particularly and unfairly hard hit by the worsening of the economic climate. At first cool to Kennedy, they responded with increasing fervor as the campaign mounted to his calls for better social and economic legislation and his illustrations of the need for action which often cited their mistreatment. Nixon, realizing that the black vote was largely Democratic by tradition anyway, concentrated more on wooing southern whites displeased with Kennedy's civil rights stand. Nixon's runningmate, who had been assigned the pursuit of minority votes, endangered this strategy by baldly promising that Nixon would appoint a Negro to his Cabinet and then embarrassed the whole ticket by vacillating on this question after horrified Nixon aides reached him.

When Negro leader Martin Luther King was jailed in Georgia on a traffic violation, an indignant Kennedy put in a sympathetic phone call to King's wife while, unbeknown to him, his brother Robert (who was his campaign manager) called the local judge. Nixon and the Administration remained silent on grounds of legal propriety, and Kennedy himself made no speech or press announcement about his action. Most of his advisors had opposed it as a useless gesture that would lose more votes than it would win. But word of his action spread rapidly among black voters, aided by a Kennedy pamphlet distributed outside Negro churches on the Sunday before election, and his symbolic action was enthusiastically received.

Race, however, was a far less divisive factor in the campaign than religion. Kennedy's Catholicism posed a difficult dilemma for both presidential nominees. Far from being "buried in the hills of West Virginia" as the senator had hoped, this issue dominated private and to a lesser extent public discussions of the campaign in a manner that only ten years later seems hard to

comprehend. Kennedy felt he had answered in the spring all legitimate questions on the subject—namely his views on such issues as education, birth control, censorship, an ambassador to the Vatican, and his own freedom of conscience and action on all public policy questions. If he remained silent in the
fall, however, the continuing charges which came from an array of Catholic-
fearing spokesmen ranging from thoughtful libertarians to right-wing bigots
would lose him the debate by default. If he spoke out again in defense of his
views, on the other hand, the Republicans would accuse him of deliberately
raising the issue in order to gain sympathy and Catholic votes, while many Catholics would resent his appearing defensive and apologetic. If Vice-President
Nixon repudiated the support of those attacking his opponent on these grounds,
he would be accused of injecting the subject in order to keep it alive in the
minds of the voters. If he remained silent, on the other hand, he was accused of
accepting or even encouraging the tactics of those who stirred this controversy.

Undoubtedly, some Nixon backers were genuinely troubled by what they
regarded as legitimate questions concerning the Catholic Church's influence
on an adherent in the White House; and undoubtedly some Kennedy supporters did play on the bigotry theme for political purposes. But there is no evidence that either candidate ever encouraged, much less personally engaged in,
such tactics. Both, to their credit, remained silent on the issue when urged by
their advisors to speak out in the closing weeks of the campaign. Both no
doubt devoutly wished the whole subject would disappear.

The most important and dramatic blow against the religious issue—which
caused it virtually to disappear from most serious (as distinguished from scurrilous) campaign discussions—was struck by Kennedy early in the campaign
in a September appearance before the Houston Ministers Association. The
previous week the issue had been brought to a boil by a highly-publicized
Washington convocation of prominent conservative Protestant clergymen,
many of them well-known Republicans, who accused the Catholic Church of
openly intervening in political affairs and of assorted other evils, all of which
they ascribed to candidate Kennedy without regard to his publicly-stated positions. Their selection of Vice-President Nixon's prominent friend, the Reverend Norman Vincent Peale of New York, as chairman and press spokesman,
increased the group's prestige and media coverage. When this challenge was
blazoned across the country, Kennedy accepted the Houston group's request
that he address the Protestant clergymen of that city on the church-state
issue.

His speech did not silence the bigots automatically opposed to any Catholic. It did not end the distribution of more than twenty million pieces of hate
literature against him. But it offered reassuring answers to all reasonable questions on this subject and was commended by Protestant and Jewish organizations as an unequivocal endorsement of constitutional church-state separation.
Television coverage of the speech, and taped replays of segments purchased
by the Kennedy campaign organization for wide distribution thereafter, made
clear to all his belief in "an America that is officially neither Catholic, Protes-

tant nor Jewish . . . where there is no Catholic vote, no anti-Catholic vote, no bloc voting of any kind . . . and where religious liberty is so indivisible that an act against one church is treated as an act against all."

Thereafter he rejected all advice to devote another campaign speech to attacks on his religion, even when his position was undermined by the Catholic hierarchy in Puerto Rico instructing all church members on that island to vote against the incumbent governor with whom the church had quarreled. This event, to the dismay of Kennedy supporters, coincided with Nixon's final two-week drive which was masterfully designed to peak his campaign on Election Day. Aided by President Eisenhower's hard-hitting speeches attacking Kennedy's inexperience, and aided as well by a stepped-up and skillful use of television, the Vice-President crammed into those two weeks an extraordinarily full traveling and speaking schedule that reached millions of people across the country. "When a President makes a decision," he cried, "it is for keeps. "He can't call a bullet back after he shoots from the hip . . . in these critical times we cannot afford to have as President of the United States a man who does not think first before he speaks or acts." Because television in general and the debates in particular had generated unusual public interest in the campaign, both candidates drew enormous, excited crowds. Both utilized every available minute to speak to every possible cluster of voters; and both were in a state of physical and mental exhaustion when election day dawned.

The turnout of voters set a record—an increase of more than 10 per cent over 1956. The Gallup Poll's final report to its readers termed the election too close for any safe prediction. The results could hardly have been closer. Kennedy's popular vote margin was less than 120,000 out of nearly 69 million votes cast. He won twelve states, including Illinois, with less than 2 per cent of the two-party vote and lost six states, including California, by an equally close margin. His electoral vote total of 303 was the same as Truman's 1948 figure; but the winner-take-all electoral system frequently magnifies tiny popular vote margins into more comfortable electoral vote results. Had fewer than 12,000 people in five states—Illinois, Missouri, Nevada, New Mexico and Hawaii—voted for Nixon instead of Kennedy, an electoral vote majority would have elected the Republican ticket.

The very narrowness of the margin made possible a variety of interpretations. The number of Negroes voting for Kennedy exceeded his edge in enough states to account for his Electoral College margin. The same can be said of the number of white southerners voting for Kennedy. The same can be said of the votes of newly unemployed workers in six industrial states. A similar conclusion could be reached regarding the millions who made up their minds on the basis of the debates, or the millions of Democrats newly registered in a major drive that fall, or those voting in the twelve (out of nineteen) most important suburban areas, which Kennedy to the surprise of most Democrats carried after an intensive campaign. Winning twenty-six of the forty largest cities, including all of those in the East, was another key reflection of his original electoral strategy.

The single factor influencing more swing-voters than any other, however, according to in-depth post-election analyses, was not unemployment or foreign policy or civil rights but Kennedy's religion. While it undoubtedly helped woo back to the Democratic column large numbers of Catholic Democrats who had voted for Eisenhower over Stevenson, these were more than offset by a loss of some 4.5 million Protestant Democrats switching from Stevenson in 1956 to Nixon in 1960. Only because large numbers of Protestants who voted for Eisenhower also switched to Kennedy—(very few long-time Republican Catholics deserted Nixon, and their votes helped him carry several states)—indeed only because large numbers of citizens in every category or in no particular category switched to Kennedy—was he able to compensate for the number of votes lost on this single issue. In the South, only an extraordinarily vigorous campaign by Johnson invoking party traditions and economic issues had stemmed an earlier tide to Nixon in that region, in which religion had been even more important than civil rights. Sympathies aroused when a right-wing crowd in Dallas, Texas, jostled the Johnsons may also have been decisive in that state.

The narrowness of the result was aggravated by the decision of 14 "free electors" elected in Mississippi and Alabama to cast their votes for a conservative Virginia Democrat, Senator Harry F. Byrd. Had the other Alabama electors, and those from Louisiana, Georgia, and South Carolina joined in this movement, Kennedy would have been denied an Electoral College majority, and the election by virtue of an archaic rule of the Constitution would have been decided by the House of Representatives under a system in which each state regardless of population casts one vote. When such a move failed in the Louisiana state democratic committee by a margin of 1 vote out of 100, this threat faded. Republican charges of voting irregularities in Chicago also faded when it was realized that even a total switch of the outcome in Illinois would not affect the final result.

Because of the votes cast for these southern "free electors" and for minor party candidates, Kennedy—like every Democratic President except Roosevelt during the preceding hundred years—received less than a majority of the total popular vote. His party's proportion of the two-party vote had shown, however, an increase over its 1956 level in every state except for six in the South and border regions. Kennedy, whose uphill fight had from the start succeeded only by his surviving a series of near-defeats (and before that near-death in wartime), commented that it was a "miracle" that he had won at all. His campaign over, he turned to the tasks before him. "The margin is narrow," he said, "but the responsibility is clear."

Election of 1964

by *John Bartlow Martin*

The 1964 election was supposed to raise the most fundamental issues of American policy—war-and-peace in the nuclear age and the proper role of government in a free society—but it turned out to be one of the silliest, most empty, and most boring campaigns in the nation's history.

The great debates it promised originated in the Republican party, and to understand this it is necessary to glance backward briefly. From the Civil War to the turn of the century, the Republican party had been the dominant party in the United States. Between 1900 and 1912, however, it began to split into two wings, and the split was along ideological lines: progressive versus conservative. In 1912 the split produced Republican disaster. The conservatives clung to power within the party during the Wilson years and, in the euphoria of the 1920's, were able to win back the Presidency. The Roosevelt revolution defeated them in the nation—but not in the party. Throughout the 1930's, the conservative wing continued to dominate the Republican party—and to lose elections. By 1940 it was clear to the party managers, even the conservative ones, that something new must be tried lest the Republican party go the way of the Whigs, and so, reluctantly, they nominated Wendell Willkie. And during the rest of the 1940's they nominated a relatively liberal candidate, Thomas E. Dewey of New York. But Dewey, like Willkie, was the choice of the eastern establishment, the men from the power centers of Wall Street, advertising agencies, public relations firms, newspaper, magazine, and book publishing houses, big business, Ivy League universities, and big law offices

— men who shuttle between New York and Washington, between New York and Paris, between government and private power; men deeply concerned about America's role in world affairs, men who had long since recognized that the larger role assigned government at home by FDR was here to stay and that the best thing for them, and for the country, was to go along with it.

These men were anathema to Republican party rank-and-file workers beyond the Alleghenies, and the farther west (and south) one went, the deeper ran the resentment of eastern power. Wendell Willkie and Tom Dewey were the choices of the eastern establishment; they were most emphatically not the choices of the county chairmen and the convention delegates from the Midwest, the Rocky Mountain states, and the South. When Dewey lost the "sure-thing" election to Harry Truman in 1948, the conservatives discerned in the loss proof that the easterners had led them astray, had forced them to nominate what the *Chicago Tribune* called "me too" candidates, candidates indistinguishable from their liberal Democratic opponents, and that as a consequence an enormous "silent" vote of disgusted conservatives had stayed home and refused to vote. They turned to their hero, Senator Robert A. Taft of Ohio, determined to nominate him in 1952. Once again, however, they were foiled: General Dwight D. Eisenhower, urged on by the eastern establishment, made himself available, and although the die-hard conservatives fought his nomination in 1952, the more realistic party managers, including many whose hearts lay with Taft, saw in Eisenhower the key to certain and overwhelming victory. They were right.

President Eisenhower, had he been a politician, might have been able to heal the ancient split in his party. But his eight years in the White House only postponed the resumption of the conservative-liberal feud. In 1960, obliged to choose a new candidate, the party turned to Vice-President Richard M. Nixon. He was opposed at the convention by Governor Nelson Rockefeller of New York, on a more liberal platform than, in all probability, the majority of delegates wanted. Nixon, anxious to heal wounds, sought to compromise with Rockefeller, thereby alienating some of his more extreme right-wing supporters. These turned to Senator Barry Goldwater of Arizona, but they were only a few, and Nixon was nominated. In the course of the ensuing campaign, Nixon tried to appease both wings of his party, and pleased neither. As the campaign progressed, ending with the narrowest of margins for John F. Kennedy, many of Nixon's own party leaders accused him of throwing the election away.

During the wrenching four years that followed, encompassing President Kennedy's assassination and the accession of Lyndon B. Johnson, the ancient feud inside the Republican party resumed. Nixon's defeat for the governorship of California in 1962 seemed to eliminate him as a candidate and the feud polarized around Rockefeller and Goldwater, with two new Republican governors, George Romney of Michigan and William Scranton of Pennsylvania, in the wings. Apparently neither Rockefeller nor Goldwater wanted to feud; they liked each other. Rockefeller wanted the Presidency and was eager to please the conserv tives. Goldwater, an amiable man, seemed not at all

sure he wanted it. He occasionally persuaded his more extreme followers not
to harass the New York governor and he met Rockefeller privately several
times seeking party unity. By 1963 Goldwater was becoming convinced that a
Rockefeller nomination might not damage the conservative cause.

Beyond them, however, in the hinterland, something more important was
going on. It was a vague unease, a malaise, a dislike of the way things were
going, an inchoate "whither are we drifting" feeling. It had many wellsprings.
The Supreme Court's school desegregation decision, and its firm implementation by John Kennedy and his brother Robert, the Attorney General, along
with civil rights legislation, had created resentment in the white South and
"white backlash" in the northern cities, where many white workingmen, particularly those of eastern European extraction, felt themselves threatened by
black men. Vestiges of the corrosive McCarthyism of the 1950's remained—a
hatred of communism, a suspicion of the Government, all further inflamed by
the frustrations of Southeast Asia and other seemingly unmanageable events.
Stretching back even further, the isolationism of the late 1930's stirred again
as America's power and foreign commitments increased. Sheer population
growth pressed people closer together and required them to have numbers so
the Federal Government and its computers could keep track of them. Bearded
youths on college campuses, along with showgirls in topless dresses, offended the small-town morality. New right-wing extremist groups kept
popping up: the John Birch Society, the Minutemen, and more, some armed
or eager to arm. At the fringe were lunatics who hated communists, Jews,
Catholics, Negroes, waste, big government (or any government, it sometimes
seemed) indiscriminately. The Wyoming legislature in 1963 called for replacing the Supreme Court with a "court of the union" composed of fifty state
chief justices, getting the United States out of the U.N. and the U.N. out of
the United States, and abolishing foreign aid. (Earlier it had favored repealing
the federal income tax.)

And at the same time the conservative rank-and-file Republican party
workers contended that what they needed was, as the slogan soon put it, "a
choice, not an echo"—that is, a candidate who would clearly oppose the
Democratic drift toward big government and internationalism and thus bring
the "silent conservative vote" to the polls to overwhelm the forces of error
and evil.

Moreover, authentic voices of intellectual American conservatism were
heard in the land, the young rightist intellectuals and older ex-communist intellectuals associated with William F. Buckley, Jr.'s *National Review*, including L. Brent Bozell, Buckley's brother-in-law, frequent contributor to the
National Review, and a Goldwater ghostwriter.

What all these troubled ordinary people, disgruntled Republican politicians, and conservative intellectuals needed was a candidate. They found him
in Barry Goldwater.

Goldwater, who for a few months in 1964 was cast in the role of fanatic,
had been anything but a fanatic throughout his life. Born January 1, 1909, in
Phoenix, Arizona, the grandson of a Polish immigrant merchant, son of an

Orthodox Jewish father and a Protestant Episcopal mother, he himself belonged to Trinity Cathedral in Phoenix but was an infrequent churchgoer. An
indifferent student but a good cadet at Staunton Military Academy in Virginia,
he spent only part of one year in college, at the University of Arizona. He
became president of the family department stores, he married the daughter of
an Indiana manufacturer, and took up hobbies—aviation, golf, photography,
Indian lore, sports cars, short-wave radio. As a conservative and well-to-do
businessman, he disliked Roosevelt's New Deal. Ineligible for combat in
World War II, he ferried bombers to India and was discharged a lieutenant
colonel. Later he became chief of staff of the Arizona Air National Guard,
and as a major general in the USAF Reserve, commanding officer of the
999th Combined Air Force Reserve Squadron, made up of Members of
Congress and congressional employees. He remained forever a friend of the
military.

In 1949 Goldwater ran on a nonpartisan reform ticket for the Phoenix City
Council and won. In 1950 he managed the successful campaign of Howard
Pyle, a popular radio announcer, for governor of Arizona. Goldwater was
widely known to Rotarians, Kiwanians, and other such groups throughout
Arizona, and had spoken to them as a businessman. He used this acquaintanceship to help the Republican cause in Arizona and was rewarded in 1952
with the party's nomination for the U.S. Senate. He rode in on Eisenhower's
coattails—Eisenhower carried Arizona by 42,000 votes, Goldwater by 7,000.

Goldwater entered the Senate as an Eisenhower Republican, having
backed Eisenhower against Taft at the bitter nominating convention. To be
sure, he favored "fiscal responsibility" but he also favored peace, workmen's
compensation, and racial reconciliation. In a campaign speech, he said he
wanted to retain the social gains made in the past twenty years, including the
Social Security system, unemployment insurance, old-age assistance, aid to
dependent children and the blind, the FHA, and stock market regulation. In
the Senate he voted to outlaw the filibuster, and at a time when Eisenhower and
Nixon were considering coming to the aid of the French in the war in Indochina, Goldwater proposed to end foreign aid to France unless she freed Vietnam, Laos, and Cambodia.

During this period, and later, Goldwater employed a breezy western manner that captivated campaign audiences. In private conversation and in public
appearances he displayed a disarming candor. He once told the Platform
Committee of his party's national convention that it ought not have a platform; instead, it ought to have a "declaration of principles," and he later explained that "principles" were easier to live with than specific platform proposals—a declaration such as "we believe in the freedom of the individual"
could be interpreted with equal ease by himself and Senator Jacob Javits, the
New York liberal. Such candor—or cynicism—is rarely displayed openly by
politicians, and is therefore attractive. When he ran for President in 1964,
Goldwater decided not to run for reelection to the Senate at the same time,
though it would have been legal in Arizona, because in 1960 he had criticized
Lyndon Johnson for seeking the Vice-Presidency and a Senate seat at the

same time. When a reporter asked about it, he said he couldn't run for both offices: "After what I said about Lyndon in 1960—they'd run me out of the country. But if I hadn't opened my big mouth so loud, I might do it." He told the same reporter, "You know, I haven't really got a first-class brain" and added that once he had read his wife a speech he planned to deliver, and when she seemed unimpressed, asked "what the hell is the matter." Mrs. Goldwater replied, "Look, this is a sophisticated audience, they're not a lot of lame-brains like you, they don't spend their time looking at TV westerns. You can't give them that corn." In 1963 a reporter asked how he felt about the possibility that he might become President, Goldwater replied, "Frankly, it scares the hell out of me." Weighing the possibility of his candidacy, he once told *Newsweek*, "If I thought I'd get my tail whipped badly, I'd say the hell with it." He was a handsome man, cheerful, amiable, agreeable, friendly. In November, 1963, heading toward the nomination, he once said, "God knows, I'm still wishing something would happen to get me out of all this. It's all a little frightening." That same year, a reporter asked why he had voted for a $6 billion agricultural appropriations bill after having ceaselessly called for a "prompt and final termination of the farm-subsidy program." Goldwater denied the action, and when shown that he had indeed supported the bill, he promptly called the clerk of the Senate and had his vote changed to no. He once said, "I know nothing about farming."

All this is wholly inconsistent with the candidate who, in 1964, and for some years before, appeared before the people of the United States as the apocalyptic Savonarola of the Republican party, scourging sin, smiting big government and all its acts, including the Social Security system and TVA, threatening nuclear war to wipe out communism everywhere. *That* Goldwater said in 1963, "I'd drop a low-yield nuclear bomb on Chinese supply lines in North Viet Nam." He said in 1960, "I do not propose to promote welfare. . . . Let welfare be a private concern." In 1963, in response to the question, "Would you, as President, favor getting out of the United Nations," he said, "I would." He suggested, in 1961, "I think TVA should be turned over to free enterprise, even if they could only get one dollar for it." But in a later book, *Where I Stand*, he wrote, "I believe the United States should make the fullest possible use of its membership in the U.N." And he added "I favor a sound Social Security system, and I want to see it strengthened," and "the Tennessee Valley Authority is an enterprise unique in our nation. Some of its elements have been successful and should be continued." However, during his whistlestop campaign in 1964 he demanded of the pretty girls who cheered him, "What good is prosperity if you are a slave," and on television, more often than not, he glowered at his audience.

It was Richard Rovere's theory that there were two Goldwaters. "There is," he wrote, "on the one hand, the Senator on the hustings, the agreeable man with the easy, breezy Aw Shucks Western manner who speaks in rightist platitudes but has only a loose grip on ideology and not, apparently, much interest in it. And there is, on the other hand, the dour authoritarian polemicist whose name is signed to *The Conscience of a Conservative, Why Not Victory?*, and to many hundreds of articles, columns, and press releases so heavily freighted with smarmy theology and invocations of Natural Law ('Right-to-work laws derive from Natural Law') that they have won for the Senator the warm approval of Archduke Otto of Austria, and the admiration of the ranking ideologues of the Franco regime in Spain. There is the Goldwater who can dispose of a large national problem by saying, 'If we get back to readin', writin', and 'rithmetic and an occasional little whack where it will help, then I think our educational system will take care of itself.' And there is the portentous Goldwater, abounding in theory: 'We have forgotten that the proper function of the school is to transmit the cultural heritage of one generation to another. . . . . The fundamental explanation of this distortion of values is that we have forgotten that purpose of education. [It] is not to educate, or elevate, *society*, but rather to educate the *individual* . . . [We must] recapture the lost arts of learning.' " Rovere believed that Goldwater was captured by the intellectuals associated with the *National Review*, among others, and that they churned out under his name unnumbered words totally out of keeping with his natural style and stance. Rovere added that the invented Goldwater was far less attractive and saleable than the original, or natural, Goldwater, a case unique in recent history. Goldwater once told Stewart Alsop of *The Saturday Evening Post*, "Oh, hell, I have ghosts all over the place." Rovere reported, "Things got so bad late in 1963 that the staff had to take on some microfilm and punch-card people to sort out what Goldwater had been saying, or had been having said for him, over the years and to determine exactly what commitments had been made for him and by him."

Precisely when the intellectual conservatives took him over is uncertain but by 1957 Goldwater had broken with President Eisenhower, claiming that Eisenhower's appropriations requests were "abominably high" and calling the Republicans' fiscal policies "a betrayal of the people's trust." Asked to comment on the President's brother Milton as a party leader, he said, "One Eisenhower in a generation is enough." In the last Eisenhower Congress he supported the President only 52 per cent of the time. He alone in the Senate voted against the Kennedy-Erwin labor reform bill of 1959 and called it "the most important [vote] of my Senate career." *Congressional Quarterly* reported, "A large portion of Goldwater's national reputation is based on his articulate and consistent opposition to 'big labor.' " Goldwater favored "right-to-work" laws, a ban on union spending in politics, mandatory secret union votes before strikes could be called, and limitations on industry-wide bargaining by any one union. "As early as his first term in Congress," *CQ* noted "Goldwater was accused by national labor publications of 'tyranny,' 'neo-fascism,' and an attempt to 'smash' organized labor." As a member of Senator McClellan's "Rackets" committee, Goldwater engaged in bitter exchanges with Walter Reuther, head of the United Auto Workers, and said that Reuther and the UAW were "a more dangerous menace than the Sputniks or anything else Russia might do."

Goldwater was also a relentless enemy of high government spending and taxation. He said he considered the 16th Amendment to the Constitution, which legalized the graduated income tax, "a very poor amendment," and, though pessimistic about the prospects of eliminating the income tax altogether, vigorously condemned its progressive nature. While favoring income tax reform, he consistently defended the oil and gas depletion allowance. In a speech to the Economic Club of New York early in 1964, Goldwater said, "We are told . . . that many people lack skills and cannot find jobs because they did not have an education. That's like saying that people have big feet because they wear big shoes. The fact is that most people who have no skill, have no education for the same reason—low intelligence or low ambition." In 1962 he said he did not think Social Security should be repealed. "I do not think it can be. I would like to see us correct it. I think it should be voluntary, for one thing." In 1963 he stuck to his guns: "I think Social Security should be voluntary. This is the only definite position I have on it. If a man wants it, fine. If he does not want it, he can provide his own." He said in a Senate speech in 1961 that he considered TVA "an unfortunate socialist adventure," and in 1963, "I am quite serious in my opinion that TVA should be sold." With admirable consistency, he favored returning offshore oil to the states and exempting independent natural gas producers from federal control, opposed the national wilderness preservation system, and favored a private communications satellite system over one run by the Government. As for education, in *The Conscience of a Conservative* he claimed "Federal intervention in education is unconstitutional" and consistently voted against programs of federal aid to education.

Similarly, Goldwater stood firm for "states' rights": "I fear Washington and centralized government more than I do Moscow," he told a political rally in Spartanburg, South Carolina, in 1960, and he took the position in *The Conscience of a Conservative* that the 10th Amendment "recognizes the states' jurisdiction" in all matters not specifically designated as federal elsewhere in the Constitution. Therefore, he wrote, the whole idea of "civil rights" was constitutionally invalid and the conflict between states' rights and civil rights was only an "imagined" one. While "it may be just or wise or expedient for Negro children to attend the same schools as white children . . . they do not have a civil right to do so." Goldwater felt that education was reserved to the states by the 10th Amendment. This was patently absurd. A great many of today's problems were not dealt with—and did not exist—when the 10th Amendment was written. Goldwater went on to say, "It so happens that I am in agreement with the objectives of the Supreme Court as stated in the *Brown* [school desegregation] decision. I believe it *is* both wise and just for Negro children to attend the same schools as whites, and that to deny them this opportunity carries with it strong implications of inferiority. I am not prepared, however, to impose that judgment of mine on the people of Mississippi or South Carolina." Goldwater himself seems to have been personally opposed to racial discrimination and introduced numerous bills intended to improve the lot of the American Indian. But when the chips were down he sided with the segregationists. In 1964· he voted against the bipartisan Civil Rights Act.

Goldwater's views on foreign policy were summed up in the title of his 1962 book, *Why Not Victory?* He believed that America's foreign policy objective should be "total victory" over "the all-embracing determination of Communism to capture the world and destroy the United States." He believed that negotiations with communists were fruitless and dangerous; he favored breaking relations with the Soviet Union, keeping mainland China out of the U.N., and considering pulling the United States out; Goldwater advocated a policy aimed at overthrowing Castro and liberating Russia's east European satellites. In a debate with Senator Fulbright, who challenged his position in 1962 as impractical and risky, he said, "The President of the United States [should] declare officially that it is our purpose to win the cold war, not merely wage it in the hope of attaining a standoff. . . . It is really astonishing that our government has never stated its purpose to be that of complete victory over the tyrannical forces of international communism." Asked what kind of total victory he envisaged, he replied, "Well, the victory would not be a military victory necessarily."

Goldwater disliked most foreign aid programs as well as disarmament negotiations and agreements. Suspecting the Soviet Union's intentions, he rejected the creation of a United States Arms Control and Disarmament agency in 1961, and he strongly opposed ratification of the limited nuclear test ban treaty in 1963. He said in 1961, "I hope the Administration will call for an immediate resumption of the [nuclear] tests. Frankly, I do not care what the rest of the world thinks about us." Goldwater frequently advocated the use of low-yield atomic weapons in certain tactical situations. At a press conference in Hartford, Connecticut, on October 24, 1963, he was quoted as saying that NATO field commanders should have the authority to use tactical atomic weapons at their discretion. He later claimed misquotation—claiming he had said only that the NATO commander should have "that authority, to some extent". His aides, seeking to "clarify" the matter further, said that when Goldwater said "commanders" he had not meant local field commanders, but rather, the string of supreme NATO commanders who succeeded each other over the years.

Goldwater seemed to have a loose grip on policy. Asked in 1964 if he stood by his 1960 suggestion that nuclear weapons should be used to help uprisings in eastern Europe, he answered "If that became necessary, if that were the only way, yes." In 1961 during the Berlin crisis he said, "I have been very much concerned about the emphasis on conventional weapons [at Berlin]. I am the first to recognize that we should have a greater mix; that we should have conventional weapons; but that we should not exclude nuclear tactical weapons in our rush toward the conventional type." In 1963 he told *Newsweek*, "I'd drop a low-yield atomic bomb on Chinese supply lines in North Viet Nam." Interviewed by *The New York Times* that year, he explained "I think we could probably return a third—maybe half—of our forces if we gave the NATO command the right to use nuclear weapons—tactical weapons —when they were attacked." Again in 1964 he added, "All NATO forces stationed in Europe, regardless of nationality, should be equipped with and trained in the use of nuclear weapons, particularly of the so-called battlefield or tactical variety."

Goldwater's Vietnam views followed a similar line: "I would strongly advise that we interdict supply routes, wherever they may be, either by sea, or most importantly, through North Viet Nam, Laos or Cambodia." He felt Chinese leaders should be told that unless they stopped delivering supplies to the Viet Cong, the United States would bomb bridges and roads leading into South Vietnam. "There have been several suggestions made. I don't think we would use any of them. But defoliation of the forest by low-yield atomic weapons could well be done. When you remove the foliage, you remove the cover." Goldwater soon claimed that this last statement had been misinterpreted—then went on to say, "I would go to the Red River Valley approaches in South China. I would first take out the bridges. If that wouldn't do the job, I would take out the railroads. I would use conventional weapons. I would not use atomic weapons when conventional weapons will do the job. But I would leave it up to the commanders." Asked by *Der Spiegel* in June, 1964, what he thought of the theory that he was an impulsive man who occasionally shot from the hip, he said, "Well, that may be so. But, every time I've shot from the hip, it has later come to be the accepted position of this country." He cited his advice to tear down the Berlin wall and give NATO forces "our modern weapons," and then added "Now I'll have to admit that I possibly do shoot from the hip. I'll have to admit also that, while I'm not the most intelligent man in the world, and a lot of people think I'm quite ignorant, that I've traveled more in this world, I've done more things probably than most men in this Congress. So I've been exposed to problems and I don't have to stop and think in details about them."

Goldwater stood loyally and consistently with the military. Although he opposed Democratic efforts to increase defense appropriations during the Eisenhower Administration, in general he supported a strong United States defense establishment and, during the Kennedy-Johnson Administration, favored increases in defense budgets, especially for continuation of the manned bomber program. It troubled him that civilians sometimes vetoed military recommendations. He once said, "I am more concerned over civilian meddlers who decide an invasion of Cuba doesn't need air support than I am over military men who recommended use of enough strength to assure the success of our venture in the Bay of Pigs."

Thus many of Goldwater's views put him outside the national consensus, but the movement which claimed him stood even farther outside the consensus. It came to be called the Goldwater movement. In the beginning, however, it was not his, but rather, a movement of rightist extremists, rightist intellectuals, super-patriots, fringe-group kooks, and conservative rank-and-file Republicans.

Among those in the movement was Robert Welch, leader of the rightist John Birch Society. Welch wrote in 1958, "I know Barry fairly well. He is a great American—I raised around $2,000 in my state and sent it to him early in 1958. . . . He is absolutely superb in his Americanism. I'd love to see him

President of the United States, and maybe someday we shall." He said later that although he personally favored Goldwater for President, the Society had taken no official position. Goldwater himself, while consistently denying he was a member of the Birch Society, refused repeatedly to repudiate the support of its members and at the 1964 national convention blocked any platform amendments repudiating extremist groups. Goldwater always saw far more danger to the country from the "radical left," mainly the Americans for Democratic Action, than from such "radical right" groups as the John Birch Society. In his 1958 Senate campaign Goldwater accepted contributions from H. L. Hunt, an extremely conservative Dallas oilman, and from Americans for America, another right-wing group. He appeared several times on the Manion Forum, run by a former Notre Dame Law School Dean, Clarence E. Manion, which fought the "confiscatory, Marxist income tax" and other wickedness. Several right-wing groups tried to promote Goldwater for the presidential nomination in 1960.

It was natural that such people would turn to Goldwater. He had been one of the staunchest supporters of Senator Joseph McCarthy, and although he privately advised McCarthy to apologize to several senators to avoid censure by the Senate, when the vote on censure came Goldwater voted against it. During the censure debate he said, "Like him or not, McCarthy is the strongest voice now speaking in America against communism. . . . To remove such a man from honor and influence in America at this juncture would be a strong victory for Moscow in the field of American public opinion . . . [and] a propaganda triumph for the Attlees, the Mendes-Frances, and the double-talking co-existence-with-Russia crowd here at home, which could be incalculable in its consequences. . . . All the discredited and embittered figures of the Hiss-Yalta period of American dishonor have crawled out from under their logs to join the efforts to get even. The news columns and the airwaves have been filled with their pious talk about 'civil liberties,' 'ethical codes,' and 'protection of the innocent,' while at the same time these people have dipped into the smut pot to discredit Senator McCarthy and his work against communism." After Senator McCarthy's death, Goldwater spoke emotionally to the Wisconsin Republican state convention: "Joe and I became friends long before either of us entered the Senate. . . . He was a faithful, tireless and conscientious American. Joe McCarthy gave himself—his life—to the service of his God and his country. . . . Because Joe McCarthy lived, we are a safer, freer, more vigilant nation today. This fact, even though he no longer dwells among us, will never perish." Goldwater's affection for McCarthy was grounded in his own strong anti-communism. He wrote in *Why Not Victory*, "Our objective must be the destruction of the enemy as an ideological force and the removal of Communists from power wherever they hold it." Opponents might point out that this would entail perpetual foreign wars and crusades for ideological ends; it was music to the ears of the John Birchers and others.

However, it was not the extremist groups that converted the movement into the effective political organization which captured control of the Republican party in 1964. It was, rather, a handful of little-known, rank-and-file, Republican backroom organization men. One was F. Clifton White, a public relations consultant from Rye, New York, who after World War II had become an important figure in New York Young Republican politics and a supporter of Governor Dewey. He developed into an expert political technician and became national chairman of the Young Republicans, an important post which he firmly held from 1950 to 1960. After the Dewey defeat in 1948, White began to drift toward conservatism; he broke with Rockefeller in a New York state contest in 1948, and Nixon's 1960 loss convinced him that the Republican party needed a new kind of candidate—a conservative one. Others felt the same way—such men as John Grenier, an urbane, bright young Birmingham lawyer who became Alabama Republican state chairman, and Peter O'Donnell, a young, rich, Dallas Texan, who soon became chairman of the Texas State Republican party. They had the active support of various business executives.

On October 8, 1961, Clifton White and a score of his friends around the country met secretly in Chicago at the Avenue Motel to see whether it might be possible to seize control of the national Republican party as White had seized the Young Republicans and then to nominate a conservative candidate who could bring out the full Republican vote in 1964. They decided to try and White told Goldwater about the decision. Goldwater seemed indifferent but at the same time unwilling to repudiate the effort. They met again on December 10—this time a few more attended, including the governor of Montana—and divided the nation into nine regions, authorized White to open an office, and set out to raise sixty thousand dollars, all aimed at mobilizing conservatives. From his office in New York, White began traveling through the nation, talking with regional volunteer directors who also were being drawn to Goldwater. On August 24, 1962, White sent an unsigned and "confidential" memorandum to his select mailing list of conservatives around the country. The memorandum did not mention Goldwater's name but it sounded notes of urgency and conspiracy: "There are four months left in 1962;" "We must be prepared to move into high gear in January of 1963;" "There are some of you from whom I have not heard since April. I am anxiously awaiting word as to your state of health." White had been in twenty-eight states at least once. He reported "many encouraging signs:" Hayes Robertson (an almost fanatic Goldwater man) had become Cook County (Chicago) chairman and had met congenially with White; White had attended a "highly successful" regional meeting in Phoenix; and a conservative county chairman had been elected in Allegheny County (Pittsburgh) in Pennsylvania and would meet shortly with White "to discuss his work and association with us." (The new Pittsburgh County chairman was an enthusiastic Goldwater man.)

This was the start of the underground movement to capture the Republican party and hand it over to Goldwater. Across the nation few state and county Republican chairmen were aware of what was going on. They—and Goldwater, Rockefeller, Romney, Scranton, and nearly everyone else—were preoccupied with the 1962 mid-term elections; White and his cabal wanted the Presidency.

It was hard going, however. In October, again at Chicago and in the same motel, at a meeting so secret that White did not mention it in his confidential memos, he and his associates discussed how to proceed in view of Goldwater's own unresponsiveness. Approached repeatedly, Goldwater had remained indifferent. Moreover, he was now praising Rockefeller. Conservative funds were drying up—White had been unable to attend the September convention in Phoenix of the National Federation of Republican Women for lack of money. They decided to go ahead anyway and hold a meeting of the entire underground organization in Chicago on December 1 and 2, 1962. White announced the plans in a confidential memorandum dated October 18: "This meeting will determine where we go—whether we are serious or dilettantes." It was held in downtown Chicago at the Essex Motor Inn, nearly one hundred strong attended, and word of a "sinister" Draft Goldwater movement finally leaked to the press. In fact, it leaked in such detail that White felt sure a tape recorder had been smuggled into the motel room. The cabal saw their prospects this way, according to one published account: solid Goldwater states—435 votes mostly from southern and Mountain states plus Indiana, Maine, Missouri, Nebraska, Oklahoma, Virginia, and Washington; "almost-as-solid" states—81 votes from Georgia, Kentucky, South Dakota, and Tennessee; states that could be won with extra effort—142 votes from Illinois, Iowa, Ohio; a total of 658 votes, plus 43 additional votes from split delegations in California, Connecticut, and Michigan, for a grand total of 701, more than enough to nominate. This seemed wildly optimistic at the time. White hoped that it would persuade Goldwater to run.

Instead, it dismayed him. Annoyed at the publicity, Goldwater told reporters he hoped the group would do nothing during 1963 and give him until January, 1964, to make up his mind. He claimed, "I don't know who the group was, where they met or what it's all about. . . . I still plan to run for the Senate two years from now. . . . Things change, and it's too early to be absolutely certain." But a little later Goldwater had already declared he would not run for the Vice-Presidency, and said that as for the Presidency, "I'd rather stay in a fluid position for the rest of this year and then see how the situation looks. . . . Assume I am interested in the Presidency. It still makes more sense for me to delay. I've done my backroom work already. Nobody's been around the country more in the last ten years than I have. I know the county chairmen. I know the potential convention delegates. Rockefeller and Romney still have to meet those people, but they're already friends of mine. Another thing. I am the only conservative in the presidential picture. The others—Rockefeller, Romney, and Scranton—are liberals. You might say, 'let them fight it out for awhile.' "

White called a highly secret meeting of the inner circle at the O'Hare Inn in Chicago for early 1963. They decided to surface and compete openly with Rockefeller, who at this time was ahead in all the polls. Peter O'Donnell, the Texas Republican state chairman, would head the effort in order to convince people that bona fide party leaders, not backroom conspirators, were in charge. And so on April 9, 1963, at a press conference in the Mayflower Hotel in Washington, D.C., O'Donnell publicly announced the formation of the National Draft Goldwater Committee. Then he and White uneasily awaited Goldwater's reaction. It came: "It's their time and their money. But they are going to have to get along without any help from me." This was all White and O'Donnell and the others needed. Soon they got more. On April 27, Goldwater, asked about the draft movement, said, "I've given up trying to stop it. It's like trying to stamp out a forest fire with your feet. It's coming up too many places, too often." He also commented when asked whether he was really running for President, "I'm doing all right just pooping around."

White, O'Donnell, and others planned a strategy to close the gap between Rockefeller and Goldwater. First, since they probably lacked time to round up enough solid Goldwater delegates to nominate him before the convention, they would try to encourage the candidacies of numerous favorite sons in order to deny delegates to Rockefeller. Second, they would propagandize to the press—and the Republican party—to prove that Goldwater could win. This was the famous "southern strategy" set forth in Draft Goldwater Committee pamphlet. It conceded to President Kennedy, then considered the certain nominee of the Democrats, fourteen states: New York, Massachusetts, Connecticut, Rhode Island, New Jersey, Delaware, West Virginia, Michigan, Minnesota, Missouri, Nevada, Oregon, Alaska, and Hawaii. It called California doubtful and claimed everything else. This would give Goldwater 301 electoral votes (270 were needed to win) and Kennedy 197. The pamphlet said, "Barry Goldwater will take all 128 electoral votes of the eleven Southern States! In 1964 Goldwater will give 'the solid South' dramatic new meaning! *This is the key to Republican success!*" To the South, Goldwater would add "the dependable Republican states of the Midwest, Rocky Mountains, and Northern New England." Thus would he win. It was, as Robert D. Novak later observed, "revolutionary doctrine." Goldwater would concede several previously vital battlegrounds—New York, Pennsylvania, Michigan, California—on the assumption that Goldwater could do what no other Republican ever had done: sweep the South. He alone, the pamphlet said, could do it. Finally, White and O'Donnell would promote the idea that Rockefeller could not win. They would show that Rockefeller's popularity in New York had declined because of his quarrels with the legislature and scandals in his administration. They even hired a polling firm to find out how Rockefeller would run against Kennedy in New York State, and the result showed Kennedy's victory by a landslide.

The attempt to cut down Rockefeller's commanding lead proved unnecessary because Rockefeller himself destroyed it that spring. On March 16, 1962, he had been divorced and on May 4, 1963, he remarried. His bride was Margaretta "Happy" Fitler Murphy. In April, before Rockefeller's remarriage, the Gallup Poll had shown that 43 per cent of rank-and-file Republicans across the nation favored Rockefeller for the nomination and 26 per cent favored Goldwater. A month later, after the wedding, Gallup found that Goldwater had pulled ahead of Rockefeller, 35 per cent to 30 per cent. Reporters soon were writing about "hysteria" over the marriage. Congressional mail was running violently against Rockefeller, they said. Clergymen took up the moral outcry, much of which concerned the new Mrs. Rockefeller's four young children by her previous marriage. The question of their custody had not been settled before her divorce from her former husband. Republican politicians heretofore friendly to Rockefeller began to desert him. Rovere has suggested that they never really supported him wholeheartedly, and only wanted an excuse to desert. Saying that Rockefeller's remarriage doomed him politically helped make it so.

About this same time the Negro revolution had begun in Birmingham and soon was spreading across the South and into the northern cities. White backlash in the North and the "southern strategy" in the South were Goldwater's meat and potatoes. By the summer of 1963 Goldwater was unquestionably the leading contender for the Republican nomination. Goldwater, who had been chairman of the Republican Senatorial Campaign Committee from 1955 to 1963, had criss-crossed the United States innumerable times, speaking to the state chairmen, the county chairmen, the precinct captains, and the party money men. He knew them all, as he often pointed out. Now on September 1, he announced a two-month schedule of speaking engagements in ten states. He had already said he would decide by January whether to be a candidate, "I'm playing this thing by ear day by day. I wouldn't want to say 'yes' or 'no' now, because I think it's much too early." He added that any candidate interested in the nomination should enter next spring's primaries.

It seemed almost certain that Goldwater intended to run. He hardly needed the twenty-three-man "advisory committee" headed by the reactionary former Senate Majority Leader, William F. Knowland of California, to help him decide whether to enter the California primary of 1964. Denison Kitchel, Goldwater's old Arizona campaign strategist, moved to Washington and set up coordinating headquarters in October. By then Goldwater supporters were claiming five hundred solid delegates and eighty-two more leaning to him. White had already undertaken a purge of extremists from the volunteer organization, for Kitchel decided that Goldwater, now about to become a serious candidate, would have a problem with extremists. The regional volunteers had formal organizations in thirty-two states. Indeed, in South Carolina the official state Republican committee passed a resolution declaring that it was now reconstituted as the state's Draft Goldwater Committee; and in several other states matters were moving in that direction. On October 24 Goldwater said he would accept the nomination if it were offered. On November 7 Rockefeller announced he would seek the nomination and would enter the March 10 New Hampshire primary. At a Republican leadership conference in Charleston, South Carolina, most delegates expressed a strong preference for Goldwater, and the Republican national chairman, William E. Miller, said Goldwater could sweep the South in 1964. Then on November 22, President Kennedy was assassinated.

Goldwater announced, on December 5, that he was reassessing his position. The accession of a southerner, Lyndon Johnson, undermined Goldwater's whole "southern strategy." Beyond politics, however, Goldwater, though opposed to President Kennedy, had liked him. He fondly recalled that once in 1961, waiting for the President in his inner oval office, he sat down in the President's rocking chair, as though to test it. Kennedy, finding him there, had asked, "Do you want this job," and Goldwater had replied, "No, not in my right mind," and Kennedy had said, "I thought I had a good thing going up to this point." After the assassination, Goldwater was hurt by abusive letters from people who blamed the President's death on right-wing elements.

Goldwater's backers asked him on December 5 to make up his mind—if he was to enter the New Hampshire primary, they had to get started. He asked for a few more days. They met again, but still he gave no definite answer, though they talked more of tactics than of whether he would run. By mid-December his managers were sure he would enter the New Hampshire primary against Rockefeller. Goldwater himself made it official, announcing that he would seek the nomination.

Unlike the primary elections of other years, those of 1964 were not decisive. The most important ones were, in order, New Hampshire, Oregon, and California, and even these were inconclusive.

In New Hampshire, Rockefeller seemed to encounter mistrust because he was a New York liberal, a governor of a big state with a reputation for big spending, and a divorced and remarried man. But Goldwater did worse. He frightened the voters half to death by calling American missiles "undependable," urging that Social Security be made voluntary (in a state which has a higher percentage of the elderly than all but three others), denounced the U.N. (New Hampshire is extremely proud of its attachment to the U.N.), declared that government couldn't stop depressions and shouldn't aid education (to an audience of students), advocated "carrying the war to North Viet Nam," and declared that the United States should send the Marines to Guantanamo to turn on the water which Castro had cut off. It was pure Goldwater, off the cuff, and Rockefeller, battling uphill for his political life, used it all mercilessly against him. Theodore H. White wrote later, "It was Rockefeller, of course, who destroyed Goldwater—not out of malice but, at this stage, out of the need of his own campaign to score through on New Hampshire conservatives."

In the end neither Rockefeller nor Goldwater won in New Hampshire—a write-in candidate, Henry Cabot Lodge, who spent the primary in the United States Embassy in Saigon, swept New Hampshire on March 10 with 35.3 per cent of the vote to 23 per cent for Goldwater and a little less for Rockefeller. Clearly, neither Rockefeller nor Goldwater had pleased New Hampshire's Republicans, who had turned to someone they thought they knew and could trust. This search by the Republicans for a *Republican* solution to their problem—not an outside movement's solution—was to continue through the summer and even into the fall.

Oregon was next. Goldwater, hurt in New Hampshire, decided not to campaign there but, rather, to concentrate on crucial California, the last big primary. Oregon citizens voted on May 15. Rockefeller won with 33 per cent of the vote, Lodge was second with 27.7 per cent. Goldwater was third with 17.6 per cent.

In California, the primary was only two weeks away. Lodge threw his support to Rockefeller, hoping to stop Goldwater. Eisenhower released a statement describing the candidate he hoped would be nominated; it was interpreted as excluding Goldwater, which Eisenhower quickly denied. The polls indicated Rockefeller was ahead in California, but California is a peculiar state, perhaps the most difficult in the union for a politician, and even more difficult in a primary than in a general election. California, an empire in itself, is almost too big to get hold of. It contains everything: endless acres of suburbs sheltering rootless people, the "little old ladies in tennis shoes," the bearded students on campuses, Negroes and Mexican-Americans, transplanted Arkansas, Oklahoma, and Texas farmers, fractured labor unions, innumerable power centers, an industrial-military complex around San Diego, and a political system whose legal structure makes organization, or machine, politics all but impossible. California politics is unstable, its electorate volatile, and nobody can count on much of anything in California.

Both Rockefeller and Goldwater threw their best men into California. Both organized excellent campaigns. In addition, Goldwater had his fanatic volunteers ringing doorbells. Rockefeller's managers went after Goldwater hard, mailing out a pamphlet entitled "Who Do You Want in the Room with the H-Bomb?", and widely distributing Goldwater quotes intended to picture him as an irresponsible bomber and enemy of Social Security. Nevertheless, Goldwater won. When California Republicans voted on June 2, they gave Goldwater 51.4 per cent of their votes—and 86 delegate votes.

Still and all, the primaries had hardly been conclusive. Lodge had won one, Rockefeller had won one and now Goldwater had won one. The rank-and-file Republican voters had given their convention no clear mandate. All spring, while public attention had been focused on these primaries, something else had been going on. The capture of the Republican party by Goldwater's men proved decisive. It had begun, as we have seen, in 1961 with the meetings of Clifton White's men. Their loyalty was not primarily to the Republican party, some of their financial backers were southwest speculators, former Democrats, with no tradition of Republicanism. The loyalty of the men of this underground was to themselves and to the conservative ideas they believed in. They transferred this loyalty to Goldwater and Goldwaterism.

They accomplished their objective quietly during this spring. They did it in precinct meetings, in county and state committee meetings, in state conventions across the country. While others were watching New Hampshire, Oregon, and California, Clifton White and his men were watching—and operating in—other places on other dates. They got twenty-five of twenty-six delegates from North Carolina in district conventions early in February before the state convention met on February 28 and 29. They got all twenty-two delegates from Oklahoma at the state convention on February 29. They got sixteen supporters for Goldwater from South Carolina on March 21. They got two new delegates on February 23 from the Fifth Congressional District of Georgia, which included Atlanta, previously a liberal stronghold. In the state of Washington, only twenty-five hundred precincts out of fifty-five hundred formerly had had Republican precinct organizations. Clifton White's men went to work, filled the rest of the precincts, and by the end of 1963, 65 per cent of the state's precincts were controlled by Clifton White. Early in 1964, when the precinct caucuses were held in homes and apartments all over the state to choose delegates to the county conventions, which in turn would choose delegates to the state convention, which in turn would choose delegates to the national convention, the Goldwater people were in command. When in June the state convention met to select twenty-four national delegates, the Goldwater people elected at least 70 per cent of them.

Such things were happening all over the country, especially in the South, the Midwest, and the West. On April 19, 1964, an Associated Press poll of GOP county chairmen and other Republican leaders reported that 526 thought Nixon the most likely nominee but said their personal preference was Goldwater. Goldwater won the Texas presidential primary with 75.3 per cent of the vote, the Indiana primary with 67 per cent, the Illinois presidential preference poll with 62 per cent. He did not win them all: Scranton won the all-write-in Pennsylvania preference primary (Goldwater ran a poor fourth); Lodge won the all-write-in Massachusetts primary with 79.5 per cent (Goldwater was second with 10.5 per cent); and Rockefeller won the West Virginia primary (Goldwater was not entered). But by the time California voted, nearly everybody agreed that Goldwater had more than 500 delegate votes. With the exception of Champ Clark in 1912, no candidate in modern times has entered a national convention with so many votes and left it without the nomination. And by June 16, when the Texas convention gave Goldwater its 56 votes, the Associated Press estimated that he had 647 pledged or favorable votes. The convention in San Francisco was less than a month away.

Almost immediately after the California primary, what looked like a stop-Goldwater movement began. Except for Lodge's managers, not one of the easterners who opposed Goldwater had seen fit to give Rockefeller any help in his desperate fight in California. Now, faced with an imminent Goldwater coup engineered by his underground cabal, they suddenly stirred themselves, invoking "Republican principles." Seldom have men in high office, or men seeking it, or men recently freed from it, behaved more foolishly.

On Saturday, June 6, Governor Scranton saw former President Eisenhower at Gettysburg and emerged from a long talk with the impression that Eisenhower had urged him to challenge Goldwater for the nomination at the Conference of Governors, due to open on Monday in Cleveland. Scranton felt that if he did, Eisenhower would openly support him for the nomination. The governors gathered in Cleveland over the weekend, Republican governors frantic at the prospect of the Goldwater coup, Democratic governors watching from the sidelines, vastly pleased. On Sunday, Governor Romney proposed to his fellow Republican governors a strong statement denouncing Goldwater; they discussed it at length. Governor Scranton arrived, prepared to announce his candidacy on a television interview show that same day, and was told that General Eisenhower was trying to reach him. He called Eisenhower, who cautioned that he hoped Scranton hadn't misunderstood him at Gettysburg. The newspapers were saying Eisenhower was supporting Scranton but, Eisenhower said, he could not lend his name to an anti-Goldwater move. Scranton must let his conscience be his guide. Scranton hastily assessed the situation among the governors, hoping to find them prepared to fall in line behind him. Instead, they were still debating Romney's proposed statement. Scranton departed for the TV studio but, in a miserable performance, failed to declare his candidacy or even to speak out against Goldwater. Romney, a determined if ineffective crusader, let loose his denunciation of Goldwater at a press conference. Rockefeller, in a sardonic mood, held a press conference too. Asked if he felt that Scranton was displaying responsibility of leadership, he answered, "Did you see him on television?" Scranton, returning to the conference, organized meeting after meeting, frantically seeking a candidate, and late that night the governors decided that Romney must be the man. Romney, however, had gone home. They telephoned him, and for two days they all squirmed, telephoned, held meetings, plotted strategies. Romney was informed he would be politically dead in Michigan if he broke his pledge to run for reelection. Herbert Brownell, Eisenhower's former Attorney General and an old Dewey and Eisenhower campaign strategist, declined to manage a Romney campaign. So did Len Hall, another eastern professional. Richard Nixon showed up in Cleveland long enough to get in trouble with everybody. The whole stop-Goldwater movement collapsed in utter confusion.

There was one more try. On June 12, two days after the Governors' Conference broke up, Governor Scranton suddenly announced his candidacy, then he set forth across the nation in a final flailing struggle to overcome Goldwater and his underground apparatus. To call the struggle uphill would be bad geography. It was up-cliffside, straight up, with nothing to latch onto. He had less than five weeks in which to campaign. Without campaign machinery, his personal staff lacked experience in national politics. And as Scranton began, Goldwater had, by the Associated Press's count, 540 first ballot votes, Rockefeller 128, Scranton 84, Lodge 45, Nixon 14, and others 109, with 204 uncommitted. Even as Rockefeller endorsed Scranton, the Texas convention gave Goldwater its 56 votes, bringing his strength to 647, by AP calculation, with 655 needed to nominate.

Yet Scranton persisted, traveling everywhere, appearing incessantly on television, visiting Republican leaders across the nation. He began to attract what looked like popular support and Lodge hurried home from Saigon to help him. What was really happening became clear when Scranton appeared before the caucus of the Illinois delegation at O'Hare Inn in Chicago. He saw it cast 48 votes for Goldwater, 8 abstentions, 2 passes, and none for himself. Senate Majority Leader Everett McKinley Dirksen of Illinois announced he would put Goldwater's name in nomination at the convention.

The convention was to open in San Francisco at the Cow Palace on July 13. During the preceding days Governor Rhodes of Ohio, who had promised

Scranton that he would hold the Ohio delegation firmly for himself as a favorite son in order to help the stop-Goldwater cause, suddenly released his delegation, and most of it went to Goldwater. Scranton knew then it was hopeless, but in San Francisco he continued his quixotic fight and, over the weekend before the convention opened, met with the eastern party leaders. The Platform Committee was clearly in Goldwater's control. Scranton's supporters decided to make a floor fight to get a stronger civil rights plank and two additional planks—one condemning extremist groups and the other pledging continued presidential control of the use of nuclear weapons. They hoped to get Eisenhower's support on the nuclear issue, and for a few hours after the old general arrived in San Francisco, they thought they had it. Then Eisenhower reaffirmed his neutrality. He claimed a former President should not discuss secret nuclear policy in public politics. Goldwater called on him, and subsequently Eisenhower said he would campaign for Goldwater if he were nominated and expressed general approval of the platform draft. Scranton appeared before delegate caucuses and on television, trying to go over the Goldwater apparatus to the people and the rank-and-file delegates. A desperate member of his staff sent a letter to Goldwater, forging Scranton's name to it, which challenged Goldwater to debate and denounced him in furious language:

> Your organization . . . feel they have bought, beaten and compromised enough delegate support to make the result a foregone conclusion. With open contempt for the dignity, integrity and common sense of the convention, your managers say in effect that the delegates are little more than a flock of chickens whose necks will be wrung at will. . . .
> You have too often casually prescribed nuclear war as a solution to a troubled world.
> You have too often allowed the radical extremists to use you.
> You have too often stood for irresponsibility in the serious question of racial holocaust.
> You have too often read Taft and Eisenhower and Lincoln out of the Republican Party.
> In short, Goldwaterism has come to stand for a whole crazy-quilt of absurd and dangerous positions that would be soundly repudiated by the American people in November.

Goldwater, of course, refused to debate and said, accurately, that Scranton himself probably had not written the letter. In a TV interview Scranton concurred but said he would stand by its contents. As Theodore White wrote later, "[The letter] made the Republican Convention the stage for the destruction of the leading Republican candidate. What Rockefeller had begun in spring, Scranton finished in June and at the Convention: the painting for the American people of a half-crazed leader indifferent to the needs of American society at home and eager to plunge the nation into war abroad."

Goldwater's managers, and Goldwater himself, confirmed the image at the convention. Many of his delegates were attending their first convention. They were not kooks, but the galleries were full of kooks. They were well-dressed, but they were not run-of-the-mill professional politicians; the spirit of compromise was alien to them. At every turning point in the convention the delegates made it plain that they were not out for mere political victory; they wanted total ideological victory and total annihilation of those who opposed them. Governor Romney proposed a civil rights amendment which could not have embarrassed Goldwater and might indeed have come from his platform committee; since it came from Romney, and was supported by Rockefeller and Lodge and Scranton, the Goldwater legions hooted it down. They were told that other platform amendments renouncing extremist groups would make it easier to carry northern industrial states. The delegates could not have cared less, for they were determined to do nothing to offend the John Birch Society. (Its lobbyist claimed that one hundred delegates belonged to the society.) When Rockefeller tried to speak, they booed him. He taunted them; the galleries raged at him, and the delegates squashed his proposals. With the hall in explosive tumult, Rockefeller said, "These things have no place in America. But I can personally testify to their existence. And so can countless others who have also experienced anonymous midnight and early morning telephone calls, unsigned threatening letters, smear and hate litera-ture, strong-arm and goon tactics, bomb threats and bombings, infiltration and take-over of established political organizations by Communist and Nazi methods." The galleries roared at him and he said, "Some of you don't like to hear it, ladies and gentlemen, but it's the truth." As they booed and yelled, all America saw a spectacle on television that could only be described as one of savage fury. The delegates got their platform, and they got their candidate, too. Goldwater was nominated on the first ballot when the roll call reached South Carolina, giving him 663 votes, 8 more than needed. He picked as his vice-presidential candidate, William E. Miller, an upstate New York con-gressman and Republican National Chairman, unknown except to Republi-can party workers, and a man whose views, far from balancing the ticket, were considered to parallel Goldwater's own.

All day after Goldwater's nomination, Eisenhower waited in his hotel suite; Goldwater did not call him. Instead, he held his first press conference as his party's nominee. He called President Johnson "the greatest faker in the United States . . . the phoniest individual that ever came around." He also struck a new note, and seemed to find a handle on the explosive race issue. General Eisenhower, in a speech to the convention, had already suggested it when he said, "Let us not be guilty of maudlin sympathy for the criminal who, roaming the streets with switchblade knife and illegal firearms seeking a help-less prey, suddenly becomes upon apprehension a poor, underprivileged person who counts upon the compassion of our society and the laxness or weaknesses of too many courts to forgive his offense." Now at his press con-ference Goldwater put crime in the cities second only to foreign policy as an issue. He told the press, "I think the responsibility for this has to start some place, and it should start at the federal level with the federal courts enforcing the law . . . . As President, I'm going to do all I can to see that women can go out in the streets of this country without being scared stiff." He sounded the theme again that night in his acceptance speech, listing "violence in our streets" as the number-two issue.

He also did something more in his acceptance speech. Two sentences, both underlined, defiantly drove the final nail into the heart of the liberal wing of the Republican Party and into the heart of Republican political pragmatism, ending any possibility of unity: "*I would remind you that extremism in the defense of liberty is no vice. And let me remind you that moderation in the pursuit of justice is no virtue.*" "I like that," Goldwater is reported to have said when he came upon it in the ghost-written speech.

Governor Rockefeller thought the passage "frightening." So did many other people. Goldwater heard that General Eisenhower was upset and made the single conciliatory gesture of the convention. He visited Eisenhower and explained that when the General had led the invasion of Normandy he had been behaving like an extremist.

The convention was over. Goldwater and his men set forth to do battle. They had gotten everything they wanted, everything they had worked for since 1960. They had also taken a stand on the race issue. Goldwater, himself no racist, had said he had opposed the civil rights bill only because he thought two sections of it usurped states' rights. He had said repeatedly that he hoped the question of race could be kept out of the campaign. Nonetheless, he had accepted the support of racists and segregationists of the most extreme sort. He wanted to hold those people; they were crucial to his "southern strategy." Goldwater wanted votes in the industrial north, too, and the best place to look for them was in the white backlash against the Negroes in northern cities. Earlier he had said he would not seek those votes either, because that would be racism. Now Goldwater—or Eisenhower, or someone who wrote speeches for one or the other of them—had suddenly found a way to seek backlash votes without ever mentioning "Blacks" or "Negroes." Even northern whites who favored school desegregation feared the newly militant blacks on the streets of the great cities. Crime was rising—though it was always rising—and Negroes were blamed by fearful whites. Goldwater would now play upon those fears. He would seek northern backlash votes by talking about "morality," "law and order," and "violence in the streets." What he could do about it if elected President was not clear. How he squared federal intervention in local law-enforcement with his states' rights doctrine was not clear either. This did not matter—he had found a stand on the race issue that would not drive away his southern segregationist supporters and might attract fearful voters in the northern industrial cities. It was a position he would use throughout the campaign, and one which Richard Nixon would use, with more success, four years later. The campaign that had begun as an underground cabal had found at last a code word for racism.

The situation of the Democratic party in 1964 was far simpler than that of the Republican party and needs only a brief description. In the days following the shattering event at Dallas on November 22, 1963, a dazed nation felt that Lyndon Johnson had somehow saved it, saved it by a single phrase in his speech to the Congress, "Let us continue." President Kennedy, in his inaugural address had said, "Let us begin." Johnson's sentence, pledging allegiance to the martyred President's program and ideals, summoning American unity, somehow seemed to help heal the wounds. In the weeks that followed, the nation looked to him for help as he looked to the nation for consensus, his favorite word. Lyndon Johnson really did want to be, as he often said, the President of all the people, and for a time, he really was.

President Kennedy had been assassinated less than a year before the next election. President Johnson had to hold his consensus together for less than a year to be elected in his own right and he succeeded. True, during the eight months between the assassination and the Democratic convention, small clouds appeared on his horizon. A number of President Kennedy's key aides resigned. To avoid being forced to take Attorney General Robert F. Kennedy as his vice-presidential candidate, President Johnson was obliged to announce that no member of his Cabinet, nor anyone who sat regularly with it, would be considered. A new coup occurred in Vietnam. Negro rioting began in the cities. George Wallace, the segregationist governor of Alabama, polled a surprisingly big vote in the Indiana Democratic primary, principally white backlash votes. Aware that his every move was compared with "what Kennedy would have done," President Johnson seemed at times uncertain. It seemed that he felt he was, somehow, a usurper in his own White House. Comparisons of his "style" with Kennedy's hurt him. People talked about his vulgar idiom, his habit of swimming nude, his dislike of intellectuals and of long position papers and analyses. And the more President Johnson attempted to hold the grip on the American imagination that John F. Kennedy had held, the more he repelled those whose imaginations Kennedy had held most firmly.

Lyndon Johnson was a vain, proud, insecure man. He required loyalty, even servility. Sensitive almost to the point of paranoia, he could charm and he could bully. He had lusted for power and had gotten it. Johnson was a master at senatorial politics and palace politics, and in his first months as President, he seemed a master, too, of national politics, an entirely different skill. He seemed a man able to weld a true national purpose, but as later events proved, he had only the loosest grasp on national politics, especially of the national mood, purpose, and will. In the end this defeated him.

Much of this was muted in the spring of 1964. The Congress gave him just about everything he asked for, including the sweeping Civil Rights Act which Kennedy had been unable to get passed and which Goldwater opposed. The nation was prosperous as never before. He asked the Congress to join him in declaring war on poverty, and the Congress assented. He asked the Congress to authorize him, in the Tonkin Gulf Resolution, to "take all necessary measures" to defend American forces and to "prevent further aggression" in Southeast Asia, and the Congress did. This last statement resulted from attacks on United States destroyers in the Gulf of Tonkin off Vietnam on August 2 and 4, just after the Republican convention and just before the Democrats met. President Johnson responded with a bold, precise, and carefully limited counter attack on North Vietnam torpedo boat bases. His restraint was used throughout the campaign to contrast with what Democrats called Goldwater's rashness. Richard Rovere has suggested that the Tonkin Gulf incident was linked to Goldwater's nomination and that the Administration, wishing to demonstrate its own restraint and firmness, had "declared the existence of a major crisis before it knew that one existed." By and large, by the time the Democrats convened at Atlantic City on August 24, their prospects, and Lyndon Johnson's, never looked better.

It was Johnson's convention all the way. The platform emphasized Johnson's new theme of the "Great Society." It proclaimed "war on poverty," and declared, "America is *One Nation, One People*. . . . Accordingly, we offer this platform as a covenant of unity. . . . We offer as the goal of this covenant PEACE for all nations and FREEDOM for all peoples." The platform was far more moderate, far less militantly liberal, than that of 1960, for this was a Johnson, not a Kennedy, platform, and Johnson wanted a tent big enough for all Americans to gather under. The platform stated that "the world is closer to peace today than it was in 1960" and that the nation had enjoyed "forty-two months of uninterrupted [economic] expansion under Presidents Kennedy and Johnson . . . the longest and strongest peacetime prosperity in modern history." It pledged "enforcement" of the Civil Rights Act (as opposed to the "full implementation and faithful execution" promised in the Republican platform). It insisted that control of nuclear weapons remain in the hands of the President alone, and condemned "extremism, whether from the right or left, including the extreme tactics of such organizations as the Communist party, the Ku Klux Klan and the John Birch Society."

The convention was one of the dullest in recent memory. The only moments of true drama came in a conflict over the seating of the Mississippi delegation. The regular all-white delegation was challenged by an insurgent, largely Negro "Mississippi Freedom Democratic party." A compromise gave the rebels two convention seats-at-large and, more importantly, established an anti-discrimination requirement for party groups naming delegates to future conventions. Both insurgents and regulars, however, rejected the compromise. In an effort to generate more drama, President Johnson toyed with various aspirants to the vice-presidential nomination, toyed with them—and with the press—publicly and for days. Then, at the last moment, went before the convention himself shortly after his own nomination and "recommended" that the convention nominate Senator Hubert H. Humphrey of Minnesota for Vice-President. It did. In their acceptance speeches, Johnson and Humphrey worked hard to preempt the middle ground of American politics. Johnson called the Democrats "a party for all Americans" and Humphrey urged Republicans to join them because their own party had been captured by men who had made it a party "of stridency, of unrestrained passion, of extreme and radical language."

It was Lyndon Johnson's convention, except for one brief moment on the last day, when Robert F. Kennedy, after standing more than twenty minutes before the convention unable to speak because of the applause and cheers of the multitude, evoked his brother's memory with a speech that ended with a quotation from Romeo and Juliet:

> . . . when he shall die
> Take him and cut him out in little stars,
> And he will make the face of heav'n so fine
> That all the world will be in love with Night
> And pay no worship to the garish Sun.

After that a film in memoriam to John Kennedy was shown; the delegates and galleries wept. Johnson's managers, however, had made sure the speech would be made and the film shown only after the nominations were over.

After the extraordinary coup at San Francisco, and after the performance of President Johnson in his first months in office, the campaign itself was an anti-climax. From the moment it began to the end, with a single brief interruption in mid-October, just about everybody knew who would win.

Barry Goldwater and his managers had hoped to raise and seriously debate the most fundamental issues of American policy, and, in doing, so, to give the voters, as his people put it, "a choice, not an echo." They wanted the voter to make a clear-cut decision between two sets of policies, even between two theories of government. In foreign affairs, they tried to make a case for "victory" over, not accommodation with, international communism. At home, they wanted to argue against federal intervention in civil rights, linking it with violence in the streets, and morality, to question the quality of American life, to decry the increase in crime and alcoholic consumption and (as they saw it) sexual immorality, including homosexuality. They had hoped to crusade successfully against all aspects of big centralized government, including its tendency, in a computerized world, to reduce individuals to numbers.

Somehow it all came out wrong. And the man responsible was, by and large, Barry Goldwater himself, with assistance from Johnson and his strategists.

Concerning the crusade against communism, Goldwater had said in Hartford in 1963 that American ground forces in Europe could probably be cut by at least one third if NATO commanders in Europe had the power to use tactical nuclear weapons on their own initiative. The Johnson people handled this extremely complicated question simply. They "hung the bomb around Goldwater's neck," as one put it, and put a one-minute spot on national television, showing a little girl picking petals from a daisy, counting them. The film then faded to a countdown at an atomic testing site and the entire scene dissolved in a mushroom cloud. Republicans, immediately aware their candidate had been badly, perhaps mortally, wounded, protested violently, and the spot was withdrawn — to be replaced by another, which showed another little girl licking an ice cream cone. In the background a voice explained Strontium-90 and said that Goldwater was against the test ban treaty. Lyndon Johnson stood for peace, nuclear control, and military restraint, while other nationally-known Democrats launched attacks on Goldwater that pictured him as the mad bomber prepared to permit "any second lieutenant" in NATO to loose holocaust upon the world. Thus, from the start, and during the cruel months of September and October, Goldwater was forever on the defensive on the issue he himself had given highest priority: victory over communism.

Goldwater's second issue was, really, a complex of issues — morality and "crime in the streets." The Democrats feared this more than the rest, since nobody really knew how many backlash voters there were in the northern cities, nor how many Goldwater could mobilize. If he succeeded here, he might hurt the Democrats badly. But again, somehow, he never made full use of the issue. Over and over he demanded, "What kind of country do we want to have?" and President Johnson replied, "The kind we've made it," and went on to talk about prosperity, progress in education, health, and welfare, and then prophesied the Great Society beyond the New Frontier. Goldwater's moral strictures soon began to sound preachy; he almost castigated Americans for their wickedness. Johnson simply said he thought America was a mighty fine place and Americans were mighty fine folks, "We're in favor of a lot of things, and we're against mighty few." Goldwater looked not only like the mad bomber, but the half-crazed moral zealot.

Goldwater's third issue, big government, was also extremely complicated, for indeed much of the bureaucratic apparatus appropriate to the Roosevelt days was obsolete. The Democrats stripped the question down to a single understandable statement: Barry Goldwater would do away with Social Security. He had never said exactly that, but he had come close enough to permit the attack. The Democrats put a spot on television showing a pair of hands tearing up a Social Security card; they showed it throughout the campaign, over and over. Johnson and other speakers hammered at the issue with the result that here, too, Goldwater was on the defensive, obliged to explain and reexplain what he had really said. The big government issue never really went anywhere at all, and the great confrontation on policies never came off.

Both campaigns were technically well organized (or at least as well organized as so huge and confused an enterprise as a presidential campaign can be). Johnson had the edge—he was an incumbent, an enormous advantage, and, like any Democrat, he could command the aid of several state and big-city organizations plus that of academics and intellectuals experienced in politics. Moreover, he had with him a party that was, for the most part, united. In 1964, the year after President Kennedy's assassination, it was more united than at any time in its recent history. Goldwater, on the other hand, was badly hurt by the profound division in his own party, a division that had been deepened by himself and his fanatic followers and by their means of winning the nomination. In state after state, leader after leader of the Republican party refused to appear with him, or appeared with him only perfunctorily. Senator Kenneth Keating of New York, whose reelection was strongly contested by Robert F. Kennedy, openly disassociated himself from the national ticket. So did Governor Romney, who even refused to appear on a platform with Goldwater. Senator Milton Young of North Dakota did the same. Charles Percy, running for governor of Illinois, boarded Goldwater's train for three joint whistle-stop appearances, but by the end of September the Republican professionals knew it was all over—Ray Bliss, Ohio state chairman, said, "As things stand right now, we face another 1936, and any goddamn fool that doesn't believe it had better." Republican candidates everywhere scattered for cover and campaigned on their own. Democratic candidates, by contrast, went to inordinate lengths to clutch Lyndon Johnson's coattails.

At the outset, Goldwater's support had been deep but very narrow; he had to broaden it. Johnson's support, on the other hand, had been broad but quite shallow; he needed to deepen it. Neither man ever really succeeded.

Goldwater scarcely tried; Johnson, however, did. Lyndon Johnson tried to keep his broad support because he wanted *all* the votes. He not only wished to win bigger than John Kennedy had won in 1960, but bigger than anybody had won ever. Moreover, he wanted people to vote *for him*, not against Goldwater; he wanted *all* the American people to vote *for* him because they *loved* him.

In these circumstances, it might be expected that it would be difficult to restrain Johnson from racing to his airplane to start campaigning the minute the convention ended. However, from the outset, Johnson's strategy for his own personal campaign—as distinguished from the campaigns of the National Committee, local organizations, labor unions, other speakers, the advertising agency's television operatives, and other battalions and divisions—and that of his senior advisors, had been to "stay presidential," that is, remain in the White House running the country, above the battle, at least through September, and see whether Goldwater would beat himself. Johnson would then reassess his position and decide his October strategy. By and large, this is what he did. It was sensible; why raise issues when you're ahead?

Far more important, however, than a hoary political truism, is the power of the incumbency. A President running for reelection need not race around the country shaking hands and making speeches in order to get his name in the paper. Everything a President does is news. The White House is constantly under TV lights and reporters' eyes. Thus Johnson, upon signing the Housing Act on September 2, permitted himself a few "remarks": "I believe that we have a commitment to assure every American an opportunity to live in a decent home, in a safe and a decent neighborhood." The same day, at the swearing-in of a member of the Council of Economic Advisers, he again allowed himself a few words: "This summer, 72,400,000 Americans have been at work, more than have ever been at work in our history." The day his Medicare Bill passed the Senate, the President issued a statement: "The vote in the Senate was a victory not only for older Americans but for all Americans. . . . In a free and prosperous society there is no need for any person, especially the elderly, to suffer personal economic disaster and become a tragic burden upon loved ones or the State through major illness when, by prudently setting aside the employers and employees contributions this can be avoided." And so on—almost daily throughout September, President Johnson uttered brief remarks on appropriate occasions. He signed the Wilderness Bill and the Land and Water Conservation Fund Bill. He signed the Nurse Training Act of 1964. He issued a statement on Labor Day and one about the North Pacific Fisheries Negotiations. He held press conferences, exchanged messages with the President of Brazil, expressed his sorrow at the death of a Finnish Ambassador serving as a U.N. mediator in Cyprus, and received a report of his Committee for Traffic Safety. He flew to Florida and Georgia to inspect damage done by a hurricane, was photographed, and issued a statement. He presented the Medal of Freedom Awards and the Harmon International Aviation Trophies. There was almost no end to what he could do—and did. He made a few campaign speeches—greeted the National Independent Committee for Johnson and Humphrey in the Cabinet room at the White House, spoke to labor unions in Detroit, at a Democratic dinner in Harrisburg, at the convention of the International Association of Machinists in Miami Beach, and inspected space facilities at Cape Kennedy. Johnson traveled to the far Southwest, to El Paso, to meet President López Mateos of Mexico and mark the settlement of the Chamizal dispute. He went to the Pacific Northwest to meet with Prime Minister Pearson of Canada to proclaim the Columbia River treaty, and took occasion on the trip to stop over in Seattle and speak at a dinner honoring "United States and Canadian Partnership in Progress." His subject that evening was the control of nuclear weapons, and he commented; "The release of nuclear weapons would come by Presidential decision alone." He also praised President Kennedy's efforts for nuclear control, declared he would work to avoid war by accident or miscalculation, and said he had worked to limit the spread of nuclear weapons. He added that the improvement of conventional weapons made unnecessary as well as unwise the use of "nuclear power to solve every problem," and pledged ceaseless work toward arms control. It was all aimed straight at Barry Goldwater's throat, but reading the text without knowledge of when it was delivered it seemed only a nonpolitical statement of American nuclear policy. Similar comments could be made of other speeches Johnson made that month, lofty, low-keyed, noncombative, above all presidential. Lyndon Johnson simply smothered Barry Goldwater.

The people were bored. One of the President's staff aides made a trip through the Midwest—which, Johnson strategists agreed, would be "the battleground"—and found that almost nobody was paying much attention to the campaign. Johnson's aide found a newspaper publisher who supported Goldwater who noted, "It's a cream puff campaign so far. There's no enthusiasm." A Democratic governor commented, "There's no fire in the campaign. They've made up their minds to vote against Goldwater. They admire Johnson, think he's safe, but they don't have the enthusiasm they had for Kennedy." A labor leader said, "There's no enthusiasm for either candidate." A cab driver: "People don't like either candidate." A housewife: "People are afraid Goldwater will take Social Security away." The President's aide found that a few Democratic backlash votes seemed to be shifting to Goldwater, but he found the backlash far less important, even in Indiana, than anticipated. He believed that many Republican votes—and independent votes—would go to Johnson because, as one put it, "Goldwater scares people. The bomb." The old FDR coalition seemed broken by prosperity, Goldwater's warlike talk, and, to some extent, the backlash. Goldwater's best issue in the Midwest was racism. Johnson's was prosperity, plus the "don't rock the boat" attitude. People did not trust Johnson personally, but they feared Goldwater. In conclusion, the President was informed that people were saying, "It's a choice between a crook and a kook"; and he was advised to go to the streets and sidewalks of the nation, particularly the Midwest, and let the people see him as he really was.

Johnson did. Bullhorn in hand, he ploughed his way through enormous crowds in state after state, in city after city, stopping his motorcade to shake hands with frantic citizens, yelling at them, "Y'all come on down to the speakin.'" In Peoria and other Midwest towns he talked pocketbook politics, telling the people how prosperous they were. Once in New Orleans he burst out with a quotation from an aging southern Senator who had said, "I would like to go back down there and make them one more Democratic speech. I just feel like I have one in me. The poor old State, they haven't heard a Democratic speech in thirty years. All they hear at election time is Negro, Negro, Negro!" In Providence and in Hartford, Johnson's crowds were enormous, bigger, Theodore H. White thought, than John Kennedy's had been in 1960. The people clutched at him; he stopped his motorcade and climbed up on the back seat of his limousine or stood on top of a closed car and grabbed a microphone or bullhorn and said, "I'm grateful to each one of you. About ten months ago there came this terrible tragedy and we lost our beloved President John F. Kennedy. Give me your help, your hand, your prayers, and I'll do the best job I can as your President." Sometimes he invited them down to the Inauguration. Sometimes he demanded, repeatedly, whether they intended to vote Democratic. And sometimes he gave them a speech straight out of his Texas Populist past. He loved it. And in those warm October days they loved him; Johnson seemed certain to get every vote there was.

Then a news story broke that threatened Lyndon Johnson's entire campaign and future. One of his closest White House aides, and one who had been with him longest, Walter Jenkins, had been arrested a week earlier with a homosexual in the basement of the Washington YMCA and charged with disorderly conduct. The Republican National Committee, at least two newspapers supporting Goldwater (the *Chicago Tribune* and the Cincinnati *Enquirer*), and Goldwater himself had heard about it, but said nothing. On Wednesday, October 14, the Washington *Star* called Jenkins to ask if the story was true. Jenkins went to Abe Fortas, a close friend and senior advisor to President Johnson, and Fortas consulted Clark Clifford, another close friend and senior advisor, Together they tried to persuade Washington editors not to print the story on grounds of humanitarianism. Jenkins, a husband and father, was hospitalized, but the United Press International sent the story over its wires. That night the west wing of the White House was alternately pandemonium and a wake, as staff aides and advisors talked about, as one put it, "how to save the election." What had looked like a landslide suddenly promised to be a debacle. This issue played straight into the hands of Goldwater. He had been focusing on the morality issue all along, sometimes coming close to attacking the President's morals, something his more extreme supporters had done with relish. Throughout the campaign, hate literature aimed at Johnson, some of it produced in Texas, circulated widely throughout the country. The underground campaign was one of the dirtiest of the century. Moreover, years ago, Senator Joseph McCarthy had warned against permitting homosexuals to have access to classified documents, since they were vulnerable to blackmail. Had Jenkins had such access? One would assume so. The issue was fearful because its effects were so hard to gauge.

Jenkins, of course, resigned, but this solved nothing. What mattered was the national security—had it been compromised? Johnson, in Washington at the Al Smith dinner, consulted with Abe Fortas by telephone and ordered an FBI investigation. Then he ordered a pollster to find out quickly and quietly how many votes this would shift. Johnson's aides debated what he should do.

Nobody will ever know what effect the Jenkins affair might have had on the election's outcome because three other events followed immediately. Within forty-eight hours, Nikita Khrushchev fell from power, the mainland Chinese exploded their first nuclear bomb, and the thirteen-year-old Tory government of England was voted out of office. The Jenkins case, as an important factor in this campaign, was over.

All election campaigns, or nearly all, are influenced by unexpected dramatic events outside the framework of the campaign itself. It is hard to recall so extraordinary a collision of events as those of mid-October in 1964. In all probability, Johnson would have been elected anyway, even with the Jenkins problem on his hands and without the help of the Soviets, the Red Chinese, and the British electorate. He might well have been elected by a lesser margin, however.

As it was, after having issued a brief statement on Jenkins, he could now devote days to CIA and Pentagon briefings on the significance of the Chinese bomb, to discussions with State Department and other advisors on the Soviet Union and Great Britain. Once again he could become, not a candidate with a deviant aide but, simply, the President. And then, after that, once more the candidate, campaigning.

Johnson had already begun to make a few serious political speeches. At Johns Hopkins University he had reiterated America's determination "to defend freedom wherever it is attacked," warned against the unrestrained use of American nuclear power, and predicted the downfall of "the ancient enemies of mankind—disease, intolerance, illiteracy, and ignorance." On national television he had attacked headon the Goldwater thesis (without naming Goldwater) that the government should withdraw from domestic affairs because it was "radical" and dangerous to prosperity and progress. He also denounced Goldwater's suggestions that we should consider using atomic weapons in Vietnam, breaking relations with Russia, and so on. All this was outside the mainstream of American foreign policy as established by both parties during the last twenty years and would gravely endanger the peace of the world.

Campaigning in New York, he heartily embraced Robert Kennedy and, as in earlier speeches, John F. Kennedy. To the Liberal party he attacked Goldwater doctrine briefly, but spent most of his time projecting the Great Society. He went on national television to report to the people on "recent events in Russia, China, and Great Britain," reassuring the people that the Soviet ambassador had informed him that Khrushchev's fall meant no change in basic foreign policy. Johnson said, "I told him that we intend to bury no one, and we do not intend to be buried." Goldwater, on the other hand, predicted that Khrushchev's fall portended a U.S.S.R.-China rapprochement.

As to the Chinese nuclear device, the President claimed the United States would continue to support the limited test ban treaty, that China should sign it, and that he would work to end all nuclear tests and to stop nuclear proliferation. As for Great Britain, "We congratulate the winners. We send warm regards to the losers. The friendship of our two nations goes on. . . . This has been an eventful week in the affairs of the world." For the rest of the campaign Johnson concentrated on the great issue of war or peace, pledging, among other things, "no wider war" in Southeast Asia.

Goldwater was swinging wildly—pulling out a copy of the communist *Worker* to belabor the Democrats for accepting communist support, hardly a great issue in this election. He held a big rally in Madison Square Garden, whistle-stopped through the Midwest, then headed west to Cheyenne, Las Vegas, Tucson, and Los Angeles. He went home to sleep in Phoenix, then off to Texas and South Carolina. On the final day before the election he went to San Francisco, but he was weary, and so were his listeners. At San Francisco he made—and said he was making—the same speech with which he had opened his campaign. "The issues have not changed. I have not changed. The challenge and the choice has not changed." However, all of them had, really. The issues—victory, big government, morality—which had sounded so good a year or so ago in the locker room of the Camelback Inn in Arizona had not sounded nearly so good on national television. Goldwater himself may not have changed but the kind of campaign he had been obliged to make—and which had been made for him—had certainly changed. As for the challenge and the choice, the challenge had hardly been made, the choice hardly presented. It was all rather sad.

The result was a Johnson landslide. Johnson carried forty-four states and the District of Columbia with 486 electoral votes; Goldwater won only six states with 52 electoral votes. Johnson received 43,128,958 votes, or 61.0 per cent of the total vote cast (compared to 60.7 per cent for Roosevelt in 1936); Goldwater got 27,176,873 (Johnson's percentage of the total two-party vote was slightly less than FDR's and, for that matter, less than Harding's in 1920) and won only his own Arizona and five Deep South states: Alabama, Georgia, Louisiana, Mississippi, and South Carolina. Johnson carried New York by more than two million, Michigan, Ohio, and California by more than a million each, and Illinois by almost a million.

What had happened? The country, still in shock after President Kennedy's assassination, had drawn together. Many voted for Johnson because they could not vote for Kennedy. Many voted less for Johnson than against Goldwater. Goldwater had frightened them. Goldwater—and the extremism of the right-wing movement—had beaten himself. The great conservative crusade of 1964 had begun with a proud slogan: "In Your Heart You Know He's Right." Democrats had responded with a jeer: "In Your Guts You Know He's Nuts." Together they composed a fitting epitaph on the 1964 campaign.

Presidential Chronology

President and political party	Born	Died	Age at inauguration	Native of—	Elected from—
George Washington	1732	1799	57	Va	Va
Do (F)			61		
John Adams (F)	1735	1826	61	Mass	Mass
Thomas Jefferson (D-R)	1743	1826	57	Va	Va
Do			61		
James Madison (D-R)	1751	1836	57	Va	Va
Do			61		
James Monroe (D-R)	1758	1831	58	Va	Va
Do			62		
John Q. Adams (N-R)	1767	1848	57	Mass	Mass
Andrew Jackson (D)	1767	1845	61	N.C.	Tenn
Do			65		
Martin Van Buren (D)	1782	1862	54	N.Y.	N.Y.
William H. Harrison (W)	1773	1841	68	Va	Ohio
John Tyler (D)	1790	1862	51	Va	Va
James K. Polk (D)	1795	1849	49	Tenn	Tenn
Zachary Taylor (W)	1784	1850	64	Va	La
Millard Fillmore (W)	1800	1874	50	N.Y.	N.Y.
Franklin Pierce (D)	1804	1869	48	N.H.	N.H.
James Buchanan (D)	1791	1868	65	Pa	Pa
Abraham Lincoln (R)	1809	1865	52	Ky	Ill
Do			56		
Andrew Johnson (R)	1808	1875	56	N.C.	Tenn
Ulysses S. Grant (R)	1822	1885	46	Ohio	Ill
Do			50		
Rutherford B. Hayes (R)	1822	1893	54	Ohio	Ohio
James A. Garfield (R)	1831	1881	49	Ohio	Ohio
Chester A. Arthur (R)	1830	1886	50	Vt	N.Y.
Grover Cleveland (D)	1837	1908	47	N.J.	N.Y.
Benjamin Harrison (R)	1833	1901	55	Ohio	Ind
Grover Cleveland (D)	1837	1908	55	N.J.	N.Y.
William McKinley (R)	1843	1901	54	Ohio	Ohio
Do			58		
Theodore Roosevelt (R)	1858	1919	42	N.Y.	N.Y.
Do			46		
William H. Taft (R)	1857	1930	51	Ohio	Ohio
Woodrow Wilson (D)	1856	1924	56	Va	N.J.
Do			60		
Warren G. Harding (R)	1865	1923	55	Ohio	Ohio
Calvin Coolidge (R)	1872	1933	51	Vt	Mass
Do			52		
Herbert C. Hoover (R)	1874	1964	54	Iowa	Calif
Franklin D. Roosevelt (D)	1882	1945	51	N.Y.	N.Y.
Do			55		
Do			59		
Do			63		
Harry S. Truman (D)	1884		60	Mo	Mo
Do			64		
Dwight D. Eisenhower (R)	1890	1969	62	Texas	N.Y.
Do			66		Pa
John F. Kennedy (D)	1917	1963	43	Mass	Mass
Lyndon B. Johnson (D)	1908		55	Texas	Texas
Do			56		
Richard M. Nixon (R)	1913		56	Calif	N.Y.

Presidential Chronology

Religion	Service	Vice-President
Episcopalian	Apr. 30, 1789 – Mar. 3, 1793	John Adams
	Mar. 4, 1793 – Mar. 3, 1797	do
Unitarian	Mar. 4, 1797 – Mar. 3, 1801	Thomas Jefferson
Liberal	Mar. 4, 1801 – Mar. 3, 1805	Aaron Burr
	Mar. 4, 1805 – Mar. 3, 1809	George Clinton
Episcopalian	Mar. 4, 1809 – Mar. 3, 1813	do
	Mar. 4, 1813 – Mar. 3, 1817	Elbridge Gerry
Episcopalian	Mar. 4, 1817 – Mar. 3, 1821	Daniel D. Tompkins
	Mar. 4, 1821 – Mar. 3, 1825	do
Unitarian	Mar. 4, 1825 – Mar. 3, 1829	John C. Calhoun
Presbyterian	Mar. 4, 1829 – Mar. 3, 1833	do
	Mar. 4, 1833 – Mar. 3, 1837	Martin Van Buren
Ref. Dutch	Mar. 4, 1837 – Mar. 3, 1841	Richard M. Johnson
Episcopalian	Mar. 4, 1841 – Apr. 4, 1841	John Tyler
Episcopalian	Apr. 6, 1841 – Mar. 3, 1845	
Presbyterian	Mar. 4, 1845 – Mar. 3, 1849	George M. Dallas
Episcopalian	Mar. 5, 1849 – July 9, 1850	Millard Fillmore
Episcopalian	July 10, 1850 – Mar. 3, 1853	
Episcopalian	Mar. 4, 1853 – Mar. 3, 1857	William R. King
Presbyterian	Mar. 4, 1857 – Mar. 3, 1861	John C. Breckenridge
Liberal	Mar. 4, 1861 – Mar. 3, 1865	Hannibal Hamlin
	Mar. 4, 1865 – Apr. 15, 1865	Andrew Johnson
Liberal	Apr. 15, 1865 – Mar. 3, 1869	
Methodist	Mar. 4, 1869 – Mar. 3, 1873	Schuyler Colfax
	Mar. 4, 1873 – Mar. 3, 1877	Henry Wilson
Methodist	Mar. 4, 1877 – Mar. 3, 1881	William A. Wheeler
Disc. of Christ	Mar. 4, 1881 – Sept. 19, 1881	Chester A. Arthur
Episcopalian	Sept. 20, 1881 – Mar. 3, 1885	
Presbyterian	Mar. 4, 1885 – Mar. 3, 1889	Thomas A. Hendricks
Presbyterian	Mar. 4, 1889 – Mar. 3, 1893	Levi P. Morton
Presbyterian	Mar. 4, 1893 – Mar. 3, 1897	Adlai E. Stevenson
Methodist	Mar. 4, 1897 – Mar. 3, 1901	Garrett A. Hobart
	Mar. 4, 1901 – Sept. 14, 1901	Theodore Roosevelt
Ref. Dutch	Sept. 14, 1901 – Mar. 3, 1905	
	Mar. 4, 1905 – Mar. 3, 1909	Charles W. Fairbanks
Unitarian	Mar. 4, 1909 – Mar. 3, 1913	James S. Sherman
Presbyterian	Mar. 4, 1913 – Mar. 3, 1917	Thomas R. Marshall
	Mar. 4, 1917 – Mar. 3, 1921	do
Presbyterian	Mar. 4, 1921 – Aug. 2, 1923	Calvin Coolidge
Congregational	Aug. 3, 1923 – Mar. 3, 1925	
	Mar. 4, 1925 – Mar. 3, 1929	Charles G. Dawes
Quaker	Mar. 4, 1929 – Mar. 3, 1933	Charles Curtis
Episcopalian	Mar. 4, 1933 – Jan. 20, 1937	John N. Garner
	Jan. 20, 1937 – Jan. 20, 1941	do
	Jan. 20, 1941 – Jan. 20, 1945	Henry A. Wallace
	Jan. 20, 1945 – Apr. 12, 1945	Harry S. Truman
Baptist	Apr. 12, 1945 – Jan. 20, 1949	
	Jan. 20, 1949 – Jan. 20, 1953	Alben W. Barkley
Presbyterian	Jan. 20, 1953 – Jan. 20, 1957	Richard M. Nixon
	Jan. 20, 1957 – Jan. 20, 1961	do
Roman Catholic	Jan. 20, 1961 – Nov. 22, 1963	Lyndon B. Johnson
Christian	Nov. 22, 1963 – Jan. 20, 1965	
	Jan. 20, 1965 – Jan. 20, 1969	Hubert H. Humphrey
Quaker	Jan. 20, 1969 –	Spiro T. Agnew

Key to Abbreviations: (D) Democrat; (D-R) Democrat-Republican; (F) Federalist; (N-R) National Republican; (R) Republican; (W) Whig.

Voting Tables for 44 Presidential Elections

(Tabulation of electoral votes for the election of 1789 will be found on page 18, and for the election of 1792 on page 29.)

THE ELECTORAL VOTE IN THE 1796 ELECTION

STATES	John Adams	Thomas Jefferson	Thomas Pinckney	Aaron Burr	Samuel Adams	Oliver Ellsworth	George Clinton	John Jay	James Iredell	George Washington	Samuel Johnston	John Henry	C. C. Pinckney
New Hampshire.	6	—	—	—	—	6	—	—	—	—	—	—	—
Vermont.......	4	—	4	—	—	—	—	—	—	—	—	—	—
Massachusetts...	16	—	13	—	—	1	—	—	—	—	2	—	—
Rhode Island...	4	—	—	—	—	4	—	—	—	—	—	—	—
Connecticut.....	9	—	4	—	—	—	—	5	—	—	—	—	—
New York......	12	—	12	—	—	—	—	—	—	—	—	—	—
New Jersey.....	7	—	7	—	—	—	—	—	—	—	—	—	—
Pennsylvania....	1	14	2	13	—	—	—	—	—	—	—	—	—
Delaware.......	3	—	3	—	—	—	—	—	—	—	—	—	—
Maryland.......	7	4	4	3	—	—	—	—	—	—	—	2	—
Virginia........	1	20	1	1	15	—	3	—	—	1	—	—	—
North Carolina..	1	11	1	6	—	—	—	—	3	1	—	—	1
South Carolina..	—	8	8	—	—	—	—	—	—	—	—	—	—
Georgia........	—	4	—	—	—	—	4	—	—	—	—	—	—
Kentucky.......	—	4	—	4	—	—	—	—	—	—	—	—	—
Tennessee......	—	3	—	3	—	—	—	—	—	—	—	—	—
	71	68	59	30	15	11	7	5	3	2	2	2	1

THE ELECTORAL VOTE IN THE 1800 ELECTION

STATES	Thomas Jefferson	Aaron Burr	John Adams	C. C. Pinckney	John Jay
New Hampshire.....	—	—	6	6	—
Vermont...........	—	—	4	4	—
Massachusetts.......	—	—	16	16	—
Rhode Island.......	—	—	4	3	1
Connecticut.........	—	—	9	9	—
New York..........	12	12	—	—	—
New Jersey.........	—	—	7	7	—
Pennsylvania........	8	8	7	7	—
Delaware...........	—	—	3	3	—
Maryland	5	5	5	5	—
Virginia............	21	21	—	—	—
North Carolina......	8	8	4	4	—
South Carolina......	8	8	—	—	—
Georgia............	4	4	—	—	—
Kentucky...........	4	4	—	—	—
Tennessee..........	3	3	—	—	—
	73	73	65	64	1

THE ELECTORAL VOTE IN THE 1804 ELECTION

STATES	PRESIDENT		VICE-PRESIDENT	
	T. Jefferson	C. C. Pinckney	George Clinton	Rufus King
New Hampshire......	7	—	7	—
Vermont.............	6	—	6	—
Massachusetts........	19	—	19	—
Rhode Island.........	4	—	4	—
Connecticut..........	—	9	—	9
New York...........	19	—	19	—
New Jersey...........	8	—	8	—
Pennsylvania.........	20	—	20	—
Delaware............	—	3	—	3
Maryland............	9	2	9	2
Virginia.............	24	—	24	—
North Carolina.......	14	—	14	—
South Carolina.......	10	—	10	—
Georgia.............	6	—	6	—
Kentucky............	8	—	8	—
Tennessee...........	5	—	5	—
Ohio................	3	—	3	—
	162	14	162	14

THE ELECTORAL VOTE IN THE 1808 ELECTION

STATES	PRESIDENT			VICE-PRESIDENT				
	James Madison	George Clinton	C. C. Pinckney	G. Clinton	J. Madison	J. Langdon	J. Monroe	Rufus King
New Hampshire..	—	—	7	—	—	—	—	7
Vermont........	6	—	—	—	—	6	—	—
Massachusetts....	—	—	19	—	—	—	—	19
Rhode Island....	—	—	4	—	—	—	—	4
Connecticut.....	—	—	9	—	—	—	—	9
New York.......	13	6	—	13	3	—	3	—
New Jersey......	8	—	—	8	—	—	—	—
Pennsylvania.....	20	—	—	20	—	—	—	—
Delaware........	—	—	3	—	—	—	—	3
Maryland.......	9	—	2	9	—	—	—	2
Virginia.........	24	—	—	24	—	—	—	—
North Carolina...	11	—	3	11	—	—	—	3
South Carolina...	10	—	—	10	—	—	—	—
Georgia.........	6	—	—	6	—	—	—	—
Kentucky*......	7	—	—	7	—	—	—	—
Tennessee.......	5	—	—	5	—	—	—	—
Ohio...........	3	—	—	—	—	3	—	—
	122	6	47	113	3	9	3	47

* One Kentucky elector did not vote.

THE ELECTORAL VOTE IN THE 1812 ELECTION

STATES	PRESIDENT		VICE-PRESIDENT	
	James Madison	De Witt Clinton	Elbridge Gerry	Jared Ingersoll
New Hampshire....	—	8	1	7
Vermont..........	8	—	8	—
Massachusetts......	—	22	2	20
Rhode Island.......	—	4	—	4
Connecticut........	—	9	—	9
New York.........	—	29	—	29
New Jersey........	—	8	—	8
Pennsylvania.......	25	—	25	—
Delaware..........	—	4	—	4
Maryland..........	6	5	6	5
Virginia...........	25	—	25	—
North Carolina.....	15	—	15	—
South Carolina.....	11	—	11	—
Georgia...........	8	—	8	—
Kentucky..........	12	—	12	—
Tennessee.........	8	—	8	—
Louisiana..........	3	—	3	—
Ohio.............	7	—	7	—
	128	89	131	86

THE ELECTORAL VOTE IN THE 1816 ELECTION

STATES	PRESIDENT		VICE-PRESIDENT				
	James Monroe	Rufus King	D. D. Tompkins	John E. Howard	James Ross	John Marshall	Robert G. Harper
New Hampshire....	8	—	8	—	—	—	—
Vermont...........	8	—	8	—	—	—	—
Massachusetts......	—	22	—	22	—	—	—
Rhode Island.......	4	—	4	—	—	—	—
Connecticut........	—	9	—	—	5	4	—
New York..........	29	—	29	—	—	—	—
New Jersey.........	8	—	8	—	—	—	—
Pennsylvania.......	25	—	25	—	—	—	—
Delaware..........	—	3	—	—	—	—	3
Maryland..........	8	—	8	—	—	—	—
Virginia............	25	—	25	—	—	—	—
North Carolina.....	15	—	15	—	—	—	—
South Carolina......	11	—	11	—	—	—	—
Georgia............	8	—	8	—	—	—	—
Kentucky..........	12	—	12	—	—	—	—
Tennessee..........	8	—	8	—	—	—	—
Louisiana..........	3	—	3	—	—	—	—
Ohio..............	8	—	8	—	—	—	—
Indiana............	3	—	3	—	—	—	—
	183	34	183	22	5	4	3

THE ELECTORAL VOTE IN THE 1820 ELECTION

STATES	PRESIDENT		VICE-PRESIDENT				
	James Monroe	J. Q. Adams	D. D. Tompkins	R. Stockton	R. G. Harper	R. Rush	D. Rodney
Maine..............	9	—	9	—	—	—	—
New Hampshire.....	7	1	7	—	—	1	—
Vermont...........	8	—	8	—	—	—	—
Massachusetts.......	15	—	7	8	—	—	—
Rhode Island.......	4	—	4	—	—	—	—
Connecticut.........	9	—	9	—	—	—	—
New York..........	29	—	29	—	—	—	—
New Jersey.........	8	—	8	—	—	—	—
Pennsylvania*.......	24	—	24	—	—	—	—
Delaware..........	4	—	—	—	—	—	4
Maryland..........	11	—	10	—	1	—	—
Virginia...........	25	—	25	—	—	—	—
North Carolina......	15	—	15	—	—	—	—
South Carolina......	11	—	11	—	—	—	—
Georgia............	8	—	8	—	—	—	—
Alabama...........	3	—	3	—	—	—	—
Mississippi*........	2	—	2	—	—	—	—
Louisiana..........	3	—	3	—	—	—	—
Kentucky..........	12	—	12	—	—	—	—
Tennessee*........	7	—	7	—	—	—	—
Ohio..............	8	—	8	—	—	—	—
Indiana...........	3	—	3	—	—	—	—
Illinois...........	3	—	3	—	—	—	—
Missouri..........	3	—	3	—	—	—	—
	231	1	218	8	1	1	4

* In each of these states, one elector died before the meeting of the electoral college.

496

THE VOTE IN THE 1824 ELECTION

STATES	POPULAR VOTE				ELECTORAL VOTE			
	Andrew Jackson	John Quincy Adams	William H. Crawford	Henry Clay	Andrew Jackson	John Quincy Adams	William H. Crawford	Henry Clay
Maine............	—	10,289	2,336	—	—	9	—	—
New Hampshire...	—	9,389	643	—	—	8	—	—
Vermont†.......	—	—	—	—	—	7	—	—
Massachusetts	—	30,687	6,616	—	—	15	—	—
Rhode Island.....	—	2,145	200	—	—	4	—	—
Connecticut......	—	7,587	1,978	—	—	8	—	—
New York†......	—	—	—	—	1	26	5	4
New Jersey.......	10,985	9,110	1,196	—	8	—	—	—
Pennsylvania......	36,100	5,441	4,206	1,690	28	—	—	—
Delaware†.......	—	—	—	—	—	1	2	—
Maryland........	14,523	14,632	3,364	695	7	3	1	—
Virginia.........	2,861	3,189	8,489	416	—	—	24	—
North Carolina....	20,415	—	15,621	—	15	—	—	—
South Carolina†...	—	—	—	—	11	—	—	—
Georgia†........	—	—	—	—	—	—	9	—
Alabama.........	9,443	2,416	1,680	67	5	—	—	—
Mississippi.......	3,234	1,694	119	—	3	—	—	—
Louisiana†.......	—	—	—	—	3	2	—	—
Kentucky........	6,455	—	—	17,331	—	—	—	14
Tennessee........	20,197	216	312	—	11	—	—	—
Missouri.........	987	311	—	1,401	—	—	—	3
Ohio.............	18,457	12,280	—	19,255	—	—	—	16
Indiana..........	7,343	3,095	—	5,315	5	—	—	—
Illinois..........	1,901	1,542	219	1,047	2	1	—	—
	152,901	114,023	46,979	47,217	99	84	41	37

† In these six states electors were appointed by the legislature.
It is the first time in the history of presidential elections that the popular votes were preserved, though no great reliance can be given to these figures.

THE VOTES IN THE 1828 ELECTION

STATES	POPULAR VOTE		ELECTORAL VOTES FOR				
	FOR PRESIDENT		PRESIDENT		VICE-PRESIDENT		
	Andrew Jackson	John Q. Adams	A. Jackson	J. Q. Adams	J. C. Calhoun	Richard Rush	William Smith
Maine.........	13,927	20,733	1	8	1	8	—
New Hampshire.	20,922	24,134	—	8	—	8	—
Vermont.......	8,350	25,363	—	7	—	7	—
Massachusetts..	6,016	29,876	—	15	—	15	—
Rhode Island...	821	2,754	—	4	—	4	—
Connecticut.....	4,448	13,838	—	8	—	8	—
New York......	140,763	135,413	20	16	20	16	—
New Jersey.....	21,951	23,764	—	8	—	8	—
Pennsylvania....	101,652	50,848	28	—	28	—	—
Delaware*......	—	—	—	3	—	3	—
Maryland......	24,565	25,527	5	6	5	6	—
Virginia........	26,752	12,101	24	—	24	—	—
North Carolina.	37,857	13,918	15	—	15	—	—
South Carolina*	—	—	11	—	11	—	—
Georgia........	19,363	No opp.	9	—	2	—	7
Alabama.......	17,138	1,938	5	—	5	—	—
Mississippi.....	6,772	1,581	3	—	3	—	—
Louisiana......	4,603	4,076	5	—	5	—	—
Kentucky.......	39,397	31,460	14	—	14	—	—
Tennessee......	44,293	2,240	11	—	11	—	—
Missouri.......	8,272	3,400	3	—	3	—	—
Ohio..........	67,597	63,396	16	—	16	—	—
Indiana........	22,257	17,052	5	—	5	—	—
Illinois.........	9,560	4,662	3	—	3	—	—
	647,276	508,064	178	83	171	83	7

* In these two states electors were appointed by the legislature.

THE VOTES IN THE 1832 ELECTION

STATES	POPULAR VOTES FOR PRESIDENT		ELECTORAL VOTES FOR PRESIDENT				ELECTORAL VOTES FOR VICE-PRESIDENT				
	Andrew Jackson, Democrat	Henry Clay,* Whig	Andrew Jackson	Henry Clay	John Floyd	William Wirt	M. Van Buren	John Sergeant	W. Wilkins	Henry Lee	A. Ellmaker
Maine...........	33,291	27,204	10	—	—	—	10	—	—	—	—
New Hampshire..	25,486	19,010	7	—	—	—	7	—	—	—	—
Vermont.........	7,870	11,152	—	—	—	7	—	—	—	—	7
Massachusetts....	14,545	33,003	—	14	—	—	—	14	—	—	—
Rhode Island.....	2,126	2,810	—	4	—	—	—	4	—	—	—
Connecticut......	11,269	17,755	—	8	—	—	—	8	—	—	—
New York.......	168,497	154,896	42	—	—	—	42	—	—	—	—
New Jersey.......	23,856	23,393	8	—	—	—	8	—	—	—	—
Pennsylvania.....	90,983	56,716	30	—	—	—	—	—	30	—	—
Delaware........	4,110	4,276	—	3	—	—	—	3	—	—	—
Maryland........	19,156	19,160	3	5	—	—	3	5	—	—	—
Virginia.........	33,609	11,451	23	—	—	—	23	—	—	—	—
North Carolina...	24,862	4,563	15	—	—	—	15	—	—	—	—
South Carolina†..	—	—	—	—	11	—	—	—	—	11	—
Georgia.........	20,750	—	11	—	—	—	11	—	—	—	—
Alabama........	—	—	7	—	—	—	7	—	—	—	—
Mississippi......	5,919	No can.	4	—	—	—	4	—	—	—	—
Louisiana........	4,049	2,528	5	—	—	—	5	—	—	—	—
Kentucky........	36,247	43,396	—	15	—	—	—	15	—	—	—
Tennessee........	28,740	1,436	15	—	—	—	15	—	—	—	—
Ohio............	81,246	76,539	21	—	—	—	21	—	—	—	—
Indiana..........	31,552	15,472	9	—	—	—	9	—	—	—	—
Illinois..........	14,147	5,429	5	—	—	—	5	—	—	—	—
Missouri.........	5,192	—	4	—	—	—	4	—	—	—	—
	687,502	530,189	219	49	11	7	189	49	30	11	7

* The figures in the Henry Clay column include the votes for the Anti-masonic candidate William Wirt.

† Electors were appointed by the legislature.

THE VOTES IN THE 1836 ELECTION

STATES	POPULAR VOTE			ELECTORAL VOTES FOR								
				PRESIDENT					VICE-PRESIDENT			
	Martin Van Buren Democrat	Whig Candidate	Name of the Whig Candidate	Martin Van Buren	William H. Harrison	Hugh L. White	Daniel Webster	Willie P. Mangum	Richard M. Johnson	Francis Granger	John Tyler	William Smith
Maine..........	22,990	15,239	Harrison	10	—	—	—	—	10	—	—	—
New Hampshire..	18,722	6,228	Harrison	7	—	—	—	—	7	—	—	—
Vermont........	14,039	20,996	Harrison	—	7	—	—	—	—	7	—	—
Massachusetts...	33,542	41,287	Webster	—	—	—	14	—	—	14	—	—
Rhode Island....	2,964	2,710	Harrison	4	—	—	—	—	4	—	—	—
Connecticut.....	19,291	18,749	Harrison	8	—	—	—	—	8	—	—	—
New York......	166,815	138,543	Harrison	42	—	—	—	—	42	—	—	—
New Jersey......	25,592	26,137	Harrison	—	8	—	—	—	—	8	—	—
Pennsylvania....	91,475	87,111	Harrison	30	—	—	—	—	30	—	—	—
Delaware.......	4,153	4,733	Harrison	—	3	—	—	—	—	3	—	—
Maryland.......	22,168	25,852	Harrison	—	10	—	—	—	—	—	10	—
Virginia.........	30,261	23,468	White	23	—	—	—	—	—	—	—	23
North Carolina..	26,910	23,626	White	15	—	—	—	—	15	—	—	—
South Carolina*.	—	—	—	—	—	—	—	11	—	—	11	—
Georgia.........	22,104	24,876	White	—	—	11	—	—	—	—	11	—
Alabama........	20,506	15,612	White	7	—	—	—	—	7	—	—	—
Mississippi......	9,979	9,688	White	4	—	—	—	—	4	—	—	—
Louisiana.......	3,653	3,383	White	5	—	—	—	—	5	—	—	—
Arkansas........	2,400	1,238	White	3	—	—	—	—	3	—	—	—
Kentucky.......	33,435	36,955	Harrison	—	15	—	—	—	—	15	—	—
Tennessee.......	26,129	36,168	White	—	—	15	—	—	—	—	15	—
Missouri........	10,995	7,337	White	4	—	—	—	—	4	—	—	—
Ohio...........	96,948	105,404	Harrison	—	21	—	—	—	—	21	—	—
Indiana.........	32,478	41,281	Harrison	—	9	—	—	—	—	9	—	—
Illinois..........	18,097	14,983	Harrison	5	—	—	—	—	5	—	—	—
Michigan.......	7,332	4,045	Harrison	3	—	—	—	—	3	—	—	—
	762,978	736,250		170	73	26	14	11	147	77	47	23

* Electors were appointed by the legislature.

TABLE 5

SUMMARY RESULTS OF THE PRESIDENTIAL ELECTION OF 1840
POPULAR AND ELECTORAL VOTE, AND STATES CARRIED
BY SECTION

SOURCE—Adapted from Svend Petersen, ed., *A Statistical History of the American Presidentia* *Elections* (New York, 1963).

	Popular Vote and Percent						Electoral Vote	
	HARRISON		VAN BUREN		BIRNEY		HA	VB
Ala.	28,471	45.6	33,991	54.4				7
Ark.	5,160	43.3	6,766	56.7				3
Conn.	31,601	55.4	25,296	44.3	174	.3	8	
Del.	5,967	55.0	4,884	45.0			3	
Ga.	40,349	55.8	31,989	44.2			11	
Ill.	45,574	48.8	47,625	51.0	159	.2		5
Ind.	65,308	55.8	51,695	44.2			9	
Ky.	58,489	64.2	32,616	35.8			15	
La.	11,297	59.7	7,617	40.3			5	
Me.	46,612	50.1	46,190	49.7	186	.2	10	
Md.	33,533	53.8	28,759	46.2			10	
Mass.	72,913	57.4	52,432	41.3	1,621	1.3	14	
Mich.	22,933	51.7	21,131	47.6	321	.7	3	
Miss.	19,518	53.5	16,995	46.5			4	
Mo.	22,972	43.6	29,760	56.4				4
N. H.	26,434	44.6	32,670	55.2	126	.2		7
N. J.	33,362	51.8	31,034	48.1	69	.1	8	
N. Y.	225,945	51.2	212,743	48.2	2,790	.6	42	
N. C.	46,379	57.9	33,782	42.1			15	
Ohio	148,157	54.1	124,782	45.6	903	.3	21	
Pa.	144,023	50.0	143,784	49.9	343	.1	30	
R. I.	5,278	61.2	3,301	38.3	42	.5	4	
S. C.								11
Tenn.	60,391	55.6	48,289	44.4			15	
Vt.	32,445	63.9	18,009	35.5	319	.6	7	
Va.	42,501	49.2	43,893	50.8				23
U.S.	1,275,612	52.9	1,130,033	46.8	7,053	.3	234	60

States Carried—New England, Harrison 5, Van Buren 1; Mid-Atlantic, Harrison 5, Van Buren 0; Old South, Harrison 2, Van Buren 2; Northwest, Harrison 3, Van Buren 2; Southwest, Harrison 4, Van Buren 2. Total States Carried, Harrison 19, Van Buren 7.

THE VOTES IN THE 1844 ELECTION

STATES	POPULAR VOTE			ELECTORAL VOTE	
	James K. Polk Democrat	Henry Clay Whig	James G. Birney Abolitionis	Polk and Dallas	Clay and Frelinghuysen
Maine..........	45,719	34,378	4,836	9	—
New Hampshire..	27,160	17,866	4,161	6	—
Vermont........	18,041	26,770	3,954	—	6
Massachusetts....	52,846	67,418	10,860	—	12
Rhode Island....	4,867	7,322	107	—	4
Connecticut......	29,841	32,832	1,943	—	6
New York.......	237,588	232,482	15,812	36	—
New Jersey......	37,495	38,318	131	—	7
Pennsylvania.....	167,535	161,203	3,138	26	—
Delaware........	5,996	6,278	—	—	3
Maryland........	32,676	35,984	—	—	8
Virginia.........	49,570	43,677	—	17	—
North Carolina...	39,287	43,232	—	—	11
South Carolina*..	—	—	—	9	—
Georgia.........	44,177	42,100	—	10	—
Alabama........	37,740	26,084	—	9	—
Mississippi.......	25,126	19,206	—	6	—
Louisiana........	13,782	13,083	—	6	—
Kentucky........	51,988	61,255	—	—	12
Tennessee........	59,917	60,030	—	—	13
Missouri.........	41,369	31,251	—	7	—
Arkansas........	9,546	5,504	—	3	—
Ohio............	149,117	155,057	8,050	—	23
Michigan........	27,759	24,337	3,632	5	—
Indiana.........	70,181	67,867	2,106	12	—
Illinois..........	57,920	45,528	3,570	9	—
	1,337,243	1,299,062	62,300	170	105

* Electors were appointed by the legislature.

THE VOTES IN THE 1848 ELECTION

STATES	POPULAR VOTE			ELECTORAL VOTE	
	Zachary Taylor Whig	Lewis Cass Democrat	Martin Van Buren Free Soiler	Taylor and Fillmore	Cass and Butler
Alabama........	30,482	31,363	—	—	9
Arkansas........	7,588	9,300	—	—	3
Connecticut......	30,314	27,046	5,005	6	—
Delaware........	6,421	5,898	80	3	—
Florida..........	3,116	1,847	—	3	—
Georgia.........	47,544	44,802	—	10	—
Illinois..........	53,047	56,300	15,774	—	9
Indiana.........	69,907	74,745	8,100	—	12
Iowa............	11,084	12,093	1,126	—	4
Kentucky........	67,141	49,720	—	12	—
Louisiana........	18,217	15,370	—	6	—
Maine..........	35,125	39,880	12,096	—	9
Maryland.......	37,702	34,528	125	8	—
Massachusetts....	61,070	35,281	38,058	12	—
Michigan........	23,940	30,687	10,389	—	5
Mississippi.......	25,922	26,537	—	—	6
Missouri........	32,671	40,077	—	—	7
New Hampshire..	14,781	27,763	7,560	—	6
New Jersey......	40,015	36,901	829	7	—
New York.......	218,603	114,318	120,510	36	—
North Carolina...	43,550	34,869	—	11	—
Ohio...........	138,360	154,775	35,354	—	23
Pennsylvania.....	185,513	171,176	11,263	26	—
Rhode Island....	6,779	3,646	730	4	—
South Carolina*..	—	—	—	—	9
Tennessee.......	64,705	58,419	—	13	—
Texas..........	4,509	10,668	—	—	4
Vermont........	23,122	10,948	13,837	6	—
Virginia.........	45,124	46,586	9	—	17
Wisconsin.......	13,747	15,001	10,418	—	4
	1,360,099	1,220,544	291,263	163	127

* Electors were appointed by the legislature.

THE VOTES IN THE 1852 ELECTION

STATES	POPULAR VOTE			ELECTORAL VOTE	
	Franklin Pierce, Democrat	Winfield Scott, Whig	John P. Hale, Free Soiler	Pierce and King	Scott and Graham
Alabama........	26,881	15,038	—	9	—
Arkansas........	12,173	7,404	—	4	—
California.......	40,626	35,407	100	4	—
Connecticut......	33,249	30,359	3,160	6	—
Delaware........	6,318	6,293	62	3	—
Florida..........	4,318	2,875	—	3	—
Georgia.........	34,705	16,660	—	10	—
Illinois..........	80,597	64,934	9,966	11	—
Indiana.........	95,340	80,901	6,929	13	—
Iowa............	17,763	15,856	1,604	4	—
Kentucky........	53,806	57,068	265	—	12
Louisiana.......	18,647	17,255	—	6	—
Maine..........	41,609	32,543	8,030	8	—
Maryland.......	40,020	35,066	281	8	—
Massachusetts....	44,569	52,683	28,023	—	13
Michigan........	41,842	33,859	7,237	6	—
Mississippi......	26,876	17,548	—	7	—
Missouri........	38,353	29,984	—	9	—
New Hampshire..	29,997	16,147	6,695	5	—
New Jersey......	44,305	38,556	350	7	—
New York.......	262,083	234,882	25,329	35	—
North Carolina...	39,744	39,058	59	10	—
Ohio...........	169,220	152,526	31,682	23	—
Pennsylvania.....	198,568	179,174	8,525	27	—
Rhode Island....	8,735	7,626	644	4	—
South Carolina*..	—	—	—	8	—
Tennessee.......	57,018	58,898	—	—	12
Texas...........	13,552	4,995	—	4	—
Vermont........	13,044	22,173	8,621	—	5
Virginia.........	73,858	58,572	291	15	—
Wisconsin.......	33,658	22,240	8,814	5	—
	1,601,474	1,386,580	156,667	254	42

* Electors were appointed by the legislature.

THE VOTES IN THE 1856 ELECTION

STATES	POPULAR VOTE			ELECTORAL VOTE		
	James Buchanan, Democrat	John C. Frémont, Republican	Millard Fillmore, Whig	Buchanan and Breckinridge.	Frémont and Dayton	Fillmore and Donelson
Alabama..........	46,739	—	28,552	9	—	—
Arkansas.........	21,910	—	10,787	4	—	—
California.........	53,365	20,691	36,165	4	—	—
Connecticut........	34,995	42,715	2,615	—	6	—
Delaware..........	8,004	308	6,175	3	—	—
Florida...........	6,358	—	4,833	3	—	—
Georgia	56,578	—	42,228	10	—	—
Illinois...........	105,348	96,189	37,444	11	—	—
Indiana...........	118,670	94,375	22,386	13	—	—
Iowa.............	36,170	43,954	9,180	—	4	—
Kentucky.........	74,642	314	67,416	12	—	—
Louisiana.........	22,164	—	20,709	6	—	—
Maine............	39,080	67,379	3,325	—	8	—
Maryland.........	39,115	281	47,460	—	—	8
Massachusetts.....	39,240	108,190	19,626	—	13	—
Michigan..........	52,136	71,762	1,660	—	⟩ 6	—
Mississippi........	35,446	—	24,195	7	—	—
Missouri..........	58,164	—	48,524	9	—	—
New Hampshire....	32,789	38,345	422	—	5	—
New Jersey........	46,943	28,338	24,115	7	—	—
New York.........	195,878	276,007	124,604	—	35	—
North Carolina.....	48,246	—	36,886	10	—	—
Ohio.............	170,874	187,497	28,126	—	23	—
Pennsylvania.......	230,710	147,510	82,175	27	—	—
Rhode Island.......	6,680	11,467	1,675	—	4	—
South Carolina*....	—	—	—	8	—	—
Tennessee.........	73,638	—	66,178	12	—	—
Texas.............	31,169	—	15,639	4	—	—
Vermont..........	10,569	39,561	545	—	5	—
Virginia..........	89,706	291	60,310	15	—	—
Wisconsin.........	52,843	66,090	579	—	5	—
	1,838,169	1,341,264	874,534	174	114	8

* Electors were appointed by the legislature.

THE VOTES IN THE 1860 ELECTION

STATES	POPULAR VOTE				ELECTORAL VOTE			
	Abraham Lincoln, Republican	Stephen A. Douglas, Democrat	John C. Breckinridge, Democrat	John Bell, Constitutional Union	Lincoln and Hamlin	Douglas and Johnson	Breckinridge and Lane	Bell and Everett
Alabama........	—	13,651	48,831	27,875	—	—	9	—
Arkansas........	—	5,227	28,732	20,094	—	—	4	—
California.......	39,173	38,516	34,334	6,817	4	—	—	—
Connecticut......	43,792	15,522	14,641	3,291	6	—	—	—
Delaware........	3,815	1,023	7,337	3,864	—	—	3	—
Florida..........	—	367	8,543	5,437	—	—	3	—
Georgia.........	—	11,590	51,889	42,886	—	—	10	—
Illinois..........	172,161	160,215	2,404	4,913	11	—	—	—
Indiana..........	139,033	115,509	12,295	5,306	13	—	—	—
Iowa............	70,409	55,111	1,048	1,763	4	—	—	—
Kentucky........	1,364	25,651	53,143	66,058	—	—	—	12
Louisiana........	—	7,625	22,861	20,204	—	—	6	—
Maine........ ..	62,811	26,693	6,368	2,046	8	—	—	—
Maryland..... ..	2,294	5,966	42,482	41,760	—	—	8	—
Massachusetts....	106,533	34,372	5,939	22,331	13	—	—	—
Michigan........	88,480	65,057	805	405	6	—	—	—
Minnesota.......	22,069	11,920	748	62	4	—	—	—
Mississippi.......	—	3,283	40,797	25,040	—	—	7	—
Missouri........ ..	17,028	58,801	31,317	58,372	—	9	—	—
New Hampshir ..	37,519	25,881	2,112	441	5	—	—	—
New Jersey......	58,324	62,801	—	—	4	3	—	—
New York.......	362,646	312,510	—	—	35	—	—	—
North Carolina...	—	2,701	48,539	44,990	—	—	10	—
Ohio............	231,610	187,232	11,405	12,194	23	—	—	—
Oregon..........	5,270	3,951	5,006	183	3	—	—	—
Pennsylvania.....	268,030	16,765	178,871	12,776	27	—	—	—
Rhode Island ..	12,244	7,707	—	—	4	—	—	—
South Carolina*.	—	—	—	—	—	—	8	—
Tennessee........	—	11,350	64,709	69,274	—	—	—	12
Texas....... ...	—	—	47,548	15,438	—	—	4	—
Vermont.........	33,808	8,649	1,866	217	5	—	—	—
Virginia.........	1,929	16,290	74,323	74,681	—	—	—	15
Wisconsin.	86,110	65,021	888	161	5	—	—	—
	1,866,452	1,376,957	849,781	588,879	180	12	72	39

* Electors were appointed by the legislature.

THE VOTES IN THE 1864 ELECTION

STATES	POPULAR VOTE		SOLDIERS' VOTE		ELECTORAL VOTE	
	Abraham Lincoln, Republican (UNION)	George B. McClellan, Democrat	Abraham Lincoln	George McClellan	Lincoln and Johnson	McClellan and Pendleton
California........	62,134	43,841	2,600	237	5	—
Connecticut.......	44,693	42,288	—	—	6	—
Delaware..........	8,155	8,767	—	—	—	3
Illinois............	189,487	158,349	—	—	16	—
Indiana...........	150,422	130,233	—	—	13	—
Iowa.............	87,331	49,260	15,178	1,364	8	—
Kansas†..........	14,228	3,871	—	—	3	—
Kentucky.........	27,786	64,301	1,194	2,823	—	11
Maine............	72,278	47,736	4,174	741	7	—
Maryland.........	40,153	32,739	2,800	321	7	—
Massachusetts.....	126,742	48,745	—	—	12	—
Michigan..........	85,352	67,370	9,402	2,959	8	—
Minnesota†.......	25,060	17,375	—	—	4	—
Missouri..........	72,991	31,026	—	—	11	—
Nevada...........	9,826	6,594	—	—	2*	—
New Hampshire....	36,595	33,034	2,066	690	5	—
New Jersey........	60,723	68,014	—	—	—	7
New York.........	368,726	361,986	—	—	33	—
Ohio.............	265,154	205,568	41,146	9,757	21	—
Oregon...........	9,888	8,457	—	—	3	—
Pennsylvania......	296,389	276,308	26,712	12,349	26	—
Rhode Island......	14,343	8,718	—	—	4	—
Vermont..........	42,422	13,325	243	49	5	—
West Virginia......	23,223	10,457	—	—	5	—
Wisconsin........	79,564	63,875	11,372	2,458	8	—
	2,213,665	1,802,237	116,887	33,748	212	21

* One of the three Nevada electors died before the election.
† The army vote from Kansas and Minnesota arrived too late and could not be counted.

THE VOTES IN THE 1868 ELECTION

STATES	POPULAR VOTE		ELECTORAL VOTE	
	U. S. Grant, Republican	H. Seymour, Democrat	Grant and Colfax	Seymour and Blair
Alabama.........	76,366	72,086	8	—
Arkansas.........	22,152	19,078	5	—
California.........	54,592	54,078	5	—
Connecticut.......	50,641	47,600	6	—
Delaware.........	7,623	10,980	—	3
Florida*.........	—	—	3	—
Georgia.........	57,134	102,822	—	9
Illinois..........	250,293	199,143	16	—
Indiana..........	176,552	166,980	13	—
Iowa............	120,399	74,040	8	—
Kansas..........	31,049	14,019	3	—
Kentucky.........	39,566	115,889	—	11
Louisiana.........	33,263	80,225	—	7
Maine...........	70,426	42,396	7	—
Maryland.........	30,438	62,357	—	7
Massachusetts.....	136,477	59,408	12	—
Michigan.........	128,550	97,069	8	—
Minnesota........	43,542	28,072	4	—
Mississippi†......	—	—	—	—
Missouri.........	85,671	59,788	11	—
Nebraska.........	9,729	5,439	3	—
Nevada..........	6,480	5,218	3	–
New Hampshire...	38,191	31,224	5	—
New Jersey.......	80,121	83,001	—	7
New York........	419,883	429,883	—	33
North Carolina....	96,226	84,090	9	—
Ohio............	280,128	238,700	21	—
Oregon..........	10,961	11,125	—	3
Pennsylvania......	342,280	313,382	26	—
Rhode Island......	12,993	6,548	4	—
South Carolina....	62,301	45,237	6	—
Tennessee.........	56,757	26,311	10	—
Texas†..........	—	—	—	—
Vermont.........	44,167	12,045	5	—
Virginia†........	—	—	—	—
West Virginia.....	29,025	20,306	5	—
Wisconsin.........	108,857	84,710	8	—
	3,012,833	2,703,249	214	80

* Electors were appointed by the legislature.
† The "unreconstructed" states of Mississippi, Texas and Virginia did not vote in this election.

THE VOTES IN THE 1872 ELECTION

STATES	Popular Vote: Ulysses S. Grant, Republican	Horace Greeley, Lib. Republican and Democrat	Charles O'Conor, Straight Democrat and Labor Reform	James Black, Prohibitionist	President: Ulysses S. Grant	Thomas A. Hendricks	B. Gratz Brown	Horace Greeley	Charles J. Jenkins	David Davis	Vice-President: Henry Wilson	B. Gratz Brown	George W. Julian	Alfred H. Colquitt	John M. Palmer	Thomas E. Bramlette	Nathaniel P. Banks	William S. Groesbeck	Willis B. Machen
Alabama	90,272	79,444	—	—	10						10								
Arkansas	41,373	37,927	—	—	6‡						6‡								
California	54,020	40,718	1,068	—	6						6								
Connecticut	50,638	45,880	204	206	6						6								
Delaware	11,115	10,206	487	—	3						3								
Florida	17,763	15,427	—	—	4						4								
Georgia	62,550	76,356	4,000	—	—		6	3‡	2		—	5		5			1		
Illinois	241,944	184,938	3,058	—	21						21								
Indiana	186,147	163,632	1,417	—	15						15								
Iowa	131,566	71,196	2,221	—	11						11								
Kansas	67,048	32,970	596	—	5						5								
Kentucky	88,766	99,995	2,374	—	—	8	4				—	8				3			1
Louisiana *	71,663	57,029	—	—	8‡						8‡								
Louisiana †	59,975	66,467	—	—	—						—	8‡							
Maine	61,422	29,087	—	—	7						7								
Maryland	66,760	67,687	19	—	—	8					—	8							
Massachusetts	133,472	59,260	—	—	13						13								
Michigan	138,455	78,355	2,861	1,271	11						11								
Minnesota	55,117	34,423	—	—	5						5								
Mississippi	82,175	47,288	—	—	8						8								
Missouri	119,196	151,434	2,439	—	—	6	8			1	—	6	5		3			1	
Nebraska	18,329	7,812	—	—	3						3								
Nevada	8,413	6,236	—	—	3						3								
New Hampshire	37,168	31,424	100	200	5						5								
New Jersey	91,656	76,456	630	—	9						9								
New York	440,736	387,281	1,454	201	35						35								
North Carolina	94,769	70,094	—	—	10						10								
Ohio	281,852	244,321	1,163	2,100	22						22								
Oregon	11,819	7,730	572	—	3						3								
Pennsylvania	349,589	212,041	—	1,630	29						29								
Rhode Island	13,665	5,329	—	—	4						4								
South Carolina	72,290	22,703	187	—	7						7								
Tennessee	85,655	94,391	—	—	—	12					—	12							
Texas	47,468	66,546	2,580	—	—	8					—	8							
Vermont	41,481	10,927	593	—	5						5								
Virginia	93,468	91,654	42	—	11						11								
West Virginia	32,315	29,451	600	—	5						5								
Wisconsin	104,997	86,477	834	—	10						10								
	3,597,132	2,834,125	29,489	5,608	286	42	18	—	2	1	286	47	5	5	3	3	1	1	1

During the counting of the electoral votes, a number of controversies arose. Objections were raised against the Arkansas and Louisiana votes, with the result that the returns of neither state were counted. The popular vote of Louisiana is given in two ways: * marks votes certified by the so-called "Custom-House" board; † marks votes certified by a returning board appointed by the Governor of Louisiana, Henry C. Warmoth, a Republican who joined the Greeley movement. The three Georgia votes for Greeley were rejected because Greeley was already dead when they were cast for him. The remaining five Greeley states cast their votes, as a complimentary gesture, for Thomas A. Hendricks.

509

THE VOTE IN THE 1876 ELECTION

STATES	S. J. Tilden Democrat	R. B. Hayes Republican	Peter Cooper Greenback	Green Clay Smith Prohibitionist	STATES	S. J. Tilden Democrat	R. B. Hayes Republican	Peter Cooper Greenback	Green Clay Smith Prohibitionist
Alabama......	102,989	68,708	—	—	Nebraska.....	17,554	31,916	2,320	1,599
Arkansas.....	58,071	38,669	289	—	Nevada.......	9,308	10,383	—	—
California....	76,468	78,322	44	—	New				
Colorado*....	—	—	—	—	Hampshire..	38,509	41,539	76	—
Connecticut...	61,934	59,034	774	378	New Jersey....	115,962	103,517	712	43
Delaware.....	13,381	10,752	—	—	New York....	521,949	489,207	1,987	2,359
Florida†......	22,927	23,849	—	—	North Carolina	125,427	108,417	—	—
Florida‡......	24,434	24,340	—	—	Ohio........	323,182	330,698	3,057	1,636
Georgia......	130,088	50,446	—	—	Oregon.......	14,149	15,206	510	—
Illinois.......	258,601	278,232	9,533	—	Pennsylvania..	366,204	384,184	7,187	1,319
Indiana.......	213,526	208,011	17,233	141	Rhode Island..	10,712	15,787	68	60
Iowa.........	112,121	171,326	9,901	36	South Carolina	90,896	91,870	—	—
Kansas.......	37,902	78,322	7,776	110	Tennessee.....	133,166	89,566	—	—
Kentucky.....	159,696	97,156	1,944	818	Texas........	104,803	44,803	—	—
Louisiana†....	70,508	75,315	—	—	Vermont......	20,350	44,428	—	—
Louisiana‡....	83,723	77,174	—	—	Virginia......	139,670	95,558	—	—
Maine........	49,917	66,300	663	—	West Virginia..	56,495	42,046	1,373	—
Maryland.....	91,780	71,981	33	10	Wisconsin.....	123,926	130,070	1,509	27
Massachusetts.	108,777	150,063	779	84					
Michigan.....	141,095	166,534	9,060	766	Total Repub-				
Minnesota....	48,799	72,962	2,311	72	lican count..	4,285,992	4,033,768	81,737	9,522
Mississippi....	112,173	52,605	—	—	Total Demo-				
Missouri......	203,077	145,029	3,498	64	cratic count.	4,300,590	4,036,298	81,737	9,522

* Electors were appointed by the legislature to avoid another election. (Colorado was admitted to the Union in August 1876.)

† Republican count.   ‡ Democratic count.

THE FINAL VOTE OF THE ELECTORAL COLLEGE

STATES	Hayes and Wheeler	Tilden and Hendricks	STATES	Hayes and Wheeler	Tilden and Hendricks
Alabama.........	—	10	Missouri........	—	15
Arkansas........	—	6	Nebraska........	3	—
California.......	6	—	Nevada.........	3	—
Colorado........	3	—	New Hampshire..	5	—
Connecticut......	—	6	New Jersey......	—	9
Delaware........	—	3	New York.......	—	35
Florida..........	4	—	North Carolina...	—	10
Georgia.........	—	11	Ohio...........	22	—
Illinois...........	21	—	Oregon.........	3	—
Indiana..........	—	15	Pennsylvania.....	29	—
Iowa............	11	—	Rhode Island....	4	—
Kansas..........	5	—	South Carolina...	7	—
Kentucky........	—	12	Tennessee......	—	12
Louisiana........	8	—	Texas..........	—	8
Maine..........	7	—	Vermont........	5	—
Maryland........	—	8	Virginia........	—	11
Massachusetts.....	13	—	West Virginia....	—	5
Michigan........	11	—	Wisconsin.......	10	—
Minnesota........	5	—			
Mississippi.......	—	8	Total.........	185	184

THE VOTES IN THE 1880 ELECTION

STATES	POPULAR VOTE				ELECTORAL VOTE	
	James A. Garfield, Republican	Winfield S. Hancock, Democrat	James B. Weaver, Greenbacker	Neal Dow, Prohibitionist	Garfield and Arthur	Hancock and English
Alabama.........	56,221	91,185	4,642	—	—	10
Arkansas.........	42,436	60,775	4,079	—	—	6
California........	80,348	80,426	3,392	—	1	5
Colorado.........	27,450	24,647	1,435	—	3	—
Connecticut......	67,071	64,415	868	409	6	—
Delaware.........	14,133	15,275	120	—	—	3
Florida..........	23,654	27,964	—	—	—	4
Georgia..........	54,086	102,470	969	—	—	11
Illinois..........	318,037	277,321	26,358	443	21	—
Indiana..........	232,164	225,522	12,986	—	15	—
Iowa............	183,927	105,845	32,701	592	11	—
Kansas..........	121,549	59,801	19,851	25	5	—
Kentucky........	106,306	149,068	11,499	258	—	12
Louisiana........	38,637	65,067	439	—	—	8
Maine...........	74,039	65,171	4,408	93	7	—
Maryland........	78,515	93,706	818	—	—	8
Massachusetts....	165,205	111,960	4,548	682	13	—
Michigan.........	185,341	131,597	34,895	942	11	—
Minnesota........	93,903	53,315	3,267	286	5	—
Mississippi.......	34,854	75,750	5,797	—	—	8
Missouri.........	153,567	208,609	35,135	—	—	15
Nebraska........	54,979	28,523	3,950	—	3	—
Nevada..........	8,732	9,613	—	—	—	3
New Hampshire...	44,852	40,794	528	180	5	—
New Jersey.......	120,555	122,565	2,617	191	—	9
New York........	555,544	534,511	12,373	1,517	35	—
North Carolina...	115,874	124,208	1,126	—	—	10
Ohio.............	375,048	340,821	6,456	2,616	22	—
Oregon..........	20,619	19,948	249	—	3	—
Pennsylvania.....	444,704	407,428	20,668	1,939	29	—
Rhode Island.....	18,195	10,779	236	20	4	—
South Carolina...	58,071	112,312	566	—	—	7
Tennessee.......	107,677	128,191	5,917	43	—	12
Texas...........	57,893	156,428	27,405	—	—	8
Vermont.........	45,567	18,316	1,215	—	5	—
Virginia..........	84,020	128,586	—	—	—	11
West Virginia.....	46,243	57,391	9,079	—	—	5
Wisconsin........	144,400	114,649	7,986	69	10	—
	4,454,416	4,444,952	308,578	10,305	214	155

Louisiana voted for two Republican tickets. Maine voted for a fusion Democratic ticket, consisting of three Democrats and four Greenbackers; it also voted for a straight Greenback ticket. Virginia voted for two Democratic tickets. Total vote, 9,218,958.

THE VOTES IN THE 1884 ELECTION

STATES	POPULAR VOTE				ELECTORAL VOTE	
	Grover Cleveland, Democrat	James G. Blaine, Republican	Benjamin F. Butler, Greenbacker	John P. St. John, Prohibitionist	Cleveland and Hendricks	Blaine and Logan
Alabama..........	93,951	59,591	873	612	10	—
Arkansas..........	72,927	50,895	1,847	—	7	—
California.........	89,288	102,416	2,017	2,920	—	8
Colorado..........	27,723	36,290	1,953	761	—	3
Connecticut.......	67,199	65,923	1,688	2,305	6	—
Delaware..........	16,964	12,951	6	55	3	—
Florida...........	31,766	28,031	—	72	4	—
Georgia...........	94,667	48,603	145	195	12	—
Illinois............	312,355	337,474	10,910	12,074	—	22
Indiana...........	244,990	238,463	8,293	3,028	15	—
Iowa.............	177,316	197,089	—	1,472	—	13
Kansas...........	90,132	154,406	16,341	4,495	—	9
Kentucky.........	152,961	118,122	1,691	3,139	13	—
Louisiana.........	62,540	46,347	—	—	8	—
Maine............	52,140	72,209	3,953	2,160	—	6
Maryland.........	96,932	85,699	531	2,794	8	—
Massachusetts.....	122,481	146,724	24,433	10,026	—	14
Michigan.........	149,835	192,669	42,243	18,403	—	13
Minnesota.........	70,144	111,923	3,583	4,684	—	7
Mississippi........	76,510	43,509	—	—	9	—
Missouri..........	235,988	202,929	—	2,153	16	—
Nebraska.........	54,391	79,912	—	2,899	—	5
Nevada...........	5,578	7,193	26	—	—	3
New Hampshire....	39,183	43,249	552	1,571	—	4
New Jersey........	127,798	123,440	3,496	6,159	9	—
New York.........	563,154	562,005	16,994	25,016	36	—
North Carolina....	142,952	125,068	—	454	11	—
Ohio.............	368,280	400,082	5,179	11,069	—	23
Oregon...........	24,604	26,860	726	492	—	3
Pennsylvania......	392,785	473,804	16,992	15,283	—	30
Rhode Island......	12,391	19,030	422	928	—	4
South Carolina....	69,890	21,733	—	—	9	—
Tennessee.........	133,258	124,078	957	1,131	12	—
Texas.............	225,309	93,141	3,321	3,534	13	—
Vermont..........	17,331	39,514	785	1,752	—	4
Virginia..........	185,497	139,356	—	138	12	—
West Virginia......	67,317	63,096	810	939	6	—
Wisconsin.........	146,459	161,157	4,598	7,656	—	11
	4,874,986	4,851,981	175,370	150,369	219	182

THE VOTES IN THE 1888 ELECTION

STATES	POPULAR VOTE				ELECTORAL VOTE	
	Benjamin Harrison, Republican	Grover Cleveland, Democrat	Clinton B. Fisk, Prohibitionist	Alson J. Streeter, Union Labor	Harrison and Morton	Cleveland and Thurman
Alabama.........	56,197	117,320	583	—	—	10
Arkansas..........	58,752	85,962	641	10,613	—	7
California........	124,816	117,729	5,761	—	8	—
Colorado..........	50,774	37,567	2,191	1,266	3	—
Connecticut.......	74,584	74,920	4,234	240	—	6
Delaware.........	12,973	16,414	400	—	—	3
Florida...........	26,657	39,561	423	—	—	4
Georgia...........	40,496	100,499	1,808	136	—	12
Illinois..........	370,473	348,278	21,695	7,090	22	—
Indiana..........	263,361	261,013	9,881	2,694	15	—
Iowa.............	211,598	179,887	3,550	9,105	13	—
Kansas...........	182,934	103,744	6,768	37,726	9	—
Kentucky.........	155,134	183,800	5,225	622	—	13
Louisiana.........	30,484	85,032	160	39	—	8
Maine............	73,734	50,481	2,691	1,344	6	—
Maryland.........	99,986	106,168	4,767	—	—	8
Massachusetts.....	183,892	151,856	8,701	—	14	—
Michigan.........	236,370	213,459	20,942	4,541	13	—
Minnesota........	142,492	104,385	15,311	1,094	7	—
Mississippi........	30,096	85,471	218	22	—	9
Missouri..........	236,257	261,974	4,539	18,632	—	16
Nebraska.........	108,425	80,552	9,429	4,226	5	—
Nevada...........	7,229	5,362	41	—	3	—
New Hampshire....	45,728	43,458	1,593	13	4	—
New Jersey........	144,344	151,493	7,904	—	—	9
New York........	648,759	635,757	30,231	626	36	—
North Carolina....	134,784	147,902	2,787	32	—	11
Ohio.............	416,054	396,455	24,356	3,496	23	—
Oregon...........	33,291	26,522	1,677	363	3	—
Pennsylvania......	526,091	446,633	20,947	3,873	30	—
Rhode Island......	21,968	17,530	1,250	18	4	—
South Carolina....	13,736	65,825	—	—	—	9
Tennessee.........	138,988	158,779	5,969	48	—	12
Texas.............	88,422	234,883	4,749	29,459	—	13
Vermont..........	45,192	16,785	1,460	—	4	—
Virginia...........	150,438	151,977	1,678	—	—	12
West Virginia......	77,791	79,664	669	1,064	—	6
Wisconsin.........	176,553	155,232	14,277	8,552	11	—
	5,439,853	5,540,329	249,506	146,935	233	168

California cast 1591 votes for Curtis, American; Illinois 150 votes, N. Y. 2668 votes for Cowdrey, United Labor. Total vote, 11,381,032.

THE VOTES IN THE 1892 ELECTION

STATES	POPULAR VOTE					ELECTORAL VOTE		
	Grover Cleveland, Democrat	Benjamin Harrison, Republican	James B. Weaver, Populist	John Bidwell, Prohibitionist	Simon Wing, Socialist-Labor	Cleveland and Stevenson	Harrison and Reid	Weaver and Field
Alabama..........	138,138	9,197	85,181	239	—	11	—	—
Arkansas..........	87,834	46,884	11,831	113	—	8	—	—
California.........	117,908	117,618	25,226	8,056	—	8	1	—
Colorado.........	—	38,620	53,584	1,638	—	—	—	4
Connecticut.......	82,395	77,025	806	4,025	329	6	—	—
Delaware.........	18,581	18,083	13	565	—	3	—	—
Florida...........	30,143	—	4,843	475	—	4	—	—
Georgia...........	129,361	48,305	42,937	988	—	13	—	—
Idaho............	•—	8,599	10,520	288	—	—	—	3
Illinois............	426,281	399,288	22,207	25,870	—	24	—	—
Indiana...........	262,740	255,615	22,208	13,050	—	15	—	—
Iowa.............	196,367	219,795	20.595	6,402	—	—	13	—
Kansas...........	—	157,237	163,111	4,539	—	—	—	10
Kentucky.........	175,461	135,441	23,500	6,442	—	13	—	—
Louisiana.........	87,922	13,281	13,282	—	—	8	—	—
Maine............	48,044	62,931	2,381	3,062	336	—	6	—
Maryland.........	113,866	92,736	796	5,877	27	8	—	—
Massachusetts.....	176,813	202,814	3,210	1,539	649	—	15	—
Michigan.........	202,296	222,708	19,892	14,069	—	5	9	—
Minnesota........	100,920	122,823	29,313	12,182	—	—	9	—
Mississippi........	40,237	1,406	10.256	910	—	9	—	—
Missouri..........	268,398	226,918	41,213	4,331	—	17	—	—
Montana..........	17,581	18,851	7,334	549	—	—	3	—
Nebraska.........	24,943	87,227	83,134	4,902	—	—	8	—
Nevada...........	714	2,811	7,264	89	—	—	—	3
New Hampshire....	42,081	45,658	292	1,297	—	—	4	—
New Jersey........	171,042	156,068	969	8,131	1,337	10	—	—
New York........	654,868	609,350	16,429	38,190	17,956	36	—	—
North Carolina....	132,951	100,342	44,736	2,636	—	11	—	—
North Dakota.....	—	17,519	17,700	899	—	1	1	1
Ohio.............	404,115	405,187	14,850	26,012	—	1	22	—
Oregon...........	14,243	35,002	26,965	2,281	—	—	3	1
Pennsylvania......	452,264	516,011	8,714	25,123	898	—	32	—
Rhode Island......	24,335	26,972	228	1,654	—	—	4	—
South Carolina....	54,692	13,345	2,407	—	—	9	—	—
South Dakota.....	9,081	34,888	26,544	—	—	—	4	—
Tennessee.........	138,874	100,331	23,447	4,851	—	12	—	—
Texas.............	239,148	81,444	99,688	2,165	—	15	—	—
Vermont..........	16,325	37,992	43	1,415	—	—	4	—
Virginia..........	163,977	113,262	12,275	2,738	—	12	—	—
Washington.......	29,802	36,460	19,165	2,542	—	—	4	—
West Virginia......	84,467	80,293	4,166	2,145	—	6	—	—
Wisconsin.........	177,335	170,791	9,909	13,132	—	12	—	—
Wyoming.........	—	8,454	7,722	530	—	—	3	—
	5,556,543	5,175,582	1,040,886	255,841	21,532	277	145	22

THE VOTES IN THE 1896 ELECTION

| STATES | POPULAR VOTE | | | | | | | ELECTORAL VOTE | | | | |
| | | | | | | | | PRES. | | VICE-PRES. | | |
	William McKinley, Republican	William J. Bryan, Democrat	Bryan and Watson, Populist	John M. Palmer, Nat. Democrat	Joshua Levering, Prohibitionist	C. E. Bentley, National	C. H. Matchett, Socialist Labor	McKinley	Bryan	Hobart	Sewall	Watson
Alabama......	54,737	131,226	24,089	6,462	2,147	—	—	—	11	—	11	—
Arkansas......	37,512	110,103	—	—	839	893	—	—	8	—	5	3
California.....	146,688	144,766	21,730	2,006	2,573	1,047	1,611	8	1	8	1	—
Colorado......	26,271	161,269	2,389	1	1,717	386	160	—	4	—	4	—
Connecticut....	110,285	56,740	—	4,336	1,806	—	1,223	6	—	6	—	—
Delaware......	20,452	16,615	—	966	602	—	—	3	—	3	—	—
Florida........	11,257	31,958	1,977	1,772	644	—	—	—	4	—	4	—
Georgia.......	60,091	94,672	440	2,708	5,716	—	—	—	13	—	13	—
Idaho........	6,324	23,192	—	—	181	—	—	—	3	—	3	—
Illinois.......	607,130	464,523	1,090	6,390	9,796	793	1,147	24	—	24	—	—
Indiana.......	323,754	305,573	—	2,145	3,056	2,267	324	15	—	15	—	—
Iowa..........	289,293	223,741	—	4,516	3,192	352	453	13	—	13	—	—
Kansas........	159,541	171,810	46,194	1,209	1,921	630	—	—	10	—	10	—
Kentucky......	218,171	217,890	—	5,114	4,781	—	—	12	1	12	1	—
Louisiana......	22,037	77,175	—	1,915	—	—	—	—	8	—	4	4
Maine........	80,461	34,587	2,387	1,866	1,589	—	—	6	—	6	—	—
Maryland......	136,978	104,746	—	2,507	5,922	136	588	8	—	8	—	—
Massachusetts..	278,976	105,711	15,181	11,749	2,998	—	2,114	15	—	15	—	—
Michigan......	293,582	237,268	—	6,968	5,025	1,995	297	14	—	14	—	—
Minnesota.....	193,503	139,735	—	3,222	4,363	—	954	9	—	9	—	—
Mississippi.....	5,123	63,793	7,517	1,071	485	—	—	—	9	—	9	—
Missouri.......	304,940	363,652	—	2,355	2,169	293	599	—	17	—	13	4
Montana......	10,494	42,537	—	—	186	—	—	—	3	—	2	1
Nebraska......	103,064	115,999	—	2,797	1,243	797	186	—	8	—	4	4
Nevada........	1,938	8,377	575	—	—	—	—	—	3	—	3	—
New Hampshire	57,444	21,650	379	3,520	779	49	228	4	—	4	—	—
New Jersey....	221,367	133,675	—	6,373	5,614	—	3,985	10	—	10	—	—
New York.....	819,838	551,369	—	18,950	16,052	—	17,667	36	—	36	—	—
North Carolina.	155,222	174,488	—	578	676	245	—	—	11	—	6	5
North Dakota..	26,335	20,686	—	—	358	—	—	3	—	3	—	—
Ohio..........	525,991	477,497	2,615	1,858	5,068	2,716	1,167	23	—	23	—	—
Oregon........	48,779	46,662	—	977	919	—	—	4	—	4	—	—
Pennsylvania...	728,300	433,230	11,176	10,921	19,274	870	1,683	32	—	32	—	—
Rhode Island...	37,437	14,459	—	1,166	1,160	5	558	4	—	4	—	—
South Carolina.	9,313	58,801	—	824	—	—	—	—	9	—	9	—
South Dakota..	41,042	41,225	—	—	683	—	—	—	4	—	2	2
Tennessee......	148,773	166,268	4,525	1,951	3,098	—	—	—	12	—	12	—
Texas.........	167,520	370,434	79,572	5,046	1,786	—	—	—	15	—	15	—
Utah..........	13,491	64,607	—	21	—	—	—	—	3	—	2	1
Vermont.......	50,991	10,607	461	1,329	728	—	—	4	—	4	—	—
Virginia.......	135,388	154,985	—	2,127	2,350	—	115	—	12	—	12	—
Washington....	39,153	51,646	—	1,668	968	148	—	—	4	—	2	2
West Virginia..	104,414	92,927	—	677	1.203	—	—	6	—	6	—	—
Wisconsin.....	268,135	165,523	—	4,584	7,509	346	1,314	12	—	12	—	—
Wyoming......	10,072	10,655	286	—	136	—	—	—	3	—	2	1
	7,111,607	6,509,052	222,583	134,645	131,312	13,968	36,373	271	176	271	149	27

The Populist vote—Bryan and Watson—is included in the Bryan column. Total vote, 13,936,957.

THE VOTES IN THE 1900 ELECTION

STATES	POPULAR VOTE								ELECTORAL VOTE	
	McKinley and Roosevelt, Republican	Bryan and Stevenson, Democrat	Wooley and Metcalf, Prohibition	Debs and Harriman, Social-Democrat	Malloney and Remmel, Socialist-Labor	Barker and Donnelly, Mid-Road Populist	Ellis and Nicholson, Union Reform	Leonard and Martin, United Christian	McKinley and Roosevelt	Bryan and Stevenson
Alabama........	55,512	97,131	2,762	—	—	4,178	—		—	11
Arkansas........	44,800	81,142	584	27	—	972	341	—	—	8
California......	164,755	124,985	5,087	7,572	—	—	—	—	9	—
Colorado.......	93,072	122,733	3,790	714	684	389	—	—	—	4
Connecticut.....	102,572	74,014	1,617	1,029	908	—	—	—	6	—
Delaware........	22,535	18,863	546	57	—	—	—	—	3	—
Florida..........	7,420	28,007	2,234	601	—	1,070	—	—	—	4
Georgia.........	35,056	81,700	1,396	—	—	4,584	—	—	—	13
Idaho...........	27,198	29,414	857	—	—	232	—	—	—	3
Illinois.........	597,985	503,061	17,626	9,687	1,373	1,141	572	352	24	—
Indiana.........	336,063	309,584	13,718	2,374	663	1,438	254	—	15	—
Iowa............	307,808	209,265	9,502	2,742	259	613	—	707	13	—
Kansas..........	185,955	162,601	3,605	1,605	—	—	—	—	10	—
Kentucky........	226,801	234,899	2,814	770	299	2,017	—	—	—	13
Louisiana........	14,233	53,671	—	—	—	—	—	—	—	8
Maine..........	65,412	36,822	2,585	878	—	—	—	—	6	—
Maryland.......	136,185	122,238	4,574	904	388	—	147	—	8	—
Massachusetts....	239,147	157,016	6,208	9,716	2,610	—	—	—	15	—
Michigan........	316,269	211,685	11,859	2,826	903	837	—	—	14	—
Minnesota.......	190,461	112,901	8,555	3,065	1,329	—	—	—	9	—
Mississippi......	5,753	51,706	—	—	—	1,644	—	—	—	9
Missouri........	314,092	351,922	5,965	6,139	1,294	4,244	—	—	—	17
Montana........	25,373	37,145	298	708	169	—	—	—	—	3
Nebraska........	121,835	114,013	3,655	823	—	1,104	—	—	8	—
Nevada.........	3,849	6,347	—	—	—	—	—	—	—	3
New Hampshire..	54,799	35,489	1,279	790	—	—	—	—	4	—
New Jersey......	221,754	164,879	7,190	4,611	2,081	691	—	—	10	—
New York......	822,013	678,462	22,077	12,869	12,621	—	—	—	36	—
North Carolina...	132,997	157,733	1,006	—	—	830	—	—	—	11
North Dakota....	35,898	20,531	731	520	—	111	—	—	3	—
Ohio...........	543,918	474,882	10,203	4,847	1,588	251	4,284	—	23	—
Oregon..........	46,526	33,385	2,536	1,494	—	275	—	—	4	—
Pennsylvania.....	712,665	424,232	27,908	4,831	2,936	638	—	—	32	—
Rhode Island....	33,784	19,812	1,529	—	1,423	—	—	—	4	—
South Carolina...	3,579	47,233	—	—	—	—	—	—	—	9
South Dakota....	54,530	39,544	1,542	169	—	339	—	—	4	—
Tennessee.......	123,180	145,356	3,860	413	—	1,322	—	—	—	12
Texas..........	130,641	267,432	2,644	1,846	162	20,981	—	—	—	15
Utah............	47,139	45,006	209	720	106	—	—	—	3	—
Vermont........	42,569	12,849	383	39	—	367	—	—	4	—
Virginia.........	115,865	146,080	2,150	145	167	63	—	—	—	12
Washington......	57,456	44,833	2,363	2,066	866	—	—	—	4	—
West Virginia....	119,829	98,807	1,692	219	—	268	—	—	6	—
Wisconsin.......	265,760	159,163	10,027	7,048	503	—	—	—	12	—
Wyoming........	14,482	10,164	—	—	—	—	—	—	3	—
	7,219,525	6,358,737	209,157	94,864	33,432	50,599	5,698	1,059	292	155

516

STATES	POPULAR VOTE						ELECTORAL VOTE	
	Roosevelt and Fairbanks, Republican	Parker and Davis, Democrat	Swallow and Carroll, Prohibition	Debs and Hanford, Socialist	Corregan and Cox, Socialist Labor	Watson and Tibbles, Populist	Roosevelt and Fairbanks	Parker and Davis
Alabama.........	22,472	79,857	612	853	—	5,051	—	11
Arkansas.........	46,860	64,434	993	1,816	—	2,318	—	9
California........	205,226	89,404	7,380	29,535	—	—	10	—
Colorado.........	134,687	100,105	3,438	4,304	335	824	5	—
Connecticut......	111,089	72,909	1,506	4,543	575	495	7	—
Delaware.........	23,712	19,359	607	146	—	51	3	—
Florida..........	8,314	27,040	5	2,337	—	1,605	—	5
Georgia..........	24,003	83,472	685	197	—	22,635	—	13
Idaho............	47,783	18,480	1,013	4,949	—	353	3	—
Illinois..........	632,645	327,606	34,770	69,225	4,698	6,725	27	—
Indiana..........	368,289	274,335	23,496	12,013	1,598	2,444	15	—
Iowa.............	307,907	149,141	11,601	14,847	—	2,207	13	—
Kansas...........	212,955	86,174	7,306	15,869	—	6,253	10	—
Kentucky.........	205,277	217,170	6,609	3,602	596	2,511	—	13
Louisiana........	5,205	47,708	—	995	—	—	—	9
Maine............	64,438	27,649	1,510	2,103	—	—	6	—
Maryland.........	109,497	109,446	3,034	2,247	—	—	1	7
Massachusetts.....	257,822	165,772	4,286	13,604	2,365	1,290	16	—
Michigan.........	364,957	135,392	13,441	9,042	1,036	1,159	14	—
Minnesota........	216,651	55,187	6,253	11,692	974	2,103	11	—
Mississippi.......	3,187	53,374	—	392	—	1,424	—	10
Missouri.........	321,449	296,312	7,191	13,009	1,674	4,226	18	—
Montana.........	34,932	21,773	335	5,676	208	1,520	3	—
Nebraska.........	138,558	52,921	6,323	7,412	—	20,518	8	—
Nevada..........	6,864	3,982	—	925	—	344	3	—
New Hampshire. .	54,163	34,074	750	1,090	—	83	4	—
New Jersey.......	245,164	164,516	6,845	9,587	2,680	3,705	12	—
New York........	859,533	683,981	20,787	36,883	9,127	7,459	39	—
North Carolina....	82,442	124,121	361	124	—	819	—	12
North Dakota.....	52,595	14,273	1,140	2,117	—	165	4	—
Ohio.............	600,095	344,674	19,339	36,260	2,633	1,392	23	—
Oregon..........	60,455	17,521	3,806	7,619	—	753	4	—
Pennsylvania......	840,949	337,998	33,717	21,863	2,211	—	34	—
Rhode Island.....	41,605	24,839	768	956	488	—	4	—
South Carolina....	2,554	52,563	—	22	—	1	—	9
South Dakota.....	72,083	21,969	2,965	3,138	—	1,240	4	—
Tennessee........	105,369	131,653	1,891	1,354	—	2,506	—	12
Texas............	51,242	167,200	3,995	2,791	421	8,062	—	18
Utah.............	62,446	33,413	—	5,767	—	—	3	—
Vermont.........	40,459	9,777	792	859	—	—	4	—
Virginia..........	47,880	80,650	1,382	218	56	359	—	12
Washington.......	101,540	28,098	3,329	10,023	1,592	669	5	—
West Virginia.....	132,628	100,881	4,600	1,572	—	339	7	—
Wisconsin........	280,315	124,205	9,672	28,240	223	530	13	—
Wyoming.........	20,489	8,930	217	1,077	—	—	3	—
	7,628,785	5,084,442	258,950	402,895	33,490	114,546	336	140

THE VOTES IN THE 1908 ELECTION

STATES	Taft and Sherman, Republican	Bryan and Kern, Democrat	Chafin and Watkins, Prohibition	Debs and Hanford, Socialist	Gilhaus and Munro, Socialist-Labor	Watson and Williams, Populist	Hisgen and Graves, Independence	Taft and Sherman	Bryan and Kern
	POPULAR VOTE							ELECTORAL VOTE	
Alabama	26,283	74,374	665	1,399	—	1,568	495	—	11
Arkansas	56,760	87,015	1,194	5,842	—	1.026	289	—	9
California	214,398	127,492	11,770	28,659	—	—	4,278	10	—
Colorado	123,700	126,644	5,559	7,974	—	—	—	—	5
Connecticut	112,815	68,255	2,380	5,113	608	—	728	7	—
Delaware	25,014	22,071	670	239	—	—	30	3	—
Florida	10,654	31,104	553	3,747	—	1,946	1,356	—	5
Georgia	41,692	72,413	1,059	584	—	16,969	77	—	13
Idaho	52,621	36,162	1,986	6,400	—	—	119	3	—
Illinois	629,932	450,810	29,364	34,711	1,680	633	7,724	27	—
Indiana	348,993	338,262	18,045	13,476	643	1,193	514	15	—
Iowa	275,210	200,771	9,837	8,287	—	261	404	13	—
Kansas	197,216	161,209	5,033	12,420	—	—	68	10	—
Kentucky	235,711	244,092	5,887	4,185	404	333	200	—	13
Louisiana	8,958	63,568	—	2,538	—	—	82	—	9
Maine	66,987	35,403	1,487	1,758	—	—	700	6	—
Maryland	116,513	115,908	3,302	2,323	—	—	485	2	6
Massachusetts	265,966	155,543	4,379	10,781	1,018	—	19,239	16	—
Michigan	333,313	174,619	16,795	11,527	1,086	—	734	14	—
Minnesota	195,843	109,401	11,107	14,527	—	—	426	11	—
Mississippi	4,363	60,287	—	978	—	1,276	—	—	10
Missouri	347,203	346,574	4,284	15,431	868	1,165	402	18	—
Montana	32,333	29,326	827	5,855	—	—	481	3	—
Nebraska	126,997	131,099	5.179	3,524	—	—	—	—	8
Nevada	10,775	11,212	—	2,103	—	—	436	—	3
New Hampshire	53,149	33,655	905	1,299	—	—	584	4	—
New Jersey	265,326	182,567	4,934	10,253	1,196	—	2,922	12	—
New York	870,070	667,468	22,667	38,451	3,877	—	35,817	39	—
North Carolina	114,887	136,928	—	345	—	—	—	—	12
North Dakota	57,680	32,885	1,496	2,421	—	—	43	4	—
Ohio	572,312	502,721	11,402	33,795	721	162	439	23	—
Oklahoma	110,558	122,406	—	21,779	—	434	244	—	7
Oregon	62,530	38,049	2,682	7,339	—	—	289	4	—
Pennsylvania	745,779	448,785	36,694	33,913	1,222	—	1,057	34	—
Rhode Island	43,942	24,706	1,016	1,365	183	—	1,105	4	—
South Carolina	3,965	62,290	—	100	—	—	43	—	9
South Dakota	67,536	40,266	4,039	2,846	—	—	88	4	—
Tennessee	118,324	135,608	300	1,870	—	1,081	332	—	12
Texas	65,666	217,302	1,634	7,870	176	994	115	—	18
Utah	61,165	42,601	—	4,890	—	—	92	3	—
Vermont	39,552	11,496	799	—	—	—	804	4	—
Virginia	52,573	82,946	1,111	255	25	105	51	—	12
Washington	106,062	58,691	4,700	14,177	—	—	249	5	—
West Virginia	137,869	111,418	5,139	3,679	—	—	46	7	—
Wisconsin	247,747	166,662	11,565	28,147	314	—	—	13	—
Wyoming	20,846	14,918	66	1,715	—	—	64	3	—
	7,677,788	6,407,982	252,511	420,890	14,021	29,146	83,651	321	162

THE VOTES IN THE 1912 ELECTION

STATES	POPULAR VOTE						ELECTORAL VOTE	
	Wilson and Marshall, Democrat	Roosevelt and Johnson, Progressive	Taft and Sherman, Republican	Chafin and Watkins, Prohibition	Debs and Seidel, Socialist	Reimer and Francis, Socialist-Labor	Wilson and Marshall	Roosevelt and Johnson
Alabama.........	82,439	22,689	9,731	—	3,029	—	12	—
Arizona.........	10,324	6,949	3,021	265	3,163	—	3	—
Arkansas........	68,838	21,673	24,297	898	8,153	—	9	—
California........	283,436	283,610	3,914	23,366	79,201	—	2	11
Colorado........	114,223	72,306	58,386	5,063	16,418	—	6	—
Connecticut......	74,561	34,129	68,324	2,068	70,056	475	7	—
Delaware........	22,631	8,886	15,998	623	556	1,260	3	—
Florida..........	36,417	4,535	4,279	1,854	4,806	—	6	—
Georgia.........	93,171	22,010	5,190	147	1,014	—	14	—
Idaho...........	33,921	25,527	32,810	1,537	11,960	—	4	—
Illinois.........	405,048	386,478	253,613	15,710	81,278	4,066	29	—
Indiana.........	281,890	162,007	151,267	10,249	36,931	3,130	15	—
Iowa............	185,325	161,819	119,805	8,440	16,967	—	13	—
Kansas..........	143,670	120,123	74,844	—	26,807	—	10	—
Kentucky........	219,584	102,766	115,512	3,233	11,647	956	13	—
Louisiana........	60,966	9,323	3,834	—	5,249	—	10	—
Maine...........	51,113	48,493	26,545	945	2,541	—	6	—
Maryland........	112,674	57,786	54,956	2,244	3,996	322	8	—
Massachusetts....	173,408	142,228	155,948	2,754	12,616	1,102	18	—
Michigan........	150,751	214,584	152,244	8,934	23,211	1,252	—	15
Minnesota.......	106,426	125,856	64,334	7,886	27,505	2,212	—	12
Mississippi.......	57,164	3,627	1,511	—	2,017	—	10	—
Missouri.........	330,746	124,371	207,821	5,380	28,466	1,778	18	—
Montana........	27,941	22,456	18,512	32	10,885	—	4	—
Nebraska........	109,008	72,689	54,216	3,383	10,885	—	8	—
Nevada..........	7,986	5,620	3,196	—	3,313	—	3	—
New Hampshire..	34,724	17,794	32,927	535	1,981	—	4	—
New Jersey......	178,289	145,410	88,835	2,878	15,801	1,321	14	—
New Mexico.....	20,437	8,347	17,733	—	2,859	—	3	—
New York.......	655,475	390,021	455,428	19,427	63,381	4,251	45	—
North Carolina...	144,507	69,130	29,139	117	1,025	—	12	—
North Dakota....	29,555	25,726	23,090	1,243	6,966	—	5	—
Ohio............	423,152	229,327	277,066	11,459	89,930	2,623	24	—
Oklahoma.......	119,156	—	90,786	2,185	42,262	—	10	—
Oregon..........	47,064	37,600	34,637	4,360	13,343	—	5	—
Pennsylvania..'...	395,619	447,426	273,305	19,533	83,164	704	—	38
Rhode Island.....	30,142	16,878	27,703	616	2,049	236	5	—
South Carolina...	38,355	1,293	536	—	164	—	9	—
South Dakota....	48,942	58,811	—	3,910	4,662	—	—	5
Tennessee........	130,335	53,725	59,444	825	3,492	—	12	—
Texas...........	221,589	26,755	28,853	1,738	25,743	442	20	—
Utah............	36,579	24,174	42,100	—	9,023	509	—	—
Vermont.........	15,350	22,070	23,305	1,154	928	—	—	—
Virginia.........	90,332	21,777	23,288	709	820	50	12	—
Washington......	86,840	113,698	70,445	9,810	40,134	1,872	—	7
West Virginia....	113,197	79,112	56,754	4,517	15,248	—	8	—
Wisconsin.......	164,409	58,661	130,878	8,467	34,168	698	13	—
Wyoming........	15,310	9,232	14,560	434	2,760	—	3	—
	6,293,019	4,119,507	3,484,956	207,828	901,873	29,259	435	88

THE VOTES IN THE 1916 ELECTION

STATES	POPULAR VOTE				ELECTORAL VOTE	
	Wilson and Marshall, Democrat	Hughes and Fairbanks, Republican	Hanly and Landrith, Prohibition	Benson and Kirkpatrick, Socialist	Wilson and Marshall	Hughes and Fairbanks
Alabama..........	99,409	22,809	1,034	1,925	12	—
Arizona...........	33,170	20,524	1,153	3,174	3	—
Arkansas..........	112,148	47,148	2,015	6,999	9	—
California........	466,200	462,394	27,698	43,259	13	—
Colorado.........	178,816	102,308	2,793	10,049	6	—
Connecticut.......	99,786	106,514	1,789	5,179	—	7
Delaware.........	24,753	26,011	566	480	—	3
Florida..........	55,984	14,611	4,855	5,353	6	—
Georgia..........	125,845	11,225	—	967	14	—
Idaho.............	70,054	55,368	1,127	8,066	4	—
Illinois...........	590,229	1,152,549	26,047	61,394	—	29
Indiana..........	334,063	341,005	16,368	21,855	—	15
Iowa.............	221,699	280,449	3,371	10,976	—	13
Kansas...........	314,588	277,658	12,882	24,685	10	—
Kentucky.........	269,990	241,854	3,036	4,734	13	—
Louisiana.........	79,875	6,466	—	292	10	—
Maine............	64,127	69,506	597	2,177	—	6
Maryland.........	138,359	117,347	2,903	2,674	8	—
Massachusetts.....	247,885	268,784	2,993	11,058	—	18
Michigan.........	285,151	339,097	8,139	16,120	—	15
Minnesota........	179,152	179,544	7,793	20,117	—	12
Mississippi........	80,422	4,253	—	1,484	10	—
Missouri..........	398,025	369,339	3,884	14,612	18	—
Montana..........	101,063	66,750	—	9,564	4	—
Nebraska.........	158,827	117,257	2,952	7,141	8	—
Nevada...........	17,776	12,127	348	3,065	3	—
New Hampshire....	43,779	43,723	303	1,318	4	—
New Jersey........	211,645	269,352	3,187	10,462	—	14
New Mexico.......	33,693	31,163	112	1,999	3	—
New York.........	759,426	869,115	19,031	45,944	—	45
North Carolina....	168,383	120,988	51	490	12	—
North Dakota.....	55,206	53,471	—	—	5	—
Ohio.............	604,161	514,753	8,080	38,092	24	—
Oklahoma.........	148,113	97,233	1,646	45,190	10	—
Oregon...........	120,087	126,813	4,729	9,711	—	5
Pennsylvania......	521,784	703,734	28,525	42,637	—	38
Rhode Island......	40,394	44,858	470	1,914	—	5
South Carolina....	61,846	1,550	—	135	9	—
South Dakota.....	59,191	64,217	1,774	3,760	—	5
Tennessee.........	153,282	116,223	147	2,542	12	—
Texas.............	286,514	64,999	1,985	18,963	20	—
Utah.............	84,025	54,137	149	4,460	4	—
Vermont..........	22,708	40,250	709	798	—	4
Virginia..........	102,824	49,356	783	1,060	12	—
Washington.......	183,388	167,244	6,868	22,800	7	—
West Virginia......	140,403	143,124	175	6,140	1	7
Wisconsin.........	193,042	221,323	7,166	27,846	—	13
Wyoming.........	28,316	21,698	373	1,453	3	—
	9,129,606	8,538,221	220,506	585,113	277	254

THE VOTES IN THE 1920 ELECTION

STATES	POPULAR VOTE					ELECTORAL VOTE	
	Harding and Coolidge, Republican	Cox and Roosevelt, Democrat	Debs and Stedman, Socialist	Christensen and Hayes, Farmer-Labor	Watkins and Colvin, Prohibition	Harding and Coolidge	Cox and Roosevelt
Alabama.........	74,690	163,254	2,369	—	757	—	12
Arizona..........	37,016	29,546	222	15	4	3	—
Arkansas.........	71,117	107,409	5,111	—	—	—	9
California........	624,992	229,191	64,076	—	25,204	13	—
Colorado.........	173,248	104,936	8,046	3,016	2,807	6	—
Connecticut......	229,238	120,721	10,350	1,947	1,771	7	—
Delaware.........	52,858	39,911	988	93	986	3	—
Florida..........	44,853	90,515	5,189	—	5,124	—	6
Georgia..........	43,720	109,856	465	—	8	—	14
Idaho............	91,351	46,930	38	6	9	4	—
Illinois..........	1,420,480	534,395	74,747	49,630	11,216	29	—
Indiana.........	696,370	511,364	24,703	16,499	13,462	15	—
Iowa.............	634,674	227,921	16,981	10,321	4,197	13	—
Kansas..........	369,268	185,464	15,511	—	—	10	—
Kentucky........	452,480	456,497	6,409	—	3,325	—	13
Louisiana........	38,538	87,519	—	—	—	—	10
Maine...........	136,355	58,961	2,214	—	—	6	—
Maryland........	236,117	180,626	8,876	1,645	—	8	—
Massachusetts.....	681,153	276,691	32,269	—	—	18	—
Michigan.........	762,865	233,450	28,947	10,480	9,646	15	—
Minnesota........	519,421	142,994	56,106	—	11,489	12	—
Mississippi.......	11,576	69,277	1,639	—	—	—	10
Missouri.........	727,521	574,924	20,924	3,291	5,142	18	—
Montana.........	109,430	57,372	—	12,204	—	4	—
Nebraska........	247,498	119,608	9,600	—	5,947	8	—
Nevada..........	15,479	9,851	1,864	—	—	3	—
New Hampshire...	95,196	62,662	1,234	—	—	4	—
New Jersey.......	615,333	258,761	27,385	2,264	4,895	14	—
New Mexico......	57,634	46,668	—	1,097	—	3	—
New York........	1,871,167	781,238	203,201	18,413	19,653	45	—
North Carolina....	232,848	305,447	446	—	17	—	12
North Dakota.....	160,072	37,422	8,282	—	—	5	—
Ohio.............	1,182,022	780,037	57,147	—	294	24	—
Oklahoma........	243,831	217,053	25,726	—	—	10	—
Oregon..........	143,592	80,019	9,801	—	3,595	5	—
Pennsylvania......	1,218,215	503,202	70,021	15,642	42,612	38	—
Rhode Island.....	107,463	55,062	4,351	—	510	5	—
South Carolina....	2,244	64,170	28	—	—	—	9
South Dakota.....	109,874	35,938	—	34,707	900	5	—
Tennessee........	219,829	206,558	2,268	—	—	12	—
Texas............	114,538	288,767	8,121	—	—	—	20
Utah.............	81,555	56,639	3,159	4,475	—	4	—
Vermont.........	68,212	20,919	—	—	774	4	—
Virginia..........	87,456	141,670	807	240	824	—	12
Washington.......	223,137	84,298	8,913	77,246	3,800	7	—
West Virginia.....	282,007	220,789	5,618	—	1,528	8	—
Wisconsin........	498,576	113,422	85,041	—	8,647	13	—
Wyoming.........	35,091	17,429	1,288	2,180	265	3	—
	16,152,200	9,147,353	919,799	265,411	189,408	404	127

Socialist-Labor, 31,175, Single Tax, 5,837.　Total vote, 26,711,183.

THE VOTES IN THE 1924 ELECTION

STATES	POPULAR VOTE			ELECTORAL VOTE	
	Coolidge and Dawes, Republican	Davis and Bryan, Democrat	LaFollette and Wheeler, Progressive Socialist, and others	Coolidge and Dawes	Davis and Bryan
Alabama........	45,005	112,966	8,084	—	12
Arizona........	30,516	26,235	17,210	3	—
Arkansas......	40,564	84,795	13,173	—	9
California......	733,250	105,514	424,649	13	—
Colorado.......	195,171	75,238	69,945	6	—
Connecticut.....	246,322	110,184	42,416	7	—
Delaware.......	52,441	33,445	4,979	3	—
Florida.........	30,633	62,083	8,625	—	6
Georgia........	30,300	123,200	12,691	—	14
Idaho..........	69,879	24,256	54,160	4	—
Illinois.........	1,453,321	576,975	432,027	29	—
Indiana........	703,042	492,245	71,700	15	—
Iowa...........	537,635	162,600	272,243	13	—
Kansas.........	407,671	156,319	98,461	10	—
Kentucky......	398,966	374,855	38,465	13	—
Louisiana......	24,670	93,218	—	—	10
Maine..........	138,440	41,964	11,382	6	—
Maryland.......	162,414	148,072	47,157	8	—
Massachusetts...	703,476	280,831	141,284	18	—
Michigan.......	874,631	152,359	122,014	15	—
Minnesota......	420,759	55,913	339,192	12	—
Mississippi......	8,546	100,475	3,494	—	10
Missouri........	648,486	572,753	84,160	18	—
Montana.......	74,138	33,805	65,876	4	—
Nebraska.......	218,585	137,289	106,701	8	—
Nevada.........	11,243	5,909	9,769	3	—
New Hampshire.	98,575	57,201	8,993	4	—
New Jersey......	676,277	298,043	109,028	14	—
New Mexico....	54,745	48,542	9,543	3	—
New York......	1,820,058	950,796	474,925	45	—
North Carolina..	191,753	284,270	6,697	—	12
North Dakota...	94,931	13,858	89,922	5	—
Ohio...........	1,176,130	477,888	357,948	24	—
Oklahoma......	226,242	255,798	41,141	—	10
Oregon.........	142,579	67,589	68,403	5	—
Pennsylvania....	1,401,481	409,192	307,567	38	—
Rhode Island....	125,286	76,606	7,628	5	—
South Carolina..	1,123	49,008	620	—	9
South Dakota...	101,299	27,214	75,355	5	—
Tennessee.......	130,882	158,537	10,656	—	12
Texas..........	130,023	483,586	42,881	—	20
Utah...........	77,327	47,001	32,662	4	—
Vermont........	80,498	16,124	5,964	4	—
Virginia........	73,359	139,797	10,379	—	12
Washington.....	220,224	42,842	150,727	7	—
West Virginia...	288,635	257,232	36,723	8	—
Wisconsin......	311,614	68,096	453,678	—	—
Wyoming.......	41,858	12,868	25,174	3	—
	15,725,003	8,385,586	4,826,471	382	136

Wisconsin gave 13 electoral votes to LaFollette and Wheeler. Faris and Brehm, Prohibitionists, received 57,551 votes. Worker's (Communists) 36,386, Socialist-Labor, 27,650, American, 23,867, Commonwealth-Land, 2778. Total vote, 29,085,292.

STATES	POPULAR VOTE				ELECTORAL VOTE	
	H. Hoover, Republican	A. Smith, Democrat	N. Thomas, Socialist	Foster, Workers	Hoover	Smith
Alabama........	120,725	127,797	460	—	—	12
Arizona.........	52,533	38,537	—	184	3	—
Arkansas........	77,751	119,196	429	317	—	9
California.......	1,162,323	614,365	19,595	216	13	—
Colorado........	253,872	133,131	3,472	675	6	—
Connecticut.....	296,614	252,040	3,019	730	7	—
Delaware........	68,860	36,643	329	59	3	—
Florida..........	144,168	101,764	4,036	3,704	6	—
Georgia.........	63,498	120,602	124	64	—	14
Idaho...........	99,848	53,074	1,308	—	4	—
Illinois..........	1,769,141	1,313,817	19,138	3,581	29	—
Indiana.........	848,290	562,691	3,871	321	15	—
Iowa............	623,818	378,936	2,960	328	13	—
Kansas..........	513,672	193,003	6,205	320	10	—
Kentucky.......	558,064	381,070	837	293	13	—
Louisiana.......	51,160	164,655	—	—	—	10
Maine..........	179,923	81,179	1,068	—	6	—
Maryland.......	301,479	223,626	1,701	636	8	—
Massachusetts....	775,566	792,758	6,262	2,464	—	18
Michigan........	965,396	396,762	3,516	2,881	15	—
Minnesota.......	560,977	396,451	6,774	4,853	12	—
Mississippi......	27,153	124,539	—	—	—	10
Missouri........	834,080	662,562	3,739	—	18	—
Montana........	113,300	78,578	1,667	563	4	—
Nebraska........	345,745	197,959	3,434	—	8	—
Nevada.........	18,327	14,090	—	—	3	—
New Hampshire..	115,404	80,715	455	173	4	—
New Jersey......	926,050	616,517	4,897	1,257	14	—
New Mexico.....	69,645	48,211	—	158	3	—
New York.......	2,193,344	2,089,863	107,332	10,876	45	—
North Carolina...	348,992	287,078	—	—	12	—
North Dakota....	131,441	106,648	842	936	5	—
Ohio............	1,627,546	864,210	8,683	2,836	24	—
Oklahoma.......	394,046	219,174	3,924	—	10	—
Oregon.........	205,341	109,223	2,720	1,094	5	—
Pennsylvania.....	2,055,382	1,067,586	18,647	4,726	38	—
Rhode Island.....	117,522	118,973	—	283	—	5
South Carolina...	3,188	62,700	47	—	—	9
South Dakota....	157,603	102,660	443	232	5	—
Tennessee.......	195,388	167,343	631	111	12	—
Texas...........	367,036	341,032	722	209	20	—
Utah...........	94,618	80,985	954	47	4	—
Vermont........	90,404	44,440	—	—	4	—
Virginia.........	164,609	140,146	250	173	12	—
Washington.....	335,844	156,772	2,615	1,541	7	—
West Virginia....	375,551	263,784	1,313	401	8	—
Wisconsin.......	544,205	450,259	18,213	1,528	13	—
Wyoming........	52,748	29,299	788	—	3	—
	21,392,190	15,016,443	267,420	48,770	444	87

Reynolds, Socialist-Labor, 21,603; Varney, Prohibitionist, 20,106; Webb, Farm-Labor, 6,390. Total vote, 36,879,414.

THE VOTES IN THE 1932 ELECTION

STATES	POPULAR VOTE			ELECTORAL VOTE	
	F. D. Roosevelt, Democrat	Herbert Hoover, Republican	Norman Thomas, Socialist	Hoover-Curtis	Roosevelt-Garner
Alabama........	207,910	34,675	2,030	—	11
Arizona.........	79,264	36,104	2,618	—	3
Arkansas........	189,602	28,467	1,269	—	9
California.......	1,324,157	847,902	63,299	—	22
Colorado........	250,877	189,617	13,591	—	6
Connecticut.....	281,632	288,420	20,480	8	—
Delaware........	54,319	57,073	1,376	3	—
Florida.........	206,307	69,170	775	—	7
Georgia.........	234,118	19,863	461	—	12
Idaho...........	109,479	71,312	526	—	4
Illinois..........	1,882,304	1,432,756	67,258	—	29
Indiana.........	862,054	677,184	21,338	—	14
Iowa...........	598,019	414,433	20,467	—	11
Kansas.........	424,204	349,498	18,276	—	9
Kentucky.......	580,574	394,716	3,853	—	11
Louisiana.......	249,418	18,853	—	—	10
Maine..........	128,907	166,631	2,489	5	—
Maryland.......	314,314	184,184	10,489	—	8
Massachusetts...	800,148	736,959	34,305	—	17
Michigan........	871,700	739,894	39,205	—	19
Minnesota.......	600,806	363,959	25,476	—	11
Mississippi......	140,168	5,180	686	—	9
Missouri........	1,025,406	564,713	16,374	—	15
Montana........	127,286	78,078	7,891	—	4
Nebraska.......	359,082	201,177	9,876	—	7
Nevada.........	28,756	12,674	—	—	3
New Hampshire..	100,680	103,629	947	4	—
New Jersey......	806,630	775,684	42,998	—	16
New Mexico.....	95,089	54,217	1,776	—	3
New York.......	2,534,959	1,937,963	177,397	—	47
North Carolina...	497,566	208,344	5,591	—	13
North Dakota...	178,350	71,772	3,521	—	4
Ohio...........	1,301,695	1,227,679	64,094	—	26
Oklahoma.......	516,468	188,165	—	—	11
Oregon.........	213,871	136,019	15,450	—	5
Pennsylvania.....	1,295,948	1,453,540	91,119	36	—
Rhode Island....	146,604	115,266	3,138	—	4
South Carolina...	102,347	1,978	82	—	8
South Dakota....	183,515	99,212	1,551	—	4
Tennessee.......	259,817	126,806	1,786	—	11
Texas...........	760,348	97,959	4,450	—	23
Utah...........	116,750	84,795	4,087	—	4
Vermont........	56,266	78,984	1,533	3	—
Virginia.........	203,979	89,637	2,382	—	11
Washington.....	353,260	208,645	17,080	—	8
West Virginia....	405,124	330,731	5,133	—	8
Wisconsin.......	707,410	347,741	53,379	—	12
Wyoming.......	54,370	39,583	2,829	—	3
	22,821,857	15,761,841	884,781	59	472

Reynolds, Socialist-Labor, 33,275; Foster, Communist, 102,991; Upshaw, Prohibitionist, 81,869; Harvey, Liberty, 53,425; Coxey, Farm-Labor, 7,309. Total vote, 39,816,522.

THE VOTES IN THE 1936 ELECTION

STATES	POPULAR VOTE				ELECTORAL VOTE	
	F. D. Roosevelt, Democrat	Alf. Landon, Republican	William Lemke, Union	Norman Thomas, Socialist	Landon and Knox	Roosevelt and Garner
Alabama........	238,196	35,358	551	242	—	11
Arizona.........	86,722	33,433	3,307	317	—	3
Arkansas........	146,765	32,039	4	446	—	9
California.......	1,766,836	836,431	—	11,331	—	22
Colorado.......	295,021	181,267	9,962	1,593	—	6
Connecticut......	382,189	278,685	21,805	5,683	—	8
Delaware........	69,702	54,014	442	172	—	3
Florida..........	249,117	78,248	—	—	—	7
Georgia.........	255,364	36,942	141	68	—	12
Idaho...........	125,683	66,256	7,684	—	—	4
Illinois..........	2,282,999	1,570,393	89,439	7,530	—	29
Indiana..........	934,974	691,570	19,407	3,856	—	14
Iowa...........	621,756	487,977	29,687	1,373	—	11
Kansas..........	464,520	397,727	—	2,766	—	9
Kentucky........	541,944	369,702	12,501	632	—	11
Louisiana........	292,894	36,791	—	—	—	10
Maine...........	126,333	168,823	7,581	783	5	—
Maryland........	389,612	231,435	—	1,629	—	8
Massachusetts....	942,716	768,613	118,639	5,111	—	17
Michigan........	1,016,794	699,733	75,795	8,208	—	19
Minnesota.......	698,811	350,461	74,296	2,872	—	11
Mississippi......	157,318	4,443	—	329	—	9
Missouri.........	1,111,043	697,891	14,630	3,454	—	15
Montana........	159,690	63,598	5,549	1,066	—	4
Nebraska........	347,454	247,731	12,847	—	—	7
Nevada.........	31,925	11,923	—	—	—	3
New Hampshire..	108,460	104,642	4,819	—	—	4
New Jersey......	1,083,850	720,322	—	3,931	—	16
New Mexico.....	105,838	61,710	924	343	—	3
New York.......	3,293,222	2,180,670	—	86,897	—	47
North Carolina...	616,141	223,283	—	21	—	13
North Dakota....	163,148	72,751	36,708	552	—	4
Ohio............	1,747,122	1,127,709	132,212	117	—	26
Oklahoma.......	501,069	245,122	—	2,221	—	11
Oregon..........	266,733	122,706	21,831	2,143	—	5
Pennsylvania.....	2,353,788	1,690,300	67,467	14,375	—	36
Rhode Island.....	165,233	125,012	19,569	—	—	4
South Carolina...	113,791	1,646	—	—	—	8
South Dakota....	160,137	125,977	10,338	—	—	4
Tennessee........	327,083	146,516	296	685	—	11
Texas...........	734,485	103,874	3,281	1,075	—	23
Utah...........	150,246	64,555	1,121	432	—	4
Vermont.........	62,124	81,023	—	—	3	—
Virginia.........	234,980	98,336	233	313	—	11
Washington......	459,579	206,892	17,463	3,496	—	8
West Virginia....	502,582	325,486	—	832	—	8
Wisconsin.......	802,984	380,828	60,297	10,626	—	12
Wyoming........	62,624	38,739	1,653	200	—	3
	27,751,597	16,679,583	882,479	187,720	8	523

Browder, Communist, 80,150; Colvin, Prohibitionist, 37,847; Aiken, Socialist-Labor, 12,777. The Roosevelt vote in N. Y. State includes 274,924 cast by the American Labor Party. Total vote, 45,646,817.

THE VOTES IN THE 1940 ELECTION

STATES	POPULAR VOTE		ELECTORAL VOTE	
	F. D. Roosevelt, Democrat	W. Willkie, Republican	Roosevelt and Wallace	Willkie and McNary
Alabama........	250,726	42,184	11	—
Arizona.........	95,267	54,030	3	—
Arkansas........	158,622	42,121	9	—
California.......	1,877,618	1,351,419	22	—
Colorado.......	265,554	279,576	—	6
Connecticut.....	417,621	361,819	8	—
Delaware........	74,599	61,440	3	—
Florida.........	359,334	126,158	7	—
Georgia.........	265,194	23,934	12	—
Idaho...........	127,842	106,553	4	—
Illinois..........	2,149,934	2,047,240	29	—
Indiana.........	874,063	899,466	—	14
Iowa...........	578,800	632,370	—	11
Kansas.........	364,725	489,169	—	9
Kentucky.......	557,222	410,384	11	—
Louisiana.......	319,751	52,446	10	—
Maine..........	156,478	163,951	—	5
Maryland.......	384,546	269,534	8	—
Massachusetts...	1,076,522	939,700	17	—
Michigan.......	1,032,991	1,039,917	—	19
Minnesota......	644,196	596,274	11	—
Mississippi......	168,267	2,814	9	—
Missouri........	958,476	871,009	15	—
Montana........	145,698	99,579	4	—
Nebraska.......	263,677	352,201	—	7
Nevada.........	31,945	21,229	3	—
New Hampshire.	125,292	110,127	4	—
New Jersey......	1,016,808	945,475	16	—
New Mexico.....	103,699	79,315	3	—
New York......	3,251,918	3,027,478	47	—
North Carolina..	609,015	213,633	13	—
North Dakota...	124,036	154,590	—	4
Ohio...........	1,733,139	1,586,773	26	—
Oklahoma.......	474,313	348,872	11	—
Oregon.........	258,415	219,555	5	—
Pennsylvania....	2,171,035	1,889,848	36	—
Rhode Island....	182,182	138,653	4	—
South Carolina..	95,470	1,727	8	—
South Dakota...	131,362	177,065	—	4
Tennessee.......	351,601	169,153	11	—
Texas...........	840,151	199,152	23	—
Utah...........	154,277	93,151	4	—
Vermont........	64,269	78,371	—	3
Virginia........	235,961	109,363	11	—
Washington.....	462,145	322,123	8	—
West Virginia....	495,662	372,414	8	—
Wisconsin.......	704,821	679,206	12	—
Wyoming.......	59,287	52,633	3	—
	27,243,466	22,304,755	449	82

Thomas, Socialist, 99,557; Browder, Communist, 46,251; Babson, Prohibitionist, 57,812; Aiken, Socialist-Labor, 14,861; other, 48,610. Total vote, 49,815,312.

THE VOTES IN THE 1944 ELECTION

STATES	POPULAR VOTE				ELECT. VOTE	
	F. D. Roosevelt, Democrat	Thomas E. Dewey, Republican	Norman Thomas, Socialist	Claude E. Watson, Prohibitionist	Roosevelt-Truman	Dewey-Bricker
Alabama........	198,918	44,540	190	1,095	11	—
Arizona.........	80,926	56,287	—	421	4	—
Arkansas........	148,965	63,551	440	—	9	—
California........	1,988,564	1,512,965	3,923	14,770	25	—
Colorado........	234,331	268,731	1,977	—	—	6
Connecticut......	435,146	390,527	5,097	—	8	—
Delaware........	68,166	56,747	154	294	3	—
Florida.........	339,377	143,215	—	—	8	—
Georgia.........	268,187	56,507	6	36	12	—
Idaho...........	107,399	100,137	282	503	4	—
Illinois..........	2,079,479	1,939,314	180	7,411	28	—
Indiana..........	781,403	875,891	2,223	12,574	—	13
Iowa............	499,876	547,267	1,511	3,752	—	10
Kansas..........	287,458	442,096	1,613	2,609	—	8
Kentucky........	472,589	392,448	535	2,023	11	—
Louisiana........	281,564	67,750	—	—	10	—
Maine..........	140,631	155,434	—	—	—	5
Maryland.......	315,490	292,949	—	—	8	—
Massachusetts....	1,035,296	921,350	—	973	16	—
Michigan........	1,106,899	1,084,423	4,598	6,503	19	—
Minnesota.......	589,864	527,416	5,073	—	11	—
Mississippi.......	158,515	3,742	—	—	9	—
Missouri.........	807,356	761,175	1,751	1,175	15	—
Montana........	112,556	93,163	1,296	340	4	—
Nebraska........	233,246	329,880	—	—	—	6
Nevada........'..	29,623	24,611	—	—	3	—
New Hampshire..	119,663	109,916	46	—	4	—
New Jersey......	987,874	961,335	3,358	4,255	16	—
New Mexico.....	81,389	70,688	—	148	4	—
New York.......	3,304,238*	2,987,647	10,553	—	47	—
North Carolina...	527,399	263,155	—	—	14	—
North Dakota....	100,144	118,535	943	549	—	4
Ohio............	1,570,763	1,582,293	—	—	—	25
Oklahoma.......	401,549	319,424	—	1,663	10	—
Oregon.........	248,635	225,365	3,785	2,362	6	—
Pennsylvania.....	1,940,479	1,835,054	11,721	5,750	35	—
Rhode Island.....	175,356	123,487	—	433	4	—
South Carolina...	90,601	4,547	—	365	8	—
South Dakota....	96,711	135,365	—	—	—	4
Tennessee........	308,707	200,311	792	882	12	—
Texas...........	821,605	191,425	593	1,013	23	—
Utah...........	150,088	97,891	340	—	4	—
Vermont.........	53,820	71,527	—	—	—	3
Virginia.........	242,276	145,243	417	459	11	—
Washington......	486,777	361,689	3,824	2,396	8	—
West Virginia....	392,774	322,819	—	—	8	—
Wisconsin.......	650,413	674,532	13,205	—	—	12
Wyoming........	49,419	51,921	—	—	—	3
Total...........	25,602,504	22,006,285	80,426	74,754	432	99

* The Democratic figure in New York includes 496,405 American Labor and 329,235 Liberal votes.
Edward A. Teichert, Socialist-Labor, 45,335; Texas Regulars, 134,439; others, 32,520. Total vote, 47,976,263.

527

THE VOTES IN THE 1948 ELECTION

STATES	POPULAR VOTE				ELECTORAL VOTE	
	Harry S Truman, Democrat	Thomas E. Dewey, Republican	Strom Thurmond, States' Right	Henry Wallace, Progressive	Truman ticket	Dewey ticket
Alabama.........	—	40,930	171,443	1,522	—	—
Arizona..........	95,251	77,597	—	3,310	4	—
Arkansas.........	149,659	50,959	40,068	751	9	—
California........	1,913,134	1,895,269	1,228	190,381	25	—
Colorado.........	267,288	239,714	—	6,115	6	—
Connecticut.......	423,297	437,754	—	13,713	—	8
Delaware.........	67,813	69,588	—	1,050	—	3
Florida..........	281,988	194,280	89,755	11,620	8	—
Georgia..........	254,646	76,691	85,055	1,636	12	—
Idaho...........	107,370	101,514	—	4,972	4	—
Illinois..........	1,994,715	1,961,103	—	—	28	—
Indiana..........	807,833	821,079	—	9,649	—	13
Iowa............	522,380	494,018	—	12,125	10	—
Kansas..........	351,902	423,039	—	4,603	—	8
Kentucky........	466,757	341,210	10,411	1,567	11	—
Louisiana........	136,344	72,657	204,290	3,035	—	—
Maine...........	111,916	150,234	—	1,884	—	5
Maryland........	286,521	294,814	2,476	9,983	—	8
Massachusetts.....	1,151,788	909,370	—	38,157	16	—
Michigan.........	1,003,448	1,038,595	—	46,515	—	19
Minnesota.......	692,966	483,617	—	27,866	11	—
Mississippi.......	19,384	5,043	167,538	225	—	—
Missouri.........	917,315	655,039	—	3,998	15	—
Montana........	119,071	96,770	—	7,313	4	—
Nebraska.........	224,165	264,774	—	—	—	6
Nevada..........	31,291	29,357	—	1,469	3	—
New Hampshire...	107,995	121,299	7	1,970	—	4
New Jersey.......	895,455	981,124	—	42,683	—	16
New Mexico......	105,464	80,303	—	1,037	4	—
New York*.......	2,780,204	2,841,163	—	509,559	—	47
North Carolina....	459,070	258,572	69,652	3,915	14	—
North Dakota.....	95,812	115,139	374	8,391	—	4
Ohio............	1,452,791	1,445,684	—	37,596	25	—
Oklahoma........	452,782	268,817	—	—	10	—
Oregon..........	243,147	260,904	—	14,978	—	6
Pennsylvania.....	1,752,426	1,902,197	—	55,161	—	35
Rhode Island.....	188,736	135,787	—	2,619	4	—
South Carolina....	34,423	5,386	102,607	154	—	—
South Dakota.....	117,653	129,651	—	2,801	—	4
Tennessee........	270,402	202,914	73,815	1,864	11	—
Texas...........	750,700	282,240	106,909	3,764	23	—
Utah...........	149,151	124,402	—	2,679	4	—
Vermont.........	45,557	75,926	—	1,279	—	3
Virginia.........	200,786	172,070	43,393	2,047	11	—
Washington.......	476,165	386,315	—	31,692	8	—
West Virginia.....	429,188	316,251	—	3,311	8	—
Wisconsin........	647,310	590,959	—	25,282	12	—
Wyoming.........	52,354	47,947	—	931	3	—
Total..........	24,105,812	21,970,065	1,169,021	1,157,172	303	189

* The Truman vote includes 222,562 Liberal Party votes.
Thomas, Socialist, 139,521; Watson, Prohibitionist, 103,343, Teichert, Socialist-Labor, 29,061; Dobbs, Socialist Workers, 13,613. Others, and blank votes, 148,971. Total vote, 48,836,579.

THE VOTES IN THE 1952 ELECTION

CANDIDATES FOR PRESIDENT AND VICE PRESIDENT

Republican—Dwight D. Eisenhower; Richard M. Nixon
Democratic—Adlai E. Stevenson; John J. Sparkman
Progressive[1]—Vincent Hallinan; Mrs. Charlotta A. Bass
Prohibition—Stuart Hamblen; Enoch A. Holtwick
Socialist Labor[2]—Eric Hass; Stephen Emery
Socialist—Darlington Hoopes; Samuel H. Friedman

STATE	Total	Rep.	Dem.	Plurality	ELEC. R	ELEC. D	Prog.[1]	Prohib.	Soc. Lab.[2]	Others[3]
Alabama......	426,120	149,231	275,075	125,844 D	—	11	—	1,814	—	—
Arizona.......	260,570	152,042	108,528	43,514 R	4	—	—	—	—	—
Arkansas......	404,800	177,155	226,300	49,145 D	—	8	—	886	1	458
California.....	5,141,849	2,897,310	2,197,548	699,762 R	32	—	24,106	15,653	—	7,232
Colorado......	630,103	379,782	245,504	134,278 R	6	—	1,919	—	352	2,546
Connecticut....	1,096,911	611,012	481,649	129,363 R	8	—	—	—	535	3,715
Delaware......	174,025	90,059	83,315	6,744 R	3	—	155	234	242	20
Florida.......	989,337	544,036	444,950	99,086 R	10	—	—	—	—	351
Georgia......	655,803	198,979	456,823	257,844 D	—	12	—	—	—	1
Idaho.........	276,231	180,707	95,081	85,626 R	4	—	443	—	—	—
Illinois.......	4,481,058	2,457,327	2,013,920	443,407 R	27	—	—	—	9,363	448
Indiana........	1,955,325	1,136,259	801,530	334,729 R	13	—	1,222	15,335	979	—
Iowa..........	1,268,773	808,906	451,513	357,393 R	10	—	5,085	2,882	139	248
Kansas........	896,166	616,302	273,296	343,006 R	8	—	—	6,038	—	530
Kentucky......	993,148	495,029	495,729	700 D	—	10	336	1,161	893	—
Louisiana......	651,952	306,925	345,027	38,102 D	—	10	—	—	—	—
Maine........	351,786	232,353	118,806	113,547 R	5	—	332	—	156	139
Maryland......	902,074	499,424	395,337	104,087 R	9	—	7,313	—	—	—
Massachusetts..	2,383,398	1,292,325	1,083,525	208,800 R	16	—	4,636	886	1,957	69
Michigan......	2,798,592	1,551,529	1,230,657	320,872 R	20	—	3,922	10,331	1,495	658
Minnesota.....	1,379,483	763,211	608,458[4]	154,753 R	11	—	2,666	2,147	2,383	618
Mississippi.....	285,532	(5)	172,566	59,600 D	—	8	—	--	—	112,966
Missouri.......	1,892,062	959,429	929,830	29,599 R	13	—	987	885	169	762
Montana......	265,037	157,394	106,213	51,181 R	4	—	723	548	—	159
Nebraska......	609,660	421,603	188,057	233,546 R	6	—	—	—	—	—
Nevada.......	82,190	50,502	31,688	18,814 R	3	—	—	—	—	—
New Hampshire	272,950	166,287	106,663	59,624 R	4	—	—	—	—	—
New Jersey....	2,419,554	1,374,613	1,015,902	358,711 R	16	—	5,589	989	5,815	16,646
New Mexico....	238,608	132,170	105,661	26,509 R	4	—	—	297	35	445
New York.....	7,128,241	3,952,815	3,104,601[6]	848,214 R	45	—	64,211	—	1,560	5,054
North Carolina.	1,210,910	558,107	652,803	94,696 D	—	14	—	—	—	—
North Dakota..	270,127	191,712	76,694	115,018 R	4	—	344	302	—	1,075
Ohio..........	3,700,758	2,100,456	1,600,302	500,154 R	25	—	—	—	—	—
Oklahoma.....	948,984	518,045	430,939	87,106 R	8	—	—	—	—	—
Oregon.......	695,059	420,815	270,579	150,236 R	6	—	—	—	—	3,665
Pennsylvania...	4,580,717	2,415,789	2,146,269	269,520 R	32	—	4,200	8,771	1,347	4,341
Rhode Island...	414,498	210,935	203,293	7,642 R	4	—	187	—	83	—
South Carolina.	341,086	168,082[7]	173,004	4,922 D	—	8	—	—	—	—
South Dakota..	294,283	203,857	90,426	113,431 R	4	—	—	—	—	—
Tennessee......	892,553	446,147	443,710	2,437 R	11	—	885	1,432	—	379
Texas.........	2,076,006	1,102,878	969,288	133,590 R	24	—	294	1,983	—	1,563
Utah..........	329,554	194,190	135,364	58,826 R	4	—	—	—	—	—
Vermont.......	153,539	109,717	43,355	66,362 R	3	—	282	—	—	185
Virginia.......	619,689	349,037	268,677	80,360 R	12	—	311	—	1,160	504
Washington....	1,102,708	599,107	492,845	106,262 R	9	—	2,460	—	633	7,663
West Virginia..	873,548	419,970	453,578	33,608 D	—	8	—	—	—	—
Wisconsin.....	1,607,370	979,744	622,175	357,569 R	12	—	—	—	—	5,451
Wyoming......	129,251	81,047	47,934	33,113 R	3	—	—	—	194	36
Total..........	61,551,978	33,824,351	27,314,987[6]	6,509,364 R	442	89	132,608	72,768	29,333	117,931

[1] Independent Progressive in California; Peace Progressive in Massachusetts; American Labor in New York. [2] Industrial Government in Minnesota, New York and Pennsylvania. [3] Breakdown of Other votes: Independent (pledged to Republican candidate in Miss.), 112,966; Socialist, 18,322; Christian Nationalist, 10,557; Socialist Workers, 8,956; write-in, 4,431; Poor Man's, 4,203; scattering, 4,040; Independent, 3,665; Constitution, 2,911; Vincent Hallinan (independent in Wis.), 2,174; People's party of Connecticut, 1,466; Farrell Dobbs (independent in Wis.), 1,350; Darlington Hoopes (independent in Wis.), 1,157; Eric Hass (independent in Wis.), 770; Social Democrat, 504; America First, 233; Independent Progressive, 225; Liberty, 1. [4] Democratic-Farmer Labor votes. [5] 112,966 Independent votes were pledged to the Republican candidate; these are shown as Other votes. [6] Includes 416,711 Liberal votes. [7] Includes 158,289 votes for separate set of electors for Republican candidates by petition.

CANDIDATES FOR PRESIDENT AND VICE PRESIDENT

Republican—Dwight D. Eisenhower; Richard M. Nixon
Democratic—Adlai E. Stevenson; Estes Kefauver
Prohibition—Enoch A. Holtwick; Edward M. Cooper
Socialist—Darlington Hoopes; Samuel H. Friedman
Socialist Labor—Eric Hass; Georgia Cozzini
Socialist Workers—Farrell Dobbs; Myra Tanner Weiss

STATE	Total	Rep.	Dem.	Plurality	ELECTORAL VOTE R	ELECTORAL VOTE D*
Alabama	496,861	195,694	280,844	85,150 D	—	10*
Arizona	290,173	176,990	112,880	64,110 R	4	—
Arkansas	406,572	186,287	213,277	26,990 D	—	8
California	5,466,355	3,027,668	2,420,135	607,533 R	32	—
Colorado	663,074	394,479	263,997	130,482 R	6	—
Connecticut	1,117,121	711,837	405,079	306,758 R	8	—
Delaware	177,988	98,057	79,421	18,636 R	3	—
Florida	1,124,220	643,849	480,371	163,478 R	10	—
Georgia	668,920	222,778	444,388	221,610 D	—	12
Idaho	272,989	166,979	105,868	61,111 R	4	—
Illinois	•4,407,407	2,623,327	1,775,682	847,645 R	27	—
Indiana	1,974,607	1,182,811	783,908	398,903 R	13	—
Iowa	1,234,564	729,187	501,858	227,329 R	10	—
Kansas	866,243	566,878	296,317	270,561 R	8	—
Kentucky	1,053,805	572,192	476,453	95,739 R	10	—
Louisiana	617,544	329,047	243,977	85,070 R	10	—
Maine	351,706	249,238	102,468	146,770 R	5	—
Maryland	932,351	559,738	372,613	187,125 R	9	—
Massachusetts	2,348,506	1,393,197	948,190	445,007 R	16	—
Michigan	3,080,468	1,713,647	1,359,998	353,749 R	20	—
Minnesota	1,340,005	719,302	617,525	101,777 R	11	—
Mississippi	248,149	56,372	144,498	88,126 D	—	8
Missouri	1,832,572	914,299	918,273	3,974 D	—	13
Montana	271,171	154,933	116,238	38,695 R	4	—
Nebraska	577,137	378,108	199,029	179,079 R	6	—
Nevada	96,689	56,049	40,640	15,409 R	3	—
New Hampshire	266,994	176,519	90,364	86,155 R	4	—
New Jersey	2,484,312	1,606,942	850,337	756,605 R	16	—
New Mexico	253,926	146,788	106,098	40,690 R	4	—
New York	7,093,336	4,340,340	2,750,769 †	1,589,571 R	45	—
North Carolina	1,165,592	575,062	590,530	15,468 D	—	14
North Dakota	253,991	156,766	96,742	60,024 R	4	—
Ohio	3,702,265	2,262,610	1,439,655	822,955 R	25	—
Oklahoma	859,350	473,769	385,581	88,188 R	8	—
Oregon	735,597	406,393	329,204	77,189 R	6	—
Pennsylvania	4,576,503	2,585,252	1,981,769	603,483 R	32	—
Rhode Island	387,609	225,819	161,790	64,029 R	4	—
South Carolina	300,583 ‡	75,700	136,372	60,672 D	—	8
South Dakota	293,857	171,569	122,288	49,281 R	4	—
Tennessee	939,404	462,288	456,507	5,781 R	11	—
Texas	1,955,168	1,080,619	859,958	220,661 R	24	—
Utah	333,995	215,631	118,364	97,267 R	4	—
Vermont	152,978	110,390	42,549	67,841 R	3	—
Virginia	697,978	386,459	267,760	118,699 R	12	—
Washington	1,150,889	620,430	523,002	97,428 R	9	—
West Virginia	830,831	449,297	381,534	67,763 R	8	—
Wisconsin	1,550,558	954,844	586,768	368,076 R	12	—
Wyoming	124,127	74,573	49,554	25,019 R	3	—
Total	62,027,040	35,581,003	26,031,322	9,549,681 R	457	73*

* Alabama's 11th electoral vote was cast for Walter B. Jones of Alabama.   † Includes 292,557 Liberal Party votes.
‡ Includes 88,509 votes for electors nominated by petition.

THE VOTES IN THE 1960 ELECTION

CANDIDATES FOR PRESIDENT AND VICE PRESIDENT
Democratic—John F. Kennedy; Lyndon B. Johnson
Republican—Richard M. Nixon; Henry Cabot Lodge

STATE	Total	Dem.	Rep.	Plurality	ELECTORAL VOTE D	R	Byrd[1]
Alabama...........	570,225	324,050	237,981	86,069 D	5	—	6[2]
Alaska.............	60,762	29,809	30,953	1,144 R	—	3	—
Arizona...........	398,491	176,781	221,241	44,460 R	—	4	—
Arkansas..........	428,509	215,049	184,508	30,541 D	8	—	—
California.........	6,506,578	3,224,099	3,259,722	35,623 R	—	32	—
Colorado..........	736,246	330,629	402,242	71,613 R	—	6	—
Connecticut.......	1,222,868	657,055	565,813	91,242 D	8	—	—
Delaware..........	195,963	99,590	96,373	3,217 D	3	—	—
Florida............	1,544,180	748,700	795,476	46,776 R	—	10	—
Georgia...........	733,349	458,638	274,472	184,166 D	12	—	—
Hawaii............	184,705	92,410	92,295	115 D	3	—	—
Idaho.............	300,450	138,853	161,597	22,744 R	—	4	—
Illinois............	4,757,409	2,377,846	2,368,988	8,858 D	27	—	—
Indiana...........	2,135,360	952,358	1,175,120	222,762 R	—	13	—
Iowa..............	1,273,810	550,565	722,381	171,816 R	—	10	—
Kansas............	928,825	363,213	561,474	198,261 R	—	8	—
Kentucky..........	1,124,462	521,855	602,607	80,752 R	—	10	—
Louisiana..........	807,891	407,339	230,980	176,359 D	10	—	—
Maine.............	421,767	181,159	240,608	59,449 R	—	5	—
Maryland..........	1,055,346	565,808	489,538	76,270 D	9	—	—
Massachusetts......	2,469,480	1,487,174	976,750	510,424 D	16	—	—
Michigan..........	3,318,097	1,687,269	1,620,428	66,841 D	20	—	—
Minnesota.........	1,541,887	779,933	757,915	22,018 D	11	—	—
Mississippi........	298,171	108,362	73,561	34,801 D	—	—	8[2]
Missouri...........	1,934,422	972,201	962,221	9,980 D	13	—	—
Montana...........	277,579	134,891	141,841	6,950 R	—	4	—
Nebraska..........	613,095	232,542	380,553	148,011 R	—	6	—
Nevada............	107,267	54,880	52,387	2,493 D	3	—	—
New Hampshire.....	295,761	137,772	157,989	20,217 R	—	4	—
New Jersey.........	2,773,111	1,385,415	1,363,324	22,091 D	16	—	—
New Mexico........	311,107	156,027	153,733	2,294 D	4	—	—
New York..........	7,380,075	3,830,085[3]	3,446,419	383,666 D	45	—	—
North Carolina.....	1,368,556	713,136	655,420	57,716 D	14	—	—
North Dakota......	278,431	123,963	154,310	30,347 R	—	4	—
Ohio..............	4,161,859	1,944,248	2,217,611	273,363 R	—	25	—
Oklahoma..........	903,150	370,111	533,039	162,928 R	—	7	1
Oregon............	775,462	367,402	408,060	40,658 R	—	6	—
Pennsylvania.......	5,006,541	2,556,282	2,439,956	116,326 D	32	—	—
Rhode Island.......	405,534	258,032	147,502	110,530 D	4	—	—
South Carolina.....	386,688	198,129	188,558	9,571 D	8	—	—
South Dakota......	306,487	128,070	178,417	50,347 R	—	4	—
Tennessee..........	1,051,792	481,453	556,577	75,124 R	—	11	—
Texas.............	2,311,845	1,167,932	1,121,699	46,233 D	24	—	—
Utah..............	374,709	169,248	205,361	36,113 R	—	4	—
Vermont...........	167,317	69,186	98,131	28,945 R	—	3	—
Virginia...........	771,449	362,327	404,521	42,194 R	—	12	—
Washington........	1,241,572	599,298	629,273	29,975 R	—	9	—
West Virginia......	837,781	441,786	395,995	45,791 D	8	—	—
Wisconsin.........	1,729,082	830,805	895,175	64,370 R	—	12	—
Wyoming..........	139,882	63,331	76,551	13,220 R	—	3	—
Total.............	68,836,385	34,227,096	34,107,646	119,450 D	303	219	15

[1] For Senator Harry F. Byrd, of Virginia.   [2] Unpledged electors.   [3] Includes 406,176 Liberal Party votes.
[4] 24 votes allocated to District of Columbia and U. S. territories.   [5] 12 votes allocated to D. C. and U. S. territories.

REVISED ELECTORAL VOTES BASED ON THE 1960 CENSUS
(States not shown have the same electoral votes as for the 1960 election)

Alabama......10	Hawaii....... 4	Maine........ 4	Mississippi.... 7	N. Carolina...13
Arizona..... 5	Illinois.........26	Maryland.....10	Missouri......12	Ohio.........26
Arkansas.... 6	Iowa......... 9	Massachusetts.14	Nebraska..... 5	Pennsylvania..29
California.....40	Kansas....... 7	Michigan.....21	New Jersey....17	Texas.........25
Florida.......14	Kentucky..... 9	Minnesota....10	New York....43	W. Virginia... 7

Total electoral votes for 1964 and 1968 elections: 538 (including 3 electoral votes for the District of Columbia as a result of the 23rd Amendment to the U. S. Constitution). The electoral vote for each state is based on the number of members in the U. S. House of Representatives, plus the two Senators.

CANDIDATES FOR PRESIDENT AND VICE PRESIDENT

Democratic—Lyndon B. Johnson; Hubert H. Humphrey
Republican—Barry M. Goldwater; William E. Miller

STATE	Total	Dem.	Rep.	Plurality	ELECTORAL VOTE		Other
					D	R	
Alabama........	689,817	210,732	479,085	268,353 R	—	10	—
Alaska..........	67,259	44,329	22,930	21,399 D	3	—	—
Arizona.........	480,783	237,765	242,536	4,771 R	—	5	482
Arkansas.......	560,426	314,197	243,264	70,933 D	6	—	2,965
California......	7,050,985	4,171,877	2,879,108	1,292,769 D	40	—	—
Colorado........	772,749	476,024	296,725	179,299 D	6	—	—
Connecticut.....	1,218,578	826,269	390,996	435,273 D	8	—	1,313
Delaware.......	201,334	122,704	78,093	44,611 D	3	—	537
D. C...........	198,597	169,796	28,801	140,995 D	3	—	—
Florida.........	1,854,481	948,540	905,941	42,599 D	14	—	—
Georgia.........	1,139,157	522,557	616,600	94,043 R	—	12	—
Hawaii..........	207,271	163,249	44,022	119,227 D	4	—	—
Idaho..........	292,477	148,920	143,557	5,363 D	4	—	—
Illinois..........	4,702,779	2,796,833	1,905,946	890,887 D	26	—	—
Indiana.........	2,091,606	1,170,848	911,118	259,730 D	13	—	9,640
Iowa............	1,184,539	733,030	449,148	283,882 D	9	—	2,361
Kansas..........	857,901	464,028	386,579	77,449 D	7	—	7,294
Kentucky........	1,046,132	669,659	372,977	296,682 D	9	—	3,496
Louisiana.......	896,293	387,068	509,225	122,157 R	—	10	—
Maine..........	380,965	262,264	118,701	143,563 D	4	—	—
Maryland.......	1,116,407	730,912	385,495	345,417 D	10	—	—
Massachusetts....	2,344,798	1,786,422	549,727	1,236,695 D	14	—	8,649
Michigan........	3,203,102	2,136,615	1,060,152	1,076,463 D	21	—	6,335
Minnesota.......	1,554,462	991,117	559,624	431,493 D	10	—	3,721
Mississippi......	409,038	52,591	356,447	303,856 R	—	7	—
Missouri.........	1,817,879	1,164,344	653,535	510,809 D	12	—	—
Montana........	278,628	164,246	113,032	51,214 D	4	—	1,350
Nebraska........	584,154	307,307	276,847	30,460 D	5	—	—
Nevada..........	135,433	79,339	56,094	23,245 D	3	—	—
New Hampshire..	286,094	182,065	104,029	78,036 D	4	—	—
New Jersey......	2,846,770	1,867,671	963,843	903,828 D	17	—	15,256
New Mexico.....	327,647	194,017	131,838	62,179 D	4	—	1,792
New York.......	7,166,015	4,913,156	2,243,559	2,669,597 D	43	—	9,300
North Carolina...	1,424,983	800,139	624,844	175,295 D	13	—	—
North Dakota....	258,389	149,784	108,207	41,577 D	4	—	398
Ohio............	3,969,196	2,498,331	1,470,865	1,027,466 D	26	—	—
Oklahoma.......	932,499	519,834	412,665	107,169 D	8	—	—
Oregon..........	783,796	501,017	282,779	218,238 D	6	—	—
Pennsylvania.....	4,818,668	3,130,228	1,672,892	1,457,336 D	29	—	15,548
Rhode Island....	390,078	315,463	74,615	240,848 D	4	—	—
South Carolina...	524,748	215,700	309,048	93,348 R	—	8	—
South Dakota....	293,118	163,010	130,108	32,902 D	4	—	—
Tennessee........	1,144,046	635,047	508,965	126,082 D	11	—	34
Texas...........	2,626,811	1,663,185	958,566	704,619 D	25	—	5,060
Utah............	400,310	219,628	180,682	38,946 D	4	—	—
Vermont.........	163,069	108,127	54,942	53,185 D	3	—	—
Virginia.........	1,042,267	558,038	481,334	76,704 D	12	—	2,895
Washington......	1,258,374	779,699	470,366	309,333 D	9	—	8,309
West Virginia....	792,040	538,087	253,953	284,134 D	7	—	—
Wisconsin.......	1,691,815	1,050,424	638,495	411,929 D	12	—	2,896
Wyoming........	142,716	80,718	61,998	18,720 D	3	—	—
Total...........	70,621,479	43,126,218	27,174,898	16,162,052 D	486	52	320,363

CANDIDATES FOR PRESIDENT AND VICE PRESIDENT
Democratic—Hubert H. Humphrey; Edmund S. Muskie
Republican—Richard M. Nixon; Spiro T. Agnew
American Independent Party—George C. Wallace; Curtis LeMay

STATE	Dem.	Rep.	AIP	All Others	Plurality	ELECTORAL VOTE D	R	AIP
Alabama*......	196,579	146,923	691,425	14,982	494,846 AIP	—	—	10
Alaska........	35,411	37,600	10,024	—	2,189 R	—	3	—
Arizona.......	170,514	266,721	46,573	3,128	96,207 R	—	5	—
Arkansas......	188,228	190,759	240,982	—	50,223 AIP	—	—	6
California.....	3,244,318	3,467,664	487,270	52,335	223,346 R	—	40	—
Colorado......	335,174	409,345	60,813	5,867	74,171 R	—	6	—
Connecticut.....	621,561	556,721	76,650	1,300	64,840 D	8	—	—
Delaware......	89,194	96,714	28,459	—	7,520 R	—	3	—
Dist. of Col.....	139,566	31,012	—	—	108,554 D	3	—	—
Florida........	676,794	886,804	624,207	—	210,010 R	—	14	—
Georgia........	334,439	380,111	535,550	—	155,439 AIP	—	—	12
Hawaii........	141,324	91,425	3,469	—	49,899 D	4	—	—
Idaho..........	89,273	165,369	36,541	—	76,096 R	—	4	—
Illinois........	2,039,814	2,174,774	390,958	14,203	134,960 R	—	26	—
Indiana........	806,659	1,067,885	243,108	5,945	261,226 R	—	13	—
Iowa..........	476,699	619,106	66,422	5,454	142,407 R	—	9	—
Kansas........	302,996	478,674	88,921	2,192	175,678 R	—	7	—
Kentucky......	397,541	462,411	193,098	2,843	64,870 R	—	9	—
Louisiana......	309,615	257,535	530,300	—	220,685 AIP	—	—	10
Maine........	217,312	169,254	6,370	—	48,058 D	4	—	—
Maryland......	538,310	517,995	178,734	—	20,315 D	10	—	—
Massachusetts...	1,469,218	766,844	87,088	8,602	702,374 D	14	—	—
Michigan.......	1,593,082	1,370,665	331,968	10,535	222,417 D	21	—	—
Minnesota......	857,738	658,643	68,931	3,198	199,095 D	10	—	—
Mississippi.....	150,644	88,516	415,349	—	264,705 AIP	—	—	7
Missouri.......	791,444	811,932	206,126	—	20,488 R	—	12	—
Montana.......	114,117	138,835	20,015	1,437	24,718 R	—	4	—
Nebraska......	170,784	321,163	44,904	—	150,379 R	—	5	—
Nevada........	60,598	73,188	20,432	—	12,590 R	—	3	—
New Hampshire.	130,589	154,903	11,173	633	24,314 R	—	4	—
New Jersey.....	1,264,206	1,325,467	262,187	23,535	61,261 R	—	17	—
New Mexico....	130,081	169,692	25,737	1,828	39,611 R	—	4	—
New York†.....	3,378,470	3,007,932	358,864	46,421	370,538 D	43	—	—
North Carolina..	464,113	627,192	496,188	—	131,004 R	—	12	1
North Dakota..	94,769	138,669	14,244	200	43,900 R	—	4	—
Ohio..........	1,700,586	1,791,014	467,495	603	90,428 R	—	26	—
Oklahoma......	301,658	449,697	191,731	—	148,039 R	—	8	—
Oregon........	358,866	408,433	49,683	2,640	49,567 R	—	6	—
Pennsylvania....	2,259,405	2,090,017	378,582	19,924	169,388 D	29	—	—
Rhode Island...	246,518	122,359	15,678	383	124,159 D	4	—	—
South Carolina..	197,486	254,062	215,430	—	38,632 R	—	8	—
South Dakota...	118,023	149,841	13,400	—	31,818 R	—	4	—
Tennessee......	351,233	472,592	424,792	—	47,800 R	—	11	—
Texas..........	1,266,804	1,227,844	584,269	489	38,960 D	25	—	—
Utah..........	156,665	238,728	26,906	269	82,063 R	—	4	—
Vermont.......	70,255	85,142	5,104	902	14,887 R	—	3	—
Virginia........	442,387	590,319	321,833	6,950	147,932 R	—	12	—
Washington.....	616,037	588,510	96,990	2,744	27,527 D	9	—	—
West Virginia...	374,091	307,555	72,560	—	66,536 D	7	—	—
Wisconsin......	748,804	809,997	127,835	4,902	61,193 R	—	12	—
Wyoming.......	45,173	70,927	11,105	—	25,754 R	—	3	—
Totals........	31,275,165	31,785,480	9,906,473	244,444	510,315 R	191	301	46

* Alabama—Humphrey total is a combination of National Democratic (54,144) and Independent Democratic (142,435) votes; the AIP Wallace vote was cast as Democratic in this state.
† New York—Humphrey total includes 311,622 votes as Liberal candidate.

About the Contributors

MARCUS CUNLIFFE is Professor of American Studies at the University of Sussex. His chief publications are The Literature of the United States; George Washington: Man and Monument; The Nation Takes Shape, 1789–1837; *and* Soldiers and Civilians: The Martial Spirit in America, 1775–1865.

NOBLE E. CUNNINGHAM, JR., is Professor of History at the University of Missouri, Columbia. He is the author of The Jeffersonian Republicans: The Formation of Party Organizations, 1789–1801; The Jeffersonian Republicans in Power: Party Operations, 1801–1909; The Making of the American Party System, 1789–1809; *and* The Early Republic, 1789–1828.

ROBERT V. REMINI is Professor of History at the University of Illinois, Chicago Circle. He has written Martin Van Buren and the Making of the Democratic Party; The Election of Andrew Jackson; Andrew Jackson; *and* Andrew Jackson and the Bank War.

Politics of the Buchanan years has been the main preoccupation of PHILIP S. KLEIN, Professor of American History at Pennsylvania State University. His main publications are President James Buchanan: A Biography *and* Pennsylvania Politics, 1817–1832: A Game Without Rules. *ROY F. NICHOLS is Professor of History at the University of Pennsylvania and is the author of* Disruption of American Democracy; The Democratic Machine, 1850–1854; Franklin Pierce; Stakes of Power: 1845–1877; *and* Blueprints for Leviathan.

ELTING MORISON is Professor of History and Master at Timothy Dwight College, Yale University. He is the author of Turmoil and Tradition: A Study of the Life and Times of Henry L. Stimson *and the editor of* Letters of Theodore Roosevelt, *an eight-volume work.*

HAROLD M. HYMAN is William P. Hobby Professor of History and Chairman of the Department at Rice University. He is the author of Era of the Oath; To Try Men's Souls: Loyalty Oaths in American History; *and the co-author of* Stanton: The Life and Times of Lincoln's Secretary of War.

SIDNEY I. POMERANTZ is Professor of History at The City College and a member of the doctoral faculty of The City University of New York. He is the author of New York: An American City, 1783–1803.

GILBERT C. FITE is George Lynn Cross Research Professor of History at the University of Oklahoma. Among his principal publications are Peter Norbeck: Prairie Statesman; George N. Peek and the Fight for Farm Parity; *and* The Farmers' Frontier, 1865–1900.

GEORGE E. MOWRY is Professor of History at the University of North Carolina at Chapel Hill. He is the author of The California Progressives; The Era of

Theodore Roosevelt: 1900–1912; Theodore Roosevelt and the Progressive Movement; *and* The Urban Nation: 1920–1960.

ARTHUR S. LINK is Edwards Professor of American History at Princeton University and editor of The Papers of Woodrow Wilson. *Among his major publications is a five-volume biography of President Woodrow Wilson. WILLIAM M. LEARY, JR., is Professor of History at Victoria University, British Columbia.*

FRANK FREIDEL is Professor of History at Harvard University. He is the author of a biography of Franklin D. Roosevelt (three volumes to date); F.D.R. and the South; *and* The Splendid Little War.

ROBERT E. BURKE is Professor of History at the University of Washington and managing editor of Pacific Northwest Quarterly. *He is the author of* Olson's New Deal for California *and the co-author of* The Federal Union; The American Nation; *and* A History of American Democracy.

BARTON J. BERNSTEIN is Associate Professor of History at Stanford University. He is the co-editor of The Truman Administration: A Documentary History. *He has edited and contributed to* Towards A New Past: Dissenting Essays in American History *and* Politics and Policies of the Truman Administration.

THEODORE C. SORENSEN is a partner in the New York law firm of Paul, Weiss, Rifkind, Wharton and Garrison. Mr. Sorensen served as counsel and advisor to President John F. Kennedy. Among his major publications are Kennedy *and* The Kennedy Legacy.

JOHN BARTLOW MARTIN, former Ambassador to the Dominican Republic, 1962–1964, is the author of numerous books. Among them are Overtaken by Events; The Pane of Glass; The Deep South Says Never; *and* Why Did They Kill.

Index

A

Acheson, Dean, 386, 387–388, 389, 417, 425
A.D.A. (*see* Americans for Democratic
  Action)
Adams, Charles Francis, Jr., on election of
  1864, 144
Adams, John:
  administration of, 35–36
  Cabinet, influence of Hamilton in, 44, 45
  Constitution, writings on, 34, 35
  Jefferson, Thomas, relations with, 34
  monarchism, accused of, 54
  political career, 34
  (*See also* election of 1796, election of
    1800)
Adams, John Quincy, 438
  Jackson, Andrew, relations with, 67
  Masons, relations with, 83–85
  (*See also* election of 1828)
Adams, Sherman, 390, 395, 397, 413, 415,
  417
Adamson Act, 312
  political consequences of, 316
  (*See also* labor unions)
Agar, Herbert, 420
Agricultural Adjustment Administration act,
  second, 355
agrarianism, election of 1800, issue in, 55
Aiken, George, 389
Albany Regency, 70
Aldrich, Winthrop, 390
Alien and Sedition Laws:
  Jefferson, Thomas, on, 45–46
  Republican newspaper editors, indicted
    under, 46
  Jeffersonian Republicans, opposition to,
    52
Alsop, Stewart, 463
Altschul, Frank, 365, 366
American Labor party (New York), 384
Americans for Democratic Action (A.D.A.),
  394, 416, 417, 467
Ameringer, Oscar, 327
Ames, Fisher, on Adams' candidacy (1800),
  48
anti-Catholicism, 323
  1960 campaign, 446, 455
  (*See also* Know Nothing party)
Anti-Masonic party:
  election of 1828, role in, 84–85
  origins of, 84
anti-Semitism, 460
Arn, Edward, 395
Arvey, Jacob, 406, 408
Atchison, David R., Kansas-Nebraska Act
  supported by, 94

B

Baker, Newton D., 338, 343, 344, 364
Ball, George, 420
Bankhead, William B., 371, 372, 374
Barkley, Alben W., 341, 342, 372–373
  presidential candidacy mentioned, 407,
    408, 409
Baruch, Bernard, 349
Bass, Mrs. Charlotta, 427
Battle of New Orleans, Andrew Jackson's
  role in, 70
Bean, Louis, 468
Belknap, William W., 174
Bell, David, 420
Bell, John:
  Compromise of 1850, supported by, 121
  election of 1860, 137–138
  national bank, supported by, 121
  secession, opposition to, 122
  on slavery, 120–123
  Whig party, national leader of, 121
Benton, Thomas Hart, opposition to
  Kansas-Nebraska Act, 94
Berdini, Gaetano Cardinal, 97, 100
Berle, Adolph A., Jr., 349, 352
bimetallism, consequences of, 228–229
Bingham, Hiram, 329
Bingham, Robert W., 341
Blaine, James G.:
  education, federal aid to, 184
  fraud, accused of, 185
  Grant, Ulysses S., opposition to, 180
  Speaker of House of Representatives, 178,
    180
Blaine, John J., 331
Blair, Montgomery, resignation as Post-
  master General, 161
Bliss, Ray C., 482
Bloom, Sol, 358, 359
"bonus army," 347
Borah, William E., 328, 358, 359, 360, 363
Bourbon Democracy (*see* Democratic
  party)
Bozell, L. Brent, 460
Bradley, Gen. Omar, 419, 424
Bradley, Joseph P., Supreme Court Justice,
  171
Breckenridge Faction (*see* Democratic
  party)
Breckenridge, John C.:
  election of 1860, 137–138
  popular sovereignty, supported by, 121
  on slavery, 120
  vice-presidential nomination of, 106
Bricker, John W., 357, 362, 368, 390, 401
Bridges, Styles, 420

537

L

T